Sex Offender Laws

About the Editor

Richard G. Wright, PhD, is a nationally known expert on the issue of sex offender laws. He has been a practitioner, researcher, scholar, public speaker, and teacher on issues of sexual offending, federal crime control, racial inequality, and domestic violence for 20 years. After many years of community organizing, policy advocacy, and program development and implementation, he received his PhD in public policy from the University of Massachusetts Boston in 2004.

He has been published in peer-reviewed journals, including *Criminology & Public Policy*, and in legal journals on federal sex offender laws such as the Walsh Act, the 2003 Protect Act, and the 1994 enactment of the Wetterling Act.

He has been interviewed and cited by numerous media outlets, including *USA Today*, *Newsweek*, the *Boston Globe*, and National Public Radio. His intellectual and scholarly agenda includes examining the growth of preventive detention, the balance between civil liberties and the War on Terror, sexual assault, and moral agency.

His scholarly output is mediated by his enthusiastic pursuit in developing new and future scholars. Several of his students have been awarded prestigious research awards. Through his mentoring, his students have conducted studies on international dimensions of sexual assault, and the relationship between gender bias, sentencing, and filicide (i.e., the act of killing one's son or daughter), presenting their work at international conferences. His vision includes a critical assessment of the role of government in crime control and reaffirming the power of young people, the individual, and the community in promoting an accountable, just, fair, and progressive democracy.

Sex Offender Laws

Failed Policies,
New Directions

Richard G. Wright, PhD

SPRINGER PUBLISHING COMPANY

NEW YORK

Springer Publishing Company, Inc.
11 West 42nd Street
New York, NY 10036
www.springerpub.com

Acquisitions Editor: Jennifer Perillo
Cover design: Steve Pisano
Composition: Monotype, LLC

09 10 11 12 / 5 4 3 2 1

Library of Congress Cataloging-in-Publication Data

Sex offender laws : failed policies, new directions / [edited by]
    Richard G. Wright. p. cm.
  ISBN 978-0-8261-1109-8
  1. Sex offenders—Legal status, laws, etc.—United States. I. Wright,
Richard Gordon, 1965–
KF9325.S493 2009
345.73′0253—dc22

                                                              2009000758

Printed in the United States of America by Bang Printing

To my wife, Becky—There are no words that will ever convey how much I love you and appreciate you. Thank you for your many, many sacrifices. You have given me more than I ever could have conceived of. Thank you.

To my daughter, Sage—I am privileged to be your daddy. I know you have and will change the world forever. I love you.

To the Wetterling family, and in particular, Patty—Because you choose to seek wisdom and knowledge when faced with tragedy and loss, you are a source of affirmation about the goodness and power of humanity. I am sorry about Jacob. I am humbled by your strength and faith in the world. Nothing will replace your loss. I hope this book reminds you that we still care.

Contents

Part III - Policy Alternatives

Contributors

Richard G. Wright	PhD	Bridgewater State College
Karen J. Terry	PhD	John Jay College of Criminal Justice
Alissa Ackerman	MS, PhD Candidate	John Jay College of Criminal Justice
Jill Levenson	PhD	Lynn University
Michelle Meloy	PhD	Rutgers, The State University of New Jersey, Campus at Camden
Shareda Coleman	PhD Candidate	Villanova University
Patricia Wetterling		Minnesota Department of Public Safety
Kim English	PhD	Colorado Dept. of Corrections, Research Division
Corey Rayburn Yung	JD	John Marshall Law School
Jo-Ann Della Giustina	JD, PhD	Bridgewater State College
Francis Williams	PhD	Plymouth State University
Cheryl Radeloff	PhD	University of Minnesota Mankato
Erica Carnes	Master's Certificate	University of Minnesota Mankato
Rachel Bandy	PhD	Simpson College
Charles Scott	MD	University of California Davis Health System
Elena del Busto	MD	Thomas Jefferson University – Jefferson Medical College
Lisa J. Sample	PhD	University of Nebraska Omaha
Andrew Harris	PhD	University of Massachusetts Lowell

that produce over-broad, poorly-considered laws are in due course followed by a decline in political and media attention to the subject and a gradual decline in application of the laws, which come to be seen by most judges and prosecutors as unwise and immoderate, and to be applied if at all only to serious and repeat offenders. And then, in due course, horrible new crimes attract media and political attention and the pattern repeats.

That cycle has been unusually protracted in our time but there are signs that the fever finally is abating in relation to crime generally and to sexual crime in particular. For crimes generally, law-and-order has by and large disappeared from election campaigns, California prosecutors have stopped invoking the three-strikes law except for really serious crimes and criminals, some states have started weakening their mandatory minimum sentence laws, and the US Supreme Court gutted the fearsome mandatory federal sentencing guidelines by making them advisory.

Most of the overreaching sex offender laws enacted in recent decades remain on the books but if Sutherland and Jenkins are right (as they are), a window of opportunity may be opening for reconsideration of the dumbest and cruelest sex offender laws of recent decades and for the development of evidence-based policies that distinguish among offenders in terms of the nature of their offenses, the risks they pose, the treatments they need, and the punishments they deserve.

Whether policy-makers pay attention to scientific evidence largely turns on whether windows of opportunity exist through which evidence can pass and be noted. There is a good chance that windows are opening in relation to crime generally and to sex offenders and sexual offenses in particular. If they do, this fine book by Richard Wright and his distinguished collaborators provides the evidence that wise policy-makers would want to consider. It covers every major field of research concerning sex offenders and sexual offenses and provides evidence of bad practices and policies in many places (and shows why they are bad) and of good ones in a few. Intellectually honest politicians should read this book.

Michael Tonry, LL.B,
Marvin J. Sonosky Professor of Law and Public Policy
University of Minnesota Law School

Acknowledgements

No volume this exhaustive, dealing with such emotionally charged subject matter, would be possible without a stellar cast of contributors, supporters, and colleagues. My deepest gratitude goes to Jennifer Perillo, my publisher at Springer. Thank you for your vision, your faith in my approach, your patience, and your overall tremendous positive nature. I wish all authors and editors would have the great fortune of working with you. Without your vision and initiative, this important work would not have happened.

This volume includes a plethora of gifted and brilliant scholars. They are both my colleagues and intellectuals I look up to. I am very appreciative of their commitment to the issue of sexual violence prevention and their willingness to take on this project. A heartfelt thank you to Karen Terry, Alissa Ackerman, Lisa Sample, Mary Evans, Jill Levenson, Rachel Bandy, Francis Williams, Michelle Meloy, Shareda Coleman, Charles Scott, Elena del Busto, Corey Rayburn Yung, Jo-Ann Della Giustina, Kim English, Andrew Harris, Cheryl Radeloff, Erica Carnes, and Patricia Wetterling. It is my sincere hope that we will continue our intellectual and scholarly paths to ending sexual violence.

I am very grateful to the support of Bridgewater State College. The support provided by the Center for the Advancement of Research and Teaching (CART), the Adrian Tinsley Program (ATP), the Office of Academic Affairs, and particularly former Vice President Ron Pitt, and the college as a whole, has been a vital part of this endeavor. A special appreciation goes to the Criminal Justice Department and most notably, Moira O'Brien, Meghan Chase, and Michelle Cubellis. As undergraduate students who assisted with this research, both Ms. Chase and Ms. Cubellis represent the best of our program. I was privileged to be your mentor, and I look forward to seeing how you change the world. Maybe I'll get to work on your book in a few years.

No editor is worth his salt without another critical pair of eyes. I am very appreciative to Barry Phillips for his help in editing my chapters. Thanks also to Nancy Ryan for her personal encouragement. Thanks are due to Carol Rose, John Reinstein, Norma Shapiro, Ann Lambert, and the Massachusetts Chapter of the American Civil Liberties Union. In this era of American history, the importance and role of the ACLU cannot be understated. A past-due thank to you Carole Upshur, who guided me through the process of becoming a scholar.

I am very appreciative of the assistance of Todd Shuster of the Zachary Shuster Harmsworth Literary Agency in making this work appear in print. Of course, no work such as this is possible without the lifetime guidance and support of one's parents. To my mother, Gertrude Wright, I offer a perpetual, humble, thank you.

Finally, it is my deepest hope to all of those who have been victims of sexual violence: This book was intended to validate your pain and loss and to call for logic, reason, patience, justice, and persistence to guide the government's response. Government's foremost responsibility is to keep people safe. We hope this book will aid in that pursuit.

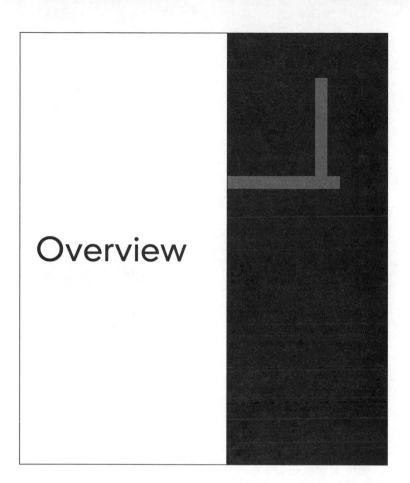

Overview

Introduction: The Failure of Sex Offender Policies

Richard G. Wright

1

The right to control one's body is one of the most fundamental, meaningful, and important human rights. How to respond when that right is violated by force, coercion, or threats is one of the most critical decisions that a government must make. In the United States, the sexual violation of children, adolescents, or adults is an all-too-common experience. Millions of women, children, and men have been sexually violated at some point in time. Yet, American policy responses to prevent or address sexual offending, particularly those enacted within the last twenty years, have largely failed. They have not done any of the following:

- reduced sex offenders' recidivism rates;
- provided safety, healing, or support for victims;

■ reflected the scientific research on sexual victimization, offending, and risk; or
■ provided successful strategies for prevention.

The central thesis of this work is that these policies have
failed by choice. Policymakers choose to focus on the most
heinous sex offenders while ignoring the most common
sexual threats that people face. Policymakers are disproportionately influenced by isolated, high-profile cases of sexual
assault committed by strangers, to the neglect of the everyday sexual violence committed by known and familiar family, friends, and acquaintances. This choice gives lawmakers
simple and clear political benefits but overall has made the
public less safe.

Misguided Policies

As is documented throughout this book, policymakers
have chosen to allow sex offender laws to be driven by the
demonization of offenders, devastating grief experienced by
a subset of victims, exaggerated claims by law enforcement,
and media depictions of the most extreme and heinous
sexual assaults. As a result of this choice, a tremendously
expensive criminal justice apparatus has been created, victims have been deprived of resources that could aid their
recovery, and efforts to treat and manage offenders have
been undermined.

A dominant factor in the passage of these inefficacious
sex offender laws is the impact of the tragic, high-profile,
stranger-predator sexual assault. Thirty years' worth of
research has shown that sexual victimization occurs primarily in the context of a preexisting relationship. This research,
described thoroughly in chapter 2, shows that the greatest risk
of sexual violation comes from one's partner, mother, father,
sister, brother, family member, or family friend. As horrific
as stranger-predator assaults are, they are far less common
than violence committed by an intimate assailant. To the det-
riment of society, stranger-predator assaults are the guiding
force behind today's ineffective sex offender laws.

As discussed throughout this text, although the
details vary, a common script can be found in the enactment of these laws. Typically, the process begins with an

influential criminal case involving the horrific abduction of a child or woman by a previously convicted sex offender, who then rapes, brutalizes, and murders the victim. Local and national media—particularly television—sensationalize the case and demonize the alleged offender. Once the identity of the perpetrator is known and proven, law enforcement officials, prosecutors, and legislators state definitively that new and amended laws would have prevented the murder from occurring. Authoritative claims are made that with legislative action, no child will be harmed in the future and offenders will be severely punished and prevented from further offenses. Grieving parents and survivors are asked to support the legislation, and many channel their trauma into the cause. New and amended sex offender laws are introduced with minimal debate, and no effective opposition is voiced, with those who do promote moderation dismissed as being soft on pedophiles. Federal and state laws are then enacted, memorialized by the name of the victim of the originating tragedy.

Cases such as the sexualized murders and abductions of Jessica Lunsford, Sarah Lunde, Polly Klaas, Megan Kanka, Alexandra Zapp, and Jetseta Gage involved all or portions of this pattern. There can be no doubt that these stranger-predator sexual attacks are horrific, tragic, and devastating. Yet in the face of such pain, the government has a responsibility to enact the laws that have the greatest chance of success. Unlike our current approach, these laws must balance grief with evidence, pain with fairness, anger with reason, and the desire for vengeance with a plan for prevention.

The Need for Effective Leadership

The government plays a critical role in defining, detecting, and punishing sexual deviance. Legislative efforts at controlling sexual behavior, scholars have noted, are strongly correlated with the mores, ethics, politics, and social conventions of each era (D'Emilio & Freedman, 1998; Jenkins, 2001). Although laws aimed at sex offenders can be traced back to the origin of the nation, the modern effort at identification of those deemed sexually dangerous began in earnest in the 1930s and '40s (Leib, 2003; Meloy, Saleh, & Wolff, 2007).

Some scholars have argued that there have been three waves of sex offender laws (Lieb, Quinsey, & Berliner, 1998). The current era of these laws began in 1994, when the Violent Crime Control and Law Enforcement Act included the Jacob Wetterling Crimes Against Children and Sexually Violent Offender Registration Act (Windlesham, 1998). This was the first federal law upon which sex offender registration and notification programs were established. The Wetterling Act was amended a number of times to include mandatory community notification provisions, a national database of registered sex offenders, and a requirement that appropriate college students register (Wright, 2004).

The Wetterling Act was superseded in 2006 by the Adam Walsh Child Protection and Safety Act, Public Law 109-248. Although the scholarly literature on the Walsh Act is scant due its newness, some authors have argued that it is a tremendously harmful expansion of federal power (Chaffin, 2008; Young, 2008; Wright, 2008). Among the numerous points within the Walsh Act are these:

- a federal requirement that states register juveniles over the age of 14 adjudicated for a sex offense;
- a conviction-based scheme distinguishing low, medium, and high-risk offenders;
- an expansion of mandatory sentences for federal sex offenders;
- an increasing role for the federal government, specifically the U.S. Marshals, in locating unregistered sex offenders (109th Congress, 2006).

According to Levinson and D'Amaro, the most common sex offender policies in use include registration, community notification, civil commitment, residence restrictions, and electronic surveillance (Levenson & D'Amaro, 2007). Meloy et al. (2007) concur with the assessment that civil commitment, registration, and notification have become common legislative responses. Yet states have gone well beyond that package of tools. States have also enacted laws requiring mandatory HIV testing of (in some cases, alleged) sex offenders; laws permitting chemical and surgical castration; and, as of July 2008, unconstitutional laws authorizing the execution of sex offenders. The scope of sex offender legislation has also reached through the Internet. As discussed in Chapter

Five, the federal government's creation of an "enticement" charge allows for proactive undercover policing to prevent sex offenders from recruiting children online. Additionally, the government has begun to use preventive detention to arrest alleged offenders before they commit a crime. With all these laws dedicated exclusively to sex offenders, this book seeks to answer one question: Are they effective?

Choosing Sensationalism Over Substance

Legislators often accept inaccurate depictions of the causes and motivations of sex offenders. In their examination of Illinois legislators' views of sex offender laws, Sample and Kadleck (2008) reported that much of legislators' understanding of sex offenders comes from mainstream media depictions, particularly those reported in the news. Their findings are consistent with Wright's interviews with Massachusetts policymakers on their sex offender laws (Wright, 2004). Levenson and D'Amaro (2007) also noted the critical role that media play in the construction, framing, and understanding of sexual offending, as did Wright's chapter on Internet sex stings.

In his commentary on juvenile sex offender laws, Chaffin (2008) argued that policymakers routinely choose to ignore empirical evidence in pursuit of punitive, simplistic policies designed to win political points. Chaffin argued that the enactment of the Walsh Act's requirement that states subject juveniles over the age of 14 to the same registration and notification mandates as adults is directly contradictory to the research findings, which point to improvements in treatments and recidivism of juvenile sex offenders. Chaffin argued that policymakers' motivations may include satisfying a public desire for revenge, or simply using these punishments as a general deterrent. He concluded his analysis with the belief that these policies have ostracized children and made their rehabilitation and recovery much more difficult.

Even with the enormous disconnect between public policy and sexual assault research, many of those who must implement these sex offender laws are trying to make them work. Meloy and colleagues (2007) noted that since this era of sex offender laws, states have varied significantly in their approaches. In their examination of eight states, Meloy et al.

reported that Vermont, Washington, Colorado, and Texas have distinguished themselves in numerous ways. Most importantly, several of these states rely on risk-assessment analysis in delineating sex offenders' dangerousness, and they integrate clinical and empirical research continually in the policy process. Terry and Ackerman's examination of Colorado, Minnesota, and Washington State in chapter 13 provides a discussion of how some states have used this era of big-government sex offender laws to incorporate critically and thoughtfully the issues of dangerousness, recidivism, and treatment.

Narrative and Structure of This Volume

This book is divided into three sections. Part 1 provides an overview of sexual assault's prevalence, incidence, and patterns; and empirical findings of the last twenty years of research on sexual assault. Specifically in chapter 1, Wright discusses the tragic and powerful impacts of sexual assault, the critical need for effective government response, and the major flaws with contemporary sex offender policies. Wright identifies several common factors influencing the passage of sex offender laws. These include an overreliance on less common, high-profile, stranger-initiated sexual assaults and murders; quick legislative action; and exaggerated claims from law enforcement about the preventive aspects of future legislation. Additionally, Wright discusses how the unmitigated pain and grief of survivors affect the policy-making process and policymakers' selective use of often-inaccurate statistics to enact and justify stranger-based sexual assault laws.

In chapter 2, Williams summarizes what researchers know about sexual assault and victimization. He looks at the national data provided by the Uniform Crime Reports, the National Crime Victimization Survey, and the National Violence Against Women Survey. Through Williams's analysis of sexual assault data and seminal studies, one of the fundamental flaws of sex offender legislation becomes apparent. His review, consistent with numerous other studies, finds that most sexual assaults are committed by someone who had a pre-existing relationship with the victim. In essence, most sexual assaults occur within a context of a relationship. The stranger-based sexual assault is a tragic, devastating, but low-frequency event. The data show that husbands, boyfriends, uncles, aunts, mothers, family friends, and dating partners represent a greater threat of sexual violence than do the stranger-predator for whom legislation is developed.

Williams also summarizes recent research on the efficacy of treatment and on specific issues associated with sexual offenses committed by juveniles and female offenders. In doing so, he provides an overview of a central issue in the sex offender debate: the question of differences among sex offenders. Critics of sex offender laws often argue that the laws are overly broad and make poor, if any, distinctions amongst sex offenders, thus overinflating the dangerousness of most (Lieb, Quinsey, & Berliner, 1998; Meloy et al., 2007; Levenson & D'Amaro, 2007; Wright, 2008; Chaffin, 2008).

In chapter 3, Terry and Ackerman analyze the evolution of major sex offender laws. They provide the historical context with an examination of early sexual psychopath laws and continue their analysis up to the 2006 passage of the Walsh Act. With their review of the voluminous literature, they provide a comprehensive understanding of the general lack of empirical support for these policies. As Welchans noted in her 2005 article on evaluations of twelve state sex offender registries, there is a disconnect between public perception and empirical efficacy. She noted that although the general public approves of the laws, there is little to no evidence of their impact in reducing recidivism. Terry and Ackerman expand on Welchans's assessments.

As with the formation of all criminal justice policies, there is an appropriate and important place for the stories, words, and experiences of victims. A common criticism of sex offender laws, however, is that policymakers have allowed a subset of victims and their tragic, heartbreaking cases to define national policy (Wright, 2004; Zgoba, 2004; Sample & Kadleck, 2008). Effective policy should balance the stories and pain of the victims with empirical evidence and evaluated best practices.

One of the most important voices in the recent sex offender debate has been Patricia (Patty) Wetterling, who, with her husband Jerry, went through the tragic and devastating experience of having their 11-year-old son, Jacob, abducted near their home in Minnesota in 1989. With their son still missing, Patty Wetterling has spent the last twenty years of her life working to end sexual violence. Chapter 4 represents Patty Wetterling in her own words. In a question-and-answer interview with this volume's editor, Ms. Wetterling discusses why these laws are enacted despite their focus on the lower-frequency stranger assault, the interface between distraught victims and policymakers, her and her family's experiences during the trauma and recovery from Jacob's disappearance, and her current work in sexual assault prevention.

Part 2 of this volume presents the evidence—the controversial, legal, and policy issues associated with specific sex offender laws. This section expands the current literature in several areas. Wright's exploratory examination of Internet sex stings in chapter 5 presents a thorough assessment of a new and complex investigative and policy tool. As he discusses, the federal government and the states created a crime known as "enticement" to allow police agencies to prevent sex offenders from using the Internet to meet and potentially assault children. Because of this legislation, law enforcement officials have utilized their undercover expertise to identify and arrest would-be sex offenders. This approach, Wright notes, is fraught with ethical problems. He argues that this strategy, well-meaning though it is, represents a form of preventive detention and net widening justified by the heinous actions of a few.

In chapter 6, Radeloff and Carnes examine an often-ignored set of sex offender laws: mandatory HIV testing and intentional transmission of HIV. With 46 of 50 states passing statutes that require those accused (or convicted) of sex crimes to undergo an HIV test, it is clear that this is a commonly used sex offender policy. Radeloff and Carnes's examination is, to the editor's knowledge, one of the first to appear in the criminological and sociological literature. They frame this issue with a review of other policy efforts at mandatory HIV testing, with an analytic look at the experiences of pregnant women and sex workers. Radeloff and Carnes raise the numerous privacy concerns of mandatory HIV testing. Turning their attention to sex offenders, they examine the issues of victim notification, due process, and the conflict between solid public health practices and the criminal justice approach. Through Radeloff and Carnes's chapter, it is apparent that this widespread policy deserves further empirical and analytic evaluation.

As previously mentioned, federal sex offender laws were expanded with the 2006 passage of the Walsh Act. Sample and Evans's chapter 7 takes a detailed look at one major provision of the new law: the Sex Offender Registration & Notification Act (SORNA). They include a discussion on the final SORNA guidelines published by Attorney General Michael Mukasey in July 2008. Sample and Evans also discuss the numerous studies on the limited and sometimes negative impact of sex offender registration and notification.

A relatively recent trend in state-level policy initiatives has been the passage of laws requiring offenders to be electronically monitored upon their probationary or parole release. In chapter 8, Meloy and Coleman review the findings about the impact of electronic monitoring, also known as GPS (Global Positioning Satellite) monitoring. They report that there are still significant issues with GPS monitoring, including public misperception, exaggerated promises from law enforcement, probation and parole, lag time, and overutilization. They conclude that, within the appropriate probation and parole settings, GPS monitoring can be an effective tool in sex offender management.

Perhaps the most popular and empirically ineffective sex offender policy is that of residence restrictions. These laws, which have been enacted at the city, county and state level, restrict where sex offenders may live. Although they vary in their specific range, these statues generally limit offenders to living outside 1,000 feet from a school, park, public pool, or other place children may congregate. In chapter 9, Levenson provides a candid discussion of residence restrictions, their efficacy, and their unintended consequences. Examining numerous local, county, and state efforts, Levenson provides the reader with a well-documented conclusion that despite their growing popularity, these laws are divisive and counterproductive. Levenson also examines the impact of these laws on offenders' ability to reintegrate and on their attempts at living an offense-free life.

As noted earlier, reliable evidence exists that another controversial set of sex offender laws may be appropriate for select offenders but is overutilized in its current form. In chapter 10, Scott and del Busto discuss state laws on chemical and surgical castration. The authors review the historical role of castration in sexual assault prevention, the biological basis for the laws, the biochemical impact on offenders, and the associated legal issues. Similar to the issues raised in Radeloff and Carnes's chapter on mandatory HIV testing, Scott and del Busto discuss the conflicts that exist between the medical community's views on the role of castration and the demands of public safety policies. Their assessment concludes that in select conditions, with a defined subgroup of offenders, castration may be an effective management strategy.

In chapter 11, Harris provides a comprehensive analysis of civil commitment legislation. Initiated in 1990 in Washington State, these laws provide for the perpetual detention of sex offenders after their criminal sentence has been completed. With the 1997 Supreme Court ruling in *Kansas v. Hendricks* upholding the constitutionality of these laws, numerous states enacted statutes focusing on the most dangerous sex offenders. As Harris notes, these states have varying criteria to determine what constitutes a "sexually violent predator" eligible for civil commitment. Harris also examines the conflict between the treatment goals of the psychiatric community and the detention demands of the criminal justice apparatus. Harris concludes his analysis with a discussion of the costs of civil commitment and the long-term viability of the policy.

In the final chapter of Part 2, Rayburn Yung discusses the timely and recent issue of the execution of sex offenders. As of 2008, six states had expanded their capital punishment statues to allow for the execution of those convicted of child rape. This policy trend was an apparent direct challenge to the Supreme Court's 1977 ruling in *Coker v. Georgia* that such laws were an unconstitutionally disproportionate punishment. Rayburn Yung discusses the Supreme Court's 2008 ruling in *Kennedy v. Louisiana*, upholding its previous decision, that these existing state statutes are unconstitutional. Rayburn Yung also discusses why many victims and victim advocates oppose expanding the death penalty to include sex offenders.

Having documented the generally poor efficacy of sex offender laws, the book examines policy alternatives in its final section. Specifically, it examines state leaders in sexual offense management, the viability of the containment model, preliminary assessments of if and how restorative justice may fit in sex offender management, and the still-unmet needs of sexual assault victims.

Terry and Ackerman return in chapter 13 to examine a handful of visionary states and programs. The authors demonstrate that Washington State, Minnesota, and Colorado turned the demands of the federal mandate into a push for empirically driven laws balanced with victim input. Since some of their efforts predated the 1994 Wetterling Act, these states have also demonstrated leadership and vision in sexual assault prevention, offending, and treatment.

The authors do not limit their discussions to state efforts. They examine the Center for Sex Offender Management, an initiative of the federal government. This training and technical assistance center utilizes research and evaluation in helping communities implement thoughtful sex offender management programs. Additionally, Terry and Ackerman profile Stop It *Now!*, a sexual abuse prevention program based in a public health framework. Summarizing the evaluative literature on this approach, they demonstrate that in the face of punitive, overreaching laws, some communities are implementing and evaluating risk-based clinically and legally sound alternatives.

In chapter 14, English discusses the containment model, a policy approach in use in select communities. This approach focuses on victim safety, interagency collaboration, and risk assessment. English provides the reader with evaluative evidence that the containment model does reduce offender recidivism.

Given the numerous problems with today's legislative onslaught, Della Giustina examines if, why, and how restorative justice can be used in addressing sexual violence. Chapter 15's examination of restorative justice and sex offending begins with an overview of the restorative justice model and its approach. The author provides insight into how reintegrative shaming may impact victims' recovery and enhance offender accountability. Given the numerous practical and ethical limits in using restorative justice in sexual offending, Della Giustina provides an interesting template for practitioners and researchers to develop and assess.

As noted earlier in discussion of chapter 4's interview with Patty Wetterling, the voices of sexual assault victims and their families are critically important in policy planning and implementation. Effective policy making includes victims and their advocates and seeks to balance their hurt and needs with constitutional limits, empirical evidence, budgetary constraints, and the input of law enforcement and the criminal justice community. In the concluding chapter, 16, Bandy provides an illuminative discussion of the unmet needs of sexual assault victims. Through interviews with advocates, victims, and victim service agencies, Bandy documents that many of those directly affected by sex offender laws do not find the laws particularly helpful. Bandy provides evidence that victims and victim advocates find sex offender laws a distraction from the dominant issues of intimate-partner and familial sexual assault. Bandy's chapter reminds the reader of the needs sexual assault victims still have and the critical importance of evidence-based policy.

It is the authors' hope that this volume of essays will help improve the United States' ability to prevent and respond to sexual assault. Given how tragic rape and molestation are, it is critical that government efforts become more effective. We believe that by incorporating the empirical evidence and the voices of all victims, and balancing those with constitutional protections, budgetary constraints, and a long-term holistic approach, sexual violence can be reduced and prevented. The U.S. government has a responsibility to make victims, their families, and their allies safer.

References

Adam Walsh Child Protection and Safety Act of 2006, Pub. L. No. 109-248. 64.

Chaffin, M. (2008). Our minds are made up—don't confuse us with the facts: Commentary on policies concerning children with sexual behavior problems and juvenile sex offenders. *Child Maltreatment, 13* (2), 110–121.

D'Emilio, J., & Freedman, E. B. (1998). *Intimate Matters: A History of Sexuality in America* (2nd ed.). Chicago: University of Chicago Press.

Jenkins, P. (2001). *Beyond Tolerance: Child Pornography on the Internet.* New York: New York University Press.

Leib, R. (2003). State policy perspectives on sexual predator laws. In B. J. Winick & J. Q. LaFond (Eds.), *Protecting Society From Sexually Dangerous Offenders* (pp. 41–60). Washington, DC: American Psychological Association.

Levenson, J. S., & D'Amaro, D. A. (2007). Social policies designed to prevent sexual violence: The emperors' new clothes. *Criminal Justice Policy Review, 18* (2), 168–199.

Lieb, R., Quinsey, R., & Berliner, L. (1998). Sexual predators and social policy (M. Tonry, Ed.). *Crime and Justice: A Review of Research, 23,* 43–114.

Meloy, M. L., Saleh, Y., & Wolff, N. (2007). Sex offender laws in America: Can panic-driven legislation ever create safer societies? *Criminal Justice Studies, 20* (4), 423–443.

Sample, L. L., & Kadleck, C. (2008). Sex offender laws: Legislators' account of the need for policy. *Criminal Justice Policy Review, 19* (1), 40–62.

Welchans, S. (2005). Megan's law: Evaluations of sexual offender registries. *Criminal Justice Policy Review, 16* (2), 123–140.

Windlesham, L. (1998). *Politics, Punishment and Populism*. New York: Oxford University Press.

Wright, R. G. (2004). *Protection or Illusion: A Policy Analysis of Massachusetts & Federal Sex Offender Legislation*. Doctoral Dissertation, University of Massachusetts Boston 2004.

Wright, R. G. (2008). Sex offender post-incarceration sanctions: Are there any limits? *New England Journal of Criminal and Civil Confinement, 34* (1), 17–50.

Young, C. (2008). Children sex offenders: How the Adam Walsh Child Protection and Safety Act hurts the same children it is trying to protect. *New England Journal of Criminal and Civil Confinement, 34* (2), 459–484.

Zgoba, K. M. (2004). Spin doctors and moral crusaders: The moral panic behind child safety legislation. *Criminal Justice Studies, 17* (4), 384–404.

2

The Problem of Sexual Assault

Francis M. Williams

This chapter summarizes major empirical data and studies on sexual assault prevalence and treatment for sex offenders and includes a discussion about issues associated with special sex offender populations (i.e., juvenile and female sex offenders). Forms of sexual assault include forcible rape, sodomy, child molestation, incest, fondling, and attempted rape. In many jurisdictions, *sexual assault* has replaced the term *rape* in most state statutes, acquiescing to the trend of defining terms with a gender-neutral approach.

Sex offender legislation is built on nonscientific premises that are skewed by public perceptions that all sex offenders are the same, that they reoffend at extremely high rates, that treatment does not work, and most importantly that most sexual assaults are committed by strangers—implying that if the public knew who the offenders were, the assaults would not occur. Almost 40 years of research into sexual victimization and offending debunk these premises. Equally as troubling is that nearly all U.S. sex offender laws are not only based on anecdotal high-profile tragedies but also go against the scientific findings on sexual victimization and perpetration.

All sex offenders are not the same; in fact, they are a heterogeneous population (Groth, Longo, & McFadin, 1982). Juveniles constitute a reasonable share of the sex offender population, according to nationwide arrest statistics, and female sex offenders represent a growing population (Vandiver & Teske, 2006). Public recognition that men can be sexual assault victims and women can be perpetrators has more recently generated closer scrutiny. The recidivism rate is relatively low for sex offenders who reoffend sexually, but it is higher for those who fail to complete treatment (Hanson & Bussiere, 1998).

There are four critical questions that this chapter addresses: What is known about sexual assault victimization? What is known about sexual assault perpetration? Does the recidivism of sex offenders justify the need for additional sex offender-specific policies? And, how effective or ineffective is sex offender treatment? These questions are addressed by presenting data and studies that have analyzed patterns of sexual victimization, sex offender recidivism, and the efficacy of treatment for both adult and juvenile offenders.

Sexual Assault Victimization

National Data

The feminist movements of the 1970s gave public voice to issues of adult sexual and domestic violence. As the political dialogue on sexual assault grew, the academic community documented previously unknown levels of abuse. One of the first seminal studies was Russell's San Francisco study. It revealed that 24% of adult women had experienced a completed rape, with 44% experiencing a completed or attempted rape (Russell, 1983, 1984). Subsequently, in a random national survey of 6,159 college women, Koss, Gidycz, and Wisniewski (1987) found that 84% of women knew their attacker, estimating that one in four women had experienced rape or attempted rape.

The Uniform Crime Report (UCR) categorizes forcible rape under the violent crimes index and categorizes sex offenses (except forcible rape and prostitution) under Part II offenses. The UCR defines forcible rape as "having carnal knowledge of a female forcibly and against her will." Assaults and attempted rape by force or threat of force are also included in this category. Preliminary 2007 UCR data (for law enforcement agencies with over 100,000 population) indicated a 2.7% drop in the number of forcible rapes (n = 92,445) reported in 2006.

A second source of sexual assault data is the National Crime Victimization Survey (NCVS). There has been a steady decline in the number of victims of sexual assault as reported in the NCVS between the years 1996 and 2006, from a high of more than 370,000 in 1999 to just fewer than 260,000 in 2006 (U.S. Department of Justice, 2006). The decline in sexual assault victimization mirrors the overall decline in violent crime victimization during the same time period, which shows a precipitous decline from over 9.5 million in 1996 to just over 6 million in 2006 (Ibid).

Sexual assault is a serious social problem that affects almost "18 million women and almost 3 million men in the United States" (Tjaden & Thoennes, 2006, p. iii). Young people, particularly young women, are being victimized at alarming rates. The 1995–1996 National Violence Against Women (NVAW) Survey reported "younger women were significantly more likely to report being raped at some time in their lives than older women" (Ibid). The report used a definition of rape that includes attempted and completed vaginal, oral, and anal penetration achieved through the use of force.

This report also found that "one of every six women has been raped at some time and that in a single year more than 300,000 women and almost 93,000 men are estimated to have been raped" (Tjaden & Thoennes, 2006, p. iii). Other significant findings from the National Violence Against Women (NVAW) report included the following: 95–96% of those who have been victimized were assaulted as children; being raped as a minor increased the probability for adulthood rape; intimate partner rape perpetrated by males on females resulted in significantly more injuries to the victim; and rape is still underreported. The satisfaction level from rape victims' contacts with police was only about 50% (Tjaden & Thoennes, 2006). The report affirms the nature of the crime as one that is mostly perpetrated against women and children and one in which most female rape victims (83.3%) and male rape victims (71.2%) know their assailant.

Children as Victims

The available information paints a disconcerting picture of sexual assault on minor children by nonstrangers; this includes family, relatives, or close family friends. The National Child Abuse and Neglect Data System (NCANDS) reported that almost 10% (9.3%) of the victims of substantiated child maltreatment cases suffered sexual abuse (U. S. Department of Health and Human Services, 2005). Using data drawn from the national Developmental Victimization Survey (DVS), Finkelhor, Ormrod, Turner, and Hamby (2005) reported that of the children and youth between the ages of 12 and 17 years, 1 in 12 (82 per 1,000) were victimized by a sexual assault. Teenagers were disproportionately victimized compared to adults, and the majority of these perpetrations were committed by acquaintances. Finkelhor and Jones (2006) later noted that there has been a consistent decline in substantiated child sexual abuse cases.

Finkelhor and Jones (2006) reviewed possible explanations for the decline of various forms of child maltreatment and victimization between 1993 and 2004 many of which included incidents of sexual abuse and sexual assault. Paralleling other crimes, the authors noted that sexual abuse declined 49% between 1990 and 2004. Sexual assault of teenagers dropped 67% between 1993 and 2004, with the subgroup of sexual assaults by known persons down even more. The authors concluded that "they [the decreases] probably reflect at least in part a real decline in sexual abuse" (p. 688). Finkelhor and Jones (2006) further proposed explanations for these declines with the caveat that little empirical evidence is available to evaluate any of the factors. They first ruled out demographic changes and capital punishment policies as being relevant to juvenile victimization, mainly because their effect on child victimization is not leveraged by research. Two other factors, gun control policies and the crack cocaine epidemic, were considered relevant only to juvenile homicide and possibly robbery trends. The authors found more plausible factors such as the impact of abortion legislation, improvement in the economy, growth in imprisonment and other serious legal sanctions, and hiring of more police and agents of social intervention.

Victim–Offender Relationship

Data from the 2005 National Crime Victimization Survey showed that 73% (128,440) of female sexual assault victims were assaulted by someone they knew (U.S. Department of Justice, 2005). Among those known assailants, 38% (66,580) of the women were assaulted by a friend or acquaintance, and 28% of the assaults were committed by intimate partners (Catalano, 2006). The survey showed that nonstranger sexual assaults (123,010) were nearly twice as frequent as stranger sexual assaults (68,670). The NCVS repeatedly finds that the majority of sexual assaults are committed by intimate and known assailants (Catalano, 2006).

Tjaden and Thoennes (2006) noted that 22.8% of male victims and 16.7% of female victims were raped by a stranger. Where males are generally raped by friends, teachers, coworkers or neighbors, females generally tend to be raped by spouses, cohabiting partners, dates, boyfriends, and girlfriends. Overall, 43% of all female and 9% of all male rape victims were raped by some type of current or former intimate partner. Nonspousal family members who perpetrated rape tended to do so while the victim was a child or adolescent. On the whole, females are at a significantly higher risk for rape than males.

Several studies have pointed out the high prevalence of sexual assault on college campuses, primarily known as acquaintance rape (Fisher, Cullen, & Turner, 2000; Koss, Gidycz, & Wisniewski, 1987; Muehlenhard & Linton, 1987). It has been estimated that one fourth of college women are victims of attempted rape or a committed rape (Koss et al., 1987). Alternately, it has been estimated that one fourth of college men have engaged in some form of sexually coercive behavior—actions that are consistent with rape or attempted rape—reemphasizing the patterns of known relationships between victims and offenders (Abbey, McAuslan, & Ross, 1998; Koss et al., 1987). In response to campus sexual assault patterns, Congress enacted several laws (e.g., the Student Right-to-Know and Campus Security Act of 1990 [The Clery Act] and the Campus Sexual Assault Victims' Bill of Rights of 1992) requiring institutions of higher education to notify students about crime on campus, publicize their prevention and response policies, maintain open crime logs, and ensure sexual assault victims their basic rights.

The victim–offender relationship has been shown to be a key factor for violence, depressive symptomatology, and other pervasive mental health disorders, such as PTSD, substance abuse, fearfulness, and other somatic complaints (Browning & Laumann, 1997; Campbell & Soeken, 1999a, 1999b; Cascardi, Riggs, Hearst-Ikeda, & Foa, 1996; DeMaris & Kaukinen, 2005; DeMaris & Swinford, 1996; Harrison, Fulkerson, & Beebe, 1997; Jasinski et al., 2000; Kilpatrick et al., 1987; Miller, Monson & Norton, 1995; Saunders et al., 1999; Stermac, Du Mont, & Dunn, 1998; Ullman & Brecklin, 2003). For example, a study of 700 women who had been violently victimized found more reports of depressive symptoms when the assailant was known to the victim.

Whether the assault occurred when the victim was a child or adolescent had no consequences on overall victim health (DeMaris & Kaukinen, 2005). Contradicting those findings is Ullman and Brecklin's 2003 study. They reported that women with both childhood and adult sexual assaults had more recent chronic medical conditions than women with assault in adulthood or childhood alone. Their subsample (n = 474) of women who had been assaulted in both life stages showed contact with health professionals for mental health/substance abuse issues over their lifetime was significantly more likely. In addition, combined child/adult victims diagnosed with PTSD and those with stressful life events had more chronic medical conditions.

Browning and Laumann (1997) found that women who experience child-adult sexual contact are more sexually active in both adolescence and adulthood, have sex at an earlier age and are more likely to bear children before they turn 19, have substantially higher numbers of sexual partners, and are more likely to contract sexually transmitted infections and experience forced sex (p. 557). Harrison et al. (1997) examined the relationship between physical and sexual abuse and substance use patterns in adolescents and found that abuse victims "use a greater variety of substances, earlier initiation of substance use, and more frequent attempts to self-medicate painful emotions" (p. 536). DeMaris and Swinford (1996) found that attempted or completed forced sexual relations were positively related to increased fearfulness in women. Similarly Campbell and Soeken (1999) found in their study of 159 primarily

(77%) African American women who were forced to have sex by an intimate partner showed significant levels of depression and also had high scores on negative health and gynecological symptoms, and risk factors for homicide.

The Relationship between Childhood and Adult Victimization

A number of studies have found that sexual assault victimization as a child increases the probability of revictimization both as an adolescent and adult. For example, Gidycz, Coble, Latham, and Layman (1993), in their study of 927 female psychology students, found that victimization was correlated with child victimization. They reported that in 28.84% (n = 830) of the sample, an adult victimization was more likely in those who had experienced a childhood victimization. Additionally, an adult victimization was dependent on an adolescent victimization in 88.31% (n = 828) of the cases. They also found that women who were victimized in both childhood and adolescence had higher rates of victimization in adulthood, and reported a link between psychological functioning and victimization experiences.

Messman-Moore and Long (2000) examined the relationship between child sexual abuse (CSA) and revictimization in three forms: unwanted sexual contact, physical abuse, and psychological maltreatment. In their sample of 648 women, they found that "more than half of the CSAS (Child Sexual Abuse Survivors) reported some form of unwanted sexual contact in adulthood (52.3%), with 26.4 percent reporting unwanted sexual intercourse" (p. 496). Still others have also found a link between childhood sexual abuse and later sexual victimization (Arata & Lindman, 2002; Briere & Runtz, 1987; Chu & Dill, 1990; Fromuth, 1986; Kessler & Bieschke, 1999; Koss & Dinero, 1989; Merrill et al., 1999; Messman & Long, 1996; Russell, 1984; Wyatt, Guthrie, & Notgrass, 1992).

It appears that once victimized, the risk for revictimization or repeat victimization[i] is greater. In a review of the existing literature on sexual revictimization, Classen, Palesh, and Aggarwal (2005) note several key points:

■ CSA is a significant risk factor. Additionally, severity of previous victimization differentiates between those who are victimized and revictimized.

- Sexual assault during adolescence places a woman at greater risk during adulthood compared to the risk associated with CSA.
- The more recent the victimization, the higher the risk for revictimization.
- Cumulative trauma increases the likelihood of revictimization—CSA coupled with physical abuse increases revictimization risks.
- Ethnic minorities and those from dysfunctional families face increased risks.
- There are correlates between sexual revictimization and certain mental health problems, such as psychiatric disorders; addictions; and interpersonal, behavioral and cognitive functioning; in addition to increased feeling of shame, blame, powerlessness, and coping strategies.

Finkelhor, Ormrod, and Turner (2007) examined revictimization patterns in a national sample (1,467) of children aged 2–17. Of particular note is that the study's analysis of "poly-victims" (a subset of the children with high levels of different types of victimizations) indicated that this group was especially susceptible to increased risk for sexual victimization, child maltreatment, and virtually all other forms of victimization. The authors note a number of implications from the study of revictimization. Most prominent is the necessity to study children across the full spectrum of childhood, most notably age ranges, in order to inform a more holistic approach to public policy concerning child and youth victimization (Ibid). Similarly there is a need to examine victimization across racial and ethnic lines in order to better understand its impact on diverse populations.

Race and Ethnicity

Tjaden and Thoennes (2006) found that those most frequently victimized for rape/sexual assault are Native American women, which is consistent with other research. The study found that 17.6% of surveyed women and 3% of surveyed men were raped at some time in their lives. They concluded that 1 out of 6 American women have been the victim or attempted victim of a rape in their lifetime, as were 1 out of 33 men. As of the year the sample was generated (1995), 17.7 million American women and 2.8 million American men have been victims or attempted victims of a completed rape. Nine of every 10 rape victims were female. Although numbers show that about 80% of victims were white, minorities were somewhat more likely to be attacked (Ibid).

Siegel and Williams (2003), using data collected from 206 predominately urban, low-income, African American women, found that CSA prior to age 13 was not by itself a risk factor for adult victimization. Rather, those who were victimized later in adolescence in combination with CSA posed a much greater risk for adult victimization; however, other risk factors such as alcohol abuse and sexual behaviors (multiple sex partners) also influenced future victimization.

Kalof's (2000) study of 383 undergraduate women found that when verbal threats or pressure was applied, African American women had the highest incidence of forced intercourse, and Asian women had the lowest in this category. Hispanic women had the highest incidence of attempted rape, whereas African American women had the lowest. African American and white women were almost three times as likely as Hispanic women to have had experiences that met the legal definition of rape. In addition ethnicity interacted with both alcohol use and early extrafamilial sexual abuse; thus based on the victims ethnicity, extrafamilial sexual abuse and alcohol abuse has a different effect on subsequent experiences of attempted rape.

Male Sexual Assault Victimization

Recent research has allowed for closer scrutiny of adult male sexual assault patterns. Contrary to popular belief, rape of adult males does not only occur in prison, although its prevalence within penal institutions may be higher than elsewhere. Although most estimates put male sexual assault victimization at around 5% to 10%, there is reason to believe that this is not quite accurate (Forman, 1982; Kaufman, Jackson, Voorhees, & Christy, 1980). Stermac, Del Bove, and Addison (2004) suggested that the prevalence of sexual assault on males is higher than traditionally believed.

Using information from the Los Angeles Epidemiological Catchment Area Project (as cited in McConaghy & Zamir, 1995) Stermac, Del Bove, and Addison (2004) reported that 7.2% of the men were sexually assaulted after the age of 15, with 39% of these men reporting that they had been forced to have intercourse. Another study found that 16% of male college students reported having at least one incident of forced sex (Struckman-Johnson, 1988). Crisis center and hospital emergency room data indicate that males make up between 1% and 10% of all reports received (Kaufman et al., 1980). Another study of male survivors found that between 5% and 10% of all reported rapes in any given year involve male victims (Scarce, 1997).

Some studies reported that for men, young white males are the most frequent victims of sexual assaults. Stermac, Sheridan, Davidson and Dunn (1996) found that sexual assaults in large urban areas target young gay males and that coercive patterns of assault similar to those seen in acquaintance sexual assaults of females was evident. Frazier (1993) found that 58% of the young males in his study of victims in a hospital-based rape crisis program were white. In Groth and Burgess's (1980) study of 22 community male rape victims, all were white. These results obviously raise methodological issues given the limited samples. Many of these studies used self-report data that were affected by cultural and social constraints that make males reluctant to disclose rape victimization. Two notable studies reported that between 36% and 71% of males who were sexually assaulted had experienced previous victimization (Mezey & King, 1989; Myers, 1989).

In comparing male and female sexual assault victims, Kaufman et al (1980) found males to be younger, more likely to have physical injuries, more likely to have been a victim of an assault in which the perpetrators were gang members, and more likely to be more socially and economically unstable than females. Frasier (1993) found similarities in race, age, prior victimization, and likelihood to have been physically harmed, but men were more hostile and depressed than female victims. Lacey and Roberts (1991) also found that men were more likely to be assaulted by more than one assailant, with weapons more typically involved, and they were more likely to be orally assaulted.

Generally men are reluctant to report their sexual assault to authorities, leading to misinformation and underreporting of its prevalence. In male-on-male rape cases, heterosexual males in particular do not want to be labeled as "homosexual." These victims fear that reporting a sexual assault subjects them to ridicule and stigmatization. One study noted that only 5 of the 40 male rape victims in the study contacted the police after the rape (Walker, Archer, & Davies, 2005). Groth and Burgess (1980) suggested that males do not report sexual assault for three primary reasons: (1) males are supposed to be able to defend themselves, (2) their sexuality becomes suspect, and, (3) recalling and describing the event brings up uncomfortable emotions. Additionally, it is not uncommon for both law enforcement officials and the public at large to be skeptical about reports of male sexual assault unless these reports involve male children.

Male Prison Rape

The incidence of male prison rape has typically been viewed as a problem for homosexual convicts or even more broadly couched under the ideology of "just desserts"—inmates are getting what they deserve. Jones and Pratt (2008) have suggested that even early researchers dismissed the issue of sexual activity between male prisoners as either being consensual or situational. All agree it is the source of much institutional violence that results in both physical and psychological trauma for the victims.

There are two prevailing views about male prison sexual victimization. One is that it is an act of sexual deprivation caused by isolation from the opposite sex. However, this view is not supported by prison officials, criminological and psychological practitioners, academic scholars, or the prisoners themselves. Instead they feel it is much more complex than that. The other view is more consistent with sexual assault as an expression of power and control rather than sexual gratification. The psychological pain of prison life, the inability to pursue personal gratification, and the limited access to appropriate means to exert power all contribute to prison rape (Jones & Pratt, 2008).

Jones and Pratt note that the wide variations (1–21%) across prevalence studies can be traced to methodological issues that encompass differences in definitions, methods of obtaining data, and the prisons selected to study; and "a lack of differentiation between incidence rates and prevalence rates of sexual victimization" (p. 284). Using a criterion established by their investigation, Jones and Pratt argue that an inclusive definition of sexual violence does not just rely on self-reports, but it uses anonymous data collection procedures and makes an effort to include multiple facilities of different types. Relying on this criterion, their investigation revealed a prevalence rate of 20%, presenting corrections officials with significant health and safety problems (Jones & Pratt).

The Prison Rape Elimination Act of 2003 (P.L. 108-79), mandated a comprehensive statistical review and analysis of the incidence of prison rape. In December 2007, the BJS published *Sexual Victimization in State and Federal Prison Reported by Inmates*, which revealed that 1,330 inmates had experienced one or more incidents of sexual victimization (U.S. Department of Justice, 2007). Overall, 3.2% (n = 24,700) of local jail inmates are estimated to have experienced sexual victimization. Most distressing is that 2.0% (n = 15,200) reported an incident involving staff, with1.6% (n = 12,100) of the 2.0% reported an incident involving another inmate, and 0.4%[ii] reported being victimized by both staff and inmates. One important finding by the report was that sexual victimization was more strongly related to inmate characteristics (e.g., female, person of two or more races, age 18–24, inmate with higher education) than to facility characteristics (U.S. Department of Justice, 2007).[iii]

A major concern for men who are raped in prison is the high percentage of HIV transmission. Maruschak (2004) found that 1.9% of men incarcerated in state and federal prison are infected with HIV but suggested that the prevalence is higher. Much of the HIV transmission in prison is passed by rape and other forms of sexual victimization. In a study of HIV acquisition due to prison rape, Pinkerton, Galletly, and Seal (2007) noted that prison rape incidents often involve multiple perpetrators and in many cases cause serious injury to the victim, which increases the risk of HIV infection. The authors developed a model to assess the acquisition rate of HIV due to prison rape and found that "approximately 68.1% of the 1.4 million men incarcerated in U.S. prisons at the end of 2003 already have or will become infected with HIV as a consequence of prison rape" (p. 302).

In addition, the scant literature attending to adult male rape suggests that the consequences of sexual assault for men are just as distressing as for female survivors. According to one study, male victims reported feelings of shock, humiliation, embarrassment, and behavioral changes and rape-related phobias persisting for a number of years after the

assault. Almost half of the male rape survivors in this investigation met criteria for a diagnosis of posttraumatic stress
disorder (PTSD). Longer term emotional reactions included
increased anger and irritability, conflicting sexual orientation, loss of self-respect, and sexual dysfunction similar to
that experienced by female rape victims (Huckle, 1995).

Impact of Sexual Assault Victimization

Sexual assault victimization has numerous costs and consequences for the victim, the offender, their families, and
society at large. Economic and societal costs of sexual victimizations are exorbitant. Criminal justice costs of sexual
violence include those incurred for law enforcement, court
proceedings, personnel, public education, and incarceration of convicted offenders. The incidence of mental illness,
debilitating physical injuries, sexually transmitted diseases,
drug use, and increased risk for other types of crimes are
some of the associated human costs.

Cohen and Miller (1998) described a 1996 National
Institute of Justice (NIJ) study that found that rape had the
highest annual total victim costs ($127 billion at $87,000
per victimization) of any crime, ultimately creating a public
health and safety concern. The cost for each sexual assault
was determined to be $110,000. Since many rape victims
are subjected to more than one sexual assault, the cost per
rape is estimated to be $87,000. The cost per sexual assault
is estimated to include $500 for short-term medical care;
$2,400 for mental health services; $2,200 for lost productiv-
ity at work; and $104,900 for pain and suffering (Cohen &
Miller, 1998).

Cost distinctions are also found in research investigating
differences in how sexual assault affects racial and ethnic
groups. For example, one study reported that as a consequence of their sexual assault, white women are more likely
to engage in problem drinking and illicit drug use. Minority women also engage in illicit drug use and heavy epi-
sodic drinking; with African American women in particular,
these behaviors are used as coping strategies (Kaukinen &
DeMaris, 2005). Additionally, 19.5% of sexual assault victims
in 1990 lost work time costing them about $1,261 dollars with
acquaintance rape victims losing even more time (DeMaris
& Kaukinen, 2005).

Medical services for sexual assault victims vary widely. Typically these costs include the initial emergency medical care, pregnancy testing, HIV and sexually transmitted diseases (STD) testing and treatment, and possibly abortions due to unwanted, rape-induced pregnancies. Miller, Cohen & Rossman (1993) found that 43% of sexual assault victims showed evidence of sexually transmitted diseases that required treatment. Though the total costs of these services are unknown, many of them are serious and chronic.

Finally, victim services have sprung up in almost every jurisdiction. There are more than 2,000 of these services operating in the United States today, and millions of dollars are dispensed each year by the federal government for victim services. Through initiatives like the Victims of Crime Act (VOCA), funds are available for use for programs that work with victims of sexual assault, domestic violence, and child abuse. VOCA was established in 1984 and between the years 1986 and 2003, VOCA distributed $3,062,972,335 in victim assistance funds to the states.[iv]

Sexual Assault Perpetration

Who are the sex offenders, and what do we know about offending behavior? There is no single typology that fits all sex offenders, though some have similar characteristics; for instance, the majority of offenders are male. Because sexual assault is so underreported, it places restrictions on developing accurate offender data. Estimates of offending prevalence are attainable through mechanisms such as the Uniform Crime Reports (UCR) and the National Crime Victimization Survey (NCVS).

For the year 2006, the UCR recorded 92,455 cases of forcible rape; arrests for rape only totaled 24,535. Of this arrest number, the UCR showed a clearance rate (i.e., either arrested or cleared by exceptional means) of only 40.9% (U.S. Department of Justice, 2008). As these numbers imply, the majority of reported rapes are never solved. What the NCVS and UCR data do reveal is that the majority of those arrested for rape are young, typically under 25 years old.

The most recent data from the Bureau of Justice Statistics (U.S,. Department of Justice, 2006) revealed that in America's prisons and jails, 148,800 inmates were serving time for rape or sexual assault; of these, 147,100 were male and 1,700 were female. Whites represented 80,800 of this number, blacks constituted 41,900, and Hispanics accounted for another 23,300 of the total. At the end of 2006, 5,035,225 adult men and women were being supervised on probation (4,237,023) or parole (798,202). Three percent (n = 127,110) were on probation for a sexual assault. African American males tend to be overrepresented in rape cases processed through the criminal justice system. Belknap (2001) suggested this attribute exists as (1) a consequence of the percentage of white males who know their victim (rape victims are less likely to report these assaults when they know the perpetrator), and (2) black males being more susceptible to prosecution in the criminal justice system. These are not necessarily the prevailing views, but there is much support for both premises.

Perpetrator Characteristics

Some have argued that individual perpetrator characteristics and rape-supportive attitudes and beliefs are widely considered to be a product of a general cultural context that objectifies women and condones the use of force by men to obtain goals, including sexual conquest (Berkowitz, 1992; Burt, 1980; Kanin, 1985, in Loh, Gidycz, Lobo, & Luthra, 2005). Loh et al. (2005) explained that these individual "characteristics include differences in socialization experiences, beliefs and attitudes about sexuality, personality, and alcohol use that have been empirically determined or hypothesized to differentiate men who are sexually aggressive from their counterparts who are sexually nonaggressive" (p. 1326).

The idea that sexual assault is related to a need to satisfy an insatiable sexual drive does comport with the literature. The stereotype of the rapist who cannot control himself often fuels bad public policy. There is no single need that compels sex offenders to rape; in fact, most offend for multiple reasons. Most of these reasons are nonsexual.

Cohen, Seghorn, and Calmas (1969) identified four types of rapists: the compensatory, the displaced aggressive, the sex-aggression diffusion, and the impulse rapist. Each type represents categories based on the relative amounts of aggression and sex present in the offense. Amir (1971) identified several types of rapists based on aberrations of their personality or as those who commit rape as a "demand of the youth culture." Similarly, Rada (1978) classified rapists by personality disorders, noting five offender types: sociopathic, masculine identity conflict, situational stress, sadistic, and psychotic.

Groth (1979) used a classification system that was based on concepts of power, control, and sexuality, and identified four types. Groth concluded that men rape for three reasons: power, anger, and sadism, noting that the majority of men rape for power, to control and possess their victim. This model categorizes offender behavior and motivations as aspects of power reassurance, power assertive, anger-retaliatory, or anger excitation. Groth's model has been adapted by the National Center for the Analysis of Violent Crime (NCAVC) to describe offender behavior, which assists in profiling.

Berlin et al. (1997) examined motivational factors and identified six types of rapists; the *opportunistic rapist* has two sub-types: (1) has prominent narcissistic personality traits, and (2) has dependent personality traits. These personality types are the *angry rapist*, who rapes out of anger or frustration. The *developmentally impaired rapist* suffers from mental retardation or is developmentally impaired. The *psychotic rapist* has an independently confirmed history of major mental illness. The *paraphilic or sexually driven rapist* has recurrent cravings for coercive sex, and the sexual assaulter has been associated with *voyeurism*. Although this is rare, it may turn violent. Essentially the way the rape is classified is by its identified motivation: whether it was sexual or nonsexual, sadistic in nature, or motivated by anger, hate, power, and control; and whether it was planned or impulsive (Robertiello & Terry, 2007).

The most comprehensive typology was developed by Prentky, Knight, and Rosenberg (1988) and consists of a model with three categories identifying eight types (later modified to nine) of offenders. This model contains biological, psychological, and cultural components of human behavior and assesses (1) the aggression of the offense, (2) the meaning of sexuality in the offense, and (3) the impulsivity reflected in the history and lifestyle of the offender.

Sexually Violent Predators

Much of our knowledge about sex offenders comes from studies on incarcerated and/or civilly committed offenders.

A common critique of contemporary sex offender policies is that they are over-inclusive (e.g., they do not allow for important distinctions amongst sex offenders). These policies are typically drawn with one type of sex offender in mind, the sexually violent predator (SVP). SVPs are defined as persons who have been convicted of or charged with sexual violence; who suffer from a mental abnormality or personality disorder; and who, as a result of the mental abnormality or personality disorder, are likely to continue to engage in predatory acts of sexual violence. There is reason to be concerned about SVPs, for they are a special group. As one study showed, SVPs "have a greater proportion of paraphilias and personality disorders (including psychopathy), along with fewer serious mental illnesses, than do other committed populations and noncommitted sex offenders" (Jackson & Richards, 2007, p. 315). This study of 190 civilly committed sex offenders in Washington State revealed that this group is at a moderate to high level for reoffending. This unique group of sex offenders is more "psychiatrically compromised" and is at a higher risk of reoffending than average sex offenders (Jackson & Richards, 2007). However, sexually violent predators constitute a small share of those subject to sex offender laws.

Predictors of Sexual Assault Perpetration

Studies of nonincarcerated sex offenders typically examine predictors or risk factors for different types of sexual assault perpetration. Abbey, Parkhill, Clinton-Sherrod, and Zawacki's (2007) study of 163 men linked several variables as predictors of sexual assault perpetration. These variables include empathy, adult attachment, attitudes about casual sex, sexual dominance, alcohol consumption in sexual situations, and peer approval of forced sex. They found that there are differences in these predictors in perpetrators and nonperpetrators. For example, the authors reported that "as compared to non-assaulters, rapists were lower in empathy and adult attachment. Rapists had expectations for sex at an earlier stage in a relationship and more casual attitudes about sex. Rapists also were more motivated to have sex as a means of achieving power over women, more frequently consumed alcohol in sexual situations, and reported greater peer approval of forcing sex on women" (p. 1575).

Prior research has already characterized rapists as a heterogeneous group with a wide range of past experiences, personality characteristics, and offense styles (Prentky & Knight, 1991). Other predictor research has provided evidence to show that sexual assault perpetrators have consensual sex at an earlier age and have more dating and consensual sex partners than do nonperpetrators (Abbey et al., 1998; Koss & Dinero, 1989; Malamuth, Sockloskie, Koss, & Tanaka, 1991; Malamuth, Linz, Heavey, Barnes, & Acker, 1995; Senn, Desmarais, Verberg, & Wood, 2000). Although attitudes, personality, and life experiences influence sexual assault perpetration, men who have committed sexual assault do not do so on every possible occasion; instead, situational factors also play a role (Abbey et al., 1998).

Abbey and her colleagues conducted a number of studies with college students, examining the role of alcohol, misperception, and sexual assault (Abbey, Ross, McDuffie, & McAuslan, 1996); alcohol, sexual intent, and sexual beliefs and experiences (Abbey et al., 1998); alcohol expectancies regarding sex, aggression, and sexual vulnerability (Abbey, McAuslan, Ross, & Zawacki, 1999; Abbey, McAuslan, Zawacki, Clinton, & Buck, 2001; Abbey & McAuslan, 2004; Abbey et al., 2007); and the use of sexually coercive behavior (Abbey et al., 1998; Koss et al., 1987). In general, the major findings in these studies provide evidence that certain behaviors contribute to sexual assault by college men. Abbey and her colleagues (1998) provided support for an earlier theoretical model[v] that sought to identity the pathways that link alcohol and sexual assault. In this sample ($n = 814$), 26% of the men reported perpetrating sexual assault. The authors supported their hypothesis that the mutual effect of beliefs and experiences with dating, sexuality, and alcohol increases the likelihood that men will misperceive the females' intentions.

Another sample of college males found that 33% ($n = 113$) reported that they had perpetrated some form of sexual assault, with 78% of those acknowledging committing more than one. Overall, 35% of the sexual assaults involved alcohol consumption, with both the man and woman drinking (Abbey et al., 2001). In all, the authors found that the represented attitudinal, experiential, and situational variables discriminated perpetrators from nonperpetrators (Ibid).

Abbey et al.'s (2007) study extended the same variables to a community sample ($n = 163$) and found that they were significant predictors of sexual assault for this population as well. Additionally, perpetrators of sexual assault have been found to exhibit less understanding of the rules of social order, less acceptance of personal responsibility, less internalization of prosocial beliefs, more immaturity, and more irresponsibility, as compared to nonperpetrators (Kosson, Kelly, & White, 1997; Rapaport & Burkhart, 1984, as cited in Loh et al., 2005).

Other risk factors for sexual offending identified by Malamuth et al. (1991, 1995) are promiscuity and hostility. Abbey et al. (1998, 2001) found that adherence to rape myths, alcohol use, and misperception of sexual cues were risk factors. A longitudinal study conducted by Malamuth et al. (1995) indicated that sexually aggressive behavior at baseline predicted conflict with women at follow-up, which included sexual and nonsexual aggression and relationship distress (Loh et al., 2005).

There are some transient factors associated with sex offenses. These include offender motivation, the victim–offender relationship, and the situational dynamics of the crime (i.e., time and place; types of weapons used; victim resistance; financial, marital and other stressor; nonpsychosexual mental disorders; and alcohol and drug use) (Laufersweiler-Dwyer & Dwyer, in Reddington & Kriesel, 2005).

Adult Perpetration and Childhood Sexual Victimization

The relationship between offense history and childhood sexual victimization has been detailed in a number of studies. Finkelhor (1994) suggests a 5% to 10% lifetime prevalence of childhood sexual victimization in men who are sex offenders. Loh and Gidycz (2006) investigated the relationship between childhood sexual assault and subsequent perpetration of dating violence in adulthood in men. They found a significant relationship between childhood sexual abuse and history of sexual assault perpetration at baseline. Prospective analyses indicated that childhood sexual assault was not predictive of perpetration during the follow-up period. These results are supportive of the idea that the effects of childhood sexual abuse may be mediated by a variety of factors.

White and Smith (2004) conducted a 5-year evaluation of college men and found that childhood victimization was associated with increased likelihood of perpetration of sexual assault in adolescence, which in turn was associated with increased likelihood of perpetrating sexually aggressive acts in college. Only adolescent sexual perpetration was predictive of perpetration during college when these variables were considered collectively.

Finally, more recently, Robertiello and Terry (2007) suggested that rather than looking at distinct unique characteristics, the best way to understand sex offender typologies is to view them along a continuum. They argued that those likely to recidivate have certain characteristics. Therefore, by identifying characteristics and motivations for offending, recidivism can be reduced. By utilizing offender interpersonal and situational characteristics and/or victim choice, information provides a distinction among types of offenders.

Female Sex Offenders

Female sex offenders are an understudied population. It is not uncommon for female sex offending to go unreported or unnoticed or even to be diverted from the criminal justice system (Allen, 1991). Part of the issue of underreporting lies with media portrayals of sex offenders. As will be discussed throughout this book, mainstream media often portray sex offenders as exclusively males. Many adult male victims will not report victimization at all and will rarely report being victimized by a female. Allen further suggested that it is only those females who have committed the more serious forms of sexual abuse who are likely to be charged.

Ramsay-Klawsnik, (1990) reported that out of 83 cases involving children who were sexually abused, only one of the accused female sex offenders was subjected to criminal prosecution. Despite the fact that the abuse was confirmed through diagnostic evaluation and was often sadistic in nature, the females were not prosecuted. In 56% of the cases, the abuse included burning, beating, biting, or pinching the breasts or genitals of the children, or tying them up during acts of sexual assault.

Female sex offenders can go unnoticed because they can easily disguise sex offending as part of the routine of child-rearing activities and boys are less likely to report it because of embarrassment (Groth & Birnbaum, 1979; Kaplan & Green, 1995). Others have noted that there is a problem with treating female sex offending as a less serious offense because it is viewed as relatively harmless (Becker, Hall, & Stinson, 2001; Broussard, Wagner, Kazelskis, 1991; Denov, 2003, 2004; Finkelhor, Williams, & Burns, 1988; Hetherton, 1999). Finally, female sex offenders can be difficult to prosecute and juries are less willing to convict females for lesser sexual offenses (Finkelhor, 1983; Mayer, 1992).

According to the Uniform Crime Reports, females represent only 10% of the sex offense cases that come to the attention of authorities. More specifically, arrests of females represent only 1% of all adult arrests for forcible rape and 6% of all adult arrests for other sex offenses (FBI, 2006).

Female sex offenders have been found to choose victims based partially on their level of access (e.g., their own children or others who are in their care) (O'Connor, 1987; Rosencrans, 1997). More recent studies have found that for convicted female sex offenders, teenagers are likely targets (Ferguson & Meehan, 2005; Vandiver, 2006; Vandiver & Kercher, 2004). They may also be acting in concert with a male accomplice (co-offender) and thus may only be serving as a tool to gain access to a victim, whereas others have their own self-interest and act on their own (solo offender) (Kaplan & Green, 1995; Vandiver, 2006).

Vandiver (2006) found that with female sex offenders, those who are co-offenders (with males) were more likely to have more than one victim, had both male and female victims, were related to the victim, and committed a nonsexual offense in addition to the listed sexual offense, as compared to solo offenders. Similar to male sex offenders, female sex offenders may seek out occupations that involve children (Faller, 1988; Finkelhor et al., 1988).

Matthews, Mathews, and Speltz (1991) developed a typology of female sex offenders based on their study of 16 women who had been sentenced to a sex offender treatment program between May 1985 and December 1987. Three types of offenders were indentified. The teacher/lover typically targeted adolescent males they believed they were in love with. The intergenerationally predisposed had been sexually abused as a child by multiple perpetrators, resulting in the inability to establish relationships, promiscuity, and exhibited abusive and self-destructive behaviors. The male-coerced offenders were passive and powerless in their interpersonal relationships and ended up usually being dominated by their partners, and thus easily coerced into offending.

Vandiver and Kercher (2004) analyzed victim and offender characteristics of 471 female registered sex offenders in Texas. They ranged in age from 18 to 78, with 88% of them being white. They also found that these offenders had known victims in 82% of those cases. They developed six categories of offenders from their analysis. Their typology was organized by the following six categories: heterosexual nurturers, noncriminal homosexual offenders, sexual predators, young child exploiters, homosexual criminals, and aggressive homosexual criminal offenders.

In their 2002 study of 40 female sex offenders in Arkansas, Vandiver and Walker (2002) found that female sex offenders cover a broad range of ages, from as young as 13 to as old as 65, though the authors note that the onset may actually be younger because these youths are not typically accessed by clinical or judicial facilities. The majority of female sex offenders also tended to be married. Oliver (2007) concurred with Vandiver and Walker but added that female sex offenders were more likely to have experienced severe and repeated sexual abuse prior to age six, were more likely victims of incest, were more likely to have attempted suicide, and were more likely to have been diagnosed with PTSD.

More recently, Strickland (2008) studied a sample of 130 incarcerated females (60 sex offenders and 70 non–sex offenders) in Georgia institutions. Her analysis revealed that sex-offending women suffered significantly higher rates of total childhood trauma. There was no difference between the groups in personality disorders, although there were significant differences found for social and sexual inadequacies. No differences were found for emotional neediness. Again, effective sex offender laws understand and accommodate for differences among sex offenders. As evidenced by this review, there appear to be significant differences between male and female sex offenders, which existing policy does not address.

Juvenile Sex Offenders

As mentioned in chapter 1, federal sex offender laws now extend to juveniles. With the enactment of the 2006 Walsh Act, juveniles are to be on par with adult sex offenders regarding registration and notification requirements. Given this change, it is important to analyze if and how juvenile sex offenders vary from adult offenders.

Juveniles are primarily versatile in their offending behavior. They are generally unpatterned and unspecialized. Purely sexual offending among juveniles is a rare phenomenon. Additionally, most juvenile sex offenders do not go on to become adult sex offenders, though there may be a subset of chronic sex offenders who may be high risk.

According to UCR data for 2006, there were 2,519 persons under the age of 18 arrested for forcible rape and 11,516 in that same age group arrested for sex offenses—14.7% and 18.2%, respectively, of the total arrests for each category. These figures represent a 9.4% decrease for forcible rapes and 8.3% decrease for sex offenses from 2005, which are consistent with the reduction in crime rates overall over the 10-year period between 1996 and 2006 (U.S. Department of Justice, 2006).

Recidivism of Sex Offenders

Underlying sex offender laws is the fear of sex offender recidivism, particularly the commission of new sexual assaults. A central assumption of these laws is the belief that sex offenders have higher recidivism rates than other criminals. The data presented below suggest that premise is false.

A 2002 BJS study of 272,111 former inmates from 15 states found that 67.5% were rearrested within a 3-year period. The majority of these rearrests were for felonies or serious misdemeanors. Of this group, 46.9% were convicted of a new crime. Rapists, who represented 1.2 % (n = 3,138) of the total of released inmates, were among those with the lowest rate (46%) of rearrest, as were other sexual assault[vi] (41.4%) prisoners. The higher end for rearrest characteristics were robbers (70.2%), burglars (74%), larcenists (74.6%), motor vehicle thieves (78%), those convicted of possessing or selling stolen property (77.4%), and possessing, using, or selling illegal weapons (70.2%). Within 3 years, 2.5% (n = 78) of released rapists were arrested for another rape. A rearrest rate of 2.5% for new sexual assaults, although a likely underestimate of actual reoffending, is still a low-frequency event (Langan & Levin, 2002).

There is evidence to suggest that nonsexual criminals rarely commit sexual offenses when they recidivate (Bonta & Hanson, 1995; Hanson, Scott, & Steffy, 1995). Scales designed to predict general criminal recidivism do not capture the true risk of sexual offending (Bonta & Hanson, 1995). Therefore, sexual offending may be different from other types of crime. Janus and Meehl's (1997) review of the literature concluded that a base rate for sexual recidivism was 20%. Consequently, in order to identify factors related to recidivism, Hanson and Bussiere (1998) conducted a meta-analysis of sex offender recidivism studies. Their examination of 61 studies showed that overall sexual offense recidivism was low at 13.4% ($n =$ 23,393) but that there were subgroups with higher recidivism rates. The best predictors for sexual recidivism were "measures of sexual deviancy (e.g., deviant sexual preferences, prior sexual offenses) and, to a lesser extent, by general criminological factors (e.g., age, total prior offenses)" (p. 348). Offenders who failed to complete treatment had higher risks for reoffending both sexually and nonsexually. However, the predictors for nonsexual violent recidivism and general criminal recidivism were similar (e.g., prior violent offenses, age, juvenile delinquency) to those of nonsexual offenders. These findings contradict the view that sex offenders inevitably reoffend because only a minority of the total sample were known to have committed a new sexual offense during the 4- to 5-year follow-up period (Hanson & Bussiere, 1998).

Recidivism rates vary significantly across studies mainly due to methodological differences. These differences include types of data sources, how recidivism is defined, and sample characteristics. Despite these issues, recidivism rates of sex offenders are relatively low. Hall (1995) conducted a meta-analysis (12 studies, $n = 1,313$) and found that 27% of untreated participants recidivated whereas only 19 % of treated participants recidivated. Later Alexander (1999), using a quasi meta-analytic framework (79 studies, $n =$ 10,988), returned a 13% recidivism rate for sex offenders who participated in a treatment program as compared to 18% for untreated participants. Hanson et al. (2002) reviewed 38 studies of released sex offenders over a 46-month follow-up period and obtained an average sexual recidivism rate of 12% for participating sex offenders and a 17% recidivism rate in a comparison group (i.e., treatment dropout, treatment refusers, untreated participants).

At the beginning of the chapter a question was posed that asked, does the recidivism of sex offenders justify the need for additional sex offender specific policies? Methodological debates notwithstanding, the literature supports the contention that sexual assault recidivism rates are lower than recidivism rates for other violent and most nonviolent crime. Still, sexual assault is an underreported crime, and any policy debate would have to factor in how this may or may not affect our responses. We must also take into account whether or not those who commit sexual offenses commit only sexual offenses or are more eclectic. However, the data do not support the rhetorical contention (often repeated in the policy debate) that sex offenders "always reoffend."

Are Sex Offenders Generalists or Specialists?

Two contrasting views have been put forward to describe the criminal activity of sex offenders in adulthood. The first view states that sex offenders are specialists who tend to repeat sexual crimes. The second argument is that sex offenders are generalists who do not restrict themselves to one particular type of crime. This debate is an important one in light of issues of public policy on how to best deal with sexual offending and recidivism in society. The variability of offenses and behavioral patterns for different types of sex offending has been documented (Bradway, 1990; Groth & Birnbaum, 1979; Knight & Prentky, 1990; Knight, Rosenberg, & Schneider 1985; Lieb & Matson, 1998). In general, studies have pointed out that there is evidence for both generality and specificity in behavioral patterns (Sample & Bray, 2003; Soothill, Francis, Sanderson, & Ackerley, 2000; Zimring, 2004). The research is inconclusive about the degree of specialization among sex offenders.

Nagayama Hall and Proctor (1987) observed sexual reoffense specialization among sex offenders with adult and child victims. In their study of 342 male sex offenders, they found that sex offenders against adults tend to reoffend sexually against adults, whereas sex offenders against children tend to reoffend against children. The authors proposed that the nonsexual criminal activity by adult rapists is symptomatic of a more generalized pattern of antisocial behavior, whereas those who assault child victims are more specialized in their reoffending. They concluded that "the best single-predictor of re-arrests is arrests for sexual offending against adults, which they say explains 12 percent of the variance in re-arrests for sexual offending against adults and 15 percent of the variance in nonsexual violent re-arrests" (p. 112).

Langan and Levin's (2002) study revealed that of the 3,138 rapists who were rearrested within the 3-year period following their release, 46% were rearrested for a new crime, 18.6% for a new violent offense, 2.5% for another rape, 8.2% for a new nonsexual assault, and 11.2% for a drug offense. These figures indicate that the majority of rearrested rapists, though arrested for something other than rape, do reflect a degree of specialization for certain offenders. Another way this can be shown is by looking at ratios. The authors explain that the odds of a released rapist being arrested for a new rape are 3.2 times greater than a nonrapist's odds.

Using national data on about 10,000 sex offenders released from prison in 1994, Miethe, Olson, and Mitchell (2006) sought to determine the specialization and persistence levels of this group. They reported that only 2% of the released rapists in this study were rearrested for a rape. A closer examination of those offenders with at least one prior sex crime arrest determined that only 5% were exclusively sex offenders (i.e., all of their arrests were for sex crimes). The authors said that "arrest cycles exhibit a predominant pattern of offense versatility and limited evidence of specialization" (p. 224). In other words, when they are rearrested, it is for a variety of offenses that are not sex crimes.

Lussier (2005) presented a developmental criminology paradigm to explore the issue of specialization versus generality. He argued that the specialization hypothesis is based on one parameter of criminal activity—recidivism—whereas the generality hypothesis focuses on participation and variety of criminal activity and does not consider the dynamic nature of criminal activity over time. Examining recidivism studies from a developmental criminology perspective—one that looks at criminal activity as it develops over time—the author suggested that specialization and generality can co-occur over the course of a criminal career. Additionally, the author stated that generalization and specialization "are two distinct processes characterizing the development of offending over time" (p. 284). This view holds that versatility in offending behavior over time tempers sex offenders' tendency to specialize in sexual crime.

Juvenile Sex Offender Recidivism

Juvenile sex offenders present unique issues when the discussion focuses on recidivism. Adolescent sex offenders are heterogeneous in that they have diverse experiences that include childhood victimization, various degrees of emotional and behavioral control issues, with varying levels of sexual interest in prepubescent children. Sexual reoffending among adolescents is also heterogeneous because the factors associated with offending for this group are so variable (Worling & Långström, 2006). Because not all juveniles who sexually offend are "high risk" for reoffending, we need to be careful how authorities and treatment providers intervene with this population. The mislabeling of juvenile sex offenders as high- or low-risk can have serious consequences on their future well-being.

Using subsequent arrests as a measure of recidivism, an early study by Doshay (1943) of 256 juvenile sex offenders who had undergone counseling for sexual offending behavior revealed that 106 juveniles with no nonsexual criminal history had only two reoffenses during the 6-year follow-up period. This was in contrast to the 24 of 148 sex offenders with other criminal histories who reoffended during that same period. Overall, 40% reoffended criminally and 7% reoffended sexually.

Another study that used subsequent referrals to the juvenile court as a measure of recidivism found that 14% of the youth were referred for sexual crimes and 35% for nonsexual crimes for an overall total 49% recidivism rate (Smith & Monastersky, 1986). Worling and Curwen (2000) evaluated the success of a specialized community-based treatment program for treating adolescent sexual offending. Working with a group of 58 sex offenders who took part in a 12-month treatment program and a comparison group of 90 adolescents, they reported that "recidivism rates for sexual, violent nonsexual, and nonviolent offenses for treated adolescents were 5.17%, 18.9%, and 20.7%, respectively. The comparison group had significantly higher rates of sexual (17.8%), violent nonsexual (32.2%), and nonviolent (50%) recidivism. Sexual recidivism was predicted by sexual interest in children. Nonsexual recidivism was related to factors commonly predictive of general delinquency such as history of previous offenses, low self-esteem, and antisocial personality" (p. 965).

A meta-analysis conducted by Reitzel and Carbonell (2006) found that the average recidivism rates for sexual, nonsexual violent, nonsexual nonviolent and unspecified nonsexual crimes were 12.53%, 24.73%, 28.51%, and 20.40%, respectively (n = 2,986, 2,604 known males) based on an average of a 59-month follow-up period across studies. Caldwell (2007) found that in a cohort of 249 juvenile sex offenders and 1,780 nonsexual juvenile offenders released from custody, the recidivism rate was 6.8% and 5.7%, respectively, during a 5-year follow-up period. It was 10 times more likely that a juvenile sex offender would be charged with a nonsexual offense as compared to a sexual offense. The non–sex offending cohort accounted for 85% of the new sexual offenses.

Worling and Långström (2006) investigated juvenile sex offender recidivism rates by examining 22 published follow-up investigations (studies of previously institutionalized juveniles) of unique samples of juveniles. (See Table 2.1 for a list of risk factors associated with recidivism.)

Recidivism rates ranged from 0% to almost 40% across studies with the follow-up periods ranging from 6 months to 9 years. Sexual assault recidivism rates using criminal charges as an estimate of reoffending were 15% (127 of 846). Those studies using more conservative estimates such as convictions, court records, self-report, or adult-only charges reported a recidivism rate of 14% (226 of 1,593). These findings echo the research on adult treatment in that most sex offenders do not inevitably reoffend, and even less do they do so perpetually, raising questions about sex offender–specific criminal sanctions.

Is Sex Offender Treatment Effective?

Questions about sex offender recidivism are invariably linked to treatment efficacy as the ultimate goal of treatment is to preclude the offender from reoffending. Treatment efficacy is often judged on whether or not there was a new sexual offense committed after treatment had been administered. Sex offenders are not a homogeneous group, as several studies have noted (Sample & Bray, 2006). Neither are they totally specialists, as some argue, though they do exhibit lower recidivism rates and have less extensive offense histories overall (Langan, Schmitt, & Durose, 2003; Sample & Bray, 2003; Soothill et al., 2000; Speir, Meredith, Johnson, Bird, & Bedell, 2001).

Identified Risk Factors for Criminal Recidivism for Adolescents Who have Offended Sexually

2.1

Empirically supported risk factors	Deviant sexual interests
	  Prior criminal sanctions for sexual offending
	  Sexual offending against more than one victim
	  Sexual offending against a stranger victim
	  Social isolation
	  Uncompleted offense-specific treatment

Promising risk factors	Problematic parent-adolescent relationships Attitudes supportive of sexual offending

Possible risk factors	High-stress family environment
	  Impulsivity
	  Antisocial interpersonal orientation
	  Interpersonal aggression
	  Negative peer associations
	  Sexual preoccupation
	  Sexual offending against a male victim
	  Sexual offending against a child
	  Threats, violence, or weapons in sexual offense
	  Environment supporting reoffending

Unlikely risk factors victimization	Adolescent's own history of sexual victimization
	  History of nonsexual offending
	  Sexual offending involving penetration
	  Denial of sexual offending
	  Low victim empathy

Continued

2.1 Identified Risk Factors for Criminal Recidivism for Adolescents Who have Offended Sexually (Cont'd)

Risk factors for adolescents vs. adults	Many empirical supported factors are the same General impulsivity, sexual preoccupation, access to potential victims are also promising factors for both groups A number of factors (denial of offense history, history of childhood sexual abuse) are not related to risk of sexual offending for both groups. However, some factors (history of nonsexual crimes, deviant arousal, marital status) are predictive of sexual reoffending risk for adults only. Other variables such as problematic parent-child relationships are unique to future risk for adolescents.
Risk factors for minority-ethnicity	No reports to date denote sexual recidivism in adolescents varies with race or ethnicity No studies have revealed distinct differences across genders for either aggressive behavior or general (including sexual) offending

Risk factors for nonsexual offending Conduct disorder symptoms prior to age 15	Number of previous convictions (for any offense)
	  Psychopathy
	  Sexual-offense related use of weapons or death threats
	  Lower Socio-economic status (SES)
	  Hostility
	  Aggression
	  Antisocial personality

Information for this table was adapted from Worling and Långström (2006)

An important question to ask is does sex offender treatment work? Or, more specifically, does sex offender treatment prevent sex offenders from recidivating? In an early study from 1989, Furby, Weinrott, and Blackshaw's comprehensive review of 42 studies concluded that there is no evidence to support the efficacy of treatment in reducing sex offender recidivism rates. Part of their conclusion was based on the fact that many of the studies evidenced multiple and serious methodological problems. Marshall, Jones, Ward, Johnston, and Barbaree (1991) asked a similar question: Can sex offenders be effectively treated so as to reduce subsequent recidivism? In their review of treatment outcomes studies, they found that comprehensive cognitive-behavioral programs and combined psychological and hormonal treatments are effective with child molesters and exhibitionists but not with rapists.

This conclusion is disputed however by Quinsey, Harris, Rice and Lalumière, (1993) in particular, who argue that narrative reviews of studies have not demonstrated that sex offender treatment is effective. Their argument centers around several factors, including methodological issues that exclude the use of comparison groups, the overestimation of treatment effectiveness by not including those who refuse or drop out of treatment as compared to outcomes of those who complete treatment with outcomes of untreated offenders, and the lack of sampling groups from the same jurisdiction and cohort. Quinsey and colleagues advocate for meta-analyses that can provide estimates of treatment effects, effect size, relationships between effect size and type of control group, and finally variability in outcome studies and mediator variables.

Marshall and colleagues' (1991) study was later followed by Alexander (1994) and still later Hall's (1995) meta-analysis of a post-Furby et al. (1989) study that provided more optimism about the efficacy of hormonal treatments and cognitive-behavioral treatments. Though Hall's meta-analysis also suffered from methodological issues, mainly because he was able to use only 12 of the original 90 identified studies (only three of which used randomly assigned subjects for both control and treatment groups), it still provided important information about the efficacy of sex offender treatment.

Since Quinsey et al's. (1993) work, much has been done in the way of addressing whether or not treatment is effective for sex offenders. Many victims of sexual assault not only seek prosecution for their attackers but also want officials to do something about treating these individuals in both institutions and communities. As pointed out earlier, the majority of perpetrators of sexual assault are known to the victim therefore a criminal justice response that does not include treatment discourages many victims from participating in the prosecution process. Nevertheless, a consensus view has emerged of how sex offenders should be dealt with. This view holds that treatment can be effective for some sex offenders, voluntary treatment is more effective, treatment reduces recidivism, and treatment must include more than just counseling (Matson, 2002).[vii]

In light of the question as to whether or not treatment works for sex offenders, there is also some debate about which treatments work best and for which offenders. Conducting research on the effectiveness of sex offender treatment has a number of obstacles both practical and methodological. Following up on released sex offenders for long periods of time is difficult and expensive. In addition, as emphasized by Quinsey and his colleagues (1993), the use of control (untreated) groups and treated groups is vital for conducting empirical research for this population. Similarities in group makeup would also be a necessary component; otherwise it would be specious to say that treatment affected recidivism rates between the groups because other factors could be involved.

The use of control groups itself presents some issues that could affect outcomes. It is typical that study subjects participate voluntarily, that is, they have some initial motivation to change. Those who do not want to participate, who are not selected to participate, or who drop out are generally used for the control group, if the study is using a control group. So the best possible candidates are selected for the treatment groups. Assigning subjects randomly to control or treatment groups presents moral and ethical issues since purposely denying treatment to released sex offenders could open up the researchers to criticism and certainly to lawsuits by future victims of the untreated group. What the research does show, given the extent of the studies, is that recidivism among sex offenders is lower (though more variable) than the general criminal offender, thus raising questions about the premise of sex offender laws (Alexander, 1999; Doren, 1998; Furby et al., 1989; Greenberg, 1998; Grubin & Wingate, 1996; Hall, 1995; Hanson & Bussiere, 1998; Hanson et al., 2002; Proulx, Tardif, Lamoureux, & Lussier, 2000; Quinsey, Lalumière, Rice, & Harris, 1995).

Sex Offender Treatment

Types of treatment that have been shown to have success come in two categories, biological (chemical or physical interventions) and psychological (behavior modification), and in most cases these are given in tandem. Biological approaches focus on reducing the sex drive; whether that is accomplished by use of pharmacology (medication) or surgical castration, the aim is to decrease or eliminate the sex drive. Several medications have been used including antiandrogens, which are used to reduce the amount of natural androgens—naturally occurring substances in the body (i.e., testosterone); hormones—medroxyprogesterone acetate (MPA), also known as Depo-Provera, help reduce the sex drive; and other antipsychotic medications have been known to dampen the sex drive, though these medications are still being tested for effectiveness (Dwyer & Laufersweiler-Dwyer, in Reddington & Kriesel, 2005). A fuller discussion of the role of medicine (e.g., chemical castration laws) in sex offender treatment can be found in Scott and del Busto's chapter 10.

Psychological approaches attempt to change offenders by modifying behaviors. These approaches include behavioral, cognitive, and psychodynamic interventions. Behavioral therapy assumes that people are conditioned by learning to act in certain ways, and that behavior can also be unlearned with appropriate behaviors replacing deviant behaviors. There are a number of behavioral methods that offer opportunities for change, these include, social skills training, systematic desensitization, assertiveness training, aversion therapy, relaxation training, and modeling amongst others (Dwyer & Laufersweiler-Dwyer, in Reddington & Kriesel, 2005).

With sex offenders, change is induced by using methods of rewards and punishments. With pedophiles, the idea is to eliminate the sexual desire for children and direct it appropriately. Cognitive methods focus on teaching offenders how

- The 2002 survey reported on 937 adolescent programs (726 community-based and 131 residential programs).[viii]
- Male to female programs were 2:1 for community-based programs and 9:1 for residential programs in 2000; in 2002 they were 2:1 and 6:1, respectively.
- In the 2002 survey respondents were allowed to rank order three theories that best represented their program's theoretical basis. Between 76 and 84% of male and female community programs and male residential programs chose cognitive-behavioral, relapse prevention, or social learning theory. In 2000, between 82% and 100% of community and residential programs had chosen some form of cognitive-behavioral (including choices of cognitive-behavioral/relapse prevention and classic cognitive-behavioral/behavioral).
- In the 2002 survey, only 64% of the female residential programs chose cognitive-behavioral, relapse prevention, or social learning. Instead 7.1% of these programs chose sexual trauma.
- Risk assessment protocols for males were more common than for females. In community-based and residential programs, 21% used ERASOR—the Estimated Risk of Adolescent Sexual Offender Recidivism—and about 31% used J-SOAP—the Juvenile Sex Offender Assessment Protocol (Burton et al., 2006).[ix]

It has been suggested that different types of sex offenders do not respond to treatment in the same ways (Holmes & Holmes, 2002). Evidence exists that shows treatment for some sex offenders is a viable option because it has been shown to reduce recidivism. What is also clear is that differences in the types of treatment have differing results and the accurate assessment of that treatment is difficult. Problems with research methodologies and differences in research methods demand that we tread carefully when drawing overall conclusions and generalizing based on any one study's results. However, public demands and the need to better "control" sex offenders' deviant behavior require a more effective response from officials. It is not enough to simply punish offenders by incarcerating them for long periods of time; more must be done to help them control their sexual desires by intervening in the behaviors that prompt them to act.

Summary and Conclusion

The problem of sexual assault is a complex and diverse topic. This chapter provides a broad yet brief overview as to the prevalence and patterns of sexual assault, its victims and perpetrators, and what is known about sex offender recidivism. It includes brief sections on issues concerning special populations like female sex offenders, male sexual assault victims, and juvenile offenders. Additionally, the chapter provides an overview of treatment that details current modalities and the efficacy of treatment.

The policy debate will continue as to whether or not sex offenders should be considered a special population of offenders warranting additional and comprehensive controls. That debate raises many questions about how we should identify, prosecute, and punish sex offenders, which makes it clear that the types of crimes committed by these offenders dredge up strong emotional and physical responses from victims, officials, and the public at large. We must be careful, however, at how we navigate these responses. More and more evidence shows us that simply punishing sex offenders for long periods of time is not the only way to respond and in fact could prove more harmful to certain sex offenders and their victims. It is more important to formulate policies that not only appropriately punish perpetrators but also policies that effectively educate the public, intervene in child abuse and neglect, provide adequate facilities for sex offenders, give guidelines for training and supervision for those who work with sex offenders, and outline treatment goals for both victims and perpetrators that are designed to reduce or eliminate the overall incidence of sexual assault.

References

Abbey, A., & McAuslan, P. (2004). A longitudinal examination of male college students' perpetration of sexual assault. *Journal of Consulting and Clinical Psychology, 72*(5), 747–756.

Abbey, A., McAuslan, P., & Ross, L. (1998, June). Sexual assault perpetration by college men: The role of alcohol, misperception of sexual intent, and sexual beliefs and experiences. *Journal of Social & Clinical Psychology, 17*(2), 167–195. Retrieved July 17, 2008, from PsycINFO database.

Abbey, A., McAuslan, P., Zawacki, T., Clinton, M., & Buck, P. O. (2001). Attitudinal, experiential and situational predictors of sexual assault perpetration. *Journal of Interpersonal Violence 16*, 784–807.

Abbey, A., McAuslan, P., Ross, L. T., & Zawacki, T. (1999). Alcohol expectances regarding sex, aggression, and sexual vulnerability: Reliability and validity assessment. *Psychology of Addictive Behaviors, 13*, 174–182.

Abbey, A., Parkhill, M. R., Clinton-Sherrod, A. M., & Zawacki, T. (2007). A comparison of men who committed different types of sexual assault in a community sample. *Journal of Interpersonal Violence, 22*(12), 1567–1580.

Abbey, A., Ross, L. T., McDuffie, D., & McAuslan, P. (1996). Alcohol, misperception and sexual assault: How are they linked? In D.M. Buss & N. M. Malamuth (Eds.). *Sex, power, conflict: Evolutionary and feminist perspectives* (pp. 138–161). New York: Oxford University Press.

Alexander, M. A. (1994, November). *Sex offender treatment: A response to the Furby et al., 1989 quasi-meta analysis II.* Paper presented at the Association for the Treatment of Sexual Abusers (ATSA) 13th Annual Conference, San Francisco, CA.

Alexander, M. A. (1999). Sex offender treatment efficacy revisited. *Sexual Abuse: A Journal of Research and Treatment, 11*(2), 101–117.

Allen, C. (1991). *Women and men who sexually abuse children: A comparative study.* Orwell, VT: Safer Society Press.

Allison, J., & Wrightsman, L. (1993). *Rape the misunderstood crime.* Newbury, Park CA: Sage Publications, Inc.

Amir, A. (1971). *Patterns in forcible rape.* Chicago: University of Chicago Press.

A Model State Sex Offender Policy. (2003). National Center for Missing and Exploited Children, (OJJDP) Office of Juvenile Justice and Delinquency Prevention. Office of Justice Programs, U.S. Department of Justice.

Arata, C. M., & Lindman, L. (2002). Marriage, child abuse, and sexual revictimization. *Journal of Interpersonal Violence, 17*, 953–971.

Becker, J. V., Hall, S., & Stinson, J. D. (2001). Female sexual offenders: Clinical, legal and policy issues. *Journal of Forensic Psychology Practice, 1*, 29–50.

Belknap, J. (2001). *The Invisible Woman,* (2nd ed.). Boulder, CO: Wadsworth.

Berlin, F. S., Lehne, G. K., Malin, H. M., Hunt, W. P., Thomas, K., & Fuhrmaneck, J. (1997). The eroticized violent crime: A psychiatric perspective with six clinical examples. *Sexual Addiction and Compulsivity, 4*(1), 9–31.

Berkowitz, A. (1992). College men as perpetrators of acquaintance rape and sexual assault: A review of recent research. *Journal of American College Health, 40*(4), 175–181.

Bonta, J., & Hanson, R. K. (1995, August). *Violent recidivism of men released from prison.* Paper presented at the 103rd Annual Convention of the American Psychological Association, New York.

Briere, J., & Runtz, M. (1987). Post-sexual abuse trauma: Data and implications for clinical practice. *Journal of Interpersonal Violence, 2*, 367–379.

Bradway, W. C. (1990). Stages of sexual assault. *Law and Order,* September: 119–24.

Browning, C. R., & Laumann, E. O. (1997). Sexual contact between children and adults: A life course perspective. *American Sociological Review, 62*, 540–60.

Broussard, S., Wagner, N. G., & Kazelskis, R. (1991). Undergraduate students' perceptions of child sexual abuse: The impact of victim sex, perpetrator sex, respondent sex, and victim response. *Journal of Family Violence, 6*, 267–278.

Burt, M. R. (1980). Cultural myths and supports for rape. *Journal of Personality and Social Psychology, 38*(2), 217–230.

Burton, D. L., & Smith-Darden, J. S. (2001). *North American survey of sexual abuser treatment and models summary data.* Brandon, VT: Safer Society Press.

Burton, D. L., Smith-Darden, J. S., & Frankel, S. J. (2006). Research on adolescent sexual abuser treatment programs. In *The Juvenile Sex Offender 2*nd *edition.* H. E. Barbaree & W. L. Marshall (Eds.) New York: The Guilford Press.

Burton, D.L., Smith-Darden, J. S. (with Levin, J., Fiske, J., & Freeman-Longo, R.). (2000). *The 1996 Safer Society Survey of sexual offender treatment programs.* Brandon, VT: Safer Society Press.

Caldwell, M. F. (2007). Sexual offense adjudication sexual recidivism among juvenile offenders. *Sex Abuse, 19*, 107–113.

Campbell, J. C., & Soeken, K. L. (1999a). Women's responses to battering over time: An analysis of change. *Journal of Interpersonal Violence, 14*(1), 21–40.

Campbell, J. C., & Soeken, K. L. (1999b). Forced sex and intimate partner violence: Effects on women's risk and women's health. *Violence against Women, 5*(9), 1017–35.

Cascardi, M., Riggs, D. S., Hearst-Ikeda, D., & Foa, E. B. (1996). Objective ratings of assault safety as predictors of PTSD. *Journal of Interpersonal Violence, 11*, 65–78.

Catalano, S. M. (2006). *Criminal Victimization 2005.* (NCJ214644) Bureau of Justice Statistics: Table 9. http://www.ojp.usdoj.gov/bjs/pub/pdf/cv05.pdf

Catalano, S. M. (2007). *Criminal Victimization 2005.* (NCJ219413) Bureau of Justice Statistics: Table 2. http://www.ojp.usdoj.gov/bjs/pub/pdf/cv06.pdf

Chu, J. A., & Dill, D. L. (1990). Dissociative symptoms in relation to childhood physical and sexual abuse. *American Journal of Psychiatry, 147*, 887–892.

Classen, C. C., Palesh, O. G., & Aggarwal, R. (2005). Sexual revictimization: A review of the empirical literature. *Trauma, Violence & Abuse, 6*(2), 103–129.

Cohen, M., & Miller, T. (1998) The cost of mental health care for victims of crime. *Journal of Interpersonal Violence, 13*(1), 93–110.

Cohen, M. L., Seghorn, T., & Calmas, W. (1969). Sociometric study of the sex offender. *Journal of Abnormal Psychology, 74*, 249–255.

DeMaris, A., & Kaukinen, C. (2005). Violent victimization and women's mental and physical health: Evidence from a national sample. *Journal of Research in Crime and Delinquency, 42*(4) November, 384–411.

DeMaris, A., & Swinford, S. (1996). Female victims of spousal violence: Factors influencing their level of fearfulness. *Family Relations, 45*, 98–106.

Denov, M. S. (2003). The myth of innocence: Sexual scripts and the recognition of child sexual abuse by female perpetrators. *Journal of Sex Research, 40*, 303–314.

Denov, M. S. (2004). The long-term effects of child sexual abuse by female perpetrators: A qualitative study of male and female victims. *Journal of Interpersonal Violence, 19*(10), 1137–1156.

Doren, D. M. (1998). Recidivism base rates, predictions of sex offender recidivism and the "sexual predator" commitment laws. *Behavioral Sciences and the Law, 16*, 97–114.

Doshay, L. J. (1943). *The boy sex offender and his later career*. New York: Grune and Stratton.

Dwyer, G., & Laufersweiler-Dwyer, D. (2005). Sex offender treatment an overview. In F.P Reddington & B.W. Kreisel (Eds.). *Sexual Assault: The victims, the perpetrators and the criminal justice system*. Carolina Academic Press: Durham, NC. 301–318.

Faller, K. C. (1988). The spectrum of sexual abuse in daycare. An exploratory study. *Journal of Family Violence, 5*(4), 283–298.

Federal Bureau of Investigation. (2006). *Crime in the United States, 2005: Uniform Crime Reports*. Washington, DC: U.S. Department of Justice, Federal Bureau of Investigation.

Ferguson, C. J., & Meehan, D. C. (2005). An analysis of females convicted of sex crimes in the state of Florida. *Journal of Child Sexual Abuse, 14*, 75–89.

Finkelhor, D. (1983). Removing the child: Prosecuting the offender in cases of sexual abuse. Evidence from the national reporting system for child abuse and neglect. *Child Abuse and Neglect, 7*(2), 195–205.

Finkelhor, D. (1994). Current information on the scope and nature of child sexual abuse. *The Future of Children, 4*(2), 31–53.

Finkelhor, D. & Jones, L. (2006). Why have child maltreatment and child victimization declined? *Journal of Social Issues, 62*(4), 685–716.

Finkelhor, D., Ormrod, R. K. & Turner, H. K. (2007). Re-victimization patterns in a national longitudinal sample of children and youth. *Child Abuse and Neglect, 31*, 479–502.

Finkelhor, D., Ormrod, R. K., Turner, H. K. & Hamby, S. L. (2005). The victimization of children and youth: a comprehensive, national survey. *Child Maltreatment, 10*(1), 5–25.

Finkelhor, D., Williams, L., & Burns, N. (1988). *Nursery crimes: Sexual abuse in day care*. Newbury Park, CA: Sage.

Fisher, B. S., Cullen, F. T., & Turner, M. G. (2000). *The sexual victimization of college women* (NCJ 182369). Washington, DC: U.S. Department of Justice.

Forman, B. D. (1982). Reported male rape. *Victimology, 7*, 235–236.

Frazier, P. A. (1993). A comparative study of male and female rape victims seen at a hospital based rape crisis program. *Journal of Interpersonal Violence, 8*, 64–76.

Fromuth, M. E. (1986). The relationship of childhood sexual abuse with later psychological and sexual adjustment in a sample of college women. *Child Abuse & Neglect, 10*, 5–16.

Furby, L., Weinrott, M. R., & Blackshaw, L. (1989). Sex offender recidivism: A review. *Psychological Bulletin, 105*, 3–30.

Gidycz, C. A., Coble, C. N., Latham, L., & Layman, M. J. (1993). Sexual assault experience in adulthood and prior victimization experiences: A prospective analysis. *Psychology of Women Quarterly, 17*, 151–168.

Greenberg, D. M. (1998). Sexual recidivism in sex offenders. *Canadian Journal of Psychiatry, 43*, 459–465.

Greenfeld, L. A., & Snell, T. L. (1999). *Women offenders*. Washington, DC: U.S. Department of Justice, Bureau of Justice Statistics.

Groth, N. A. (1979). *Men who rape: the psychology of the offender*. New York: Plenum Press.

Groth, A. N., & Burgess, A. W. (1980). Male rape: Offenders and victims. *American Journal of Psychiatry, 137*, 806–810.

Groth, N., Longo, R., & McFadin, J. (1982). Undetected recidivism among rapists and child molesters. *Crime and Delinquency, 28*, 450–458.

Grubin, D., & Wingate, S. (1996). Sexual offense recidivism: prediction versus understanding. *Criminal Behaviour and Mental Health, 6*, 349–359.

Hall, G. C. N. (1995). Sexual offender recidivism revisited: A meta-analysis of recent treatment studies. *Journal of Consulting and Clinical Psychology, 63*, 802–809.

Hanson, R. K. m, & Bussiere, M. T. (1998). Predicting relapse: A meta-analysis of sexual offender recidivism studies. *Journal of Consulting and Clinical Psychology, 66*(2), 348–362.

Hanson, R. K., Gordon, A., Harris, A. J. R., Marques, J. K., Murphy, W. Quinsey, V. L., & Seto, M. C. (2002). First report of the collaborative outcome data project on effectiveness of psychological treatment for sex offenders. *Sexual Abuse: A Journal of Research and Treatment, 14*(2), 169–194.

Hanson, R. K., Scott, H., & Steffy, R. A. (1995). A comparison of child molesters and nonsexual criminals: Risk predictors and long-term recidivism. *Journal of Research in Crime and Delinquency, 32*, 325–337.

Harrison, P. A., Fulkerson, J. A., & Beebe, T. J. (1997). Multiple substance use among adolescent physical and sexual abuse victims. *Child Abuse & Neglect, 21*, 529–39.

Hetherton J. (1999). The idealization of women: Its role in the minimization of child sexual abuse by females. *Child Abuse and Neglect, 23*(2), 161–174.

Holmes, S., & Holmes, R. (2002). *Sex crimes patterns and behavior* (2nd ed.). Thousand Oaks, CA: Sage.

Huckle, P. L. (1995). Male rape victims referred to a forensic psychiatric service. *Medicine, Science,and the Law, 35*, 187–192.

Jackson, R. L., & Richards, H. J. (2007). Diagnostic and risk profiles among civilly committed sex offenders in Washington State. *International Journal of Offender Therapy and Comparative Criminology, 51*(3), 313–323.

Janus, E. S., & Meehl, P. E. (1997). Assessing the legal standard for predictions of dangerousness in sex offender commitment proceedings. *Psychology, Public Policy and Law, 3*.

Jasinski, J. L., Williams, L. M., & Siegel, J. (2000). Childhood physical and sexual abuse as risk factors for heavy drinking among African American women: A prospective study. *Child Abuse & Neglect, 24,* 1061–71.

Jones, T. R. & Pratt, T. (2008). The prevalence of sexual violence in prison: The state of the knowledge base and implication for evidence-based correctional policy making. *International Journal of Offender Therapy and Comparative Criminology. 52*(3), 280–295.

Kalof, L. (2000) Ethnic differences in female sexual victimization. *Sexuality & Culture, 4,* 75–97.

Kanin, E. J. (1985). Date rapists: Differential sexual socialization and relative deprivation. *Archives of Sexual Behavior, 14*(3), 219–231.

Kaplan, M. S., & Green, A. (1995). Incarcerated female sex offenders: A comparison of sexual histories with eleven female sex offenders. *Sexual Abuse: A Journal of Research and Treatment, 7,* 287–300.

Kaufman, A., Jackson, R., Voorhees, R., & Christy, J. (1980). Male rape victims: Noninstitutionalized assault. *American Journal of Psychiatry,* 137, 221–223.

Kessler, B. L., & Bieschke, K. J. (1999). A retrospective analysis of shame, dissociation, and adult victimization in survivors of childhood sexual abuse. *Journal of Counseling Psychology,46,* 355–341.

Knight, R. A., & Prentky, R. A. (1990). Classifying sexual offenders: The development and corroboration of taxonomic models. pp. 23–52 in *Handbook of Sexual Assault:* 228, *Journal of Research in Crime and Delinquency Issues, Theories, and Treatment of the Offender,* edited by W. L. Marshall, D. R. Laws, and H. E. Barbaree. New York: Plenum.

Knight, R. A., Rosenberg, R., & Schneider, B. A. (1985). Classification of sexual offenders: Perspectives, methods, and validation, pp. 222–93. In *Rape and Sexual Assault: A Research Handbook,* edited by Ann Walbert Burgess. New York: Garland.

Koss, M. P., & Dinero, T. E. (1989). Discriminant analysis of risk factors for sexual victimization among a national sample of college women. *Journal of Consulting and Clinical Psychology, 57*(2), 242–250.

Koss, M. P., Gidycz, C. A., & Wisniewski, N. (1987). The scope of rape: Incidence and prevalence of sexual aggression and victimization in a national sample of higher education students. *Journal of Consulting and Clinical Psychology,55,* 162–170.

Lacey, H. B., & Roberts, R. (1991). Sexual assault on men. *International Journal of STD & AIDS, 2,* 258–260.

Langan, P. A., & Levin, D. J. (2002). *Recidivism of prisoners released in 1994.* Bureau of Justice Statistics. June 2002, NCJ 193427. Washington DC: U.S. Department of Justice.

Langan, P. A., Schmitt, E. L., & Durose, M. R. (2003) *Recidivism of sex offenders released from prison in 1994.* Bureau of Justice Statistics Special Report, November 2003, NCJ 198281. Washington, DC: U.S. Department of Justice.

Lieb, R., & Matson, S. (1998). *Sexual predator commitment laws in the United States: 1998 update.* Olympia: Washington State Institute for Public Policy.

Loh, C., & Gidycz, C. (2006). A prospective analysis of the relationship between childhood sexual victimization and perpetration of dating violence and sexual assault in adulthood. *Journal of Interpersonal Violence, 21*(6), 732–749.

Loh, C., Gidycz, C., Lobo, T. R., & Luthra, R. (2005). A prospective analysis of sexual assault perpetration: Risk factors related to perpetrator characteristics. *Journal of Interpersonal Violence, 20*, 1325–1348.

Lussier, P. (2005). The criminal activity of sexual offenders in adulthood: Revisiting the specialization debate. *Sexual Abuse: A Journal of Research and Treatment, 17*(3), 269–292.

Malamuth, N. M., Linz, D., Heavey, CL., Barnes, G., & Acker, M. (1995). Using the confluence model of sexual aggression to predict men's conflict with women: A ten year follow–up study. *Journal of Personality and Social Psychology, 69*, 353–369.

Malamuth, N. M., Sockloskie, R. J., Koss, M. P., & Tanaka, J.S. (1991). Characteristics of aggressors against women. *Journal of Consulting and Clinical Psychology, 59*, 670–681.

Marshall, W. L., Jones, R., Ward, T., Johnston, P., & Barbaree, H. E. (1991). Treatment outcomes with sex offenders. *Clinical Psychology Review, 11*, 465–485.

Maruschak, L. M. (2004, December). HIV in prisons and jails, 2002. *Bureau of Justice Statistics Bulletin,* pp. 1–11.

Matson, S. (2002). Sex offender treatment: A critical management tool. *Corrections Today.* October, 114–117.

Matthews, J. K., Mathews, R., & Speltz, K. (1991). Female sex offenders: A typology. In M. Quinn (Ed.), *Family sexual abuse: Frontline research and evaluation* (pp. 199–210). Newbury Park, CA: Sage.

Mayer, A. (1992). *Women sex offenders.* Holmes Beach, FL: Learning Publications.

McConaghy, N.,& Zamir, R. (1995). Heterosexual and homosexual coercion, sexual orientation and sexual roles in medical students. *Archives of Sexual Behavior, 24*, 489–502.

McGrath, R. J., Cumming, G. F., & Burchard, B. L. (2003). *Current practices and trends in sexual abuser management: Safer Society 2002 nationwide survey.* Brandon VT: Safer Society Press.

McGuire, T. (2000). Correctional Institution based on sex offender treatment: A relapse behavior study. *Behavioral Sciences and the Law, 18*, 57–71.

Merrill, L. L, Newell, C. F., Thomsen, C. J., Gold, S. R., Milner, J. S., & Koss, M. P.(1999). Childhood abuse and sexual revictimization in a female navy recruit sample. *Journal of Traumatic Stress, 12*, 211–225.

Messman, T. L., & Long, P. J. (1996). Child sexual abuse and its relationship to revictimization in adult women: A review. *Clinical Psychology Review, 16*, pp. 397–420.

Messman–Moore, T. L., & Long, P. J. (2000) Child sexual abuse and revictimization in the form of adult sexual abuse, adult physical abuse, and adult psychological maltreatment. *Journal of Interpersonal Violence, 15*, (5): pp. 489–502.

Mezey, G., & King, M. (1989). The effects of sexual assault: A survey of 22 victims. *Psychological Medicine, 19*, pp. 205–209.

Miethe, T. D., Olson, J., & Mitchell, O. (2006). Specialization and persistence in the arrest histories of sex offenders: A comparative analysis of alternative measures and offense types. *Journal of Research in Crime and Delinquency, 43*(3), 204–229.

Miller, B. C., Monson, B. H., & Norton M. C. (1995). The effects of forced sexual intercourse on white female adolescents. *Child Abuse & Neglect 19*, 1289–301.

Miller, T. R., Cohen, M. A., & Rossman, S. B. (1993). Victim costs of violent crime and resulting injuries. *Health Affairs*, Winter, 1993.

Muehlenhard, C. L., & Linton, M. A. (1987). Date rape and sexual aggression in dating situations: Incidence and risk factors. *Journal of Counseling Psychology, 34*(2): pp.186–196.

Myers, M. F. (1989). Men sexually assaulted as adults and sexually abused as boys. *Archives of Sexual Behavior, 18*, 203–215.

Nagayama Hall, G. C. N., & Proctor, W. M. (1987). Criminological predictors of recidivism in a sexual offender population. *Journal of Consulting and Clinical Psychology, 55*(1), 111–112.

O'Connor, A. A. (1987). Female sex offenders. *British Journal of Psychiatry, 150, 615–620.*

Office for Victims of Crime (OVC) Office of Justice Programs, U.S. Department of Justice. Retrieved July 9, 2008, from http://www.ojp.usdoj.gov/ovc/welcovc/scad/factshts.htm

Oliver, B.E. (2007). Preventing female–perpetrated sexual abuse. *Trauma, Violence & Abuse, 8*(1), 19–32.

Pinkerton, S. D., Galletly, C. L., & Seal, D.W. (2007). Model–based estimates of HIV acquisition due to prison rape. *The Prison Journal. 87*(3), 295–310.

Prentky, R. A., & Knight, R. A. (1991). Identifying critical dimensions for discriminating among rapists. *Journal of Consulting and Clinical Psychology, 59*, pp. 643–661.

Prentky, R., Knight, R., & Rosenberg, R. (1988). Validation analyses on the MTC taxonomy for rapists: Disconfirmation and reconceptualization. In Prentky's & Quinsey's (Eds.) *Human Sexual Aggression: Current Perspectives.* New York: Annals of the New York Academy of Sciences.

Proulx, J., Tardif, M., Lamoureux, B., & Lussier, P. (2000). How does recidivism risk assessment predict survival? In D.R. Laws, S.M. Hudson, & T. Ward (Eds.). *Remaking relapse prevention with sex offenders: A sourcebook.* Thousand Oaks: Sage.

Quinsey, V. L., Harris, G. T., Rice, M. E., & Lalumière, M. L. (1993). Assessing treatment efficacy in outcome studies of sex offenders. *Journal of Interpersonal Violence, 8*(4), 512–523.

Quinsey, V. L., Lalumière, M. L., Rice, M. E., & Harris, G. T. (1995). Predicting sexual offenses. In J.C. Campbell (Ed.). *Assessing dangerousness: Violence by sexual offenders, batterers, and child abusers.* (pp.114–137). Thousand Oaks: Sage.

Rada, R. T. (1978). *Clinical aspects of the rapist.* New York: Grune & Stratton.

Ramsay–Klawsnik, H. (1990). *Sexual abuse by female perpetrators: Impact on children.* Paper presented at the National Symposium on Child Victimization, Atlanta, GA.

Reddington, F. P. & Kreisel, B. W. (Eds.) (2005). *Sexual assault: the victims, the perpetrators, and the criminal justice system.* Carolina Academic Press, Durham, NC.

Reitzel, L. R., & Carbonell, J. L. (2006). The effectiveness of sexual offender treatment for juveniles as measured by recidivism: A meta–analysis. *Sex Abuse, 18*, 401–421.

Robertiello, G & Terry, K. J. (2007). Can we profile sex offenders? A review of sex offender typologies. *Aggression and Violent Behavior, 12*, 508–518.

Rosencrans, B. (1997). *The last secret: Daughters sexually abused by mothers*. Orwell, VT: Safer Society Press.

Russell, D. E. H. (1983). The prevalence and incidence of forcible rape and attempted rape of females. *Victimology: An International Journal, 7*, 1–4.

Russell, D. E. H. (1984). *Sexual exploitation: Rape, child sexual abuse, and workplace harassment*. Beverly Hills, CA: Sage

Sample, L. L. & Bray, T. M. (2003). Are sex offenders dangerous? *Criminology and Public Policy 3*(1), 59–62.

Sample, L. L., & Bray, T. M. (2006). Are sex offenders different: An examination of rearrest patterns. *Criminal Justice Policy Review, 17*(1), 83–102.

Scarce, M. (1997). *Male on male rape: The hidden toll of stigma and shame*. New York: Plenum.

Senn, C. Y., Desmarais, S., Verberg, N., & Wood, E. (2000). Predicting coercive sexual behavior across the lifespan in a random sample of Canadian men. *Journal of Social and Personal Relationships, 17*, 95–113.

Siegel, J. A., & Williams, L. M. (2003). Risk factors for sexual victimization of women. Results for a prospective study. *Violence against Women, 9*(8), 902–930.

Smith, W., & Monastersky, C. (1986). Assessing juvenile sexual offenders risk for reoffending. *Criminal Justice and Behavior 13*, 115–140.

Soothill, K., Francis, B., Sanderson, B., & Ackerley, E. (2000). Sex offenders: specialists, generalists—or both? A 32–Year criminological study. *British Journal of Criminology, 32*, 325–37.

Speir, J., Meredith, T., Johnson, S., Bird, C., & Bedell, H. (2001). *Informing crime control strategies with criminal career research*. A Report of the Georgia Statistical Analysis Center. June 7, 2001. Atlanta: Georgia Statistical Analysis Center.

Stermac, L., Del Bove, G. & Addison, M. (2004). Stranger and acquaintance sexual assault of adult males. *Journal of Interpersonal Violence, 19*(8), 901–915.

Stermac, L., Du Mont, J., & Dunn, S. (1998). Violence in known–assailant sexual assaults. *Journal of Interpersonal Violence, 13*, 398–412.

Stermac, L., Sheridan, P., Davidson, A., & Dunn, S. (1996). Sexual assault of adult males. *Journal of Interpersonal Violence, 11*, 52–64.

Strickland, S. M. (2008). Female sex offenders: Exploring issues of personality, trauma, and cognitive distortions. *Journal of Interpersonal violence, 23*(4), 474–489.

Struckman–Johnson, C. (1988). Forced sex on dates: It happens to men too. *Journal of Sex Research, 24*, 234–241.

Tjaden, P. & Thoennes, N. (1998). *Prevalence, Incidence, and Consequences of Violence against Women: Findings from the National Violence Against Women Survey (NVAW)*. Washington, D.C.: National Institute of Justice, U.S. Department of Justice.

Tjaden, P. & Thoennes, N. (2006). *Extent, Nature, and Consequences of Rape Victimization: Findings From the National Violence Against Women Survey*, Washington, DC: U.S. Department of Justice and U. S. Department for Health and Human Services, Centers for Disease Control Prevention, National Institute of Justice, NCJ 210346.

Ullman, S. E., & Brecklin, L. R. (2003). Sexual assault history and health–related outcomes in a national sample of women. *Psychology of Women Quarterly, 27*, 46–57.

U.S. Department of Justice, Bureau of Justice Statistics. (2005). *Criminal Victimization in the United States,* Retrieved April 27, 2008, from http://www.ojp.usdoj.gov/bjs/cvictgen.htm

United States Department of Justice (2006). Uniform Crime Reports *Crime in the United States.*, Federal Bureau of Investigation. Released September 2007. Retrieved April 27, 2008, from http://www.fbi.gov/ucr/cius2006/offenses/violent_crime/forcible_rape.html

U.S. Department of Justice (2008). Uniform Crime Reports (2007). *Crime in the United States.* Federal Bureau of Investigation. Released June 9, 2008. Retrieved July 9, 2008, from http://www.fbi.gov/ucr/2007prelim/index.html

U.S. Department of Justice (2007). *Criminal Victimization* 2006, Bureau of Justice Statistics Bulletin, December 2007. Retrieved July 9, 2008, from http://www.ojp.usdoj.gov/bjs/pub/pdf/cv06.pdf

U.S. Department of Justice (2007). *Sexual Victimization in Local Jails 2007,* Bureau of Justice Special Report, June 2008. NCJ 221946. Retrieved July 21, 2008, from http://www.ojp.gov/bjs/pub/pdf/svljri07.pdf

U.S. Department of Health and Human Services, Administration on Children, Youth and Families. *Child Maltreatment 2005* (Washington, DC: U.S. Government Printing Office, 2007). Retrieved, July 9, 2008 from http://www.acf.hhs.gov/programs/cb/stats_research/index.htm#can

Vandiver, D. M. (2006). Female sex offenders: A comparison of solo offenders and co–offenders. *Violence and Victims, 21*(3), 339–354.

Vandiver, D. M., & Kercher, G. (2004). Offender and victim characteristics of registered female sex offenders in Texas: A proposed typology of female sexual offenders. *Sexual Abuse: A Journal of Research and Treatment, 16,* 121–137.

Vandiver, D. M. & Teske, R. (2006). Juvenile female and males sex offenders: A comparison of offender, victim, and judicial processing characteristics. *International Journal of Offender Therapy and Comparative Criminology. 50*(2), 148–165.

Vandiver, D. M., & Walker, J.T. (2002). Female sex offenders: An overview and analysis of 40 cases. *Criminal Justice Review, 27*(2), 284–300.

Walker, J., Archer, J., & Davies, M. (2005). Effects of rape on male survivors: A descriptive analysis. *Archives of Sexual Behavior, 34,* pp.69–80

White, J.W., & Smith, P. H. (2004). Sexual assault perpetration and reperpetration: From adolescence to young adulthood. *Criminal Justice and Behavior,* 2004, *31,* pp.182–202.

Worling, J. R., & Curwen, T. (2000). Adolescent sexual offender recidivism: Success of specialized treatment and implications for risk prediction. *Child Abuse & Neglect, 24*(7), 965–982.

Worling, J. R., & Långström, N. (2006). Risk of sexual recidivism in adolescents who offend sexually, correlates and assessment. In H.E Barbaree & W. L. Marshall, (Eds.), *The juvenile sex offender* (2nd ed.). New York: The Guilford Press.

Wyatt, G. E., Guthrie, D., & Notgrass, C. M. (1992). Differential effects of women's child sexual abuse and subsequent sexual revictimization. *Journal of Consulting and Clinical Psychology, 60,* pp. 167–173.

Zimring, F. E. (2004). *An American travesty: Legal responses to adolescent sexual offending.* Chicago: University of Chicago Press.

[i] Finkelhor, Ormrod, and Turner (2007) refer to the different meanings and conceptualizations of the term *revictimization*. The authors note that in some studies the term revictimization has meant a connection between childhood victimization (CSA) and adult victimization (rape), two victimizations (repeat victimizations) in close proximity, and the recurrence of child maltreatment at the hands of the same perpetrator.

[ii] N not reported

[iii] This report can be found at http://www.ojp.gov/bjs/pub/pdf/svljri07.pdf

[iv] Information retrieved from Office for Victims of Crime and can be accessed at: http://www.ojp.usdoj.gov/ovc/welcovc/scad/factshts.htm

[v] See Abbey et al., 1996

[vi] Other sexual assault is defined as (1) forcible or violent sexual acts not involving intercourse with an adult or minor, (2) nonforcible sexual acts with a minor (such as statutory rape or incest with a minor), and (3) nonforcible sexual acts with someone unable to give legal or factual consent because of mental or physical defect or intoxication.

[vii] For more on this, go to The Association for the Treatment of Sexual Abusers (ATSA) http://www.atsa.com/index.html

[viii] The 2002 survey included previously unrecorded individual practitioners, the removal of which would bring respondent totals similar to the 2000 numbers.

[ix] Risk assessment for nonsexual offenses was not determined in McGrath's analyses.

A Brief History of Major Sex Offender Laws

Karen J. Terry &
Alissa R. Ackerman

Since the early 1990s, there has been a proliferation of laws enacted to increase sentences for sex offenders, permit the state to involuntarily commit them to secure facilities, and regulate the behavior of those living in the community. Most of these legislative acts are "memorial laws," enacted after a tragic kidnapping, sexual assault, and/or murder of a child. The aim of these laws is to protect the community from certain sex offenders who are at risk for repeating their offenses, and they have been upheld as constitutional because they promote the state's interest in preserving public safety (Janicki, 2007). To date, however, few evaluation studies have assessed the efficacy of these laws, and the studies that have been conducted produced mixed results.

Since the 1990s, the primary policies to regulate sex offenders are the Jacob Wetterling Crimes Against Children and Sexually Violent Offender Registration Act,[i] "Megan's Law,"[ii] and the Adam Walsh Child Protection and Safety Act of 2006.[iii] Although these provide states with a core set of regulatory policies for sex offenders, many states and local jurisdictions have enacted additional policies to further protect communities from sex offenders. These supervision, management, and treatment polices include residence restrictions, civil commitment, mandatory chemical castration of sex offenders, GPS tracking, and community supervision for life. The aim of this chapter is to show the development of sex offender legislation at the local, state, and federal level and provide a brief overview of the policies throughout the last century.

History of Sex Offender Laws

Although most sex offender policies currently in place were enacted within the last twenty years, the regulation of sexual behavior is not a new concept. Sexual behavior has been regulated since ancient times, though the behaviors and methods of regulation have varied. Attitudes toward sex offenders have fluctuated historically, and acts defined as sexual offenses vary across time and culture. Sexual behavior that is considered "normal" or, alternatively, "deviant," is a socially constructed reality that is always adapting (Jenkins, 1998).

Sexual behavior in ancient times was detailed extensively in art, literature, poetry, mythology, and theater (Breiner, 1990; Dover, 1978; Mondimore, 1996). Many types of sexual behavior were considered acceptable at that time, including homosexuality and intergenerational sexual relationships. Strict regulations of sexual behavior emerged in the Middle Ages, when there was a shift in moral thinking about the purpose of sexual behavior. This shift, influenced by religion, led to the regulation of any sexual behavior whose primary purpose was not procreation (Mondimore, 1996). By the 18th century, moral courts had been created to evaluate cases such as those involving incest, which was declared an ecclesiastical offense, and incestuous marriages were dissolved (Thomas, 2000). Other sexual behaviors, such as homosexuality, bestiality, and intergenerational sexual relationships, were brought before the criminal courts and were punishable by sentences as severe as death.

At the beginning of the 20th century, the Industrial Revolution allowed young women to enter the marketplace and the Progressive Era led to the rise of social activities for women outside the home for the first time. Groups such as the Women's Christian Temperance Union (WCTU), which were interested in controlling the sexual mores of young women, began lobbying for an increase in the age of consent (Odem, 1995). The group argued that older men were seducing young girls, and supported their claims by citing the increasing frequency of sexual attacks upon women and adolescents and the spread of venereal diseases. Largely as a result of their efforts, the age of sexual consent was raised from 16 to 18 in every state by 1920 (Ibid).

At the same time that the WCTU was focusing on "male seducers," there was a more general concern about serious "sex fiends" and "perverts" preying on children (Jenkins, 1998). With few explanations for this behavior, researchers began classifying their behavior as the result of psychopathology or more general psychological problems. The medicalization of the problem of deviant sexual behavior led to far-reaching policies in the early part of the 20th century.

Medicalization of the Sex Offender Problem

Before the beginning of the 20th century, few researchers studied deviant sexual behavior. When researchers did turn their attention to this issue, it was psychologists who tried to understand and explain it. Krafft-Ebing (1965) believed that deviant sexual behavior was attributable to psychopathological problems in the individual and that sexual disorders were a permanent part of a person's character. His work focused primarily on homosexual activity, paraphilias, and masturbation. He concluded that sexual deviants were pathological and a threat to social hygiene. Other researchers, such as Haverock Ellis (1942) and Sigmund Freud (1953) also focused on issues of sexual deviancy from a psychological perspective. Both believed that deviant sexual behavior was rooted in psychopathology, though Ellis thought deviant sexual mores such as homosexuality could not be cured, whereas Freud thought any treatment would have to be of significant depth to identify the core of the neuroses and potentially change the person.

This research, as well as criminological research by Lombroso and others at the time, was important because the medical explanations for deviant sexual behavior became part of the justification for laws implemented against sex offenders. Many criminological researchers thought that deviant behavior was genetic or applied some type of physiological explanation for the deviancy. As such, most states had policies allowing eugenics, or sterilization of criminals who were deemed genetically unfit for procreation. This practice continued until 1942, when the Court declared the sterilization of habitual criminals unconstitutional in *Skinner v. Oklahoma* (1942). The medical explanations for criminal behavior also led to widespread policies on hospitalization of offenders, particularly sex offenders.

As with many of the sex offender policies today, emotionally charged cases of sexual abuse against children led to strict policies against sex offenders in the 1930s. One of the more prominent cases involved Albert Fish, who claimed to have sexually assaulted more than 400 children and murdered at least six people from 1910 to 1930 (Schecter, 1990, 1994). Also striking was his interest in sexually deviant practices of sadism and masochism, as well as his practice of cannibalism. The media constantly reported about the dangers of Fish and the details of his horrific crimes, injecting fear into the hearts of those living in New York City. ("Fish Held," 1935; "Plea of Insanity," 1935). Though not typical, it was cases like this that led to widespread support for the arrest and incapacitation of sexual "defectives" ("Isolation," 1937).

Despite the decreasing number of sexual crimes at this time, arrests for sex offenders increased dramatically. This increase resulted from a change in policing practices, specifically a focus on minor sexual nuisances such as homosexual acts in public (Karpman, 1954; Tappan, 1950). In fact, arrests for sodomy in New York City nearly doubled in the 1930s because officers were required to crack down on all homosexual activity in the subway and other public places (Jenkins, 1998). By 1937, these "habitual sexual offenders" became known as sexual psychopaths.

Because of the perceived psychological nature of their offenses, states began implementing policies to indefinitely incapacitate sexual psychopaths into mental health facilities instead of prison. In 1937, Michigan became the first state to implement Mentally Disordered Sex Offender (MDSO) legislation, though 28 states eventually followed suit (Schwartz, 1999). Based on the idea that sexual psychopathy was a disorder that could be diagnosed and treated, MDSO laws allowed states to civilly commit sex offenders until they were "cured" (Alexander, 1993). This practice of civil commitment of sex offenders continues today and is a focus of state and federal policy. (Civil commitment is discussed in more detail in chapter 11 of this volume.)

The definition of sexual psychopathy differed by state, and was variably defined as anything from "an utter lack of power to control impulses" to having the "criminal propensities towards the commission of sex offences" (Grubin & Prentky, 1993, p. 383). However, all states required that in order to be committed, sexual psychopaths had to have a mental illness and be a danger to themselves or others. Even if an offender was mentally ill, once he was no longer deemed dangerous he was to be released. Yet, there was no consistent way in which to assess dangerousness, so the diagnoses were made subjectively and inconsistently. Dangerousness was also a concept subject to changing perceptions of sexual behavior and often reflected the sexual mores of the times. For example, homosexual men were considered dangerous in the 1950s, when the legislation was intended to incapacitate truly dangerous offenders such as Albert Fish. The implementation of these laws also reflected a lack of understanding about "nuisance" sexual behaviors; offenses such as exhibitionism were considered a "gateway" into more severe types of offending.

The use of civil commitment under sexual psychopath laws increased throughout the 1940s and early 1950s. At this time mental hospitals accepted many types of offenders, with a focus on those perceived as a social threat. Commitment could result from acts defined as felonies or misdemeanors, as well as both statutory and forced offenses. Many of the sex offenders committed at this time were accused of acts such as peeping, lewdness, impairing morals, or offenses related to homosexuality such as sodomy.

Knowledge about sexual behavior and identity was still in its infancy mid-century, and homosexuality was considered socially unacceptable and deemed a mental disorder. Despite Kinsey, Pomeroy, and Martin's (1948) report on

Sexual Behavior in the Human Male, which indicated that many men had homosexual thoughts or had committed acts of a homosexual nature, the American Psychiatric Association (APA) listed homosexuality as a sexual deviation until 1973 in the Diagnostic and Statistical Manual of Mental Disorders (APA, 1968, p. 44). Additionally, it was only in 1992 that the World Health Organization removed homosexuality from its list of diseases. Researchers at this time differed on their views about homosexuality. Some linked homosexuality to deviant sexual behaviors such as pedophilia, whereas others noted that homosexual sex offenders were not particularly dangerous as a group and that they were not likely to escalate in the types of behaviors they committed (Karpman, 1954, p. 38). Homosexual acts were also considered illegal in most states. Illinois became the first state to repeal sodomy laws in 1962, but in 1986 the U.S. Supreme Court upheld Georgia's antisodomy laws in *Bowers v. Hardwick* (1986), stating that there was no fundamental right to engage in sodomy. Though this ruling also affected heterosexual couples who committed such acts, the substantial majority of offenders arrested for these crimes were homosexual. It wasn't until 2003 that the U.S. Supreme Court ruled that sodomy laws were unconstitutional (*Lawrence v. Texas*, 2003).

By the late 1940s, many researchers began to oppose the idea of civil commitment for those deemed sexual psychopaths. Tappan (1950) published a report on the problems of sexual psychopathy legislation, noting that the statutes are largely based upon erroneous views of sex offenders. He listed 10 primary fallacies concerning the sex offender, as shown in Table 3.1 (Tappan, 1950, pp. 13–16; Terry, 2006, pp. 30–31). Tappan (1950, p. 37) also noted that nearly all psychiatrists believed there was not sufficient knowledge about sex offenders to justify legislation for sexual psychopaths. He argued that sexual psychopath legislation set a dangerous precedent because it allowed for civil adjudication of individuals without due process and for indefinite commitment to hospitals for offenders who are neither insane nor seriously psychologically impaired; and that the treatment justification for hospitalization was erroneous and the cost of commitment was extraordinary to the taxpayers (Terry, 2006, p. 31).

Tappan's (1950) 10 Key Criticisms of the Paranoia about Sex Ofenders, which Inspired the Sexual Psychopath Laws

3.1

Facts About Sex Offenders	Criticism of Sexual Psychopath Laws, Based Upon Sex Offender Facts
Most sex offenders are not homicidal, stranger sex fiends	Citing Sutherland (1950), he noted that there is a greater danger of murder by an acquaintance or relative than by an unknown sex fiend. He also noted that most sex offenders only commit minor offenses.
Sex offenders have a low rate of recidivism	Sex offenders repeat their offenses less frequently than other property or violent offenders except for those convicted of homicide.
Sex offenders rarely escalate their behavior	Though escalation does occur in some serious offenders, most find a sexual act which gives them satisfaction (e.g., exhibitionism) and persist in that behavior.
It is not possible to predict dangerousness	He cited many psychiatrists who supported this point, noting that sexual psychopath laws were based upon assessments of risk
There is no agreement as to the definition of "sex psychopathy"	"Sexual psychopaths" exhibited a variety of psycho-logical problems, and there is no clear definition as to what did or should constitute a sexual psychopath.
Sex offenders are not simply "over-sexed" individuals	Organic treatments such as castration are not likely to be effective remedies for deviant sexual behavior since sexual urges are not the driving force of the offender.
Sex offenders cannot be "cured"	Commitment to a mental hospital does not mean that sex offenders will be effectively treated.
Most individuals committed are minor offenders	Though sexual psychopathy legislation was passed in order to incapacitate the serious sexual fiend, this rarely happens. Instead, they most often incapacitate those with moral offenses, such as homosexual behavior.

Continued

Tappan's (1950) 10 Key Criticisms of the Paranoia about Sex Ofenders, which Inspired the Sexual Psychopath Laws (Cont'd)

3.1

Due process rights are disregarded in commitment process	Because the commitment procedure is of a civil nature. Tappan asserts that there is a violation of human rights and due process in the commitment procedure, stating that, "regardless of the type of court employed to attain this result, it is in effect a serious punishment in which liberty and due process are vitally involved. Reasoning to the contrary is founded in a technical legalism of the most vicious sort."
The "sex offender problem" will go away because a law was passed	The only purpose of the statute is to satisfy the public, and that experience with these laws "reveals the futility of ineffectual legislation."

Over the next few decades, several psychiatric and mental health organizations suggested that these laws should be repealed, and by 1990 sexual psychopath laws existed in only 13 states (American Psychiatric Association, 1999). Although medical solutions for sexually deviant behavior continued in the 1960s—for example, with the development of chemical castration and the rise of behavioral treatment for sex offenders—much of the research and laws turned towards social explanations of sexual offending in the 1970s and 1980s.

Sex Offender Laws in the 1970s and 1980s

Much of the shifting focus on explanations of sexual violence in the 1970s and 1980s was due to the rise of feminist researchers in the late 1960s. They began to focus on sexual behavior and the reactions to victims of sexual abuse. There was a prevailing negative view of victims of sexual violence, and the police, courts, and even academic research viewed the victims of sexual abuse as partially or primarily responsible for their victimization (see Amir, 1971). The women's movement against sexual violence arose because, as Scully (1990, p. 2) noted, male and female constructions of social reality differed. Sexual assault and child sexual abuse were discussed more openly and honestly at this time, and for the first time it became apparent that child sexual abuse was not primarily a "stranger danger." Instead, the focus was on abuse within the home. This new discourse modified the stereotype that the victims of abuse were to blame rather than the perpetrators.

As knowledge about the true nature of child sexual abuse began to surface, it was also becoming socially acceptable to speak to therapists about negative feelings and behaviors. This combination of factors led to an interesting discovery: many adults began claiming that they had been victims of sexual abuse when they were younger but had repressed the memories of abuse until adulthood. There was an influx of lawsuits in the 1980s from women claiming that they only remembered the child sexual abuse after several therapy sessions. As a result of the repressed memories that were surfacing across the United States, many states extended their statutes of limitations because the abuse was often recalled years after the abuse allegedly occurred.

Many of the therapists were using recall methods such as hypnosis and truth serums (Green, 1994). Allegations eventually began to surface that such methods of recall, used in conjunction with leading questions by therapists, led patients to "remember" false events. Many therapists were unintentionally planting false memories, based upon the disorders experienced by the "victims" (e.g., eating disorders, depression). At their extreme, the repressed memory cases included claims of childhood sexual abuse in conjunction with ritualistic satanic abuse. A widely known case at the time was the McMartin preschool case, which resulted in the most expensive trial in California history, lasting over six years and ending with no convictions. Since that time, many states have passed laws allowing children to testify about sexual abuse allegations via closed circuit television so that they do not have to face their accusers.

The debate over repressed and false memories has continued for well over a decade. The topic is controversial; many clinicians believe that highly traumatic experiences in childhood can lead to repressed memories that, when recovered, are vividly truthful (Bartol & Bartol, 2004). However, Elizabeth Loftus, having conducted extensive research on the topic, has persistently challenged this notion (Lillienfeld & Loftus, 1998; Loftus, 1979). Research on repressed memories has shown that some memories can be recovered, but that what is remembered is not necessarily what happened. Indeed, the American Psychological Association Working Group on Investigation of Memories of Child Abuse (1998) concluded that although most victims of child sexual abuse remember the events that ensued, some memories of abuse could be forgotten and later remembered. However, the group cautioned that sometimes false memories of events, which never took place, are constructed. It is essential that policy makers and practitioners understand both sides of this debate and proceed with caution as policy related to child abuse is written.

1990s–Present: The Emergence of Current Sex Offender Laws

The late 1990s and early 2000s saw the emergence of several high-profile cases involving sexual offenses against children. As a result, public policies began to focus once again on protecting the public from stranger danger.

Washington became the first state to pass comprehensive laws regulating the management, supervision, and commitment of sex offenders in 1990. It did so largely because of two heinous cases of sexual assault and torture against children. The first case involved Wesley Allan Dodd, who sexually molested, tortured, and murdered three young boys. The second involved Earl Shriner, who kidnapped a 7-year-old boy, sexually assaulted him, cut off his penis, and left him for dead. Both men had made statements prior to their offenses that they intended to commit such acts, and Dodd even noted that if he had the chance he would do it again. Because both men had served finite sentences, the state of Washington could do nothing to keep them incapacitated or to monitor their whereabouts in the community. Dodd was eventually executed (see Ostrom & Broom, 1993), but the case of Shriner prompted the implementation of a comprehensive legislative act for serious sex offenders who could potentially be released form prison one day.

The Community Protection Act of 1990, as it was called, contained 14 separate provisions for ensuring community safety against predators such as Earl Shriner. Many of these statutory regulations were later enacted in other states (e.g., sexually violent predator legislation) or on a federal level (e.g., registration and community notification). This brought about an emergence of "memorial laws," named after children who were sexually assaulted and killed.

Though this era has been defined by the memorial laws passed, other laws had a broader scope aimed at protecting children. Most notable is the PROTECT[iv] Act of 2003 (117 STAT. 650), whose stated goal was to prevent the abduction of children and to eliminate sexual exploitation of children. Accordingly, the act provided new and expanded ways to investigate, prosecute, and sentence federal sex crimes:

- Creating a national AMBER Alert Program that would allow better coordination between local and state programs
- Allowing the interception of all wire, oral, and electronic communications related to sexual abuse and sex trafficking and the interception of all oral and electronic communications related
- Lifting the 25-year statute of limitations for sexual and physical abuse
- Authorizing the term of supervised release, after incarceration, to range from any specified number of years to life for sex crimes against children
- Increasing the penalty for child abduction to a minimum of 20 years in prison
- Increasing the penalty for using a child for the production of pornography to 15–30 years
- Decreasing pretrial release for offenders charged with certain crimes involving children
- Decreasing the authority of judges to provide reduced prison sentences to certain sex offenders
- Creating "Two Strikes" laws that would provide lifetime imprisonment for offenders convicted of two serious sex offenses against children
- Strengthening the provisions on "virtual" child pornography and current obscenity laws

With an increased knowledge about the extent of commercial sexual exploitation of children, some states have attempted to enact policies to help those children who are in danger of harm. For example, The Safe Harbor for Exploited Youth Act (A. 5258-c, S.3175-c.) in New York would remove prostitution as a crime for girls 16 and under, focusing instead on how to help them find safe housing and protection from pimps or others who have exploited them. Unfortunately, such laws face many obstacles and have yet to be shepherded through on a state level.

Table 3.2 shows a summary of the most influential sex offender statutes currently in place. Even though there are

3.2	Groundbreaking Policies Related to the Management and Supervision of Sex Offenders		
Name of Statute	**Federal or State**	**Brief Description**	
Community Protection Act of 1990	Washington State	Act that contained 14 sections related to the punishment and management of sex offenders. Includes America's first community notification statute, as well as a provision for civil commitment of sexual predators. Allows law enforcement to notify the public about released sex offenders in the community.	
Jacob Wetterling Crimes Against Children and Sexually Violent Predator Program (1994)	Federal	Required each state to create a registry for offenders convicted of sexual offenses against and other certain other offenses against children.	
Megan's Law (1996)	Federal (initiated in New Jersey)	Subsection of the Jacob Wetterling Act that requires notification about sex offenders in the community. Together, these are referred to as Registration and Community Notification Laws (RCNL). The two Acts required all states to implement RCNL by the end of 1997 or risk losing federal funding for state and local law enforcement.	

3.2 Groundbreaking Policies Related to the Management and Supervision of Sex Offenders (Cont'd)

Pam Lychner Sexual Offender Tracking and Identification Act of 1996	Federal	Subsection of the Jacob Wetterling Act. Established a national database at the Federal Bureau of Investigation (FBI) to track the whereabouts of all those who have been convicted of an offense against a minor or a sexually violent offense.
Jimmy Ryce Involuntary Civil Commitment for Sexually Violent Predators Treatment and Care Act (1998)	Florida	Allows for long-term civil commitment of sex offenders who are assessed to be at high risk to recidivate. Many other states have similar commitment statutes, though this memorial law is based upon a high-profile case in Florida.
Campus Sex Crimes Act (2000)	Federal	Requires sex offenders to provide information about institutions of higher education that they attended for school or for employment. This information is provided to law enforcement agencies in the jurisdiction of the institution and entered into state registry records
PROTECT Act (2003)	Federal	Enacted to prevent the abduction of children and to eliminate sexual exploitation of children. Employs strategies such as the AMBER Alert, increases penalties for offenders, increases statute of limitation, and strengthens laws on child pornography.

Continued

3.2 Groundbreaking Policies Related to the Management and Supervision of Sex Offenders (Cont'd)

Jessica Lunsford Act (2005)	Initiated in Florida (Subsequently passed in majority of states)	State law that increased penalties for sexually based offenses against minors; requires fingerprinting and identification of all individuals working at schools; requires GPS tracking of offenders; and increases supervision of registrants. Florida was the first state to pass this law, but other states have "Jessica's laws" that are very similar to the Florida law, most notably California's Proposition 83.
Adam Walsh Child Protection and Safety Act (2006)	Federal	Act that sets national standards on the following measures: registration and notification, civil commitment, child pornography prevention, and Internet safety, and makes failure to register as a sex offender a deportable offense. It is one of the most comprehensive acts ever created to supervise and manage sex offenders. States that do not comply risk losing 10% of federal funding.

hundreds of memorial laws, these have had a national influence in the supervision and management of sex offenders. They focus primarily on the enhanced supervision of sex offenders in the community, as well as the incapacitation of offenders who are at the highest risk of reoffense.

Registration and Community Notification Laws

In 1989, 11-year-old Jacob Wetterling, his 10-year-old brother, and an 11-year-old friend were riding their bikes home from a convenience store in St. Joseph, Minnesota. A masked gunman came out of a driveway and ordered the boys to throw their bikes into a ditch, turn off their flashlights, and lie face down on the ground. After asking the boys their ages, the gunman told Jacob's brother and friend to run into the woods and he threatened to shoot them if they looked back. Despite the warning, both boys looked back in time to see the gunman take Jacob by the arm. By the time they reached the wooded area, both Jacob and the gunman were gone (see Jacob Wetterling Resource Center, 2008). Despite the efforts of friends, family members, and the local community, Jacob has never been found.

Although it is not known who abducted Jacob, many assume that the perpetrator was one of the sex offenders living in a halfway house in St. Joseph. Patty Wetterling, Jacob's mother, became a leader in the community effort to implement sex offender registration requirements in Minnesota and, subsequently, nationally. In 1994, Congress passed the Jacob Wetterling Crimes Against Children and Sexually Violent Offender Registration Act, part of the Federal Violent Crime Control and Law Enforcement Act of 1994, in Jacob's honor. Ms. Wetterling, a national figure on sexual violence prevention, presents her view of the history and evolution of these laws in chapter 4.

The Jacob Wetterling Act required each state to create a registry for offenders convicted of sexual and certain other offenses against children. States had a specified time period within which to enact this legislation, along with guidelines established by the Attorney General. If states failed to comply, the states would forfeit 10% of federal funds from the Omnibus Crime Control and Safe Streets Act of 1968.

Another emotionally charged case of sexual abuse led to a modification of the Jacob Wetterling Act. On July 29, 1994, Megan Kanka, a 7-year-old girl from Hamilton Township, New Jersey, was raped and killed by a recidivist pedophile living across the street from her. Jesse Timmendequas, who had been convicted of two previous sexual offenses against children, lived with two other child sexual abusers. Jesse lured

Megan into his house with promises of seeing his puppy, and then he raped and killed her. Megan's parents and community members wondered how recidivist sex offenders could be living in the community without the community's knowledge and awareness.

Maureen Kanka went on a crusade to change the law, arguing that registration as established by the Wetterling Act was not a sufficient form of community protection from sex offenders. Her goal was to mandate community notification, which under Wetterling had been at the discretion of law enforcement. She said that if she had known that a sex offender was living across the street, she would have warned Megan and Megan would still be alive today. Eighty-nine days after her death, New Jersey enacted "Megan's Law." On May 17, 1996, less than two years later, President Bill Clinton enacted a federal version of Megan's Law that set guidelines for the state statutes (Terry & Furlong, 2008).

The federal Megan's Law was a subsection of the Jacob Wetterling Crimes Against Children and Sexually Violent Offender Registration Law. Together, these were referred to as Registration and Community Notification Laws (RCNL). The two acts required all states to implement RCNL by the end of 1997 or risk losing federal funding for state and local law enforcement. Prior to Megan's death, only five states had enacted laws requiring sex offenders to register their personal information with a law enforcement agency (Earl-Hubbard, 1996.) On August 5, 1996, Massachusetts was the last of the 50 states to enact its version of Megan's Law. Since that time, those two laws have been supplanted by the Sex Offender Registration and Notification Act (SORNA) provisions with the Walsh Act (discussed below).

In 2000, Congress again amended the Violent Crime Control and Law Enforcement Act of 1994 (42 U.S.C. 14071) to include a new subsection with respect to sex offender registration requirements. The new section was titled "The Campus Sex Crimes Prevention Act of 2000" (Section 170101) and would take effect two years from the date of enactment. Under the amended act, registered sex offenders would now be required to provide information about institutions of higher education that they attended for school or for employment. This information would be provided to law enforcement agencies in the jurisdiction of the institution and would be entered into state registry records. Schools could request information at any time.

Registration and community notification statutes and guidelines differ by state, though after a dozen years there is greater uniformity than upon their inception. Table 3.3 shows the differences in registration and notification statutes by state, including the number of years the offenders must remain on the registry, whether the state mandates DNA collection for sex offenders, whether juveniles have to register, whether there are special provisions for homeless registrants, and whether there are state residence restrictions. (Chapter 7 discusses sex offender registration and notification in more detail.)

RCNL has been challenged on a number of constitutional and other bases, generating a substantial amount of case law (see Terry & Furlong, 2008). Those challenging the statutes have claimed violations of ex post facto, due process, cruel and unusual punishment, equal protection, search and seizure, and failure of the state to notify the offender of his duty to register. Cases have also covered issues such as inappropriate triggering offense (e.g., kidnapping a child with no sexual offense), failure to register (for a regulatory law) as a criminal offense, inappropriate risk assessment procedures, lack of jurisdiction by the courts, the lack of clarity in laws as they apply to homeless and juvenile offenders, and the broad scope of Internet notification.

Few RCNL challenges have been met with success. The courts have unanimously decided that RCNL is appropriate state regulation, not punishment, and that it is not an onerous burden. The Supreme Court has even upheld challenges to the most broad notification systems. In *Connecticut Department of Public Safety v. Doe* (2003) and *Smith v. Doe* (2003), the Court stated that Internet notification, even if applied ex post facto, is constitutional because injury to reputation alone is not a deprivation of liberty. Within these two Supreme Court cases, heard together, the Court also upheld Alaska's provision, which required that the registry be retroactive.

One of the problems with the original wave of registration and community notification laws is that there are variations amongst the states, creating logistical and interagency barriers. The first law that attempting to unify state statutes was the Pam Lychner Sexual Offender Tracking and Identification

3.3 Overview of the Differences in Registration and Notification Requirements by State

State/Federal	Year RCNL Initially Enacted	Number of Years to Remain on Registry	DNA	Juvenile Registration	Quarterly Verification for High Risk/Homeless Registrants	Residency Restrictions
Federal[v]	1996	10–life	√	*	√	*
Alabama	1996	Life[vi]	√	√		2000
Alaska	1994	15–life	√		√	
Arizona	1996	10–life	√	√		
Arkansas	1997	Life	√	√	√[vii]	2000[viii]
California	1997	Life	√	√	√[ix]	1 mile
Colorado	1994	Life	√	√	√	
Connecticut	1994	10–life	√	√	√	
Delaware	1994	15–life	√	√	√	
Florida	1995	Life	√	√	√	1000

State	Year	Sentence				
Georgia	1994	10–life			√	1000
Hawaii	1997	Life	√		√[x]	
Idaho	1993	Life[xi]		√	√	
Illinois	1996	10–life	√	√	√	500
Indiana	1994	10–life		√	√	1000
Iowa	1995	10–life	√	√	√	2000
Kansas	1994	10–life	√	√	√[xii]	
Kentucky	1994	20–life		√	√	1000
Louisiana	1992	10–life	√	√	√	1000
Maine	1996	10–life			√	
Maryland	1995	10–life			√	
Massachusetts	1996	20–life		√		
Michigan	1994	25–life[xiii]		√		1000
Minnesota	1996	10–life		√	√	√[xiv]
Mississippi	1995	Life	√	√	√[xv]	

Continued

3.3 Overview of the Differences in Registration and Notification Requirements by State (Cont'd)

State	Year	Duration				
Missouri	1997	Life	✓	✓	✓	1000
Montana	1991	10–life	✓	✓	✓	
Nebraska	1997	10–life	✓	✓	✓	500
Nevada	1995	15–life		✓	✓	
New Hampshire	1996	10–life	✓	✓	✓	
New Jersey	1994	15–life	✓	✓	✓	
New Mexico	1995	10–life	✓		✓	
New York	1996	20–life	✓	✓	✓	
North Carolina	1995	10–life	✓	✓	✓	
North Dakota	1991	15–life	✓	✓	✓	
Ohio	1997	10–life	✓		✓	1000
Oklahoma	1995	10–life	✓	✓	✓	2000[xvi]

State	Year					
Oregon	1993	10–life		√	√	√xvii
Pennsylvania	1995	10–life			√	
Rhode Island	1996	10–life		√	√	
South Carolina	1994	Life		√	√	√xviii
South Dakota	1994	10–life	√	√		500
Tennessee	1994	10–life			√	1000
Texas	1995	10–life	√	√	√	√xix
Utah	1996	10–life	√	√	√xx	1000
Vermont	1996	10–life			√	
Virginia	1994	10–life	√	√	√	
Washington	1990	10–life	√	√	√	880
West Virginia	1996	10–life		√	√	1000
Wisconsin	1996	15–life			√	
Wyoming	1997	15–life	√		√	

(Source: Terry & Furlong, 2008)

Act of 1996, which was another amendment to the Jacob Wetterling Act named after the victim of a violent sexual assault. Pam Lychner was a real estate agent in Houston, Texas, who was on her way to show a home to a prospective client. However, a recidivist violent offender was at the home waiting for her. He attacked her and would have killed her, but her husband arrived in time to save her. She subsequently formed the victims' rights advocacy group "Justice for All," which lobbied for tougher sentences for violent and sexual criminals. Sadly, Lychner and her two daughters were killed in the explosion of TWA Flight 800 in July 1996. In her memory, Congress passed the Pam Lychner Sexual Offender Tracking and Identification Act later that year (Levenson & D'Amora, 2007).

The Pam Lychner Act established a national database at the Federal Bureau of Investigation (FBI) to track the whereabouts of all those convicted of an offense against a minor or a sexually violent offense. Although a functional national database is an important goal for an effective system of notification, thereby reducing the problem of linkage blindness, there are problems with the current system. Namely, the information in the database is derived from information on the state databases. The frequent relocation of sex offenders, particularly now with the implementation of residence restrictions (discussed below), leads to information on the database often being outdated.

Civil Commitment

Several states have passed legislation allowing for the civil commitment of "sexually violent predators" (SVP) to a psychiatric facility if they are assessed as having a mental abnormality or personality disorder and are dangerous to themselves or others. The goal of this legislation is to incapacitate recidivist sex offenders who are at high risk to reoffend until they are deemed rehabilitated (Seling, 2000). Like the sexual psychopath legislation before them, SVP laws assume a relationship between mental disorder, risk, and sexual violence. SVP legislation is essentially a modification of the sexual psychopathy laws, though there are a few significant variations. Most importantly, civil commitment is not intended to replace incarceration, but instead supplement it. Upon completion of a criminal sentence, sex offenders who have a mental disorder and are deemed dangerous can be committed to some type of secure mental hospital until they

are "rehabilitated," although there is no agreed-upon definitive treatment for sexual offending.

SVP legislation is controversial for many reasons, including the cost of commitment, type of commitment facility, and
concern that the commitment is punishment under the guise
of rehabilitation. Most importantly, however, is the issue of
risk assessment, because sex offenders are incapacitated for
acts that they might commit based upon their perceived risk.
The risk assessment process is faulty, as predicting human
behavior is a nearly impossible task (Hood & Shute, 1996).
One key concern is that assessment is not a uniform phenomenon, and the ability to predict a person's actions depends
largely upon who is being assessed and the quality of the
assessment (Lidz & Mulvey, 1995). Predictions of violence
tend to be most accurate for certain types of cases, such as
when there is a history of repeated violence (Litwack, 1993),
there is evidence of psychopathy (Hemphill, Hare, & Wong,
1998; Quinsey, Lalumiere, Rice, & Harris, 1995), or there is a
previous conviction for a sexual offense (McGrath, 1994).

As of 2006, there were 4,534 sex offenders civilly committed in the United States. Though most often individuals can be
held indefinitely, 494 people have been discharged or released
(very few of these were deemed "rehabilitated"; rather, they
were released as a result of technical issues related to the
case or the commitment) (Gookin, 2007). Civil commitment
has been criticized for how expensive it is. The national average cost for commitment is approximately $94,000, whereas
the typical cost for incarceration in prison is roughly $26,000
(Ibid). Despite the challenges against it, new laws (such as
the Walsh Act, discussed below) encourage states to create
commitment procedures if they have not already done so.
See chapter 11 for more on civil commitment.

Residence Restrictions

State and local legislators recently enacted many regulations
in local jurisdictions to monitor offenders in the community,
such as GPS monitoring and the use of special identifiers on
sex offender's drivers' licenses (Vitiello, 2008). The most common of these policies is residence restrictions, which limit the
places where sex offenders can live, work, or loiter. The policies are based upon the premise that geographical proximity
to offense opportunities (e.g., child victims) increases the likelihood that an offender will recidivate. This is concordant with

the criminological literature, which indicates that criminal offenses are dependent upon situational opportunities, and potential offenders will use the environment to their advantage in the commission of a crime (Cohen & Felson, 1979).

The goal of residency restriction statutes is to increase public safety protection by limiting sex offenders' access to the places "where children congregate." The places of congregation and the length of the restriction vary by jurisdiction. Residence restrictions typically bar offenders from living within a 1,000- to 2,500-foot distance from schools, day care centers, parks, or other places densely populated by children (Nieto & Jung, 2006). Some states have gone so far as to say that children congregate at bus stops, and thus have included those within the residency limitations. Most residence restrictions have been implemented on a local rather than state level. Nieto and Jung (2006) noted that 22 states have some form of residence restrictions, though the Minnesota Department of Corrections (2007) explained that these are generally applied on a case-by-case basis.

Sex offenders have challenged residence restrictions in court, and in 2005 the Eighth Circuit Court of Appeals upheld an Iowa statute that prohibited sex offenders from living within 2,000 feet of designated places where children congregate (*Doe v. Miller*, 2005). The Court ruled that residence restrictions are not, on their face, unconstitutional. In a petition to the Supreme Court, the Association for the Treatment of Sexual Abusers (ATSA) (2005) argued that residence restrictions may deprive sex offenders of housing options, may force offenders to move from supportive environments and employment opportunities, and, subsequently, could increase rather than decrease recidivism risk.

Few empirical studies have thus far addressed the outcome of this legislation, and the empirical studies that do exist have produced conflicting results. The Minnesota Department of Corrections (2003) reported that residence restrictions create a shortage of available housing alternatives for sex offenders, which they said may force them into isolated areas that lack services, employment opportunities, and/or adequate social support. Walker, Golden, and VanHouten (2002) mapped the addresses of 170 sex offenders in a metropolitan Arkansas county and found that a higher percentage of child sex offenders (48%) lived within 1,000-foot buffer zones around schools, day care centers, and parks than did non–child sex offenders (26%). A New York City study indicated that indicated that 85% of New York City's highest risk offenders lived within five blocks of a school (Weiner, 2007). Wartell (2007) found that only 27% of available living space within the city of San Diego was available to sex offenders. A fuller discussion of residence restrictions and their efficacy and unintended consequences can be found in chapter 9.

The Jessica Lunsford Act

After the kidnapping, rape, and murder of Florida resident Jessica Lunsford by a repeat sex offender, the legislature moved quickly to change current legislation. In 2005, Governor Jeb Bush signed the Jessica Lunsford Act into legislation. Some of the highlights of the act include the following

- The penalty for failing to respond to an address-verification increased and is now a third-degree felony punishable by incarceration.
- Any individual who has information regarding a sex offender or predator, who fails to notify law enforcement, may be charged with a felony offense.
- Any individual over the age of 18 who commits the aforementioned offense against a child under 12 will be given a life felony and a mandatory minimum 25-year sentence.
- When sex offenders and predators are rearrested for any reason, the court must make an informed decision to determine dangerousness before the individual can be released on bail.
- Any person who commits a sex crime against a minor will, after release from incarceration, be subject to GPS monitoring for the remainder of his or her life.
- The law requires the Florida Department of Law Enforcement to have equipment that reads fingerprints, with the ability to immediately identify individuals when they report to probation officers. Similarly, the equipment will immediately alert probation departments when individuals are rearrested.
- The law demands mandatory fingerprinting and background checks for all noninstructional or contractual personnel working at schools. (see Florida Department of Education, 2005)

The problem with Jessica's Law, like many of the policies enacted before it, is that it treats sex offenders as a homogeneous group and does not differentiate those at high and low risk of recidivating (Melkonia, 2007). There are currently no published studies assessing the efficacy of Jessica's Law in the states where it has been enacted. The policies in place prior to Jessica Lunsford's death were not a deterrent to her killer or others who committed such heinous crimes, and the law has consistently tried to respond to such deficiencies. For instance, registration did not deter sexual crimes against children, so the legislature added notification requirements; to respond to the deficiencies of RCNL, many states enacted sexually violent predator statutes; when these did not deter, Jessica's Law emerged (Mortensen, 2006). Though Jessica's Law is structured as a response to sexual crimes like the policies before it, some legal scholars speculate that provisions such as GPS tracking will actually deter known offenders from recidivating (Ibid).

According to the Jessica Lunsford Foundation site (Jessica Marie Lunsford Foundation, 2008), 33 states have enacted some version of Jessica's Law. Most notably, California passed Proposition 83 in November 2006 with 76% of the vote, allowing for the enactment of the Sexual Predator Punishment and Control Act (SPPCA). The SPPCA allows for the enhancement of criminal penalties for child sexual abusers, GPS monitoring, more sex offender eligible for civil commitment, and residence restrictions of 2,000 feet (creating "predator free" zones) (Dacey, 2007). Unfortunately, California and other states that have enacted such sweeping restrictions have given little credence to the problems now faced in states such as Iowa that have had residence restrictions in place for years. Whereas many groups in Iowa are calling for such restrictions to be repealed because they are seemingly causing more harm than good, more states are imposing the same or more severe restrictions.

The Adam Walsh Act

The Adam Walsh Child Protection and Safety Act of 2006 (H.R. 4472), also referred to as the "Child Protection Act," was signed into legislation by President Bush in 2006. It is one of the most comprehensive acts ever created to supervise and manage sex offenders.

Epitomizing the memorial laws before it, the Adam Walsh Act is specifically geared toward preventing the brutal abductions, rapes, and murders of victims by strangers. The act sets national standards on the following measures: registration and notification, civil commitment, child pornography prevention, and Internet safety; and it makes failure to register as a sex offender a deportable offense for immigrants. Additionally, the Office of the Attorney General has agreed to establish grants to support pilot programs for the monitoring of released sex offenders as well as for numerous other initiatives (e.g., combating sexual abuse of children, fingerprinting programs, online safety programs).

One of the most significant components of the act is that it clarifies national standards for all sex offenders regardless of the state they live in. Table 3.4 shows the key features of the Sex Offender Registration and Notification Act (SORNA), which is Title I of the Adam Walsh Act.

3.4 Key Provisions of SORNA

Tier 3, or the highest risk offenders, will be registered on a national database for life

Tier 2 (moderate-risk) and Tier 1 (low-risk) offenders will be required to register for 25 and 15 years, respectively

Failure to register or accurately & regularly update home and work (and if appropriate, school) information can result in felony charges, punishable by 10 years in prison

In-person verification of registry information will be 12 months for Tier 1 offenders, 6 months for Tier 2 offenders, and 3 months for Tier 3 offenders

All state registry Web sites must include information for all sex offenders in their database—not just that of high-risk (Tiers 2 and 3) offenders

DNA samples will be required of all registrants

All juvenile sex offenders will be required register and those who are least 14 years of age at the time of the offense and who have been adjudicated for aggravated sexual abuse or some comparable offense will be subject to community notification provisions

Section 301 of the Adam Walsh Act establishes grants for the development of civil commitment programs for sexually violent predators. Called the Jimmy Ryce State Civil Commitment Program for Sexually Dangerous Persons, this section is named after the Florida statute of the same name. States are eligible for support if, within a 2-year compliance period, they have established a civil commitment program or submitted a plan for such a program. The act creates guidelines for the civil commitment process, including the institution of proceeding, the psychiatric examination, the hearing, the determination and disposition, and discharge procedures.

Sex Offender Legislation: A Moral Panic

After nearly two decades of federal sex offender laws, it is well past time for critical and widespread assessment and reevaluation. Reentry and reintegration of offenders into the community should be a key goal of sex offender legislation. However, it is unclear if the sex offender laws implemented so far accomplish this goal. Before implementing any more such laws, it is necessary to thoroughly evaluate the policies currently in place. Feel-good legislation may not be the most effective for sex offenders; sex offenders constitute a heterogeneous group of individuals who offend for a variety of reasons, and current legislation imposes substantial criminal penalties and other collateral consequences on sex offenders through one-size-fits-all policies (Vitiello, 2008). There are, of course, some very serious sex offenders who are repeat offenders with many victims. It is important to identify those individuals and make any efforts to keep them from committing future offenses that might have been preventable. The question is, do sex offender laws appropriately target those offenders and protect the community from them, or do they cast a wide net, effectively losing the most dangerous offenders?

Sex offenders are often scrutinized because of the fear that they will inevitably commit new sex crimes. In fact, many state legislatures have stated that sex offenders pose a high risk of reoffending in their laws. As discussed in chapter 2, the majority of recidivism studies provide findings that are contrary to this belief. A meta-analysis by Hanson and Morton-Bourgon (2005) provided a 13.7% recidivism rate for a new sex crime over a 5-year period and a study by the

Bureau of Justice Statistics (BJS) found a 5.3% recidivism rate for sex offenders over 3 years (BJS, 2003). Because of the low reporting and conviction rates, as well as varying definitions of recidivism and follow-up periods, caution should always be given when looking at official recidivism statistics. However, recent criminological literature consistently shows that when sex offenders do reoffend, they are more likely to commit a nonsexual offense than a sexual one (see Lussier, LeBlanc, & Proulx, 2005; Miethe, Olson, & Mitchell, 2006; Simon, 2000; Smallbone & Wortley, 2004; Soothill, Francis, Sanderson, & Ackerley, 2000; and Zimring, Piquero, & Jennings, 2007). This is an important shortcoming of the legislation, because all sex offender legislation is based on the assumption that sex offenders will recidivate with new sexual offenses.

The aim of all sex offender legislation is to protect the community. However, much of the legislation is based upon flawed assumptions about sex offenders or it is based upon the high-profile cases of stranger abduction and murder of children—rare occurrences. These occurrences cause a moral panic in the community, resulting in knee-jerk legislation that is not supported by the research. It is true that this legislation might prevent some tragic cases of abuse. For instance, had the Kankas known that Jesse Timmendequas lived across the street from them, Megan would have been instructed not to go near his house. However, sound national policy should not be based on rare but tragic occurrences but on the most common experiences supported by empirical data.

Sex offender legislation has been criticized for providing a false sense of security and for potentially increasing, rather than decreasing, risk in the community. Harsher regulations, such as residence restrictions, might cause offenders to abscond from registration requirements. Evidence of this is seen in the fact that states that have more restrictive policies have lower compliance rates (Bedarf, 1995). Recent research suggests that sex offender laws make treatment compliance difficult and other collateral consequences, such as inability to find suitable employment or housing, put offenders at a greater risk of reoffending (Earl-Hubbard, 1996; Levenson & Hern, 2007; Tewskbury, 2004, 2005).

These laws also pose difficulties for the general criminal justice system. For instance, when working with an alleged sex offender, the defense attorney must discuss the implications of pleading guilty that go far beyond traditional punishments. In such cases, the defendant may choose to go to trial and risk a harsher sentence to avoid being subject to sex offender laws. The fear of such consequences will only increase after full implementation of the Adam Walsh Act. For those offenders who plead or are found guilty, they are subject to increased sentencing under the Jessica Lunsford Act or similar legislation regardless of the future risk they may pose. Such legislation, which increases mandatory minimum sentences for child sexual abusers, reduces the discretion of judges in sentencing based upon individual cases and can result in low-risk sex offenders serving extensive and unnecessary prison sentences (Melkonia, 2007; Vitiello, 2008).

Since the early 1990s, our interest in sex offenders has been heightened by highly publicized cases that have caused public outrage and a subsequent moral panic. This is not only from cases that invoke fear of sexual "monsters" abducting children, but from offenses involving people we trust, such as priests, coaches, teachers, and scout leaders. When sex crimes against children occur, harsher, more punitive laws are enacted. This pattern of emotionally driven legislative escalation appears inevitable. Although any sexually based offense is tragic, sex offender legislation should focus on the empirical basis for sexual offending, as well as the rights and needs of victims, offenders, and their families. New sex offender policies must bypass the need for short-term symbolic victories. Questions remain as to how this can be accomplished, and future research and evidence-based policy are a necessity.

References

Alexander, R. (1993.) The civil commitment of sex offenders in light of Foucha v. Louisiana. *Criminal Justice and Behavior, 20,* 371–387.

American Psychiatric Association. (1999). *Dangerous Sex Offenders: A Task Force Report of the American Psychiatric Association.* Washington, DC: APA.

American Psychiatric Association. (1968). *Diagnostic and Statistical Manual of Mental Disorders* (2nd Ed.). Washington, DC: APA.

American Psychological Association Working Group to Investigate Memories of Child Abuse. (1998). Final conclusions. *Psychology, Public Policy, and Law, 4,* 933–940.

Amir, M. (1971). *Patterns in Forcible Rape.* New York: Columbia University Press.

Association for the Treatment of Sexual Abusers (ATSA) as amicus curiae in support of petitioner, *Doe v. Miller,* filed on November 3, 2005, with the United States Supreme Court.

Bartol, C. R. & Bartol, A. M. (2004). *Psychology and Law: Theory, Research, and Application* (3rd Ed.). Belmont: Thompson Wadsworth.

Bedarf, A. R. (1995). Examining Sex Offender Notification Laws. *California Law Review, 83*, 885, 907–908.

Breiner, S. J. (1990). *Slaughter of the innocents: Child abuse through the ages and today*. New York: Plenum.

Bureau of Justice Statistics. (2003). *Recidivism of Sex Offenders Released From Prison in 1994*. Washington, DC: U.S. Department of Justice.

Cohen, L.E. & Felson, M. (1979). Social change and crime rate trends: A routine activities approach. *American Sociological Review, 44*, 588–608.

Dacey, J. (2007). Sex offender residency restrictions: California's failure to learn from Iowa's mistakes. *Journal of Juvenile Law, 28*, 11–29.

Dover, K. J. (1978). *Greek homosexuality*. Cambridge: Harvard University Press.

Earl-Hubbard, M. (1996). The Child Offender Registration Laws: The Punishment, Liberty Deprivation, and Unintended Results Associated with the Scarlet Letter Laws of the 1990s. *Northwestern University Law Review, 90*, 788, 790.

Ellis, H. (1899/1942). *Studies in the psychology of sex* (2 vols.). New York: Random House.

Fish held legally sane; Two alienists report alleged Budd slayer has some abnormalities. (December 28, 1934). *New York Times*.

Florida Department of Law Enforcement (2005). Highlights from the Jessica Lunsford Act, Retrieved March 31, 2008, from http://www3.fdle.state.fl.us/sopu/citizeninfo.asp.

Florida Department of Education (2005). Technical Assistance Paper – Jessica Lunsford Act, Retrieved March 31, 2008, from http://info.fldoe.org/docushare/dsweb/Get/Document-3151/k12_05-107a.pdf.

Freud, S. (1905/1953). *Three essays of the theory of sexuality. The complete psychological works of Sigmund Freud* (Standard ed., vol. 7). London: Hogarth.

Gookin, K. (2007). *Comparison of state laws authorizing involuntary commitment of sexually violent predators: 2006 Update*. Olympia: Washington State Institute for Public Policy.

Green, R. (1994). Recovered memories of sexual abuse: The unconscious strikes back or therapist induced madness? *Annual Review of Sex Research, 5*, 101–121.

Grubin, D., & Prentky, R. (1993). Sexual psychopathy laws. *Criminal Behaviour and Mental Health, 3*, 381–392.

Hanson, R.K, & Morton-Bourgon, K. (2005). The characteristics of persistent sexual offenders. *Journal of Consulting and Clinical Psychology, 73*, 1154-1163.

Hemphill, J. F., Hare, R. D, & Wong, S. (1998). Psychopathy and recidivism: A review. *Legal and Criminological Psychology, 3*, 139–170.

Hood, R, & Shute, S. (1996). Protecting the public: Life sentences, parole, and high risk offenders. *Criminal Law Review, 788–800.*

Isolation advised for sex criminals; Dr Lichtenstein would keep defectives off the streets and out of prison. (October 14, 1937). *New York Times*.

Jacob Wetterling Resource Center (2008) Retrieved on May 22, 2008, from http://www.jwrc.org/.

Janicki, M. A. (2007). Better seen than herded: Residency restrictions and global positioning system tracking laws for sex offenders. *The Boston University Public Interest Law Journal, 16*, 285–311.

Jenkins, P. (1998). *Moral panic: Changing concepts of the child molester in modern America*. New Haven: Yale University Press.

Karpman, B. (1954). *The sexual offender and his offenses: Etiology, pathology, psychodynamics and treatment*. New York: Julian.

Kinsey, A., Pomeroy, W.B. & Martin, C.E. (1948). *Sexual behavior in the human male*. Bloomington: Indiana University Press.

Krafft-Ebing, R. V. (1886/1965). *Psychopathia sexualis*. New York: Putnam.

Levenson, J. and D'Amora, D., (2007). Social policies designed to prevent sexual violence: The Emperor's new clothes? *Criminal Justice Policy Review, 18*, 168–199.

Levenson, J.S. and A. Hern. 2007. Sex offender residence restrictions: Unintended consequences and community re-entry. *Justice Research and Policy, 9*, 60–73.

Lidz, C. W, & Mulvey, E. P. (1995). Dangerousness: From legal definition to theoretical research. *Law and Human Behavior, 19*, 41–48.

Lillienfeld, S.O. & Loftus, E. (1998). Repressed memories and World War II: Some cautionary notes. *Professional Psychology: Research and Practice, 29*, 471–478.

Litwack, T. R. (1993). On the ethics of dangerousness assessments. *Law and Human Behavior, 17*, 479–482.

Loftus, E.F. (1979). *Eyewitness Testimony*. Cambridge: Harvard University Press.

Lussier, P., LeBlanc, M., & Proulx, J. (2005). The generality of criminal behavior: A confirmatory factor analysis of the criminal activity of sex offenders in adulthood. *Journal of Criminal Justice, 33*, 177–189.

McGrath, R.J. (1994). Sex offender risk assessment and disposition planning: A review of clinical and empirical findings. *International Journal of Offender Therapy and Comparative Criminology, 35*, 328-350.

Melkonia, K. (2007). Michigan's sex offender registration act: Does it make communities safer? The implications of the inclusion of a broad range of offenders, a review of statutory amendments and thoughts on future changes. *University of Detroit Mercy Law Review, 84*, 355–381.

Miethe, T.D., Olson, J. & Mitchell, O. (2006). Specialization and persistence in the arrest histories of sex offenders: A comparative analysis of alternative measures and offense types. *Journal of Research in Crime and Delinquency, 43*, 204–229.

Minnesota Department of Corrections. (2003) *Level three sex offenders residential placement issues, 2003 report to the legislature*. St. Paul: Minnesota Department of Corrections.

Minnesota Department of Corrections. (2007). *residential proximity & sex offense recidivism in Minnesota*. St. Paul: Minnesota Department of Corrections.

Mondimore, F. M. (1996). *A natural history of homosexuality*. Baltimore: Johns Hopkins University Press.

Mortensen. M.L. (2006). GPS monitoring: An ingenious solution to the threat pedophiles pose to California's children. *Journal of Juvenile Law, 27*, 17–32.

Nieto, M., & Jung, D. (2006). *The impact of residency restrictions on sex offenders and correctional management practices: A literature review.* California Research Bureau: Sacramento, CA.

Odem, M.E. (1995). *Delinquent daughters: Protecting and policing adolescent female sexuality in the United States.* Chapel Hill: University of North Carolina Press.

Ostrom, C.M. & Broom, J. (January 3rd 1993). Wesley Dodd: A long, steady slide into dark desperation. *The Seattle Times.* Retrieved on July 17, 2008 from http://community.seattletimes.nwsource.com/archive/?date=19930103&slug=1677933.

Plea of insanity entered for Fish; Attorney admitted slayer of Grace Budd asks for a lunacy commission. (January 8, 1935). *New York Times.*

Quinsey, V. L., Lalumiere, M. L., Rice, M. E, & Harris, G. T. (1995). Predicting sexual offences. In J. C. Campbell (ed.), *Assessing Dangerousness: Violence by Sexual Offenders, Batterers and Child Abusers.* Thousand Oaks, CA: Sage.

Schechter, H. (1990). *Deranged: the shocking true story of america's most fiendish serial killer.* New York: Pocket Books

Schechter, H. (1994). *Depraved: The Shocking True Story Of America's First Serial Killer.* New York: Pocket Books.

Schwartz, B. K. (1999). The case against involuntary commitment. In A. Schlank & F. Cohen (eds.), *The Sexual Predator: Law, Policy, Evaluation and Treatment, Vol. 2.* Kingston, NJ: Civic Research Institute.

Scully, D. (1990). *Understanding sexual violence: A study of convicted rapists.* Cambridge: Unwin, Hyman.

Seling, M. (2000). *A treatment program overview.* Steilacoom, WA: Special Commitment Center.

Simon, L.M.J. (2000). An examination of the assumptions of specialization, mental disorder, and dangerousness in sex offenders. *Behavioral Sciences and the Law, 18,* 175–308.

Smallbone, S.W. & Wortley, R. K. (2004). Criminal diversity and paraphilic interests among adult males convicted of sexual offenses against children. *International Journal of Offender Therapy and Comparative Criminology, 48,* 175–188.

Soothill, K., Francis, B., Sanderson, B. & Ackerley, E. (2000). Sex offenders: Specialists, generalists – or both? *British Journal of Criminology, 40,* 56–67.

Tappan, P. W. (1950). *The Habitual Sex Offender: Report and Recommendation of the Commission on the Habitual Sex Offender.* Trenton: Commission on the Habitual Sex Offender.

Terry, K.J. (2006). *Sexual Offenses and Offenders: Theory, Practice, and Policy.* Belmont: Wadsworth.

Terry, K. J, & Furlong, J. (2008). *Sex Offender Registration and Community Notification: A "Megan's Law" Sourcebook.* Kingston: Civic Research Institute.

Tewksbury, R. (2004). Experiences and attitudes of registered female sex offenders. *Federal Probation, 68,* 30–33.

Tewksbury, R. (2005). Collateral consequences of sex offender registration. *Journal of Contemporary Criminal Justice, 21,* 67–81.

Thomas, T. (2000). *Sex Crime: Sex Offending and Society.* Devon: Willan.

Vitiello, M. (2008). Punishing Sex Offenders: When Good Intentions Go Bad. *Arizona State Law Journal, 40,* 651–690.

Walker, J.T., Golden, J.W. & VanHouten, A.C. (2002). *Poverty and crime in the Arkansas Mississippi River delta.* Little Rock: Arkansas Crime Information Center.

Wartell, J. (2007, March). *Sex offender laws: Planning for an election.* Presented at the National Institute of Justice 9th Annual Crime Mapping Research Conference.

Weiner, A. D. (2007, January). Sex offenders near schools: A review of the sex offender database. Retrieved June 22, 2007 from http://www.house.gov/weiner/report39.htm.

Zimring, F.E., Piquero, A.R., & Jennings, W.G. (2007). Sexual delinquency in Racine: Does early sex offending predict later sex offending in youth and young adulthood? *Criminology & Public Policy, 6,* 507–534.

---

[i] 42 U.S.C. § 14071

[ii] 42 U.S.C. § 14071(e)

[iii] Pub. L. 109–248,§501(1)(A), 120 Stat. 587, 623 (July 27, 2006)

[iv] Prosecutorial Remedies and Other Tools to end the Exploitation of Children Today Act of 2003

[v] There are no specific provisions in the federal statute for the boxes that are starred. Rather, the issues are dependent upon the state in which the offender resides.

[vi] Juveniles required to register for 10 years.

[vii] Quarterly for SVPs, every 6 months for all other sex offenders.

[viii] Level III or IV offenders only.

[ix] Quarterly for SVPs, every 30 days for those with no fixed address.

[x] Quarterly verification for all sex offenders.

[xi] Juveniles required to register until 21 years of age, unless transferred to adult registry.

[xii] Quarterly verification for all sex offenders.

[xiii] 10 years after release from prison or up to 25 years including the time of incarceration, whichever is longer.

[xiv] No actual distance restriction, the agency responsible for supervision of the Level III sex offender shall mitigate the concentration of such offenders near schools.

[xv] Quarterly verification for all sex offenders.

[xvi] Level II sex offenders required to register may not reside in the same individual dwelling.

[xvii] The Department of Corrections decides where and how close a sex offender can live from a school or day care.

[xviii] Individuals who are required to register cannot live in student housing at an institution of higher education supported in whole or in part by the state.

[xix] The state parole board decides where and how close a sex offender can live or go near a child safety zone.

[xx] Lifetime parolees must verify their addresses every 60 days pursuant to a parole agreement.

The Politics of Sex Offender Policies: An Interview with Patricia Wetterling

4

Patricia Wetterling &
Richard G. Wright

Editor's Note: In October 1989, 11-year-old Jacob Wetterling
was abducted at gunpoint from his hometown in St. Joseph,
Minnesota, by a masked man. Jacob and his younger brother,
Trevor, were on their way home from a convenience store with
another boy when the gunman took Jacob and told Trevor
and his friend to run into the woods or he would shoot them
(Johnson, 1989).

On February 17, 2008, the Wetterling family honored Jacob
on what would be his 30th birthday (Associated Press, 2008).
Despite national press attention; extensive searching by family,
friends, and law enforcement; and tremendous advocacy by the
Wetterling family and friends, Jacob still has not been found. In
the past 19 years, the Wetterling family has survived. During
that time, Patty Wetterling, Jacob's mother, has become a policy

maker, activist, and educator—and has found herself at the center of the continuing debate over sex offender laws.

As discussed earlier in this book, the first federal sex offender law ushering in this current era was named after Patty's son. The Jacob Wetterling Crimes Against Children and Sexually Violent Offender Registration Act was enacted in 1994 as a part of the Violent Crime Control and Law Enforcement Act (Wright, 2004). This law required released sex offenders to provide their home and work addresses and personal information to local police departments. As mentioned in chapter 3, the Wetterling Act was amended numerous times and eventually supplanted by the 2006 Adam Walsh Act.

Patty Wetterling has a unique and extraordinary perspective in the debate about the efficacy of sex offender laws. In 1990 she and her husband created the Jacob Wetterling Foundation, which works with law enforcement agencies and grieving parents in cases of child abduction and sexual violation. She has served on the Board of Directors for the National Center for Missing and Exploited Children (NCMEC) and is recognized as an expert in child abduction.

Ms. Wetterling ran unsuccessfully for Congress twice, narrowly losing in 2006. In her campaign for the House of Representatives seat in the Sixth District of Minnesota, she lost to Michele Bachmann (R) 50.05% to 42.1%. Her 2004 campaign against House incumbent Rep. Mark Kennedy (R) resulted in a 54% to 46% loss (Federal Elections 2004: Election Results for the U.S. President, the U.S. Senate, and the U.S. House of Representatives).

Over the last several years, Ms. Wetterling has become an outspoken opponent of some sex offender laws, essentially arguing that they do not reflect the more common sexual violence committed by family members, friends, and known assailants. Her experience was recently chronicled in a 2007 report by Human Rights Watch (Human Rights Watch, 2007). Today, Ms. Wetterling works as the Sexual Violence Prevention Program Director for the Minnesota Department of Health.

On June 27, 2008, this volume's editor interviewed Ms. Wetterling in an attempt to understand her personal journey through this tragic, complex, and painful social problem. After reviewing the transcripts, it was decided to include the interview in full in this volume so that readers could benefit from her unique view into sex offender policy.

Interview with Patty Wetterling — June 27, 2008

Richard Wright: Let's start where we are today and work backwards. Obviously you know we are operating under the Adam Walsh Act, which is the major rewrite of sex offender federal laws from a few years ago. What are your general thoughts about the Adam Walsh Act?

Patty Wetterling: Well, I had great concerns about some of what they were trying to do when they proposed the bill. I kept raising questions about treating juveniles the same way we treat adults. It makes no sense at all, and that was one provision that I had concerns over. I was told not to worry about the juvenile provisions because that would get thrown out. I was told there was no way that would pass. Also, when we worked on the Jacob Wetterling Act, we were told that we couldn't make it retroactive, and yet the Adam Walsh Act has done that. One of the other clear pieces that I had concerns over was the amount of money that we are spending on GPS monitoring.

This law applies to a very, very tiny percentage of our general population. There are many pieces to it that are very costly and don't necessarily work. I worked with a family where the offender was on house arrest and he convinced his girlfriend to go over to his house. While he was on house arrest with a bracelet, he murdered her and took off. These laws don't necessarily stop crimes from happening, and they cost a ton of money. Those are two issues I have great concerns over. Additionally The AWA allocates zero dollars for prevention.

Wright: And the specific juvenile provision you are talking about is the fact that under the new law, if a juvenile gets adjudicated after the age of 14 for a sex offense, he or she has to register like an adult offender.

Wetterling: Yes, and there's a tremendous amount of research that finds that children's brains aren't developed until their mid-20s, and so they are incapable of making some of those decisions. They don't know or don't think about long-term consequences of their behaviors. There are also Romeo and Juliet cases where these kids are having a relationship that may not be violent. Yet even in those instances where it is not violent, they are still treated exactly the same as a violent adult offender. I think that's the biggest challenge that I have with sex offender laws. They tend to treat all sex offenders the same, and they're not the same.

Wright: One of the ways the laws have changed in the last decade or so is that we no longer focus primarily on registration and notification. We have civil commitment, chemical castration laws, residency restrictions, mandatory HIV testing, and, as you've mentioned, GPS monitoring. Which do you think are the most helpful or harmful of these laws?

Wetterling: I still think that sex offender registration can be a helpful tool for law enforcement. When my son was kidnapped they didn't have a clue who was in the area. It can absolutely work. It doesn't have to work against sex offenders; it can clear them very quickly. Community notification, the way we do it in Minnesota, I think is respectful because they not only notify the community about the offender, but they also educate people about dangerous behaviors—for example, anybody who is maybe giving your child too much attention or giving them presents, gifts, money, trying to spend a lot of time with them. That's preventive information that can stop a bad relationship or a bad situation from happening. Then, law enforcement briefly spends about 5 minutes talking about the one guy who is coming out. It deemphasizes the absolute anger and energy that's usually thrown at one person, when most people victimize somebody who is very close to them, somebody in their family or a neighbor, somebody who has their trust.

Wright: If I understand you correctly, you still think that registration can be pretty helpful and that when notification is done well, it can be helpful. What do you think about all these issues around residency restrictions and chemical castration and all these other types of laws?

Wetterling: Let's take these one at a time. But first of all, I don't believe in registering juveniles. I don't see any, not one redeeming quality in doing that. The goal is to interrupt the behaviors if they've done something wrong, get them some help so they can live a normal, healthy, wonderful life. Registering juveniles takes away everything that would allow them a normal, healthy, happy life. It takes away any stability and sense of support. Registering juveniles is ludicrous and wrong always.

Residency restrictions are also wrong and ludicrous and make no sense at all. We're putting all of our energy on the stranger, the bad guy, and the reality is it's most sex offenses are committed by somebody that gains your trust, or is a friend or relative, and so none of these laws address the real, sacred thing that nobody wants to talk about.

Wright: Let me ask you about a recent development. There are about six states right now that have enacted laws that would authorize the execution of individuals convicted for child rape. Recently in the case of *Kennedy v. Louisiana*, the Supreme Court came out in a 5-4 vote saying that the Louisiana law was unconstitutional. It upheld its previous decision in *Coker v. Georgia*, which said that the death penalty for rape was a disproportionate and unconstitutional punishment. Since the ruling, there's been quite a bit of backlash, particularly by the states with those statutes. How do you feel about executing sex offenders?

Wetterling: First of all, I don't believe in the death penalty. But if you made it possible to use the death penalty for a child rape situation, the perpetrator might as well kill the child because there's the same consequence, and if offenders are cognizant of those kinds of consequences, then they have no motivation to keep the child alive.

Wright: So your argument is that if the offender realizes that they may get executed by this rape, then they're just going to go ahead and commit the murder.

Wetterling: Right, because they could possibly get away with it. If the child lives, he or she might tell. Here's the question that I always want to ask, when we pass these laws. Will this make our communities safer? Will this make our children safer? No. Executing child rapists may, may stop one rapist, one time, but it's not a discouraging factor. These guys don't think they're going to get caught in the first place, so it doesn't discourage the behavior. It would take one guy off the street, but we're putting all of our energy into the smallest piece of the puzzle.

Wright: I want to ask you a couple questions now about your specific journey, because there are so many things that are compelling about the decisions that you've made and how you responded to Jacob's disappearance. How have your views about sexual offending and sexual assault changed over the years from the time that Jacob first disappeared to now? How have your own thought process and feelings about sexual assault and sexual offending changed?

Wetterling: Oh gosh, I think so much has changed over the years. We live in a small town, and we were absolutely shocked and horrified with Jacob's abduction. We should be always shocked and horrified, every time it happens. What concerns me now, and what I think has grown progressively worse, is that we are no longer shocked and horrified over the sexualization of our children.

The video games—for example, Grand Theft Auto, you get points for picking up a prostitute, you get points for going back and killing her. We're grooming our children to be sexualized; you know the "pimp-ho" mind-set genre, glamorizing that kind of dominance and objectification of young girls. They sell pole dancing kits to young girls, so we are encouraging these behaviors. Then when our children do what we've taught them to do, and act the way we've taught them to act, the only answer we have is to arrest them, register them as a sex offender, and change their lives forever so they have no possibility of regaining themselves. It makes no sense.

Wright: You've been dealing with this now for over 18 years. When you think back to what you thought about sexual offending and sex offenders 18 years ago and what you know now today, how do you think your views have changed?

Wetterling: I ask a lot of questions. I've always asked a lot of questions. I feel that, when Jacob was kidnapped, I was angry—as you can imagine. I've been angry; I know fear and I know anger, and I don't like living my life like that. I believe that much of the legislation and much of the initiative in this country is to use fear and anger to keep people on guard. I honestly believe—and this is consistent, this is what I felt in 1989 and what I feel today—that there are more good people in the world than bad. We need to pull together and design a world that is safer and better. Just having this absolute anger and pointing our fingers at one or two people as the bad guys, we're denying the realities of sexual offending. We're denying it.

I've learned a lot. I didn't know that most of the time sexual offenses are committed by someone that the child knows. I learned that by being investigated. Law enforcement always looks at the family, friends, and relatives. They always look very closely at the family. I understand that. It was painful, but I do understand that now. Knowing that, why are we always putting all this stuff under this "stranger danger" mind-set? That's not the solution to this problem.

Wright: Let me expand on part of what you just said. From watching your response to these sex offender laws, one of the things that's been amazingly unique about your experience, it seems to me, is that you have never really been focused on vengeance or retaliation. Many of the policies and the public attitude toward sex offenders tends to be very much about demonization, revenge, and retribution. But as someone who has gone through it, you've had a very different response. You have not focused on vengeance and retaliation but on prevention and a positive outlook. Can you talk a little bit about your healing process? Why you are able to get past rage and anger, and not operate with a sense of vengeance?

Wetterling: It was a process of gaining support. I gained a lot of support from law enforcement and a lot of support from the community. The more I learned about this issue, the more I was committed to change and to resolving and doing what I could to stop it. I couldn't hang on to that anger. It was destroying me inside. It was. I've seen people do that. They become very bitter. They can also be very effective at changing laws, but it's unhealthy. I couldn't do it. The other thing is that I have three other kids, and I didn't want them walking around distrusting everybody and afraid to talk to a new person just because that would be a stranger. Nothing made sense to me, and I still wrestle with it.

I don't know the answer, I just know that we spend so much time telling our kids don't talk to strangers, and then we put them on a school bus with a new driver every fall. We send them off to summer camp with camp counselors. We're full of inconsistencies, and I think it is good we put them on a school bus and send them off to camp. I don't think we should teach them to fear strangers. I think we should instead be teaching them how to talk to people, how to have respectful relationships, how that interaction can work, because then they'll know when somebody has bad intentions, when they're treating them in a way that makes them uncomfortable. I don't know why I thought about it differently than other people. I know I do and it's hard.

Wright: I want to expand on that a little bit. One of the things I do think is remarkable about your approach and your choices is that they have never really focused on demonizing offenders or blaming. I would like to understand why. How have you managed to not do that?

Wetterling: I don't exactly know when it started, but it took a long time. At first I didn't want to talk to offenders. I got asked to speak at victims' rights weeks or speak in the prisons, but I didn't want to have anything to do with it. I couldn't do it. But then I met a woman. She and her daughter were camping when an offender slit a hole in their tent and snatched her daughter, kidnapped and murdered her. This woman made an appeal. She said she wanted to talk to the offender. She was a very Christian, very forgiving woman. The offender did call, and she spent a long time talking to him. She found the man and he was charged, convicted, and sentenced.

I was amazed by that story. I couldn't do that. At that point in my journey, I was not that open and forgiving. Not that I wouldn't like to be, I just wasn't. It began a process for me. I decided I would write a letter to the man who took Jacob. The only way I could do that was to think of this man as once a child. As a child, something really bad must have happened to this man that he would then act out and do these things to other children.

Registering and treating them as demons and animals, not even human, that doesn't do anything. It destroys the person. It would destroy me internally and it would not help solve the problem. The problem is how do we treat our kids? If they are victims, we need to get them help right away so that they don't continue the behavior. We've got to build a culture that values and protects its kids.

Wright: Now you are the program director for sexual violence prevention in the Minnesota health department. It sounds like you have been explaining this a little bit all along, but it sounds like this is a next phase in your own growth and your own journey. Why are you so focused on the prevention of sexual offending?

Wetterling: Because of the sheer volume of sexuality involving our children. Twenty-five percent of our teenage girls have an STD or STI. That's a phenomenal public health problem. If we view sexual offending as a public health problem, we would look at it like we do other health issues. When people start getting really sick, the medical field doesn't say, we've got to build more hospitals and that will solve it. They do lot of research in trying to figure out what is causing people to become sick. But with sex offenses, all we can think of is to build more prisons. It doesn't solve the problem, so what we have to do is look at it. What are the contributing factors to somebody becoming a perpetrator? Some of the juvenile offenders that they're arresting are not sadistic killers. They're not the same as the man who took Jacob. They're kids. They are acting out in a sexualized culture, doing the things we've taught them to do. We need to better define the problem. We need to look at what works and then we need to get that out to the general population. Many sex offender laws really don't work. They don't solve a thing.

Wright: You have had access to hundreds of legislators who've passed these laws. Some of these laws have been fairly thoughtful and some have been fairly reactive. Having dealt with so many legislators, how would you characterize their understanding of the problem?

Wetterling: Overall I would say they have very little understanding of the problem. That's why I ran for Congress. I don't think they want to. Nobody wants to look at the problem. You don't want your child to be a victim. I have said this a lot. In Minnesota, everybody wants to find Jacob and everybody wants to find the man who took him. We've been overwhelmed with just amazing, amazing support, but at the same time nobody wants to find the man who took Jacob... in their family. They don't want to find him in their church, in their school community, in their neighborhood. These people are not monsters. They're living and functioning amongst us, and we've got to figure out a way for them to live amongst us and not harm another. There are many things that need to be looked at, including the effect of pornography. We have a "pornified" culture. It affects the way men view women and they way men view girls. The amount of violence with pornography has greatly grown. We're nurturing that, we are putting that in beer ads and that's everywhere. We are so used to it that we aren't even shocked anymore, and that's sad to me.

Wright: I want talk about your Congressional campaigns in a minute, but I want to go back to this question about the legislator's role....

Wetterling: First of all, they don't understand the problem. Second of all, they usually propose legislation after another really horrific crime. So they've got public sentiment and demand. People demanding that they do something. These are people who have to get reelected, and the goal is to look like they are the toughest on crime, that they've done the most to go after these bad boys. They name laws that are either compelling, compassionate, like after the child, or the

PROTECT Act. The Adam Walsh Act is named after a child. There are so many named after children, Dru's Law, Jessica's Law. It gives the sense that this is compassionate and caring and that it will make the world safer. Often, it doesn't.

Wright: So, when a legislator meets with the parents of the victim, and the victim wants a new law and he introduces a bill, what do you think his intent is?

Wetterling: Well, first of all, I would venture to guess that maybe I'm different on this one, too, but when Jacob was abducted, I didn't want a law. It upset me. We had state legislators come to us right at the beginning and say, we want to do something, we're going to pass a law. I thought, why are you talking about laws? I'm looking for Jacob. I didn't want a law named after Jacob, I wanted my son.

I didn't have the time or energy to put any thought into that. But over time I began looking, and I asked law enforcement, what would have helped you? They said it would have helped to know who was in the area. From a law enforcement perspective, that makes sense. It would have helped to have a central repository of information because we have a very fluid society. Those I think are two valid law enforcement tools, but when they expanded it to community notification, I wasn't even sure if I liked that. It made me very nervous about people not handling that information well.

On an intellectual level, when these guys are released from prison, we want them to succeed. That's the goal. Then you have no more victims. All of these laws they've been passing make sure that they're not going to succeed. They don't have a place to live; they can't get work. Everybody knows of their horrible crime and they've been vilified. There is too much of a knee-jerk reaction to these horrible crimes.

Wright: You ran for Congress twice and briefly for the Senate. Those campaigns were very close. If you had won those campaigns, how would you have changed federal sex offender laws? What would you have done?

Wetterling: That's a really good question. I would have suggested a study on sex offender treatment. What works? There are a lot of programs out there, and I think that some of them in fact do work. The Good Lives Model is one I'm intrigued by. I think it's fascinating and if we could use the model across our general population with young kids, then possibly we could have fewer perpetrators. Let's invest in our youth, early investment in treatment for juveniles. People are also of the mind-set that treatment doesn't work, and I think it does. I think that many of the treatment programs, especially for young people, do work. I would have done that. I would have always asked the questions that nobody is asking, so that we could make sure that a particular piece of legislation was indeed going to do what we intend it to do.

Wright: As you know, the media has a major impact on all of these stories. There are times when the media can report on sexual offending in a very thoughtful way, in a very deliberate way, and there are times when they can be very sensational. Can you think of examples from your experience where the media dealt very well with Jacob's disappearance or in some cases where they dealt very poorly with it?

Wetterling: We had one TV station which did a series. It was a 5-night series on the problem, the victims, the perpetrators, the hopes. Actually it might have had one part on solutions or treatments and the hope. They really took time to show the depth of it. It was really, really well done and very thoughtful. We did a lot of shows on the national level, too, that were hour-long programs, that I thought delved into the reality that we as families are facing and the challenges. My basic statement for years has been somebody knows who took Jacob, somebody did this and you know, somebody knows. They may have a piece of information that we still need. We have got to find the man who took Jacob. There is somebody out there who steals kids. He's got my son. Did he do it again? I don't know.

I'm not soft on these guys, but I just know that they're not all the same. They're not all the same and we can't treat them as such. There was one time when a man was arrested in St. Paul. My mother called—we were all up at the lake—and she said, "There's a break in your case." I said, "I don't think so. I've talked to the sheriff's department. They know where we are and they haven't called." She said, "Well they've been promoting it all day on TV. There's a break in your case. Watch the news tonight." So we did.

This man was arrested in St. Paul and they said that he had knowledge of Jacob's kidnapping. The media said that when the police did a search they found pornography. They found a digital camera. They found movies. They found clothing. They found a container which appeared to be a container with testicles. They said that the suspect had been involved in a search for Jacob done at Fort Snelling. I'm sitting there with kids and

I'm like, "What the hell?" I was livid. I was livid, because, first of all, that our sheriffs didn't know about it. The sheriff didn't call because he didn't know about this media report.

The St. Paul police officer didn't seal the search warrants. The reporter didn't verify their facts. The testicles were dog testicles. I was really worried about my other son. He wasn't with us; he was staying with a friend. I was so scared Trevor was going to watch and see that report, and what would Trevor think? I didn't sleep for days.

It was absolutely glamorizing the horrible act that could have happened. We went through 6 months of anxiety because the man who had been arrested had a boy's jock strap. We went through 6 months of waiting for DNA. Today they act like you get DNA back in 10 minutes or in an hour. We waited 6 months, and that's still not uncommon.

Wright: From your experience, what distinguishes the news media that do a responsible, sensitive, thorough job from the sensational?

Wetterling: The wording. They tend to right away call someone a rapist, or a child molester. The wording that they use is very inflammatory. I'm not thinking of good examples right now, but I know you'll know them when you hear them. They often suggest it being a stranger. They only report the stranger cases. The sad reality is, they so overemphasize the stranger cases, it suggests that those are the only thing that's happening. There are stations that do a better job. Some really address sexual violence by talking to victims. They know that most cases aren't reported to police and that most of the time it's not a stranger.

The ones that do, the strangers that do make those high-profile cases are often very bad. I think we have to work out some of the kinks of civil commitment, because there's got to be a way for some of these people to not get out. We've had cases where the offender told people they were going to reoffend. They told them who they were going to go after and how they going to do it. Now these people are clearly not safe. I don't believe they should be out. So we have to have a place for discerning the differences between these people. They are still human beings.

Wright: One other question about your process and your journey. One of the things again that I think is so amazing about your journey is that you've gone through this tragedy, and one of the ways you've chosen to deal with it is by better understanding the issue. I mean it would be a very completely normal response for someone who has gone through this to say, I don't want to talk about this. I don't want to deal with this anymore; I can't deal with it anymore. But you've kind of gone the opposite way, in choosing to live a very public life, understanding sexual assault, understanding sexual offending. Why did you make that choice?

Wetterling: I don't know. I think it was because that's who I am, and when Jacob was kidnapped, I made a very hard decision. It's not that I went through something. I still deal with this. I refuse to let the man who took Jacob take anything else. You can't take my marriage. You can't take my other children. You can't take my sense of goodness with the world. You can't take away the world that Jacob believed in. You can't have it. I've fought very hard to rebuild the world that I know it could be. The way the world can be when people care about one another and they reach out. When somebody does something wrong, you get them the help that they need so that they can turn their lives around. I just couldn't go to the very punitive way and stay there. It wasn't me.

Wright: Let me ask you just a few final questions. So as a fellow parent—I have a 3 ½-year-old daughter—if something like what happened to Jacob, what was done to Jacob, happened to my daughter, what advice would you give me?

Wetterling: Never give up. I still hope that one day we'll find Jacob. We'll find out what happened, we'll find out where he is. I don't know that he's not alive. There is no proof to show that he's not alive. I wish that I would have told him that I would search forever. I didn't. I didn't know. I would just encourage parents to hang on, hold onto who you are and do what you can. What we really want, what we really want, all of us, even the really angry, vindictive parents want is for it to never happen again.

Parents are very vulnerable when legislators approach them. They tell them things like "if we had had this law, your child would be home safe." That's not true, so often that's not true. But the parents are hurting and they are very vulnerable. They feel like it will make my child's life have meaning to the rest of the world. Nobody will forget that there's a law. We are very vulnerable.

Wright: You know, you used the word that was exactly what I was searching for and I think it's a brilliant choice of words, is this question around vulnerability. How can we help people in the healing process? When you talk to families, or rape victims, sexual assault victims, the process is a lifelong healing process.

Wetterling: Absolutely. If we as a community or as a state have a strategy for managing sex offenders, let's use the best practices. Let's educate our law enforcement to be better prepared and to have a plan to address these concerns in our community.

Wright: Does your family have any lessons learned about healing or about the journey? What you would say to other families, should they have to go through this?

Wetterling: One of my best friends described it as looking to the light. It can turn into a very dark place, and you have to find some vision of how it can be better, and how you see yourself going forward. You have to find something outside of the very dark experience. I tell parents that you will find the strength to find the sunshine again. There are steps. There are support groups. There are a lot of people that can help you along the way, but you have to know that it's there because at the time you don't see it, you don't feel it. All you know is the dark and the pain.

Wright: Is there anything else that you can think of that you would want to say about assault laws and sexual assault policy?

Wetterling: Yes. I think that one thing that is so sorely missing in all of this—with all of our anger and all of our tough laws, there is no safe place for these guys. There are a lot of people who succeed. They do these terrible offenses and they go to jail and do their time. Then they get out and never reoffend. There is no place to share their stories, because you can't say, well, yeah I was a sex offender once and then I got some help, and I got off alcohol and drugs and I'm cured. As a culture, we don't tolerate that. We have not built into the system any means for success, and I think that's really sad. If I were the parent, the second worst thing to having your child kidnapped, would be to be the parent of someone who did this. I just can't imagine if you are the parent of a juvenile who did something wrong and you get them some help. You want them to lead a healthy, full life, and we've not built that into the equation at all.

Wright: I just want to thank you again, Patty. I have to say the more I talk to you, the more I learn about this from you, your perspective, and the more I watch you, I am just amazed at the journey you've taken. You have uncovered some insights into this from the perspective that I haven't seen too many people who have. I just want to thank you again for doing this and choosing to live a very public life.

Wetterling: Well, it wasn't at first a choice, it became very public because I was begging the whole world to help us, and pretty soon they were. The side effect is the public side. I am pretty shy and quiet. If I lived my life the way I was nobody would have ever heard of me, ever. But with that comes a responsibility, and I'm trying to do the best I can with it.

References

Associated Press. (2008, February 17). Jacob Wetterling would turn 30 today. Retrieved August 20, 2008, from http://www.startribune.com/15703727.html

Federal Elections 2004: Election results for the U.S. President, the U.S. Senate, and the U.S. House of Representatives. (n.d.). Retrieved September 13, 2008, from http://fec.gov/pubrec/fe2004/federalelections2004.shtml

Human Rights Watch. (2007, September). No easy answers: Sex offender laws in the U.S. *19* (4), 141.

Johnson, D. (1989, October 30). Small town is shaken by child's abduction. *The New York Times*. http://query.nytimes.com/gst/fullpage.html?res=950DE0DE163CF933A05753C1A96F948260&sec=&spon=&pagewanted=1

Wright, R. G. (2004, December). *Protection or Illusion? A Policy Analysis of Massachusetts and Federal Sex Offender Legislation*. 297. Boston: University of Massachusetts Boston.

---

[1] Interview transcribed by Michelle Cubellis, Bridgewater State College.

Sex
Offender
Policies

Internet Sex Stings

Richard G. Wright

"The bogeyman is real and he lives on the Net. He lived in my computer and he lives in yours. While you are sitting here, he's at home with your children." 19-year old rape survivor, Alicia Kozakiewicz, from her 2006 Congressional testimony. (C-SPAN, 2006)

These words were uttered by a young woman who as an underage child was kidnapped, raped, and tortured by an adult man she met over the Internet. As tragic as Alicia Kozakiewicz's Congressional testimony was, it was surpassed in its impact by the testimony of Justin Berry. Berry testified about a series that profiled his Internet activities in the *New York Times* in late 2005. The 19-year-old Berry spoke about his role in performing sexual acts broadcast via his webcam when he was a minor. Berry also detailed his development of a child pornography business involving photographs of himself and others in response to sexual solicitations from adult male strangers, all occurring over the Internet (U.S. House of Representatives Energy & Commerce Committee Investigations Subcomittee, 2006).

These tragic cases, and similar ones, raised the nation's attention to the problem of children being enticed over the Internet into sexually abusive relationships with adults. Given the heinousness of these offenses and the emotional volatility of the issue, it is critical to analyze the research, policies, and legal aspects of Internet sexual solicitation.

Those arrested for Internet sexual solicitation come from all walks of life. Despite the stereotype of sex offenders as strangers and predators, reputable professionals have been accused and convicted of these crimes. Examples include a minister, a rabbi, a federal criminal prosecutor who would commit suicide, a New York City police detective, a university professor, a mayor, a church pastor, a state trooper, an Iraq and Afghanistan veteran, a teacher, an official from the Department of Homeland Security, and a former executive with Disney, among many others. All these individuals were arrested via an Internet sex sting for the crime of intent to recruit a minor via the Internet for sexual purposes (The Associated Press, 2006a; Associated Press, 2006b; The Associated Press, 2008a; Associated Press, 2008b; Ballou, 2007; Edwards, 2008; Goodnough, 2007; Jenkins, 2001; Semple, 2004).

The statutory language includes variants such as enticement of a minor for sexual purposes, attempts to solicit a minor, and so forth, yet the underlying crime is one of attempting to lure a minor, via the Internet, into a sexual relationship with an adult. The most controversial manner to achieve convictions for these charges is investigations and arrests via an Internet sex sting. This chapter examines several factors influencing the use and impact of the sex sting. Although this specific strategy is a relatively new law enforcement practice, some have argued that the use of undercover stings (and deception) is broadly supported in the private and public sectors (Hay, 2003).

Internet sex stings are a law enforcement practice in which federal, state, and local police monitor select Internet chat rooms and social networking sites. The structure of the sting/ investigation varies with important and critical details (to be discussed), but the essential script includes the following:

A police officer signs into a chat room or social networking site with an alias, pretending to be a minor. An adult signs into the chat room identifying as an adult. At some point, the underage child (police officer) and the adult (almost always a male) begin to communicate with one another.

Over a period of time that varies between days, weeks, and months, the two parties routinely chat and exchange e-mails and instant messages. The adult may initiate a picture exchange, which may include child pornography. The content of the discussion gradually includes sexual desires, wishes, and behaviors. At some point in time, one of the parties suggests an in-person meeting. Both eventually agree to the meeting (presumably for sexual purposes). At the in-person meeting, the adult is shocked to learn that the person he or she has been communicating with is actually an adult law enforcement official. At that meeting, the adult is then arrested on state or federal charges of intent to solicit/recruit a child for sexual purposes.

Despite their broad popular, legislative support and well-meaning intent, Internet sex stings present numerous ethical problems including the following:

- Distorting the research on online sexual solicitation to focus on adult predators rather than on the more common sexual solicitations and harassment committed by peers and young adults
- Expanding the power of the state to punish people for deviant thoughts, not actions
- Shifting our legal system from an adversarial one, assuming innocence, to an inquisitorial one, assuming guilt
- Net widening by utilizing preventive arrest and prosecution of innocent people (e.g., people who, although they arranged a meeting, would not have followed through and had sex with the minor)
- Fueling ineffective public policies that focus on the high-profile, less frequent stranger sexual assaults instead of the more common sexual violence committed by known assailants (e.g., husbands, boyfriends, brothers, extended family friends)

It is only by examining the drawbacks as well as the benefits of this practice and its associated issues that we can come to an informed perspective as to whether or not (and if so, when and under what conditions) this tactic should be employed as a means of sexual assault prevention.

The first portion of this chapter illustrates the public perception of Internet sexual solicitation, discusses what an Internet sex sting is, and illuminates the myriad of problems created by this approach. The second part examines the research on Internet sexual solicitations, uncovering the central fallacy in the policy debate: a misplaced focus on adult predators. Next the chapter discusses the federal response, including the use of symbolism and again the misrepresentation of scientific research. The chapter then demonstrates the dramatic framing power of the media and the role of the high-profile tragedy. It then examines the legal issues raised by Internet sex stings, including why enticement and Internet sex stings shift our most valued legal belief from one of a presumed innocence to a presumed guilt. It further demonstrates that this shift results in a problematic act of net widening. The final part proposes a call for an analytical research and public critique of this approach.

The Internet and Sex Offenders

Internet Sexual Solicitation

How often are children contacted online for sexual purposes by adults? Are young people at significant risk of online adult sexual solicitation? Underlying the move toward prevention of online-initiated sex crimes is an assumption that adult predators are the most serious threat facing young people. The research to date suggests that is not the case.

In June 2000, Finkelhor and associates reported their findings on the first national study on online child sexual solicitation. In their seminal study, they reported that nearly 20% of children aged 10 to 17 received at least one sexual solicitation in the previous year. Their initial study also reported that 3% of young people who regularly used the Internet were the recipients of "aggressive" sexual solicitations including requests to meet in person (Finkelhor, Mitchell, & Wolak, June 2000). As will be discussed shortly, the latter statistic has consistently been inaccurately used in the debate about online sex offenders (Wolak, Finkelor, & Mitchell, 2007).

An additional 3% of these young people reported that they had developed close relationships with adults online. In those cases, 24% of sexual solicitations came from adults, and juveniles were responsible for another 48% of online sexual solicitations. An important finding was the limited awareness by parents of their children's Internet-based relationships. In the 2000 study, Finkelhor et al. reported that parents did not know about three quarters of their child's online relationships.

In nearly one third of these adult–child online friend-ships, a public meeting took place with the child's friend present. This initial study reported that adult–child sexu-ally exploitive relationships, although troubling when they do occur, "seem to be few in a much larger set of seemingly benign relationships" (Finkelhor, Mitchell, & Wolak, 2000, p. 6). A secondary concern addressed by this study was young people being encouraged to run away from home by preda-tory adults. Seven young people (0.4% of the study) reported experiencing this type of online communication. The research argued that although the stereotype of lecherous men going online to find child victims does occur, it does not occur near-ly as frequently as the public is led to believe. In fact, they reported that the majority of online sexual communications which young people will be subjected to resembles what they hear from their in-person peer group.

Interestingly, Finkelhor et al. stated that even though their study did not identify any cases of online sexual solici-tation which resulted in an in-person meeting, Internet sex stings are "certainly a good thing" (Finkelhor, Mitchell, & Wolak, June 2000, p. 35). They assumed sex stings are oper-ating as a deterrent. This is an important though uncritical endorsement of this law enforcement strategy, which sits on a questionable ethical ledge, as will be discussed shortly. Yet the primary importance of the study was that it was the first of its kind and became repeatedly misused in the policy debate.

A final thought from their initial study is the lack of com-munication between children and parents. In virtually all forms of distressing, upsetting, or unwanted Internet com-munications, it was quite common for children not to tell their parents. As with all child protection issues, the primary responsibilities for children's safety resides with their par-ents and primary caretakers. Clearly beyond the scope of their study, an important field of inquiry is how to increase children's communications/trust with their parents about their online activities.

Finkelhor and colleagues were commissioned by Congress to update their survey in 2005. In the second implementation of the Youth Internet Safety Survey (YISS-2), they found that the proportion of young people who received unwanted sexual solicitations decreased from the initial 2001 survey (13% down from 2001's 19%). Yet those who had received "aggressive" sexual solicitations, including a request to meet in person, did not substantially deviate (4% in 2005; 3% in 2001). One of the new concerns highlighted in YISS-2 was the proportion of young people (4%) who received online requests for nude or sexually explicit photographs of themselves (Wolak, Finkelhor, & Mitchell, 2006).

They also reported that young people were increasingly exposed to unwanted sexual material and online harassment when compared to their 2001 findings. They reported that 9% of young people who regularly used the Internet were harassed (Ybarra, Mitchell, Wolak, & Finkelhor, 2006). This telephone survey with 1,500 young people (aged 10–17) also reported that fewer young people were communicating online with people they did not know and that they also reduced their use of Internet chat rooms (Wolak et al., 2006, p. 7). Regarding aggressive sexual solicitations, girls experienced an increase (4% to 7%) in the types of communications most likely to result in an in-person meeting. It is important to note that in both the 2001 and 2005 studies, Finkelhor et al. argued that type of Internet predator these stings are designed to detect, is fairly rare.

Within the 4% of young people "aggressively sexually solicited," 80% were aged 14 and over and the majority (70%) were girls. In an attempt to understand those who were initiating aggressive sexual solicitations, the study asked respondents about their knowledge of their online partner. Respondents reported that 39% of those who "aggressively sexually solicited" a child were adults. In assessing the frequency of this behavior it is important keep in mind the study's 4% positive finding. It is clear that this low prevalence is in sharp contrast to media and political imagery, suggesting a common and frequent phenomenon. Additionally, of those respondents who were "aggressively sexually solicited," the majority of the offenders were adolescents.

In both the 2000 and 2005 surveys, there were few instances of solicited youth who were sexually assaulted by someone they met online. In 2000 no youths reported this experience and in 2005, two girls reported this experience (Wolak et al., 2006, p. 18). Overall the report shows that between 2000 and 2005, fewer young people were establishing online relationships with adults they previously did not know.

They noted that young people are increasingly prone to divulge personal information online, demonstrating an ever decreasing desire for personal privacy. In the 2000 study, 11% of youth posted personal information online (e.g., names, addresses, telephone numbers, personal photographs). By 2005, over one third (34%) of young people disclosed such information, particularly on social networking sites (Wolak et al., 2006). This growing desire to divulge person information into cyberspace reflects other ongoing social voyeuristic trends, including the growth of reality television, increases in the number and popularity of social networking sites (e.g., Facebook, MySpace) and blogs, and may reflect a general disinterest by young people in traditional views about privacy (Dretzin, 2008).

Finally, one interesting finding/recommendation proposed by this Congressional report focused on Internet "grooming." Grooming is a process in which an adult initiates a nonsexual relationship with a child with the intent to gain his or her trust for later sexual exploitation. The 2005 YISS-2 found that adolescents were more likely to be sexually solicited by adults under the guise of seeking companionship, mentoring, etc. These activities by the adults may in fact be grooming (Wolak et al., 2006, p. 59).

In a different 2005 study examining those who were arrested for online enticement of a minor (and equivalent statutory variations), Finkelhor and associates supported and recommended the use of Internet sex stings. Additionally, they argued that law enforcement posing as juveniles may be having a deterrent effect on potential sex offenders (Mitchell, Wolak, & Finkelhor, 2005).

Despite their endorsement of the utilization of Internet sex stings as a strategy to prevent child sexual abuse, Wolak, Finkelhor, Mitchell, and Ybarra (2008) stated that the adult-stranger predatory stereotype is largely inaccurate. They argued that the majority of sexual encounters originating from an online relationship are typically nonviolent relationships of adults with adolescents under the age of legal consent (e.g., statutory rape). They argued that offline-initiated molestation of children under the age of 12 is more common than online-initiated assaults (Wolak et al., 2008).

Even though adult-predator/online-child exploitation cases are low-frequency events, it is still important to understand which young people are at higher risk for being "groomed" by online sex offenders. Wolak et al. (2008) reported that children and young adults who tend to use chat rooms, have histories of sexual or physical victimization, or are lonely and talk to online strangers about sex are at a greater risk of online sexual victimization than those who do not (Wolak et al., 2008, p. 116).

In his examination of 31 convicted sex offenders in the Bureau of Prisons, Malesky (2007) reported that nearly half tried to meet an underage child they had met online. He argued that these offenders are fairly sophisticated and relentless in their online pursuit of child sexual activity. The generalizability of Malesky's study is limited due to the small and unique sample of federal offenders. Other scholars have argued that online child molesters are typically are not violent (Wolak, Finkelhor, Mitchell, & Ybarra, 2008).

In summation, Finkelhor and associates note that they believe their findings have been "misunderstood." They state that although 13% of youth received online sexual solicitations, many of those solicitations may have come "from other youth." They report that when the young people believed they knew who solicited them, they said about "half" were other youth (Wolak et al., 2007). The fact is that researchers are concerned that their findings are being misrepresented and manipulated in the justification for sex offender laws.

Online Child Pornography

One concern of those supporting Internet sex stings is an associated issue of child pornography. A segment of those arrested via Internet sex stings are also convicted on child pornography charges (Jenkins, 2001). Once the individual has been arrested, law enforcement often secures a warrant for home and work computers, occasionally finding virtual and/or "real" child pornography. In those cases, the individuals will often be prosecuted on child pornography charges in addition to the enticement charges. Yet Jenkins noted that there are no definitive data examining the relationship between child porn use and child molestation (p. 129).

In his study of child pornography users on the Internet, Jenkins argued that the subculture organizes itself like any other deviant subculture, with its own mores, rules, jargon, and rationalizations. He noted that child porn users often invoke a rationale similar to those arrested in Internet sex stings: passive curiosity. Jenkins noted that child porn users often argue that they are simply interested in viewing the material, not actually harming a child (Jenkins, 2001, pp. 120–131). Some defendants in Internet sex stings argue a very similar point in that they were simply chatting or curious and would never actually harm a child.

In their review of the literature on sex offender typologies, Robertiello and Terry (2007) noted that cyber sex offenders may fall into one of three categories. Although the categories are not mutually exclusive, they noted that online offenders may be child porn producers, child porn distributors or sexual solicitors (Ibid). It is important in assessing the utility of the Internet sex sting to determine what type(s) of Internet sex offenders these defendants are. The research examining Internet sexual activity, deviant online speech and behavior and contact (or in-person) offending is just emerging. No definitive typologies have been developed and scientific predictions as to when contact offending emerges from an online relationship are far from reliable.

The Government's Response: The Creation of Enticement

As mentioned earlier by the cases, high-profile horrific cases of children such as Justin Berry and Alicia Kozakiewicz being seduced and brutalized by online predators captured the nation's attention. These rare but tragic cases inspired a political call to "do something."

The federal government has played a leadership role in responding to the problem of online sexual solicitation and in utilizing the Internet sex sting. Marion and Oliver (2006) have argued that the federal government often passes crime control policies that are primarily "symbolic" and that have little empirical impact (p. 169). Although federal policies designed to prevent online sexual solicitation may also be symbolic, two of the most influential laws were passed in 1988 and 2006. Despite their symbolism, federal law has tremendous implications for state and local communities that are charged with implementing the laws, which can include financial, legal, and ethical problems.

Protection of Children from Sexual Predators Act of 1988

The central law in which federal offenders captured via Internet sex sting are charged with was enacted in 1988. Public Law 105-314 creates an offense in the U.S. code of "enticement and coercion." The specific language of the law is as follows:

> "Whoever, using the mail or any facility of means of interstate or foreign commerce, or within the special maritime and territorial jurisdiction of the United States knowingly persuades, induces, entices or coerces any individual who has not attained the age of 18 years, to engage in prostitution or any sexual activity for which any person can be charged with a criminal offense or attempts to do so, shall be fined under this title, imprisoned not more than 15 years, or both." (105th Congress of the United States, 1998)

Additional related crimes created in the 1998 bill include transporting a minor for sexual purposes and corresponding child porn charges. Although the actual law is uninstructive regarding the crime of enticement, the underlying policy rationales can be gleamed from a review of the Congressional Record, prior to the bill's passage. The following are telling excerpts from this report:

> Rep. Dunn from Washington State claimed,

> The McCollum-Dunn bill tells cyber-predators that the information superhighway is not a detour for deviant behavior, but, rather a dead end ... Our message is clear. We will not stop until every mother and father has the peace of mind that their children are safe from sexual predators. (House of Representatives, 1988, p. H4492)

Rep. Weller from Illinois modestly stated,

> I particularly want to compliment the gentleman from
> Florida (Mr. McCollum) and the gentlemen from Michi-
> gan (Mr. Conyers) for their bipartisan efforts in bringing
> this important legislation to the floor, legislation designed
> to protect children from **the weirdos, the wackos and
> slimeballs [emphasis added]** who use the latest tech-
> nology to prey on children and their families. (House of
> Representatives, 1988, p. H4494)

Rep. McCollum, cosponsor of the bill, crystallized the
problem the bill attempted to solve:

> Current laws at the Federal level do not allow for the
> arrest and the conviction of somebody until they have
> actually induced in some manner the child to actually go
> meet with them somewhere to engage in a sexual activity.
> The key portion of this bill, and there are a lot of other
> things in it, is to make sure when there is contact made
> over the Internet for the first time by a predator like this
> with a child, with the intent to engage in sexual activity,
> whatever that contact is, as long as the intent is there to
> engage in that activity, he can be prosecuted for a crime.
> (House of Representatives, 1988, p. H4497)

It is worthwhile to note that the focus in the law is on the
individual's intent. As will be discussed later, one criticism of the
enticement charges/Internet sex sting is that the focus is not on
what an offender **did, but on what he or she might do**.

Libertarian-leaning Rep. Ron Paul of Texas opposed
the bill. Separate from the question of whether or not it was
appropriate for the federal government to become involved,
he raised the questions of efficacy and political popularity:

> In the name of the politically popular cause of protecting
> children against sex crimes, the Members of Congress
> will vote on whether to move the Nation further down
> the path of centralized-Government implosion by appro-
> priating yet more Federal taxpayer money and brandish-
> ing more U.S. prosecutors at whatever problem happens
> to be brought to the floor by any Members of Congress

hoping to gain political favor with those embracing some politically popular cause ...

Who, after all, can stand on the House floor and oppose a bill which is argued to make the world safer for children with respect to crimes? [emphasis added] It is a sad commentary when members of this body only embrace or even mention federalism when it serves their own political purposes and, at the same time, consciously ignore federalism's implications for these politically popular causes. **It seems to no longer matter whether governmental programs actually accomplish their intended goals or have any realistic hope of solving problems ... All that now seems to matter is that Congress pass a new law [emphasis added].** (House of Representatives, 1988, p. H4499)

Once enacted, the enticement charges would later be enhanced in 2006 through the Walsh Act.

Adam Walsh Child Protection & Safety Act of 2006

In June 2006, President George W. Bush signed into law the Adam Walsh Child Protection & Safety Act. As discussed elsewhere in this volume, this is the most comprehensive and far-reaching set of sex offender laws the nation has ever passed. Specific to the issue of enticement and Internet sex stings, the new legislation requires that offenders convicted of the enticement charge be registered as "Tier II" sex offenders, with a minimum registration period of 25 years. Additionally, federal sex offenders convicted of the enticement charge are subject to a mandatory minimum 10-year sentence (Wright, 2008).

It is important to examine the legislative debate in assessing how perceptions evolved since 1988. Senator Orin Hatch noted one of the key changes:

The bottom line is that sex offenders have run rampant in this country and now Congress and the people are ready to respond with legislation that will curtail the ability of sex offenders to operate freely. It is our hope that programs like NBC Dateline's *To Catch A Predator* series will no longer have enough material to fill an hour or even a minute. (United States Senate, 2006, p. S8012)

Senator Joseph Biden of Delaware made several claims about the bill's purpose and origin:

The Adam Walsh Child Protection and Safety Act takes direct aim at this problem [sex offenders]. Plain and simple, this legislation I can say will save children's lives ... This has to be a bittersweet moment for John Walsh. For what we are doing here today? We are naming a bill that will save the lives of hopefully thousands of other young people after a beautiful young boy who was victimized and killed. (United States Senate, 2006, p. S8014)

Senator Allen from Virginia repeated the often-used, but totally false, mantra about recidivism rates to support the law:

Some may wonder, why there is such a focus on sex offenders? Why is there such a focus on pedophiles and sex offenders and rapists? The reason is, if you look at the statistics—and it is not unique to Virginia it is that way it is across the country—the highest recidivist rate, or the highest repeat offender rate of any crime—even higher than murderers, even higher than armed robbers—is sex offenders. (United States Senate, 2006, p. S8018)

One provision in the 2006 bill required the expansion of the Internet Crimes against Children (ICAC) Task Forces. ICAC Task Forces are the dominant form in which law enforcement agencies are trained in how to conduct Internet sex stings.

The Internet Crimes Against Children (ICAC) Task Forces.

Federal law enforcement agencies have a significant role in the use of the Internet sex sting in addressing enticement/solicitation charges. When it was created in 1998, the purpose of the Internet Crimes against Children (ICAC) program was "to help State and local law enforcement develop an effective response to cyberenticement and child pornography cases" (Medaris & Girouard, 2002). Among the several initiatives that these task forces conduct are Internet sex stings. As of late 2007, through federal funding, all 50 states had a state or local task force, with 59 throughout the nation. In 2007, the Office of Juvenile Justice and Delinquency Prevention (OJJDP) provided $17 million to these task forces (U.S. Department of Justice, 2007). Training and technical assistance on how to conduct these stings is provided by the federal government (Internet Crimes Against Children Task Force Training & Technical Assistance Program, 2008). In addition, the FBI runs the Innocent Images program, which investigates the child pornography trade, including individuals who may be arrested via an Internet sting (Jenkins, 2001).

In 2006, Attorney General Alberto Gonzales created Project Safe Childhood, which included the ICAC program. Gonzales depicted the problems of Internet sexual solicitations and child pornography as a war (U.S. Department of Justice, 2006). Utilizing the war metaphor creates a dramatic framing. As will be argued later, this metaphor allows the government tremendous power, particularly in the form of preventive policing. As evident in the War on Terror, a key operational assumption is that those accused are guilty until proven innocent (Cole, 2003; Mayer, 2008). Later in this chapter, I argue that the war against online sex offenders has key and dangerous parallels to the War on Terror.

The Media's Impact in High-Profile Stranger-Predator Cases

A common finding in the enactment of problematic sex offender laws is the impact of high-profile sex crimes committed by strangers, many of whom had previous convictions for sex crimes. The role of the media in identifying, framing, and covering these select cases should not be underestimated.

Jenkins (2001) has argued that the framing of a social problem is inextricably linked with government response and media coverage. He has noted that the online threats to children have been primary framed as online sexual solicitation and cyber stalking to the ignorance of other issues, including child pornography (Ibid, p. 7).

This view is contrasted by the work of Alexy, Burgess, and Baker (2005). Their study of published news cases involving Internet sexual offending against children found that nearly

60% of the cases involved individuals trading in child pornography. Nearly 22% (21.8%) of their sample involved convictions and arrests for "traveling" to meet a child met over the Internet. A fifth of media-reported cases involved individuals charged with both sets of offenses (Ibid).

Below is a discussion of major media events affecting the popularization of the Internet sex sting and its associated issues. These include the 2004–2007 television show *To Catch a Predator*, the advocacy group *Perverted Justice*, the case of Justin Berry, the role of the *New York Times*, and several dramatic Congressional hearings.

To Catch a Predator

In 2004, executives at MSNBC first aired this derivative of their "newsmagazine," *Dateline*. In this variation, the television show identifies an adult male who has developed an online relationship with a fictional child. The fictional child is actually an adult member of an online-advocacy group known as Perverted Justice, posing as this underage child. Once this online relationship becomes sexual, an in-person meeting is scheduled. At this juncture, local law enforcement then arrests the adult male once he appears at the agreed-upon location. *To Catch a Predator* would film the entire scene with the on-screen moderator, Chris Hansen, acting as the alleged offender's moral compass, just prior to the arrest.

To Catch a Predator became a major success for both MSNBC and Hansen. The 2006–2007 series attracted an average of 11 million viewers, a significantly larger audience than MSNBC's other *Dateline* programs (Stelter, 2007). Through the show, Hansen became a frequent public speaker about online child sexual solicitations, including providing testimony to Congress. Pervereted-Justice.com, as discussed below, gained significant financial benefits and international recognition for their assistance in the show. As of late 2007, the group reached an agreement with MSNBC to be paid $70,000 an episode for consultation services (Salkin, 2006).

Among the many controversial issues the show raised, the most complex revolved around the case of Louis Conradt Jr. In November 2006, Mr. Conradt, then an assistant district attorney for Rockwall County, Texas, shot himself in his home as he was about to be arrested in an Internet sex sting, facilitated by *To Catch a Predator*, Perverted Justice, and the local police (Eaton, 2006). The episode, including the after-math of Conradt's suicide, aired in February 2007.

This practice raised the question of journalistic ethics and whether *To Catch a Predator* was reporting the news or creating news. McCollam (2007) argued that this action and type of journalism is nothing more than "public humiliation." Other media critics concur with this assessment (Cohen, 2008). Additionally, McCollam (2007) effectively argued that the show blurred the lines between reality television and broadcast news and transformed Chris Hansen into an expert and "pop-culture icon." Other journalists have also identified numerous ethical issues with *Dateline*'s approach and role (Farhi, 2006).

The effect of the Conradt case may have been to facilitate the demise of the popular show. The victim's sister, Patricia, argued that *Dateline* was directly responsible for her brother's death, launching a $100 million lawsuit (Cohen, 2008). In allowing the suit to proceed, Federal Judge Denny Chin stated that "a reasonable jury could find that NBC crossed the line from responsible journalism to irresponsible and reckless intrusion into law enforcement" (Conradt against NBC Universal, 2008).

In addition, Judge Chin noted that a jury could also find that NBC encouraged the police to over-respond by using a "heavily armed SWAT team to extract a 56-year old prosecutor from his home when he was not accused of any violence" (Conradt against NBC Universal, 2008). Ironically, this particular sting, in which 24 other men were arrested and Conradt committed suicide, resulted in no convictions, as the district attorney could not prosecute the cases due to evidentiary problems (Conradt against NBC Universal, 2008). In his opinion, permitting the suit to proceed, Judge Chin stated that NBC might have been involved in "planning the execution of the warrants," thus clearly (if proven) crossing a line (Conradt v. NBC Universal, 2008, p. 23).

In his article on the Conradt sting and *To Catch a Predator*, Dittrich (2008) reported that a law enforcement officer serving as an on-the-set consultant was uncomfortable with *Dateline*'s maneuvers. Dittrich also reported that *Perverted Justice*, not local law enforcement, informed the district attorney's office of the sting. He also noted that Chief Myrick of the Murphy Police claimed that the decision to raid the house with a SWAT team was not his. Dittrich also claimed that Chris Hansen said he did not have any regrets about the Murphy, Texas, sting.

On June 24, 2008, the *Los Angeles Times* reported, prior to trial, that the parties reached an undisclosed settlement (Gold, 2008). According to the *Times* report, the show ended its run in December 2007, in part due to this type of litigation. Despite the end of the show, one of its lasting effects was the promotion of Hansen as an expert in pedophiles and Internet sexual solicitation.

In a hearing of the House Committee on Energy & Commerce, Rep. Bart Stupak (D-MI) cited Hansen's testimony that studies underestimate the prevalence of online sexual solicitation. According to Rep. Stupak and Hansen as many as one out every three children are sexually solicited when online (C-SPAN, 2006). This complete distortion of the available data, as discussed earlier, fuels the perception of an increased prevalence, thus enhancing the perceived "need" for the stings.

Perverted Justice

Next to the television show *To Catch a Predator*, perhaps the most controversial aspect of Internet sex stings is the advocacy group known as Perverted Justice (PJ). Founded in 2003 by Xavier Von Erck, the online organization consists of 41,000 registered users and 65 volunteers who act as underage decoys in aiding law enforcement in Internet sex stings. As discussed earlier, in 2004, the group developed a business arrangement with NBC's *To Catch A Predator*, in which PJ would provide the "decoys," (e.g., volunteers performing as underage minors) aiding law enforcement in their online stings. Reports have estimated that NBC paid Perverted Justice between $70,000 per episode and $2 million in total (Salkin, 2006; Zetter, 2007).

As described in their web biography, they argue their goal is to "create a 'chilling effect' in regional chat rooms and other easy targets of opportunity online such as through social networking sites." Additionally, their self-described intent is to turn "the website into a conviction machine with as many first agreements with police as possible" (Frequently Asked Questions: Partially Submitted by Readers, 2008).

Critics of the organization argue that these volunteers have no training in police work, psychiatry, sexual assault prevention, sexual offending, the law or due process (Salkin, 2006). One of the many questions raised by the role of *Perverted Justice* is that of vigilantism. Several studies have documented that vigilantism against sex offenders has led to their harassment, victimization, and even murder (Human Rights Watch, 2007; Levenson, 2005; Wright, 2008; Zevitz & Farkas, 2000).

Yet Jenkins has written that PJ is not the first web group of its kind. A few years prior to the creation of PJ, Jenkins reported, several private web-based advocacy groups took on the charge of stopping electronic child pornography. A few of these group collaborated with local law enforcement (similar to PJ), whereas some operated alone. Several of the groups took to launching denial-of-service (DOS) attacks on known child pornography bulletin boards. Jenkins (2001) noted that, although it was a short-term victory, these web groups had more success eliminating child pornography than did law enforcement (pp. 169–177).

Justin Berry and the New York Times

Online child sexual solicitation becomes more complex and potentially dangerous when it involves the use of a webcam. These cameras, which allow real-time photography/video to be broadcast over the Internet, add a level of graphicness and explicitness, and may fuel sex offenders' fantasies. In late 2005, the front-page story of Justin Berry had an effect similar to that of *To Catch a Predator*, by providing a real-life case study of criminal adolescent-adult online sexuality.

As reported by *New York Times* reporter Kurt Eichenwald, from the age of 13 to 19, Berry became both a victim and a perpetrator of child abuse and pornography. After setting up a webcam in his home bedroom, Berry was sexually solicited numerous times online by adult men. These sexual solicitations included not only sexual demands and requests for in-person meetings but specific, graphic sexual requests which Berry would comply with via his webcam (Eichenwald, 2005).

Over the years, Berry met various men from his online encounters. In a Congressional hearing, called as a result of the *New York Times* investigation, Berry testified that he had been molested by several adult men he had originally met online (U.S. House of Representatives Energy & Commerce Committee Investigations Subcomittee, 2006). According to the *New York Times*, Berry also organized an online business involving sexual exposure of himself and in the process violated numerous federal anti-child pornography laws (Eichenwald, 2005).

After initially identifying himself as a "fan" of Berry's, the *New York Times* reporter, Eichenwald, requested a meeting with him. After meeting Berry, Eichenwald developed a nonsexual relationship with him. Eichenwald, whose methods and actions would later raise concerns about the role of journalists in crime control, intended to aid Berry in getting out of the Internet child pornography trade, while simultaneously reporting the news story and aiding federal prosecutors in investigating and prosecuting these cases (France, 2007).

Through the assistance of Eichenwald, Berry cooperated with federal law enforcement authorities, releasing information on numerous "clients" (i.e., adults who had purchased or aided in production and distribution of child porn). In describing Berry's role and the nexus of Internet child pornography, online sexual solicitation and adolescent sexual exposure, Eichenwald's article initiated tremendous political response. Shortly thereafter, Eichenwald and Berry appeared on national programs, including *Oprah, Larry King Live*, and *Today* (France, 2007).

Eichenwald's role, which included giving Mr. Berry $2,000 (which would later be repaid by Berry's family), drew comparisons to Hansen's role in *To Catch a Predator* in that instead of reporting the news, journalists are influencing the news (France, 2007). Compounding the problem was that his editors at the *New York Times* were unaware of the financial relationship between the two parties, apparently in violation of ethical standards of the newspaper (Eichenwald, 2007). The Justin Berry case grew in importance, in part due to his testimony before Congress (discussed below).

Congressional Hearings on Sex Crimes and the Internet

As previously mentioned, Congress has played a leadership role in the problem of enticement and in the use of the Internet sex sting. One vehicle at Congress's disposal is that of the Congressional hearing. Congressional hearings often have multiple goals, functions and motivations. They may provide oversight to an existing problem. They may be used as an information-gathering process. They may be used to support or defeat forthcoming legislation.

Congress held several hearings on Internet sexual solicitations in 2006 and 2007. The House Judiciary Committee held a hearing on "Sex Crimes and the Internet," on October 17, 2007. In his introductory remarks, Representative Bobby Scott (Georgia) tried to offer moderate and reasonable criticism of new responses to the problem of online sexual solicitation. Immediately after, Rep. Ric Keller (Florida) lauded the efforts of *To Catch a Predator*, taking the stereotypical "tough" on crime control position (Judiciary Committee of the United States House of Representatives, 2007).

Following testimony from law enforcement officials, Internet providers, and others, the most dramatic moments occurred with the testimony of Alicia Kozakiewicz. When Kozakiewicz was 13, she met Scott Tyree online. Tyree would later be convicted for the kidnapping, rape, and torture of Kozakiewicz (Jaffee, 2007).

The then-19-year-old Kozakiewicz described her experience and her belief that the ICAC Task Forces saved her life. She claimed that at a moment when she expected to be killed, she "saw the most beautiful letters in the alphabet, FBI, in bold yellow on the back of their jackets and I knew that I was safe." She described the FBI and ICAC as her "angels" and said that they could "walk on water" (C-SPAN, 2006).

Toward the end of her testimony, she said that the "bogeyman is real and he lives on the Net. He lived in my computer and he lives in yours. While you are sitting here, he's at home with your children." At the end of her 10-minute testimony, Rep. Debbie Wasserman-Schulz, a member of the Committee, cried (C-SPAN, 2006). The dramatic effect of Kozakiewicz's testimony was clear.

Justin Berry testified to Congress on April 4, 2006, in a hearing held by the Investigations Subcommittee of the House Committee on Energy and Commerce. Among the numerous issues Berry testified about was the allegedly slow response from the Child Exploitation and Obscenity Section (CEOS) of the Department of Justice to his case and his offer of assistance. Berry claimed that after his (and the *New York Times'*) disclosure about his crimes and the adult predators, he wanted to work with prosecutors to shut down other child porn rings. During the negotiations, in which through his lawyer he sought immunity, he claimed that the CEOS seemed very slow and uninterested in the case:

> I informed them that I had names, credit card numbers, and IP addresses, of approximately 1500 people who paid to watch child pornography from my websites ... Weeks passed seemingly without progress. I cannot describe the agony of that time. Each night I wondered ... Were the children I knew being molested that night? Were they being filmed? Why was no one stopping this? I knew it would take time to grant me immunity or not. But why couldn't they rescue the children in danger? (U.S. House of Representatives Energy & Commerce Investigations Subcommittee, 2006)

Once immunity was granted and an initial prosecution conducted, Berry stated that he was still afraid:

> I wish I could say the prosecution story had a happy ending. It did not. At that time I was afraid that I would be killed by the adults who would be harmed by my testimony and who were frantically searching for me ... I do not trust CEOS to protect me. (U.S. House of Representatives Energy & Commerce Investigations Subcommittee, 2006)

At the very end of his testimony, there was a stunning exchange in its simplicity and brevity. The exchange occurred between Rep. Greg Walden from Oregon and Justin Berry:

> Rep Walden: Mr. Berry, is there anyone in this room that you believe molested you?

> Berry: Yes. Ken Gorelay.

> Rep. Walden: Thank you. (U.S. House of Representatives Energy & Commerce

> Investigations Subcommittee, 2006)

It is important to understand the significance of that interchange. In a Congressional hearing with one person alleging a violation of federal and state law, an elected official (not a prosecutor, judge, or police officer) asked a witness under oath whether he had been criminally sexually molested. The alleged molester (Ken Gorelay) was subsequently called to testify. He invoked his right against self-incrimination and was dismissed by the committee. The exchange, which arguably should have been conducted in a courtroom but instead was made live on national television, could have easily been misinterpreted as a scene out of a Hollywood television show.

Finally, Chris Hansen of NBC's *To Catch a Predator* testified at the same June 2006 Congressional hearing. After discussing the process his show utilized and the role of *Perverted Justice*, he described one of the dozens of men who were "investigated":

> After five investigations in five different States, we thought we had seen it all, but no one was prepared for what we saw in Fort Myers. Late on a sunny Sunday afternoon, our hidden cameras were rolling when a 40-year-old man parked his SUV in front of our home. He had set up a date for sex with a decoy posing as a 14-year-old boy. We watched as he got out and walked around the rear passenger door. We suspected he may be grabbing some beer or food, as we had seen other visitors do. **Instead he takes his 5-year-old son out of the car seat and led him by the hand up the driveway towards the back door of the house. There was an audible gasp inside the house. [emphasis added]** After he walked in, I told him who I was and what *Dateline* was doing. I didn't want to scare his son. (Subcommittee on Oversight and Investigations of the Committee on Energy and Commerce, 2006)

The implication Hansen was drawing was that the father had allegedly brought his 5-year-old son to watch, participate, or somehow be involved in this possible sexual encounter. During the following question-and-answer session with Mr. Hansen, the question was raised about the show's relationship with law enforcement:

> Mr. Walden: And talk to me about the relationship with law enforcement … Is law enforcement interested in participating?

Mr. Hansen: *Perverted Justice* was contacted by the Riverside County Sheriff's Department and they said, "Look, if you are willing to work with us, we are willing to work with you. And if Dateline wants to do their parallel investigation that is fine too." And obviously we don't want to be an arm of law enforcement.

Mr. Walden: Of course not.

Mr. Hansen: And law enforcement doesn't want to be an arm of journalism.

Mr. Walden: Right.

Mr. Hansen: So, we felt that with *Perverted Justice* kind of acting as the Chinese wall in the middle, if you will, we were able to preserve our integrity and they were able to preserve theirs, and we were able to operate. (Subcomittee on Oversight and Investigations of the Committee on Energy and Commerce, 2006, pp. 30–31)

Hansen provided the committee with *Dateline's* most disturbing case while also explaining how their actions didn't violate journalistic or law enforcement ethics. As successful as *To Catch a Predator* became, it is fair to assume that Hansen understands dramatic effect.

Griffin and Miller (2008) argued that policies aimed at high-profile cases of stranger–child abductions (which Internet sex stings are theoretically designed to prevent) are simply no more than *crime-control theater*, often replete with unintended consequences and little efficacy. Griffin and Miller proposed the following definition of *crime control theater:* "a public response or set of responses to crime which generate the appearance but not the fact of crime control" (p. 167). The focus of their study was the impact of the AMBER alert system, a broadcasting system in which the notification of a missing/abducted child is broadcast regionally and nationally.

Enacted in 1996 after the abduction and murder in Texas of Amber Hagerman, Griffin and Miller (2008) argued that proponents of the law (most notably law enforcement, child advocacy programs and the National Center for Missing and Exploited Children [NCMEC]) repeatedly use the infrequent, sensational success of the program as evidence of its overall impact. Their assessment of the policy also argued that it has a racialized component, focusing heavily on the symbolic victimizations of young, white girls (Ibid, p. 169).

Using Griffin and Miller's model, it is reasonable to view Internet sex stings as another form of crime control theatre, and it is instructive to add the Congressional crime hearing as another element to their conceptualization of crime control theater.

There is no question that these graphic, public testimonies are very dramatic and emotional. Again expanding Griffin and Miller's concept, dramatic depictions of actual violence may fuel the desire for crime control theater policies. The theatricality of the Congressional hearing, which often leads to new legislation, is an important factor in the drive for new and expanded sex offender laws.

Public dramatizations of online child sexual solicitation and the Internet sex sting are hardly limited to the above examples. Feature-length depictions have appeared in the *Atlantic Monthly*, *Oprah*, and *America's Most Wanted* (Flanagan, 2007; Harpo Productions, 2008; Springer, 2007). Even nontraditional crime-fighting allies including Miss America Lauren Taylor and NBA All-Star Shaquille O'Neal have become a part of the Internet sex sting scene (Associated Press, 2005; Springer, 2007).

As is documented throughout this book, sex offender policies are often disproportionately influenced and illuminated by rare, high-profile tragedies. As discussed, the *New York Times*, NBC, and Perverted Justice and Congressional hearings have played significant roles in the glamorization of the Internet sex sting and its associated issues.

Legal Issues—Free Speech, Entrapment, and Factual Impossibility

As mentioned earlier, one of the concerns about Internet sex stings and the crimes of enticement is that they are actually prosecuting constitutionally protected speech. In addition to this legal argument, those accused of this crime will use several other strategies to defeat the charge. In addition to the free speech argument, defendants will also raise the issues of entrapment and factual and legal impossibility. Supporters of Internet stings will argue that they are no different than drug and prostitution stings and other forms of undercover police work, which are largely uncontroversial. Below is a limited discussion of each of those issues, beginning with the question of free speech.

Are Internet Sex Stings a Violation of Free Speech?

The intent of these stings is to capture and arrest an alleged offender before they have sex with a minor. Opponents of these stings argue that what is actually being criminalized is speech; in essence, the sexually explicit dialogue between an adult and the make-believe "minor" (i.e., police officer). Do Internet sex stings prosecutions punish sexual expression, which is protected as a form of free speech?

During these investigations and prosecutions, a central point of evidence is the chat room logs, transcripts, e-mails, and instant messages. The prosecution presents the written words of the defendant as evidence that they intended to have sex with a child (had the recipient of the e-mails been an actual child). The prosecution argues that it is only the proactive and ingenious work of law enforcement which prevented the defendant from finding an actual potential victim.

One legal scholar has argued that that is what is being prosecuted and that **the speech itself** (outside of any action taken by the defendant—e.g., showing up at an arranged meeting place) **should be** criminalized. Utilizing the previously discussed case study of Justin Berry, Lovejoy argued that cyber-sex between adults and minors, in and of itself, is harmful enough to warrant a federal and/or state statute. Not surprisingly, Lovejoy (2008) condoned the use of the Internet sex sting as appropriate and necessary.

Lovejoy further argued that Supreme Court decisions dismissing the "free speech" defense of child pornography would also apply to prohibiting cyber-sex between adults and perceived minors. Yet he also acknowledged that the court ruled in *Ashcroft v. Free Speech Coalition* (2002) that the "government cannot prohibit speech on the ground that it may encourage pedophiles to engage in illegal conduct" (p. 31).

These concerns are a central reason why law enforcement agencies conduct the arrest at an alleged meeting. When a defendant takes steps to meet with a believed minor, his or her actions bolster the prosecutors' efforts to demonstrate criminal intent.

Paralleling the distortion of the media coverage of and federal laws on Internet child sexual abuse, Lovejoy ignored the fact that much of the sexual communication a minor receives is facilitated by other minors or young adults (Wolak et al., 2006). Given this research, should adolescents be prosecuted for sending sexually provocative e-mails and instant messages to their peers? As mentioned previously, assuming that the person sexually soliciting a minor is always an adult predatory sex offender is erroneous and problematic.

The Question of Entrapment: Inducement & Predisposition

One legal argument made by those arrested via Internet sex stings is that they were entrapped. For a defendant to successfully argue that he or she was entrapped into the commission of a crime, the defendant must combat two issues: inducement and predisposition.

Inducement is the argument that the government's actions (i.e., law enforcement) persuaded, manipulated, or coerced the defendant into commission of the crime (Boggess, 2007). An inducement argument needs to demonstrate that not only did the government provide an opportunity to commit the crime, but also the government provided an **excessive opportunity**.

A hypothetical example of inducement may be helpful. An undercover narcotics agent for a local police department is involved in a drug buy in an attempt to arrest a suspected dealer. The "true" or real street price for 2 kg of heroin is (roughly) $2,000. If the officer offers to buy the heroin from the suspected dealer for $2,200, he has not induced the defendant. If the officer offers the suspect $10,000 for the same heroin, inducement may have occurred. One of the central findings in the overturned Internet sex sting conviction in the 2000 case of *United States v. Mark Douglas Poehlman* was that the law enforcement officer's responses to Poehlman were "excessive" in their initiation and sexual explicitness (U.S. v. Poehlman 2000).

Predisposition shifts the focus from the government's behavior to the defendant's. Generally, predisposition can be established when the defendant has taken active steps to commit a crime before coming in contact with law enforcement agents (Hay, 2003). For example, in Internet sex sting cases, child pornography on an offender's computer is often introduced as evidence of predisposition. E-mails or Web site visits looking for child sexual activity, *prior to* contact with the law enforcement officer, may also demonstrate predisposition. Prior convictions for child sexual assault or enticement may be allowed as evidence of predisposition.

Inducement and the second factor, predisposition, have an inverse relationship with one another. For an entrapment defense to be successful, the defendant must prove that the government induced him AND that he did not have predisposition. This combination, along with widespread acceptance of Internet sex stings, makes this defense often unsuccessful.

Federal courts are generally upholding convictions won through Internet sex stings. Both on the question of entrapment and the defendant's "intent," federal appellate courts have generally rejected the defendant's arguments. One case in which the conviction was reversed is discussed below.

In the 2005 case of the *United States v. Kevin Eric Curtin*, Kevin Curtin was arrested and convicted for attempting to engage with a minor he had recruited over the Internet. The Ninth Circuit Court of Appeals reversed his conviction and remanded the case for a new trial. Via an Internet sex sting, Curtin was arrested for his plan to meet an underage minor (in actuality, Las Vegas Detective Michael Castaneda) whom he wanted to have sex with in Las Vegas. Upon his arrest, Curtin's laptop and personal digital assistant (PDA) were found to contain 140 stories of adults having sex with children and chat channels Curtin had used in the past.

The three judge panel of the Ninth Circuit Court ruled that stories on the defendant's PDA should not have been admitted as evidence in the trial, thus creating a "prejudicial effect" on the jury (U.S. V. Curtin, 2006). In his dissenting opinion, Judge Stephen Trott argued that Curtin was not only aware of his actions but specifically asked if "Christy" (Detective Castaneda) was working with police (Wallace, 2006, p. 3689). Trott disputed Curtin's assertion that he was "role-playing" online and actually looking for an adult. Trott also noted that the trial court did not err by allowing a sample (i.e., five) of the stories on the defendant's PDA to be entered as evidence. In his dissent Trott also noted that the stories on Curtin's PDA demonstrated a **predisposition** toward adult–child criminal sex and were correctly allowed during the trial (p. 3716).

The appeal was not concluded at this point. It was subsequently reheard en banc with 15 judges of the Ninth Circuit Court of Appeals on October 3, 2006. Upon its hearing before the 15-judge panel (as opposed to the 3-judge panel which had previously ruled), the conviction was again reversed but with instructions that in the retrial the district court review the relevance of the stories on Curtin's PDA before they could be introduced to the jury as evidence of his predisposition (U.S. v. Curtin 2007).

Case law has found that the use of the entrapment defense does not appear to be very successful in reversing convictions. However, the aggressive behavior of the government in Internet sex stings raises an ethical question. By this aggressive focus on intent (as primarily determined by the offender's words) and the use of deception by the police, is the underlying belief one that the defendant is guilty until proven innocent? Elucidated shortly, I argue that this approach does make a dangerous presumption of guilt.

The Question of Factual/Legal Impossibility

Another 2005 case from the Tenth Circuit Court of Appeals presents a different interpretation of legal arguments against Internet sex stings. Stanley Howard Simms, of New Mexico, met with and engaged in sexually explicit chat and e-mails with two (assumed) underage girls. The "girls" were not law enforcement agents but Michael Walker, a resident of Missouri. Sims was convicted on three charges, two of which were related to the issues of enticement. The third charge Simms was convicted on was a child porn charge because he shared sexually explicit electronic images of himself and other children in his online relationship (United States v. Simms, 2005).

On appeal, Sims argued that conviction of the two counts of enticement should be overturned due to the "factual impossibility" argument (explained below). In addition, the defendant argued that the child porn conviction should be overturned due to the fact that the government could not prove that the sexually explicit images were of "real" and not virtual children. The Tenth Circuit affirmed the conviction but reversed his 37-month sentence and remanded it to the original trial for resentencing. In this case, the appellate court upheld the enticement conviction despite the defendant's claim of factual impossibility (Ebel, 2005).

Defendants arguing factually impossibility state that because the underage minor receiving the sexual solicitations is actually an adult, there can be no violation of "enticing a minor." The minor, in fact, does not exist. They argue that they could not break the law, because there was no actual minor or victim. The Tenth Circuit, consistent with other federal court rulings, has found that as long as the defendant "believed a minor to be involved," factual impossibility is not a valid defense (Ebel, 2005).

Boggess (2007) argued that there is a consensus emerging among the federal circuit courts that a minor is not necessary for an enticement/inducement conviction to be sustained and that the argument of factual impossibility is not a successful strategy to defeat Internet sex sting convictions. She reported that 9 of the 11 federal circuit courts have upheld enticement convictions, acquired via Internet sex stings. She also noted that states (including Missouri) are modeling state enticement laws consistent with recent case law. Should Boggess' interpretation prove correct, state-level convictions may increase along with a corresponding utilization of the Internet sex sting by state and local law enforcement.

Boggess (2007) noted the distinctions between factual and legal impossibility defenses. Specifically, she noted that under the factual impossibility argument, the defendant claims that the act cannot physically be accomplished. Legal impossibility, she argued, occurs when a crime could not have occurred because an element of the crime has not been satisfied. She also noted that factual impossibility cannot be applied to "attempt" or "intent" charges as those focus on the defendant's preliminary actions and thoughts (Ibid). As noted earlier, one danger of prosecutions based on one's thoughts is the shift away from a presumption of innocence toward one of guilt.

Boggess (2007) stated that defendants may also argue that the government's conduct in an Internet sex sting was so outrageous that it inevitably violated the defendant's due process rights. A similar argument is often made in cases to the government's treatment of detainees at Guantanamo Bay. This parallel will be explored later in this chapter. A fourth possible defense against the Internet sex sting conviction is that the government violated wiretap laws regarding the authorized or unauthorized recordings of one's communications (Ibid).

Another question in the legal debate is the question of the age of the "victim." Defendants will claim that they actually didn't believe the "victim" when they said they were a minor and that they went to meet the victim to see if they were over the age of 18 (Lovejoy, 2008; United States v. Curtin, 2007; United States v. CurtinWallace, 2006). Jenkins (2001) has stated that this rationalization is also used by those charged with possession of child pornography.

Although case law appears to be clear, an ethical question is raised. Is it just to argue that a law can be broken although the intended crime cannot actually be accomplished? When the actual victim of a crime does not exist are convictions and arrests an act of net widening or an act of punishment?

Aren't Internet Sex Stings the Same as Drug and Prostitution Stings?

Proponents of Internet sex stings argue that this type of deception is necessary to capture would-be pedophiles and is no different than drug, prostitution, and other types of law enforcement stings. Jenkins (2001) has written that the federal government deployed similarly deceptive stings to detect child porn, 15 years prior to the enticement sting (p. 40). Even opponents of Internet sex stings have accepted the use and appropriateness of in-person drug and prostitution stings (Fulda, 2002). The most obvious and significant difference is the nature of the medium employed.

By the nature of its diffuse structure, easy access, and worldwide proliferation, the Internet is very conducive for anonymity. Screen names, e-mail addresses, in fact nearly all information communicated online can be easily fabricated and falsified. The anonymity of drug and prostitution stings is limited due to their requirement of face-to-face transactions. The would-be buyer and the would-be seller are conducting a transaction with a long-standing knowledge of its illegality. Thus, for the transaction to take place, it must occur in a face-to-face setting. Contrary to these stings, the world of the Internet sex sting is fraught with the vagaries of intent, sexual innuendo, fantasy, exaggeration, and bravado.

Hay (2003) stated that all stings lower the crime rate by identifying offenders and deterring crime. His view was that stings have a dual purpose. First is their informational purpose, which identifies the likely offenders. The second purpose is a behavioral function, more accurately known as the general deterrent function. These functions are both valid but often contradict one another (Ibid).

Hay (2003) also countered the argument that stings are unnecessary. An alternative that law enforcement might be able to use is covert surveillance. Once enough evidence is gathered by secret monitoring, an arrest warrant may be issued and may be conducted. His position was that stings are preferable because they require fewer resources and risk less infringement on the accused's privacy (Ibid, p. 13).

Hay noted that the nature of the Internet sex sting often involves individuals who have no prior history of child sexual abuse (p. 20). He acknowledged that stings occasionally produce false positives, individuals who are innocent (p. 39). In the case of the Internet sex sting, the "innocent" is the defendant who would not have had sex with an actual child. Hay concluded with an assessment that the Internet sex sting is no different than other type of law enforcement stings and provides an overall benefit by reducing crime. As discussed in the following section, there are numerous logical flaws in the assumptions that Internet sex stings always prevent sex crimes.

Shifting of Our Legal Principles to Widen the Net?

Despite their broad popular and legislative support, Internet sex stings present numerous ethical problems. Our nation is built on an adversarial system of justice, where one is assumed innocent until proven guilty. Internet sex stings assume the man who would chat with the (imagined) child would commit child sexual abuse, unless he is stopped. This move toward an inquisitorial system of justice, one in which one must prove one's innocence, is not justified by a series of heinous, low-frequency offenses (Inciaridi, 2008, p. 129).

A central danger in moving away from the legal bedrock that is "innocent until proven guilty" is that innocent people will be wrongfully arrested and punished. The most blatant example of a parallel is the American response to terrorists. The Bush Administration's decision to detain people without trial at Guantanamo Bay is the contemporary example of an inquisitorial system. As numerous scholars have argued, the heinous and devastating actions of a few do not justify jettisoning core legal principles (Ball, 2007; Cole, 2003; Mayer, 2008). Given the public disdain and fear of sex offenders and terrorists, the comparison is valid. When one moves toward an inquisitorial system, innocent people will inevitably be captured within the criminal justice system's net. Although the public approves of this net widening, it does violate the principles under which our laws operate.

This conflict illustrates our struggle between balancing moral imperatives and the law. This underlying tension of enticement charges and Internet sex stings is between our desire to use any actions to protect our children with a legal system that assumes innocence and punishes conduct. The presumption of innocence proposes human control of our emotions. It assumes that we are rational beings who can moderate strong and powerful emotions. Given the choice between acting on irrational desires, we calculate the moral costs and benefits and choose not to commit crime. As noted earlier, supporters of Internet sex stings believe that would-be offenders cannot control their emotions, inevitably leading to child rape. This overgeneralization based upon the deviance of a few promotes a view of causality not supported by research.

A second problem created by enticement charges and Internet sex stings is elucidated by further analyzing the relationship between a person's words and their actions. At the core of Internet sex stings is an assumption that the adult would inevitably follow through on their sexual comments and have unlawful sex with a child (Hay, 2003). This assumption is critically flawed for many reasons.

The first logical flaw in this thought pattern is an inaccurate understanding of the role of the Internet in sexual development. For example, doesn't the anonymous nature of the Internet encourage the exploration of sexual fantasies that one may actually never engage in? Doesn't this anonymous exploration of sexuality apply to both adults and adolescents? Does the act of sexually deviant online speech inherently lead to in-person sexually deviant and criminal behavior?

Human behavior is fraught with distinctions between what one says and the actions one takes. Whether verbally lashing out a child, a bad driver, or the romantic partner who is an hour late, we support and encourage instantaneous emotions to be modified by one's reflection and delayed behavior.

Sexuality and sexual fantasies are replete with instances of curiosity, desire, testing of boundaries, fears, guilt, excitement, and moral calculations. Whether it involves marriage partners of 40 years or a young adult with many sexual partners, there are many cases in which an individual **does not** always act on their sexual feelings. In fact, due to the nature of the Internet, it promotes both healthy and unhealthy sexual fantasies (Boies, Knudson, & Young, 2004).

Sheldon and Howitt (2008) studied the sexual fantasies of convicted sex offenders. Their exploratory work provides us some insight into the relationships between sexual fantasies and sexual offending. One of their surprising findings was that most common sexual fantasies these sex offenders had were of adult women and consensual acts, not forced child sex (p. 151). This finding undermines the causative relationship that supporters of Internet sex stings assume: that an offender's deviant fantasies are fed by online chats, escalating their desire to commit an in-person offense.

Sheldon and Howitt noted that studying the relationship between sexual fantasy and offending is very problematic. They cited earlier research documenting that nonoffending adults often have sexual thoughts which include the use of force and involve children, yet they do not act on those feelings (Langevin et al., 1998, and Kirkendall & McBride, 1990, as cited in Sheldon & Howitt, 2008). Finally, they reported that "we are unable to say how many, or if any, Internet offenders will go on to contact offend against children" (Sheldon & Howitt, 2008).

In their exploratory case study with a convicted pedophile, Wilson and Jones (2008) examined the relationship between the offender's fantasies and his actions. Their conclusion provided modest support for Internet sex stings in that "the inter-relations between psychological, physical, and importantly virtual, provide an almost indisputable link between 'thinking' and 'doing' in the sexual offender" (Ibid).

However, they discussed the difficulties in generalizing this possible causality:

> The proposed model also does not suggest that every individual who has sexual fantasies will act upon those fantasies ... Or that any deviant fantasy will transit into anything more than a fleeting sexual thought or desire ... The societal rules, the conducts of behavior and **self-regulation prevent [emphasis added]**, for the great majority, extreme fantasies ever being played out in the real world. (Wilson & Jones, 2008)

Law enforcement agents, prosecutors, and supporters of Internet sex stings assume that Internet sexual curiosity about adult–child sex will in a definitive causal chain lead to child sexual abuse. They assume that fantasy inevitably causes action. Their argument is centered, statically, on the Internet communications and the fact that the defendant showed up at a meeting place. This is an inherent flaw in logic. There are cases in which the would-be perpetrator pulls back from the brink, reflecting on his or her actions and the possible consequences.

In fact, by accepting that adults interested in child sex **might not** commit the act (based on their own fears, moral unease, self-regulation, etc.), the proponents would lose a central concept in their arguments. Proponents argue that it is **only** the undercover officer who stopped a child sexual assault from occurring. In order to justify this form of proactive/preventive policing, the public must be convinced that there is no other alternative. By demonizing sex offenders and repeating factually incorrect statistics about recidivism, treatment, offense histories, etc., proponents have created an uncontrollable enemy. This enemy, the would-be Internet child molester, can only be stopped by undercover cops.

An additional logical/ethical flaw in the debate about Internet sex stings and online child sexual solicitation is a poor, static, dated, and nostalgic view of young people and adolescent sexuality. Numerous reports are finding that today's youth do not have traditional boundaries of public and private spheres and that they generally view the Internet as an extension melding the two spheres (Dretzin, 2008). A central factor in understanding the impact of the Internet in sexual solicitation is essentially to understand that Internet addictions may apply to not only hardcore, lonely pedophiles but to everyday, "normal" adolescents (Dretzin, 2008). Additionally, there can be tremendous immediate gratification by broadcasting one's life in a forum that is never "off" (Ibid). As supported by the research of Wolak and associates, young people commonly use the Internet to discuss sexuality (Wolak et al., 2008).

In the ever-expanding political tendency to simplify problems, policy and political descriptions of Internet sex stings become a one-dimensional image of a convicted pedophile sitting in a dark room at a keyboard desperately seeking potential victims. Media and political portrayals such as these most notably illustrated by *To Catch a Predator* ignore a major central, dynamic factor: an adolescent's agency and desire for sexual exploration.

Some of these online sexual solicitations are initiated by adolescents and preteens pretending they are older than they are, making sexually explicit comments and questions to seek information and to demonstrate their newfound sexual power. Some scholars argue that these concerns about Internet sexual solicitations and possible sexual assaults are an exaggeration and are more accurately a moral panic focused on fears of adolescent female sexuality.

Cassell and Cramer (2008) argued that the obsession with young girls online is similar to earlier technological changes (e.g., telegraph and telephone) and previous attempts to control female development and sexuality. They postulated that the online sexuality is an important marker for healthy adolescent female sexuality (p. 69).

Another important omission in the Internet predator debate is the lack of critical understanding in gendered uses of the technology. Several reports showed that girls are at greater risk for online sexual victimization than boys (Cassell & Cramer, 2008; Wolak et al., 2008). Boys who are gay or questioning their sexual orientation are also at greater risk (Wolak et al., 2008). Adding any significant differences in Internet usage into the policy debate about online dangers clouds the waters on discussions about the lurking Internet sex offender.

Fulda's 2002 study reported that those arrested in Internet sex stings were far more likely to have no criminal history and no concurrent charge other than "intent to recruit or solicit." Fulda went as far to state the intended targets of these stings (e.g., pedophiles) are not being captured by this technique. Wolak and associates also reported that those arrested in Internet sex stings tended to have a shorter criminal history than those arrested for a child sexual assault. Yet these scholars did not find that Internet sex stings arrestees were completely "clean" of sexually deviant behavior or criminality (Wolak et al., 2008).

By allowing the government to generalize a subset of horrific cases into a perpetual fear, we condone a dangerous strategy. By not questioning the assumption that adults who contact youth online will inexorably lead to child rape, we accept an unfounded fear. That fear becomes the justification for assuming guilt before innocence, thus making the Internet sex sting seem a necessary tool. When jettisoning our legal principles for an unsubstantiated generic fear, which **only** the government can prevent, we lose more than our sense of safety. We lose our sense of agency and our sense of control.

Conclusion

Some scholars have argued that Internet sex stings are a new and dangerous precedent. This practice, though quite popular among policy makers, the general public, and mainstream media, is a form of preventive detention (Wright, 2008). The centerpiece of the American legal system is that one is innocent until proven guilty. Secondly, our system is designed to punish actions, not thoughts. This growing use of preventive detention focused on a low-frequency, yet horrible, offense raises significant questions about the growth of preventive policing, a shift to a presumption of guilt, and a public that has uncritically accepted a demonization of sex offenders.

As Fulda (2002) argued, totalitarian nations operate with assumptions that individuals are presumed guilty, thus those who are deemed "dangerous" need to be detained. Although I would not agree with Fulda's characterization, I do believe that Internet sex stings sit along a continuum comparable to holding enemy combatants at Guantanamo without trial.

We are willing to capture and prosecute the many, for fear of the actions of a few. This represents a continuing escalation of net widening and a general decrease in privacy protections resulting in less safety and freedom for everyone.

Hoffman noted that it is critical that criminologists and other researchers convey and construct their work in ways emphasizing a child (and adolescent's) agency and away from the media construction of the menacing predator (Hoffman, 2008). Although the utilization of the Internet sex sting is unlikely to end, some scholars have called for a greater focus on prevention efforts targeted toward adolescents, not parents (Wolak et al., 2008).

Given the popularity of this investigative technique, public disdain for sex offenders, and the ever-increasing utilization of the Internet, it is unlikely that federal and state laws will be modified to reflect the most common online risks young people face. Case law, the rare but horrific adult Internet predator case, and the powerful role of the media to shape public sentiment influence the likelihood that the Internet sex sting will persevere.

However, in our perpetual struggle between balancing freedom and safety, we must continually assess the following questions:

- How many innocent people have been and will be harmed by this presumption of guilt?
- Will the scientific research into online sexual activity continue to be misrepresented by the media, policy makers, and the tragic high-profile offense?
- Can increased support for parents and improvements in technology provide greater control of Internet dangers than increasing the role of government?
- Under the well-meaning auspices of child protection, is an individual's right to an exploration of his or her sexual fantasies being eroded?
- Similar to the War on Terror, are we placing too much trust in government to decide the balance between safety and security?

Finally, as illustrated by Alicia Kozakiewicz and Justin Berry, there are rare but tragic cases of adult Internet predators finding and brutalizing children. This exploratory critique is in no way meant to trivialize the pain and grief those victims and their families have suffered. Consistent with this book is our view that the pain of sexual assault victims can be most effectively addressed by balancing research, law, and a holistic response with their voices. With this call for moderation and analysis, our future may be one in which we trust one another instead of perpetually fearing the unknown.

References

105th Congress of the United States. (1998, October 30). H.R. 3494. Protection of Children From Sexual Predators Act of 1988, p. 20. Washington, DC.

108th Congress. (2003, April 30). Public Law 108-21. Prosecutorial Remedies and Other Tools To End The Exploitation of Children Today Act of 2003. Washington, DC.

Alexy, E. M., Burgess, A. W., & Baker, T. (2005). Internet offenders: Traders, travelers and combination traders-travelers. *Journal of Interpersonal Violence, 20* (7), 804–812.

Associated Press. (2005, May 25). Shaq goes undercover for Justice Dept. probe. Retrieved July 18, 2008, from http://sportsillustrated.cnn. com/2005/basketball/nba/specials/playoffs/2005/05/25/shaq/

The Associated Press. (2006a, April 5). Homeland official arrested for solicitation. Retrieved July 10, 2008, from www.msnbc.msn. com/id/12159118

Associated Press. (2006b, December 1). Rabbi gets 6 years in prison after being caught in sex sting. Retrieved July 10, 2008, from http://www. usatoday.com/news/nation/2006-12-01-rabbi_x.htm.

The Associated Press. (2008a, January 14). *Mayor/Pastor Held in Online Sex Sting.* Retrieved June 27, 2008, from www.msnbc.msn. com/id/22655404/

Associated Press. (2008b, May 16). Texas megachurch minister busted in Internet sex sting. Retrieved July 10, 2008, from http://www.foxnews. com/story/0,2933,356467,00.html

Ball, H. (2007). *Bush, the Detainees and the Constitution: The Battle over Presidential Power in the War on Terror.* Lawrence, KS: University of Kansas Press.

Ballou, B. R. (2007, February 28). Ex-trooper Gets 5 Years for Soliciting Sex. *The Boston Globe.* Boston: The New York Times Company.

Boggess, B. M. (2007, Fall). Atempted Enticement of a Minor: No Place for Pedophiles to Hide Under 18. USA 2442(b). *Missouri Law Review.*

Boies, S. C., Knudson, G., & Young, J. (2004). The Internet, Sex, and Youths: Implications for Sexual Development. *Sexual Addiction & Compulsivity, 11,* 343–363.

Cassell, J., & Cramer, M. (2008). High tech or high risk: Moral panics about girls online. In T. McPherson (Ed.), *Digital Youth, Innovation and the Unexpected* (pp. 53–76). Cambridge, MA: The MIT Press.

Cohen, A. (2008, March 10). Editorial Observer: What's on TV Tonight? Public Humiliation to the Point of Suicide. *The New York Times.* New York: The New York Times. http://www.nytimes.com/2008/03/10/ opinion/10mon4.html?_r=1

Cole, D. (2003). *Enemy Aliens: Double Standards and Constitutional Freedoms in the War on Terror.* New York, NY, USA: The New Press.

C-SPAN. (2006, June 28). Making the Internet Safe for Children, Day 2. Washington, D.C.

Dittrich, L. (2008, June 26). Tonight on Dateline this man will die. Retrieved July 18, 2008, from http://www.esquire.com/features/predator0907

Dretzin, R., Maggio, J. (Producers), Dretzin, R. (Writer), Dretzin, R., & Maggio, J. (Directors). (2008). *Growing Up Online* [Motion Picture]. USA: Frontline.

Eaton, T. (2006, November 7). Prosecutor Kills Himself in Texas Raid Over Child Sex. *The New York Times.* New York, NY, USA: The New York Times.

Edwards, H. (2008, May 14). Seattle University Professor Held in Online Sex Sting. *The Seattle Times.* Seattle, WA, USA: The Seattle Times Company.

Eichenwald, K. (2005, December 19). Through his webcam, a boy joins a sordid online world. *The New York Times.* New York: The New York Times Company.

Eichenwald, K. (2007, 6 March). Reporter's Essay: Making A Connection with Justin - Editor's Note Appended. *The New York Times.* New York, NY, USA: The New York Times Company.

Farhi, P. (2006, April 9). 'Dateline' Pedophile Sting: One More Point. *Washingtonpost.com.* Washington, DC, USA: The WashingtonPost Company.

Finkelhor, D., Mitchell, K. J., & Wolak, J. (June 2000). *Online Victimization: A Report on the Nation's Youth.* Crimes Against Children Research Center'. Washington, D.C.: National Center for Missing & Exploited Children.

Flanagan, C. (2007, July/August). Babes in the Woods. *The Atlantic Monthly , 300* (1), pp. 116–133.

France, D. (2007, October 28). Saving Justin Berry. *New York Magazine.* http://nymag.com/guides/money/2007/39957/#

Frequently Asked Questions: Partially Submitted by Readers. (2008, January). Retrieved 8 July, 2008, from Perverted-Justice.Com: http://www.perverted-justice.com/index.php?pg=faq#cat1

Fulda, J. (2002). Do Sting Operations Directed at Pedophiles Capture Offenders? *Sexuality & Culture, 6* (4), 73–100.

Gold, M. (2008, June 24). *NBC Resolves Lawsuit Over "To Catch A Predator" Suicide.* Retrieved June 30, 2008, from Los Angeles Times: http://latimesblogs.latimes.com/showtracker/2008/06/nbc-resolves-la.html

Goodnough, A. (2007, October 6). U.S. Prosecutor Held in a Child Sex Sting Kills Himself. *New York Times.* Miami, FL, USA: The New York Times Company.

Griffin, T., & Miller, M. K. (2008). Child Abduction, AMBER Alert, & Crime Control Theater. *Criminal Justice Review, 33* (3), 159–176.

Harpo Productions. (2008). *Child Predator Watch List.* Retrieved July 16, 2008, from Oprah.com: http://www.oprah.com/presents/2005/predator/predator_main.jhtml

Hay, B. (2003). *Sting Operations, Undercover Agents and Entrapment.* Harvard Law School, John M. Olin Center for Law, Economics and Business Discussion Paper Series. The Berkeley Electronic Press.

Hoffman, B. (2008). The Science and Politics of Reducing Child Victimization. *Journal of Contemporary Criminal Justice, 24* (2), 103–113.

House of Representatives. (1988). *Child Protection and Sexual Predator Punishment Act of 1988 (House of Representatives - June 11, 1998).* House of Representatives. Washington, D.C.: THOMAS - Library of Congress.

Human Rights Watch. (2007, September). No easy answers: Sex offender laws in the US. *19* (4), 141.

Inciaridi, J. A. (2008). *Criminal Justice* (8th ed.). New York, NY, USA: McGraw-Hill.

Internet Crimes Against Children Task Force Training & Technical Assistance Program. (2008, June 18). *Internet Crimes Against Children Task Force Training & Technical Assistance Program.* Retrieved July 3, 2008, from http://www.icactraining.org/default.htm

Jaffee, M. (2007, October 17). *ABC News: Teen Tells of Online Sex Pred Nightmare.* Retrieved July 8, 2008, from abcnews: http://abcnews.go.com/Politics/Story?id=3742297

Jenkins, P. (2001). *Beyond Tolerance: Child Pornography on the Internet.* New York, New York: New York University Press.

Judiciary Committee of the United States House of Representatives. (2007, October 17). Sex Crimes and the Internet. Washington, DC.

Levenson, J. S. (2005). The Effect of Megan's Law on Sex Offender Reintegration. *Journal of Contemporary Criminal Justice, 21* (1), 49–66.

Lovejoy, T. P. (2008, Winter). Comment: A new playground: Sexual predators and pedophiles online: Criminalizing cybersex between adults & minors. *St. Thomas Law Review.* Vol. 20 No.2

Malesky, L. A., Jr. (2007). Predatory Online Behavior: Modus Operandi of Convicted Sex Offenders in Identifying Potential Victims and Contacting Minors Over the Internet. *Journal of Child Sexual Abuse, 16* (2), 23–32.

Marion, N. E., & Oliver, W. M. (2006). *The Public Policy of Crime and Criminal Justice.* Upper Saddle River, New Jersey, USA: Pearson - Prentice Hall.

Mayer, J. (2008). *The Dark Side: The Inside Story of How the War on Terror Turned Into A War on American Ideals.* New York, NY, USA: Doubleday.

McCollam, D. (2007, January/February). The Shame Game. *Columbia Journalism Review,* pp. 28–33.

Medaris, M., & Girouard, C. (2002). *Protecting Children in Cyberspace: The ICAC Task Force Program.* Office of Juvenile Justice and Delinquency Prevention, U.S. Dept. of Justice. Washington, D.C.: OJJDP.

Mitchell, K. J., Wolak, J., & Finkelhor, D. (2005). Police Posing as Juveniles Online to Catch Sex Offenders: Is It Working? *Sexual Abuse: A Journal of Research and Treatment, 17* (3), 241–267.

National Center Missing and Exploited Children. (2008). *What is the Cyber Tipline?* Retrieved July 15, 2008, from NCMEC: http://www.missingkids.com/missingkids/servlet/PageServlet?LanguageCountry=en_US&PageId=2446

Patricia Conradt, as Administratrix of the Estate of Louis William Conradt, Jr., Deceased, Plaintiff against NBC Universal, Inc., Defendant, 07 Civ. 6623 (DC) (United States District Court Southern District of New York February 26, 2008).

Robertiello, G., & Terry, K. J. (2007). Can We Profile Sex Offenders? A Review of Sex Offender Typologies. *Aggression and Violent behavior, 12*, 508–518.

Salkin, A. (2006, December 13). Web Site Hunts Pedophiles, and TV Goes Along. *The New York Times*. New York, NY, USA: The New York Times Company.

Semple, K. (2004, August 17). Detective Caught In Internet Sting Over Child Sex. *The New York Times*. New York, NY, USA: The New York Times Company.

Sheldon, K., & Howitt, D. (2008). Sexual Fantasy In Paedophile Offenders: Can Any Model Explain Satisfactorily New Findiings From A Study of Internet and Contact Sexual Offenders? *Legal and Criminological Psychology, 13*, pp. 137–158.

Springer, J. (2007, April 27). Miss America, Walsh on online sting. Retrieved July 18, 2008, from MSNBC: http://www.msnbc.msn.com/id/18329652

Stelter, B. (2007, August 27). 'To Catch A Predator' Is Falling Prey to Advertisers' Sensibilities. *The New York Times*. New York, NY, USA: The New York Times Company.

Subcomittee on Oversight and Investigations of the Committee on Energy and Commerce. (2006). *Making the Internet Safe for Kids: The Role of ISP's and Social Networking Sites.* United States House of Representatives. Washington: United States Government Printing Office.

U.S. Department of Justice. (2007, October 15). Department of Justice Announces Internet Crimes Against Children Task Forces in All 50 States. Washington, D.C.

U.S. Department of Justice. (2006). Project Safe Childhood. Washington, DC, USA.

U.S. House of Representatives Energy & Commerce Committee Investigations Subcomittee. (2006, April 4). Exploitation of Children Over the Internet, Day 1. Washington, D.C., USA.

U.S. House of Representatives Energy & Commerce Investigations Subcommittee. (2006, April 4). Exploitation of Children Over the Internet - Day 1. Washington, D.C., USA.

United States of America v. Kevin Eric Curtin, 04-10632 (United States Court of Appeals for the Ninth Circuit April 4, 2006).

United States v. Kevin Eric Curtin, 04-10632 (9th Cir. 2007).

United States v. Mark Douglas Poehlman, 98-50631 (9th Cir. 2000).

United States of America V. Stanley Howard Simms, 03-2151, 03-2177 (United States Court of Appeals Tenth Circuit November 9, 2005).

United States Senate. (2006). *Children's Safety and Violent Crime Reduction Act of 2006 (Senate - July 20, 2006)*. U.S. Senate. Washington, D.C.: THOMAS (Library of Congress).

Wilson, D., & Jones, T. (2008, May). 'In My Own World' : A Case Study of a Paedophile's Thinking and Doing and His Use of the Internet. *The Howard Journal, 47* (2), pp. 107–120.

Wolak, J., Finkelhor, D., & Mitchell, K. (2006). *Online Victimization of Youth: Five Years Later.* Crimes Against Children Research Center of the University of New Hampshire. Washington, D.C.: National Center for Missing & Exploited Children.

Wolak, J., Finkelor, D., & Mitchell, K. (2007, December). *1 in 7 Youth: The Statistics about Online Sexual Solicitations.* Retrieved August 14, 2008, from Crimes Against Children Research Center: http://www.unh.edu/ccrc/internet-crimes/factsheet_1in7.html

Wolak, J., Finkelhor, D., Mitchell, K. J., & Ybarra, M. (2008). Online "Predators" and Their Victims. *American Psychologist, 63* (2), 111–128.

Wright, R. G. (2008). Sex Offender Post-Incarceration Sanctions: Are There Any Limits? *New England Journal of Criminal and Civil Confinement, 34* (1), 17–50.

Ybarra, M. L., Mitchell, K. J., Wolak, J., & Finkelhor, D. (2006, October). Examining Characteristics and Associated Distress Related to Internet Harassment: Findings From the Second Youth Internet Safety Survey. *Pediatrics, 118* (4), pp. e1169–e1777.

Zetter, K. (2007, November 7). *NBC Contracted to Pay "Perverted Justice" Vigilantes Nearly $2 Million to Pose as Children for Online Stings.* Retrieved June 8, 1008, from Wired: http://blog.wired.com/27bstroke6/2007/11/perverted-justi.html

Zevitz, R. G., & Farkas, M. A. (2000). *Sex Offender Community Notification: Assessing the Impact in Wisconsin.* National Institute of Justice. Washington, DC: U.S. Department of Justice.

Sex Offenders, Mandatory HIV Testing, and Intentional Transmission

Cheryl Radeloff & Erica Carnes[i]

During the 1990s, two complementary types of morality-based policies emerged to further exert governmental control over bodies and sexuality. In this chapter we will be looking at criminal statutes that mandate HIV testing for sex offenders and penalties for individuals who "intentionally transmit" HIV. These policies have been able to draw upon both state power and public fear about sexual deviance. Yet the policies that emerged were neither based on scientific research nor necessarily effective at reducing the spread of HIV or sexual offenses.

Risk behaviors, such as consensual sex and injectable drug use, have been associated with the spread of HIV making it difficult and controversial to criminalize. In comparison, intentional transmission has been theorized to be a minor factor in the spread of HIV/AIDS. Conviction rates for those charged with HIV-related crimes are low and tend to serve as additional charges toward offenses that are already illegal (sex crime, assault, or prostitution related) (Lazzarina, Bray, & Burris, 2002, p. 247). Instead these policies further stigmatize HIV-positive persons and continued to perpetuate the surveillance and containment of those accused and/or convicted of sexually related offenses.

We contend that one of the driving social forces behind these laws is a coinciding moral sex panic regarding sexual deviancy and the spread of disease. Moral panics often result in legislation that aims to not only protect groups deemed innocent in society, but punish those seen as dangerous. The ensuing legislation has been referred to as symbolic policies. This has led to a process that has resulted in the social construction of a particular icon for which most members of a society readily identify, yet seldom can define. From media headlines which chronicled the tumultuous sex and drug-riddled era of the late twentieth century, popular stereotypes like the "crack whore," "patient zero," and "the stealth infected sex offender" emerged (Corrigan, 2006).

This chapter will explore the types of HIV testing policies that have emerged toward sex offenders in the United States. This includes previous efforts in controlling HIV in populations identified as vulnerable or dangerous including women, people of color, and sex workers; the legal arguments that surround mandatory testing for those arrested and convicted of sexual offenses; and the classification of intentional transmission as a sexual offense. Although we agree that regulatory policies are needed in a democratic society, one must question at what point do regulatory policies stop protecting people and start limiting their constitutionally protected privacy rights and legislating morality. The women's movement has argued that the government should have a limited role in reproductive rights, the current gay rights movement has most recently questioned the government's refusal to acknowledge and legitimize same sex relationships through legal marriage, and in this chapter we will outline another contested role the government has taken on: mandatory testing for HIV (Cossman, 2007; Eskridge, 1996; Pateman, 1988, Seidman, 2003). These movements challenge the extent to which the government should control the bodies and lives of "bad" sexual citizens.

Two approaches have been used by state governments in an attempt to control the HIV/AIDS pandemic.[ii] In the first approach, public health entities sought to curtail transmission through measures that required the cooperation of individuals deemed as high-risk. High-risk groups have traditionally included injectable drug users, hemophiliacs, and homosexuals. Inclusion in these groups is ascribed to behavior or inherent medical conditions causing dramatically higher rates of contracting the virus. Public health measures have promoted voluntary testing, assurances of confidentiality of results, and the destigmatization of disease status. These were achieved through the Americans with Disabilities Act of 1990 (ADA)[iii] and access to state benefits (1990).

The second approach utilized control and containment powers of the state through both public health and criminal justice entities to curtail and limit the behavior of individuals whose bodies were labeled as dangerous, uncontrollable, or irrational. These coercive measures involved the mandatory testing of certain groups, contact tracing (the identification and notification of all persons who have had body fluid contact with an infected person), restriction of activities/behaviors that might lead to the transmission of HIV, and the possibility of quarantine for infected individuals. Historically marginalized within society, the groups targeted for the enactment of these coercive measures included sex offenders, prostitutes, immigrants, prisoners, and mothers.

Many scholars (Baldwin, 2005; Gostin, 2004; Smith, 1998) have contended that two federal pieces of legislation passed in the 1990s had a significant impact in prompting and shaping mandatory testing policies toward sex offenders at the state level. They were the Ryan White Comprehensive AIDS Resources Emergency (CARE) Act (1990) and the amended Omnibus Crime and Control Act of 1968. The CARE Act, as amended in 1996, required states to mandate HIV testing for charged or convicted sex offenders (Webber, 1997, p. 81). The Omnibus Crime and Control Act, as amended by the 101st Congress, made block grants available for crime prevention at the state level. The U.S. Department of Justice Formula Grant Programs (established in 1992 and enforced in 1994) required HIV testing for all people convicted of certain sexual acts (U.S. Department of Justice, n.d.). Without the predesignated state statutes that required testing of sex offenders, states could lose 10% of their awarded grant money.

Yet unlike public health responses to the HIV epidemic, few to no voluntary or preventive measures were directed toward potential sex offenders or their victims. Instead, government policies increased and mandated sentencing towards sex offenders and instituted surveillance systems. Although policy responses of preventive control of HIV and sex offender statutes are seemingly unrelated, legislators began instituting mandatory HIV testing towards those either arrested or convicted of sexual offenses. Proponents of these policies utilized rhetoric that invoked protection for victims.[iv]

An example of this rhetoric is seen in Kuiper (1998/1999) when she examines the rise of intentional transmission policy. In 1997, 20-year-old Nushawn Williams, an African American man living in rural New York, was accused of intentionally preying on young women with offers of sex in exchange for drugs. "Sixteen confirmed cases of HIV have been linked to the suspect, including two babies born to infected mothers. As many as 100 women, one as young as 13, were exposed to HIV over just two years, authorities reported. Two of the man's victims are pregnant, and it is estimated that an additional 70 people have been exposed to the virus, with one confirmed case of one of the women subsequently infecting another" (Ibid). The rhetoric of the account focuses on the age and gender of the victims and concludes by focusing on the infection of an "innocent" man by one of the original victims. These polices have tended to frame HIV transmission as one-dimensional and ignore the possibility of a "victim" being positive prior to the incident in question. For example, whereas mandatory HIV testing policies for prostitution-related offenses in Nevada include solicitation as a crime in which mandatory testing is proscribed, the original law focused on the prostitute rather than the customer side of the interaction (Radeloff, 2004).

These policies increased the state's criminal justice and health division's control of sexualized bodies. In addition, longstanding public health laws were reinvoked that increased the state's power to punish individuals and groups who were deemed public menaces both due to the disease status and their "unwillingness" to police their own sexual behavior.

In response to the federal government's ever-increasing "war on crime," sex offenders became increasingly targeted as dangerous populations to be managed (Smith, 1998). For purposes of this chapter, sex offenders will be defined as adults (aged 18 and over) who have committed or used force, coercion, or threats to obtain access to another's sexuality. To scholars like Jenkins (1998), the term *sex offender* has evolved (usually with a male face) from a behavior (the rapist, child molester, and homosexual) to a constructed identity (the sexual predator and pedophile). This is not unintentional. The very conceptualization of the "sex offender" is part and parcel of very public, media-promoted moral panics that involved child abduction, sexual assault, and murder. Through social activism, the gay liberation movement has been very effective in de-linking homosexuality from sexual deviance.

Moral Panics and Symbolic Policies

Theories of moral panics attempt to explain how social policy develops during a state of excitement over perceived transgressions of moral boundaries. The term "moral panics" was coined by Cohen (1972) to characterize the reactions of policy makers, the general public, the police, and the media to a specific social issue. According to Schneider and Jenness (1997), moral panics can be defined as "a widespread feeling on the part of the public or some relevant public that something is terribly wrong in society because of the moral failure of a specific group of individuals" and that something must be done to control this problem (p. 473). Based on the work of Goode and Ben-Yehuda (1994a, 1994b), Thompson (1998) succinctly described the intrinsic pattern of moral panics: someone or something is defined as a threat, the threat is portrayed in an easily recognizable form by the media, there is a exponential rise in public concern, and eventually the panic recedes and/or results in public or social policy. As characterized by Goode and Ben-Yehuda (1994a, 1994b), moral panics are defined through five criteria: concern, hostility, consensus, disproportional, and volatility.

The influence of the media and political actors in contributing to a climate that produces moral panics is important when thinking about HIV/AIDS and sex offenders. Rubin (1989, 1993) and Schneider and Jenness (1997) contended that the biological and medical elements of the AIDS pandemic have effectively been translated into a moral panic. The difference between contemporary and past moral panics is that rather than focusing on one group of people as the cause of a problem, contemporary moral panics question the status of the very institutions or social relations that traditionally are thought to provide stability (Thompson, 1998, p. 2).

A key aspect of moral panic theory is its association with morality. Goode and Ben-Yehuda said that when examining the groups involved in a moral panic, it is important to discuss the issue of motive. Do policy actors, special interest groups, the media, and citizens become involved in a moral panic because they deeply and genuinely share a common worldview, ideology, or morality about an issue or situation; or do these policy players have ulterior motives, such as economic gain as a result of involvement? The questions of motive and morality are important questions; like gender and sexuality, they might not be as separate as one would like. Many policy makers participate in the moral panic mentality not only because it fits their worldview and their morality, but as politicians, it fits their constituents' perceptions as well. One could question if a lack of participation on a moral panic piece of legislation might be detrimental to the policy makers involved.

In addition, these theorists believe that moral panics are more likely to emerge from those in middle to lower levels of "the power and status hierarchy" (Goode & Ben-Yehuda, 1994a, p. 19). Groups that may be vested within these positions include "professional associations, police departments, the media, religious groups, educational organizations" (Ibid). These types of interest groups differ from what Goode and Ben-Yehuda labeled "established lobbies" or "established pressure groups" by having different access to formal policy makers. Established lobbies "employ a paid professional staff who represent their interest, or the interests of their clients" (Ibid, p. 117). This perspective is important for examining the influence of middle-level actors and organizations on social policy. It proposes that diverse groups that are not always associated as prime power brokers may have a role in policy formulation, the causes of panics, and may act as moral entrepreneurs who create crusades. Moral panics question what is considered normal, moral, and natural in social relations involving the family (Thompson, 1998, p. 72).

To Schneider and Jenness (1997), the AIDS epidemic has inspired the reform of existing public policy. The authors argued that the public policy responses have expanded social control mechanisms and denied civil liberties to those groups deemed the cause or threat (p. 472).

For example, by 1988, legislation was being proposed and passed in Georgia, Florida, Utah, and Nevada that required the routine testing of arrested prostitutes. In conjunction with this legislation, judges, district attorneys, and other policy institutors began supporting criminal charges for prostitutes who tested HIV positive (Radeloff, 2004). Criminal policies targeting HIV-positive prostitutes, similar to later testing policies toward sex offenders, reflect the moral, political, and economic interests of the policy makers proposing this legislation. Law enforcement officials seek to control and contain dangerous populations through increasing their police powers. This public safety approach is in direct contrast with the public health approach to HIV management and prevention. The findings of Backstrom and Robins (1995, 1996) indicated that public health officials reflect their orientations toward prevention and treatment. Less than 40% of legislative health chairs and chief state health officers supported proposals of legislation that would criminalize continued high-risk behaviors of people who test HIV positive.

The legislative response to moral panics has been the passage of symbolic policies. According to Marion (1997), "symbolic policies are legislative acts that do not provide any tangible change, but serve to evoke a particular response from the public. Many symbolic policies make voters 'feel good' by giving the appearance that something is being done about a problem" (pp. 1–2). These policies are passed for a variety of reasons including increased approval ratings for elected officials, a created and oftentimes false sense of public safety, moral guidance, and education for elected officials and the public (Marion, 1997). Symbolic policies are not created as a means to a solution but as a way to reassure and show the public that something is being done. These policies can oversimplify the problem and are a collection of short-term fixes and not long-term solutions (Ibid).

Recent examples of federal legislation that can be categorized as symbolic policies are the Walsh Act, which created a tier system for ranking risk levels of sex offenders; Megan's Law, which created the sex offender registry; and the proposed Jessica's Law, which would create GPS monitoring of sex offenders. Each of these laws was the response to a horrific crime against a child, committed by a stranger; and each was the result of not only intense media attention, but also social activism on the part of parents and other children's advocacy groups to increase state power of surveillance and containment of sex offenders. Whereas on the surface it appears that this legislation will protect the public, in reality these policies have low rates of effectiveness and do not deter sexual offenses. Central to their failing is a mischaracterization of sexual threats, as discussed by Williams in chapter 2 and throughout this book, specifically that the majority of sexual assaults are committed by known assailants, not strangers. Sex offender policies, including HIV policies, emphasize the unknown stranger as the primary threat of sexual danger.

Arguments against these policies are rich and point to their many flaws. Symbolic policies are passed for reasons of comfort, whether it is comfort of the legislators, of victims' families, or even of the general public. Constituents of elected officials play heavily on the legislators' decisions to vote for symbolic policies. A wrong vote could be played out in the media and could potentially cost a legislator reelection. Although the bill may be ineffective, unenforceable, or even unconstitutional, the public will never hear those reasons, but what they will hear is that a particular legislator voted against a bill that would have theoretically protected their children.

Background and History of Mandatory Testing

Criminal Law

Criminal law as a means for stemming the incidence and public fears around disease has largely been critiqued for ineffectiveness (Brandt, 1987, 1988a, 1988b, 1988c; Kenney, 1992). Some of the earliest examples of mandatory testing were the British Contagious Disease Acts of 1864, 1866, and 1869. Enacted largely to serve military interests, they were the first policies that formally associated prostitutes with the spread of disease and called for regulations to detain them

(Bell, 1994; Butler, 2004; Radeloff, 2004; Walkowitz, 1980). In subsequent times of war, Brandt (1988c) contended, the incidence of venereal disease actually increased during World War I when similar measures were instituted. Voluntary confidential testing measures and government-supported programs (public education and contact tracing) have been cited as more effective in reducing rates of infectious sexually transmitted disease as opposed to mandatory testing (Gostin, 2004; Lazzarina et al., 2002). Therefore, besides symbolic assurances of safety, the only real accomplishment of criminal laws was the widespread curtailment of civil liberties.

As fears about the spread of HIV/AIDS heightened in the United States, instead of mandating widespread testing for the general population, many states began to consider criminal prosecutions under laws and special statutes related to HIV transmission. Lazzarina et al. (2002) outlined three types of criminal law that address the risk behavior of HIV-positive individuals: HIV-specific exposure and transmission laws, public health statutes prohibiting behavior that exposes others to communicable diseases such as sexually transmitted infections, and criminal law that covers homicide and assault. Criminal law is thought to be effective as a deterrent to disease-transmitting behavior due to the threat of punishment (Ibid, p. 239).

Typically, two classifications of criminal law—homicide and assault—have been applied to HIV transmission. Homicide, either actual or attempted, may range from cases involving sexual conduct to exposing others to bodily fluids. Homicide prosecutions for HIV transmissions are rare because they require the death of the victim. HIV infection may take years to result in AIDS and the opportunistic infections that may lead to death. Prosecutions for attempted homicide, although still rare, rest on the assumption that the accused acted with the specific intent to cause the death of the victim regardless of the level of significant risk posed by the actions.

Three examples of attempted homicide include cases in which an individual injected a partner with HIV-contaminated blood to avoid alimony payments or behaviors that have been identified by health authorities, such as the Centers for Disease Control, as constituting a lower risk for HIV transmission—such as spitting, biting, or salvia. In 1998, Dr. Bruce Schmidt was found guilty of trying to kill his lover by exposing him to HIV through an infection. While being transported in 1988, incarcerated HIV-positive inmate Curtis Weeks spit on guards and was subsequently convicted of attempted murder. A 1987 suicide attempt by Donald Haines led to his conviction for attempted murder of numerous police officers and emergency responders; and finally, Willie Campbell, a homeless individual, assaulted a police officer by spitting in his eyes and mouth, and was subsequently convicted of attempted murder for an intentional transmission of HIV (Kovach, 2008).

While homicide prosecutions for HIV are rare, assault charges are more common. Assault is classified as either simple or aggravated. Those convicted of HIV-related assault charges have engaged in practices such as spitting, biting, and the spread of bodily waste. Aggravated assault refers to crimes that either cause or have the potential to cause serious bodily injury. One of the problems with proving assault, whether simple or aggravated, is proof of prior knowledge or motive for causing bodily injury or harm. This is where intentional transmission becomes problematic. When one attempts to prosecute for transmission, it can be hard to prove it was intentional, thus making the law arguable and perhaps useless. Because the specific risks of transmission from a single act are variable (and often incalculable), it is uncertain that a particular act may result in bodily harm. Sexuality is especially problematic in this regard in that taking risk (emotional, social, psychological, physical) is often inherent in the behavior. To ascertain that one partner acted with the intent to harm requires an examination of public sphere behavior, often of actions and consent that are nonarticulated.

Reckless endangerment, as a criminal offense, avoids the requirement to prove intent or motive in the transmission of HIV. Under this misdemeanor charge, one commits reckless endangerment if engaging in conduct that places or may place another in danger of death or serious bodily harm. An example of reckless endangerment would be the behavior of an HIV-positive person who knew of not only his or her HIV-positive status, through testing and counseling, but the ramifications of behavior that may put others at risk. Many states have created alternative statutes as a way to criminalize this behavior. These statutes can be classified under general communicable disease exposure laws, HIV-specific exposure laws, and HIV-specific statutes that increase penalties for circumstances, such as sex offenses, solicitation and prostitution, and actions intended to harm emergency response personnel (Lazzarina et al., 2002, p. 240). Gostin (2004) contended that HIV-specific offenses may have some advantages over existing criminal law, such as less pressure on the prosecution to demonstrate knowledge or intent to harm (p. 194).

Communicable disease exposure laws and state-sanctioned public health responses have a long-standing legacy in the United States. Originally directed at diseases such as cholera, tuberculosis, the plague, smallpox, yellow fever, syphilis, and gonorrhea, a few states have statutes that criminalize any behavior that risks transmission of any disease, typically as a misdemeanor. Others created disease-specific statutes that addressed the epidemic of the day. Gostin (2004) said that many of these laws represent the bias and prejudices of their creators and helped to further stigmatize certain individuals and groups for their illness and risk to society (p. 190). Most public health statutes that do address the risk of transmitting venereal or sexually transmitted disease do not specifically include HIV/AIDS.

In theory, when public health regulations and criminal laws are being proposed, four factors influence the decision: the nature of the risk, the duration of the risk, the probability of harm, and the severity of harm (Gostin, 2004, p. 95–96). Each of the risk components should be supported by scientific evidence. Ideally, the state evaluates regulation policy through a "means/ends" test. This evaluative tool measures the four factors involved in formulating policy and determines its effectiveness. The purpose of evaluation is to see if the benefits that are gained by a society outweigh the personal burdens and costs of the regulatory policy. Control measures associated with the regulation of disease and criminal behavior tend to be oriented around control and containment measures. These range[v] from mandatory sexually transmitted infection testing, mandatory sentencing, surveillance through reporting, registration, and monitoring to state agencies, and zoning regulations restrict activities and residence. These measures are officially established and sanctioned by the state and the various institutions that support it.

Mandatory Testing

Disease screening is one of the most basic tools of modern public health and preventive medicine. Screening programs have a long and distinguished history in efforts to control epidemics of infectious diseases and targeting treatment for chronic diseases ... In practice when screening is conducted in contexts of gender inequality, racial discrimination, sexual taboos, and poverty, these conditions shape the attitudes and beliefs of health system and public health decision-makers as well as patients, including those who have lost confidence that the health care system will treat them fairly. Thus, if screening programs are poorly conceived, organized or implemented, they may lead to interventions of questionable merit and enhance the vulnerability of groups and individuals. (Committee on Perinatal Transmission of HIV, Institute of Medicine, Youth, and Families Board on Children, and National Research Council, 1999).

According to Gostin (2004) and Webber (1997), currently under federal law, mandatory HIV testing is required for recruits and members of the armed forces, immigrants,[vi] the Foreign Service, and other federal programs like the Peace Corps. State laws have imposed mandatory testing within the criminal justice system primarily for prisoners, sex offenders, and pregnant women. Under a 1994 provision enacted by the 101st Congress, states were required to enact and enforce statutes that provided for the testing of certain convicted sex offenders for HIV if the state was to be eligible to receive federal funding. Thus the federal government mandated testing for sex offenders through more indirect means—the loss of grant funds (U.S. Department of Justice, n.d.).

In 1995, the Newborn Infant HIV Notification Act was introduced in Congress to require HIV testing of pregnant women. Although this measure was not ratified, it has been widely implemented at the state level. Pretest counseling and voluntary HIV testing for pregnant women were included in the 1996 CARE Act. The CARE Act amendments required states that received and wanted continued funding for HIV counseling and testing programs to have certification that they (states) had adopted Center for Disease Control recommendations for the HIV counseling and voluntary testing of pregnant women (as cited in Webber, 1997, p. 81).

In the private sector, mandatory HIV testing is primarily required within the insurance industry (life or disability insurance) and blood and body tissue banks. Other individuals who are indirectly mandated for HIV testing include emergency responders along with partners of HIV-infected persons. Rationales for testing within the private sector include notions of national security and protection for vulnerable populations from harm.

Outside of the private sector, the benefit of mandatory public HIV testing would be to potentially decrease the spread of HIV and bring a sense of comfort for the person being tested. By making testing mandatory, citizens become aware of their status, can seek education and counseling, take precautions to avoid spreading the virus, and utilize the state's resources. Mandatory testing may also decrease the stigma surrounding the process itself. No longer limited to "at risk" populations, HIV testing becomes a normalized medical procedure, much like blood tests for diabetes and cholesterol. For example, New Jersey recently increased their requirements for prenatal testing. Although there was some questioning of the policy by advocacy groups, for the most part, these policies passed into law with little to no controversy (Richburg, 2007).

Testing: Upon Arrest or Conviction

Without widespread public testing, concerns have been raised over the restriction of civil liberties for both the accused and the victims. The controversy over mandatory HIV testing for sexually related offenses involves the phase at which testing is required for the offender and the parties who have access to the offender's test results. As of 2001, 45 states had statutes authorizing compulsory HIV testing of sex offenders (Gostin, 2004, p. 209). Currently, 47 states (and several U.S. territories) have passed statutes mandating HIV testing for persons charged or convicted of sexual offenses. Testing for sex offenders is mandated either at the time of arrest or upon conviction, or both, depending on the state.

Testing during any stage of the arrest phase (e.g., accusation of victim(s), hearing, or formal charges) has the potential to be challenged for violating due process and probable cause, whereas conviction does not. States that allow testing during the arrest phase have attempted to address issues of probable cause by either ordering HIV testing based on the written request of the victim and the subsequent issue of a search warrant for purposes of obtaining a blood sample, or after a probable cause hearing. The hearing, held within the 30 days after a written request, must demonstrate that an offense was committed, the person charged was the person who committed the crime, and the crime involved the transmission of bodily fluids that might expose the victim to the HIV virus (Smith, 1998). Therefore, even though probable cause and due process rights of the accused are protected with testing upon conviction, efforts to minimize the violation of rights have been attempted by several states.

For example, Table 6.1 shows Arkansas, Arizona, California, Florida, Georgia, Idaho, Kansas, Louisiana, Michigan, New Jersey, New Mexico, New York, Oklahoma, Tennessee, Wisconsin, and the Virgin Islands as some of the states that have required HIV testing of sex offenders in both the arrest and conviction stages of the criminal justice system. Yet as Table 6.1 shows, of the states that mandated HIV testing during the arrest phase, the majority required either a written request from the victim or a formal motion of the court in order to obtain blood samples from the accused.

Even after conviction, Connecticut, the District of Columbia, Florida, Maine, Maryland, Minnesota, Montana, Nebraska, New Jersey, New York, Pennsylvania, Rhode Island, Utah, Virginia, and the Virgin Islands still required a written request of the victim in order to test a sex offender for HIV.

Many convictions are achieved months after an arrest. A problem with testing post conviction is that victims are unable to have a baseline of their perpetrator's disease status in order to take proactive measures. Thus even though they may acknowledge the time period it takes for a seropositive status to appear via testing, victims must undergo the mental stress of possible HIV infection, along with the mental, physical, and emotional stress of sexual assault for themselves, and fears of infection for intimate partner(s) and dependent family members.

One concern of mandatory HIV testing during the arrest phase of the criminal justice process is whether it violates the offender's Fourth Amendment rights against unreasonable search and seizure. Courts have generally sustained blood tests as long as a search warrant can be issued based on findings of reasonable cause (Smith, 1998, p. 4).

6.1   U.S. State and Territory Mandatory HIV Testing and Sexual Offenses—1998[vii]

Testing during Accusation/Arrest Phase			
Mandatory	Request of Victim	Probable Cause /Motion of the Court	Other
CT, ID, KY, MI[vii], NV, OK, OR, TN	AK, CA, DE, FL, GA, KS, MD, NJ, SD, TX, WI, VI	AK, AR, CA, GA, LA, MD, NY, SD, TX, VA, VI	CO[ix], MD[x], NM[xi], NY[xii], OH[xiii], VA[xiv], WI[xv]

Testing after Conviction			
Mandatory	Request of Victim	Probable Cause /Motion of the Court	Other
AL, AK[xvi], AZ, CA, FL, GA, IL, IN, IA, KS, LA, MS, MO, NH, NM, ND, OK, SC, WA, WI	CT, DC, FL, ME, MD, MN, MT, NE, NJ, NY, PA, RI, UT, VA, VI	GA, MI, WV	ID[xvii], TN[xviii], VA[xix]

A second concern of mandating testing during the arrest phase is maintaining the confidentiality of both the offender and the victims' HIV status. Although HIV/AIDS are protected categories under the Americans with Disability Act (ADA), the potential risk of discrimination and or harm due to disclosure of an HIV-positive status exists for those arrested or convicted of sexual offenses.

Many states allow disclosure of an offender's HIV status to a variety of vested groups including the offender, victim, victim's partners and family, as well as court, state health, and corrections personnel. Smith (1998) recommended that besides safeguards for maintaining confidentiality, model

6.2 U.S. State and Territory Mandatory HIV Testing and Sexual Offenses—Additions 2008[xx]

Arrest/Indicted	Conviction
AK, AR, CO, DE, FL, ID, KS, LA, MI, NV, NJ, NC, ND, OH, OK, TN, VA, WI	AL, AK, AZ, CA, CT, DC, FL, GA, HI, IL, IN, IA, KS, KY, LA, ME, MD, MI, MN, MS, MO, ND, NE, NH, NJ, NM, MT, NY, OR, PA, PR, RI, SC, UT, VA, VT, WA, WV, WI, WY

Testing during Accusation/Arrest Phase			
Mandatory	Request of Victim	Probable Cause/ Motion of the Court	Other
WY	ND, NC	ND, NC	

Testing after Conviction			
Mandatory	Request of Victim	Probable Cause/ Motion of the Court	Other
ND, PR, WY	HI, VT		

testing initiatives also should create civil liability statutes against individuals who disclose test results to unauthorized or unrecognized parties (p. 6).

A third concern for mandatory HIV testing for pretrial detainees is the tenet of presumed innocence. In the eye of the public, one could argue, there is a direct correlation between testing and guilt, therefore creating a false assumption that mandatory testing of sex offenders implies guilt.

Yet through rulings such as *Bell v. Wolfish* (1979), the U.S. Supreme Court has maintained that pretrial containment conditions, such as mandatory testing, do not violate presumption of innocence as long as other constitutional conditions are met (p. 6).

Typically the disease status of an infected individual is considered confidential and only available to the tested individual, any contacts that individual may have had (contact tracing), and the appropriate state health officials for statistical purposes. Mandatory testing has the ability to release positive test results to legally recognized parties while at the same time potentially violating the accused's right to confidential health care.

Public health agencies are able to disclose information only in the following circumstances:

> Directly to the individual, to appropriate federal agencies or authorities, health care personnel in a medical emergency or to protect the life of a person who is subject to the information from serious, imminent harm, pursuant to court order sought exclusively by public health agencies in light of a clear danger to an individual or public health which can be mitigated by disclosure by the public health agency to appropriate public or private agencies. (Gostin, 2004, p. 105)

Yet criminally mandated testing is able to bridge this information and makes it publicly available to designated parties. Another problem with mandated criminal testing is that often state agencies are not always able to obtain or transmit the HIV serostatus of individuals due to confidentiality in health care and patient rights. Whereas public health organizations are better equipped to provide pre- and post-test counseling, criminal justice entities may not have the adequate resources for disseminating results to offenders and victims.

Intentional Transmission

One report challenging the application of criminal laws as a method of curtailing HIV transmission is the 1988 Presidential Commission on the Human Immunodeficiency Virus Epidemic. According to the *Report of the Presidential Commission on the Human Immunodeficiency Virus Epidemic*, the commission found "traditional criminal laws are not well suited to prevention of HIV transmission" and instead recommended criminal prosecution for circumstances involving intentional or reckless conduct deserving of punishment because of the high potential for HIV transmission (as cited in McColgin & Hey, 1997, p. 263–265).

McColgin and Hey (1997, p. 287) and Closen et al. (1994) contended that no other contagious disease has warranted criminal laws the way HIV has. Since 1989, 28 states and the federal government have adopted HIV-specific criminal statutes (Gostin, 2004, p. 190). Most of these are classified as a felony offense. These laws criminalize exposure or transmission of HIV through at least one of the following behaviors: sexual contact, sharing equipment used for injecting substances, and donated blood or body organs. Statutes developed by states to criminalize HIV-transmission behaviors tend to enhance or expand the severity and sentencing of acts already addressed under criminal law. Specifically crimes such as solicitation and prostitution, rape and sexual assault, and assaulting an emergency responder can be punished individually or with harsher sentences when the accused person or perpetrator knows he or she is HIV positive (Lazzarina et al., 2002, p. 244). These additional charges have become known as intentional transmission.

An intentional transmission label applies to individuals who choose not to disclose their disease status and continue to have unprotected sex. Previously, public health law allowed officials to quarantine individuals who were deemed public health menaces. In *Disease and Democracy: the Industrialized World Faces AIDS,* Baldwin (2005) discussed state public health laws that gave police powers to public health authorities, enabling them to control and contain contagious disease patients. Emerging in the 19th Century, these laws included epidemiological investigation and the ability to remove and isolate contagious individuals. Some examples of institutionalization involved campaigns toward tuberculosis, leprosy, and smallpox. Besides institutionalization, contagious individuals could also be barred from certain occupations such as food handling and childcare.

Although the state's ability to control and contain bodies through quarantine has been curtailed, current legislation focuses on an increased level of state surveillance and government intrusion that monitors the activities of HIV-positive

individuals and sex offenders. Intentional transmission statutes differ from mandatory testing for sex offenders in that
(1) the individual is already aware of his or her status and
(2) that engaging in sexual high-risk behavior that places
another at risk for acquiring HIV can result in a sex offender
status. For example, in 2001, William Brian Freeman was
charged with intentionally exposing a partner to HIV after
having unprotected sex with a partner in Las Vegas. Freeman
had unprotected oral and anal sex in a vehicle with a partner
he originally met at a bar and failed to disclose to his partner that he was HIV positive. Freeman's seropositive status
was questioned after a driving-under-the-influence traffic
stop, and police officers found antiviral medication in his car
(Children's AIDS Fund, 2001).

Typically, most criminal statutes involve three criteria for
the charge of intentional transmission: knowledge of serologic status, behavior risking transmission, and failure to inform
(Gostin, 2004, p. 192). Referring to Freeman's case, not only
was Freeman negligent of informing his partner of his HIV
status, but he knew of his HIV seropositivity and engaged in
behavior that could risk transmission. Had Freeman recently
committed this act in South Dakota, the crime would remain
the same but his legal status would change. Based on the
2008 enactment of Senate Bill 65, the law requires people
convicted of intentionally transmitting HIV to register as sex
offenders after their release from prison. The label of sex
offender mandates registration to law enforcement agencies
for addition to the state sex offender registry. Failure to register as a sex offender carries an additional prison term of 2
years (The Associated Press, 2008).

Thus, the main issue surrounding intentional transmission is knowledge of serologic status. Knowledge ranges from
the receipt of a positive HIV test result, partnership with an
HIV-infected person, to engagement in high-risk behavior.
The problem with assumed knowledge involves whether the
testing is voluntary (for personal knowledge versus insurance), for a workplace occupation, or due to incarceration.
Additionally, individuals may avoid testing because of disease stigma, a perceived lack of high-risk behavior, a denial
of identity or membership in "high risk" behavior groups, and
notions of immunity based on age, income, or other factors.

Although civil and criminal law at the state level punishes offenders for the intentional transmission of HIV, it is

6.3 State Criminal Statutes on HIV Transmission—2008

This chart. updated in 2008. is based on earlier compilations by the ACLU's National Prison Project and Lambda Legal.[1]

State	Statute	Type of Crime	Summary	Notes
Alabama	Ala. Code § 22-11A21 (c)	Class C misdemeanor	Persons who knowingly engage in activities likely to transmit their STD are guilty of a Class C misdemeanor.	
Alaska	Alaska Stat. § 11.41.420	May be considered an aggravating factor in a felony conviction, allowing for imposition of a sentence beyond the presumptive range.	Where offense was a felony specified in A.S. § 11.41.410 — 11.41.455 (sexual offenses), it can be considered an aggravating factor if the defendant had been previously diagnosed as having or having tested positive for HIV or AIDS, and the offense either (A) involved penetration, or (B) exposed the victim to a risk or a fear that the offense could result in the transmission of HIV or AIDS.	
Arizona	N/A	N/A	N/A	N/A

State	Statute	Classification	Description	Notes
Arkansas	Ark. Code Ann § 514-123	Class A felony	It is a Class A felony for a person who knows he/she is HIV positive to expose another person through the parenteral transfer of blood or blood products or engaging in sexual penetration without informing his/her partner of his/her HIV status. Sexual penetration includes intercourse, cunnilingus, fellatio, anal intercourse, or any other intrusion of any body part or object into the genital or anal openings of another person's body. Emission of semen is not required to violate the statute.	There is an exception for consenting partners. If convicted, defendant is required to register as a sex offender. A.C.A. §12-12 903(12)(A)(i)(p)
	Ark. Code Ann. § 20 -15-903	Class A misdemeanor	Persons who are HIV positive must inform their physician or dentist of their HIV status.	
California	Cal. Health & Saf. Code § 120291	Felony punishable by imprisonment for 3. 5. or 8 years	Any person who, knowing he/she is HIV positive, engages in unprotected sexual activity without disclosing his/her status to his/her partner and acts with specific intent to infect the other person is guilty of a felony.	Exceptions for protected sex and informed consent to unprotected sex. Defendant must have specific intent to infect. Knowledge of HIV status is not enough to convict.

Continued

6.3 State Criminal Statutes on HIV Transmission—2008 (Cont'd)

State	Statute	Type of Crime	Summary	Notes
	Cal. Health & Saf. Code § 120290	Misdemeanor	A person afflicted with any contagious, infectious, or communicable disease who willfully exposes him/herself to anther person is guilty of a misdemeanor.	
	Cal. Health & Saf. Code § 1621.5	Felony punishable by imprisonment for 2, 4, or 6 years	Persons who know they are HIV positive and donate blood, semen, breast milk, organs, or other tissues to a medical center are guilty of a felony.	Does not apply to an individual who "self defers" her blood or plasma or to one who donates her blood for an autologous donation.
	Cal. Pen Code § 12022.85	3-year sentencing enhancement	Persons who commit a sexual offense with knowledge that they were HIV positive at the time of commission will receive a 3-year sentencing enhancement.	Includes rape, statutory rape, spousal rape, sodomy, and oral sex.
	Cal. Health & Saf. Code § 1621.5	Felony punishable by imprisonment for 2, 4, or 6 years	Persons who know they are HIV positive and donate blood, semen, breast milk, organs, or other tissues to a medical center are guilty of a felony.	Does not apply to an individual who "self defers" her blood or plasma or to one who donates her blood for an autologous donation.

	Cal. Pen Code § 12022.85	3-year sentencing enhancement	Persons who commit a sexual offense with knowledge that they were HIV positive at the time of commission will receive a 3-year sentencing enhancement.	Includes rape. statutory rape. spousal rape. Sodomy. and oral sex.
	Cal. Pen. Code § 647f	Felony (penalty enhancement)	A person convicted of soliciting or engaging in prostitution under Cal. Pen. Code §647(b) who was previously convicted one or more times of a violation of that subdivision or of any other sex offense. and in connection with one or more of those convictions a blood test was administered pursuant to § 1202.1 or 1202.6 with positive test results, of which the defendant was informed. is guilty of a felony.	
Colorado	Colo. Rev. Stat § 187-201.7	Class 5 felony	Persons who commit prostitution with knowledge of being HIV positive commit a class 5 felony.	
	Colo. Rev. Stat § 187-205.7	Class 6 felony	Patronizing a prostitute with knowledge of being HIV positive is a class 6 felony.	Includes sexual intercourse or entering place of prostitution with intent to engage in prostitution.
Connecticut	N/A	N/A	N/A	N/A
Delaware	Del. Code Ann. 16 § 2801	Class E felony	Knowing. reckless. or intentional use of HIV-infected human tissue or organs is a Class E felony.	N/A

Continued

State Criminal Statutes on HIV Transmission—2008 (Cont'd)

State	Statute	Type of Crime	Summary	Notes
District of Columbia	N/A	N/A	N/A	N/A
Florida	Fla. Stat. Ann. § 384.24		It is unlawful for any person, knowing him/herself to be HIV positive and knowing the risk of transmission through sexual intercourse, to have intercourse without informing his/her partner of his/her HIV status and receiving consent.	Explicit exception for informed consent.
	Fla. Stat. Ann § 381.0041 (11)(b)	3rd-degree felony punishable by not more than 5 years.	Any person who, knowing him/herself to be HIV positive and knowing that HIV may be transmitted through donating blood, plasma, organs, skin, or other human tissue, donates blood, plasma, organs, skin, or other human tissue is guilty of a felony of the 3rd degree.	

Georgia	Ga. Code Ann. § 165-60(c)	Felony punishable by imprisonment for not more than 10 years	A person with knowledge that he/she is HIV positive who knowingly 1) engages in sexual intercourse or any sexual act involving the sex organs of one person and the mouth or anus of another person without prior disclosure of HIV status 2) shares hypodermic needles 3) offers or consents to perform sexual intercourse with another person for money without disclosing HIV status 4) solicits another person to perform or submit to an act of sodomy without disclosure of HIV status 5) donates blood, blood products, other body fluids, or any body organ or body part without disclosing HIV status to the person drawing blood or collecting body parts or fluid, is guilty of a felony.	Exception for informed consent.
	Ga. Code Ann. § 165-60(d)	Felony punishable by imprisonment for not less than 5 and not more than 20 years	Any person knowing him/herself to be HIV positive who commits an assault with the intent to transmit HIV or hepatitis using body fluids (blood, semen, or vaginal secretions), saliva, urine, or feces upon which they are engaged in official duties or "on account of the officer's performance of peace officer or a correctional officer his/her official duties" commits a felony.	
Hawaii	N/A	N/A	N/A	N/A

Continued

6.3 State Criminal Statutes on HIV Transmission—2008 (Cont'd)

State	Statute	Type of Crime	Summary	Notes
Idaho	Idaho Code § 39-608	Felony punishable by imprisonment for a period not to exceed 15 years or by fine not in excess of $5,000 or by both.	Any person knowing he/she is HIV positive who transfers or attempts to transfer body fluid, body tissue, or organs to another person is guilty of a felony.	Consent with full disclosure is an affirmative defense.
Illinois	720 Ill. Comp. Stat. 5/1216.2	Class 2 felony	Any person knowing that he/she is HIV positive who 1) engages in intimate contact with another, 2) transfers, donates, or provides his or her blood, tissue, semen, organs, or other potentially infectious body fluids for transfusion, transplantation, insemination, or other administration to another, 3) dispenses, delivers, exchanges, sells, or in any other way transfers to another any nonsterile intravenous or intramuscular drug paraphernalia, is guilty of a felony.	Informed consent is an affirmative defense. Statute does not require that the other party must contract HIV. "Intimate contact" is defined as "the exposure of the body of one person to the bodily fluid of another person in a manner that could result in the transmission of HIV."
Indiana	Ind. Code Ann. § 35-42-1-7	Class C felony for committing the act. Class A felony if the act results in transmission of HIV.	A person who recklessly, knowingly, or intentionally donates, sells or transfers blood, blood component, or semen that contains HIV is guilty of a felony.	Does not apply to a person who first notifies the blood center that the blood or blood component must be disposed of and not used for any purpose or to a person who donates fluid for research purposes.

| Ind. Code Ann. § 35-42-2-6(c) | Class D felony for committing the act. Class C felony if the defendant knew or recklessly failed to know that the bodily fluid or waste was infected with Hepatitis B, HIV, or TB. Class B felony if the person knew or recklessly failed to know that the fluid or waste was infected with Hepatitis B or TB and the offense results in transmission. Class A felony if the person knew or recklessly failed to know that the bodily fluid or waste was infected with HIV and the offense resulted in transmission. | A person who knowingly or intentionally, in a rude, insolent, or angry manner, places blood or another body fluid or waste on a law enforcement or corrections officer commits battery by bodily waste. | Applies to officers identified as such and engaged in the performance of official duties. Includes firefighters and first responders. |

Continued

6.3 State Criminal Statutes on HIV Transmission—2008 (Cont'd)

State	Statute	Type of Crime	Summary	Notes
Iowa	Iowa Code § 709 C	Class B felony	A person who knows he/she is HIV positive and a) engages in intimate contact with another person, b) transfers, donates, or provides blood, tissue, semen, organs, or other potentially infectious bodily fluids for transfusion, transplantation, insemination, or other administration to another person, or c) dispenses, delivers, exchanges, sells, or in any other way transfers to another person any non-sterile intravenous or intramuscular drug paraphernalia previously used is guilty of a felony.	Informed consent is an affirmative defense. Actual transmission of HIV is not necessary for conviction.

Continued

| Kansas | Kan. Stat. Ann. § 21-3435 | Class A misdemeanor | It is a Class A misdemeanor for an individual who knows him or herself to be infected with a life threatening communicable disease to knowingly: engage in sexual intercourse or sodomy (defined as penetration with the male sex organ only) with another individual with the intent to expose that individual to that disease: to sell or donate his or her own blood, blood products, semen, tissue, organs or other body fluids with the intent to expose the recipient to a life-threatening communicable disease: or to share with another individual a hypodermic needle, syringe, or both for the introduction of drugs or any other substance or for the withdrawal of blood or body fluids with the intent to expose another person to a life-threatening communicable disease. |
| Kentucky | Ky. Rev. Stat. § 529.090 | Class D felony | Anyone who knows him/herself to be HIV positive and commits, offers, or agrees to commit prostitution by engaging in sexual activity in a manner likely to transmit HIV is guilty of a class D felony. |

6.3 State Criminal Statutes on HIV Transmission—2008 (Cont'd)

State	Statute	Type of Crime	Summary	Notes
	Ky. Rev. Stat. § 529.090 (4)	Class D felony	Any person who knows he/she is HIV positive and procures another to commit prostitution in a manner likely to transmit HIV is guilty of a class D felony.	
	Ky. Rev. Stat. § 311.990 (24) (b)	Class D felony	A person who knows he/she is HIV positive and has been informed that HIV can be transmitted through tissue donation, and then donates organs, skin, or other human tissue, is guilty of a class D felony.	
Louisiana	La. Rev. Stat. § 43.5	Fined not more than $5,000 or imprisoned for not more than 10 years or both. If the victim is a police officer acting in the line of duty, then the fine increases by $1,000 and imprisonment for not more than 11 years.	No person shall expose another to the AIDS virus through sexual contact or any means or contact without the knowing and lawful consent of the victim.	"Means or contact" is defined as "spitting, biting, stabbing with an AIDS contaminated object, or throwing of blood or other bodily substances."

State	Statute	Classification	Description	Notes
Maine	N/A	N/A	N/A	N/A
Maryland	Md. Code Ann. Health-General § 18-601.1	Fine of $2,500 or imprisonment not exceeding 3 years or both.	A person with HIV may not knowingly transfer or attempt to transfer HIV to another person.	N/A
Massachusetts	N/A	N/A	N/A	N/A
Michigan	Mich. Comp. Laws § 333.5210	Felony	A person who knows he/she has HIV and engages in sexual penetration (sexual intercourse, cunnilingus, fellatio, anal intercourse, or any other intrusion, however slight, of any part of a person's body or of any object into the genital or anal openings of another person's body, but emission of semen is not required) without first informing the other party of his/her HIV status is guilty of a felony.	Exception for informed consent.
Minnesota	N/A	N/A	N/A	N/A
Mississippi	Miss. Code Ann. § 97 27-14(1)	Felony	A person who knowingly exposes another person to human immunodeficiency virus (HIV) is guilty of a felony.	Prior knowledge and willing consent to the exposure is a defense.

Continued

State Criminal Statutes on HIV Transmission—2008 (Cont'd)

State	Statute	Type of Crime	Summary	Notes
	Miss. Code Ann. § 97 27-14(1)	Felony	A person who knows he is HIV positive who attempts to cause or knowingly causes a corrections employee, a visitor to a correctional facility or another prisoner or offender to come into contact with blood, seminal fluid, urine, feces, or saliva is guilty of a felony.	
Missouri	Mo. Rev. Stat § 191.677	Class B felony. Class A felony if transmission occurs.	It is unlawful for a person who is HIV positive to 1) be or attempt to be a blood, blood products, organ, sperm, or tissue donor except as deemed necessary for medical research, 2) act in a reckless manner by exposing another person to HIV without that person's knowledge and consent through contact with blood, semen, or vaginal secretions in the course of oral, anal, or vaginal sexual intercourse, the sharing of needles, biting, or purposely acting in any other manner which causes the HIV infected person's semen, vaginal secretions, or blood to come into contact with the mucous membranes or non-intact skin of another person.	Exception for informed consent. Use of condom is not a defense. "Recklessness" includes (1) knowledge of infection when other person does not know or does not consent; (2) evidence of infection with primary and secondary syphilis, gonorrhea, or Chlamydia; or (3) another person provides evidence of sexual contact with the HIV-infected person after a diagnosis of HIV infection.

State	Statute	Penalty	Description	Defense/Exception
Montana	Mont. Code Ann. § 50 18-112	Misdemeanor	A person with a sexually transmitted disease may not knowingly expose another person to infection.	N/A
Nebraska	N/A	N/A	N/A	N/A
Nevada	Nev. Rev. Stat. § 201.205	Category B felony punishable by imprisonment for not less than 2 years and not more than 10 years or by a fine of not more than $10,000 or both.	A person who has received actual notice that he/she tested positive for HIV and intentionally, knowingly, or willfully engages in conduct that is intended or likely to transmit the disease to another person is guilty of a class B felony.	Affirmative defense when other person knew of infection, knew exposure could result, and consented.
	Nev. Rev. Stat § 201.358	Category B felony punishable by imprisonment for not less than 2 years and not more than 10 years or by a fine of not more than $10,000 or both.	A person who works as a prostitute who tests positive for HIV and continues to engage in prostitution is guilty of a Category B felony.	
New Hampshire	N/A	N/A	N/A	N/A
New Jersey	N.J. Stat § 2C:34-5	3rd-degree crime punishable by up to 5-year imprisonment and up to $15,000 fine.	A person who knows he/she is HIV positive and commits an act of sexual penetration without the informed consent of the other party is guilty of a crime in the 3rd degree.	Exception for informed consent.

Continued

6.3 State Criminal Statutes on HIV Transmission—2008 (Cont'd)

State	Statute	Type of Crime	Summary	Notes
New Mexico	N/A	N/A	N/A	N/A
New York	NY Public Health Law § 2307	Misdemeanor	Any person who, knowing him/herself to be infected with an infectious venereal disease, has sexual intercourse with another is guilty of a misdemeanor.	
North Carolina	N/A	N/A	N/A	N/A
North Dakota	N.D. Cent. Code § 12 1-20-17	Class A felony	A person who knows he/she is infected with HIV and willfully transfers body fluid to another person is guilty of a class A felony.	Affirmative defense for informed consent with the use of an appropriate prophylactic device. Violations of this statute are sex crimes.
Ohio	Ohio Rev. Code Ann. § 2927.13	4th-degree felony	A person, knowing him/herself to be HIV positive, who donates blood, plasma, or product of blood that the person knows or should know is being accepted for the purpose of transfusion to another individual, is guilty of a 4th-degree felony.	

Oklahoma	Okla. Stat. § 1192.1	Felony punishable by imprisonment for not more than 5 years.	It is unlawful for any person, knowing he/she has HIV and with intent to infect another, to engage in conduct reasonably likely to result in the transfer of the person's own blood, bodily fluids containing visible blood, semen, or vaginal secretions into the bloodstream of another or through the skin or other membranes of another person except during in-utero transmission of blood or bodily fluids.	Exception for informed consent. Exception for any transmission that occurs as a result of pregnancy or birth.
	Okla. Stat. § 1031	Felony punishable by imprisonment for not more than 5 years.	Any person who engages in prostitution with knowledge that he/she is HIV positive is guilty of a felony.	
	Okla. Stat. § 1-519	Felony	Any person, after being infected and before being discharged and pronounced cured by a physician in writing, who marries any other person or exposes any other person by the act of copulation or sexual intercourse to such venereal disease or to liability to contract the venereal disease, is guilty of a felony.	
Oregon	N/A	N/A	N/A	

Continued

6.3 State Criminal Statutes on HIV Transmission—2008 (Cont'd)

State	Statute	Type of Crime	Summary	Notes
Pennsylvania	18 Pa .Cons. Stat. § 2703	2nd-degree felony	A person who is confined in or committed to any local or county detention facility, jail, prison, state penal or correctional institution is guilty of a 2nd-degree felony if he/she intentionally or knowingly causes another to come into contact with blood, seminal fluid, saliva, urine, or feces when at the time the person knew, had reason to know, or should have known or believed, such material to be infected with a communicable disease, including but not limited to HIV.	

Citation	Penalty	Description	Notes
18 Pa. Cons. Stat. § 2704	Penalty shall be the same for murder in the 2nd degree, which is punishable by death or life imprisonment.	A person who already has been sentenced to death or life imprisonment and who intentionally or knowingly causes another to come into contact with blood seminal fluid, saliva, urine, or feces by throwing, tossing, spitting, or expelling such fluid or material when at the time of the offense the person knew, had reason to know, should have known, or believed such fluid or material to have been obtained from an individual infected with a communicable disease including but not limited to HIV, is guilty of a crime (penalty same as murder in the 2nd degree).	
18 Pa. Cons. Stat. § 5902(a)	Felony of the 3rd degree	Any person who commits prostitution knowing he/she is HIV positive is guilty of a felony.	
18 Pa. Cons. Stat. § 5902(b)	Felony of the 3rd degree	A person who knowingly promotes the prostitution of another who is HIV positive is guilty of a felony.	
18 Pa. Cons. Stat. § 5902(e)	Felony of the 3rd degree	A person who knows he/she is HIV positive and patronizes a prostitute is guilty of a felony.	Second or more offenses require publication by court of sentencing order in newspaper.
Rhode Island N/A	N/A	N/A	N/A

Continued

6.3 State Criminal Statutes on HIV Transmission—2008 (Cont'd)

State	Statute	Type of Crime	Summary	Notes
South Carolina	S.C. Code Ann. § 4429-145	Felony punishable by fine of not more than $5,000 or imprisonment for not more than 10 years.	It is unlawful for a person who knows he/she is infected with HIV to knowingly engage in sexual intercourse (vaginal, anal, or oral) with another person without first informing them of their HIV status, to knowingly commit an act of prostitution, to forcibly engage in vaginal, anal, or oral sex without the consent of another person including one's legal spouse, to knowingly sell or donate blood, blood products, semen, tissue, organs, or other bodily fluids, and/or to knowingly share a hypodermic needle, syringe or both without first informing them of their HIV status.	Exception for informed consent.

| South Dakota | S.D Codified Laws § 22-18-31 | Class 3 felony | Any person who, knowing him/herself to be infected with HIV, intentionally exposes another person to infection by (1) engaging in sexual intercourse or other intimate physical contact with another person: (2) transferring, donating, or providing blood, tissue, semen, organs, or other potentially infectious body fluids or parts for transfusion, transplantation, insemination or other administration to another in any manner that presents a significant risk of HIV transmission; (3) dispensing, delivering, exchanging, selling or in any other way transferring to another person any non-sterile intravenous or intramuscular drug paraphernalia that has been contaminated by himself/herself; or (4) throwing, smearing, or otherwise causing blood or semen to come in contact with another person for the purpose of exposing that person to HIV infection, is guilty of criminal exposure to HIV. | Affirmative defense for informed consent. Actual transmission is not necessary for conviction. |

Continued

State	Statute	Type of Crime	Summary	Notes
Tennessee	Tenn. Code Ann. § 39 13-109	Class C felony	A person, knowing that he/she is HIV positive, who knowingly (1) engages in intimate contact with another: (2) transfers, donates or provides blood. tissue. semen, organs, or other potentially infectious body fluids or parts for transfusion, transplantation, insemination, or other administration to another in any manner that presents a significant risk of HIV transmission: or (3) dispenses, delivers, exchanges, sells, or in any other way transfers to another any nonsterile intravenous or intramuscular drug paraphernalia. is guilty of a class C felony.	Informed consent is an affirmative defense. Actual transmission of HIV is not necessary for a conviction.
	Tenn. Code Ann. § 68 10-107	Class C misdemeanor	Any person infected with an STD who exposes another to such infection commits a violation.	

Texas	N/A	N/A	N/A	Weeks v. State (1992, Tex App Eastland) 834 SW2d 559, petition for discretionary review ref (Oct 14, 1992) (Upholding attempted murder conviction of HIV positive defendant who spat twice in face of prison guard was supported by evidence where record showed that (1) defendant knew he was HIV positive, (2) defendant had stated that he was going to take as many with him as he could, (3) defendant believed that he could kill victim by spitting on him, and (4) experts had not entirely ruled out possibility of transmitting HIV through saliva.).
Utah	Utah Code Ann § 7610-1309	Felony of the 3rd degree	N/A	A person who has actual knowledge that he/she tested positive for HIV and then committed prostitution, patronized a prostitute or committed sexual solicitation is guilty of a 3rd degree felony.
Vermont	N/A	N/A	N/A	N/A

Continued

State	Statute	Type of Crime	Summary	Notes
Virginia	Va. Code Ann § 18.2-67, 4:1(A)	Class 6 felony	Any person who, knowing he/she is infected with HIV, syphilis, or Hepatitis B. has sexual intercourse, cunnilingus, fellatio, analingus, or anal intercourse with the intent to transmit the infection to another person is guilty of a class 6 felony.	
	Va. Code Ann § 18.2 -7, 4:1(B)	Class 1 misdemeanor	Any person who, knowing he/she is infected with HIV, syphilis or Hepatitis B. has sexual intercourse, cunnilingus, fellatio, analingus, or anal intercourse with another person without having previously disclosed his or her HIV status is guilty of a class 1 misdemeanor.	Exception for informed consent.
	Va. Code Ann § 32.1-289.2	Class 6 felony	Any person who donates or sells, attempts to donate or sell, consents to the donation or sale of blood, other body fluids, organs and tissues, knowing that the donor is or was infected with HIV and who knows that such material may transmit the infection, is guilty of a class 6 felony.	Exception for use in medical or scientific research.

	Rev. Code Wash. § 9A.36.011(1)(b)	Class A felony	A person is guilty of assault in the 1st degree if he or she. with intent to inflict great bodily harm. administers, exposes, or transmits to another the human im-munodeficiency virus.
Washington			
West Virginia	N/A	N/A	N/A
Wisconsin	N/A	N/A	N/A
Wyoming	N/A	N/A	N/A

not as concerned with providing adequate care and support for those who test positive. It may seem rational for a person with a positive test result to take proper precautions to prevent transmission, but in reality for many people who are being tested, a lack of counseling leaves those tested uninformed. They continue their lives as though nothing has changed. Thus sexual partners are at risk for contracting HIV, making them vulnerable for increased government surveillance and regulation.

Adversely Affected Populations

One critique of mandatory testing laws toward sex offenders is that they pay undue attention to traditionally oppressed groups. Historically these populations have been subjected to more aggressive police intervention, racist and sexist public policy, and stereotypes that are falsely thought to represent large populations of people. As Kai Wright (2005) reported in "Super Infector," through sensationalized media reporting, overzealous police forces, and pressured prosecutors, criminalization of HIV transmission has achieved all of the above. Wright defined the super infector as a person who is HIV positive and is intentionally transmitting the virus to multiple people. The media has portrayed super infectors as young men of color from urban areas that prey upon young white women in rural settings. Alongside the media, public officials and law enforcement officers have assisted in making this demographic the most prosecuted under criminal transmission statutes (Ibid, p. 20).

Another category of vulnerable or dangerous populations warranting additional HIV measures is pregnant women. According to Wright and Hatcher (2006), a sex offender is "any individual who, because of his or her sexual behavior, has come into contact with the legal system" (p. 159). In December 2007, the state of New Jersey passed into law mandatory HIV testing for all pregnant women. Under the rhetoric of controlling mother-to-child HIV transmission, New Jersey tests women in the beginning of the pregnancy and again in the third trimester, unless the mother objects. New Jersey joins four other states in mandated HIV testing for pregnant women (Richburg, 2007). New Jersey's current law requiring mandatory HIV testing for all pregnant women indicates a disturbing shift in law and public opinion. Prior to this law, no other state mandated HIV testing for all pregnant women.

According to Riki E. Jacobs, executive director of a New Jersey nonprofit that advocates for the rights of people with AIDS, prior to the mandate, approximately 98% of pregnant women in New Jersey were being tested. Jacobs critiqued the law for minimal effectiveness and invasion of privacy (Richburg, 2007). The legislation of testing, rather than increasing prenatal care, discourages women from seeking medical support (Nicholson, 2002, p. 180).

Simpson and Forsyth's (2007) exploratory research reinforced findings from Nelms (2005) and Nicholson (2002), which indicated that HIV-positive women not only experience not only higher rates of verbal and physical abuse but also increased levels of partner abandonment. In addition, the partners of HIV-positive women may be "serial infectors" who are not tested for HIV at the time of pregnancy. This gendered policy not only allows fathers to escape state surveillance, but in essence puts women at further risk for intimate partner violence in a system that offers little to no support for women and children.

In defense of mandated testing of pregnant women, the state has claimed that it has a compelling interest in the protection of the public and unborn children from sex-related health risks. In the same vein, the state has claimed a vested stake in the mandated testing of prostitutes. It is a widely accepted misconception that female prostitutes carry disease and that loose morals are the source of HIV infection. Prostitute seropositivity studies generally show low positivity rates in prostitutes who consistently use safer sex methods. Results from studies (Centers for Disease Control, 1987; Elifson, Boles, Darrow, & Sterk, 1999; Treichler, 1999) showed female prostitutes have rates of infection similar to women in the general population. In addition, both pregnant women and prostitutes can be classified as sex offenders under Wright and Hatcher's (2006) proceeding definition, thus placing them under the rubric of sex offender laws and leaving them with little to no ability to challenge these policies.

In the 1980s, many states enacted legislation that mandated testing upon arrest for sexual solicitation. These laws not only increased punishment for prostitution, but also enabled the state to increase surveillance and control over the bodies of prostitutes and directly reestablish the link between prostitution and disease. McColgin and Hey (1997) questioned the effectiveness of laws that not only criminalize prostitution but add on HIV-specific charges such as manslaughter and assault. Laws prohibiting prostitution are generally viewed as ineffective, tend to drive the sexual exchange of money or drugs underground, and make education efforts for prostitutes and clients more difficult. In addition, laws that criminalize HIV may thwart testing efforts as well as safer sex practices. In February 2007, Sakinah Floyd, a 36-year-old, HIV-positive woman, was accused of having unprotected sex for money with at least 10 male college students at Cheyney University (suburban Philadelphia). Police found drugs commonly used by HIV-positive people in her bag. While in custody, Floyd faced charges of prostitution, solicitation, aggravated assault, and reckless endangerment (NBC 10, 2007).

Floyd's case also calls into question the matter if an HIV-positive prostitute negotiates a sexual act with a condom. Can he or she still be charged with the intentional transmission of HIV? Through statutes specifically targeting prostitution, the answer is yes. Another shortcoming of statutes that attempt to regulate prostitution is the risk that prostitutes face from HIV-positive customers. This oversight reflects a sexist societal bias towards prostitution as an occupation that primarily provides services for men. Prostitutes who are targeted for intentional transmission may face legal as well as societal barriers from defending themselves in such cases.

Conclusion

At first glance, it seems that increased surveillance and testing of sex offenders is the most effective way to protect the public's well-being, but throughout this chapter we have outlined some of the less visible and non articulated drawbacks that may arise with mandatory testing and federal policing of people's bodies. It seems almost incomprehensible to question whether this criminal type should be required to be tested for HIV. Lack of mandatory testing could be construed as negligence on behalf of the state. Perceived to be dangerous and deviant, the regulation and surveillance of this population protects the vulnerable subjects of a society from further exploitation and abuse. Yet at the same time, this country values the right to privacy; freedom from unreasonable search and seizure; and, at one time, the ability for offenders to do penance for their crimes and become autonomous, productive citizens.

Mandatory HIV testing for sex offenders was the result of the shifting policy response to the HIV/AIDS pandemic from a moral panic mentality into tangible state policy. This was embedded into federal law. This chapter defined what is meant by mandatory testing, intentional transmission, and outlined the major types of laws and policies that contribute to the body of legislation. It also discussed the legal precedents and civil liberties rhetoric, which have shaped the laws and sociological issues contextualizing these policies. Instead of reducing HIV transmission rates and empowering individuals and groups who are at risk for HIV through sexual assault and other involuntary forms of acquisition, these policies threaten civil liberties and privacy rights, and are disproportionately aimed at men of color, prostitutes, pregnant women, and anyone who perpetuated what might be labeled as a "sex offense."

In essence, courts have overwhelmingly supported the reduction of individual civil liberties with hopes of greater public protection. Although the state's role in protecting citizens is of the utmost priority, we must continue to reexamine the role fear plays in making policy. Sound social policy should be based on rational, empirical evidence rather than the unsubstantiated demands of the most active and organized segments of society.

References

Americans with Disabilities Act of 1990. (1990). Pub. L. No. 101-336, §2, 104 Stat. 328.

The Associated Press. (2008). Governor signs HIV bill. *The Rapid City Journal.* Retrieved June 2, 2008, from http://www.rapidcityjournal. com/articles/2008/03/13/news/top/doc47d9431e9823d676396066.txt

Backstrom, C. & Robins, L. (1995/1996). State AIDS policy making: Perspectives of legislative health committee chairs. *AIDS and Public Policy Journal,* Winter, *10,* 238–248.

Baldwin, P. (2005). *Disease and Democracy: The Industrialized World Faces AIDS.* Berkeley: University of California Press.

Bell, S. (1994). *Reading, Writing, and Rewriting the Prostitute Body.* Bloomington: Indiana University Press.

Bell v. Wolfish, 441 U.S. 520 (1979).

Brandt, A. (1987). *No magic bullet: A social history of venereal disease in the United States since 1880*. Oxford, UK: Oxford University Press.

Brandt, A. (1988a.) AIDS: From social history to social policy. *Law, Medicine, and Health Care, 14*, 231–233.

Brandt, A. (1988b). The syphilis epidemic and its relation to AIDS. *Science, 239*, 375–379.

Brandt, A. (1988c). AIDS in historical perspective: Four lessons from the history of sexuality transmitted diseases. *American Journal of Public Health, 78*, 367–370.

Butler, J. (2004). Letter to my countrywomen, dwelling in the farmsteads and cottages of England. In W. K. Kolmar and F. Bartkowski *(Eds.), Feminist Theory: A Reader. Second Edition*. Pp. 86-91. New York: McGraw Hill. (Original work published in 1871)

Centers for Disease Control.(1987).Antibody to human immunodeficiency virus in female prostitutes. *Morbidity and Mortality Weekly Report, 36*, 157–61

Children's AIDS Fund. (2001). Nevada man accused of intentional HIV exposure. *Las Vegas Review Journal*. Retrieved May 18, 2008, from http://www.childrensaidsfund.org/resources/upd0246.htm

Closen, M., Bobinski, M., Hermann, D., Hernandez, J., Schultz, G., & Strader, J. (1994). Criminalization of an epidemic: HIV-AIDS and criminal exposure laws. *Arkansas Law Review, 46*, 921–983.

Cohen, S. (1972). *Folk Devils and moral panics: The creation of the mods and the rockers*. London, UK: MacGibbon and Kee.

Committee on Perinatal Transmission of HIV, Institute of Medicine, Youth, and Families Board on Children, and National Research Council. (1999). *Reducing the odds: Preventing perinatal transmission of HIV in the United States*. Washington, DC: National Academies Press.

Corrigan, R. (2006). Making Meaning of Megan's Law. *Law and Social Inquiry, 31*, 267–312.

Cossman, B. (2007). Sexual Citizens: The Legal and Cultural Regulation of Sex and Belonging. Palo Alto, CA: Stanford University Press.

Elifson, K.W., J. Boles, W.W. Darrow, & Sterk, C.E. (1999). HIV seroprevalence and risk factors among clients of female and male prostitutes. *Journal of Acquired Immunodeficiency Syndrome Human Retrovirology, 20*, 195-200.

Eskridge, W. (1996). *Case For Same Sex Marriage: From Sexual Liberty to Civilized Commitment*. Glencoe, IL: Free Press.

Goode, E. & Ben-Yehuda, N. (1994a). *Moral panics: The social construction of deviance*. Oxford, UK: Blackwell.

Goode, E. & Ben-Yehuda, N. (1994b). Moral panics: Culture, politics, and social construction. *Annual Review of Sociology, 20*, 149-171.

Gostin, L. (2004). *The AIDS pandemic: Complacency, injustice, and unfulfilled expectations*. Chapel Hill, NC: University of North Carolina Press.

Hodge, J. G. (2008) Advancing HIV prevention initiative-A limited legal analysis of state HIV statutes. Initial assessment for the Centers for Disease Control and Prevention. *The Center for Law and Public Health at Georgetown and Johns Hopkins Universities*. Retrieved September 30, 2008, from http://www.publichealthlaw.net/Research/PDF/AHP%20Report%20-%20Hodge.pdf

Jenkins, P. (1998). *Moral panic: Changing concepts of the child molester in modern America.* New Haven, CT: Yale University Press.

Kenney, S. (1992). Comment: Criminalizing HIV transmission: Lessons from history and a model for the future. *Journal of Contemporary Health Law and Policy. 8,* 245-255.

Kovach, G. (2008). Prison for man with H.I.V. who spit on a police officer. *The New York Times.* Retrieved May 18, 2008, from http://www.nytimes. com/2008/05/16/us/16spit.html?partner=rssnyt&ampemc=rss

Kuiper, J. (1998). The Need for Tougher Standards in Washington Imposing Criminal Liability for the Intentional Exposure to HIV. *Gonzaga Law Review, 34,* 185-199.

Lazzarina, Z., Bray, S., & Burris, S. (2002). Evaluating the impact of criminal laws on HIV risk behavior. *Journal of Law, Medicine, and Ethics, 30,* 239-253.

Marion, N. (1997). Rethinking federal criminal law: Symbolic policies in Clinton's crime control Agenda. *Buffalo Criminal Law Review, 1,* 67-108.

McColgin, D. & Hey, E. (1997). Criminal law. In D. Webber (ed.), *AIDS and the law, 3rd Edition.* New York, NY: John Wiley and Sons, Inc.

The National HIV/AIDS Clinicians Consultation Center. (2007) State HIV testing laws compendium-2008. *University of California San Francisco National HIV/AIDS Clinicians' Consultation Center (NCCC) at UCSF/SFGH.* Retrieved September 30, 2008, from http://nccc.ucsf. edu/StateLaws/

NBC 10 Philadelphia. (2007). Police issue warning about HIV-positive prostitute. *NBC 10 Philadelphia.* Retrieved May 26, 2008, from http://www.nbc10.com/education/10979750/detail. html?dl=mainclick

Nelms, T.P. (2005). Burden: The phenomenon of mothering with HIV. *Journal of the Association of Nurses in AIDS Care, 16,* 3-13.

Nicholson, E. (2002). Mandatory HIV testing on pregnant women: Public health policy considerations and alternatives. *Duke Journal of Gender Law and Politics,* 9, 175-191.

Omnibus Crime Control and Safe Streets Act of 1968, tit. I, § 506, 42 U.S.C. §3756 (1995)

Pateman, C. (1988) *The Sexual Contract.* Palo Alto, CA: Stanford University Press.

Radeloff, C. (2004). Vectors, polluters, and murderers: HIV testing policies for prostitutes in Nevada (Doctoral dissertation, University of Nevada Las Vegas, Las Vegas, 2004.

Richburg, K. (2007). N.J. orders HIV testing for pregnant women. *The Washington Post.* Retrieved May 26, 2008, from http://www.washingtonpost. com/wpdyn/content/article/2007/12/27/AR2007122702136.html

Rubin, G. (1989). Thinking Sex: Notes for a Radical Theory of the Politics of Sexuality. In C.S. Vance (ed.), *Pleasure and Danger: Exploring Female Sexuality,* London, UK: Pandora Press.

Rubin, G. (1993). Thinking sex: Notes for a radical theory of the politics of sexuality. In H. Abelove, M. A. Barale, and D. M. Halperin (eds.), *The Lesbian and Gay Studies Reader* (pp. 3-44). New York, NY: Routledge.

Ryan White CARE Act of 1990, 42 U.S.C § 300ff-47 (1994)

Schneider, B.& Jenness,V.(1997). Social control, civil liberties, and women's sexuality. In L. Richardson, V. Taylor, and N. Whittier (eds.), *Feminist Frontier IV* (pp. 472-484). New York, NY: The McGraw-Hill Companies.

Seidman, S. (2003). *Beyond the Closet: The Transformation of Gay and Lesbian Life.* New York, NY: Routledge.

Simpson, J., & Forsyth, B. (2007). State-mandated HIV testing in Connecticut: Personal perspectives of women found to be infected during pregnancy. *Journal of the Association of Nurses in AIDS Care, 18,* 34-46.

Smith, K. (1998). Mandatory HIV testing for convicted or accused sex offenders: Toward a model scheme. *Buffalo Women's Law Journal, 6,* 52-101.

Thompson, K. (1998). *Moral panics.* London, UK: Routledge.

Treichler, P. (1999). *How to have a theory in an epidemic: Cultural chronicles of AIDS.* Durham, NC: Duke University Press.

U.S. Department of Justice. (2000). Sexual Assault of Young Children as Reported to Law Enforcement: Victim, Incident, and Offender Characteristics. Bureau of Justice Statistics. Retrieved June 10, 2008, from http://www.ojp.usdoj.gov/bjs/pub/pdf/saycrle.pdf

U.S. Department of Justice. (n.d.). Testing Certain Offenders for HIV. Bureau of Justice Assistance. Retrieved May 27, 2008, from http://www.ojp. usdoj.gov/BJA/txt/chap12.txt

Walkowitz, J. (1980). *Prostitution and Victorian society: Women, class, and the state.* Cambridge, UK: Cambridge University Press.

Webber, D. (1997). HIV/AIDS in the workplace. In D. Webber (ed.) *AIDS and the Law, 3ʳᵈ Edition.* New York, NY: John Wiley and Sons, Inc.

Wright, K. (2005). Super infector. *Colorlines, 8,* 16-20.

Wright, L.& Hatcher, A. (2006). Treatment of sexual offenders. In R. D. McAnulty and M. M. Burnette (eds.) *Sex and Sexuality. Volume 3: Sexual Deviation and Sexual Offenses.* Westport, CT: Praeger Publishers.

---

[i] Special thanks are due to Meghan Chase, Bridgewater State College, for her research assistance in identifying mandatory HIV testing state statutes.

[ii] *AIDS* as a term was first introduced in July 1982. Almost five years later, in 1986, the term HIV (Human Immunodeficiency Virus) was introduced as a replacement for "AIDS virus." The choice of this term was deliberate. According to Treichler (1999), the choice of HIV was credited to its promise of unification of the scientific establishment and to promote the idea of a single etiology or agent hypothesis (p. 30). Eventually, the diagnosis and thus identity of AIDS is assigned when a person has a CD4, or white blood count, below 200, and or an opportunistic infection. It was also around this time in the public's mind that one could be infected with a virus (HIV) and not have a diagnosis of AIDS.

[iii] The Americans with Disabilities Act of 1990 (ADA) is considered one of the most significant pieces of civil rights legislation besides the Civil Rights Act of 1964 and the Rehabilitation Act of 1973. While HIV/AIDS is not directly mentioned in the text of the legislation, its charge of providing nondiscrimination standards in employment provides coverage against HIV/AIDS discrimination (ADA, 1990).

iv For the purpose of this chapter, the term *victim* will be used rather than *survivor*. Self-identifying as a survivor is recognized as a rhetorical device to initiate the healing process. Unfortunately, within institutional systems, individuals often have little to no power.

v *STI*, or sexually transmitted infections, has become the preferred term in public health rhetoric, replacing STD and venereal disease.

vi Since 1987, immigration has been denied to HIV-positive individuals unless granted a special waiver of inadmissibility granted on a case-by-case discretionary basis by the Department of Homeland Security and the U.S. Department of State for visa permission.

vii Adapted from Smith, K., 1998.

viii The legal events include prostitution, criminal sexual conduct, and intravenous drug use (IVDU)

ix After a hearing

x Committing same offense

xi If formally charged

xii Previous conviction within the same year

xiii Requested by prosecutor, victim, or court approved requestor

xiv Request by prosecutor

xv After a hearing

xvi Within 90 days

xvii Upon entering correctional facility

xviii Certain offenses

xix Requested by prosecutor

xxUpdated state laws and statutes were compiled from a variety of sources including The National HIV/AIDS Clinicians Consultation Center, 2008,and Hodge, 2008.

Sex Offender Registration and Community Notification

Lisa L. Sample & Mary K. Evans

Although sex offenders and sexual offenses have received an extraordinary amount of legislative attention over the past two decades, few policy reforms have been as far-reaching as sex offender registration and community notification. What began as individual state laws, requiring sex offenders to register their addresses with local law enforcement agencies, quickly grew into federal mandates for all states to not only gather information on sex offenders and their whereabouts, but also to release this information to the public. It has now been over a decade since states were mandated to acquire and release sex offender information to the public. It is, therefore, an appropriate time to revisit the assumptions behind these laws, the goals for which they where intended, and the degree to which these goals have been realized.

In this chapter, we review the historical evolution of sex offender registration and community notification laws, and the current state of this legislation. We remind readers of the assumptions and goals underlying these policies and examine their application and implementation. Finally, we review empirical investigations of both the manifest and latent consequences of these laws and conclude with a discussion on the controversial nature and future direction of sex offender policy reforms.

Evolution of Sex Offender Reforms

To many, registration laws are new and innovative policy reforms that address the behavior of sex offenders, but in actuality, registration laws are simply old polices that have been repackaged for a different era (Tewksbury, 2002). For instance, in 1937, Florida became the first state to enact a criminal registration statute that required offenders of all types to register their addresses with law enforcement agencies upon criminal convictions in an effort to prevent reoffending. This law used registration to target those persons convicted of felonies "involving moral turpitude" living in the three most populous counties of the state. California followed suit in 1947, when the state enacted the nation's first statewide sex offender registration law, requiring all criminal offenders to provide their whereabouts to police (Ibid). Arizona followed, passing its own sex offender registration law in 1951; Florida, Alabama, Ohio, and Nevada all enacted sex offender registration laws statewide during the decade of 1957–1967 (Ibid). Little is known about the application of these early registration laws or the degree to which they affected criminal behavior. Despite this lack of information, states began re-embracing the notion of sex offender registration in the 1980s.

Current Sex Offender Registration Laws

Beginning in 1986, Illinois became one of the first states to officially revisit offender registration passing the Habitual Child Sex Offender Registration Act (Sample & Kadleck, 2008). The act was intended to protect children from the crimes of repeat sex offenders and required persons convicted of a second offense of criminal sexual assault or abuse against persons under 18 years of age to register their residency information with local law enforcement agencies for a period of 10 years (730 ILCS 150/1). Moreover, this act applied to not only adults but also juvenile offenders convicted of crimes against children.

In the 1990s, Illinois legislators expanded their 1986 registration requirements to include all offenders convicted of sex crimes against both children and adults. Additionally, the law expanded the definition of sex crimes to include nonviolent offenses such as possessing child pornography and luring a child over the Internet (730 ILCS 150/1). The catalysts of the expansion of the Illinois law, and the diffusion of registration laws nationwide, can be traced to three specific incidents of sexually related homicide against children.

In October of 1989, Jacob Wetterling, 11, was abducted near his home in Minnesota by an armed, masked stranger (Finn, 1997). To date, Jacob has not been found. His case resembled that of a boy in a neighboring town who was abducted and sexually attacked earlier that year. Both incidents are believed to have been committed by the same man, thus leading police to conclude they were searching for a repeat sex offender. Although the Wetterling abduction drew attention to the repetitiveness of sex offenders' behaviors, it was the homicides of Polly Klaas and Megan Kanka that brought this issue to the forefront of the national policy agenda (Jenkins, 1998).

In 1993, the media widely disseminated the story of Polly Klaas, a 12-year-old girl who was abducted from her bedroom in California, sexually assaulted, and subsequently killed. One year later, the media reported that 7-year-old Megan Kanka was missing from her New Jersey home. She was later found sexually assaulted and murdered. Both Polly Klaas and Megan Kanka were murdered by previously convicted sex offenders who had been released from prison. The parents of these children actively lobbied state and federal legislators for remedies to address the repeat behavior of sex offenders. The results of their efforts have become the centerpiece of modern federal and state sex offender policies.

In 1994, the federal Jacob Wetterling Crimes Against Children and Sexually Violent Offender Registration Act, buried deep in the Violent Crime Control and Law Enforcement Act, mandated that 10% of a state's funding under

the Edward Byrne Memorial State and Local Law Enforcement Assistance grant program be used for establishing a
statewide system for registering and tracking convicted sex
offenders (Finn, 1997). The act also "strongly encouraged"
states to collect DNA samples from registered sex offenders, which would be typed and stored in databases, and used
to clear crimes (Ibid, p. 7). States quickly began complying
with the Wetterling Act by requiring blood samples and
registry information from only those sex offenders convicted
of violent sex acts against children. To date, every state has
created and/or expanded their registry, and applicable DNA
laws, to include persons convicted of violent or nonviolent
sex crimes[i] against persons regardless of their age (Sample
& Bray, 2003).

Contemporary Community Notification Laws

In 1989, Earl Shriner drew national media attention for
sexually assaulting a 7-year-old Seattle boy, mutilating
his genitals, and leaving him for dead. Shriner had been
hospitalized for murder in the 1960s and convicted of child
molestation in 1977, 1987, and 1988 (Jenkins, 1998, p. 191).
These crimes committed by Shriner influenced Washington's
Community Protection Act (1990), which was the nation's first
community notification law that permitted the dissemination
of sex offenders' personal information to the community
in which registrants reside (Matson & Lieb, 1996). Shortly
thereafter, in 1994, as a result of the Kanka sexually related
homicide, New Jersey rapidly adopted similar legislation,
entitled "Megan's Law," which was passed with the belief that
parents should have the right to know if a dangerous sexual
predator moves into their neighborhood. The idea of notify-
ing community members of sex offenders' whereabouts was
embraced by federal legislators, as evidenced by the passage
of a federal version of Megan's Law.

The initial Wetterling Act was amended to include
Megan's Law in 1996, which required states to make relevant
information on released sex offenders available to the
general public. This federal legislation, however, did not
provide detailed instructions to states concerning how to
notify the public. As a result, states differ in their implementation of Megan's Law. Community notification dissemination
procedures can include, but are not limited to, print media

reports in newspapers, neighborhood flyers, phone calls, door-to-door campaigns, community meetings, and/or state sponsored Web sites (Adams, 2001; Levenson, 2003).

Despite the lack of federal guidance on how notification procedures should occur, Megan's Law was fairly exact in addressing the types of information that should be released to the public. Specifically, sex offenders are required to provide a photograph and register their addresses, offenses, and other relevant information, such as their telephone numbers, social security numbers, employment information, and fingerprints to local authorities when they move into a new community (Adams, 2001; Levenson, 2003). Additionally, sex offenders are required to proactively update this information if anything changes; therefore, the accuracy of information disseminated to the public is heavily reliant on the coopera- tion of convicted sex offenders.

It should be noted that not all convicted sex offenders are listed on registries. For instance, sex offenders convicted prior to the enactment of Megan's Law and offenders who commit sexual crimes but plead guilty to nonsexual offenses are often not reflected in state registries. Those who have fulfilled the term limit of registration, which varies by crime type and state, would no longer be reflected on registration lists. Similarly, the information for those offenders who have absconded will not be accurate on registry listings. Moreover, some states require only the most "dangerous" offenders (i.e., Tier III) to be listed publicly, meaning that those with no prior history of sex crimes are not subject to notification procedures, whereas other states require that all sex offend- ers, including juveniles, regardless of prior history, be listed. Given the variability of registry requirements across states, there have been numerous constitutional challenges against the requirement of registration and notification.

Some landmark constitutional challenges to sex offend- er registration and community notification statutes have included allegations that they violate the *Ex Post Facto* clause and due process guarantees of the United States Constitu- tion (see, *Connecticut Dept. of Public Safety v. Doe. (2003)*. 538 U.S.; *Smith v. Doe*, 538 U.S. 84 (2003). Besides these two court cases in particular, there have been many other constitu- tional challenges; however, defendants have not prevailed, and sex offender registration and notification laws continue to persist and evolve. As new registration and notification policies develop, there will inevitably be additional constitutional issues raised and challenged.

Recent Policy Reforms to Amend Community Notification

Past amendments to the Wetterling Act have set the stage for our most recent sex offender policy reforms. For instance, the Wetterling Act was amended in 1996 by the Pam Lychner Sexual Offender Tracking and Identification Act, which was the first step toward a national registration system, allowing for the creation of a central federal database to facilitate the tracking of registrants from state to state by the FBI and state law enforcement agencies. Ms. Lychner was attacked by a twice-convicted felon but survived the attempted rape and teamed up with U.S. Senators to craft the bill that created the National Sex Offender Registry (NSOR).

States have also passed additional laws in response to victimizations. In 2005, Florida's Governor signed the Jessica Lunsford Act into law, which established more stringent mandatory sentencing and tracking of convicted sex offenders. Jessica Lunsford, 9 years old, was raped and murdered by John Couey, a convicted sex offender who lived in Jessica's neighborhood. Jessica's Law not only doubles the mandatory sentences for sex offenders, but also requires extensive electronic monitoring of Florida's sex offenders for the rest of their lives. Since the enactment of Jessica's Law in Florida, a majority of states have not waited for a federal response to tighten sex offender registration requirements and have enacted similar legislation. Recently, however, the Wetterling Act and its amendments have been replaced with more comprehensive and uniform federal legislation.

The Walsh Act

Twelve years after the initial Wetterling Act, President George W. Bush signed the Adam Walsh Child Protection Act of 2006 (Walsh Act, 2006). The new law greatly expanded federal sex offender policies by enhancing penalties for those who sexually exploit children, expanding Internet investigations and prosecution for child pornography, and most importantly adding a central compilation of all state sex offender registries into one uniform national sex offender registry.

Many legislators have stressed the importance of the Walsh Act while others have objected to its provisions. Senator Bill Frist (R-TN), for example, suggested that even though the Walsh Act cannot prevent all sex crimes, "[some]… can be prevented by arming the American people with the tools that can help catch these predators and once they are caught, making sure they are kept away from children, and that children are kept out of their reach" (Congressional Record, 2006, p. S4089). Likewise, Senator Mark Foley (R-FL) strongly backed such legislation, stating, "It used to be that we tracked library books better than we do sex offenders, but this bill will even the score" (Congressional Record, 2006, p. H5725). Ironically, Senator Foley, known to be a leader in preventing child exploitation, resigned from Congress in 2006 after allegations emerged about him sending sexually explicit Internet messages with then-current and former congressional pages under the age of 18 (Babington & Weisman, 2006).

Outspoken critics such as Representative Scott of Virginia (D-VA) have not discounted the suffering of the victims or the families but have warned against passing legislation "that merely panders to our emotions." Scott further blasted the Act's mandatory minimum sentencing requirements and registration of juveniles, stating, "Many studies have shown that mandatory minimum sentencing wastes taxpayers money, are unfairly applied to minorities, and violate common sense." He went on to say that he has seen "no study that suggests that the policy of posting the name of juvenile delinquents, as this bill does, on the Internet, serves any constructive purpose" (Congressional Record, July 25, 2006: H5723). Debates continue regarding the overall purpose of the Walsh Act and its provisions; however, the proponents of the legislation are winning the battle.

Generally, the Walsh Act imposes mandatory minimum penalties for the most serious federal crimes against children, increases penalties for crimes such as sex trafficking of children and child prostitution, distributes grants to states to help civilly commit sex offenders, authorizes new regional Internet Crimes Against Children task forces to combat the sexual exploitation of minors on the Internet, and creates a National Child Abuse Registry, requiring investigators to do background checks on adoptive and foster parents. All of these sex offender reforms listed as general objectives of the act are noteworthy; however, the most relevant to our discussion of registration and community notification is the Walsh Act's Title I, which is referred to as the Sex Offender Registration and Notification Act (SORNA, 42 USC §16911).

Sex Offender Registration and Notification Act

The Sex Offender Registration and Notification Act (SORNA) establishes federal comprehensive standards for sex offender registration and community notification. The purpose of such legislation is to establish and maintain a nationwide network of sex offender registries and notification procedures in an attempt to inform the public and thereby prevent victimizations. SORNA is thought to build on existing state law in a number of ways. First, it expands states' jurisdictions to federally recognize and register sex offenders on American Indian reservations. It also increases penalties and expands the types of crimes for which registration is required. For example, the Walsh Act establishes a 20-year mandatory prison sentence for members of a child exploitation enterprise, provides a 10-year consecutive mandatory penalty for any federal sex offender who commits an offense against a child, and authorizes additional resources to prosecute child pornographers.

Additionally, the Walsh Act normalizes the requirements for registration nationwide, in terms of duration and accuracy of information. The law requires that sex offenders provide more extensive personal registration information to be publicly released, and requires sex offenders to frequently verify registration information and update information within 3 days of changes. Failure to comply with registration requirements is a felony punishable by up to 10 years in prison. Further, the Walsh Act mandates juvenile registration (i.e., juveniles above the age of 14). Some states (e.g., Illinois) have long required the registration of juveniles, so the Walsh Act simply creates uniformity nationwide. In sum, the Sex Offender Registration and Notification provision in the Walsh Act standardizes the ways in which states have previously responded to the Wetterling Act and Megan's Law of the 1990s. This standardization can be seen in the ways in which sex offenders are defined, when sex offenders must register upon convictions, the types of information states must gather about released sex offenders, and the types of punishments for offenders upon failures to comply.

Under the SORNA, sex offenders must register before they are released from prison or within 3 days of a nonimprisonment sentence. Sex offenders are to provide the following information: name (including alias), social security number, address or multiple addresses, employer and address, school (if a student), and license plate number and description of any vehicle owned or operated (Adam Walsh Child Protection and Safety Act of 2006, Pub. L. No. 109–248, 120 Stat. 587). Additionally, each jurisdiction must include the following information for every offender in the registry: a physical description of the sex offender; the convicted offense; the criminal history of the offender, including dates of arrests and convictions and correctional or release status; a current photograph; fingerprints and palm prints; a DNA sample; a photocopy or a valid driver's license or identification card; and any other information required by the attorney general (Ibid, Sec. 112). If sex offenders fail to comply with these requirements, they can be tried in federal court and convicted of a felony, for which sanctions can range from monetary penalties to a maximum imprisonment that is greater than 1 year.

The Walsh Act also defines and requires a three-tier classification system for sex offenders (Sec. 111). Unlike systems in roughly 15 states, this tier system does not classify offenders based on individualized assessments of risk for reoffending but rather by the type of crime for which offenders are committed. Under this highly debated "conviction-based" approach, all persons required to register are subject to community notification (via the Internet, at a minimum) regardless of assessed risk to the community. The tier levels established are as follows:

- Tier I sex offenders are those other than Tier II or Tier III sex offender (required to register for a period of 15 years).
- Tier II are those other than Tier III with an offense punishable by imprisonment for more than 1 year and comparable to or more severe than the following federal offenses involving a minor: sex trafficking, coercion and enticement, transportation with intent to engage in criminal sexual activity, abusive sexual conduct. Also included are any offenses involving the use of a minor in a sexual performance, solicitation

of a minor to practice prostitution, or production or distribution of child pornography (required to register for a period of 25 years).

■ Tier III are sex offenses punishable by imprisonment for more than 1 year and comparable to or more severe than the following federal offenses: sexual abuse or aggravated sexual abuse, abusive sexual contact against a minor less than 13 years old, offenses involving kidnapping of a minor (parent or guardian excepted), or any offense that occurs after one has been designated a Tier II sex offender (required to register for life).

Although all tiers proscribe a mandatory duration for registration, these durations can be mitigated. If Tier I sex offenders maintain what the act refers to as a "clean record" for 10 years, there is a 5-year reduction of registration time. Tier II sex offenders do not get a reduction and must register for fixed period of 25 years, whereas Tier III sex offenders must register for life, with no exceptions (Adam Walsh Child Protection and Safety Act of 2006, Pub. L. No. 109–248, 120 Stat. 587). Additionally, the tiers determine the time intervals in which registration information must be verified. Tier I sex offenders must verify information once a year, those in Tier II every 6 months, whereas those in Tier III must verify information every 3 months (Ibid, Sec. 116).

An additional requirement of the Walsh Act is to have each jurisdiction in the United States provide registry information to the public via the Dru Sjodin National Sex Offender Public Web site. Much of the personal information regarding sex offenders is displayed on this Website; however, victim information is not made available to the community. Also not displayed are offenders' social security numbers, references to arrests of offenders that did not result in conviction, and any other information exempted from disclosure. Moreover, states have the option of excluding any information about Tier I sex offenders convicted of an offense other than a specified offense against a minor, the name of employers of sex offenders, the name of educational institutions sex offenders attend, and any other information exempted from disclosure by the attorney general.

Beyond Internet notification of sex offender information, the Walsh Act mandates that community notification be conducted by various jurisdictional law enforcement agencies (i.e., parole officers, state patrol). When sex offenders move or update their information, law enforcement agencies are required to notify social service agencies, volunteer organizations (e.g., Boy Scouts), schools, public housing agencies, or any other organization or company that requests such notification (Adam Walsh Child Protection and Safety Act of 2006, Pub. L. No. 109–248, 120 Stat. 587).

Through the above provisions, SORNA theoretically will decrease victimization rates and increase public safety through improved monitoring and tracking mechanisms for sex offenders. Proponents argue that SORNA closes gaps and potential loopholes in current sex offender programs by holding offenders accountable for updating registration information through increasing the sanctions for violating registration requirements and requiring the registration of both adult offenders and juveniles over 14 years of age. It must be noted that only juveniles at least age 14 who are adjudicated delinquent for offenses equivalent to rape or attempted rape are required to register, but not for those adjudicated delinquent for lesser sexual assaults or nonviolent sexual contact. By July 27, 2009, all states are expected to implement SORNA requirements.

Potential Implications of the Sex Offender Registration and Notification Act

To date, it is unclear how states with varying financial resources, juvenile justice systems, and philosophies, and states with "risk-based" classification and notification procedures, will respond to the new "conviction-based" approach, will adapt to the registration of juveniles, or will financially comply will SORNA. Many of these issues have previously been contemplated by scholars, however, as states began embracing and expanding contemporary sex offender laws (Levenson, 2006; Petrosino & Petrosino, 1999; Sample & Bray, 2006).

Scholars have suggested that the deterrent effects of sex offender registration and notification laws may be hampered by the extension of these policies to more people and behaviors (Levenson, 2006; Sample & Bray, 2003). Sex offender laws require law enforcement agencies to register sex offenders, track their residences, notify the public of their whereabouts, and apprehend registration violators in addition to the traditional crime-fighting and community-service functions they are already expected to perform. Probation and parole officers have also accepted additional duties as they have been forced to go to extraordinary lengths to monitor sex offenders and find them housing and employment in communities that are opposed to their presence. The additional duties that sex offender laws require from law enforcement, probation, and parole officers undoubtedly tax the time and attention of these already overworked criminal justice agents (Zevitz & Farkas, 2000b). The expansion of sex offender laws to juveniles and those who have committed nonviolent sex crimes against children further increases the duties of these agents and possibly affects their ability to perform any of their duties effectively.

Criminal justice agents are not the only group to be affected by the expansion of sex offender laws to all sex offender types. Current sex offender policies require a substantial financial commitment from taxpayers. In 1999, for instance, the Illinois State Police received approximately $500,000 from the legislature to maintain the sex offender registry and place this information on the World Wide Web (Sample, 2001). Although this may sound like a large sum, it did not fully cover the costs of the computer mainframe, software, servers and printers, personnel salaries, training, and research needed to support registration and community notification laws. In addition, the Illinois Department of Corrections requested $115,000 to supplement the costs of the photography and computer equipment, development fees, and personnel salaries needed to take the photographs of sex offenders that are posted on the registration Web site.

The additional financial commitment to existing states' laws now required by the passage of the Walsh Act has been acknowledged by federal legislators. The Congressional Budget Office estimates that implementing the Walsh Act will cost about $1.5 billion over the 2006–2011 period (Congressional Budget Office Cost Estimate, 2006). Any additional costs to states would be incurred voluntarily as a condition of receiving the allocated federal aid. Therefore, if states fail to comply with the Walsh Act within 3 years of the required implementation date, the consequence is a 10% reduction to Byrne law enforcement assistance grants. Critics argue that, in fact, it may be more expensive for states to implement the Walsh Act than suffer the 10% reduction in Byrne funds. Representative Jim McReynolds (TX), for example, opposes provisions of the Walsh Act and states, "It would cost local communities more to enact the stringent requirements than what the state would earn if it complied. It's a financial loser … an unfunded mandate" (Sandberg, 2008).

With every classification of offender that policy makers add to sex offender registries, they substantially increase the money required for this policy and the number of people law enforcement, probation, and parole agencies must monitor. For example, under a 1986 Illinois statute, 3,609 sex offenders with child victims were potentially subject to registration, based on the 1990 arrest data (Sample & Bray, 2003). After the 1995 extension of this statute to include all sex offenders with child or adult victims, the number grew to 5,483, an increase of 52%. How effectively can criminal justice agents respond to this increase in workload? How effectively can they monitor a rapidly growing population of offenders? How are states expected to pay for the increase in personnel and equipment needed to monitor offenders and inform the public? It seems reasonable to assume that the effectiveness and efficiency of sex offender laws may be diminished with their expansion to more sex offender types. It is for this reason that scholars have long embraced a "risk-based" approach to registration and notification as opposed to a more general, all-encompassing approach (Levenson, 2006; Sample & Bray, 2003).

Evidence that suggests sex offenders are not a homogeneous group and do not possess an equal risk of reoffending (Hagan & Cho, 1996; Sample & Bray, 2006; Sample, 2006). To this end, given the financial costs and personnel resources required, it is likely that sex offender laws have a greater likelihood of successfully reducing victimization if they are targeted toward those offenders who pose the most risk for reoffending. A risk-based approach uses validated assessment instruments to determine individuals' likelihood of future offending. Those assessed most at risk for reoffending should be registered and have their information released to the public, thereby focusing scant resources on those most likely to endanger the public. We acknowledge that current sex offender laws and risk assessment instruments can do little to predict or prevent an initial sex crime, but there is little evidence to suggest that a "conviction-based" approach will have any greater likelihood of protecting the public than one based on scientific assessments of risk.

Beyond the costs of implementing the Walsh Act and SORNA, and the abandonment of scientific assessments of risk, there are the implications for juvenile sex offenders forced to register their information. Scholars have documented the rehabilitation emphasis upon which the juvenile justice system was founded (Bernard, 1992; Bishop, 2006; Leonard & Sample, 2000). States' juvenile justice systems have long used programming and assessment in the hope of turning delinquent youth into productive, law-abiding adults. Juvenile proceedings are often closed, juvenile offenders' names are often not released to the public, and juveniles' dispositions are often not released to the media, unless they are tried as adults—all in an effort to allow youthful offenders to reform. The inclusion of juvenile sex offenders in a national sex offender registry appears to counter over 100 years of juvenile justice philosophy and the justice procedures in several state systems. It is unclear to what degree the release of juvenile offender information will affect the programming these youth receive or inhibit their likelihood of reform. To the degree that the release of juvenile information further isolates youthful sex offenders, prevents them from creating positive social networks, inhibits their ability to receive an education, or prevents them from maintaining contact with family and friends, it is possible that the Walsh Act could exacerbate juveniles' behavior and ensure future offending.

Other implementation problems with the Walsh Act arise from the inability to locate the approximately 100,000 sex offenders who are not currently registered because they have absconded or failed to update registration information with law enforcement agencies (Congressional Record, May 4, 2006: S4090). The Governmental Accountability Office (GAO) has noted this challenge by investigating techniques to triangulate information with the motor vehicle departments and the New Hires Data (GAO, 2006; GAO, 2008). Understandably, this may facilitate confirmation of offender information, but one must remember that will not locate those offenders who do not have cars or jobs. Therefore, these techniques may prove to be limited in their ability to accurately complement registration information.

A more critical implementation issue with the enactment of the Walsh Act is the ability of states to enact such polices because registered sex offenders are challenging them as a violation of civil liberties. In 2008, in the case of *Evans v. Ohio,* the Court upheld that the Walsh Act violates both the retro-activity clause of the Ohio Constitution and the Ex Post Facto clause of the United States Constitution (*Evans v. Ohio*, 2008). Challenges like these to state enforcement of the Walsh Act could prove to slow the full enactment and implementation of the laws by the appropriate, mandated time frame.

There are many challenges to, and potential consequences of, the implementation of the Walsh Act. Theoretically, if SORNA is successfully implemented at the state and federal level, the provisions will enhance public safety and prevent future victimization by increasing public awareness of sex offenders living in communities, all while holding offenders accountable with more stringent requirements than past legislation. In their examination of sex offender recidivism, however, Soothill, Francis, Sanderson, and Ackerley (2000) warned about the dangers of exaggerating the risk of sexual reoffending to an entire population of offenders. They stated, "Potential outcomes of such exaggeration may be to unnec-essarily increase the fear of the public, hinder the genuine rehabilitation of offenders who have changed their ways, while wasting valuable resources on those who do not need increased surveillance" (p. 63). It seems to us that public safety would be better served and the public's fear put more at ease by applying registration and notification laws to individual offenders based on their specific likelihood of reoffending and allowing juvenile offenders to rehabilitate.

The Walsh Act is skewed toward efforts to increase pen-alties for offenders and create more restrictive laws in lieu of addressing the underlying issues that lead to sex offend-ing behavior. Much of this may be based on the assumptions upon which the laws are based—assumptions about both the causes of sex offending and the likelihood of future criminal behavior. By analyzing the historical path to the Walsh Act and reviewing the consequences thereof, we can draw infer-ences about the assumptions policy makers hold toward sex offenders and offending, and the goals of the legislation.

Assumptions and Goals of Registration and Notification Laws

The catalysts for much of contemporary sex offender laws are legislative assumptions about the behavior of sex offenders.

The four most common assumptions about sex offenders include that they inevitably reoffend, that they have a propensity to kill their victims, that they most frequently choose children as victims, and that they are often strangers to their victims (Sample, 2009). Moreover, these laws infer ways in which sex offenders' behavior can be prevented and the role of the public in fulfilling these control strategies.

Legal scholars and researchers have long been highlighting what they believe to be the assumptions of sex offenders and offending that prompted much of the legislation we have today (Levenson, Brannon, Fortney, & Baker, 2007; Sample & Bray, 2003, 2006; Sample, 2006; Shajnfeld & Krueger, 2006). Sample and Bray (2003) suggested that the requirements found in sex offender registration and community notification laws imply an assumption that sex offenders will inevitability reoffend, or at the very least, reoffend with greater frequency than other types of offenders. Also, given that registration and notification laws often apply to all sex offenders, regardless of the age of their victims or the nature of their crimes, these laws seem to imply that all sex offenders have an equally high probability of recommitting sex offenses (Sample & Bray, 2006). In this way, current sex offender legislation assumes that sex offenders are a homogeneous group of offenders who exhibit similar offending patterns irrespective of their type.

Another assumption inherent in registration and notification is that sex offenders often kill their victims. The naming of many federal sex offender laws after murdered children, such as Megan's Law and the Walsh Act, have only reaffirmed the assumption that sex offending and homicide are almost inevitably intertwined. They also infer that children are the individuals most at risk for sexual victimization and death at the hands of sex offenders.

Registration laws, and the recent Walsh Act mandating notification nationwide, make much sex offender information available to law enforcement agencies and the general public. As mentioned previously, citizens are given physical descriptions of the offenders and their pictures, in addition to addresses, places of employment, and vehicles owned. The disclosure of this information implies that victims seldom know their attackers. Indeed, if victims were acquainted with their offenders, they would already know what they looked like and where they lived. Although it is likely that sex offenders may be strangers to law enforcement agents, for whom they would need this detailed information, the disclosure of such details to the public inherently implies that citizens do not know whom they should be monitoring, and thus offenders are presumed to be strangers to their families and communities.

Given that requirements for registration include disclosing offender information to law enforcement agencies, it is easy to assume that law enforcement personnel are solely responsible for controlling sex offenders' behaviors. After all, the information provided to law enforcement agencies theoretically makes it easier for police to monitor sex offenders' whereabouts and watch their activities. Notification laws, however, imply that the public is responsible for some surveillance of sex offenders as well. By providing sex offender information to communities, notification laws imply that citizens should be vigilant in determining the whereabouts of convicted sex offenders and should take some preventive measures to guard against personal victimization and the victimization of their children (Anderson & Sample, 2008).

In sum, registration and notification laws suggest that sex offenders of all types will equally and inevitably reoffend and will often kill their victims. Those most likely to be victimized and murdered are children, and they are often attacked by strangers. If law enforcement agencies and community members have identifying information about sex offenders, they will be better able to prevent future victimizations, especially against children, through formal and informal surveillance techniques and by developing protective measures to prevent attacks. With these assumptions in mind, the goals of registration and notification become clear. The laws are intended to protect the public, particularly children, from sexual victimization; but to some degree, the laws are also intended to prevent homicide. These goals are to be accomplished by gathering and providing information to law enforcement agencies, so they may formally monitor sex offenders' whereabouts. These laws also provide law enforcement agencies with the tools (i.e., information) with which to solve crimes more quickly. The goals of these laws, however, are also to be attained through private-citizen action as well. Armed with information about sex offenders, the public can informally monitor sex offenders' activities and provide greater protection to children within the community.

The degree to which any criminal justice policy can achieve its goal rests on the assumptions on which it is built. To this end, we now compare the assumptions of sex offenders and offending inherent in registration and notification laws to empirical examinations of sex offenders' behaviors in order to determine the likelihood of registration and notification achieving the goals for which they were intended.

Assumptions versus Empirical Realities

Sex offender registration and notification policy makers seem to embrace the notion that sex offenders will inevitably reoffend; however, an examination of empirical research on the recidivism of sex offenders seems to refute this notion. Several researchers have investigated, both retrospectively and prospectively, sexual reoffending patterns among offenders hospitalized, incarcerated, or under treatment for sex crimes (for reviews see Furby, Weinrott, & Blackshaw, 1989; Becker & Hunter, 1992; Hanson & Bussiere, 1998). These scholars typically find variability in rates of reoffending from 3% to 55%, but most conclude, "The present findings contradict the popular view that sexual offenders inevitably reoffend. Only a minority of the total sample ... were known to have committed a new sexual offense" (Hanson & Bussiere, 1998, p. 357). Despite methodological difficulties, differences in sample size, and variability in follow-up lengths, most studies find some level of sexual reoffending among sex offenders, but generally, recidivism rates tend to be much lower for sex offenders than those found for other offender groups, and sex offense recidivism rates tend to be much lower than sex offender laws imply. Clearly, not all sex offenders inevitably reoffend.

Although these findings may seem to refute assumptions regarding the compulsivity of sexual reoffending, it is possible that some types of sex offenders exhibit higher rates of sexual recidivism than others. Scholars have noted variability in the rates of general reoffending for sex offenders with adult, as opposed to child, victims. Most have found that rapists or offenders with adult victims recidivate at a higher rate than child molesters (Marques, Day, Nelson, & West, 1994; Quinsey, Khanna, & Malcolm, 1998; Quinsey, Rice, & Harris, 1995). With regard to rearrests for another sexual offense, Sample and Bray (2006) found that those arrested for child pornography (10%) and those arrested on an "other" sex crime (such as juvenile pimping or soliciting a juvenile prostitute, 9%) were more frequently rearrested within 5 years for another sex crime than those arrested for rape, child molestation, pedophilia (sexual assault of a child 12 or younger), or hebophilia (sexual assault of a teen 13 to 18). Marques et al. (1994) also examined sexual recidivism among sex offenders with child and adult victims and found that a greater proportion of rapists were rearrested for another sex crime (9.1%) than child molesters (4%). Despite this information regarding the variability in recidivism rates across sex offender types, these data continue to suggest that sex offenders, irrespective of type, do not reoffend with great frequency.

Concerning sex offenders' propensity to murder their victims, scholars suggest that sex offenders rarely kill (Francis & Soothill, 2000; Sample, 2006). Francis and Soothill (2000) followed 7,436 convicted sex offenders in England and Whales in 1973 over a 21-year period and found that only 2.55% (or 19 of 7,436) were convicted for killing another person. Of these 19 people reconvicted, 11 had committed sex crimes against children (persons 16 or younger) in 1973. In regard to offenders' simultaneous raping and killing of their victims, Sample (2006) found that 3% of arrests in Illinois from 1990 to 1997 included a sex offense charge and a charge for homicide. When data were disaggregated by charges for specific sex crime types, the findings indicated no homicide charges were enacted in conjunction with arrests for child molestation, child pornography, or hebophilia, and only 1% of pedophilia charges were accompanied by a homicide charge. The findings seem to refute popular and legislative notions regarding the compulsivity of sex offenders and the degree to which their behavior turns increasingly toward murder. The studies also suggested that sex offenders are not a homogeneous group of offenders exhibiting similar recidivism patterns. This should be kept in mind when evaluating broad-based laws, such as registration and notification, that are intended to curb the likelihood of all sex offenders' reoffending equally and prevent child homicide.

The notions that children are often the targets of sex offenders' attention and that sex offenders are often strangers to their victims are also challenged by empirical evidence. Information on those most likely to be the victims of sex crimes is mixed. For instance, Snyder (2000) used National

Incident-Based Reporting System (NIBRS) data from 12 states to examine the victims of sex crimes and found that children 18 years or younger represented over two thirds of the victimizations of sexual attacks from 1991 through 1996. In contrast, an examination of all persons arrested in Illinois for any offense from 1990 to 1997 revealed that the majority of arrests for sex crimes (63%) were for raping an adult 18 years or older, not for crimes against children (Sample & Bray, 2006).

Several factors make it difficult to accurately assess trends in sex crimes against children. Most states and countries, when reporting arrests or crimes known to the police for sex crimes, do not differentiate between sexual crimes against adults or children. Data on sexual assaults are simply represented in the aggregate, irrespective of whether the crime was against someone over or under the age of 18. Moreover, the U.S. National Crime Victimization Survey (NCVS) does not interview anyone under the age of 12, making it impossible to discern the degree to which juveniles, 12 years or younger, experience sexual victimization. These deficiencies in data collection make conclusions about trends in offending against children virtually impossible to ascertain. There is agreement across data sources, however, with regard to the relationship between victims of sex crimes and offenders.

A review of the NCVS from 1996 to 2005 suggested that the majority of victims of sex crimes knew their attackers (Bureau of Justice Statistics, 2005). Only about one third of victims were assaulted by a stranger. Snyder's (2000) study of NIBRS data from 12 states reaffirmed these results, suggesting that only approximately 14% of his sample were assaulted by strangers, whereas slightly over one quarter were assaulted by a family member, and the vast majority of victims were attacked by an acquaintance. Given the information presented about sexual victimization, it appears that assumptions regarding children as frequent victims of sexual assault are difficult to validate. Undoubtedly, despite the impediments in obtaining reliable data on the age of victims, children do seem to be falling victim to sex crimes. What is known, however, is that most victims of sex crimes, both children and adults, know their attackers, calling into question the assumption of sex offenders as strangers to their victims. The information provided to the public by registration and notification is likely already known to victims and community members; therefore, although citizens search Web sites to discern information on potential strangers who may offend against their children, it is more likely that they already know likely offenders. While seeking out strangers, the public may overlook those family members, friends, or acquaintances who are more likely to victimize their children.

Given the way in which legislative assumptions comport to empirical information, the likelihood of registration and notification achieving their goals of protecting children and preventing future sexual victimizations and/or death appears bleak. However, empirical examinations of these laws' public acceptance and evaluations of effectiveness may prove otherwise.

Effectiveness of Registration and Notification Laws

Most scholars acknowledge that registration and notification laws were passed on misinformation and faulty assumptions about sex offenders and their behaviors, with no research-based evidence of their effectiveness, and with little thought to their long-term consequences for offenders (Cohen & Jeglic, 2007; Levenson, 2006; Levenson, et al., 2007; Sample, 2006; Sample & Bray, 2003, 2006; Sample & Kadleck, 2008; Shajnfeld and Krueger, 2006; Tewksbury, 2002, 2005; Zevitz, 2003; Zevitz & Farkas, 2000a). Nevertheless, researchers have recently begun investigating the effectiveness of community notification laws and the degree to which they inform the public and affect sex offenders' behavior.

Much has been written about contemporary registration and notification laws (Cohen & Jeglic, 2007) and what we know about the public's knowledge and acceptance of the laws (Levenson, 2003; Levenson et al., 2007; Phillips, 1998; Tewksbury, 2002, 2005; Zevitz & Farkas, 2000a). Several scholars, for example, have found widespread public knowledge and support for sex offender registration and community notification laws (Levenson et al., 2007; Martin & Marinucci, 2006; Phillips, 1998). Phillips (1998), for example, found that 80% of residents surveyed in 1997 were familiar with Washington's notification law and believed it was very important for improving public safety. Moreover, the majority of the 400 residents sampled reported feeling safer when armed with sex offender addresses and information. Levenson et al. (2007) also reported that the majority of respondents from their survey generally knew how notification of sex offenders was achieved by law enforcement agencies, believed that the public should have access to this information, and felt that notification strategies are effective at reducing sexual victimization. Despite the seemingly widespread support for registration and notification laws, this support may diminish, however, depending on the occupations of the residents surveyed.

Redlich (2001) surveyed community members, law enforcement officers, and law students to discern their attitudes toward notification laws. She found the groups significantly differed in their support for this legislation, with law students having less favorable opinions. Moreover, Malesky and Keim (2001) surveyed mental health professionals and found that over 80% of the respondents did not believe that notification would affect child victimization rates. Although there appears to be public support for notification laws, this support may be tempered by the educational level and occupation of respondents.

Despite the public support for these laws, scholars have suggested that few citizens may access sex offender information or act upon the information learned (Anderson & Sample, 2008). Anderson and Sample (2008) surveyed approximately 1,800 Nebraska residents and found that, although the overwhelming majority of residents knew of the registry and the availability of this information, only about one third of citizens accessed registry information, and most of these received their information from the newspaper as opposed to the registry Web site. Moreover, of those who accessed registry information, only one third took any preventive measures for themselves or their children as a result. Nevertheless, of those who did and did not access sex offender information, most (88%) felt personally safer, and safer for their families, knowing this information was available. Despite public support for registration and notification laws, it seems that few people may access this information, yet the knowledge that this information exists may make people feel safer. Other scholars, however, suggest these laws may do little to reduce public fear of victimization or reduce reoffending (Avrahamian, 1998; Petrosino & Petrosino, 1999; Tewksbury, 2002; Zevitz & Farkas, 2000a).

The utility of community notification laws is premised on the accuracy of sex offender information, yet empirical and journalistic investigations consistently reveal a significant amount of error in descriptions of sex offenders and their addresses (Lees & Tewksbury, 2006; Tewksbury, 2002). Not only is incorrect descriptive information about offenders often included on registry Web sites, but sex offenders also provide false addresses for their residences, which should not be surprising given the magnitude of their past crimes. To this end, on their very surface, these laws may be ineffective at informing the public, increasing the surveillance of offenders, and preventing future assaults simply because people do not access the information or the information that is accessed is inaccurate.

Even when information on sex offender registries is assumed to be correct, and notification procedures occur as intended, there are scholars that are still skeptical of these laws' ability to reduce offending (Adkins, Huff, & Stageberg, 2000; Avrahamian, 1998; Petrosino & Petrosino, 1999; Schram & Milloy, 1995; Tewksbury, 2002; Walker, Maddan, Vasquez, VanHouten, & Ervin-McLarty, 2005; Zevitz, 2003; Zevitz & Farkas, 2000a). After a review of the literature, Lovell (2007) concluded, "There is no evidence that community notification has resulted in a decreased number of assaults by strangers on children" (p. 3), and there is little evidence that the laws have had an effect on reducing intra-familial sexual abuse, which represents the majority of assaults against children. More specifically, Zevitz (2003) examined sex offenders who were subject to notification procedures. He tracked their rates of return to prison over a 4 ½-year period and found that, after controlling for demographic and criminal history variables, notification had no direct effect on the likelihood of being recommitted to prison. These findings reaffirm those of Walker et al. (2005) who suggested notification may do little to reduce incidents of rapes reported to police.

Despite these findings of ineffectiveness, other scholars have suggested that notification laws may have an effect on changing offenders' attitudes toward reoffending (Elbogen, Patry, & Scalora, 2003; Levenson & Cotter, 2005). Levenson and Cotter (2005) surveyed convicted sex offenders and found that some respondents noted an increased motivation to prevent reoffending as a function of notification laws and an increased honesty with friends and family regarding their past behaviors. To the degree that attitudes affect behavior, these studies offer some hope concerning notification laws' ability to reduce reoffending.

Beyond notification laws' impact on individual behavior, some researchers have begun investigating the effect of these laws on communities (Mustaine, Tewksbury, & Stengel, 2006; Telpner, 1997; Zevitz, 2003, 2004). Mustaine, Tewksbury, and Stengel (2006), for example, noted that sex offenders are often relocated after release from prison in communities characterized by greater levels of social disorganization, and by implication, communities with fewer resources to monitor and prevent deviant behavior. Zevitz (2003) also noted that sex offenders' relocation in the community often targets already fragile communities. Although the presence of sex offenders represents an initial destabilizing effect on neighborhoods, this destabilization may not be of such a magnitude that it permanently weakens a community's ability to recover and protect itself. Moreover, the knowledge of the presence of sex offenders in a community increases residents' fear of crime, and the strengthening of social ties among residents produces virtually no reduction in fear of child victimization (Zevitz, 2004). In sum, Telpner (1997) argued that notification laws potentially enable citizens to build communities on the premise that these neighborhoods are free from sexually dangerous persons. This soothes citizens' psyches and permits a vision of their neighborhood as safe from crime. These notions are contradicted, however, by findings that suggest notification may increase residents' fear of crime and destabilize community organization.

Although it remains unclear the degree to which notification laws achieve their intended goal of reducing reoffending and promoting community safety, most scholars agree that these laws have created unintended or latent consequences, mainly for offenders. Researchers have begun noting the adverse effects that registration and notification may have on offenders and their behaviors (Levenson & Cotter, 2005; Mustaine et al., 2006; Tewksbury, 2005; Tewksbury & Lees, 2006; Zevitz, 2003). Sex offenders reported experiencing harassment, social isolation, stigmatization, and feelings of vulnerability as a result of sex offender laws, all of which are associated risks of sexual offending (Levenson & Cotter, 2005; Tewksbury, 2005; Tewksbury & Lees, 2006). Moreover, offenders have experienced loss of employment, loss of housing, loss of social relationships, and property damage as a result of notification procedures (Ibid). Sex offenders are not the only individuals experiencing unintended consequences of notification, however. A study of probation and parole officers in Wisconsin revealed that these laws are accompanied by increased responsibilities and greater expectations for criminal justice agents (Zevitz & Farkas, 2000b). These authors concluded that any gains in public awareness and community protection resulting from notification laws come at a high cost for corrections in terms of personnel, time, and budgetary resources.

Registration and notification laws are intended to inform the public as to the whereabouts of convicted sex offenders with the hope of preventing reoffending. In fact, several scholars have directly examined notification's ability to reduce reoffending, but they have not found any significant effects of community notification on sex offenders' behavior (Adkins et al., 2000; Levenson, 2006; Schram & Milloy, 1995; Walker et al., 2005; Zevitz, 2003). Although notification may not promote significant reductions in recidivism, it appears to somewhat inform the public. However, rather than easing the public's fear of victimization, it seems that notification meetings may have the opposite effect and may increase public angst about sexual crimes (Zevitz & Farkas, 2000a). To the degree that registration and notification laws' manifest consequences were intended to reduce reoffending and ease public fear, these laws appear to be falling short of these goals. They have, however, succeeded in creating unanticipated, or latent, consequences for offenders.

Conclusions and Future Directions

The recently passed Sex Offender Registration and Notification Act housed within the broader Walsh Act, makes claims about the goals that registration and community notification can achieve. These claims have little foundation in light of the numerous studies discussed, which have indicated that registration and notification have had little to no influence on the rates of sex crimes in general or recidivism rates more specifically (Adkins et al., 2000; Schram & Milloy, 1995; Walker et al., 2005; Welchans, 2005; Zevitz, 2003). Not surprisingly, there has been criticism regarding the ability of the Walsh

Act to achieve its stated goals; however, three specific provisions yield significant controversy: the mandated juvenile registration provisions, the impact of a conviction-based schema versus a risk-classification schema, and the requirement to make failure to register a felony offense.

The Walsh Act has been suggested to be over-inclusive because it is conviction based, in that it mandates community notification for virtually all offenders, both adults and juveniles. Research findings demonstrate that sex offenders are not a homogeneous group of equal levels of offenders, and public disclosure of sex offenders' information can disrupt the stability of offenders in ways that may interfere with successful reintegration, thereby exacerbating risk for recidivism (Levenson & Cotter, 2005; Levenson, D'Amora, & Hern, 2007; Sample & Streveler, 2002; Tewksbury, 2004, 2005; Tewksbury & Lees, 2006, 2007; Zevitz & Farkas, 2000c).

Moreover, it could be argued that over-inclusion in sex offender laws is being achieved by the registration and community notification of juveniles 14 years or older, as required by the Walsh Act. This provision mandates that juvenile sex offenders be treated in a similar fashion as adult sex offenders and thereby negates longstanding goals of rehabilitation originally inherent in the creation of the juvenile justice system. This could have the effect of making a permanent class of sex offenders, whose behaviors were established in their youth and more firmly entrenched by institutional procedures of public notification.

Juvenile sex offenders will not only be subject to the intended consequences associated with being a registered sex offender, but they will also likely face the many unintended consequences that scholars have found. Stigmatization at school, inability to secure employment or higher education, harassment, and social isolation are just as likely for the juvenile offender as for the adult. Furthermore, the requirement of registration for juveniles may actually prevent parents from coming forward to report intrafamilial sexual assaults due to the fear that their child will have to register. Elizabeth Letourneau, professor at the Medical University of South Carolina, best summarized when she said, "If kids can't get through school because of community notification, or they can't get jobs, they are going to be marginalized, and marginalized people commit more crimes" (Jones, 2007).

Although the recently passed Walsh Act mandates a conviction-based system of classifications for notification, most scholars embrace the notion of a risk-based classification system, one that notifies the public of those assessed to pose the greatest risk to society (Levenson, 2006; Sample & Bray, 2006; Shajnfeld & Krueger, 2006). Community protection policies are more likely to succeed when used in a targeted manner rather than when broadly applied (Levenson, 2006). Also, as discussed in chapter 14, the containment model of supervision may be more effective at monitoring and preventing behavior.

A few sexually related homicides of children committed by strangers to their victims have left the public with the impression that they are at greater risk of victimization from strangers than acquaintances. Empirical data, however, suggest that this is not the case. The myth of the stranger sex offender has likely affected the techniques by which citizens protect themselves from victimization and possibly has left them vulnerable to the potential offenders they know. To this end, public safety may be enhanced through public education campaigns that better informing the public of trends in sex offending and victimization. As citizens are informed of the whereabouts of sex offenders, they should also be educated on preventive strategies and techniques. Scholars have noted increased levels of fear among the public after learning of sex offender information (Zevitz & Farkas, 2000a), yet few community notification procedures include information on preventive techniques. In light of the potential fear community notification may cause, public awareness policies should be accompanied by prevention campaigns with empirically driven information about the causes of offending and trends in victimization.

Beyond the stated criticisms regarding this new round of sex offender legislation, empirical evidence suggests that, in their current forms, registration and notification have little hope of making children and adults safer from sexual victimization and murder. Given the trends in victimization, the rates of recidivism and homicide among offenders, and the findings of evaluations of current registration and notification laws, scholars have begun to suggest moving toward evidence-based social policies for sex offenders (Lees & Tewksbury, 2006; Levenson, 2006; Shajnfeld & Krueger, 2006). Given the complex nature of the causes of offending, some have suggested multidisciplinary commissions be established to investigate the effects of sex offender polices on offenders' behavior and their reintegration into the community (Shajnfeld & Krueger, 2006).

The suggestions above are meant to help enhance the effectiveness of current registration and notification laws. They are not meant to dismiss the threat of sex offending, make light of the harm that victims endure, or demean the tragedy of sexually assaulted and/or murdered children. Nor are they intended to question or demean the desires and intentions of public officials that lie behind sex offender laws—primarily that of protecting the public from sexual harm and easing public fear (Sample & Kadleck, 2008). Rather our observations in this chapter are simply based on the history of sex offender laws, the assumptions therein, and evaluations of their effectiveness.

Sex offending is a reprehensible behavior with long-lasting consequences for the victims; therefore, this behavior needs to be managed, controlled, and prevented. This we cannot deny. Moreover, sex offenders' crimes invoke strong, fearful feelings from legislators and the public at large, which often prompt public officials into quick legislative action. Before enacting further policies to control this behavior, however, we need a careful examination of the laws currently enacted, a thorough review of the empirical evidence we currently possess, more research on the causes of the behavior, and a thoughtful synthesis of all this information. To the degree that we can pass policies that are empirically driven and address some of the causes of sex offending, rather than simply reaffirming misplaced assumptions about offenders, we may be able to enact laws that enhance public safety and achieve their goals.

References

Adam Walsh Child Protection and Safety Act of 2006, Pub. L. No. 109–248, 120 Stat. 587.

Adams, D. B. (2001). *Summary of State Sex Offender Registries, 2001.* Washington, DC: U.S. Department of Justice.

Adkins, G., Huff, D., & Stageberg, P. (2000). *The Iowa Sex Offender Registry and Recidivism.* Des Moines: Iowa Department of Human Rights.

Anderson, A. L., & Sample, L. L. (2008). Public awareness and action resulting from sex offender community notification laws. *Criminal Justice Policy Review.* Forthcoming.

Avrahamian, K. A. (1998). A critical perspective: Do ' Megan's Laws' really shield children from sex-predators? *Journal of Juvenile Law, 19,* 301–317.

Babington, C., & Weisman, J. (2006, October 2). FBI to examine Foley's email. *The Washington Post.* Retrieved August 11, 2008, from http://www.washingtonpost.com

Becker, J. V., & Hunter, J. A., Jr. (1992). Evaluation of treatment outcomes for adult perpetrators of child sexual abuse. *Criminal Justice and Behavior, 19*(1), 74–92.

Bernard, T. J. (1992). *The Cycle of Juvenile Justice.* New York: Oxford University Press.

Bishop, D. M. (2006). Public opinion and juvenile justice: Myths and misconceptions. *Criminology and Public Policy, 5*(4), 653–664.

Bureau of Justice Statistics. (2005). Washington, DC: U.S. Department of Justice.

Cohen, M., & Jeglic, E. L. (2007). Sex offender legislation in the United States: What do we know? *International Journal of Offender Therapy and Comparative Criminology, 51*(4), 369–383.

Congressional Budget Office Cost Estimate. (2006, March 8). H.R. 4472 Children's Safety and Violent Crime Reduction Act of 2005.

Connecticut Dept. of Public Safety v. Doe. (2003). 538 U.S. 1.

Elbogen, E. B., Patry, M., & Scalora, M. (2003). The impact of community notification laws on sex offender treatment attitudes. *International Journal of Law and Psychiatry, 26,* 207–219.

Evans v. Ohio, CV-08 646797 (2008).

Finn, P. (1997). *Sex Offender Community Notification* (NCJ 162364). Washington, DC: U.S. Department of Justice.

Francis, B., & Soothill, K. (2000). Does sex offending lead to homicide? *The Journal of Forensic Psychiatry, 11*(1), 49–61.

Furby, L., Weinrott, M. R., & Blackshaw, L. (1989). Sexual offender recidivism: A review. *Psychological Bulletin, 105*(1), 3–30.

Governmental Accountability Office, GAO (2006). National sex offender registry: New hires data has potential for updating addresses of convicted sex offenders. GAO-06-766.

Governmental Accountability Office, GAO (2008). Convicted sex offenders: Factors that could affect the successful implementation of driver's license related processes to encourage registration and enhance monitoring. GAO-08-116.

Hagan, N. E., & Cho, N. E. (1996). A comparison of treatment outcomes between adolescent rapists and child sexual offenders. *International Journal of Offender and Comparative Criminology, 34*(2), 105–113.

Hanson, K. R., & Bussiere, M. T. (1998). Predicting relapse: A meta-analysis of sexual Offender recidivism studies. *Journal of Consulting and Clinical Psychology, 60*(2), 348–362.

Jacob Wetterling Crimes Against Children and Sexually Violent Offender Registration Act, Pub. L. No. 103–322 (1994).

Jenkins, P. (1998). *Moral panic, changing concepts of the child molester in modern America.* New Haven CT: Yale University Press.

Jones, M. (2007, July 18). "How can you distinguish a budding pedophile from a kid with real boundary problems?" New York Times.

Lees, M., & Tewksbury, R. (2006). Understanding policy and programmatic issues regarding sex offender registries. *Corrections Today, 68*(1), 54.

Leonard, K. K., & Sample, L. L. (2000). Disparity Based on Sex: Is Gender-Specific Treatment Warranted? *Justice Quarterly 17*(1), 8–128.

Levenson, J. S. (2003). Policy interventions designed to combat sexual violence: Community notification and civil commitment. *Journal of Child Sexual Abuse, 12,* 17–52.

Levenson, J. S. (2006). "The New Scarlet Letter: Sex Offender Policies in the 21st Century." In David Prescott (ed.) Applying Knowledge to Practice: Challenges in the Treatment and Supervisions of Sexual Abusers. Forthcoming.

Levenson, J. S., Brannon, Y., Fortney, T., & Baker, J. (2007). Public perceptions and community protection policies. *Analyses of Social Issues and Public Policy, 7*(1), 1–25.

Levenson, J. S., & Cotter, L. P. (2005). The effects of Megan's Law on sex offender reintegration. *Journal of Contemporary Criminal Justice, 21*(1), 49–66.

Levenson, J. S., D'Amora, D. A., & Hern, A. L. (2007). Megan's Law and its impact on community re-entry for sex offenders. *Behavioral Sciences and the Law, 25*(4), 587–602.

Lovell, E. (2007). Megan's Law: Does it protect children? London: Policy and Public Affairs, NSPCC. Report retrieved 8/9/2007 at http://www.evidencenetwork.co.uk

Malesky, A., & Keim, J. (2001). Mental health professionals' perspectives on sex offender registry web sites. *Sexual Abuse: A Journal of Research and Treatment, 13*(1), 53–63.

Marques, J. K., Day, D. M., Nelson, C., & West, M. A. (1994). Effects of cognitive-behavioral treatment on sex offender recidivism preliminary results of a longitudinal study. *Criminal Justice and Behavior, 21*(1), 28–54.

Martin, M., Marinucci, C. (2006, July 18). "Support behind Tough Sex Offender Initiative." San Francisco Chronicle.

Matson, S., & Lieb, R. (1996). *Community notification in Washington State: A 1996 survey of law enforcement.* Olympia: Washington State Institute for Public Policy.

Mustaine, E. E., Tewksbury, R., & Stengel, K. M. (2006). Social disorganization and residential locations of registered sex offenders: Is this a collateral consequence? *Deviant Behavior, 27*(3), 329–350.

Petrosino, A. J., & Petrosino, C. (1999). The pubic safety potential of Megan's Law in Massachusetts: An Assessment from a sample of criminal sexual psychopaths. *Crime and Delinquency, 45*(1), 140–158.

Phillips, D. M. (1998). *Community notification as viewed by Washington's citizens.* Washington, DC: Washington State Institute for Public Policy.

Quinsey, V. L., Khanna, A., & Malcolm, P. B. (1998). "A Retrospective Evaluation of the Regional Centre Sex Offender Treatment Program." *Journal of Interpersonal Violence, 13*(5): 621–644.

Quinsey, V. L., Rice, M. E., & Harris, G. T. (1995). "Actuarial Prediction of Sexual Recidivism. *Journal of Interpersonal Violence. 10*(1): 85–105.

Redlich, A. D. (2001). Community notification: Perceptions of its effectiveness in preventing child sexual abuse. *Journal of Child Sexual Abuse, 10*(3), 91–116.

Representative Scott (VA). "Adam Walsh Child Protection and Safety Act of 2006." *Congressional Record* 152: 99 (July 25, 2006) p. H5723. Available from: Lexis Nexis Congressional; Accessed 11/9/08.

Sample, L. L. (2009). Sex Crimes and Policies. In Michael Tonry (ed.) *Handbook on Crime and Public Policy*. Oxford University Press, forthcoming.

Sample, L. L. (2001). The Social Construction of the Sex Offender. Unpublished Dissertation. University of Missouri – St. Louis.

Sample, L. L. (2006). An examination of the degree to which sex offenders kill. *Criminal Justice Review, 31*(3), 230–250.

Sample, L. L., & Streveler, A. J. (2002). Latent Consequences of Community Notification Laws. in *Controversies in Criminal Justice and Criminology*. Scott H. Decker, Leanne Fiftal Alarid, and Charles Katz (eds.). Los Angeles, CA: Roxbury Publishing. 353–361.

Sample, L. L., & Bray, T. M. (2003). Are sex offenders dangerous? *Criminology & Public Policy, 3*(1), 59–82.

Sample, L. L., & Bray, T. M. (2006). Are sex offenders different? An examination of re-arrest patterns. *Criminal Justice Policy Review, 17*(1), 83–102.

Sample, L. L., & Kadleck, C. (2008). Sex offender laws: Legislators' accounts of the need for policy. *Criminal Justice Policy Review, 19*(1), 40–62.

Sandberg, L. (2008). "Sex registry called too harsh for juveniles: New offender law groups teens with adults, regardless of recidivism risk." *Houston Chronicle Austin Bureau*. Accessed online 5/27/08 at: http://www.chron.com/disp/story.mpl/front/5549287.html

Schram, D., & Milloy, C. D. (1995). *Community Notification: A Study of Offender Characteristics and Recidivism*. Olympia, WA: Washington State Institute for Public Policy.

Senator Foley (FL). "Adam Walsh Child Protection and Safety Act of 2006." *Congressional Record* 152: 99 (July 25, 2006) p. H5725. Available from: Lexis Nexis Congressional; Accessed 11/9/08.

Senator Frist (TN). "Sex Offender and Registration and Notification Act." *Congressional Record* 152: 52 (May 4, 2006) p. S4089. Available from: Lexis Nexis Congressional; Accessed 11/9/08.

Shajnfeld, A., & Krueger, R. B. (2006). Reforming (purportedly) non-punitive responses to sexual offending. *Developments in Mental Health Law, University of Virginia, 26*(1), 31–53.

Smith v. Doe, 538 U.S. 84 (2003).

Snyder, H. N. (2000). Sexual Assault of Young Children as Reported to Law Enforcement: Victim, Incident, and Offender Characteristics. Washington D.C.: American Statistical Association. U.S. Department of Justice, Bureau of Justice Statistics.

Soothill, K., Francis, B., Sanderson, B., & Ackerley, E. 2000. Sex Offenders: Specialists, Generalists—or Both? A 32-year Criminological Study. *British Journal of Criminology*, 40, 56–67.

Telpner, B. J. (1997). Constructing safe communities: Megan's Law and the purposes of punishment. *Georgetown Law Journal, 85*(6), 2039–2068.

Tewksbury, R. (2002). Validity and utility of the Kentucky Sex Offender Registry. *Federal Probation, 66*(1), 21–27.

Tewksbury, R. (2004). Experiences and attitudes of female registered sex offenders. *Federal Probation, 68*(3), 30–33.

Tewksbury, R. (2005). Collateral consequences of sex offender registration. *Journal of Contemporary Criminal Justice, 21*(1), 67–81.

Tewksbury, R., & Lees, M. (2006). Perceptions of Sex Offender Registration: Collateral Consequences and Community Experiences. *Sociological Spectrum, 26*(3), 309–334.

Tewksbury, R., & Lees, M. (2007). Perceptions of punishment: How registered sex offenders view registries. *Crime & Delinquency, 53*(3), 380–407.

Walker, J. T., Maddan, S., Vasquez, B. E., Van Houten, A.C., & Ervin-McLarty, G. (2005). The Influence of Sex Offender Registration and Notification Laws in the United States. Retrieved December 15, 2005, from www.acjc.org

Welchans, S. (2005). Megan's Law: Evaluations of sexual offender registries. *Criminal Justice Policy Review, 16*(2), 123–140.

Zevitz, R. G. (2003). Sex offender community notification: Its role in recidivism and offender reintegration. *Criminal Justice Studies, 19*(2), 193–208.

Zevitz, R. G. (2004). Sex offender placement and neighborhood social integration: The making of a scarlet letter community. *Criminal Justice Studies, 17*(2), 203–223.

Zevitz, R. G., & Farkas, M. A. (2000a). *Sex Offender Community Notification: Assessing the Impact in Wisconsin.* Washington, DC: U.S. Department of Justice.

Zevitz, R. G., & Farkas, M. A. (2000b). The impact of sex-offender community notification on probation/parole in Wisconsin. *International Journal of Offender Therapy and Comparative Criminology, 44*(1), 8–21.

Zevitz, R. G., & Farkas, M. A. (2000c). Sex offender community notification: Managing high-risk criminals or exacting further vengeance? *Behavioral Sciences & the Law, 18*(2/3), 375–391.

---

[i] Nonviolent sex crimes refer to crimes such as possessing, viewing, or manufacturing child pornography, enticing a child, soliciting a minor, and other such offenses for which offenders must register upon conviction.

GPS Monitoring of Sex Offenders

Michelle L. Meloy &
Shareda Coleman

Background

The use of electronic technology as part of community supervision dates back to 1964, when it was first used in Boston (and Cambridge), Massachusetts (Crowe, Sydney, Bancroft, & Lawrence, 2002). Perhaps it is no coincidence that the city first experimenting with electronic systems to monitor criminals in the community was also the permanent home to John Augustus, a 19th-century boot maker who is often cited as the United States' pioneer of probation. Although a private citizen, Augustus's belief in the harms of alcohol and the social ills of drunkenness led him to bail out a "common drunkard" from a police court. Augustus convinced the judge to release the man into his custody and promised to return him to court for his next hearing. Three weeks later, Augustus's probationer appeared before the judge as a reformed man. Thus began Augustus's nearly 20-year career as a volunteer officer of the court, keeping hundreds of wayward criminals out of trouble by helping them secure housing, treatment, and employment. Augustus's success with his clients prompted the State of Massachusetts, in 1859, to formalize probation as a legitimate part of the criminal justice system (Friedman, 1993).

Other states followed, and today all 50 states and many countries around the world have similar systems. Parole, a form of conditional release from prison, was established during the same time period. Both probation and parole departments supervise offenders residing in the community and are the most likely criminal justice agencies to utilize electronic technologies for monitoring purposes. As a matter of fact, most convicted sex offenders spend at least some portion of their criminal sentence on probation or parole (Greenfield, 1997).

Although electronic monitoring first appeared on the criminal justice landscape over 40 years ago, it was not until the 1980s that electronic surveillance of offenders by way of "house arrest" was commonly used (Burks, 1989, as cited in Crowe et al., 2002). In 1988, the U.S Parole Commission and many state and local jurisdictions began experimenting with the use of electronic monitoring (EM) on releases. By 1991, the Federal Pretrial-Probation and Parole Systems had adopted the practice nationally (Gowan, 2000, as cited in Crowe et al., 2002). It was enthusiastically embraced by applied criminal justice professionals, the judiciary, and policy makers alike (Corbett, 1989). "Electronic supervision was heralded as a solution for many prevailing problems, including large caseloads, crowded jails and prisons, and the high costs of incarceration and supervision" (Crowe et al., 2002, p. 3).

Today, one of the fastest-growing areas of electronic monitoring is the use of Global Positioning Systems (GPS) to track the whereabouts of offenders on community-based supervision (Brown, Mccabe, & Wellford, 2007). This chapter describes what GPS monitoring is, the nuts and bolts of its operation, and some of the most important issues associated with its use. We then discuss sex offender laws and policies and how GPS is affecting this area of law, and we conclude with what is known about electronic monitoring, sex offenders, and community-based supervision.

GPS Costs and Other Issues

GPS is a worldwide navigational system that uses orbiting satellites to track a cell phone-size receiver's location, updating the position every few seconds (Brown et al., 2007). There are essentially three types of GPS used for community-based monitoring: active, passive, and hybrid. Active systems function via cellular technologies to transmit the tracked GPS data points to a software system for processing. These transmissions of data occur every couple of minutes, resulting in almost real-time offender tracking, but they are used in less than 20% of cases (Ibid). Passive GPS, the most commonly used system, tracks an offender's movements each day and downloads these data into the charger base each night (Ibid). This information is then transmitted to the supervising agency using telephone land lines. With passive GPS monitoring, probation and parole officers view the map points retroactively to assess the presence of a violation (i.e., an offender has entered exclusion zones, has exited the inclusion zones, or is near an address where a crime occurred).

A hybrid GPS system has evolved specifically to respond to the needs of the criminal justice system. The primary distinction of the hybrid system is the frequency with which GPS tracking points are transmitted back to the supervising department or vendor. In the hybrid tracking model, data are transmitted in a programmable, but less frequent, manner than in the active system, but the hybrid system automatically changes to an active monitoring mode at the first sign of a violation (Brown et al., 2007; Jannetta, 2006; New Jersey State Parole Board, 2007; Tennessee Board of Probation and Parole, with Middle Tennessee State University, 2007). The blended GPS tracking approach is generally less expensive than its real-time tracking counterpart.

The cost of GPS, for the state and for the offender, varies by jurisdiction. To illustrate, in 2007, the State of Tennessee charged offenders monitored with GPS a $50 monthly fee. Additionally, the state absorbed $2.2 million in expenses for 2 years of operational costs for the program (Turner et al., 2007). According to Brown and colleagues (2007), the average total cost per unit, per day is about $15 for active GPS and $13 for passive tracking systems, whereas other research has reflected a lower average daily rate of $8 for active real-time tracking systems and half that price for passive GPS (see Turner et al., 2007).

Aside from these direct expenses, other indirect costs are associated with the use of global positioning system monitoring. For example, many additional municipality or state workers may be needed to augment the existing work force to keep up with the increases in offenders sentenced to community based GPS programs (Brown et al., 2007.) Some critics argue that the high costs of electronic monitoring are unwarranted given that it can only reveal an offender's whereabouts, not prevent crime. However, even the highest daily cost estimates are far less expensive than incarceration rates that exceed $80 daily or nearly $30,000 annually (Brown et al., 2007). Given the outcomes comparing failure rates of sex offenders on community-based sanctions versus those who serve prison terms only (see forthcoming section), if electronic monitoring is a successful augmentation to probation and parole, it is likely to be a cost-effective criminal justice policy.

Goals and Limitations of GPS Monitoring

The most commonly cited goals of GPS monitoring of offenders are increased public safety, client compliance, and deterrence from additional crimes (Brown et al., 2007). Rational choice theorists would argue that GPS can deter criminal activity because of the offender's perceived certainty of getting caught because the offender believes that he or she is always being watched when wearing the GPS device. Social learning theories would suggest that the GPS tracking deters crime because it will likely discourage criminogenic associates from spending time with the monitored offender (i.e., these criminogenic associates do not want their actions watched or whereabouts tracked). The theory purports that it is this deviant association among peers that encourages and reinforces their illegal behavior. The socialization or clustering of sex offenders is of great concern to many officials. Thus, the states of Maryland, Minnesota, Oregon, and Wisconsin specifically forbid sex offenders from residing near one another (Meloy, Miller, & Curtis, 2008).

A "no victim contact" order or "no contact with minors" condition is common for sex offenders on probation or parole

(Meloy, 2006), and these mandates would be easier to monitor with GPS tracking. Having precise map points for an offender's whereabouts at any given time can also assist law enforcement agents in criminal investigations because these data can confirm an offender's presence near a crime scene at a critical time or exclude him or her from consideration (New Jersey State Parole Board, 2007). Under certain circumstances, GPS software can be programmed to signal an alert if an offender is in range of his or her victim's residence or other excluded locations such as parks or schools. Others have noted that GPS can also help alleviate jail or prison overcrowding conditions by providing judges or criminal justice officials with a more intensive, community-based supervision option, making probation or parole a viable option for more offenders (Brown et al., 2007; Renzema & Mayo-Wilson, 2005).

Despite the potential strengths of GPS monitoring, it cannot prevent crimes; rather, it serves only as a warning of an offender's location and enhances community supervision by making it easier for officers to monitor an offender's whereabouts (Brown et al., 2007). According to *USA Today* (2006), Wright argued that empirical data do not support the notion that GPS technology prevents sexual assaults (Koch, 2006, p. 2). In reality, the only way the criminal justice system can ensure that offenders do not recidivate is through lifetime incarceration or the implementation of the death penalty. Both of these options are problematic on fiscal, legal, and moral grounds.

There are several pragmatic limitations on today's use of GPS as a crime prevention tool. For example, equipment failure, lack of tamper-proof bracelets, and loss of GPS signals are all common problems. As a result of these factors, and others, a survey of criminal justice agencies found that investigating the actual cause for a GPS violation (i.e., offender rule breaking or technical failure) can be difficult, if not impossible. Furthermore, some geographical areas and/or offender employment positions are not conducive to GPS tracking. "Depending on the client's work, the client may need to continually go outside to acquire a signal, or the equipment may be cumbersome for such jobs as construction" (Brown et al., 2007, p. 63). Thus, a lost GPS signal may be the result of geographical or technological constraints, as opposed to offender tampering or other rule-breaking behavior.

Additionally, responding to every alert as though it were a serious threat to public safety results in undue stress for officers and victims. In Denver, Colorado, for instance, notification to potential victims of an offender's presence unnecessarily alarmed victims and resulted in the emotional fatigue of officers:

> This was due to responding to so many alerts (most of which were presumably benign) and the associated stress of possibly missing one. The agency realized that while GPS is an effective tool in assisting with a client's supervision, GPS itself is incapable of always ensuring a victim's safety. When the focus of the program changed from "protecting the victim" to simply ensuring more effective supervision, both officers and victims were happier. Victims are now only notified of [offender] alerts that pose potential alerts that pose potential threats (such as the [offender] venturing into the victim's exclusion zone). (Brown et al., 2007, p. 27)

Also, given that most offenders will be responsible for at least some of the fiscal requirements associated with GPS tracking, it could prove cost-prohibitive for some, thus regressively restricting the release options of offenders with lower socioeconomic status. In addition to the direct daily out-of-pocket offender expenses associated with GPS, individuals may be required to have a telephone land line and/or have access to cellular technologies, as well as a place to reside that will accommodate those. There are indications that a growing number of convicted sex offenders are becoming homeless as a result of restrictions on where offenders can reside (see Levenson & Hern, 2007). Obviously, living under highway viaducts or other common locales for homeless persons is not conducive to supporting the technological requirements of various GPS monitoring systems.

Finally, a significant limitation on today's GPS tracking of offenders is the inability to adequately measure its deterrent impact on a large scale. Most agencies do not have measures suitable for this type of analysis (Brown et al., 2007). Furthermore, random assignment to GPS tracking versus another sanction type or control group is required to make definitive statements regarding efficacy outcomes.

Unintended Consequences of GPS Usage

"With more information, comes more responsibility" (Brown et al., 2007, p. 25). One of the more serious implications for jurisdictions that use GPS is the potential increased liability should a victim be reinjured or a new crime committed. What is the legal responsibility of a department that has violation information for an offender who enters the exclusionary zone surrounding a victim's home? How long does an agency have to respond to this information? These important and difficult issues have yet to be answered by the courts.

The state of Texas encountered one such situation when a parolee who had been on passive GPS recidivated with another violent crime. When his previous whereabouts were reviewed retrospectively, it became clear by his patterns that he had been searching for new victims while being electronically monitored. This case resulted in numerous departmental changes in how GPS data are reviewed by officers, including the introduction of supervisor oversight (Brown et al., 2007).

The Tennessee Board of Probation and Parole, with Middle Tennessee State University (2007), in one of the few available outcome studies of sex offenders on GPS monitoring, reported that their officers were working as many as 60 hours per week and had nearly double the normal workload as a result of GPS tracking. This dramatic increase in manpower was not expected. The 24/7 nature of the job resulted in many officers feeling strained and overworked. One community-based supervision specialist discussed the impact on his personal life:

> We [GPS officers] are unable to enjoy our free time off. Our free time is interrupted by alerts...We cannot go hiking due to cellular coverage, cannot mow the lawn, we cannot leave the state to visit family or friends on our weekend off because of the response time, going out to dinner is often interrupted, and even taking a long bath. We are constantly on edge waiting for our next alert. Concerning our sleep, we may get a call at 2:00 a.m., and by the time we have cleared the latter, it is 5:00 a.m. or 6:00 a.m. and we have to get ready to come to the office for our regular scheduled shift. It can be exhausting. (pp. 30–31)

The lesson learned is that active GPS monitoring can dramatically increase officer workloads and should be considered when determining caseload sizes and the type of tracking system an agency will adopt, and the types of offenders to whom GPS monitoring will apply (Turner et al., 2007). Also, because the type of work required of GPS monitoring is more data-driven than traditional supervision, officers may perceive they have an increased workload even if the actual time spent on a case is the same (Brown et al., 2007).

Anecdotal evidence has indicated other unexpected outcomes: vigilante justice and employment barriers. For instance, one offender reported being accosted and threatened in the parking lot of a retail store because his GPS unit outed him as a sex offender, and others have reported a decrease in job offers because prospective employers frowned upon the GPS unit in the workplace (Tennessee Board of Probation and Parole, with Middle Tennessee State University, 2007).

Finally, the commonly perceived notion that GPS tracking can prevent crimes can lead to a false sense of security (Brown et al., 2007). As one released sex offender pointed out in a *USA Today* article "[monitoring] tells you where the offender is, not what he's doing" (Koch, 2006, p. 2). Furthermore, in the same article, Dr. Wright noted that some sex offenders will recidivate even with GPS monitoring. Extant literature and independent survey data collected here from criminal justice officials (forthcoming section) support the idea that the public needs to be properly educated about GPS tracking: that it can be an invaluable tool to community supervision but not a magic wand to ending sexual violence.

Sex Offender Legislation and GPS Monitoring

Keeping pace with sex offender laws at all levels of government is an almost impossible feat. Several factors affect the ever-changing legal landscape of sex offender legislation: public conceptions of "stranger danger," media presentations of sexual violence and the engendering of a moral panic over sex offenders, a "nothing works" treatment mentality, jail overcrowding, new technologies, and increasing pressure on policy makers to ensure community safety from released sex offenders (Meloy, Saleh, & Wolff, 2007).

Mandated GPS tracking of released sex offenders is the newest sex offender legislation to enjoy widespread popularity with lawmakers and the public. In an attempt to gain a real-time understanding of these laws and their geographical dispersion, we accessed all published materials on the subject and augmented these data with original research. A summary of our work is presented here.

The Interstate Commission for Adult Offender Supervision (ICAOS) published a 2007 report documenting survey results on each state's use of GPS tracking of released sex offenders. The report identified 35 states that, in some way, utilize this form of electronic monitoring.

We assumed that any validity threats to the information contained in the ICAOS report would be in the form of a Type II error (i.e., failure to identify a state that is actually using GPS tracking). To address this potential validity constraint, we contacted all of the 15 states identified in the 2007 report as non–GPS offender tracking jurisdictions and learned that as of 2008, most of them are now using GPS tracking for some sex offenders (see Table 8.1). Thus, based upon published materials and our independent research, it was determined that all 50 states require sex offender registration and community notification. Moreover , as of this writing there are 46 states that report using GPS monitoring and 35 state-level proximity laws restricting where sex offenders can reside or be physically present. Finally, 19 states have civil commitment procedures for (adult) sex criminals (see Interstate Commission for Adult Offender Supervision, 2007; Meloy, Miller, & Curtis, 2008; Meloy et al., 2007; Scott & Gerbasi, 2003).

The recent proliferation of GPS tracking appears heavily influenced by high-profile child victimizations by released sex offenders, a generalized public fear over sexual predators, exaggerated promises and claims of GPS technology, and technological advances that have made its use increasingly possible. The federal government (via the Adam Walsh Act) and nearly every state now use GPS tracking for released sex offenders.

In 2005, the Florida legislature passed the Jessica Lunsford Act (Stat. § 948.06) an influential piece of legislation named after a young girl who was kidnapped, raped, and murdered by a convicted neighborhood sex offender. Among other conditions, the law stipulates that released child molesters will be on active lifetime GPS surveillance,

8.1 Sex Offender Laws

State	Sex Offender Registration	Community Notification	Civil Commitment	Proximity Restrictions	Gps Monitoring
Alabama	X	X		X	X**
Alaska	X	X			
Arizona	X	X	X	X	X
Arkansas	X	X		X	X**
California	X	X	X		X
Colorado	X	X			X
Connecticut	X	X			X**
Delaware	X	X			X**
Florida	X	X	X	X	X
Georgia	X	X		X	X
Hawaii	X	X			
Idaho	X	X		X	X
Illinois	X	X	X	X	X
Indiana	X	X		X	X
Iowa	X	X	X	X	X
Kansas	X	X	X	statewide law prohibiting residency restrictions (2006)	
Kentucky	X	X		X	X**
Louisiana	X	X		X	X
Maine	X	X		X*	X
Maryland	X	X		X	X**
Massachusetts	X	X	X		X
Michigan	X	X		X	X

Minnesota	X	X	X	X	X**
Mississippi	X	X		X	EM
Missouri	X	X	X	X	X
Montana	X	X		X	X
Nebraska	X	X	X	X	X
Nevada	X	X		X	X**
New Hampshire	X	X	X		X
New Jersey	X	X	X		X
New Mexico	X	X			X
New York	X	X	X	X*	X
North Carolina	X	X		X	X
North Dakota	X	X	X	X*	X
Ohio	X	X		X	X
Oklahoma	X	X		X	X
Oregon	X	X		X	X
Pennsylvania	X	X	juveniles only		X
Rhode Island	X	X			X**
South Carolina	X	X	X		X
South Dakota	X	X		X	X
Tennessee	X	X		X	X
Texas	X	X	X	X*	X
Utah	X	X		X*	X
Vermont	X	X			
Virginia	X	X	X	X	X
Washington	X	X	X	X	X
West Virginia	X	X		X	X**
Wisconsin	X	X	X	X	X
Wyoming	X	X			

X* = Mobility-only restrictions

X** = Independent research identified these states as also using GPS at the offender's expense. Although using electronic technology to monitor convicted offenders was not a new concept, Jessica's victimization and Florida's law catapulted GPS legislation into high gear. Although many states have developed and implemented their own versions of Jessica's Law, the majority maintain a condition requiring GPS surveillance of offenders. As a result, global positioning system monitoring continues to gain popularity as a supervisory tool.

A review of Table 8.1's summary of sex offender laws and policies reflects that 15 states have all five forms of major sex offender policies (registration, community notification, civil commitment, proximity restrictions, and GPS tracking). These states are Arizona, California, Florida, Illinois, Iowa, Minnesota, Missouri, Nebraska, New York, North Dakota, South Carolina, Texas, Virginia, Washington, and Wisconsin. The geographical dispersion indicates that western, middle-west, and southern regions of the country are the most legislatively active in this area of policy. It would require additional measures to substantiate the legal punitiveness of a state's sanctioning of sexual criminals, but it is reasonable speculation that having all of the major forms of sex offender legislation is correlated with increased punitiveness ratings.

Content analysis of these categorical data reveals other noteworthy trends. For example, all 35 of the states with some form of state-level restrictions on residence or mobility also have GPS tracking of sex offenders. Even though neither proximity restrictions nor GPS tracking were created in the last 3 years, the implementation rates of both have experienced a notable increase since 2005. Residence restrictions and GPS tracking are both examples of the most recent era of sex offender laws and policies. Accordingly, states that already have one of these newest sex offender laws are significantly more likely to have the other type, suggesting that a cumulative effect or "more is more" mentality may be present.

Perceptions of Lawmakers and Practitioners about GPS

In an attempt to get a better understanding of how policy makers and criminal justice practitioners view issues related to GPS tracking of sex offenders, the authors conducted a nonrandom survey of representatives in several key states across the country. We identified 20 practitioners and policy makers to survey. We slightly overrepresented legislative officials (n = 12) in our sample and contacted eight community-supervision directors or GPS-tracking specialists (see Exhibit 8.1). All respondents were guaranteed anonymity in the analysis process. In total, we had a 50% response rate. Thus, the analysis provided herein is based on n = 10 surveys, representing six different states from the middle-west part of the country and the northeastern corridor that currently have GPS tracking.

Exhibit 8.1: Practitioner and Policy maker Survey for GPS Monitoring of Sex Offenders

1. Why does your state support the use of GPS for sex offender supervision? Public opinion, high-profile sexual crimes in your area, scientific backing in support of the technology, or something else?
2. How is GPS used in your state? For example, is its use mandated by the court? Is a court order required? Are other classes of offenders considered for GPS monitoring, or is it used only on sexual criminals? Does your state use a passive or active system?
3. To what extent do you believe your state's policy makers are aware of the science on sex offenders, sexual violence, recidivism, or deterrence? In other words, if and how are they informed of the studies pertaining to the causes of sexual violence, failure/success rates, risk factors for abuse and victimization, treatment issues for these offenders, and/or best practices for keeping communities safe from sex offenders?
4. What are the selection criteria of candidates for GPS monitoring? In other words, is it mandated for all convicted sex offenders or used only on some sex offenders? Do parole (or probation) officers determine who is appropriate for GPS? If so, how?
5. Do you believe GPS supervision is an effective deterrent? Why or why not? Has your state conducted any outcome studies on the effects of GPS supervision with sex offenders? If so, what are the results?
6. What other laws or techniques does your state use in response to sex crimes and sex offenders?
7. If you could design the perfect strategy to reduce rates of sexual violence in your state, what would it entail?

Analysis indicated that sex offender supervision is a priority for practitioners and policy makers. Yet, there appears to be a difference of opinions in terms of the best method for monitoring this population. Criminal justice professionals benefit from firsthand knowledge and experience with sex offenders, whereas lawmakers may not be privy to this type of practical data. Additionally, policy makers are accountable to their constituency in ways that practitioners are not. The marriage of these factors means that lawmakers are often criticized for being uninformed about the issues upon which they create laws.

As one Illinois community-supervision director put it, "there is a huge need to educate all elected officials [at the] local, state, and national [levels]." Similarly, a practitioner from the Utah Department of Corrections admits "difficulty in educating...our state legislature on the realities of sex offender deterrence and recidivism issues." It is impossible to create sound laws if legislatures are not aware of the sex offender research on prevalence, risks, recidivism, and deterrence.

Many of the legislative respondents perceived sexual violence as a stranger-danger crime committed by serial predators. This rationale motivated their desire for constant supervision of sex offenders upon release. In contrast, all of the practitioners had a more empirically based understanding of victim–offender relationships (i.e., known offenders, family members, intimate partners) and recidivism issues (i.e., only certain typologies of offenders have a propensity to be rearrested for sex crimes).

As previously noted, lawmakers are under tremendous pressure from the public at large to secure and protect the communities in which they are elected. In a recent survey, a Maine representative admitted, "Lawmakers...are strongly pressured by the public, which is very under-informed and emotional on the subject of sex offenders." Another criminal-justice practitioner, a GPS-tracking specialist from Pennsylvania, claimed, "It is mainly public pressure put on politicians" that motivates some of their policy-making decisions.

However, lawmakers see themselves as well versed on the issues pertaining to sex offenders. To illustrate, a state representative in a northeastern state informed the authors that, "Policy makers are very informed about sex offender issues. Policy makers understand that there are sick people out there, looking to harm our children, and in doing so, increase the potential for lifelong psychological and physical damages. That's why it is important to make sure that sex offenders don't re-offend," said the respondent. Whether GPS surveillance can accomplish this is an unresolved issue. Therefore, efforts must be made to bridge the gap between observations and expectations in order to prioritize evidence-based policies.

Ironically, some states that utilize GPS monitoring have not conducted analyses as to the value of its use. For example, representatives from both Maine and Utah admitted to a lack of outcome studies regarding GPS monitoring of sex offenders. While both states claimed to be in the early stages of implementing this supervisory tool, substantiated evidence would only benefit their pursuits. However, in other states, limited research has been conducted. In a recent New Jersey six-page report, the state claimed a deterrent effect to GPS monitoring of high-risk sex offenders (New Jersey State Parole Board, 2007). The 'success' of New Jersey's sex offender GPS tracking is one of the reasons the state representative we surveyed stated that he "enthusiastically supported" the state's GPS law because it will "help protect our communities from dangerous sexual predators," said this representative.

It is important to note that both policy makers and especially practitioners acknowledge that GPS monitoring is a tool in the arsenal of sex offender supervision and not a panacea to all the problems posed by convicted sex offenders. As such, it may not be used as a universal sanction. In fact, a Maine representative claimed the state is "currently limiting intensive surveillance tools to only high risk offenders for whom the technology serves a useful purpose." In restricting the application of GPS, officials may reduce its potential net-widening effect. Indeed, all sex offenders are not created equal and as such warrant consideration on a case-by-case basis. When used in conjunction with other supervision tools, many agree that GPS can be an effective and cost efficient program. To illustrate, one of our respondents, a Utah practitioner of sex offender probation, agrees that GPS is merely a "supplement [to] traditional supervision techniques." Despite the different motivations of policy makers and practitioners, they share a common goal of reducing recidivism. To that end, it is necessary to first engage in more research regarding the efficacy of electronic monitoring, with particular attention paid to GPS. Secondly, it is necessary to make policy makers aware of the results of these outcome studies so they can ensure evidence-based practices. Equally important is the education of the public at large, perhaps through mass media and other sources. Doing so will undoubtedly affect the demands the public often places on state and national legislatures.

Research on GPS Monitoring and Sex Offenders

The criminal justice system is increasingly reliant on community-based sanctions for monitoring of known sex offenders (Center for Sex Offender Management, 2002). "Sex offenders are being sentenced to probation and parole in record numbers, for increasingly long periods of time, and under more stringent conditions than ever before" (Meloy, 2006, p. 8). Technological advancements in electronic monitoring and GPS tracking are likely to increase the trend of placing sex offenders on community-based supervision. But isn't supervising sex offenders in the community the equivalent of risky business?

Actually, many experts believe that collaborative, surveillance-intensive, multifaceted approaches to probation and parole with a prioritization on sex offender group treatment produce the best chances of reducing sexual recidivism rates (Center for Sex Offender Management, 2002; Meloy, 2006; Meloy et. al., 2007). Reasons for this include low official recidivism rates for most types of sex offenders, especially when compared with other convicted felons (see Langan & Levin, 2002; Langan, Schmitt, & Durose, 2003); positive outcomes associated with successful completion of sex offender treatment (see Alexander, 1999; Aos, Phipps, Barnoski, & Lieb, 2001; Hall, 1995; Hanson et al., 2002; Lösel & Schmucker, 2005); and the lack of therapeutic intervention received by most prisoners (Turner, Bingham, & Andrasik, 2000).[i]

Studies specifically addressing sex offender recidivism during intensive community supervision found that offenders have recidivism rates comparable to or lower than other types of felons on probation and than sex offenders receiving jail or prison terms only (see Berliner, Schram, Miller, & Milloy, 1995; McGrath, Hoke, & Vojtisek, 1998; Meloy, 2005, 2006; Stalans, Seng, & Yarnold, 2002). For instance, Berliner et al. (1995) found that sex offender probationers were less likely to be rearrested for a new sex crime within a 24-month follow-up period, compared to the sex offenders who served only jail time (as cited in Stalans, 2004).

Further, the State of Vermont investigated the impact of specialized sex offender supervision by comparing sex offender probationers sentenced to standard probation and individual therapy sessions with a second sample of convicted sex offenders sentenced to specialized probation and man-dated group therapy that embraced a cognitive-behavioral modification focus. The probationers in the specialized pro-bation and treatment group had much lower failure rates (i.e., any new arrest) than the men sentenced to standard proba-tion and individual therapy (McGrath et al., 1998).

In another study, Stalans et al. (2002) investigated three counties in one midwestern state that utilized the contain-ment approach (English et al., 1996) to sex offender proba-tion by comparing sex offenders sentenced to specialized sex offender probation with sex offenders on standard pro-bation in each of three counties. Results indicated that in two of the three jurisdictions that were evaluated, recidivism rates were lower for some types of sex offenders on intensive community-based supervision where all of the stakeholders (i.e., officers, therapists, police, courts) worked collaborative-ly instead of using the more isolated strategy associated with traditional supervision (Stalans et al., 2002).

Meloy (2005) investigated the failure rate of a national sample of felony sex offender probationers, with an average follow-up period of 36 months. The sexual recidivism rate of the probationers was 4.5%, and the nonsexual recidivism rate was 12%. These failure percentages were lower than the recidivism rates for non–sex offenders on probation (see Langan & Cunniff, 1992), and slightly less than a national sample of sex offenders sentenced directly to prison (see Langan et al., 2003). Using a separate population of sex offenders sentenced to specialized community supervision, and combining qualitative and quantitative data, Meloy (2006) found that nearly 90% of the offenders in the study had no signs of sexual recidivism during the roughly 2-year observation period. Collectively, research outcomes support the use of intensive community-based supervision for most sex offenders.

There have been three studies to date that specifically examine sex offender supervision within the context of GPS tracking. These results are less conclusive. Turner et al. (2007) used a quasi-experimental design in their GPS sex offender research. The researchers ended up with a sample size of 95 parolees on GPS monitoring (treatment group) and a comparable (control) group of 88 sex offenders who were on parole but not assigned to GPS tracking. After 6 months, approximately 40% of offenders without GPS and slightly over 37% of offenders with GPS committed a new violation (i.e., technical infractions and new crimes). The failure rates between the groups were not significant. The one notable difference between the two groups concerned a significant drop in the percentage of parolees who absconded while on the GPS monitoring (2.1%) compared with 9.9% of the control group who absconded. In the end, the Center for Evidence-Based Corrections at the University of California, Irvine, found "GPS monitoring appeared to have little effect on parolee recidivism" in San Diego County (Turner et al., 2007, p. 34).

The State of Tennessee collected GPS data on nearly 900 sex offenders from September 2006 through October 2007. Of the total, 493 parolees were on GPS tracking (treatment group) and 370 "comparable" offenders were not (control group). Though they did not supply the raw data used in their statistical calculations, the researchers concluded that there was "no statistically significant difference" between the treatment and control groups (Tennessee Board of Probation and Parole, with Middle Tennessee State University, 2007). Although researchers controlled for most offender variables, many differences remained between the control and treatment groups. For example, the treatment group had a higher mean education level, and the offenders in the control group had a lower mean age of conviction. Despite these important differences in the groups, the conclusion of the Tennessee Board of Probation and Parole (2007) was that there were no statistically significant differences in the performance of parolees with or without GPS tracking.

The New Jersey State Parole Board released a report on the GPS tracking of sex offenders on December 5, 2007, totaling six pages in length. The report contained limited information on the research methodology used in a pilot study comprising upwards of 225 parolees on GPS tracking. Findings indicated that only one offender committed a new sex crime within the 2 year observation period and that 19 others committed a nonsexual offense or had a technical violation. No specificity was provided with regard to how many of the 19 offenders committed a new nonsexual offense or how many of these men had technical charges. However, these profoundly positive results should be interpreted with more caution than the other GPS studies because methodological information was not available for review, no control group was used in the study, and researchers did not appear to account for an offender's time at risk. In other words, only a portion of the subjects in the GPS pilot study were followed for the full 24 months. Furthermore, it is impossible to determine how many of the 225 subjects were observed for the full observation period. Although these results are encouraging, more reliable replication studies are needed.

A few more studies examined the impact of electronic monitoring on community supervision more broadly by either including heterogeneous populations of offenders in the analysis (sex and non–sex offenders) or by including different forms of electronic surveillance. Padgett, Bales, and Blomberg's (2006) study included over 75,661 Florida offenders over a 2-year span to "estimate the effect of radio frequency (RF) and GPS monitoring on the likelihood of revocation and absconding from supervision" (p. 63). In their analysis, Padgett et al. (2006) divided offenses by seriousness level into three categories: violent, property, and drug offenses. Results generally showed that those sentenced to EM were more likely to have been convicted of a violent offense (including, but not limited to, a sex offense) than those not on EM at all. Generally, results indicated that those sentenced to electronic monitoring while on home confinement were both less likely to commit technical violations and less likely to commit a new offense.

In terms of the differences between the two types of supervision, those on GPS were found to "have risk levels significantly higher than those on RF" (Padgett et al., 2006, p. 75). The real-time tracking associated with GPS may make it more applicable for serious offenders. Ironically, Padgett et al.'s (2006) study found RF only "slightly more effective" than GPS at reducing the likelihood of revocation for a new offense and for absconding from supervision. With regard to violent offenders, for example, RF monitoring was responsible for a 98.1% reduction in failure outcomes, compared to

91.5% for GPS monitoring. However, the modest difference between these two types of supervision does not undermine the utility of GPS. Although these results paint a relatively positive portrait of GPS monitoring, finding its use a significant cause of lower recidivism, "policy makers cannot conclude from this study that EM 'works'" (Mair, 2006, p. 57). On the contrary, these findings are far too insignificant and lack generalizability.

In their review of the literature surrounding electronic monitoring, Renzema and Mayo-Wilson (2005) identified empirically valid studies that focused on moderate- to high-risk offenders. The authors concluded, "After 20 years of EM, we have only a few clues as to its impact" (p. 233). This dismal forecast is due in large part to the manner in which electronic monitoring is implemented; that is, as an "intervention that is typically quite short, applied in a standard fashion, and applied to a diverse group of offenders for whom it may or may not have any relevance to their motives for offending" (p. 232).

The authors highlighted a study by Finn & Muirhead-Steves (2002) wherein the latter two researchers explored the impact EM has on high-risk, violent male parolees in Georgia. Notwithstanding intervening variables, recidivism rates were slightly reduced for the small subgroup of sex offenders in the study.[ii] However, overall results show electronic monitoring had "no direct effect on the likelihood of recommitment to prison or time until failure" (Finn & Muirhead-Steves, 2002, p. 293). In fact, within about three years of release, nearly a quarter of the electronic monitoring group and a quarter of the non-electronically monitored comparison group were returned to prison (Renzema & Mayo-Wilson, 2005). Therefore, there was no significant difference in outcomes between the two groups.

Similarly, Bonta, Wallace-Capretta, & Rooney's (2000) research found EM only somewhat useful when used in conjunction with a court order. For probationers under EM supervision, the results indicate an 87% compliance rate with treatment as opposed to a 52.9% rate for those not under supervision. It must be noted, however, that "it is impossible to gauge whether higher completion rates were due to EM or due to the threat of revocation" (Renzema & Mayo-Wilson, 2005, p. 230). Combined, the studies listed above demonstrated "no overall impact on recidivism at the longest follow-up period for each study, periods that ranged from one to three years" (Ibid). What is clear is the need for more research.

Conclusion

GPS monitoring of sex offenders is a common sex offender policy being used in most states. This chapter discussed some of the strengths and limitations associated with GPS monitoring, with a particular focus on its efficacy and what is known about the outcomes associated with the growing trend of sentencing sex offenders to community-based sanctions. Criminal justice experts and policy makers were questioned about their perceptions of GPS tracking. Surveyed practitioners were positive about its use, assuming it was implemented and managed responsibility. Still, they were quick to point out its limitations and state that GPS is simply another tool to aid practitioners, not a magic bullet to end the problem of sexual violence. Policy makers were less restrained in their optimism regarding GPS surveillance's ability to deter sex crimes.

Extant literature on community-based sanctions for sex offenders indicated that probation and parole is a reasonable, if not preferable, sentencing option for most sex offenders. To what extent GPS might add to these favorable results is unclear. Thus far, the effects of electronic monitoring in general, and GPS monitoring specifically, are inconclusive. Although a few studies have declared its deterrent appeal, at best it appears that GPS surveillance for sex offenders has a null effect on sex offender recidivism. Thankfully, results do not indicate a criminogenic effect upon the offender, although some concerns are raised (e.g., vigilante justice, employment barriers, fiscal discrimination against the poorest offenders). Methodologically rigorous outcome studies must be prioritized, as well as educating policy makers and the public regarding the realistic strengths and limitations of GPS tracking.

We would be remiss if we did not address the potential influence that the commercialization of GPS technologies might have on criminal justice practices. According to Mair (2006), "[v]endors of EM equipment are out to make money...the marketing of a product can, of course, involve claims about 'effectiveness' that have no empirical grounding that would be acceptable to academic standards" (p. 58). If profit-seeking vendors put revenue over empirical validity, they perpetuate a flow of misinformation to both policy makers and the public at large. Other factors must also be considered when evaluating GPS supervision. For instance, is GPS most effective for low-, moderate-, or high-risk offenders? Is it better at reducing new sex crimes or just technical violations? The limited research has failed to adequately address these and other issues surrounding GPS monitoring. This dearth of information must be addressed before best practices in sex offender supervision can be achieved.

References

Alexander, R., Jr. (2004). The United States Supreme Court and the civil commitment of sex offenders. *The Prison Journal, 84*(3), 361–378.

Alexander, M. (1999). Sex offender treatment efficacy revisited. *Sexual Abuse: A Journal of Research and Treatment, 11*, 101–116.

Aos, S., Phipps, O., Barnoski, R., & Lieb, R. (2001). The comparative costs and benefits of programs to reduce crime. Olympia: Washington State Institute for Public Policy.

Berliner, L., Schram, D., Miller, L., & Milloy, C. (1995). A sentence alternative for sex offenders: A study of decision making and recidivism. *Journal of Interpersonal Violence, 10*, 487–502.

Bonta, J., Wallace-Capretta, S., & Rooney, J. (2000). Can electronic monitoring make a difference? An evaluation of three Canadian programs. *Crime and Delinquency, 46*(2), 61–75.

Brown, T., McCabe, S., Wellford, C. (2007). Global positioning system (GPS) technology for community supervision: Lessons learned. Washington, D.C., National Institute of Justice, Office of Justice Programs, U.S. Department of Justice.

Center for Sex Offender Management. (2002). *Managing sex offenders in the community: A handbook to guide policymakers and practitioners through a planning and implementation process*. Washington, DC: U.S. Department of Justice.

Corbett, R. (1989). Electronic Monitoring. *Corrections Today, 51*, 6.

Crowe, A., Sydney, L., Bancroft, P., Lawrence, B. (2002). Offender supervision with electronic technology: A user's guide. Washington, DC: U.S. Department of Justice.

English, K, Pullen, S., Jones, L. (1996). *Managing adult sex offenders*: A containment approach. Lexington, KY: American Probation and Parole Association.

Finn, M. A., & Muirhead-Steves, S. (2002). The effectiveness of electronic monitoring with violent male parolees. *Justice Quarterly, 19*(2), 293–312.

Florida statute § 948.06

Friedman, L. (1993). *Crime and punishment in American history*. New York: Basic Books.

Greenfield, L. (1997). Sex offenses & offenders: An analysis on data of rape and sexual assault. Washington, DC: U.S. Department of Justice. Bureau of Justice Statistics.

Hall, G. (1995). Sex Offender Recidivism Revisited: A Meta-analysis of Recent Treatment Studies. *Journal of Consulting and Clinical Psychology*, 63, 802–809.

Hanson, R., Gordon, A., Harris, A., Marques, J., Murphy, K., Quinsey, V., et al. (2002). First Report of the Collaborative Outcome Data Project on the Effectiveness of Psychological Treatments of Sex Offenders. *Sexual Abuse: A Journal of Research and Treatment*, 14, 169–194.

Interstate Commission for Adult Offender Supervision. (2007). GPS Update Survey. Retrieved February 19, 2007, from http://www.interstatecompact.org/LinkClick.aspx?fileticket=lU6GvRmuPwM%3d&tabid=105&mid=431

Jannetta, J. (2006). GPS monitoring of high-risk sex offenders [Working paper]. Retrieved January 24, 2008, from http://ucicorrections.seweb.uci.edu/pubs

Koch, W. 2007. More sex offenders tracked by satellite. *USA Today*. Retrieved electronically on August 2, 2008 from http://www.usatoday.com/tech/news/techinnovations/2006-06-06-gps-tracking_x.htm.

Langan, P., & Cunniff, M. (1992). Recidivism of Felons on Probation, 1986–1989. Washington, D.C.: U.S. Department of Justice.

Langan, P., & Levin, D. (2002). Recidivism of Prisoners Released in 1994. Washington, D.C.: U.S. Department of Justice.

Langan, P., Schmitt, E., & Durose, M. (2003). Recidivism of Sex Offenders Released from Prison in 1994. Washington, D.C.: U.S. Department of Justice.

Lösel, F., & Schmucker, M. (2005). The Effectiveness of Treatment for Sexual Offenders: A Comprehensive Meta-Analysis. *Journal of Experimental Criminology*, 1, 117–14.

Levenson, J., & Hern, A. (2007). Sex Offender Residence Restrictions: Unintended consequences and community reentry. *Justice Research & Policy*, 9–59–73.

McGrath, R., Hoke, S., & Vojtisek, J.E. (1998). Cognitive-behavioral Treatment for Sex Offenders: A Treatment Comparison and Long-Term Follow-Up Study. Criminal Justice and Behavior, 25, 203–205.

Mair, G. (2006). Electronic Monitoring, Effectiveness, and Public Policy. *Criminology and Public Policy*, 57–60.

Meloy, M.L. (2005). The Sex Offender Next Door: An Analysis of Recidivism, Risk Factors and Deterrence of Sex Offenders on Probation. *Criminal Justice Policy Review*, 16, 211–236.

Meloy, M.L. (2006). Sex *Offenses and the Men Who Commit Them*. Boston: Northeastern University Press.

Meloy, M.L., Miller, S., Curtis, K.M. (2008). Making Sense out of Nonsense:

The Deconstruction of State-Level Sex Offender Residence Restrictions. *American Journal of Criminal Justice*, 33, 209–222.

Meloy, M.L., Saleh, Y., & Wolff, N. (2007). Sex Offender Laws in America: Can Panic Driven Legislation ever Create Safer Societies? *Criminal Justice Studies*, 20(4), 423–443.

New Jersey State Parole Board (2007). Report on New Jersey's GPS Monitoring of Sex Offenders. Accessed March 1, 2007 from www.state.nj.us/parole/docs/reports/gps.pdf

Padgett, K. G., Bales, W.D., & Blomberg, T.G. (2006). Under Surveillance: An Empirical Test of the Effectiveness and Consequences of Electronic Monitoring. *Criminology & Public Policy*, 5(1), 61–92.

Renzema, M., & Mayo-Wilson, E. (2005). Can Electronic Monitoring Reduce Crime for Moderate to High-risk Offenders? *Journal of Experimental Criminology*, 1, 215–237.

Scott, C., & Gerbasi, J. (2003). Sex Offender Registration and Community Notification Challenges: The Supreme Court Continues Its Trend. *The Journal of the American Academy of Psychiatry and the Law*, 31, 494–501.

Stalans, L., Seng, M., & Yarnold, P. (2002). Long-term Impact Evaluation of Specialized Sex Offender Probation Programs in Lake, DuPage, and Winnebago Counties. Chicago: Illinois Criminal Justice Information Authority.

Stalans, L. (2004). Adult Sex Offenders on Community-based Supervision: A Review of Recent Strategies and Treatment. *Criminal Justice and Behavior*, 31, 564–608.

Tennessee Board of Probation and Parole, with Middle Tennessee State University (2007). Monitoring Tennessee's sex offenders using global positioning systems: A project evaluation. Retrieved February 8, 2008 from http://www2.state.tn.us/bopp/Press%20Releases/BOPP%20GPS%20Program%20Evaluation,%20April%202007.pdf

Turner, B., Bingham, J., & Andrasik, F. (2000). Short-term Community-based Treatment for Sexual Offenders: Enhancing Effectiveness. *Sexual Addiction & Compulsivity*, 7, 211–223.

Turner, S., Jannetta, J., Hess, J., Myers, R., Shah, R., Werth, R., & Whiltby. (2007). Implementation and Early Outcomes for the San Diego High Risk Sex Offender (HRSO) GPS PilotProgram. University Of California, Irvine. Center For Evidence-Based Corrections (Irvine, Ca). Retrieved February 6, 2008 from http://ucicorrections.seweb.uci.edu/pubs

---

The authors recognize the extraordinary assistance of Rutgers University students Michael Moncil, Lisa Descano, and especially Kristin M. Curtis. Their collective dedication to this project and commitment to the pursuit of identifying best practices in sex offender policy were invaluable to the completion of this research.

[i] Readers should be mindful that these figures are likely an underestimation of the true extent of sexual reoffending. Most studies use official data sources (arrests and reconvictions) to compile failure rates. Sex crimes are believed to be significantly underreported by victims, so there are undoubtedly sex crimes committed by these offenders that go undetected by law enforcement or community-based officers.

[ii] According to Renzema and Mayo-Wilson (2005), sex offender desistance may be explained by the additional year EM offenders spent under supervision, compared to the control group. This extension possibly granted these offenders "extensive and more competent overall treatment" needed for desistance (p. 228).

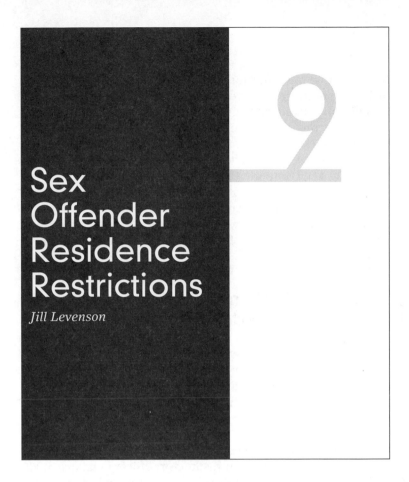

Sex Offender Residence Restrictions

Jill Levenson

9

National sex offender registration began in 1994 with the passage of the Wetterling Act. It was not until 1996, however, with the implementation of Megan's Law, that information regarding sex offenders and their whereabouts was made public. Over the past decade, the availability of online sex offender registries has enabled widespread awareness of sex offenders living in the community, increasing concerns for the safety of children and leading politicians to pass laws restricting where sex offenders can live. Residence restrictions typically prohibit individuals convicted of sex crimes from residing within 500 to 2,500 feet of schools, parks, playgrounds, day care centers, bus stops, and other places where children are commonly present.

Popular with citizens and politicians, these laws are not without controversy. The prospect of sexual predators living in residential neighborhoods is frightening. The proliferation of increasingly restrictive zoning laws, however, has led to homelessness and transience for many offenders, provoking calls for reconsideration of the laws' utility. This chapter will first describe the range of housing laws commonly enacted in states, counties, and cities across the United States. Subsequently, their intended goals will be explored, as will the congruence of such intentions with available research data. The unanticipated and collateral consequences of housing restrictions will be reviewed, and the chapter will conclude with recommendations for evidence-based sex offender management strategies.

History and Implementation of Residence Restrictions in the United States

Currently, at least 30 state laws have been passed to prohibit sex offenders from residing near places frequented by children (Meloy, Miller, & Curtis, 2008). About half are associated with registration statutes and apply to all registered sex offenders, regardless of the victim's age. Other statutes apply to convicted sex offenders who are under some sort of probationary supervision, and some apply only to those with minor victims. The most common distance requirements are 1,000 to 2,000 feet, with a handful of states designating smaller buffer zones. Protected venues typically include schools, parks, playgrounds, and day care centers, but some laws include other facilities such as arcades, amusement parks, movie theaters, youth sports facilities, school bus stops, and libraries. Though 60% of states have enacted such legislation, state laws are absent in some regions of the country such as the far northeast and the central states (Ibid).

The first state law restricting where sex offenders can live was passed in Florida in 1995. Applying only to sex offenders on probation who abused minor victims, this law created 1,000-foot buffer zones around schools, parks, playgrounds, day care centers, and other places where children congregate. By 2004, 15 states (Alabama, Arkansas, California, Delaware, Florida, Georgia, Illinois, Indiana, Iowa, Kentucky, Louisiana, Ohio, Oklahoma, Oregon, and Tennessee) had enacted similar legislation. In 2005, after the murder of 9-year-old Jessica

Lunsford by a convicted sex offender living near her home in Florida, fear of sex offenders reached a new level. Strategies for protecting children from sexual predators were a top priority for politicians, and between 2005 and 2007, the number of states with housing restrictions doubled (Meloy et al., in press; Nieto & Jung, 2006).

Perhaps the most notorious of these laws are found in Iowa, Georgia, and California. In 2002, Iowa passed one of the strictest state laws in the nation, banning sex offenders from living within 2,000 feet of schools and day care centers. A judge ruled the law unconstitutional, declaring that it amounted to ex post facto punishment (*Doe v. Miller and White*, 2004). The ruling was later overturned by the Eighth Circuit Court of Appeals (*Doe v. Miller*, 2005), and the law was upheld as well by the Iowa Supreme Court (*State v. Seering*, 2005). When the law was reinstated in 2005, it was retroactively applied to its original implementation date in 2002, and thousands of sex offenders were forced to relocate, creating a crisis of transience for sex offenders and law enforcement officials. In response, Iowa prosecutors, victim advocates, and law enforcement personnel lobbied for reforms, asserting that housing laws create more problems than they solve and undermine the purpose of sex offender registries because homeless sex offenders are more difficult to track and monitor (CALCASA, 2006; Iowa County Attorneys Association, 2006; NAESV, 2006).

In Georgia, a 2006 statewide ban on living or working within 1,000 feet of schools, day care centers, and bus stops threatened to displace 15,000 registered sex offenders. The law was quickly challenged, and in December 2007 the Georgia Supreme Court struck down the law as unconstitutional due to protection of property rights (*Mann v. Georgia Department of Corrections et al.*, 2007). According to the Southern Center for Human Rights, the decision was interpreted as applying only to homeowners but will again be challenged by the Southern Center for Human Rights (Southern Center for Human Rights, 2008).

In California in 2006, voters overwhelmingly passed Proposition 83 (which was named *Jessica's Law* for Jessica Lunsford) despite being publicly opposed by the state's victim advocacy group (CALCASA, 2006). The law includes, among other initiatives, a 2,000-foot residential restriction law. Concerns were voiced that the law would displace the nearly 100,000 sex offenders on California's registry, but the statute was later interpreted by the attorney general not to be retroactive. Legal challenges are pending in the California Supreme Court.

On the other hand, the state of Kansas took a more cautious approach to implementing housing restrictions and in November of 2006 solicited testimony from nationally recognized sexual violence experts during a judiciary committee hearing. As a result, the Kansas Sex Offender Policy Board issued a report recommending against housing laws but noting that "residency restrictions are extremely popular with the general public, thus making policy makers' decision on this issue a difficult one" (Kansas Sex Offender Policy Board, 2007, p. 26). The board recognized the dilemma of lawmakers:

> The appeal of residence restrictions is to protect public safety, and more specifically, the safety of children. The fundamental issues to consider are whether residence restrictions for sex offenders have been proven to protect public safety, whether the theory behind residence restrictions is consistent with research and best practices in the fields of corrections and law enforcement, the viability of enforcing the restrictions, and whether the resources utilized for such an effort would be best directed toward alternative measures that would protect a larger segment of the population and/or one that is at a higher risk of victimization. (pp. 26–27)

After considering the potential benefits and detriments of sex offender buffer zones, the Kansas State Legislature elected not to enact a statewide law and prohibited local municipalities from establishing their own ordinances.

In 2005, a new phenomenon swept across the country— the passage of municipal sex offender housing ordinances. These laws are passed by local jurisdictions (cities, towns, and counties) and often exceed state laws by expanding restricted areas to 2,500 feet (almost a half mile) surrounding places where children commonly congregate. The first local ordinance in the country was passed in Miami Beach, Florida, in June 2005, fashioned after zoning laws preventing the operation of adult establishments within 2,500 feet of schools. By 2008, over 133 municipal ordinances had been passed in Florida.

Local restrictions have emerged throughout the nation, and can be found in most states, even those without statewide statutes. City and county councils appear to fear that if they do not enact laws similar to those of their neighbors, their towns will become a dumping ground for sex offenders. This tends to produce a domino effect as surrounding towns and counties create protected zones in an effort to keep exiled sex offenders from migrating to their communities. As Commissioner Peter Bober, from Hollywood, Florida, told the *South Florida Sun Sentinel* in May 2007, "Other cities already have them and if we fail to act, then we put a big target on ourselves as being a desirable place for sex offenders to reside" (Rodriquez, 2007).

Legislative Intent of Residence Restrictions

Residence restrictions are well-intentioned policies designed to protect children from sexual assault. For example, consider the background section of California's Proposition 83, passed by 70% of voters in November 2006, which states,

> Sex offenders have very high recidivism rates. According to a 1998 report by the U.S. Department of Justice, sex offenders are the least likely to be cured and the most likely to reoffend, and they prey on the most innocent members of our society. More than two-thirds of the victims of rape and sexual assault are under the age of 18. Sex offenders have a dramatically higher recidivism rate for their crimes than any other type of violent felon. (California Secretary of State, 2006)

Likewise, the city of Jacksonville, Florida, adopted a local ordinance, and the City Council set forth a number of assertions (City of Jacksonville, 2005), including the following:

> **WHEREAS**, the City of Jacksonville is deeply concerned about the numerous recent occurrences in our state and elsewhere, whereby convicted sex offenders who have been released from custody repeat the unlawful acts for which they had originally been convicted; and **WHEREAS**,

the City finds from the evidence the recidivism rate for released sex offenders is alarmingly high, especially for those who commit crimes on children. (p. 1)

Furthermore, legislators often refer to high recidivism rates to explain the need for sex offender policies. ""What we"re up against is the kind of criminal who, just as soon as he gets out of jail, will immediately commit this crime again at least 90 percent of the time ... that percentage is one of the sad givens of this kind of illegal activity,"" Assemblyman Bill Hoge of Pasadena, sponsor of a proposed California castration bill, told the New York Times (Drummond Ayres Jr., 1997).

Lobbyist Ron Book, who pioneered the enactment of municipal housing laws in Florida, proclaimed to the *South Florida Sun Sentinel* newspaper in February 2008:, "When an individual gets convicted for sexually deviant behavior, at the end of the day nobody wants them living in their apartments."

The *New Hampshire Valley News* reported that Attorney General Kelly Ayotte asked lawmakers to strengthen penalties against sex offenders in 2006, using a familiar argument: "I don't want you to be fooled ... sex offenders are committing the same type of offense over and over" (Tillman, 2006).

The *Columbus Dispatch,* in October 2007, quoted Delaware County Prosecutor David Yost, who supports residency restrictions: "Keeping sex offenders away from schools is just an obvious thing to do," Yost said (Lane, 2007). "I'm concerned that a lot of people in public policy are being put off by the argument that there's no evidence that these kinds of restrictions help. There are times we have laws and there is not empirical proof that they help something, yet we don't throw common sense out."

Similarly, in a criminal justice committee meeting of the Florida House of Representatives on March 19, 2008, Rep. Luis Garcia said, "As long as it saves one [child] from being abused or molested, so be it ... if they want to sue us for protecting our kids, let them do that. If it was up to me, I wouldn't put them 2,500 feet away, I'd put them in the next country" (*Florida House of Representatives,* March 19, 2008).

A recent study of legislators from Illinois shed light on the political rationale for sponsoring sex crime prevention bills (Sample & Kadleck, 2008). The authors interviewed

25 state legislators and found several common themes. Sex offenders were often described as perverted, sick, compulsive, and untreatable, with 78% of the politicians opining that sex criminals will almost surely reoffend. They expressed pessimism about treatment effectiveness and often spoke of rape and murder simultaneously, indicating that these were indeed the types of events they hoped to avert by enacting legislation. Though we would expect lawmakers to consult with experts when developing bills, all of the politicians interviewed by Sample and Kadleck acknowledged that the media were by far their primary sources of information about sex offenders. Although many were unconvinced that current sex offender laws would achieve goals of public safety, almost all viewed themselves as having a duty to respond to their constituents' demand for action.

It is clear that these policies are driven by public perceptions fueled by media attention to sensational sex crimes. Surveys of citizens have revealed that the general public is somewhat misinformed about the realities of sexual violence. When nearly 200 residents were surveyed in Florida, a majority of subjects opined that 80% of sex offenders will reoffend and that many child sex abuse victims have been assaulted by strangers (Levenson, Brannon, Fortney, & Baker, 2007a). Most respondents were rather skeptical about the rehabilitative potential of sexual perpetrators. Females indicated more fear compared to males, and parents reported higher levels of anger and lower levels of tolerance for sex offenders living in communities. A subsequent analysis of these data compared public perceptions to published research, and revealed statistically significant differences between public perceptions and documented rates of recidivism, stranger assault, and treatment effectiveness (Fortney, Levenson, Brannon, & Baker, 2007).

Are Legislative Assumptions Accurate?

Sex offense recidivism statistics are frequently declared without citing a source, and even when properly attributed, the statistics given are sometimes misrepresented. For example, some New York politicians quote a 49% recidivism rate, drawn from a New York Department of Corrections report that studied 556 sex offenders released from prison (Canestrini, 1996). Within 9 years of their release, 49% were returned to prison (most commonly for probation violations and drug charges), but only 6% were convicted of a new sex crime.

The National Center for Missing and Exploited Children backs its support of "tougher sex offender legislation" (which ultimately became the 2006 Walsh Act), by stating on its website that "according to statistics from the U.S. Department of Justice ... released sex offenders were four times more likely to be rearrested for a sex crime than non–sex offenders." This statement, though it is an accurate quote from the Department of Justice (DOJ) report, can easily be misinterpreted when taken out of context. Within 3 years of release from prison in 1994, 5.3% of released sex offenders were rearrested for a new sex crime, and 1.3% of non–sex offenders were rearrested for a new sex crime (Bureau of Justice Statistics, 2003). It is true that the sex offenders, as is the case with most criminal offenders, were four times more likely to be arrested again for their crimes of choice. However, it is noteworthy that the DOJ report found that new sex crimes were more than six times more likely to be committed by other types of criminals (3,328) than by previously identified sex offenders (517).

The most compelling sex offense recidivism studies, conducted by Canadian researchers and involving over 20,000 sex offenders from North America and England, reported an average rearrest rate of 14% over 4 to 6 years (Hanson & Bussiere, 1998; Hanson & Morton-Bourgon, 2005). Recidivism rates fluctuate according to risk factors such as criminal history, victim preferences, and offender age. Longer follow-up studies have revealed that pedophiles who molest boys are at highest risk (35% over 15 years) and that rapists of adults also tend to reoffend more frequently (24% over 15 years) (Harris & Hanson, 2004). But, sex offenders are more likely to be rearrested for nonsexual crimes than sex offenses (Bureau of Justice Statistics, 2003; Hanson & Bussiere, 1998; Sample & Bray, 2003, 2006) and are among the least likely criminals to kill their victims (Sample, 2006).

There is no dispute that some sex offenders are extremely dangerous or violent and pose a severe threat to public safety. But most residence restrictions laws broadly apply to all individuals with felony sex offense convictions, despite extensive research suggesting that a majority will not be rearrested for new sex crimes. Although official recidivism rates do underestimate true offense rates, Harris and

Hanson (2004) concluded, "Most sexual offenders do not re-offend sexually over time ... this finding is contrary to some strongly held beliefs. After 15 years, 73% of sexual offenders had not been charged with, or convicted of, another sexual offence. The sample was sufficiently large that very strong contradictory evidence is necessary to substantially change these recidivism estimates" (p. 17).

Residence laws also imply that children are at risk from predators lurking in school yards or playgrounds. The myth of "stranger danger" persists despite the fact that most sexual perpetrators are well known to their victims. According to the Department of Justice, most child sexual abuse victims are molested by family members (34%) or close acquaintances (59%) (Bureau of Justice Statistics, 2000). About 40% of crimes take place in the victim's own home, and 20% take place in the home of a friend or relative (Bureau of Justice Statistics, 1997). A Wisconsin study revealed that in 200 cases of recidivistic sex offenses, none involved predatory sex crimes against strangers (Zevitz, 2006). In Minnesota, only 8 of 224 repeat offenses (3.6%) were perpetrated by a neighbor and most reoffenses committed against strangers involved an adult victim (Duwe, Donnay, & Tewksbury, 2008). Laws tend to be passed in response to anomalous cases rather than the statistical probabilities reported by researchers.

Another assumption underlying sex offender laws is that sexual criminals cannot be rehabilitated. It is true that there is no cure for pedophilia, just as there is no cure for many medical and mental disorders such as diabetes or schizophrenia. But there is evidence to suggest that many sex offenders benefit from cognitive behavioral interventions that focus on helping them to change their thinking patterns and manage their impulses. For some sex offenders, as with other individuals suffering from addictions or compulsions, recovery can be a lifelong process. Some controlled experimental designs have failed to detect differences in recidivism rates between treated and untreated offenders (Hanson, Broom, & Stephenson, 2004; Marques, Wiederanders, Day, Nelson, & van Ommeren, 2005). Other meta-analyses, however, have found that rates of sexual reoffending drop by about 40% after participation in contemporary cognitive-behavioral therapies (Hanson et al., 2002; Losel & Schmucker, 2005), and Marques et al. (2005) reported that successful completers demonstrated significantly reduced rates of recidivism.

In summary, sex crime recidivism estimates reflect complex issues that cannot be conveyed and understood without a comprehensive and thoughtful examination. Sex crime policies are often justified by simplistic assumptions that all sex offenders reoffend, that treatment does not work, and that strangers who lurk in playgrounds pose an unprecedented threat to children. These erroneous beliefs are widely propagated by the media, creating strongly held but largely inaccurate public perceptions (Levenson et al., 2007a; Sample & Kadleck, 2008). These beliefs, in turn, prompt the expansion of sex crime policies based on "common knowledge" that often lacks empirical support.

Effectiveness of Residence Restrictions

Residence restriction laws are relatively new, so little research to date exists to actually ascertain whether these laws "work" to prevent recidivism. Some related research has been conducted, however, to elucidate the issues surrounding the premises and intentions of these laws. In fact, in order to fully understand the impact of residential restrictions on public safety, it is critical to clarify our knowledge regarding some of the foundations on which these laws were passed. For instance, do sex offenders tend to live within close proximity of potential victims? Do recidivists live closer to schools or parks than nonrecidivists? And, if so, do sex offenders prey on young children near parks or schools? The answers to these questions would help to justify the logic behind housing laws and the benefits of prohibiting sex offenders from living in close proximity to children. An assessment of the limited research in these areas follows.

A study in Newark, New Jersey revealed that sex offenders lived significantly closer (on average, 1,094 feet closer) to schools than did community members, but that those who had abused children lived significantly farther from the schools than offenders of adults (Chajewski & Mercado, 2008). In another New Jersey study in Camden, 88% of sex offenders lived within 2,500 feet of schools, parks, day care centers, or churches, compared with 80% of community members (Zgoba, Levenson, & McKee, in press). An analysis of the locations of registered sex offenders in an Arkansas county found that child abusers were more likely than other sex offenders to live near schools, day care centers and parks (Walker, Golden, & VanHouten, 2001).

Some authors have postulated that these findings might be explained by routine activities theory, suggesting that sex offenders might purposefully place themselves in close proximity to potential victims (Walker et al., 2001). Others, however, have contended that economic considerations are the primary factor in residential choices (Tewksbury & Mustaine, in press; Tewksbury & Mustaine, 2006). Underemployment can force sex offenders to reside in less affluent communities, and lower-income neighborhoods are often found in densely populated urban areas where residents are naturally going to live in closer proximity to schools and other child-oriented venues. Registered sex offenders are likely to live in communities that have higher levels of social disorganization (Tewksbury & Mustaine, 2008). Child abusers tend to live in somewhat less socially disorganized neighborhoods than other sex offenders, though these neighborhoods tend to have lower incomes and greater minority populations when compared with communities in general (Tewksbury, Mustaine, & Stengel, 2008). Such neighborhoods may attract criminals because they are more affordable, but they are also characterized by community neglect and a lack of resources, which may make their citizens more vulnerable to crime.

It may seem sensible to keep sex offenders away from schools or parks in an effort to prevent recidivism. Research suggests, however, that sex offenses are not associated with most measures of proximity to available victims. Though in general, sex offenses occur more frequently in census tracts with larger proportions of young children, the presence of schools is not associated with a greater prevalence of sex offenses (Tewksbury et al., 2008). Also, Tewksbury et al. (2008) found that a higher concentration of registered sex offenders in a neighborhood had no significant correlation with the number of sex offenses that occurred.

In Colorado, sex offense recidivists were randomly scattered throughout the geographical area and were not more likely to live near schools than nonrecidivists (Colorado Department of Public Safety, 2004). A Minnesota study of 329 high-risk sex offenders revealed that recidivism occurred in only 13 cases, and only two reoffenses took place in parks.

In both of these cases, the perpetrators lived miles from the crime scene and drove a vehicle to commit the offense (Minnesota Department of Corrections, 2003).

More recently, researchers in Minnesota analyzed 224 recidivistic sex offenses and concluded, "Not one of the 224 sex offenses would likely have been deterred by a residency restriction law" (Duwe et al., 2008; Minnesota Department of Corrections, 2007, p. 2). The majority of these sex offenders (79%) victimized someone known to them, and half of the assaults against strangers occurred more than 1 mile from the offenders' homes. Of the 16 minor victims with whom contact was made within a mile of the offender's home, none of these relationships were established near a school, park, or playground. Most of the offenses against children were perpetrated by offenders who were well acquainted with the victims; they were parents, caretakers, paramours of the mother, babysitters, or friends of the family. Only 3.6% of the cases involved a neighbor. The authors concluded that in child sexual abuse cases, residential proximity is not nearly as important as social or relationship proximity (Duwe et al., 2008).

The hypothesis that sex offenders who live within closer proximity to schools, parks, or playgrounds have an increased likelihood of sexually reoffending remains unsupported by research. No empirical evidence exists to suggest that residential restrictions are likely to be a successful strategy for deterring sex crimes, preventing recidivism, or protecting children.

Unintended Consequences of Residence Restrictions

The reintegration problems commonly faced by criminal offenders are exacerbated for registered sex offenders. The stigma of sex offender registration and community notification is well documented, as are the ways in which they can impede community reentry and adjustment (Levenson & Cotter, 2005a; Levenson, D'Amora, & Hern, 2007b; Mercado, Alvarez, & Levenson, 2008; Sample & Streveler, 2003; Tewksbury, 2004, 2005; Tewksbury & Lees, 2006, 2007; Zevitz, 2006; Zevitz & Farkas, 2000). For instance, sex offenders surveyed in Florida, Indiana, Connecticut, Wisconsin, Oklahoma, Kansas,

New Jersey, and Kentucky reported adverse consequences such as unemployment, relationship loss, threats, harassment, physical assault, and property damage, as well as psychological symptoms such as shame, embarrassment, depression, or hopelessness as a result of public disclosure. Housing difficulties are also commonly noted by registered sex offenders, and the proliferation of residential restriction laws compounds this problem in several important ways.

Housing Availability

Residence laws greatly diminish housing options for sex offenders, especially in major metropolitan areas (Carlson, 2005; Zandbergen & Hart, 2006). In Orange County, Florida (the greater Orlando region), researchers found that 95% of over 137,000 residential properties were located within 1,000 feet of schools, parks, day care centers, or school bus stops, and over 99% of housing fell within 2,500 feet of these locations. Restrictions of 1,000 feet resulted in only 4,233 potentially available dwellings; and 2,500-foot buffer zones eliminated all but 37 properties in the entire county. School bus stops were found by far to be the most problematic restriction (99.6% of properties were within 2,500 feet of a bus stop) (Zandbergen & Hart, 2006).

In Colorado, researchers found that in heavily populated areas, residences farther than 1,000 feet from a school or child care center were virtually nonexistent (Colorado Department of Public Safety, 2004). In Newark, New Jersey, 98% of sex offenders live within 2,500 feet of a school and 65% live within 1,000 feet. Moreover, after analyzing the availability of residential housing in Newark, the authors concluded that 93% of the city's territory is located within 2,500 feet of a school and would therefore be unavailable to sex offenders (Chajewski & Mercado, 2008).

When residence restrictions are enacted, the results quickly become evident. Six months after the implementation of Iowa's 2,000-foot housing zone, thousands of sex offenders became homeless or transient, making them more difficult to track and monitor. The number of registered sex offenders in Iowa who could not be located more than doubled, damaging the reliability and validity of the sex offender registry (Rood, 2006). Similarly, the abundance of local 2,500-foot ordinances in South Florida has led to homelessness for many sex offenders who were forced to live under bridges as a result. The *Miami Herald* reported on April 8, 2008, that 245 of 2,050 registered sex offenders in Miami have absconded and cannot be located (*Miami Herald*, 2008).

In California, the Sex Offender Tracking Program in Sacramento reported that the number of sex offenders registered as transient has increased steadily since the passage of Proposition 83, from 2,049 in July 2007 to 3,229 in July of 2008 (California sex offender registration, 2008). Ironically, unstable and transient living arrangements are associated with increased criminal recidivism.

Criminal Reentry, Housing Instability, and Recidivism

Released prisoners and convicted felons are faced with many reentry challenges, including the need to obtain affordable housing (La Vigne, Visher, & Castro, 2004; Petersilia, 2003; Travis, 2005). After being separated from their families while in prison, criminal offenders often find themselves without social supports, financial resources, housing, employment, and transportation. Barriers to employment often thwart financial stability, and even so-called affordable housing may be beyond their reach. An empirical relationship between housing instability and criminal recidivism has been documented. In Georgia, the likelihood of rearrest increased by 25% each time a parolee relocated (Meredith, Speir, Johnson, & Hull, 2003). Criminal offenders in New York shelters were more likely to have drug and alcohol abuse problems, to be unemployed, and to abscond from probation or parole (Nelson, Deess, & Allen, 1999). Unstable living arrangements were identified as the strongest predictor of absconding in a study of over 4,000 parolees in California (Williams, McShane, & Dolny, 2000); and in a national sample (n = 2,030), probationers who moved multiple times over the course of their supervision were nearly twice as likely to have a disciplinary action against them (Schulenberg, 2007). Offenders themselves have reported that housing is a crucial link to community adjustment and reintegration (La Vigne et al., 2004).

Housing and property ownership lead to intensified social bonds, which contribute to crime desistance through exposure to pro-social activities, law-abiding peers, conformity, and development of a nondeviant identity (Laub & Sampson,

2001). Employment and relationships, especially marriage, are consistent predictors of crime desistance (Ibid), whereas lifestyle instability has been correlated with both general and sexual recidivism (Andrews & Bonta, 2007; Hanson & Harris, 1998). In fact, sex offenders with pro-social support systems have fewer violations and new offenses than those who have negative or no support (Colorado Department of Public Safety, 2004). Thus, housing laws resulting in instability and subsequent disengagement from family and community have the potential to increase rather than to deter criminal recidivism.

Psychosocial Consequences of Residence Restrictions

The impact of residence restrictions on sex offenders is just becoming known. Only a few studies have been published to date, though others are forthcoming. Levenson and Cotter (2005b) surveyed 135 sex offenders about the impact of Florida's 1,000-foot statewide exclusionary zone on their reintegration. About one quarter of offenders reported that they were forced to move from a home that they owned or rented, or were unable to return home following their release from prison, because of residential restriction laws. Almost half (44%) said that they were not allowed to live with supportive family members, 57% found it difficult to obtain affordable housing, and 60% reported emotional distress as a result of housing restrictions. New Jersey sex offenders reported similar experiences, with many of them saying that housing restrictions have led to financial hardship, depression, hopelessness, and anger, and pushed them farther away from employment, treatment, and family support (Mercado et al., 2008). Sex offenders have rarely opined that housing laws would help them prevent offending and often have indicated that if they were motivated to reoffend, they would be able to do so despite residential restrictions (Levenson & Cotter, 2005b; Levenson & Hern, 2007; Mercado et al., 2008).

In Kansas and Oklahoma, 54% of registered sex offenders surveyed said that a residence-restriction law forced them to move (Tewksbury & Mustaine, 2007). In Indiana, 26% of sex offenders surveyed were unable to return to their homes after being released from prison, 37% were unable to live with family members, and nearly a third said that a landlord refused to rent to them or to renew a lease (Levenson & Hern, 2007). Many (38%) reported that affordable housing was less available due to restrictions on where they could live, and that as a result they lived farther away from employment, social services, and mental health clinics. When sex offenders relocate, they typically move to communities with higher levels of social disorganization (Mustaine, Tewksbury, & Stengel, 2006).

Young adults seem particularly vulnerable to the consequences of these laws; age was significantly inversely correlated with being unable to live with family and having difficulties securing affordable housing (Levenson, 2008; Levenson & Hern, 2007). This is especially salient given the new federal requirements of the Adam Walsh Act, which requires juvenile sex offenders as young as 14 to be placed on public registries. Residence restrictions are generally tied to sex offender registration status, so we are likely to see a growing housing crisis for a substantial number of youth with sexual behavior problems who may be prevented from living with their families.

When Levenson and Cotter (2005b) collected their data in 2004, city ordinances had not yet been passed in Florida. Since that time, however, 26 of the 30 independent cities in Broward County, Florida (the Fort Lauderdale metropolitan area), enacted local sex offender zoning laws increasing buffer areas to 2,500 feet (about one half mile). A more recent study of 109 sex offenders in Broward revealed escalating problems of homelessness and transience, with 39% of the subjects reporting at least 2 days of homelessness or living with someone else, and 22% saying they were forced to relocate more than twice (Levenson, 2008). Almost half said that a landlord refused to rent to them, and 13% reported that they were arrested and jailed for a residence violation. Again, age was inversely correlated with intensification of adverse consequences, and larger buffer zones were associated with increased transience and homelessness and reduced employment opportunities.

These laws can also lead to family separation or relocation, creating unintended consequences for offenders' family members including financial hardships and job and school disruption for spouses and children. Residence laws aggravate the scarcity of housing options for sex offenders, forcing them out of metropolitan areas and farther away from the social support, employment opportunities, and social services that are known to aid offenders in successful community reentry. Because residence restrictions have the potential to disrupt stability and contribute to psychosocial stressors, they may increase dynamic risk (Hanson & Harris, 1998) associated with sex offense recidivism. Clearly, this outcome is not what lawmakers intended, and is not in the best interest of public safety.

Conclusions and Recommendations

Available evidence does not suggest that residence restrictions will reduce sex crime recidivism or protect children. Most registered sex offenders do not reoffend, and those who do have not been noted to live in closer geographical proximity to children than nonrecidivists. Residential zoning laws significantly diminish housing availability and create psychosocial consequences that are likely to challenge the coping skills of many sex offenders as they face transience and instability. Treatment providers and parole agents should be cognizant of the stress created by housing problems and be prepared to assist offenders with coping strategies as well as referrals for case management services. Attention to dynamic risk factors, which fluctuate according to environmental conditions, should be a salient part of ongoing assessment and treatment planning. Ironically, the instability and psychosocial stress created by housing laws may exacerbate risk.

Social stability and support increase the likelihood of successful reintegration for criminal offenders, and public policies that create obstacles to community reentry may compromise public safety (Petersilia, 2003). Sex offenders who have a positive support system have significantly lower recidivism rates and fewer rule violations than those who have negative or no support (Colorado Department of Public Safety, 2004). Social bonds of stable employment and family relationships also lead to lower recidivism rates for sex offenders (Kruttschnitt, Uggen, & Shelton, 2000). It is well established that the stigma of felony conviction can inhibit participation in pro-social roles such as employment, education, parenting, and property ownership (Tewksbury & Lees, 2007; Uggen, Manza, & Behrens, 2004). Uggen et al. (2004) highlighted that self-concept, civic engagement, and social capital are essential to an offender's identity as a conforming citizen and to desistance from crime.

Social capital is described as an asset derived from and facilitated by social ties through the sharing of information and resources. Sex offenders often live in disadvantaged communities with less social capital—schools, churches, and stores have deteriorated; unemployment and poverty flourish; few nondeviant role models exist; informal neighborhood supervision is less salient; and residents have less pride in and sense of responsibility for their community. On the other hand, studies of prisoner reentry consistently emphasize that access to jobs and affordable housing helps them reintegrate into local social networks and sustain legitimate opportunities for social conformity.

Applying a theory of social capital, Burchfield and Mingus (2008) interviewed sex offenders in Illinois, who described how stigma led to withdrawal from pro-social activities, how informal social controls created barriers to social capital in the community, and how parole restrictions prevented them from establishing relationships and engaging in positive peer culture. Policies such as residence restrictions can disrupt the stability of sex offenders and interfere with the potential to sustain social capital, raising concerns that such laws might be ultimately counterproductive (Levenson, Zgoba, & Tewksbury, 2007c).

Iowa prosecutors and victim advocates recognized pitfalls of residential zoning laws and publicly denounced such restrictions, asserting that they generate more problems than they solve (Iowa County Attorneys Association, 2006; NAESV, 2006). Prosecutors observed a reduction in plea bargains, for instance, causing some cases to go unadjudicated, leaving victims at risk and perpetrators without treatment or punishment (Iowa County Attorneys Association, 2006). Victim advocates warned that transience undermines the validity of registries, making it more difficult to track the whereabouts of sex offenders and to supervise their activities.

Understandably, sex offenders find little sympathy in politicians and citizens. It is important for scholars and researchers, however, to enlighten stakeholders regarding the challenges these restrictions create, and the potential for increased risk. Some sex offenders do indeed pose a threat of violence to communities, and neighborhood residents have a legitimate interest in protecting children from sexual assault.

From a public safety standpoint, however, it is more efficient to implement policies that do not inadvertently contribute to the risk for reoffense. Professionals and policy makers alike are encouraged to consider a range of options available for building safer communities and to endorse those that are most likely to achieve their stated goals while minimizing collateral consequences.

For instance, empirically derived risk assessment models are recommended to classify offenders into relative risk categories with concordant restrictions and intensity of supervision. Such a model is in stark contrast to the offense-based classification system required by the Adam Walsh Act. Offense-based categories are likely to be overly inclusive, in many cases inflating risk, but will underestimate the risk of offenders who pled down to lesser offenses. The result will be a registry with so many seemingly high-risk offenders that the public's ability to truly identify sexually dangerous persons will be significantly diluted. In addition, overly inclusive registries aggravate the collateral consequences of registration for lower-risk offenders, perhaps inadvertently obstructing any deterrent effect.

Residence restrictions should not be legislated, but should be a case management decision best left to the discretion of supervision officers and treatment providers. Some jurisdictions have instead instituted "child safety zones" or "loitering zones." Rather than restricting where sex offenders reside, such initiatives prohibit them from hanging around in places where they can easily cultivate relationships with children and engage in grooming tactics. In some cases, loitering laws are supplemented with GPS monitoring devices that alert officials when a sex offender enters a forbidden area without a legitimate reason. These types of laws seem better equipped to manage the daily activities of sex offenders at risk for abusing children than housing laws, which dictate primarily where sex offenders sleep.

Diminishing access to potential victims is an appropriate component of sex crime prevention, and interventions should be tailored to the offender's risk, offense patterns, and victim preferences. Treatment should be included as part of any comprehensive strategy for preventing recidivistic sexual violence. Collaborative approaches such as containment models, in which treatment providers, probation officers, and polygraph examiners work together to manage the risk of registered sex offenders, should be emphasized as a paradigm for community protection. These strategies are more likely to be successful in achieving our common goal of preventing sexual violence and creating safer communities.

References

Andrews, D. A., & Bonta, J. (2007). *The psychology of criminal conduct* (4th ed.). Cincinnati: Anderson Publishing.

Burchfield, K. B., & Mingus, W. (2008). Not in my neighborhood: Assessing registered sex offenders' experiences with local social capital and social control. *Criminal Justice and Behavior, 35*, 356–374.

Bureau of Justice Statistics. (1997). *Sex offenses and offenders: An analysis of Data on rape and sexual assault.* (No. NCJ-163392). Washington, DC: U.S. Department of Justice.

Bureau of Justice Statistics. (2000). *Sexual assault of young children as reported to law enforcement: Victim, incident, and offender characteristics* (No. NCJ 182990). Washington, DC: U.S. Department of Justice.

Bureau of Justice Statistics. (2003). *Recidivism of sex offenders released from prison in 1994* (No. NCJ 198281). Washington, DC: U.S. Department of Justice.

CALCASA. (2006). Opposition to California's Jessica Lunsford Act, from http://www.calcasapublicpolicy.org/

California Secretary of State. (2006). Proposition 83. Retrieved August 8, 2008, from http://vote2006.sos.ca.gov/voterguide/pdf/prop83_text.pdf

California sex offender registration. (2008). Retrieved August 8, 2008, from http://www.ccoso.org/library_articles.php#Sex+Offender +Registration

Canestrini, K. (1996). Profile and follow-up of sex offenders released in 1986. Albany, NY: State of New York Department of Correctional Services.

Carlson, M. (2005, August 25). Not in my city. *Orlando Weekly.*

Chajewski, M., & Mercado, C. C. (2008). An analysis of sex offender residency restrictions in Newark, New Jersey. *Sex offender law report, 9*, 1–6.

City of Jacksonville. (2005). Ordinance 2005-629. Retrieved August 8, 2008, from http://citycirc.coj.net/docs/2005-0629/Original%20Text/2005-629.doc

Colorado Department of Public Safety. (2004). Report on safety issues raised by living arrangements for and location of sex offenders in the community. Denver: Sex Offender Management Board.

Doe v. Miller, 405 F. 3d 700 (8th Circuit 2005).

Doe v. Miller and White (U.S. District Court, Southern District of Iowa 2004).

Drummond Ayres, B., Jr. (1997, August 26). California Child Molesters Face "Chemical Castration." *New York Times.* Retrieved August 8, 2008, from http://query.nytimes.com/gst/fullpage. html?res=9402E1DC1339F934A1575BC0A960958260

Duwe, G., Donnay, W., & Tewksbury, R. (2008). Does residential proximity matter? A geographic analysis of sex offense recidivism. *Criminal Justice and Behavior, 35*(4), 484–504.

Florida House of Representatives. (2008, March 19). Retrieved 8/8/08, from http://www.flsenate.gov/Session/Index. cfm?Mode=Video&Submenu=8&Tab=session.

Fortney, T., Levenson, J. S., Brannon, Y., & Baker, J. (2007). Myths and facts about sex offenders: Implications for practice and public policy. *Sex Offender Treatment, 2*(1), 1–17.

Hanson, R. K., Broom, I., & Stephenson, M. (2004). Evaluating community sex offender treatment programs: A 12-year follow-up of 724 offenders. *Canadian Journal of Behavioural Science, 36*(2), 85–94.

Hanson, R. K., & Bussiere, M. T. (1998). Predicting relapse: A meta-analysis of sexual offender recidivism studies. *Journal of Consulting and Clinical Psychology, 66*(2), 348–362.

Hanson, R. K., Gordon, A., Harris, A. J. R., Marques, J. K., Murphy, W., Quinsey, V. L., & Seto, M. C. (2002). First report of the collaborative outcome data project on the effectiveness of treatment for sex offenders. *Sexual Abuse: A Journal of Research and Treatment, 14*(2), 169–194.

Hanson, R. K., & Harris, A. J. R. (1998). Dynamic predictors of sexual recidivism (No. 1998-01). Ottawa: Department of the Solicitor General of Canada.

Hanson, R. K., & Morton-Bourgon, K. (2005). The characteristics of persistent sexual offenders: A meta-analysis of recidivism studies. *Journal of Consulting and Clinical Psychology, 73*(6), 1154–1163.

Harris, A. J. R., & Hanson, R. K. (2004). *Sex offender recidivism: A simple question* (No. 2004 03). Ottawa: Public Safety and Emergency Preparedness Canada.

Iowa County Attorneys Association. (2006). *Statement on sex offender residency restrictions in Iowa*. Des Moines: Author.

Kansas Sex Offender Policy Board. (2007). *Annual report*. Topeka: Kansas Criminal Justice Coordinating Council.

Kruttschnitt, C., Uggen, C., & Shelton, K. (2000). Predictors of desistance among sex offenders: The interaction of formal and informal social controls. *Justice Quarterly, 17*(1), 61–88.

La Vigne, N., Visher, C., & Castro, J. (2004). *Chicago Prisoners' Experiences Returning Home*. Washington, DC: Urban Institute.

Lane, Mary Beth (2007, October 7). Sex-offender ghettos. *Columbus Dispatch*. Retrieved August 8, 2008, from http://www.dispatchpolitics. com/live/content/local_news/stories/2007/10/07/sexoff.new.ART_ ART_10-07-07_A1_8884374.html?sid=101

Laub, J. H., & Sampson, R. J. (2001). Understanding desistance from crime. *Crime and Justice, 28*, 1–69.

Levenson, J. S. (2008). Collateral consequences of sex offender residence restrictions. *Criminal Justice Studies, 21*(2), 153–166.

Levenson, J. S., Brannon, Y., Fortney, T., & Baker, J. (2007a). Public perceptions about sex offenders and community protection policies. *Analyses of Social Issues and Public Policy, 7*(1), 1–25.

Levenson, J. S., & Cotter, L. P. (2005a). The effect of Megan's Law on sex offender reintegration. *Journal of Contemporary Criminal Justice, 21*(1), 49–66.

Levenson, J. S., & Cotter, L. P. (2005b). The impact of sex offender residence restrictions: 1,000 feet from danger or one step from absurd? *International Journal of Offender Therapy and Comparative Criminology, 49*(2), 168–178.

Levenson, J. S., D'Amora, D. A., & Hern, A. (2007b). Megan's Law and its Impact on Community Re-entry for Sex Offenders. *Behavioral Sciences & the Law, 25*, 587–602.

Levenson, J. S., & Hern, A. (2007). Sex offender residence restrictions: Unintended consequences and community re-entry. *Justice Research and Policy, 9*(1), 59–73.

Levenson, J. S., Zgoba, K., & Tewksbury, R. (2007c). Sex offender residence restrictions: Sensible crime policy or flawed logic? *Federal Probation, 71*(3), 2–9.

Losel, F., & Schmucker, M. (2005). The effectiveness of treatment for sexual offenders: A comprehensive meta-analysis. *Journal of Experimental Criminology, 1*, 117–146.

Mann v. Georgia Department of Corrections et al. (Supreme Court of Georgia 2007).

Marques, J. K., Wiederanders, M., Day, D. M., Nelson, C., & van Ommeren, A. (2005). Effects of a relapse prevention program on sexual recidivism: Final results from California's Sex Offender Treatment and Evaluation Project (SOTEP). *Sexual Abuse: A Journal of Research & Treatment, 17*(1), 79–107.

Meloy, M. L., Miller, S. L., & Curtis, K. M. (2008). Making Sense Out of Nonsense: The Deconstruction of State-Level Sex Offender Residence Restrictions. *American Journal of Criminal Justice*.

Mercado, C. C., Alvarez, S., & Levenson, J. S. (2008). The impact of specialized sex offender legislation on community re-entry. *Sexual Abuse: A Journal of Research & Treatment, 20*(2), 188–205.

Meredith, T., Speir, J., Johnson, S., & Hull, H. (2003). *Enhancing Parole Decision-Making through the Automation of Risk Assessment*. Atlanta: Applied Research Services, Inc.

Miami Herald. (2008). For Sexual Predators, It's A Camp of Isolation. (April 8), Page A1.

Minnesota Department of Corrections. (2003). *Level three sex offenders residential placement issues*. St. Paul: author.

Minnesota Department of Corrections. (2007). *Residential proximity and sex offense recidivism in Minnesota*. St. Paul, MN: MN Department of Corrections.

Mustaine, E. E., Tewksbury, R., & Stengel, K. M. (2006). Residential location and mobility of registered sex offenders. *American Journal of Criminal Justice, 30*(2), 177–192.

NAESV. (2006). *Community management of convicted sex offenders: Registration, electronic monitoring, civil commitment, mandatory minimums, and residency restrictions*. Retrieved 4/2/06, from www.naesv.org

Nelson, M., Deess, P., & Allen, C. (1999). *The First Month Out: Post-Incarceration Experiences in New York City*. New York: Vera Institute of Justice.

Nieto, M., & Jung, D. (2006). *The impact of residency restrictions on sex offenders and correctional management practices: A literature review*. Sacramento, CA: California Research Bureau.

Petersilia, J. (2003). *When Prisoners Come Home: Parole and prisoner reentry*. New York, NY: Oxford University Press.

Rodriquez, Ihosvani (2007, May 17). "Hollywood Takes Steps to Curb Sex Offenders." *South Florida Sun – Sentinel*, pg. B.1.

Rood, L. (2006, January 23). New data shows twice as many sex offenders missing. *Des Moines Register*.

Sample, L. L. (2006). An examination of the degree to which sex offenders kill. *Criminal Justice Review, 31*(3), 230–250.

Sample, L. L., & Bray, T. M. (2003). Are sex offenders dangerous? *Criminology and Public Policy, 3*(1), 59–82.

Sample, L. L., & Bray, T. M. (2006). Are sex offenders different? An examination of rearrest patterns. *Criminal Justice Policy Review, 17*(1), 83–102.

Sample, L. L., & Kadleck, C. (2008). Sex Offender Laws: Legislators' Accounts of the Need for Policy. *Criminal Justice Policy Review, 19*(1), 40–62.

Sample, L. L., & Streveler, A. J. (2003). Latent consequences of community notification laws. In S. H. Decker, L. F. Alaird & C. M. Katz (Eds.), *Controversies in criminal justice* (pp. 353–362). Los Angeles: Roxbury.

Schulenberg, J. L. (2007). Predicting noncompliant behavior: Disparities in the social locations of male and female probationers. *Justice Research and Policy, 9*(1), 25–57.

Southern Center for Human Rights. (2008). *Georgia Sex Offender Law back in Federal Court moments after being signed by Governor Perdue*. Retrieved August 8, 2008, from http://www.schr.org/about-thecenter/pressreleases/HB1059litigation/PressReleases/press_lawsuitHB1059_SB1signed.htm

State v. Seering, No. 34 / 03-0776 (Iowa Supreme Court 2005).

Tewksbury, R. (2004). Experiences and Attitudes of Registered Female Sex Offenders. *Federal Probation, 68*(3), 30–34.

Tewksbury, R. (2005). Collateral consequences of sex offender registration. *Journal of Contemporary Criminal Justice, 21*(1), 67–82.

Tewksbury, R., & Lees, M. (2006). Consequences of sex offender registration: Collateral consequences and community experiences. *Sociological Spectrum, 26*(3), 309–334.

Tewksbury, R., & Lees, M. (2007). Perception of Punishment: How Registered Sex Offenders View Registries. *Crime and Delinquency, 53*(3), 380–407.

Tewksbury, R., & Mustaine, E. (2008). Where Registered Sex Offenders Live: Community Characteristics and Proximity to Possible Victims. *Victims and Offenders, 3*(1), 86–98.

Tewksbury, R., & Mustaine, E. (in press). Collateral consequences and community re-entry for registered sex offenders with child victims: Are the challenges even greater? *Journal of Offender Rehabilitation*.

Tewksbury, R., Mustaine, E., & Stengel, K. M. (2008). Examining Rates of Sexual Offenses from a Routine Activities Perspective *Victims and Offenders, 3*(1), 75–85.

Tewksbury, R., & Mustaine, E. E. (2006). Where to find sex offenders: An examination of residential locations and neighborhood conditions. *Criminal Justice Studies, 19*(1), 61–75.

Tewksbury, R., & Mustaine, E. E. (2007). Stress and collateral consequences for registered sex offenders. *under review*.

Tillman, Jodie (2006). "Recidivism: It's Not Open-and-Shut." *New Hampshire Valley News*. Retrieved August 8, 2008, from http://www.vnews.com/sexcrimes/recidivism.htm

Travis, J. (2005). *But the all come back: Facing the challenges of prisoner reentry*. Washington, D.C.: Urban Institute Press.

Uggen, C., Manza, J., & Behrens, A. (2004). Less than the Average Citizen: Stigma, Role Transition, and the Civic Reintegration of Convicted Felons. In S. Maruna & R. Immarigeon (Eds.), *After Crime and Punishment: Pathways to Offender Reintegration* (pp. 261–293). Devon, UK: Willan Publishing.

Walker, J. T., Golden, J. W., & VanHouten, A. C. (2001). The Geographic Link Between Sex Offenders and Potential Victims: A Routine Activities Approach. *Justice Research and Policy, 3*(2), 15–33.

Williams, F. P., McShane, M. D., & Dolny, M. H. (2000). Predicting parole absconders. *Prison Journal, 80*(1), 24–38.

Zandbergen, P. A., & Hart, T. C. (2006). Reducing housing options for convicted sex offenders: Investigating the impact of residency restriction laws using GIS. *Justice Research and Policy, 8*(2), 1–24.

Zevitz, R. G. (2006). Sex offender community notification: Its role in recidivism and offender reintegration. *Criminal Justice Studies, 19*(2), 193–208.

Zevitz, R. G., & Farkas, M. A. (2000). *Sex offender community notification: Assessing the impact in Wisconsin*. Washington, DC: U.S. Department of Justice.

Zgoba, K., Levenson, J. S., & McKee, T. (in press). Examining the Impact of Sex Offender Residence Restrictions on Housing Availability. *Criminal Justice Policy Review*.

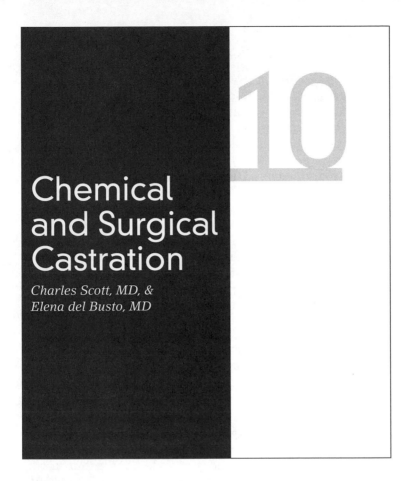

10

Chemical and Surgical Castration

*Charles Scott, MD, &
Elena del Busto, MD*

As discussed throughout this text, sexual assaults in general and high-profile attacks on children in the 1980s and the 1990s led to the development of various laws intended to prevent future deviant sexual acts against members of society. The public outcry against the 2005 brutal kidnapping and killing of 9-year-old Jessica Lunsford by known sex offender John Cooey reflects the outrage and animosity toward sex offenders evoked by such heinous crimes. In lobbying for legislation to better track and follow released sex offenders, Jessica's father, Mark, echoed the sentiments of many in society when he stated, "I want these predators and these offenders to know one thing ... I'll get you before you get me" (Johnson, 2008).

Castration has emerged as one type of sentencing and/or legislative treatment option for sex offenders. The goal of castration legislation has been to decrease the risk of future sexual offenses by altering an offender's hormone and/or neurotransmitter levels, either chemically or surgically. In signing Louisiana's 2008 castration statute, Governor Bobby Jindal provided a voice to his constituents' belief that castrating offenders will make the world a safer place with this statement:

> The Sex Offender Chemical Castration Bill is a good bill, and I am especially glad to sign it into Louisiana law today ... Those who prey on our children are among the very worst criminals imaginable. Not only as the governor of this great state, but as a father of three children, I believe that sexually assaulting a child is one of the worst crimes, and I am glad we have taken such strong measures in Louisiana to put a stop to these monsters' brutal acts—make no mistake about it, if anyone wants to molest children and commit sexual assaults on kids, they should not do so here in Louisiana. Here, we will do everything in our power to protect our children, and we will not rest until justice is won and we have fully punished those who harm them. (Office of the Governor, 2008)

Does castration of offenders represent the magic bullet wished for by our society? Critics of castration laws argue that a one-size-fits-all approach represents a political, not scientific, solution that includes offenders for whom castration is not effective, and as a result of such policies, more harm than good may result. To help understand key issues in this debate, this chapter reviews the following areas important in understanding recent castration statutes: (1) a historical perspective of castration, (2) key definitions, (3) or "the proposed mechanism of action of castration" castration's proposed mechanisms of action, (4) a comparison of state castration statutes, (5) potential legal challenges, (6) public policy implications, and (7) future public policy directions.

A Historical Perspective of Castration

The word *castrate* originates from the Latin word *castratus,* which means to remove the testicles of a man or ovaries of a woman. *Castratus* is similar to the Greek word *keazein,* which means "to split." Greek mythology refers to castration in the story of Uranus, the Greek god known as Father Sky. According to this legend, Uranus was castrated by his son, who threw his father's testicles into the Mediterranean Sea, from which Aphrodite (the god of love, lust, and beauty) arose. Throughout history, castration has been used for various purposes, including protecting the chastity of royalty, ridding mankind of unwanted or inappropriate genetic traits, or punishing persons for their sexual crimes (Breitenberger, 2007).

The practice of castration to create eunuchs can be traced to the early Greek and Roman empires, where castrates were used as the guardians of the royal court. The term *eunuch* comes from two Greek words, *eune* ("bed") and *ekhein* ("to keep"), which literally translates as "keeper/guardian of the bedchamber" or "chamberlain" (Glass & Watkin, 1997). Romans clearly knew that castrates were infertile, as described by the Roman poet Juvenal when he wrote, "There are girls who adore unmanly eunuchs—so smooth, so beardless to kiss and no worry about abortion!" (Juvenal, 1974)

Eunuchs also gained an important role in the Renaissance and in the baroque musical world. During that time, young boys were selectively chosen, based on their musical talent and voice, to be castrated prior to puberty. These eunuchs or castrati would maintain the high-pitched voice of a prepubertal boy, despite developing the lung capacity and strength of an adult male. The high-pitched, forceful voices of castrati became very popular, so much so that composers such as Handel and Scarlatti wrote pieces specifically for them. Castrati remained an important part of the Renaissance and Baroque musical worlds until the Roman Catholic Church, which always viewed castration as a form of mutilation, banned the practice in 1880 (Glass & Watkin, 1997).

The use of castration as punishment or to deter sex offenders is not a recent trend. The *lex talionis* code of justice (an eye for an eye) castrated rapists for centuries as punishment for their crime (R. D. Miller, 1998). In 1892, a Swiss patient diagnosed with "imbecility," and "neuralgic pain of the testis," and hypersexuality was treated with surgical castration (Sturup, 1971). During colonial times in America, black slaves were castrated for allegedly having sexual relations or for raping white women (Druhm, 1997). The surgical castration of prisoners was performed in the late 1800's by Dr. Harry Sharp of Indiana, in an effort to reduce sexual urges. This method became so effective that Indiana passed the first law allowing for sterilization of mental defectives (R. D. Miller, 1998).

The eugenics movement quickly followed. Eugenics focused on selective breeding, encouraging forced sterilization of people with undesirable traits that were believed to be transmitted genetically. This movement eventually led to the sterilization of approximately 60,000 mentally handicapped, incarcerated women (Druhm, 1997). When the U.S. Supreme Court upheld a state law that sterilized the "mentally infirm," Justice Oliver Wendell Holmes noted, "Better for all the world, if instead of waiting to execute degenerate offspring for crime, or to let them starve for their imbecility, society can prevent those who are manifestly unfit from continuing their kind ... three generations of imbeciles are enough" (*Buck v. Bell*, 1927). American efforts at regulating and punishing sexual behavior have often correlated with the political and cultural norms of the times. Thus the question of whether the underlying sexual behavior is truly offensive or damaging often cannot be separated from a cultural understanding of that era's sexual mores. This view explains the punishment of interracial sexual relations (at least black male sexual behavior) and the views of the mentally handicapped.

In 1929, Denmark passed the first law legalizing surgical castration for the treatment of sex offenders and continued this practice until 1972. Soon thereafter, many other European nations followed suit, leading to reports of marked reduction in sexual recidivism of those sex offenders who were surgically castrated (Sturup, 1968). Following World War II, the use of surgical castration as a form of punishment for criminal behavior fell out of favor, in large part because of humanitarian concerns resulting from the Nazi regime's forced castration of sex offenders and other groups of individuals (Gawande, 1997; Vanderzyl, 1994; Wong, 2001).

Key Definitions

Castration statutes provide either chemical or surgical castration for individuals who are convicted sex offenders. *Sex offender* is not a medical term; instead these words represent a legal category of men or women convicted of an unlawful sexual activity. Under this definition, sex offenders may be individuals convicted of crimes such as rape, sexual assault, child molestation, lewd and lascivious acts upon a child, public nudity or exhibitionism, or the possession of certain types of pornography. The phrase *sexually violent predator* is also a legal term and generally designates a person who has committed one or more specific sex offenses, has been diagnosed with a mental disorder or abnormality, and as a result of this condition is likely to engage in future dangerous acts. Both sex offenders and sexually violent predators are potential candidates for mandatory castration.

In contrast, the term *paraphilia* is a medical term used to describe any deviant sexual behavior that is required to achieve sexual excitement (Atkinson, Atkinson, Smith, Bem, & Nolen-Hoeksema, 1993). Diagnoses for paraphilias are defined in the Diagnostic and Statistical Manual of Mental Disorders, Text Revision, 2000 (American Psychiatric Association, 2000) as "recurrent, intense sexually arousing fantasies, sexual urges, or behaviors generally involving (1) nonhuman objects, (2) the suffering or humiliation of oneself or one's partner, or (3) children or other non-consenting persons that occur over a period of at least six months." Eight specific paraphilias listed in the DSM-IV-TR include the following: exhibitionism, fetishism, frotteurism (touching and rubbing against a nonconsenting person), pedophilia, sexual masochism, sexual sadism, transvestic fetishism, and voyeurism. Paraphilia not otherwise specified (NOS) is also included to code for those paraphilias that do not meet criteria for any one of the other eight categories. Examples of paraphilia NOS include telephone scatology (obscene phone calls) and zoophilia (sexual gratification achieved in conjunction with an animal) (American Psychiatric Association, 2000).

Although one may suffer from a DSM-IV-TR paraphilia, a paraphiliac does not necessarily engage in an unlawful activity that leads to an arrest or conviction as a sex offender. For example, a person who is sexually gratified only by fantasizing about women's shoes would likely qualify for fetishism but may never violate any law if his or her behavior remains restricted to fantasy life. Similarly, a person can engage in unlawful sexual offenses that do not equate with a mental disorder. Consider the case of an 18-year-old boy who is in a relationship with a 17-year-old girl who voluntarily consents to sexual intercourse even if such sexual contact could be considered unlawful statutory rape in certain jurisdictions.

The diagnosis pedophilia is often used interchangeably with child molestation or in reference to some other sexual activity involving a juvenile. However, important distinctions exist between the two terms. Pedophilia is listed in the DSM-IV-TR as a mental disorder that does not require an overt act (and therefore is not necessarily criminal), whereas child molestation is a legal term describing a criminal act, regardless of its motivation. According to the DSM-IV-TR, pedophilia requires that the individual has "recurrent, intense sexually arousing fantasies, sexual urges, or behaviors involving sexual activity with a prepubescent child or children (generally age 13 years or younger)" (p 572). This definition also requires that the person has acted on these sexual urges or that their fantasies cause marked distress or interpersonal difficulty. Finally, the DSM-IV-TR delineates specific age requirements to diagnose pedophilia. In particular, the person must be at least 16 years old and at least five years older than the targeted child, although for older adolescents with pedophilia, no precise age difference is specified (American Psychiatric Association, 2000).

In contrast to the DSM-IV-TR definition of pedophilia, statutory definitions of sexual offenses involving children do not require a prepubertal status. For example, a 19-year-old male who becomes sexually involved with a 15-year-old girl would *not* qualify as a pedophile based solely on this activity but could be legally classified as a sex offender. Likewise, the fact that an adult has unlawful sexual activity with another adult does not automatically establish that this person has any type of mental disorder or abnormality. An emerging area of controversy is whether or not certain rapes or forced sexual activity should be considered a type of paraphilia. Because paraphilia includes individuals who experience recurrent arousing sexual fantasies that involve the suffering of another nonconsenting person, are there some rapists who might qualify for a diagnosis of paraphilia under this definition? In other words, is there a subgroup of rapists who commit their crimes primarily because of recurrent and sexually deviant, arousing fantasies that involve force on an unwilling partner?

In studies that measure male rapists' erections when exposed to images suggestive of forced sexual activity, some rapists demonstrate sexual arousal, whereas others do not (Doren, 2002). In distinguishing which rapists might qualify as having a paraphilia, Doren (2002) outlined three overt behaviors that could serve as indicators: (1) repetitive patterns of actions, (2) sexual arousal during the rape that may lead to ejaculation, and (3) most if not all of the individual's criminal behavior being sexual in nature. Future studies may provide further information as to whether this proposed subgroup of rapists represents a meaningful distinction, particularly related to any potential response to castration as a mechanism to decrease their risk of sexual recidivism.

Castration's Proposed Mechanisms of Action

Concerns regarding the risk of sex offenders reoffending in the community appear well grounded. In a large meta-analysis examining 29,000 sex offenders, the sexual recidivism rate ranged between 10% and 15% after 5 years (Hanson & Bussiere, 1998). Furthermore, in a study comparing 9,691 sex offenders to non–sex offenders released from U.S. prisons in 1994, sex offenders were four times more likely to be arrested for a sex crime over the 3-year follow-up period. Forty percent of new sex crimes after release were committed within the first 12 months. Approximately 5% of all child molesters and rapists released were arrested for a new sex crime during the 3 years after their release (Langan, Schmitt, & Durose, 2003).

Due to the apparent increased risk of harm posed by sex offenders, castration holds an obvious appeal for communities searching to find an effective intervention to protect society. Can medications or surgery actually decrease the risk of sexual reoffending? The following sections review the proposed mechanisms of both chemical and surgical castration and summarize studies examining the effects of castration and their impact on decreasing sex offender recidivism.

Physiological Effects of Castration

Sexual drive is regulated by complex interactions between both neurotransmitters and sex hormones in the body (Saleh & Berlin, 2003). Castration's goal is to chemically or surgically alter a person's sex drive by targeting one or more of these various systems. Historically, the most frequently targeted hormone to lower male sex drive has been testosterone. Testosterone is a steroid hormone (in the androgen group of hormones) found in both sexes, although in higher concentrations in men. Testosterone is essential in the regulation of sexuality, aggression, cognition, emotion, and personality (Rubinow & Schmidt, 1996) and is largely responsible for the frequency and magnitude of spontaneous erections (Sturup, 1968). For these reasons, testosterone's role in sexual violence is of crucial importance in the understanding and potential treatment of sex offenders. In males, testosterone is primarily produced in the testes (i.e., testicles) and to a lesser extent by cells located in the adrenal glands near the kidneys. Testosterone levels remain relatively low until the onset of puberty. This increase in testosterone is responsible for male pubertal development and continues until early adulthood (Saleh & Berlin, 2003).

Regulation of testosterone is primarily carried out by a sensitive feedback loop known as the hypothalamic-pituitary-gonadal axis. Briefly stated, testosterone production is responsive to hormones released by the anterior pituitary gland located in the brain. These hormones include luteinizing hormone (LH) and follicle-stimulating hormone (FSH) and provide an indirect target for medications designed to alter the body's testosterone level (Saleh & Berlin, 2003).

Although sexually deviant individuals were once believed to have increased levels of testosterone, this theory has not been consistently supported by research. Studies have shown that individuals with sexually deviant thoughts have, on average, the same blood levels of testosterone as normal adult males (Rosler & Witztum, 1998; Seim & Dwyer, 1988). Some researchers now theorize that sexual deviants experience abnormal responses to normal testosterone levels. Therefore, one premise for the castration of sex offenders is that a lowering of their testosterone will result in a decrease in abnormal sexual thoughts and behaviors (Hendricks et al., 1988; Howard, 1995). Two forms of castration to accomplish this goal are chemical castration and surgical castration.

Chemical Castration

As noted above, the purpose of chemical castration is to alter a person's sexual drive and sexual behavior through the use of a medication. Sexual drive is influenced by a range of factors that include the body's neurotransmitters and hormones. The medications most commonly used for the purposes of chemical castration are generally divided into two categories:

(1) those that lower testosterone; and (2) those that change the body's serotonin levels (Saleh & Berlin, 2003).

Drugs that Lower Testosterone. The lowering of a person's testosterone level has been shown to impact a person's sexual desire and behavior. As a result of a lowered testosterone level, the individual typically experiences a reduction in libido, sexual potency, erections, sperm count, and masturbation frequency (Craissati, 2004; Donovan, 1984). In essence, chemical castration creates a temporary, yet reversible, impotence. Agents that have been shown to lower testosterone levels include compounds known as progestins, antiandrogens, luteinizing hormone-releasing hormone agonists, and gonadotropin-releasing hormone agonist analogues. None of the medications currently used for purposes of chemical castration have received approval from the U.S. Food and Drug Administration (FDA) (Saleh & Berlin, 2003).

Medroxyprogesterone (MPA) is the synthetic progesterone analogue most commonly used for chemical castration in the United States. MPA decreases plasma blood levels of testosterone using three mechanisms. First, it activates the enzyme testosterone-A-reductase, which is responsible for breaking down testosterone in the body. Second, MPA binds to plasma globulins, resulting in testosterone being cleared from the body more quickly. Third, MPA inhibits the pituitary gland from releasing hormones that signal the testes to produce testosterone (Albin, Vittek, & Gordon, 1973; Berlin & Schaerf, 1985; Saleh & Berlin, 2003). MPA is available in two forms: the oral form known as Provera, which is typically prescribed in doses of 50–300 mg a day, and the intramuscular injection known as Depo-Provera, which is commonly administered at a dose of 300 mg once a week. Complete suppression of testosterone secretion has been noted in individuals who receive doses of MPA in the range of 500–1000 mg once a week. Oral administration of MPA is prescribed less often because of its erratic absorption by the gut (Rosler & Witztum, 2000).

Kravitz et al. (1995) found that suppression of sexually deviant fantasies and behaviors occurred within the first 2 weeks of MPA treatment. Heller, Laidlaw, Harvey, and Nelson (1958) demonstrated that MPA could lower the sexual drive in normal males. Money (1968) described the first successful use of Depo-Provera in a reported treatment of a transvestite pedophile. In subsequent studies, Money described nine paraphiliacs whom he treated with intramuscular MPA at weekly dosages of 300–400 mg with a resulting decrease in erectile frequency, sexual drive, and orgasms (Money, 1970, 1972). MPA has also been reported as effective in controlling a variety of paraphilias, including pedophilia, exhibitionism, and voyeurism (Rosler & Witztum, 2000).

One study often cited to demonstrate the benefits of MPA compared sex offenders treated with MPA with sex offenders receiving therapy alone. Meyer, Cole, & Emory (1992) compared the efficacy of depot MPA (400 mg every week) in 40 men with a range of paraphilias (23 pedophiles, 7 rapists, 10 exhibitionists) to the reactions of 21 patients who refused medications but received psychotherapy. The follow-up period for both groups ranged from 6 months to 12 years. The rate of recidivism was an outcome measure for both groups. Recidivism rate was defined as arrest or self-reported inappropriate sexual behavior. Results were dramatically different between the two groups. The men treated with MPA had an 18% recidivism rate, versus a 58% recidivism rate for the control group, who received only psychotherapy (Meyer et al., 1992).

Do paraphiliacs require lifelong treatment with MPA? Some studies suggest that after control of sexual deviant urges has been maintained, the dose of MPA may be lowered (Walker & Myer, 1981; Walker, Meyer, Emory, & Rubin, 1984) or discontinued altogether without a recurrence of sexually deviant behaviors (Cooper, 1987). At the same time, caution should be considered with this approach because some individuals continue to have deviant sexual thoughts or behaviors regardless of low testosterone levels (Ibid) or with a lowering of the MPA dose.

Despite MPA's reported efficacy in reducing deviant sexual fantasies, several side effects have been reported from this treatment. Dose-related adverse side effects that have been described include abdominal pain, increased blood cortisol levels, depression, diabetes mellitus, increased production of breast milk, insomnia, gallstones, hot flashes, hypertension, and the formation of blood clots (Zonana et al., 1999). Serious, irreversible side effects that have been reported include breast enlargement, abnormal sperm production (which may be reversible) and liver damage (Weiss, 1999). In 2004, Pfizer added a "black box warning" to the drug label for Depo-Provera concerning the possible side effect of weakened bone tissue. The label includes the following statement:

> Bone loss is greater with increasing duration of use and may not be completely reversible. It is unknown if use of Depo-Provera Contraceptive Injection during adolescence or early adulthood, a critical period of bone accretion, will reduce peak bone mass and increase the risk for osteoporotic fractures in later life. (U.S. Food and Drug Administration, 2004)

The progesterone derivative cyproterone acetate (CPA) has been used for chemical castration in Canada and Europe since the 1970s but is not currently available in the United States (Rosler & Witztum, 2000). CPA works by blocking testosterone from binding to certain cell receptors, thereby effectively nullifying testosterone's effects (Neumann & Kalmus, 1991). CPA also has significant progesterone-like activity (approximately 100 times more potent then progesterone itself) and inhibits the pituitary from secreting FSH and LH levels with a subsequent decrease in testosterone levels (Rosler & Witztum, 2000). Like MPA, CPA's effects are largely dose dependant (Zonana et al., 1999).

CPA can be administered orally in a dose of 50–200 mg a day or via an intramuscular injection (depot) 300 to 700 mg weekly or biweekly (Reilly, Delva, & Hudson, 2000). Physiologically, there is a documented decrease in testosterone levels as well as sperm production at doses greater than 150 mg a day (Rosler & Witztum, 2000). Doses of 100 mg or less appear to partially inhibit testosterone, but not at levels sufficient to suppress sexually deviant tendencies (Rosler & Witztum, 2000). Patients taking CPA have reported diminishing deviant sexual interest and desire along with decreases in spontaneous erections (Bradford & Pawlak, 1993; Cooper, Sandhu, Losztyn, & Cernovsky, 1992).

In the first clinical study examining the effectiveness of CPA treatment of sex offenders, Laschet & Laschet (1971) followed more than 100 men who were diagnosed with a paraphilia for periods lasting from 6 months to 4 years. Exhibitionism was the most common paraphilia in this group, but other diagnoses included pedophilia and sexual sadism. CPA at a dose of 100 mg a day prevented approximately 80% of individuals from being able to achieve an erection or have an orgasm and eliminated their sexual drive. At a lower dose of 50 mg a day, a diminished sexual drive was reported, but individuals were still able to obtain an erection. Bradford & Pawlak (1993) conducted a double-blind placebo crossover study of CPA and found that self-reported sexual activity, sexual, drive, sexual fantasies, and masturbation frequency all decreased when the individuals were taking CPA. Multiple studies have demonstrated that individuals' rate of sexual recidivism is substantially less following treatment when compared with the pre-treatment period (Zonana et al., 1999). However, many of these studies have been criticized because they are case reports, lack objective measures of sexual interest, or do not include comparison groups of matched offenders who did not receive CPA treatment (Ibid).

Associated side effects that have been reported from CPA include depression, weight gain, shortness of breath, nausea, vomiting, weakness, weight gain, thromboembolism, enlarged breast tissue (gynecomastia), and irreversible liver damage (Bradford, 1983; Gijs & Gooren, 1996). In addition, the long-term use of CPA has been associated with a decrease in mineral bone density with osteoporosis as a potential result (Neumann & Kalmus, 1991).

CPA has been described as having less reported feminization, fatigue, and weakness when compared to MPA (Davies, 1974). Cooper et al. (1992) compared the effects of MPA to CPA in a placebo controlled double-blind crossover study, thus providing the first direct comparison of the two drugs (Cooper et al., 1992). Both drugs where equally effective in their suppression of sexual fantasies, masturbation habits, erections, and testosterone levels (Grossman, Martis, & Fichtner, 1999). Although some research has shown equivalent efficacy between MPA and CPA, other studies examining reoffense rates have demonstrated that individuals taking MPA have a higher recidivism rate (27%) compared to those taking CPA (3%) (Meyer & Cole, 1997).

Because MPA and CPA do not completely inhibit testosterone production or activity (Rosler & Witztum, 1998), drugs with other mechanisms of action in lowering the body's testosterone have been investigated as alternative forms of chemical castration. Synthetic analogues of a hormone known as gonadotropin-releasing hormone (GnRH) have received increasing attention because of their ability to substantially decrease the body's testosterone through their influence on the pituitary gland (which also helps regulate testosterone production). These agents are also referred to as luteinizing hormone-releasing hormone agonists (LHRH-A).

Prior to consideration for their use with sex offenders, these compounds were most commonly used in the treatment of prostate cancer (Bourget, 2008; Conn & Crowley, 1991). Four GnRH/LHRH agonists that have been used to decrease testosterone include triptorelin, nafarelin, and leuprolide acetate, and a subcutaneous implant known as goserelin acetate. Because these agents have demonstrated efficacy in some individuals who have not responded to either MPA or CPA, this treatment intervention has been recommended as an important alternative to the more traditional hormonal agents (Briken, Nika, & Berner, 2001).

Initial administration of these medications yields an acute increase in testosterone levels for the first 4 to 6 weeks of treatment. Therefore, CPA is often administered concomitantly until the testosterone levels wane to prepubescent levels (Bourget, 2008). The associated side effect profile of GnRH agonists is reportedly less than those of CPA or MPA (Grasswick & Bradford, 2002; Rosler & Witztum, 2000). Such side effects may include enlarged breast tissue, hot flashes, weight gain, and a decrease in bone density with long-term use (Grasswick & Bradford, 2002; Hoogeveen & Van der Veer, 2008). To help manage a potential decrease in bone mass, some physicians recommend the administration of calcium and vitamin D or biphosphonates (Liberman et al., 1995) and even small doses of testosterone (Rosler & Witztum, 2000).

Some authors have described potential advantages of the use of GnRH agonists as compared to MPA or CPA. First, they can be used in individuals where CPA and/or MPA are contraindicated or not effective (Hill, Briken, Kraus, Strohm, & Berner, 2003; Rosler & Witztum, 1998). Second, some individuals report experiencing fewer side effects from GnRH agonists compared to MPA or CPA (Rosler & Witztum, 2000). Third, they can be used in conjunction with CPA if there is suspicion that an offender is surreptitiously taking testosterone to increase levels reduced by CPA (Hill et al., 2003). Rosler & Witztum (1998) report that they have treated over 40 paraphiliac men with triptorelin who failed to respond to CPA or serotonergic drugs. According to their research, not one recurrence of sexually deviant behavior was noted over a 5-year follow-up period.

Drugs that Alter Serotonin Levels. Other medications used clinically to decrease the sexual drive include medications that alter neurotransmitters, particularly serotonin. These medications include classes of antidepressants known as tricyclic antidepressants (TCA) and the serotonin-specific reuptake inhibitors (SSRIs) (Saleh & Berlin, 2003). SSRIs are the most commonly used antidepressants for paraphiliacs. Theoretical mechanisms of SSRIs in treating paraphilias include a reduction in sexual drive and impulsiveness, the lowering of recurrent sexually obsessive deviant thoughts, the treatment of underlying depressive symptoms, and an indirect lowering of testosterone (Hill et al., 2003). Some authors suggest that SSRIs only help those individuals with sexually compulsive symptoms (Stein et al., 1992), whereas others have described patients with comorbid mood symptoms experiencing benefit from an SSRI drug (Kafka & Prentky, 1992). Systematic studies examining the use of these agents in managing paraphilias are currently lacking, though there have been a number of case reports and retrospective reviews that have described their potential efficacy. Greenberg and Bradford (1997) described a study they conducted that compared 95 men with paraphilias treated with SSRIs with 104 subjects who were treated only with psychosocial interventions. According to this research, paraphiliac fantasies and urges were significantly reduced in the men receiving SSRIs, though both groups demonstrated a decrease in paraphilic behavior over the 12-week follow-up period.

The use of SSRIs in the treatment of paraphilias requires further research to substantiate long-term efficacy (Rosler & Witztum, 2000). However, because these agents have been described as having fewer reported side effects, they may play an important role in the treatment of individuals who are not considered highly dangerous, are not likely to reoffend, and whose behavior is significantly connected to their sexually compulsive thoughts.

Surgical Castration

Like chemical castration, the goal of surgical castration is to decrease the body's testosterone level. In men, surgical castration involves the actual removal of the testicles, the primary organs responsible for making testosterone. The procedure is also known as an orchiectomy. Although the testes produce the vast majority of testosterone, a small amount of testosterone is also made by the adrenal glands, which are located on top of the kidneys. Therefore, surgical castration does not totally prohibit the production of all testosterone in the body, although it does result in a dramatic drop in the testosterone level. In addition, individuals who have been surgically castrated can take hormones to increase their testosterone levels back to normal.

A vasectomy is not the same procedure as surgical castration. A vasectomy involves cutting, tying, or cauterizing the tubes, known as the *vas deferens*, that carry sperm from the testes. As a result, sperm is blocked from exiting the male body, thereby preventing the impregnation of females. Unlike with surgical castration, the testes are not removed as part of a vasectomy procedure. A vasectomy does not diminish testosterone production or an offender's deviant sexual thoughts or behaviors. Finally, surgical castration does *not* involve amputation of the male penis.

Unlike chemical castration, surgical castration is irreversible and is generally restricted to more severe cases or those that do not respond to other forms of treatment (Hill et al., 2003). However, like chemical castration, surgical castration has demonstrated a significant effect on lowering sex offenders' sexual drive and sexual reoffense rates. Researchers found, in one study of 900 convicted sex offenders who underwent surgical castration and were followed for several years, that a significant number reported a decrease in their sex drive. In addition, the sexual reoffense rate was less than 3%, a relatively low number in comparison to reoffense rates of noncastrated offenders (Sturup, 1968).

In a comprehensive review of the literature comparing outcomes between treated and untreated groups of sex offenders ($n = 22,181$) Schmucker and Losel (2008) found that offenders who received surgical castration compared with those who did not demonstrated the most dramatic decrease in sexual recidivism. After surgical castration, chemical castration demonstrated the highest mean effect of all treatments in decreasing recidivism for a sexual offense. Although this review examined studies mainly in North America (31 studies from the United States and 17 from Canada), this analysis also included eight studies from German-speaking countries, eight from Great Britain, and five from other countries.

Comparison of State Castration Statutes

On September 17, 1996, California became the first state to authorize the use of either chemical or physical castration for certain sex offenders who were being released from prison into the community (Cal. Pen. Code. § 645, 2003). At the signing ceremony for this new legislation, Governor Pete Wilson expressed the public sentiment toward sex offenders when he said,

> I have a message for those skulking in the shadows. You better stay in the shadows or leave this state, because we will not tolerate your conduct ... We are going to win this fight. We are not going to concede one inch of any playground in any neighborhood to vicious predators. (Stone, 1996)

Although this legislation was considered extremely controversial at the time, at least eight additional states have subsequently passed laws that provide some form of castration for individuals who have been convicted of a sex offense and are being considered for parole or probation. Of the nine states authorizing castration for convicted sex offenders, four (Georgia, Montana, Oregon, and Wisconsin) permit the use of chemical castration only (Ga. Stat. Ann. § 16-6-4, 2002; Ga. Stat. Ann. § 42-9-44.2, 2002; Mont. Code Ann. § 45-5-512, 2002; Ore. Rev. Stat. § 144.625, 2001; Ore. Rev. Stat. § 144.627, 2001; Ore. Rev. Stat. § 144.629, 2001; Ore. Rev. Stat. § 144.631, 2001; Wis. Stat. Ann. § 301.03, 2002; Wis. Stat. § 304.06, 2002; Wis. Stat. § 980.08, 2002; Wis. Stat. § 980.12, 2002), four (California, Florida, Iowa, and Louisiana) allow either chemical castration or voluntary surgical castration (Cal. Pen. Code. § 645, 2003; Fla. Stat. Ann. § 794.011, 2002; Fla. Stat. Ann. § 794.0235, 2002; Iowa Code § 903B.1, 2003; La. Adm. Code 22:I.337, 2000; La. Rev. Stat. Ann. § 15:538, 2003), and one (Texas) (Tex. Gov. Code § 501.061, 2003; Tex. Gov. Code § 508.226, 2003) provides voluntary surgical castration as the only treatment option.

Several important similarities and differences are noted when comparing elements among these nine statutes. First, although all statutes apply to individuals who have been convicted of a sex offense, all nine states vary regarding the sexual behavior that triggers application of their castration statutes.

In Louisiana, for example, a conviction for any 1 of 10 specific sex offenses renders an individual eligible for castration, whereas Oregon notes only that chemical castration will be administered to "suitable" offenders who are convicted of "sex crimes" (La. Adm. Code 22:I.337, 2000; La. Rev. Stat. Ann. § 15:538, 2003; Ore. Rev. Stat. § 144.625, 2001; Ore. Rev. Stat. § 144.627, 2001; Ore. Rev. Stat. § 144.629, 2001; Ore. Rev. Stat. § 144.631, 2001). Second, in five states, castration is authorized only when the victim is younger than a specified age. Two states—Louisiana and Montana—permit castration regardless of the victim's age for repeat offenders (La. Adm. Code 22:I.337, 2000; La. Rev. Stat. Ann. § 15:538, 2003; Mont. Code Ann. § 45-5-512, 2002). Two states—Florida and Oregon—allow castration regardless of the victim's age, even for first-time offenders (Fla. Stat. Ann. § 794.011, 2002; Fla. Stat. Ann. § 794.0235, 2002; Ore. Rev. Stat. § 144.625, 2001; Ore. Rev. Stat. § 144.627, 2001; Ore. Rev. Stat. § 144.629, 2001; Ore. Rev. Stat. § 144.631, 2001).

Third, states differ regarding whether the proposed castration is discretionary, mandatory, or voluntary. Only Louisiana and Oregon mandate chemical castration for eligible first-time offenders. In contrast, five of the nine states mandate chemical castration for designated repeat sex offenders, three allow discretion by the court in whether chemical castration will be required, and Texas requires complete voluntary consent for surgical castration under all circumstances (La. Adm. Code 22:I.337, 2000; La. Rev. Stat. Ann. § 15:538, 2003; Ore. Rev. Stat. § 144.625, 2001; Ore. Rev. Stat. § 144.627, 2001; Ore. Rev. Stat. § 144.629, 2001; Ore. Rev. Stat. § 144.631, 2001; Tex. Gov. Code § 501.061, 2003; Tex. Gov. Code § 508.226, 2003). Fourth, states are nearly equally divided in their designation of who pays for the costs of castration treatment and subsequent monitoring. Four of the nine statutes require the state to pay costs, four require the offender to bear some or all of the financial burden, and one state (Wisconsin) (Wis. Stat. Ann. § 301.03, 2002; Wis. Stat. § 304.06, 2002; Wis. Stat. § 980.08, 2002; Wis. Stat. § 980.12, 2002) does not specify who pays for treatment. Finally, at least four of the states identify consequences for treatment noncompliance, ranging from revocation of probation (Louisiana) to potential incarceration for up to 100 years (Montana) (La. Adm. Code 22:I.337, 2000; La. Rev. Stat. Ann. § 15:538, 2003; Mont. Code Ann. § 45-5-512, 2002). Oregon is the only state that specifically includes violation of parole for those individuals who use chemicals to counteract the effect of chemical castration (Ore. Rev. Stat. § 144.625, 2001; Ore. Rev. Stat. § 144.627, 2001; Ore. Rev. Stat. § 144.629, 2001; Ore. Rev. Stat. § 144.631, 2001). It is critical to note that no state currently mandates surgical castration, perhaps due to the increased likelihood of successful legal challenges resulting from this permanent intervention. Table 10.1 compares and contrasts general elements of all nine statutes authorizing some form of castration.

The nine statutes also vary considerably in how they address the assessment and treatment of sex offenders. First, states are not uniform on what specific chemical agents are recommended for treatment. Of the eight statutes that authorize chemical castration, seven specifically identify MPA as a treatment option, and seven allow the use of other pharmaceutical agents in addition to MPA. Whether a medical or psychiatric evaluation is required prior to castration (either chemical or surgical) represents a second important area that is treated very differently among these nine statutes. California requires no medical or psychiatric evaluation of the offender prior to mandatory chemical castration (Cal. Pen. Code. § 645, 2003). As a result, both male and female offenders, rapists and child molesters, and psychotic and nonpsychotic offenders are all eligible for mandated treatment, whether or not such treatment is clinically appropriate. The Montana statute does not specifically require a mental health or medical assessment, but does specify that the treatment must be "medically safe drug treatment" (Mont. Code Ann. § 45-5-512, 2002). The Wisconsin statute is exceptionally vague about the type of evaluation, if any, required prior to treatment. This statute notes that the decision to grant supervised release may not be based on the fact that the person is a "proper subject" for antiandrogen treatment (Wis. Stat. Ann. § 301.03, 2002; Wis. Stat. § 304.06, 2002; Wis. Stat. § 980.08, 2002; Wis. Stat. § 980.12, 2002).

This statement implies that some form of evaluation is warranted to determine which offenders are appropriate for chemical castration. However, the nature and extent of any such evaluation remains unclear. For example, does the evaluation include a clinical interview only or does it also involve standardized actuarial risk assessment instruments specifically designed to evaluate a person's risk of recidivism? Moreover, do these evaluations require more objective

10.1 General Overview of Castration Statutes*

State	Included Offenses	Victim Age	Castration Method	Discretionary (D) Mandatory (M) Voluntary (V)	Person/Agency Financially Responsible	Consequences of Non Compliance
California	Sodomy, aiding/abetting sodomy, lewd and lascivious act with force/menace, oral copulation, aiding/abetting oral copulation, sexual penetration (with a foreign object)	<13	Chemical or voluntary surgical	D—First offense M—Second offense	State	Not specified
Florida	Sexual battery	Any	Chemical or voluntary surgical	D—First offense M—Second offense	State	Second-degree felony
Georgia	Child molestation, aggravated child molestation (involving physical injury to the child or sodomy)	<17	Chemical only	D—First offense aggravated child molestation D—Second offense child molestation	Offender pays for counseling. Unclear regarding who pays for MPA.	Not specified

Continued

General Overview of Castration Statutes* (Cont'd)

State	Included Offenses	Victim Age	Castration Method	Discretionary (D) Mandatory (M) Voluntary (V)	Person/Agency Financially Responsible	Consequences of Non Compliance
Iowa	Sexual abuse, lascivious acts, assault with intent, indecent contact, lascivious conduct, exploitation by a counselor, sexual exploitation of a minor	<13	Chemical or voluntary surgical	D—First "serious sex offense" M—Second offense unless determined "not effective"	Offender pays "reasonable fees"	Not specified
Louisiana	Aggravated rape, simple rape, forcible rape, sexual battery, aggravated sexual battery, oral sexual battery, aggravated oral sexual battery, incest, aggravated incest, aggravated crimes against nature	<13 years or any repeat sex offender	Chemical or voluntary surgical	M—If specified in mental health treatment plan	Offender pays costs of evaluation, treatment plan, and treatment	Revocation of probation, parole, or suspension of sentence. Good time earned may be forfeited.

State	Offense	Victim age	Type	Designation	Costs	Notes
Montana	Sexual assault, sexual intercourse without consent, incest	<16—first offense Any age—second offense	Chemical only	D—First offense if victim <16 and offender ≥3 years older D—Second offense	State	Criminal contempt of court with incarceration between 10 and 100 years.
Oregon	Pilot program of 40—50 persons each year convicted of "sex crimes"	Any	Chemical only	M—For all offenders deemed "suitable" without a medical contraindication	Offender (All costs)	Parole violation: "subject to sanctions" if fails to cooperate with program or takes any chemical to counteract treatment
Texas	Indecency with a child, sexual assault Aggravated sexual assault	<17 <14	Surgical only	V—All offenses	State	Not applicable
Wisconsin	Sexual assault of a child Second-degree sexual assault of a child	<13 13–15	Chemical only	D—All offenses	Not described	Not described

*Based on corresponding state statutes (see pp. 306–316)

measurements of sexual arousal, such as a polygraph or plethysmography, in addition to the offender's self report of sexual interest? Without a standardized, state-of-the-art evaluation process, the real risk arises that offenders who don't need treatment will be recommended for castration and those who might be more appropriate candidates could be missed.

In those six states that mention a pretreatment evaluation, the stated qualifications of the examiners vary. For example, Georgia requires a "psychiatrist or qualified mental health professional," Oregon specifies that a "competent physician" is necessary, and Texas mandates both a "psychiatrist and psychologist who have experience in treating sex offenders" (Ga. Stat. Ann § 16-6-4, 2002; Ga. Stat. Ann. § 42-9-44.2, 2002; Ore. Rev. Stat. § 144.625, 2001; Ore. Rev. Stat. § 144.627, 2001; Ore. Rev. Stat. § 144.629, 2001; Ore. Rev. Stat. § 144.631, 2001; Tex. Gov. Code § 501.061, 2003; Tex. Gov. Code § 508.226, 2003).

How states choose to address informed consent for both chemical and surgical castration represents a third important clinical component of this legislation. Of the nine statutes, three states—Iowa, Florida, and Oregon—do not address whether any element of informed consent is required prior to administration of a chemical agent (Iowa Code § 903B.1, 2003; Fla. Stat. Ann. § 794.011, 2002; Fla. Stat. Ann. § 794.0235, 2002; Ore. Rev. Stat. § 144.625, 2001; Ore. Rev. Stat. § 144.627, 2001; Ore. Rev. Stat. § 144.629, 2001; Ore. Rev. Stat. § 144.631, 2001). The informed consent process in the remaining five chemical castration statutes requires only that the offender be informed regarding the side effects. Three of these five states require that the offender acknowledge receipt of this information, and Georgia specifies that the offender must consent to treatment in writing (Ga. Stat. Ann. § 16-6-4, 2002; Ga. Stat. Ann. § 42-9-44.2, 2002). The Texas statute provides the most detailed process for obtaining informed consent for surgical castration. For example, the inmate must be at least 21 years old and must meet with a psychiatrist and psychologist as part of the informed consent evaluation. A "monitor" with a background in mental health law and ethics is appointed and assists the inmate with understanding the risks and benefits, to ensure that the consent is informed and voluntary. Furthermore, the inmate must request surgical castration in writing, may change his mind at any time, and should he ever withdraw consent, is no longer eligible for the procedure in the future (Tex. Gov. Code § 501.061, 2003; Tex. Gov. Code § 508.226, 2003).

The fourth clinical issue raised by chemical castration statutes involves whether psychological counseling is required in conjunction with chemical or surgical castration. Georgia is the lone state that mandates some form of psychological counseling for all designated sex offenders (Ga. Stat. Ann. § 16-6-4, 2002; Ga. Stat. Ann. § 42-9-44.2, 2002). Louisiana requires counseling only if the counseling is specified in the individual's treatment plan but otherwise does not require additional treatment (La. Adm. Code 22:I.337, 2000; La. Rev. Stat. Ann. § 15:538, 2003). The remaining seven states do not require counseling in addition to chemical or surgical castration.

The specific duration of medication treatment in the eight chemical castration statutes is a fifth important treatment component of these laws. Because six of the eight statutes mandate that either the state or offender demonstrate that the chemical castration is no longer necessary prior to cessation of treatment, chemical castration is potentially lifelong for some offenders. Finally, six of the nine statutes are silent regarding whether liability immunity applies to those providers who comply with the standards as set forth in their state statute. Both Georgia and Louisiana note that providers are not civilly or criminally liable if they act in good faith (Ga. Stat. Ann. § 16-6-4, 2002; Ga. Stat. Ann. § 42-9-44.2, 2002; La. Adm. Code 22:I.337, 2000; La. Rev. Stat. Ann. § 15:538, 2003). The Texas surgical castration statute provides the most explicit immunity for providers and specifies that physicians are "not liable for an act or omission related to the procedure" unless they are negligent in their care (Tex. Gov. Code § 501.061, 2003; Tex. Gov. Code § 508.226, 2003). Table 10.2 compares and contrasts these clinical questions as addressed in the nine castration statutes.

Legal Challenges to Castration Statutes

Several constitutional challenges to castration legislation may emerge as increasing numbers of offenders become eligible for court-imposed castration. Challenges to this legislation may include alleged violations of the First, Eighth, and Fourteenth Amendments to the federal Constitution.

10.2 Clinical Issues and Castration Statutes*

State	Chemical Agent Specified	Required Medical or Psychiatric Evaluation	Informed Consent Issues	Required Counseling	Cessation of Treatment	Provider Liability Immunity
California	MPA or its chemical equivalent	No	Must inform regarding side effects	No	Until no longer necessary (until DOC demonstrates to Board of Prison Terms that it's not necessary)	Not specified
Florida	MPA	Yes—Court-appointed "medical expert"	Not mentioned for MPA Described for voluntary physical castration	No	Until no longer necessary Court order specifies duration—either a specific term of years or for life	Not specified

State	Drug	Assessment	Informed consent	In treatment plan	Duration	Liability
Georgia	MPA or its chemical equivalent	Yes—Psychiatrist or qualified mental health professional for aggravated child molestation	Must be informed regarding side effects and consent to treatment in writing	Yes	Defendant must demonstrate no longer necessary	Not liable civilly or criminally if provider acts in good faith
Iowa	MPA or "approved pharmaceutical agent"	Yes—"Appropriate assessment" required to determine if treatment would be effective	Not addressed	No	Until the agency in charge of supervising the treatment determines that it is no longer necessary	Not specified
Louisiana	MPA or its chemical equivalent	Yes—"Qualified mental health professional with experience in treating sexual offenders"	Must inform regarding uses and side effects with written acknowledgement of information	Yes (If in treatment plan)	Shall continue unless it is determined that the treatment is no longer necessary.	Not liable civilly or criminally if provider acts in good faith
Montana	MPA or chemical equivalent or other medically safe drug treatment	No—But treatment must be "medically safe drug treatment"	Must inform regarding side effects	No	Until DOC determines that the treatment is no longer necessary	Not specified

Continued

10.2 Clinical Issues and Castration Statutes* (Cont'd)

State	Chemical Agent Specified	Required Medical or Psychiatric Evaluation	Informed Consent Issues	Required Counseling	Cessation of Treatment	Provider Liability Immunity
Oregon	"Hormone or antiandrogen, such as MPA"	Yes—By a "competent physician"	Must inform regarding side effects and offender must acknowledge receipt of the information	No	"State … shall require … treatment … during all or a portion of parole or post—prison supervision"	Not specified
Texas	Not applicable—Surgical castration only option	Yes—Physician, psychiatrist, and psychologist who have experience in treating sex offenders evaluate inmate for "suitability"	Detailed informed consent, counseling by a psychiatrist and a psychologist, and appointed monitor Inmate must request procedure in writing	No	Not applicable	Physician "not liable for an act or omission relating to the procedure" unless negligent
Wisconsin	Antiandrogen or its chemical equivalent	Unclear—Decision to grant supervised release "may not be based on the fact that the person is a proper subject" for antiandrogen treatment	Not addressed	No	Not described	Not specified

*Based on corresponding state statutes (see pp. 306–316)

First Amendment and Castration Legislation

The First Amendment protects a person's freedom of speech, (U.S. Constitution, amend. VIII), which involves consideration of two important components: the right to formulate an idea; and the right to communicate that idea once created (Stelzer, 1997). Because castration reportedly decreases sexual fantasies and thoughts, could an offender challenge imposed castration as violating his or her First Amendment right to generate ideas? In other words, does a sex offender have a right to create sexual fantasies deemed deviant? As described above, lowering a paraphiliac's testosterone level has been associated with a decrease in deviant sexual thoughts and urges.

The U.S. Supreme Court has not specifically ruled that the First Amendment's right to free speech prohibits a government intervention that restricts a citizen's ability to form thoughts. However, lower courts have discussed that a right to free speech incorporates a right to generate ideas. For example, in *Kaimowitz v. Department of Mental Health* (1976), the Michigan court ruled that the state could not perform experimental psychosurgery offered to an involuntarily detained sexual psychopath. The court specifically noted that such psychosurgery could affect the person's ability to generate ideas. As a consequence, without the ability to generate ideas, the person would be unable to effectively express ideas as protected by the First Amendment.

The Supreme Court has held that the right to *receive* ideas, in contrast to generating ideas, is protected by the First Amendment, regardless of the idea's social worth. In 1969, the Supreme Court addressed the right of individuals to receive ideas without government interference as it related to the possession of pornography. In the case of *Stanley v. Georgia* (1969), police found pornographic materials in the defendant's home and a Georgia court subsequently found the defendant guilty of possessing obscene matter. On appeal, the U.S. Supreme Court reversed the conviction on the grounds that the Constitution protects the right to receive information and ideas. Writing for the majority, Justice Marshall stated:

If the First Amendment means anything, it means that a state has no business telling a man, sitting alone in his own house, what books he may read or what films he may watch ... Our whole constitutional heritage rebels at the thought of giving government the power to control men's minds. (*Stanley v. Georgia*, 1969)

A counterargument to a First Amendment challenge emphasizes that sex offenders have committed a sex crime and therefore lack mastery over their fantasies. As a consequence, the government is not suppressing all thoughts but only those thoughts connected with illegal behavior.

Eighth Amendment and Castration Legislation

A second potential constitutional challenge involves whether forced castration violates the Eighth Amendment. The Eighth Amendment to the U.S. Constitution, made applicable to the states through the Fourteenth Amendment, prohibits cruel and unusual punishment (U.S. Constitution, amend. VIII). The U.S. Supreme Court has interpreted cruel and unusual punishment to include punishments that are excessive and not graduated and proportioned to the offense (*Weems v. U.S.*, 1909) and those that do not consider the defendant's degree of criminal culpability (*Enmund v. Florida*, 1982). In determining which punishments are so disproportionate as to be cruel and unusual, the U.S. Supreme Court established in *Trop v. Dulles* (1958) the importance of analyzing "the evolving standards of decency that mark the progress of a maturing society." The *Trop* Court also noted that the Eighth Amendment is aimed at preserving "nothing less than the dignity of man. While the State has the power to punish, the Amendment stands to assure that this power be exercised within the limits of civilized standards" (*Trop v. Dulles*, 1958). In essence, whether or not a punishment is considered cruel and unusual is partly related to the acceptance of the punishment by society as one that is just and appropriate.

Proponents of chemical castration for sex offenders argue that castration is not inherently cruel and that this treatment assists the offender in desisting from behavior that could result in further crimes and future punishments. Furthermore, castration is not excessive when considering an offender's previous harm to society and the importance of preventing future sexual victimization. Finally, because the offender is afforded increased freedom as a result of castration treatment, the state cannot achieve its objective in a less restrictive manner (Berlin, 1997).

How have courts analyzed mandated medical interventions that affect an offender's sexual functioning as a potential cruel and unusual punishment? In *Feilen v. Washington* (1912), the Supreme Court of Washington upheld a trial court's requirement that a man convicted of raping a young girl must undergo a vasectomy to prevent procreation. The Washington State Supreme Court commented that a vasectomy was a relatively painless procedure without a marked degree of physical torture, suffering, or pain. In addition, the court emphasized that vasectomies had been used by several states to sterilize "idiots, insane, imbeciles, and habitual criminals" as an exercise of the state's police power to prevent future criminal acts. The court concluded that in comparison to barbaric acts such as burning an accused at the stake, a vasectomy did not violate the Eighth Amendment's ban on cruel and unusual punishment (*Feilen v. Washington*, 1912).

Two years later, an Iowa court reached the opposite conclusion regarding the constitutionality of court-ordered vasectomies. In the 1914 case of *Davis v. Berry* (1914), the Iowa Board of Parole ordered a prison inmate (who was a repeat felon) to undergo a vasectomy in accordance with the state statute. Regarding the effects of a forced vasectomy, the court wrote, "The physical suffering may be so great, but that is not the only test of cruel punishment; the humiliation, the degradation, the mental suffering are always present and known by all the public, and will follow him wheresover [*sic*] he may go." The court held that a mandated vasectomy violated the Eighth Amendment. In addition, the court noted that castration represented an even greater degree of punishment than that resulting from a vasectomy (*Davis v. Berry*, 1914).

Although the U.S. Supreme Court has yet to rule whether or not castration represents cruel and unusual punishment, the South Carolina Supreme Court has rendered an opinion on this issue. In the case of *State v. Brown*, three defendants pleaded guilty to first-degree criminal sexual conduct in connection with a vicious gang rape. Their 30-year sentences were suspended, contingent on the defendants' completion of surgical castration as a condition of a recommended 5-year parole. In reviewing the case on appeal, the South Carolina Supreme Court determined that surgical castration was a form of mutilation and as such was cruel and unusual punishment prohibited by the South Carolina Constitution (*State v. Brown*, 1985).

Not all states have agreed with South Carolina that castration represents cruel and unusual punishment. In the case of *People v. Foster* (2002), Steven Foster challenged a California court's imposition of chemical castration as part of his plea bargain agreement as a violation of the state and federal constitutional ban on cruel and unusual punishment. Foster was convicted of sexually abusing the 12-year-old daughter of his girlfriend and agreed to plead guilty to 5 of 41 various charged sexual offenses. At the time he accepted his plea bargain, Foster acknowledged that he understood the possible consequences of his plea to include chemical castration. He also agreed to waive his right to appeal any sentence specified in the plea agreement. The trial court sentenced him to a 30-year prison term and ordered him to undergo hormone-suppression treatment upon parole. Following his conviction and sentencing, Foster claimed that the portion of the judgment requiring hormone-suppression treatment was grossly disproportionate and therefore violated state and federal constitutional prohibitions against cruel and unusual punishment (*People v. Foster*, 2002).

The appellate court's majority opinion noted that Foster had acknowledged that he understood the consequences of his plea to include the possibility of mandatory MPA, and that he had agreed to waive his right to any appeal. Justice McIntyre wrote,

> In other words, having bargained for a 30-year sentence that included the possible imposition of hormone suppression treatment in exchange for the dismissal of myriad serious felony charges, Foster cannot then maintain on appeal that such treatment cannot be imposed because it would violate prohibitions against cruel and unusual punishment. To do so would be to have his cake and eat it too. (*People v. Foster*, 2002)

The court majority disagreed with the sole dissent's opinion that the trial court was not authorized to mandate chemical castration because the statute noted that such treatment was, for all practical purposes, a condition of parole to be determined by the Board of Prison Terms, not by the trial court. The majority emphasized that such treatment was "not a mere condition of parole; it is a form of punishment, the imposition of which is part of a defendant's sentence" (*People v. Foster*, 2002). The ruling in this case clearly held that castration was for purposes of punishment rather than treatment and this punishment had been agreed upon when Foster accepted his plea bargain.

Does the Eighth Amendment argument apply if the offender waives his or her Eighth Amendment protection? In other words, is castration cruel and unusual punishment if the individual volunteers for castration? The U.S. Supreme Court has held that constitutional rights may be waived if the waiver is voluntary, "intelligent, and knowing" and "with sufficient awareness of the relevant circumstances and likely consequences" (*Brady v. United States*, 1970).

Whether or not the individual volunteers for a treatment does not determine whether such treatment is considered cruel and unusual punishment by the court. In fact, as discussed above, in *State v. Brown*, the South Carolina Supreme Court held that surgical castration violated the state's constitutional ban on cruel and unusual punishment. In addressing whether such punishment remained unconstitutional if the individual waived this constitutional right, the court noted, "Notwithstanding that the defendant accepted the condition, thereby attempting to waive his right to be free from cruel and unusual punishment, the condition was void because a state cannot impose conditions which are illegal and void as against public policy" (*State v. Brown*, 1985).

Batchoo (2007) presents three arguments for allowing sex offenders to volunteer for surgical castration. These arguments include the following:

1. When the offender volunteers for surgical castration, the need for an Eighth Amendment protection is diminished and the dignity of the offender's request should be respected.
2. Waiving one's Eighth Amendment right in sex offender cases is similar to a defendant's waiver of other rights, which often occurs during the trial process. For example, a defendant may accept a plea bargain to receive a lesser sentence thereby waiving his constitutional right to a jury trial. Similarly, a sex offender may waive his or her Eighth Amendment rights in hopes of receiving a lesser

sentence that may or may not involve a desire for treatment of sexually deviant behaviors.
3. Waiving one's Eighth Amendment rights in a sex offender case is not the same as waiving such rights when one is facing the death penalty. Sex offenders who volunteer for castration may receive an earlier release from prison and may have improved functioning in contrast to a capital defendant, whose waiver may result in death (Batchoo, 2007).

Even if an offender voluntarily consents to castration in order to prove that he or she has lowered his or her risk of future sexual offending, there is no guarantee that accepting castration will result in community release. In the California case of *People v. Flores* (2006), Edward Flores was a 46-year-old man who had been committed as a sexually violent predator to Atascadero State Hospital in 1997. Flores began his history of sexually victimizing children at the age of 13 or 14 and had a total of 15–18 victims prior to his hospital commitment. While hospitalized, Flores voluntarily underwent chemical and surgical castration in hopes of showing at his recommitment hearing that he was no longer likely to engage in sexually violent criminal behavior. The state's expert administered an actuarial instrument known as the Static-99. The Static-99 provides estimates of a person's future risk of sexual recidivism based on historical factors that have been demonstrated as associated with an increased risk of sexual recidivism. According to this expert, Flores's score predicted a 52% likelihood of reoffending within 15 years. Flores' expert witnesses challenged the use of the Static-99 in predicting behavior of a castrated offender, noting that this instrument had not been developed on castrated individuals. A defense expert further testified that castration was highly effective in reducing recidivism, and evidence was presented that Flores no longer demonstrated deviant sexual arousal when shown images of children that had previously been sexually stimulating for him.

The state's expert countered that Flores's motivation for sexual offending was not purely sexual and also involved an emotional connection with the children through his sexual acts. This expert testified that even if Flores's testosterone level was lowered, he could continue to molest children with his hands: "A man does not need to have an erection to molest a child" (*People v. Flores*, 2006). The jury rejected Flores's contention that his castration made him not likely to reoffend. On appeal, the California Court of Appeals upheld the jury's verdict, noting that castration was only one factor to be considered in assessing Flores's risk.

Fourteenth Amendment and Castration Legislation

Convicted sex offenders may also challenge forced castration under the Fourteenth Amendment's guarantee of both due process and equal protection. The Fourteenth Amendment prohibits a state from depriving its citizens of "life, liberty, or property, without due process of law" (U.S. Constitution, amend. XIV). In examining what procedural due process is warranted, the procedures surrounding either chemical or surgical castration must be sufficient to protect the offender's interests against those of the state (*Parham v. J.R.*, 1974). Various U.S. Supreme Court cases have addressed procedural protections for an inmate refusing treatment, and an analysis of procedural due process in this arena includes four general considerations (Beckham, 1998). There must first be a determination that a mental illness or abnormality is present (*Kansas v. Hendricks*, 1997). Next, the proposed treatment must be in the inmate's medical interest. Third, the mandated treatment must be essential for the inmate's safety or the safety of others. Finally, less intrusive treatments, such as psychotherapy, should be tried first before ordering medication (*Riggins v. Nevada*, 1992).

The California castration statute appears potentially vulnerable under this analysis. In particular, under the California statute, mandated treatment is based solely on the offender's having committed an enumerated offense, does not require a mental disorder or abnormality, and does not provide an assessment process to determine the appropriateness of castration treatment (Cal. Pen. Code § 645, 2003).

Substantive due process "involves a definition of the protected constitutional interest, as well as identification of the conditions under which competing state interests might outweigh it" (*Mills v. Rogers*, 1982). In *Washington v. Glucksberg* (1997), the U.S. Supreme Court emphasized that the Due Process Clause specially protects those fundamental rights and liberties that are "objectively, deeply rooted in this

Nation's history and tradition." The court also noted that the Fourteenth Amendment forbids the government to infringe on fundamental liberty interests unless the infringement is narrowly tailored to serve a compelling state interest (*Washington v. Glucksberg*, 1997).

Does mandated castration affect a fundamental right to procreation? In *Skinner v. Oklahoma* (1942), Justice Douglas (writing for the court majority) described procreation as one of the "basic civil rights of man," which is "fundamental to the very existence and survival of the race." All eight chemical castration statutes apply equally to men and women; therefore, the impact of hormonal therapy on future fertility must be considered.

Proponents of castration legislation argue that although castration may decrease a male's fertility, castrated men remain able to procreate and therefore no constitutional violation has occurred. More serious, substantive due process claims are raised in reference to female offenders. Antiandrogens, such as MPA, have not been shown to diminish significantly the likelihood that women will reoffend, thereby weakening the argument that forced chemical castration of females furthers a compelling government interest.

Chemical castration statutes may also be vulnerable to constitutional challenges under the Equal Protection Clause of the Fourteenth Amendment. The Fourteenth Amendment prohibits states from "denying to any person within its jurisdiction the equal protection of the laws" (U.S. Constitution, amend. XIV §1). Two distinct arguments can be made that castration statutes violate equal protection. First, chemical castration statutes may represent gender discrimination, based not on unequal treatment, but on unequal effect: the physiologic gender-related effect of antiandrogen treatment on women. In males, antiandrogen treatment decreases sexual urges primarily by lowering testosterone levels that occur at higher levels in men than in women. In females, medroxyprogesterone acetate reduces libido in less than five percent of cases and is associated with unique side effects in women that include irregular menses and breast swelling (Schwartz, 1994). Second, those statutes that do not require an assessment of the offender potentially represent an unconstitutional classification among male offenders. In particular, equal protection rights are violated because sex offenders are required to undergo chemical treatment without differentiating between those offenders who would benefit from treatment and those who would not (Beckham, 1998).

Finally, in the controversial case of *Roe v. Wade* (1973), the U.S. Supreme Court determined that the unwritten constitutional right to privacy was embedded in the Fourteenth Amendment and protected a woman's right to have an abortion. Fourteenth Amendment challenges could also be made that sex offenders have a right to privacy regarding their own bodies, a right that would be violated by legislated castration. In response, the state would likely respond that such privacy rights are not absolute and that no less-restrictive means are available to more effectively manage the risk of future harm posed by these individuals.

Castration Legislation and Public Policy Implications

In reviewing current trends regarding the castration of sex offenders, several issues are important to address. These issues include the following: (1) an offender's ability to provide informed consent to castration, (2) the government's role in diagnosing individuals and mandating castration, (3) the financial costs to society with and without castration, and (4) castration legislation's impact on sexual reoffending.

An Offender's Ability to Provide Informed Consent to Castration

Informed consent requires that the individual has voluntarily agreed to the treatment, has the information necessary to understand the recommended treatment, and has the capacity to make the treatment decision. If voluntary castration is not viewed by the court as cruel and unusual punishment, what potential concerns remain regarding an offender voluntarily accepting castration? Voluntary waiver of a constitutional right has been described as present when there is "no physical or mental coercion" that prompts the defendant to waive the right (Beckman, 1998).

Are sex offenders inherently coerced to accept castration when faced with a longer incarceration should they refuse this intervention? In *Kaimowitz v. Department of Mental*

Health (1976), a Michigan circuit court addressed whether or not a sexual psychopath could give voluntary informed consent to experimental psychosurgery to treat his aggression. The court commented that an involuntarily detained mental patient lived in an inherently coercive atmosphere, which affected his ability to give true consent.

However, there are important distinctions to be made between the circumstances described in the *Kaimowitz* case and castration. First, unlike the experimental brain surgery proposed in *Kaimowitz*, castration has reported efficacy in decreasing sexual recidivism and is unlikely to be considered an experimental procedure. Second, various risks of both chemical and surgical castration have been defined, unlike with the psychosurgery, where the risks were unknown. Third, for individuals undergoing chemical castration, the process is reversible unlike that of permanent brain surgery.

The informed consent process also involves the provider giving information about the proposed treatment to the adult receiving the treatment. In general, informed consent requires that the person be informed of the nature of their illness, the recommended treatment for the illness, the risks and benefits of the proposed treatment, alternatives to the treatment, and risks of not receiving the treatment. Some castration statutes define eligibility for treatment based solely on a legal classification without the requirement of a mental health diagnosis or evaluation. Therefore, some offenders may face mandatory castration in the absence of having a recognized medical or mental disease for which treatment is warranted. Some of the statutes allow information regarding potential risks to be communicated to the offender. However, when offenders are subjected to mandatory castration, they cannot apply this knowledge to decide whether or not to accept such treatment, nor do they have a choice as to alternate treatments.

The Government's Role in Diagnosing Offenders and Mandating Castration

Although castration has demonstrated therapeutic value in certain types of paraphiliacs, court-ordered castration raises concerns for the medical community as a key participant in this mandated government intervention. In particular, the American Medical Association (AMA) has issued a position statement that reads (in part),

The AMA (1) opposes physician participation in castration and other surgical or medical interventions initiated solely for criminal punishment; (2) physicians can ethically participate in court-initiated medical treatments only if the procedure being mandated is therapeutically efficacious and is therefore undoubtedly not a form of punishment or solely a mechanism of social control; (3) while the court has the authority to identify criminal behavior, the court does not have the ability to make a medical diagnosis or to determine the type of treatment that will be administered; (4) in accordance with ethical practice, physicians should treat patients based on sound medical diagnoses, not court defined behaviors ... (5) a national specialty society or national medical society should approve preestablished scientifically valid treatment for medically determined diagnoses. (n.d.)

The AMA guidelines above do not prohibit a physician from providing chemical or surgical castration, but they do emphasize the importance of prescribing such treatments only if they are effective in treating an identified diagnosis.

Several competing agendas may arise between members of the medical community and persons who pass and enact castration legislation. Medical providers expected to provide castration as "treatment" often have a minimal role in the design and implementation of these laws. In particular, issues related to the type of evaluation conducted, the information provided during the informed consent process, the coordination of psychotherapy in combination with castration, the monitoring of ongoing treatment, and the criteria for discontinuation of treatment are not clearly defined in the vast majority of the statutes. Without significant medical input into the crafting of castration statutes, the resulting outcome can be criticized as representing the practice-by-proxy of medicine by elected officials who have no medical license. In this situation, legislators, not doctors, determine who is appropriate for castration and under what circumstances castration will be implemented. These determinations are generally based on the specific offense committed and/or the age of the victim rather than the appropriateness or potential benefit of castration.

There are likely situations where medical providers will not agree that castration is appropriate. In many states, it is unclear who provides the information, treatment, and monitoring of castrated offenders should members of the medical community refuse to participate in the court-ordered process. Under California's castration statute, certain sex offenders are mandated to undergo MPA "or its chemical equivalent" upon parole and MPA treatment is mandated to begin one week prior to release from confinement. Interestingly, the statute also reads, "Nothing in the protocols shall require an employee of the Department of Corrections who is a physician and surgeon ... to participate against his or her will in the administration of the provisions of the section" (Cal. Pen. Code § 645, 2003). What happens when there is no physician willing to prescribe chemical castration but chemical castration is required by law? Who orders the medication under this circumstance? What if other medications are determined as medically appropriate but are not the "chemical equivalent" of MPA? Is the physician required to only use MPA when another treatment may be a more appropriate intervention?

Some of the castration statutes provide immunity from civil and/or criminal liability to the professional who provides castration. This immunity is important in addressing concerns by providers that they will face malpractice claims for adverse side effects associated with castration or should the person reoffend despite treatment. Although immunity may reassure providers that they will not face legal liability for their participation in court ordered castration, Stone, Winslade, and Klugman (2000) expressed concerns that such immunity could protect practitioners who engage in unethical or unlawful practices. Such practices could include the failure to provide informed consent or to provide treatment without the presence of a diagnosis appropriate for castration.

Financial Costs to Society With and Without Castration. The potential cost savings to society for an effective treatment of sex offenders are substantial. In a comprehensive report analyzing the economic costs of crimes, the United States Department of Justice estimated that the tangible and intangible costs per child sex abuse victim was approximately $100,000 (T. Miller, Cohen, & Wiersma, 1996). The cost of incarcerating a single sex offender is also substantial, particularly under involuntary indeterminate civil commitments. Reported estimates of incarceration have ranged from $68,000 per year per offender in Washington State's civil commitment program to Florida's projected cost of $100,000 a year to incarcerate a single sex offender (Friedland, 1999). In contrast, the estimated cost of daily pills or monthly injections of Depo-Provera range from $2,300 to $7,000 annually (Flack, 2005). Additional costs may also include blood tests to monitor serum testosterone levels, medical monitoring, and physician and counseling fees.

Some of the castration statutes require the offender to pay for castration as well as follow-up treatment and counseling. Although a state may view this policy as a cost-saving tactic, could this particular requirement actually increase the risk of sexual recidivism? Many offenders have few or no financial resources upon release. Their conviction as a sex offender also limits their employability. With few funds to pay for mandated medications, blood tests, physician appointments, and psychological counseling, there is a serious concern that released offenders will stop taking their medicine or not participate in counseling. Therefore, although requiring the offender to take financial responsibility for his or her own treatment may be an understandable and honorable goal, this approach could also undermine adherence to treatment, thereby increasing the risk of reoffense (Stone et al., 2000).

Castration's Impact on Sexual Reoffending

Several studies of paraphiliac individuals who have undergone chemical or surgical castration have demonstrated a decrease in sexual offending as a result of this intervention. Has recent castration legislation also met the goal of decreasing sex offender recidivism? This question is difficult to answer for several reasons. First, information on offenders eligible for castration is not readily available for public analysis. Second, it is virtually impossible from the available data to readily determine how many eligible offenders have refused castration. Third, castration legislation is relatively recent and only a limited number of castrated offenders appear to have been released into the community. Therefore, the outcome of these individuals for a period longer than 5 years is not yet known. Fourth, many states do not require a psychological examination prior to an offender receiving castration. Because motivation to participate in treatment is an important outcome predictor, perhaps those offenders who choose castration represent a sample more likely to respond and less likely to reoffend than those who refuse.

Fortunately, the Oregon State Legislature included a provision in their castration legislation that required selected offenders to be evaluated prior to release to determine whether medical treatment with MPA was indicated to reduce their risk. As a result, outcomes of those sex offenders who received MPA and were released have been analyzed. Maletzky, Tolan, and McFarland (2006) studied 275 men evaluated under the Oregon depo-Provera Program between 2000 and 2004. Over half (51.3%) of these men were evaluated and determined as not needing MPA treatment. Characteristics of this group included individuals who did not have true deviant interests, who had committed statutory rapes, and who were assessed as not posing an immediate risk. In contrast, among the 134 inmates (48.7%) assessed as appropriate for MPA treatment, many had repeatedly molested children (especially boys), committed multiple rapes, or demonstrated an inability to control their deviant sexual behaviors.

Of the 134 inmates recommended as needing MPA treatment, 79 (59%) received the medication but 55 (41%) did not. These researchers collected information on the diagnoses and outcomes of three groups. The majority of these offenders had been out of custody for over 2 years. These three groups included the following:

1. Male offenders assessed as needing MPA who eventually received it
2. Male offenders assessed as needing MPA but who did not receive it
3. Male offenders evaluated but determined not to need MPA

Measures of recidivism included reoffending, parole violations, and reincarcerations, and whether any of these offenses or violations were sexual in nature. Of the 79 men who actually received MPA, none had committed a new sexual offense. In marked contrast, nearly one third of offenders recommended for MPA who did *not* receive it committed a new offense, and approximately 60% of these were sexual in nature. In evaluating differences between those offenders recommended for MPA who received it and those who did not, researchers found that supervising officers were significantly more likely to make certain homosexual pedophiles received MPA than they were for either heterosexual pedophiles or men who raped (Maletzky et al., 2006).

The authors also compared men recommended to receive MPA who did not take the medication to those men assessed as not needing MPA. Curiously, men evaluated as not needing MPA were nearly as likely to have committed a new offense as those for whom MPA was recommended but never took it. These violations were also as likely to be sexual in nature. This finding suggests that continued improvement in establishing evidence-based guidelines is needed to determine which offenders are appropriate for castration so that appropriate candidates are not overlooked.

Future Public Policy Directions

A laudable goal of castration legislation is to decrease the risk of future sexual victimization by known offenders. Future public policy efforts designed to reach this goal should consider the following components when designing a castration statute:

1. Individuals responsible for drafting castration legislation should consult with appropriate medical and mental health experts. Caution is warranted in the use of statutory language that is overly broad in the application of castration and is narrowly limited in medication treatment options.
2. Chemical and/or surgical castration should be recommended only for individuals appropriate for this intervention. For example, mandating castration for an individual whose sexually offending behavior is unrelated to testosterone level may provide a false sense of security, expose the offender to unnecessary medical risks, and fail to prevent harm to future victims.
3. Medical and/or mental health professionals should be involved in the assessment of offenders identified as potential castration candidates. Such determinations should use current evidence-based approaches by providers who have the appropriate training and experience in the evaluation of sex offenders.

4. Treatment providers in various settings (such as a prison or outpatient parole clinic) should not be required to provide castration or ongoing monitoring if this participation violates established treatment guidelines or ethical practices. Particular concerns arise when the treatment is involuntary and the provider has not provided appropriate informed consent to the offender.

5. Castration legislation should include funding for an outcome evaluation component that follows castrated individuals upon release. This follow-up program could create a database that includes (among many potential items) demographic data, diagnoses, violations of parole, sexual and nonsexual reoffense rates, adherence to treatment, costs of treatment, barriers to treatment, and reported side effects of treatment. Comparisons of castrated sex offenders to sex offenders who were not castrated could provide valuable information as to the utility and cost-effectiveness of this approach.

6. Castration legislation should include funding for the costs of castration, medical monitoring, and appropriate lab work paid for by the state. A desire to require offenders to pay for their treatment is understandable. However, the inability of many offenders to pay for treatment increases the likelihood of continued incarceration or failure to continue treatment if released. Disruptions in treatment increase the risk of reoffense and/or reincarceration along with the costs of treating additional victims and their families. The state's economic burden for assuming treatment costs is minimal compared to the financial costs of incarceration and the financial and emotional costs to future victims.

7. Education and training for community supervisors and/or parole officers regarding the importance of their ensuring that all offenders receiving chemical castration adhere to their prescribed medication regime is extremely important, as demonstrated by the Oregon Depo-Provera follow-up project.

8. The development of a statewide training program for mental health professionals and physicians in the assessment and monitoring of castrated offenders should be strongly considered. The lack of available providers competent to manage castrated offenders poses a substantial barrier to the maintenance of these individuals in the community.

9. The need for ongoing psychological counseling of sex offenders combined with castration should not be ignored. For most offenders, cognitive behavioral therapy or other effective psychotherapies would be an important requirement of a treatment program.

Regarding emerging castration legislation, governments will need to balance the need to protect society with the needs of the mental health community to provide treatment in a safe and ethical manner. To date, no case challenging the constitutionality of these statutes has reached the U.S. Supreme Court. Future cases will help determine whether these current statutes have struck the appropriate balance between sex offenders' rights and society's right to be free of their criminal behavior.

References

Albin, J., Vittek, J., & Gordon, G. (1973). On the mechanism of the antian-drogenic effect of medroxyprogesterone acetet. *Endocrinology, 93,* 417–422.

American Medical Association. (n.d.). H-140.955 Court-ordered castration. Retrieved March 25, 2008, from http://www.ama-assn.org/apps/pf_new/pf_online?f_n=browse&doc=policyfiles/HnE/H-140.955.HTM

American Psychiatric Association. (2000). *Diagnostic and statistical manual of mental disorders (Text revision)* (4th ed.). Washington, DC: American Psychiatric Association.

Atkinson, R. L., Atkinson, R. C., Smith, R. C., Bem, D. J., & Nolen-Hoeksema, S. (1993). *Introduction to psychology* (11th Edition). Fort Worth: Harcourt Brace Jovanovich.

Batchoo, L. (2007). Note: Voluntary surgical castration of sex offenders: Waiving the Eighth Amendment protection from cruel and unusual punishment. *Brooklyn R. Rev, 72,* 689–719.

Beckham, L. (1998). Chemical castration: constitutional issues of due process, equal protection, and unusual punishment. *West Virginia Law Review., 100,* 853–894.

Berlin, F. S., & Schaerf, S. W. (1985). Laboratory assessment of the paraphilias and their treatment with antiandrogenic medication. In R. C. W. Hall & T. P. Beresford (Eds.), *Handbook of Psychiatric Diagnostic Procedures* (pp. 273–305). New York: Spectrum Publications.

Berlin, J. (1997). Chemical castration of sex offenders: "A shot in the arm" towards rehabilitation. *Whittier Law Review, 19,* 169–213.

Bourget, D. (2008). Evidential basis for the assessment and treatment of sex offenders. *Brief Treatment and Crisis Intervention, 8*(1), 130–146.

Bradford, J. M. (1983). The hormonal treatment of sexual offenders. *Bulletin of the American Academy of Psychiatry and the Law, 11*(2), 159–169.

Bradford, J. M., & Pawlak, A. (1993). Double-blind placebo crossover study of cyproterone acetate in the treatment of the paraphilias. *Archives of Sexual Behavior 22*(5), 383–402.

Brady v. United States, 397 U.S. 742 (1970).

Breitenberger, B. M. (2007). *Aphrodite and Eros: The development of erotic mythology in early Greek poetry and cult.* Florence, Kentucky: Routledge.

Briken, P., Nika, E., & Berner, W. (2001). Treatment of paraphilia with luteinizing hormone-releasing hormone agonists. *Journal of Sexual and Marital Therapy, 27*(1), 45–55.

Buck v. Bell, 274 U.S. 200 (1927).

Cal. Pen. Code. § 645 (2003).

Conn, P. M., & Crowley, W. F. (1991). Gonadotropin-releasing hormone and its analogues. *The New England Journal of Medicine, 324*(2), 93–103.

Cooper, A. J. (1987). Medroxyprogesterone acetate (MPA) treatment of sexual acting out in men suffering from dementia. *Journal of Clinical Psychiatry, 48*(9), 368–370.

Cooper, A. J., Sandhu, S., Losztyn, S., & Cernovsky, Z. (1992). A double-blind placebo controlled trial of medroxyprogesterone acetate and cyproterone acetate with seven pedophiles. *The Canadian Journal of Psychiatry, 37*(10), 687–693.

Craissati, J. (2004). *Managing high risk sex offenders in the community: A psychological approach.* New York: Routledge.

Davies, T. S. (1974). Cyproterone acetate for male hypersexuality. *Journal of International Medical Research, 2*(2), 159–163.

Davis v. Berry, 216 Fed 413 (S.D. Iowa 1914).

Donovan, B. T. (1984). *Hormones and human behavior.* London: Cambridge University Press.

Doren, D. M. (2002). Diagnostic issues within sex offender civil commitment assessments: defining relevant paraphilias. In N. Hale & M. H. Seawell (Eds.), *Evaluating sex offenders: A manual for civil commitments and beyond.* London: Sage Publications.

Druhm, K. A. (1997). A welcome reaction to draconia: California's penal law section 645. The castration of sex offenders and the Constitution. *Albany Law Review, 61*(1), 285–343.

Enmund v. Florida, 458 U.S. 782 (1982).

Feilen v. Washington, 70, Wash. 65 (1912).

Fla. Stat. Ann. § 794.011 (2002).

Fla. Stat. Ann. § 794.0235 (2002).

Flack, C. (2005). Chemical castration: an effective treatment for the sexually motivated pedophile or an impotent alternative to traditional incarceration? *The Journal of Law in Society, 173*

Friedland, S. I. (1999). On treatment, punishment, and the civil commitment of sex offenders. *University of Colorado Law Review, 70.*

Ga. Stat. Ann. § 16-6-4 (2002).

Ga. Stat. Ann. § 42-9-44.2 (2002).

Gawande, A. (1997). The unkindest cut: the science and ethics of castration. Retrieved March 8, 2008, from http://www.papillonsartpalace.com/unkindes.htm

Gijs, I., & Gooren, L. (1996). Hormonal and psychopharmacological interventions in the treatment of paraphilias: An update. *Journal of Sex Research, 33,* 273–290.

Glass, J. M., & Watkin, N. A. (1997). From mutilation to medication: the history of orchiectomy. *British Journal of Urology, 80*(3), 373–378.

Grasswick, L. J., & Bradford, J. B. (2002). Osteoporosis associated with the treatment of paraphilias: a clinical review of seven case reports. *Forensische Psychiatrie und Psychotherapie, 9* (Suppl), 40.

Greenberg, D. M., & Bradford, J. M. W. (1997). A review of the role of selective serotonin reuptake inhibitors. *Sex Abuse, 9,* 349–361.

Grossman, L. S., Martis, B., & Fichtner, C. G. (1999). Are sex offenders treatable? A research overview. *Psychiatric Services, 50*(3), 349–361.

Hanson, R. K., & Bussiere, M. T. (1998). Predicting relapse: A meta-analysis of sexual offender recidivism studies. *Journal of Consulting and Clinical Psychology, 66*(2), 348–362.

Heller, C. G., Laidlaw, W. M., Harvey, H. T., & Nelson, W. O. (1958). Effects of progestational compounds on the reproductive processes of the human male. *Annals of the New York Academy of Sciences, 71*(5), 649–665.

Hendricks, S. E., Fitzpatrick, D. F., Hartmann, K., Quaife, M. A., Stratbucker, R. A., & Graber, B. (1988). Brain structure and function in sexual molesters of children and adolescents. *Journal of Clinical Psychiatry, 49*(3), 108–112.

Hill, A., Briken, P., Kraus, C., Strohm, K., & Berner, W. (2003). Differential pharmacological treatment of paraphilias and sex offenders. *International Journal of Offender Therapy and Comparative Criminology, 47*(4), 407–421.

Hoogeveen, J., & Van der Veer, E. (2008). Side effects of pharmacotherapy on bone with long-acting gonadorelin agonist triptorelin for paraphilia. *The Journal of Sexual Medicine, 5*(3), 626–630.

Howard, R. C. (1995). The neurophysiology of sexual desire, with particular reference to paedophilia. *The Annals, Academy of Medicine, Singapore, 24*(5), 724–727.

Iowa Code § 903B.1 (2003).

Johnson, J. N.C. latest to embrace Jessica's Law. Retrieved, August 19, 2008, from http://news14.com/content/top_stories/597791/n-c--latest-to-embrace-jessica-s-law/Default.aspx

Juvenal, P. (1974). *The sixteen satires.* London: Penguin Books.

Kafka, M. P., & Prentky, R. (1992). Fluoxetine treatment of nonparaphilic sexual addictions and paraphilias in men. *Journal of Clinical Psychiatry, 53*(10), 351–358.

Kaimowitz v. Department of Mental Health, 1 (Mich. Cir. Ct. 147 1976).

Kansas v. Hendricks, 117 (S. Ct. 2072 1997).

Kravitz, H. M., Haywood, T. W., Kelly, J., Wahlstrom, C., Liles, S., & Cavanaugh, J. L., Jr. (1995). Medroxyprogesterone treatment for paraphiliacs. *Bulletin of American Academy of Psychiatry and the Law, 23*(1), 19–33.

La. Adm. Code 22:I.337 (2000).

La. Rev. Stat. Ann. § 15:538. (2003).

Langan, P. A., Schmitt, E. L., & Durose, M. R. (2003). *Recidivism of Sex Offenders Released from Prison in 1994*. U.S. Department of Justice, Office of Justice Programs, Bureau of Justice Statistics, NCJ 198281, Washington, DC. Retrieved May 2, 2008, from http://www.ojp.usdoj.gov/bjs/abstract/rsorp94.htm

Laschet, U., & Laschet, L. (1971). Psychopharmacotherapy of sex offenders with cyproterone acetate. *Pharmakopsychiatrie Neuropsychopharmakologie, 4*, 99–104.

Liberman, U. A., Weiss, S. R., Broll, J., Minne, H. W., Quan, H., Bell, N. H., Rodriquez-Portales, J., Downs, R. W., Dequeker, J., Favus, M. (1995). Effect of oral alendronate on bone mineral density and the incidence of fractures in postmenopausal osteoporosis. The Alendronate Phase III Osteoporosis Treatment Study Group. *The New England Journal of Medicine, 333*(22), 1437–1443.

Maletzky, B. M., Tolan, A., & McFarland, B. (2006). The Oregon depo-Provera program: a five-year follow-up. *Sex Abuse, 18*(3), 303–316.

Meyer, W. J., Cole, C., & Emory, E. (1992). Depo provera treatment for sex offending behavior: An evaluation of outcome. *Bulletin of the American Academy of Psychiatry and the Law, 20*(3), 249–259.

Meyer, W. J., & Cole, C. M. (1997). Physical and chemical castration of sex offenders: A review. *Journal of Offender Rehabilitation, 25*(3/4), 1–18.

Miller, R. D. (1998). Forced administration of sex-drive reducing medications to sex offenders: treatment or punishment? *Psychology, Public Policy, and Law, 4*(1-2), 175–199.

Miller, T., Cohen, M., & Wiersma, B. (1996). *Victim costs and consequences: a new look*. U.S. Department of Justice, National Institute of Justice Research Report, NCJ 155282, Washington, DC. Retrieved May 2, 2008, from http://www.ojp.usdoj.gov/nij/pubs-sum/155282.htm

Mills v. Rogers, 457 U.S. 291 (1982).

Money, J. (1968). Discussion of the hormonal inhibition of libido in male sex offenders. In M. R. London (Ed.), *Endocrinology and Human Behavior*. London: Oxford University Press.

Money, J. (1970). Use of androgen depleting hormone in the treatment of male sex offenders. *Journal of Sex Research, 6*, 165–172.

Money, J. (1972). The therapeutic use of androgen-depleting hormone. *International Psychiatry Clinics, 8*, 165–174.

Mont. Code Ann. § 45-5-512, (2002).

Neumann, F., & Kalmus, J. (1991). Cyproterone acetate in the treatment of sexual disorders: Pharmacological base and clinical experience. *Experimental and Clinical Endocrinology, 98*(2), 71–80.

Office of the Governor, Bobby Jindal. Governor signs chemical castration bill, authorizing the castration of sex offenders in Louisiana. Retrieved August 19, 2008, from http://www.gov.louisiana.gov/index.dfm?md=newsroom&=detail&articleID=270).

Ore. Rev. Stat. § 144.625 (2001).

Ore. Rev. Stat. § 144.627 (2001).

Ore. Rev. Stat. § 144.629 (2001).

Ore. Rev. Stat. § 144.631 (2001).

Parham v. J.R., 442 U.S. 584 (1974).

People v. Flores, 144 (Cal. App. 4th 625 2006).

People v. Foster, 101 (Cal. App. 4th 247 2002).

Reilly, D. R., Delva, N. J., & Hudson, R. W. (2000). Protocols for the use of cyproterone, medroxyprogesterone, and leuprolide in the treatment of paraphilia. *The Canadian Journal of Psychiatry, 45*, 559–563.

Riggins v. Nevada, 504 U.S. 127 (1992).

Roe v. Wade, 410 U.S. 113 (1973).

Rosler, A., & Witztum, E. (1998). Treatment of men with paraphilia with a long-acting analogue of gonadotropin-releasing hormone. *The New England Journal of Medicine, 338*(7), 416–422.

Rosler, A., & Witztum, E. (2000). Pharmacotherapy of paraphilias in the next millennium. *Behavioral Sciences & the Law, 18*(1), 43–56.

Rubinow, D. R., & Schmidt, P. J. (1996). Androgens, brain, and behavior. *The American Journal of Psychiatry, 153*(8), 974–984.

Saleh, F. M., & Berlin, F. S. (2003). Sex hormones, neurotransmitters, and psychopharmacological treatments in men with paraphilic disorders. *The Journal of Child Sexual Abuse, 12*(3-4), 233–253.

Schmucker, M., & Losel, F. (2008). Does sexual offender treatment work? A systematic review of outcome evaluations. *Psicothema, 20*(1), 10–19.

Schwartz, H. I. (1994). Informed consent and competency. In R. Rosner (Ed.), *Principles and practice of forensic psychiatry* (pp. 103–110). New York: Chapman & Hall.

Seim, H. C., & Dwyer, M. (1988). Evaluation of serum testosterone and luteinizing hormone levels in sex offenders. *Family Practice Research Journal, 7*(3), 175–180.

Skinner v. Oklahoma, 316 U.S. 535 (1942).

Stanley v. Georgia, 394 U.S. 557 (1969).

State v. Brown, 284 S.C. 407 (1985).

Stein, D. J., Hollander, E., Anthony, D. T., Schneider, F. R., Fallon, B. A., Leibowitz, M. R., et al. (1992). Serotonergic medications for sexual obsessions, sexual addiction and paraphilias. *Journal of Clinical Psychiatry, 53*, 267–271.

Stelzer, G. L. (1997). Chemical castration and the right to generate ideas: Does the First Amendment protect the fantasies of convicted pedophiles? *Minnesota Law Review,* 1687–1709.

Stone, K. Wilson issues warning, endorses castration bill. Daily News (Los Angeles, California), September 18, 1996.

Stone, T. H., Winslade, W. J., & Klugman, C. M. (2000). Sex offenders, sentencing laws and pharmaceutical treatment: a prescription for failure. *Behavioral Sciences & the Law, 18*(1), 83–110.

Sturup, G. K. (1968). Treatment of sexual offenders in Herstedvester Denmark. The rapists. *Acta Psychiatrica Scandinavica Supplement, 204*, 5–62.

Sturup, G. K. (1971). Treatment of the sex offender. Castration: the total treatment. *International Psychiatry Clinics, 8*(4), 175–196.

Tex. Gov. Code § 501.061 (2003).

Tex. Gov. Code § 508.226 (2003).

Trop v. Dulles, 356 86 1958).

U.S. Constitution, amend. VIII,

U.S. Constitution, amend. XIV,

U.S. Constitution, amend. XIV § 1.

U.S. Food and Drug Administration. (2004). Black box warning added concerning long term use of Depo-Provera contraceptive injection. *FDA Talking Paper*. Retrieved April 28, 2008, from www.fda.gov/bbs/topics/ANSWERS/2004/ANS01325.html

Vanderzyl, K. A. (1994). Castration as an alternative to incarceration: An impotent approach to the punishment of sex offenders. *Illinois University Law Review, 15*(107–140).

Walker, P. A., Meyer, W. J., Emory, L. E., & Rubin, A. L. (1984). Antiandrogen treatment of the paraphilias. In H. C. Stancer, P. E. Garfinkel & V. M. Rakoff (Eds.), *Guidelines for the use of psychotropic drugs* (pp. 427–443). New York: Spectrum Publications.

Walker, P. A., & Meyer, W. J. (1981). Medroxyprogesterone acetate treatment for paraphilic sex offenders. In J. R. Hayes, T. K. Roberts & K. S. Soloway (Eds.), *Violence and the violent individual*. New York: Spectrum Publications.

Washington v. Glucksberg, 117 (S. Ct. 2268 1997).

Weems v. U.S., 217 U.S. 349 (1909).

Weiss, P. (1999). Assessment and treatment of sex offenders in the Czech Republic and in Eastern Europe. *Journal of Interpersonal Violence, 14*(4), 411–421.

Wis. Stat. Ann. § 301.03 (2002).

Wis. Stat. § 304.06 (2002).

Wis. Stat. § 980.08 (2002).

Wis. Stat. § 980.12 (2002).

Wong, C. M. (2001). Chemical castration: Oregon's innovative approach to sex offender rehabilitation, or unconstitutional punishment? *Oregon Law Review, 80*(1), 267–301.

Zonana, H., Abel, G., Bradford, J., Hoge, S. K., Metzner, J., Becker, J., Bonnie, R., Fitch, L., Hughes, L. (1999). Pharmacological treatment of sex offenders. In *Dangerous sex offenders: A task force report of the American Psychiatric Association*. Washington, DC: American Psychiatric Association.

The Civil Commitment of Sexual Predators: A Policy Review

11

Andrew J. Harris

In 1990, Washington's Governor Booth Gardner signed into law the Community Protection Act, establishing the nation's first contemporary civil commitment law for individuals designated as sexually violent predators (SVPs).[i] Following Washington's lead, a succession of states moved to adopt similar laws, with 20 states establishing civil commitment policies as of 2008, and many others considering their passage (Fitch & Hammen, 2004).[ii] Although the majority of these states adopted civil commitment legislation during the 1990s, interest in the laws has surged in recent years, as reflected by California's expansion of civil commitment criteria pursuant to Proposition 83, the passage of new civil commitment laws in New York and New Hampshire, and the 2006 congressional passage of a federal civil commitment statute under provisions of the Adam Walsh Child Protection and Safety Act.

Typically applied following completion of a criminal sentence, SVP civil commitment permits the state to retain custody of individuals found by a judge or jury to present a risk of future harmful sexual conduct by virtue of a mental abnormality or personality disorder. Following commitment, states remand individuals to the custody of mental health authorities or in some cases correctional agencies, which ostensibly provide treatment for the condition that makes the individual likely to engage in acts of sexual violence. In most states, commitments are for an indeterminate period, with mental health authorities retaining custody until the individual is determined to no longer pose a threat to society. As of mid-2007, over 4,500 individuals had been committed under state SVP statutes (Gookin, 2007).

Since their inception, civil commitment policies have engendered significant controversy. Proponents of the laws have maintained that civil commitment represents a necessary stop-gap measure to protect society from a small but dangerous group of individuals who continue to pose a threat to society following completion of their formal criminal sanctions. Criticisms of the policies have emerged primarily within two sectors: the legal establishment, where debate has focused on constitutional concerns related both to civil commitment's fundamental premises and to its application; and the mental health community, where many have cited concern over the limitations of treatment and risk-assessment technology. Mental health professionals and advocates have also expressed concerns regarding the co-opting of the psychiatric profession to fulfill a criminal justice function, the misappropriation of public mental health resources, and the effects of the laws on compounding stigmatization of individuals with serious mental illness (Mental Health America, 2006). Further, some have questioned the policies' long-range sustainability, considering the significant and mounting costs of the policy (Harris, 2006; La Fond, 2003).

This chapter examines the social, political, legal, and practical dimensions of SVP civil commitment, evaluating the policies' promises, limitations, and viability as sustainable elements of sex offender management practice. As set forth in Figure 11.1, this examination is framed within three domains:

11.1

Framework for Examining SVP Civil Commitment Policies

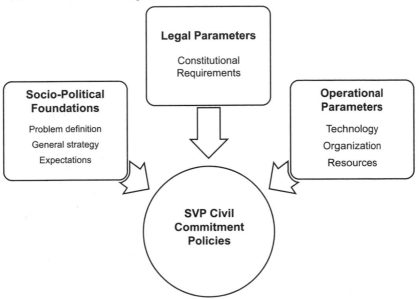

- The sociopolitical domain, in which the core problem is defined, general strategies set forth, and expectations framed through legislative action
- The legal domain, in which policies and practices are circumscribed in accordance with constitutional parameters
- The operational domain, in which the policies are implemented in response to organizational challenges, financial resource limitations, and technological constraints

Following a consideration of each of these three areas, the chapter concludes with an assessment of the policy outlook for SVP civil commitment, considering the role of the policies within the context of criminal justice and sex offender management policy.

Sociopolitical Context

Early Precursors to SVP Civil Commitment

The concept of using the mental health system as a response to sexual crime and deviance dates back to the early 20th century. As news coverage of violent sexual crimes fueled the public's sense of vulnerability, positivist criminological thought and the ideology of the progressive movement converged to reconstruct crime and deviance as manifestations of both social and individual pathology. Simultaneously, the burgeoning field of psychiatry set forth a framework for understanding the problem of the "sexual psychopath" and offered the promise of therapeutic technology that might address that problem.

Summarizing the prevailing sentiments of the era, Jenkins (1998) cited a 1915 *New York Times* editorial:

> Moral degenerates are easily discoverable without waiting until acts of violence put them in the category of criminals. [It is simply wrong to permit such men] to roam the State without any attempt to segregate them ... It is high time that the State provide adequate places of custody where they may have treatment by skilled physicians. (p. 41)

These ideas found their way into the realm of public policy with the passage of the Massachusetts Briggs Act, a law that permitted the indefinite civil commitment of "defective delinquents"—a class of individuals deemed to be at high risk of committing criminal offenses based on prior acts. Adopted in 1911 and amended in 1921, the Briggs Act set forth a hybrid of civil and criminal procedures permitting the preventive detention and treatment of individuals determined by psychiatric experts to pose a threat of committing criminal acts.[iii]

Beginning in the 1930s, a succession of states, building on the Briggs Act's core model, adopted a series of laws targeting a class of individuals designated as "sexual psychopaths." In his seminal study of the proliferation of sexual psychopath legislation, criminologist Edwin Sutherland cited a series of conditions related to the passage of these laws. Notably, Sutherland (1950) cited the responses of the media, citizenry, and political establishment to high-profile sexual crimes, and noted the convergence of these concerns with the "solution" offered by the field of psychiatry and its attendant therapeutic ideal.

Although the passage of sexual psychopath legislation was most commonly justified on the grounds of preventing heinous acts of sexual murder, the laws as implemented were often applied as a generalized response to sexual deviance. With behaviors such as homosexuality designated as psychiatric disorders, the statutes permitted the roundup and preventive detention of many individuals who presented little or no imminent danger for committing sexually violent acts (Miller, 2002).

The use of sexual psychopath laws reached its zenith in the 1950s, by which time 28 states had adopted active sexual psychopath laws (Zonana & Norko, 1999). By the 1960s, however, the numbers of individuals committed to state custody as sexual psychopaths had begun a steady decline, amidst the growing influence of civil rights law and mounting concerns over the cost, efficacy, and conditions of large state institutions.

On a more specific level, the demise of sexual psychopath laws was also inextricably linked to a growing sense within psychiatry—the field upon whose therapeutic promise the policies had once been based—that sexual psychopath civil commitment had largely failed to achieve its once-stated goals of individual treatment and rehabilitation. These reservations were accompanied by a growing body of research and commentary that called into question the ability of psychiatric "experts" to accurately predict future violent behavior (Ennis & Litwack, 1975; Steadman & Cocozza, 1974).

Reflecting these concerns, the Group for the Advancement of Psychiatry (1977) adopted a formal position statement in 1977 disavowing psychiatry's role in such civil commitment schemes, citing the limitations of treatment technology and suggesting that the problem of sexual offending behavior was more appropriately addressed through the criminal justice system. By the 1980s, sexual psychopath statutes had been repealed or fallen into disuse in most states.

Beginning in the early 1990s, a series of social and political developments converged to resurrect the mental health system's role in managing individuals at risk of committing future sexual offenses. Whereas some of these developments closely paralleled the phenomena described by Sutherland a half century earlier, others reflect a decidedly different dynamic, rooted in contemporary views of crime, punishment, mental health, and the role of government.

Role of Seminal Events and Citizen Mobilization

Writing about the diffusion of sexual psychopath laws in 1950, Sutherland noted that the laws "are customarily enacted after a state of fear has been aroused in a community by a few serious sex crimes committed in quick succession" (p. 143). Jenkins, in his historical analysis (1998) of societal responses to the sexual victimization of children, evoked Cohen's (2003) concept of "moral panic," suggesting that the phenomenon described by Sutherland reflected a dominant and recurring theme throughout the 20th century.

Consistent with these phenomena, the passage of Washington's groundbreaking law was prominently linked to the 1989 abduction, rape, and mutilation of a 7-year-old Tacoma boy by a man named Earl Shriner, who had been released from prison two years earlier, following a 10-year sentence for sexually assaulting two teenage girls.[iv] Regarding Sutherland's reference to "crimes committed in quick succession," the Shriner incident occurred in the wake of two other high-profile cases—a murder committed by Gene Kane, a convicted rapist on community work release who raped and killed a Seattle woman in the fall of 1988; and the case of Gary Minnix, another released rapist who committed a brutal attack in December of that year (Boerner, 1992).

The linkage between seminal events and SVP civil commitment legislation is not limited to Washington, but rather represents a fairly pervasive theme across states. In a series of case studies published in 2005, Harris established that the passage of SVP legislation was consistently associated with the social and political convergence surrounding particular cases. This research also noted the profound role that citizens' groups—often spearheaded by the parents of victims—played in both the crafting of the legislative policy response and the assurance of its passage (Harris, 2005).[v] Although the precise circumstances and dynamics within each of these states varied, the main elements of the political landscape were similar—a specific name and face attached to the legislation, an active victim-advocate constituency, and tremendous pressure on the political establishment to provide a quick and viable solution to the problem.

Table 11.1 highlights some key examples from this study.

11.1 SVP Legislation and Seminal Events[1]

State	SVP Legislation's Antecedent Events
Washington	▪ Series of high-profile sexual crimes during 1988–89, including murder of Diane Ballasiotes by convicted rapist Gene Kane, and sexual assaults committed by Gary Minnix and Earl Shriner ▪ Community Protection Task Force convened pursuant to the lobbying initiative of a group called the "Tennis Shoe Brigade," which was led in part by the mothers of Kane and Shriner's victims
Minnesota	▪ In 1992, state resurrects use of its then-dormant depression-era sexual psychopath law in the wake of the July 1991 abduction, rape, and murder of a university student by twice-convicted sex offender Scott Stewart ▪ In 1994, after convicted rapist Dennis Linehan successfully challenges his pending commitment under the antiquated statute, legislature blocks prison release through the passage of a new "sexually dangerous persons" law modeled on Washington's
Wisconsin	▪ State passes civil commitment law in 1994 amidst a litany of partisan recriminations related to the pending prison release of Gerald Turner, who had served just less than 18 years in prison for the Halloween 1973 abduction, rape, and murder of a 9-year-old girl
Kansas	▪ Task force convened following the 1993 abduction and murder of 19-year-old Stephanie Schmidt by convicted rapist Don Gideon ▪ Passage of the Kansas statute, as well as the subsequent adoption of neighboring Missouri's SVP civil commitment law, linked to efforts of Gene and Peggy Schmidt, the parents of Stephanie Schmidt

Continued

11.1 SVP Legislation and Seminal Events[1] (Cont'd)

California	▪ SVP legislation emerges following a massive citizen mobilization in response to the pending release of a convicted rapist named Reginald Muldrew in Covina, California ▪ In October 1995, Governor Pete Wilson signs the civil commitment bill into law on the steps of Covina City Hall, surrounded by victims groups and community activists
Florida	▪ Jimmy Ryce Civil Commitment for Sexually Violent Predators Treatment and Care Act passed in 1998, named for a young boy who had been abducted, sexually assaulted, and killed by a released sex offender in September 1995 ▪ Statute's passage inextricably linked to the advocacy of Don and Claudia Ryce, the parents of the young boy for whom the act was named

[1]Adapted from Harris (2005)

Role of Contextual Developments

Although seminal events and related citizen mobilization undoubtedly provided significant impetus for the passage of SVP laws, these factors do not fully explain why civil commitment—a strategy that had been abandoned by psychiatry and most states as a failed experiment less than two decades earlier—reemerged so extensively during the 1990s. A more complete understanding of this renewed interest in civil commitment requires examining a broader constellation of developments in both the criminal justice and the mental health fields.

First, the rise of SVP laws coincided with a general shift in both the public's view and policy makers' responses to crime and punishment. Concern over violent crimes had led voters and legislators to toughen penalties and to reduce judicial and parole discretion in sentencing and release decisions. This trend reflected states' departure from indeterminate sentencing and the adoption of measures such as mandatory minimums, truth-in-sentencing requirements, and selective incapacitation strategies such as "three strikes" laws. Stemming from this, incarceration rates, which had begun climbing in the mid-1980s, witnessed particularly accelerated growth throughout the 1990s.

These developments heralded the emergence of a "new penology" that emphasized "abandonment of the previous focus on the individual in favor of one emphasizing the group in which the individual is categorized" (Feeley & Simon, 1992). Applied to civil commitment, this emerging paradigm was reflected in a critical deviation between earlier sexual psychopath laws and the newer SVP laws—namely a shift from a hope of reforming aberrant individuals, and toward the labeling and management of high-risk populations (Simon, 1998).

The influence of the new penology is reflected in a significant disciplinary shift related to the roles and functions of the mental health professions in civil commitment schemes. As noted earlier, the reemergence of SVP civil commitment in the 1990s was met with significant voices of dissent within organized psychiatry, a field that—with its therapeutic promise—had been central to the passage of previous generation of sexual psychopath commitment policies (Appelbaum, 1997; Maier, 1999; Wettstein, 1992; Zonana, 1997). Yet whereas the earlier laws were based on psychiatry's therapeutic ideal, the new generation of civil commitment laws placed the assessment and management of risk front and center, shifting the disciplinary focus to the field of psychology.[vi]

A second major contextual development facilitating the rise of SVP commitment policies was the significant transformation of the public mental health system, particularly regarding its role in managing forensic populations. Although the shifting locus of care from psychiatric institutions into the community began in the 1960s, the patient profile in public institutions has changed dramatically over the past two decades. With the advent of managed care contributing to a decline in civilian hospital populations, and with rising proportions of individuals with serious mental illness becoming involved with the justice system, forensic patients (i.e., those who have entered the mental health system pursuant to criminal justice involvement) have steadily supplanted traditional institutional clients. Reflecting this trend, the proportion of state hospital expenditures connected to forensic mental health patients rose steadily from 7.6% in 1983 to 33%

in 2005 (National Association of State Mental Health Program Directors, 2007).

Although this trend remains a considerable source of concern among mental health advocates, it nonetheless remains a vital part of the landscape. With public mental health agencies increasingly viewing forensic services as part of their core mission, the development of inpatient programs for sex offenders emerges as a natural extension of the increasingly blurred lines separating the criminal justice and mental health systems.

Finally, the political advent of SVP civil commitment laws must be viewed through the lens of expanded public, media, and legislative focus on the problem of sex offending in general. Media coverage throughout the 1990s transformed the names of Megan Kanka, Polly Klaas, Adam Walsh, and Jacob Wetterling into household names. As described throughout this book, the rise of SVP civil commitment laws coincided with a broad-based expansion of containment-oriented sex offender legislation at both the state and federal levels, with the issue of sex offenders remaining at the top tier of state legislative agendas (National Conference of State Legislatures, 2006). The term *sexual predator*—barely used in news reports prior to 1990—rapidly worked its way into the popular lexicon, being referenced 924 times in major newspapers in 1995 (Jenkins, 1998).

Whether viewed as a warranted response to a profound threat, or as a renewed wave of a "moral panic," these developments suggest that the move toward SVP civil commitment is far from an isolated phenomenon, but rather an outgrowth of increasing calls for an expanded government role in managing the actions and behaviors of previously convicted sex offenders.

Implications for Policy and Practice

The sociopolitical etiology of SVP laws carries significant implications for those charged with implementing the civil commitment strategy. Whereas from a statistical vantage, the events that prompted civil commitment legislation are extremely low-probability occurrences, the emotionally charged nature of the legislative debate and the active role of the victim-advocacy community contributes to an implementation environment that has little or no tolerance for error.

Commenting on the deliberative process undertaken by Washington's Community Protection Task Force, David Boerner wrote, "From the beginning, we knew that any reform proposals would be tested against one fundamental question. If the reform had been in effect in 1987, would it have given the state the power to act to prevent Earl Shriner from committing future violent acts?" (p. 550)

Although in certain respects one might fairly conclude that the general conceptual basis for civil commitment of people like Shriner is sound and defensible, in the realm of politics and public opinion, the rather circumscribed problem statement articulated by Boerner becomes significantly less refined. Examining the political conditions surrounding the passage of civil commitment legislation, it appears likely that the statutes have been guided less by the pragmatism characterized in Boerner's approach, and more by a broader sense of societal vulnerability to acts of sexual violence.

Paradoxically, the cogent and compelling rationale for Washington's civil commitment policy may be partially responsible for SVP civil commitment's major conceptual hurdle—a divergence between the policy's intellectual justification and its political foundations. We ultimately emerge with two potential perspectives on the problem—an expansive perspective, as developed in the political arena and applied as a "catch-all" remedy to a range of system failures, and a selective perspective focused on a handful of extreme and exceptional cases.

These divergent perspectives have a direct bearing on the likely actions of policy implementers. Under an expansive orientation, those charged with implementing the policies may be expected to cast a relatively broad net to fulfill the policies' fundamental public safety mandate. This approach brings a greater likelihood of false positive or Type II errors, in which individuals who would not commit the types of acts that drove the legislation will be designated as SVPs and committed to state custody, perhaps indefinitely.

Alternatively, if one adopts the selective perspective, implementing agents would be charged with minimizing the number of false positives and selecting an extremely narrow group for commitment. Under these circumstances, the policies would operate under the specter of potential Type I errors, in which the system fails to intervene in the case of an individual who proceeds to commit an extreme act of violence.

Placed in the context of political calculus, the selective approach carries with it potentially significant organizational risks, whereas the expansive orientation represents a relatively safe and conservative approach. A Type I error means that an innocent citizen is victimized, bringing the threat of substantial negative consequences for those deemed responsible for the system failure. Under a Type II error, the victim is a previously convicted sex offender held in state custody under erroneous pretenses—a circumstance that is unlikely to attract any significant attention. Assuming that innocent victims of crime represent more potent players in the political arena than perpetrators of sexual violence, it is reasonable to establish that SVP civil commitment policies, from the outset, are oriented toward an expansive view of the target population.

Legal Context

The second prong of this chapter's analysis considers the effects of legal parameters, as embodied in case law, in shaping SVP civil commitment policy and practice. Whether validating existing practice or mandating reform, legal rulings have emerged as central elements in the SVP civil commitment narrative.

From the day in March 1991 that Washington's first SVP commitment—a convicted rapist named Andre Young—appealed his commitment to the Washington Supreme Court, the courts have played a pivotal role in shaping the course of SVP commitment policies. Since Young's initial appeal, SVP civil commitment laws have been the subject of three U.S. Supreme Court rulings, hundreds of lower court rulings in federal and state courts, and countless legal analyses in the pages of law reviews and journals.

Legal issues associated with SVP civil commitment may be grouped into three main areas:

- SVP civil commitment's fundamental constitutionality
- The criteria for civil commitment and the manner in which they are applied
- Postcommitment constitutional requirements, including treatment, conditions of confinement, and transition and release provisions

Fundamental Constitutionality of Civil Commitment

From the outset, the crafters of Washington's Community Protection Act implicitly recognized that they walked a constitutional tightrope as they sought to balance individual liberty interests with an expanded power of the state (Boerner, 1992). In the wake of the act's passage, the battle lines were swiftly drawn in the pages of the nation's law reviews and within a short period of time found their way into the state and federal courts.

Initial constitutional challenges to civil commitment fell into two major categories—those related to the allegedly punitive intent of the laws, and those related to the state's civil power to exert custody of individuals. The former stemmed from what might be termed the fig leaf argument—the assertion that the laws are essentially designed to extend the police powers of the state under the guise of treatment. This view suggested that the basis for commitment, although nominally civil, in fact represented a form of criminal sanctions, and in turn asserted that the laws violated constitutional prohibitions against double jeopardy and ex post facto lawmaking.[vii]

The second type of challenge suggested that, by adopting an overly broad and nonclinical construct of "mental abnormality," the laws overstepped the state's authority to civilly retain custody of individuals who did not have a diagnosable mental illness, and in so doing violated Fourteenth Amendment provisions governing substantive due process. These arguments cited the Supreme Court's ruling in *Foucha v. Louisiana,* which established that presumed dangerousness alone, in the absence of a diagnosable mental illness, was insufficient to justify psychiatric civil commitment.

Recognizing these potential issues, Washington prosecutors reviewed and rejected multiple potential cases in 1991 before King County Prosecutor Norm Maleng—who had chaired the Community Protection Task Force—selected Andre Young as his test case for the new law. Although the Washington Supreme Court upheld Young's commitment, Young filed a successful habeas corpus petition in U.S. District Court, leading to a 1995 Ninth Circuit ruling that the punitive nature of Young's detention in fact violated the U.S. Constitution (*Young v. Weston,* 1995). Young was held by the

State of Washington under a temporary injunction pending appeal to the U.S. Supreme Court.

That same year, the Kansas Supreme Court ruled on the case of a twice-convicted child molester named Leroy Hendricks, who, like Young, had been the first individual in his state to be successfully committed under his state's new civil commitment statute. In its 1995 ruling, the Kansas Supreme Court ruled that Hendricks' commitment violated substantive due process, and it further cited the inconsistency between the law's implicit intent and its purported civil nature, stating, "It is clear that the primary objective of the act is to continue incarceration and not to provide treatment" (In Re Hendricks, 1996).

Kansas immediately sought injunctive relief from the federal courts, and both the Young and Hendricks cases headed to the U.S. Supreme Court. In June 1997 the Court issued a 5-4 ruling in *Kansas v. Hendricks*, overturning the lower court's ruling and essentially ushering in a new stage in the application of SVP civil commitment in Kansas and elsewhere. The court ruling stated,

> As a threshold matter, commitment under the Act does not implicate either of the two primary objectives of criminal punishment: retribution or deterrence. The Act's purpose is not retributive because it does not affix culpability for prior criminal conduct. Instead, such conduct is used solely for evidentiary purposes, either to demonstrate that a "mental abnormality" exists or to support a finding of future dangerousness ... Nor can it be said that the legislature intended the Act to function as a deterrent. Those persons committed under the Act are, by definition, suffering from a "mental abnormality" or a "personality disorder" that prevents them from exercising adequate control over their behavior. Such persons are therefore unlikely to be deterred by the threat of confinement. (*Kansas v. Hendricks*, 1997)

The *Hendricks* ruling, coupled with the court's subsequent determination in the case of Andre Young (*Seling v. Young*), effectively put to rest initial suggestions that the laws fundamentally violated substantive due process and constitutional prohibitions against double jeopardy and ex post facto lawmaking. In the immediate wake of

Hendricks, several states, including Florida and Massachusetts, adopted new civil commitment laws, and those with existing laws witnessed a surge in new commitment activity (Harris, 2005).

Challenges to Commitment Criteria

With the initial round of constitutional challenges essentially put to rest by the *Hendricks* and *Young* rulings, the attention of legal analysts shifted to the legal criteria related to commitment and, more specifically, the application of those criteria to individual cases.

As reflected in Table 11.2, SVP civil commitment statutes generally delineate three categories of criteria to support commitment: qualifying events or behaviors, mental condition, and dangerousness. Statutes also may specify a required nexus between the specified mental condition and the dangerousness criterion.

Events and Behaviors. Regarding events and behaviors, types of qualifying offenses vary from state to state, with enumerated offenses typically ranging from indecent liberties with a child to adult rape, covering a relatively diverse population of offenders.[viii] Although behavioral criteria are typically operationalized in terms of arrest and conviction on a specific

11.2 SVP Civil Commitment Criteria

Criterion	Definitional Elements
Events and/or Behaviors	At least one prior qualifying offense Imminent release from custody and/or act of "harmful sexual conduct" by individual not in custody
Mental Condition	Mental abnormality or personality disorder Volitional impairment
Dangerousness	Likely to engage in acts of violence if not confined

listing of offenses, states may also include individuals whose history includes past harmful sexual conduct or offenses for which the individual has been adjudicated delinquent or found not guilty by reason of insanity.[ix]

Of the three noted criteria, events and behaviors tend to be the most straightforward, with adherence to these criteria typically established pursuant to bureaucratic determination and rarely contested in legal proceedings. In contrast, both the mental condition and dangerousness criteria contain significant shades of gray and therefore have formed the basis for considerable debate among forensic psychologists and legal experts.

Mental Condition. The adoption of the term *mental abnormality* rather than the clinical designation of *mental illness* emerged as a prominent element of the substantive due process challenges set forth in *Hendricks*. This argument essentially maintained that the designation of mental abnormality was an arbitrary concept with no medical or other scientific basis. The *Hendricks* court dismissed this argument, ruling that clinical acceptance of the designation was not constitutionally required.

The concept of volitional impairment, and the requirement that states establish the individual's inability to control his or her impulses as part of civil commitment proceedings, has continued to engender significant debate in both legal and clinical circles (Hamilton, 2002). Organized psychiatry has long maintained that volitional impairment is an untenable concept, and that distinguishing an "irresistible impulse" from an "impulse not resisted" remains beyond the scope of professional judgment (Group for the Advancement of Psychiatry, 1977). This argument was central to the case made by the State of Kansas before the U.S. Supreme Court in October of 2001 (*Kansas v. Crane*, 2002) and featured prominently in amicus briefs filed with the court on both sides of the case (American Psychiatric Association, 2001; Association for the Treatment of Sexual Abusers, 2001a).

The court's ruling in the *Crane* case, issued in the spring of 2002, agreed that although an "absolutist" approach was unworkable, finding of "some" volitional impairment was required. The court failed, however, to clarify a workable definition or standard for lack of control, effectively ceding these determinations to state and federal district courts. In the months following the ruling, courts throughout the country addressed the "lack of control" issue, generally yielding opinions supporting wide latitude in applying the concept.[x] One federal court ruling in Arizona concluded, "If the state establishes not only that a person is dangerous, but also that a mental illness or abnormality caused the dangerousness, the state has met its burden to show a lack of control" (*In Re Leon G.*).

Hence, the *Crane* ruling effectively relegated *volitional impairment* to a rhetorical concept with little substantive bearing on the commitment process. Just as the concept of mental abnormality may be driven largely by the nature of the individuals' prior behaviors, the volitional impairment criterion may in turn be viewed as similarly circular in its logic and application.

Dangerousness. In light of the above issues, it remains questionable whether the criteria considered thus far—qualifying events and mental condition—substantively narrow the population eligible for SVP civil commitment. Considering this, we are therefore left with one final definitional element in the quest for limiting principles: the idea of dangerousness, or, put into causal terms, the likelihood of future acts of sexual violence.

Legal determinations of dangerousness have typically fallen to psychologists, psychiatrists, and related professionals, who are assumed to possess specialized knowledge and technology that makes their assessments superior to those that might be made by a layperson. Otto (1994) noted that technical capacity and legal admissibility are independent concepts, suggesting that questions regarding the **ability** of mental health professionals to differentiate levels of dangerousness should be separated from those regarding the **appropriate role** of such professionals in legal proceedings.

Regarding the former, the past two decades have produced considerable developments in the field of specialized risk assessment for sex offenders. Dozens of studies have contributed to a growing evidence base regarding recidivism risk factors and the potential efficacy of treatment interventions (Hanson & Bussiere, 1998; Hanson & Morton-Bourgon, 2004). On the basis of these findings, a broad array of specialized actuarial and guided clinical assessment instruments have been introduced and continue to be tested and refined (Doren, 2004).

Yet despite these advances, the application of sex offender risk assessment in the context of SVP civil commitment proceedings has engendered a good deal of controversy among forensic professionals. One commonly cited concern relates to the reliance on predictive factors that are static or highly stable in nature (e.g., number of prior offenses, age, and victimization history). Although the field has developed a fairly good sense of the immutable case characteristics that might place certain populations at higher risk of reoffense than others, it has a much more limited understanding of the influence of dynamic characteristics associated with sexual recidivism risk within individuals—factors that may include responses to treatment, situational stressors, availability of social supports, and employment or housing status (Craissati & Beech, 2003; Hanson & Harris, 2000).

A second set of issues relates to the ability of general violence risk assessment tools to meet the unique legal requirements associated with SVP commitment criteria. Research on the predictive accuracy of SVP forensic evaluations suggests that, although forensic psychologists show some ability to predict general violence, predictions regarding sexual violence may be no more accurate than chance (Jackson, Rogers, & Schuman, 2004). Further, existing actuarial and guided clinical tools designed for use with the sex offender population generally do not address the unique, multidimensional constellation of legal standards associated with SVP commitment, particularly the required interrelationship between dangerousness, mental condition, and volitional impairment (Rogers & Jackson, 2005).

Despite these limitations, however, it appears that the threshold for admissibility of expert predictions of future violence in SVP proceedings is quite low, with research suggesting a general absence of uniform legal standards of dangerousness for purposes of SVP civil commitment (Janus & Meehl, 1997).

In determining the admissibility of expert testimony, the courts have generally applied two types of standards—the *Frye* standard, which considers testimony admissible if it is found to have general acceptance in the particular field in which it belongs (*Frye v. United States*, 1923); and the *Daubert* standard, in which testimony is evaluated based on its relevance to the issues at hand and its reliability, or the extent to which it is grounded in scientific methods (*Daubert v. Merrell Dow Pharmaceuticals*, 1993).

Citing a number of cases, Petrila and Otto (2001) suggested that courts considering SVP cases have rarely applied *Frye* and *Daubert* rules with any real force, focusing more on preponderance of evidence than on a critical review of scientific principles:

> [The courts] appear content to characterize concerns about the reliability and validity of assessment techniques as going to the weight of the evidence—a matter for the discretion of the trial court ... even if a court questions the reliability of a particular instrument in a particular case, the tendency is to find evidence 'in the overall record' sufficient to establish that a defendant meets SVP criteria. (pp. 3–20)

To summarize, the commitment criteria established by statute and applied by the courts generally lend themselves to the casting of a fairly wide net in establishing the commitment-eligible population. Qualifying offenses are relatively straightforward as definitional matter, but are clearly insufficient to adequately distinguish the SVP population from the broader universe of sex offenders. The concepts related to mental condition—mental abnormality and volitional impairment—remain amorphously construed as matters of technical and legal definition. Finally, legal thresholds for determinations of dangerousness appear to be relatively expansive in their interpretation, providing considerable latitude to forensic experts and prosecutors in establishing the parameters of commitment.

Postcommitment Activities

The third major legal arena related to SVP civil commitment concerns the requirements associated with the activities following commitment, specifically those involving treatment, conditions of confinement, and provisions for transition and discharge from commitment.

From a legal perspective, *Hendricks* established the legitimacy of civil commitment based on the presumption of therapeutic intent. Thus, for a civil commitment to be legal, the conditions of confinement must comport with the legal justification for custody—to provide committed individuals with treatment for the condition that presumably makes them dangerous, with the presumed intent of ameliorating that condition. Absent therapeutic intent, the terms of confinement begin to approximate preventive detention, significantly undermining the legal basis for commitment.

This requirement—which essentially translates into the need to ensure that commitment facilities more closely resemble a psychiatric hospital than a prison—has formed the basis for a series of federal civil rights cases challenging conditions of confinement (*Turay v. Seling*; *Hargett et al. v. Baker et al.*; *Canupp et al. v. Butterworth*). In the most prominent instance, Washington operated its civil commitment program under an extensive injunction until 2005,with the court providing ongoing oversight of facility conditions, treatment programming, staffing, safety, and a range of related issues, and with the court imposing financial sanctions for lack of compliance (*Turay v. Seling*; Lieb, 2003).

Beyond addressing conditions of treatment and confinement, the courts have also influenced the manner in which states address the issues of transition and release. The federal judge presiding over the Washington case wrote,

> A continuing major flaw in the SCC program is the lack of what experts on both sides have called the light at the end of the tunnel. Mental health treatment, if to be anything more than a sham, must give the confined person hope that if he gets well enough to be safely released, he will be transferred to some less restrictive alternative.[xi]

There are two plausible routes toward effectuating release: the earning of release through treatment compliance and substantive progress, or release through the court's determination that the individual no longer meets commitment criteria.

The first avenue toward release is consistent with the phased program approach commonly employed in sex offender treatment programs (Association for the Treatment of Sexual Abusers, 2001b; Marques, 2001), in which treatment program professionals or external evaluators grant conditional release privileges based on clinical progress assessments. As a practical matter, this form of release is relatively rare within civil commitment programs (Gookin, 2007).

The second route to release involves a court determination, generally informed by expert testimony, that the behavioral and psychological factors that initially supported commitment are no longer present. Although more common than treatment-driven releases, such determinations are significantly confounded by what Grisso (2000) described as the "tyranny of static variables"—a circumstance stemming from the reliance of sex offender risk assessment practice on immutable factors such as the nature or frequency of prior offenses or victim characteristics. Basing commitment on static factors effectively makes "improvement" logically impossible, and compromises any efforts towards effectuating release. Hanson (1998) confirmed this, indicating, "We have much more evidence to justify committing offenders than we have for releasing them."

The legal complexities involved in release determinations are illustrated by the California case of Patrick Ghilotti, who in 2001 became the first committed SVP to successfully complete the state's treatment program. In accordance with statutory requirements and agency operating practice, the case was reviewed by two independent examiners, each of whom concluded that Ghilotti met the clinical and statutory criteria for conditional release. The pending release produced an immediate barrage of press reports in Marin County, where Ghilotti had been convicted of a series of rapes in the 1970s and 1980s (Chabria, 2002).

Ghilotti's discharge was blocked by the state's mental health commissioner, who sought to overrule the opinions of treatment staff and independent evaluators recommending release. Although the courts ultimately determined that the commissioner acted beyond his statutory authority in blocking Ghilotti's discharge, the state was permitted to set forth a series of stringent terms and conditions for release. Ghilotti ultimately chose to remain committed rather than agree to the terms and conditions put forward by the state and accepted by the courts (Chabria, 2002).

Operational Context

Having considered both the sociopolitical foundations of SVP commitment and the manner in which policy and practice have been circumscribed by the courts, the third and final prong of this chapter's analysis addresses the operational domain in which the policies must be carried out.

From an implementation vantage point, SVP civil commitment policies entail significant operational complexity, requiring multiple decision points, extensive cross-system collaboration, and significant resource demands. Implementation is further complicated by a factor discussed earlier: the persistent tension between the implicit political rationale for civil commitment and the policy's legal justification and ostensible purpose.

Figure 11.2 delineates the principal operational functions of SVP civil commitment, which may be grouped into three major domains of activities:

11.2

Operational Elements of SVP Civil Commitment

Commitment Decision			
Screening	Filing Decision	Probable Cause	Commitment

Custody and Treatment		
Secure Custody	Treatment	LRA/Release Decisions

Transition and Release	
Transition/LRA	Post-Release Activity

- Those leading up to and including the commitment decision
- Those associated with care, custody, and treatment of those committed
- Those associated with transition and release back into the community

Commitment Decision

Civil commitment is predicated, first and foremost, on the ability to identify a small but dangerous group of high-risk individuals suitable for commitment. Although ultimately a judicial or jury determination, the winnowing down of the potential SVP population from the broader universe of sex offenders released from correctional custody involves multiple decision points prior to the commitment proceeding—a screening decision determining which cases get referred to prosecutors; a prosecutorial filing decision regarding which cases should be pursued for commitment; and a judicial probable cause determination to assess which cases are suitable for commitment proceedings.

The process leading to commitment therefore generally involves two broad phases: a screening process, which separates potential commitment candidates from the broader population of sex offenders; and a legal process, under which civil commitment is effectuated. The former involves a combination of bureaucratic and clinical determinations based on offender profiles and risk assessments. The latter involves the filing of a petition, a judicial determination of probable cause, and a trial seeking commitment.

States vary in their approaches to the resource intensity and organizational locus of initial screening evaluations. Some delegate authority to mental health agencies, others centralize screening activities with correctional officials, and still others rely on independent, multiagency boards or commissions. In most cases, the screening comprises multiple stages, beginning with bureaucratic determinations based on record reviews and progressing to more extensive clinical evaluations. Approaches range from streamlined reviews using in-house staff specialists, to more resource-intensive systems requiring multiple levels of review and consensus and extensive use of contracted evaluators (Harris, 2005).

Similar variation may be found in the legal process, with state civil commitment laws varying across such dimensions as prosecutor jurisdiction, and methods of funding mechanisms for prosecutors, public defenders, and the courts. Approaches include decentralized systems relying solely on regional or county prosecutors (e.g., Massachusetts, Florida, and California), centralized legal activities in the office of state attorneys general (Kansas), and hybrid approaches involving both attorneys general and selected county prosecutors (Washington, Wisconsin).

As civil commitment policies evolve over time, many states experience a net-widening effect, particularly within the initial stages of the screening process. Often prompted by perceived system failures and related statutory changes, it is common for the referred population to become more expansive over time, as correctional authorities and others gravitate toward more inclusive referral policies. Two examples of this phenomenon may be seen in the experiences of Minnesota and California.

Prior to 2003, Minnesota's civil commitment system involved a significant screening role for the state correctional agency, which sent only a small proportion of offenders on to prosecutors for possible commitment. Following the nationally publicized murder of college student Dru Sjodin by an individual who had slipped through the cracks of Minnesota's screening system, referrals from the Department of Corrections (DOC) to county prosecutors jumped nearly twentyfold, from 13 cases in 2002 to 246 cases in 2003 (Governor's Commission on Sex Offender Policy, 2005). Along similar lines, statutory changes made pursuant to the passage of California's Proposition 83 (i.e., Jessica's Law), which both expanded commitment criteria and diminished the screening role of the California Department of Corrections and Rehabilitation in the commitment screening process, referrals to the state's mental health authorities for SVP evaluations jumped from 676 referrals between November 2005 and November 2006 to 9,312 referrals the following year—a nearly fifteenfold increase.[xii]

This net-widening effect contributes to a related intersystem issue related to commitment systems, namely that associated with significant downstream resource demands. The referral practice changes in Minnesota not only placed considerable demands upon prosecutors unequipped to deal with the influx of new cases (Hennepin County Criminal Justice Coordinating Committee, 2004), but also ultimately led to a dramatic increase in the numbers of new commitments to the state's Department of Human Services, from 15–18 new commitments per year prior to 2004 to an estimated 58 per year in 2006 (Minnesota Department of Human Services, 2006). In California, the changes brought about through Proposition 83 created a sizable workload backlog within California's screening system, requiring an infusion of new resources to keep pace with the increased demand (California Legislative Analyst's Office, 2006). Similar bottleneck effects have been seen in Florida virtually since the inception of that state's civil commitment policy in 1999, manifested in significant demands on the courts, delays in time to trial, and substantial numbers of noncommitted civil detainees housed within the system (Florida Office of Program Policy Analysis and Governmental Accountability, 2004).

Custody and Treatment

The downstream resource demands just described are manifested most prominently in the institutional requirements associated with custody and treatment of the SVP population. In 2006, states spent a total of $454 million on housing and treating civilly committed individuals, exclusive of debt service or bed construction costs. Annual costs per resident averaged $94,000, with seven states spending over $100,000 per resident. These costs were generally four to five times higher than the costs associated with housing a state prison inmate in those states (Gookin, 2007).

Despite these significant costs, the matter of what to do with individuals once they are committed generally commands minimal initial interest among lawmakers, whose primary impetus is simply to keep sexual predators off of the streets. Hence, in contrast with commitment processes, which tend to be fairly circumscribed by statute, determining the means of custody and treatment is typically ceded to administrators who must not only establish requisite systems for providing legally-mandated services, but also must make the case for significant levels of resources related to staffing, physical facilities, and an array of contracted services ranging from food to medical care. Reflecting the comparative lack of legislative focus, it is common to witness significant initial bureaucratic uncertainty over agency roles, facility development, and resource levels as implementing agencies struggle to develop viable systems of custody and treatment (Harris, 2005).

The significant resource intensity of custody and treatment as noted above is essentially driven by two factors:

1. A substantial cost per bed, largely driven by the profile of the population and the legal and practical imperatives for a therapeutic environment
2. Demand for a substantial (and growing) number of beds, linked to a steady flow of new commitments and negligible numbers of discharges

Regarding the former, this chapter's earlier review of legal issues noted that the legitimacy of civil commitment is based on establishing conditions of confinement that comport with therapeutic intent. Accordingly, commitment facilities must be equipped, staffed, and operated more along the standards of secured inpatient psychiatric institutions than prisons.

The costs of providing these services may be further exacerbated by limited pools of available labor, particularly in the remote areas in which many commitment facilities are based. Further, the demographics of the sex offender facilities relate to medical costs, particularly for the aging segment of the population. Washington reports that one third of the residents in its commitment center are over age 50, with 43% of these individuals suffering from serious chronic and debilitating illnesses (such as heart disease, pulmonary disease, cancer, and diabetes) requiring frequent emergency care and hospitalizations (Washington Department of Social and Health Services, 2006).

Although the costs per bed are indeed significant, the most pressing challenge to civil commitment's financial sustainability may have less to do with the per-unit cost than with the number of units required. As explored throughout this chapter, the policies are implicitly structured to encourage the use of commitment and to discourage release from custody. Accordingly, the operating budgets of institutional programs have witnessed steady annual increases in response to an ever-increasing population (Harris, 2006).

Moreover, beyond the significant operating expenses, the steady growth of the committed population inevitably leads to demands for additional bed space. In 2004, California invested $350 million in a 1,500-bed SVP facility at a construction cost of $350 million—a construction cost of $233,000 per bed. In 2007, Minnesota's Department of Human Services submitted a capital budget request for $90 million for the second phase of a planned multiyear, 800-bed capacity expansion. Combined with a previously authorized $44 million, this translates into a construction cost of $180,000 per bed. Similarly expansive projects have been undertaken in states such as Wisconsin, Florida, Kansas, and Washington, many of which appear to revisit their facility needs every 5–7 years (Harris, 2006).

Transition and Release

Considering the significant fiscal ramifications of unchecked population growth, policy makers are left with two choices beyond simply absorbing these costs: curtailing new commitments or increasing the rate of system discharges. The latter option, in turn, ultimately rests on developing means of safe and effective means of community transition and release.

From a political standpoint, the prospect of releasing a previously convicted sex offender into the community represents a high-risk proposition. Once that particular individual has been designated as a sexually violent predator or a sexually dangerous person for purposes of commitment, the potential stakes of release are ratcheted even higher. It is therefore not surprising that communities and legislators are rarely enthusiastic about setting forth transition and release provisions.

From a treatment perspective, the intent of the transition phase is to reintroduce the individual to life within the community and to monitor the individual's ability to maintain institutional treatment gains when functioning in a community-based context. From a public safety vantage point, the primary emphasis is to maintain sufficient control over the individual's activities and behaviors. Ultimately, a successful transition program must address both of these goals while simultaneously placating an exceedingly anxious public.

Evaluating policy provisions pertaining to transition and release, the experience of Washington proves particularly instructive. As noted earlier in this chapter, the civil commitment program's oversight by the federal court drew particular attention to what the judge in the case referred to as the "light at the end of the tunnel." With court-imposed fines mounting by the day, the state had little choice but to embark on an ambitious and earnest effort to establish a viable means of structured release.

The state's efforts to develop a less restrictive alternative (LRA), chronicled extensively in court documents produced between 1997 and 2001, was considerably hampered by an inability to locate appropriate housing sites. In response, the 1999 legislature directed the Department of Social and Human Services (DSHS) to develop guidelines for the siting and development of LRA facilities. These guidelines, produced by DSHS in October of 2000, set forth the parameters for a complex series of rules and procedures providing for extensive public review, equitable geographic distribution of LRA facilities, considerable siting restrictions, and systems of financial mitigation for communities (Washington Department of Social and Health Services, 2000).

The 2001 legislature, in response to the DSHS report, adopted a series of statutory modifications pertaining to the siting, staffing, operations, and release provisions pertaining to community transition programs. These measures, in large part, were designed to respond to the needs of two audiences—the federal court, which was requiring proactive steps to develop an LRA, and Washington's communities that demanded assurances that public safety would not be compromised.

Washington's proactive efforts to address the concerns of the courts while simultaneously responding to community demands came with a hefty price tag. In contrast to institutional methods of control, in which individuals are contained by facility walls, the state's community-based systems for sexually violent predators require higher levels of staff supervision, technological costs, and payment of community mitigation funds to offset public safety concerns. As a result, Washington estimated the cost of maintaining an individual in its secure community transition program at approximately $400,000 per year, compared to the estimated $125,000 the state pays to house an individual in its institutional commitment program (Washington Department of Social and Health Services, 2006).

In sum, although transition and release emerges as both a legal and fiscal imperative affecting the viability of SVP civil commitment, the potent political overlay adds a significant source of complexity to the equation.

Policy Directions and the Future of Civil Commitment

In her essay *Risk and Justice*, cultural anthropologist Mary Douglas wrote, "A risk is not only the probability of an event but also the probable magnitude of its outcome, and everything depends on the value that is set on the outcome.

The evaluation is a political, aesthetic, and moral matter" (1992, p. 31).

Across multiple dimensions, the story of SVP policies and their implementation is a story of risk—the societal risk linked to the unknown future actions of sex offenders; the political risk associated with the actions or inactions of public officials or their agents; the legal risk associated with the constitutional tightrope walked by SVP civil commitment policies; and the financial risk associated with a steady flow of new commitments and a negligible number of system discharges.

The idea of risk—not just in an actuarial sense, but also in the broader context as framed by Douglas—permeates every aspect of SVP civil commitment policies, accounting for both the policies' most limiting obstacles and their most integral strengths.

On a conceptual level, the social construction of risk concerning perpetrators of sexual violence provides the basis for the policies' exceptional levels of support from policy makers and the general public. It also accounts for the policies' most fundamental conceptual limitation, namely an ambiguity concerning the target population, the means to be employed in identifying it, and ultimately the outcomes we hope to achieve by the civil commitment strategy.

In terms of implementation practice, we cannot ignore the prominent role that this broadened construction of risk plays in the everyday decisions connected to the civil commitment process. With prediction of dangerousness at the forefront of the policy, with statutes crafted in a manner that broadly delegates the rules and standards for such prediction, implementers are forced to employ their own risk calculus to commitment and release decisions. In such a situation, the political, moral and aesthetic consequences of failure to act are significantly greater than those of acting, creating immense incentives for those involved in the process—corrections officials, psychologists, prosecutors, judges, juries—to push the process as far as the law will allow. Although the courts have accepted the laws within general boundaries, this acceptance does not strip the laws of their moral and political pretext, nor does it speak to the policies' significant, long-term resource demands.

In this context, the sustainability of SVP civil commitment policies appears to depend on a critical examination of the policies' sociopolitical influences and the manner in which those influences have shaped the policies' expectations and implementation practices. This examination, coupled with careful consideration of alternative means of addressing the risks presented by high-risk sex offenders, may ultimately define a sustainable role for SVP civil commitment within a rational system of sex offender management.

References

American Psychiatric Association. (2001). *Amicus curiae brief submitted to U.S. Supreme Court in support of respondent in Crane v. Kansas.*

Appelbaum, P. (1997). Law and psychiatry: Confining sex offenders. *Psychiatric Services, 48*(10), 1265.

Association for the Treatment of Sexual Abusers. (2001a). *Amicus curiae brief submitted to U.S. Supreme Court in support of respondent in Crane v. Kansas.*

Association for the Treatment of Sexual Abusers. (2001b). *Practice standards and guidelines for members of the association for the treatment of sexual abusers.* Beaverton, OR: Association for the Treatment of Sexual Abusers.

Boerner, D. (1992). Confronting violence: In the act and in the word. *University of Puget Sound Law Review, 15*(3), 525–577.

California High Risk Sex Offender and Sexually Violent Predator Task Force. (2006). *Report to the governor.* Sacramento: California State Legislature.

California Legislative Analyst's Office. (2006). *Analysis of 2006–07 budget bill: Department of mental health.* Sacramento: California State Legislature.

Canupp et al. v. Butterworth, 2008 U.S. Dist. Lexis 75381

Chabria, A. (2002, April 14). The bureaucrat and the bogeyman. *Los Angeles Times Magazine,* 21.

Cohen, S. (2002). *Folk devils and moral panics:* (3rd ed.). New York: Routledge.

Commitment of W.Z. (173 NJ 109).

Craissati, J., & Beech, A. (2003). A review of dynamic variables and their relationship to risk prediction in sex offenders. *Journal of Sexual Aggression, 9*(1), 41–55.

Daubert v. Merrell Dow Pharmaceuticals, 509 579 (1993).

Doren, D. M. (2004). *Bibliography of published works relative to risk assessment for sexual offenders. accessed August 23, 2007 at www. atsa.com/pdfs/riskAssessmentBiblio.pdf*

Douglas, M. (1992). *Risk and blame* (Paperback ed.). New York, London: Routledge.

Ennis, B., & Litwack, T. (1975). Psychiatry and the presumption of expertise: Flipping coins in the courtroom. *Cal L Rev., 62,* 693–723.

Feeley, M. M., & Simon, J. (1992). The new penology: Notes on the emerging strategy of corrections and its implications. *Criminology, 30*(4), 449–474.

Fitch, W. L., & Hammen, D. (2004). Sex offender commitment in the United States. *National Association of Mental Health Program Directors—Forensic Division,* September 2004.

Florida Office of Program Policy Analysis and Governmental Accountability. (2004). *Sexually violent predator program is reducing backlog, but still not timely (Report # 04-63).*

Foucha v. Louisiana 504 U.S. 71 (1992)

Frye v. United States, 54 App. D. C. 46, 293 F. 1013 (1923).

Gookin, K. (2007). *Comparison of state laws authorizing involuntary commitment of sexually violent predators: 2006 update, revised.* (No. 2008). Olympia: Washington State Institute for Public Policy.

Governor's Commission on Sex Offender Policy. (2005). *Final report.* St. Paul: Minnesota Office of the Governor.

Grisso, T. (2000). Ethical issues in evaluations for sex offender re-offending. *Sinclair Seminars, March 2000,* Madison, WI.

Group for the Advancement of Psychiatry. (1977). *Psychiatry and sex psychopath legislation: The 30s to the 80s.* New York: Mental Health Materials Center.

Hamilton, G. (2002). Casenote: The blurry line between "mad" and "bad": Is "lack-of-control" a workable standard for sexually violent predators? *University of Richmond Law Review, 36*(May 2002), 481.

Hanson, R. A. (1998). What do we know about sex offender risk assessment? *Psychology, Public Policy, and Law, 4,* 50–72.

Hanson, R. K., & Bussiere, M. T. (1998). Predicting relapse: A meta-analysis of sexual offender recidivism studies. *Journal of Consulting and Clinical Psychology, 66,* 348–362.

Hanson, R. K., & Harris, A. J. R. (2000). Where should we intervene? Dynamic predictors of sex offense recidivism. *Criminal Justice and Behavior, 27,* 6–35.

Hanson, R. K., & Morton-Bourgon, K. (2004). *Predictors of sexual recidivism: An updated meta-analysis.* Ottawa, Canada: Public Safety and Emergency Preparedness Canada.

Hargett v. Baker, 2002 U.S. Dist Lexis 13721Harris, A. (2005). *Civil commitment of sexual predators: A study in policy implementation.* New York: LFB Scholarly Publishing.

Harris, A. J. (2006). Cost and resource allocation in the implementation of civil commitment laws: A guide for policymakers. In A. Schlank (Ed.), *The sexual predator: Volume 3.* Kingston, NJ: Civic Research Institute.

Hennepin County Criminal Justice Coordinating Committee. (2004). *Sex offenders in Hennepin county: Issues and recommendations.* Hennepin County Criminal Justice Coordinating Committee.

In Re Hendricks, 259 Kansas 246 (1996).

In re Leon G., 200 Ariz. 298, 26 P.3d 481 (2001).

Jackson, R. L., Rogers, R., & Schuman, D. (2004). The adequacy and accuracy of sexually violent predator evaluations: Contextualized risk assessment in clinical practice. *International Journal of Forensic Mental Health, 3,* 115.

Janus, E., & Meehl, P. (1997). Assessing the legal standard for prediction of dangerousness in sex offender commitment proceedings. *Psychology, Public Policy, and the Law, 3*(March 1997), 33.

Janus, E. S., & Walbek, N. H. (2000). Sex Offender Commitments in Minnesota: A Descriptive Study of Second Generation Commitments. *Behavioral Sciences & the Law, 18*, 343–374.

Jenkins, P. (1998). *Moral panic: Changing concepts of the child molester in modern America*. New Haven: Yale University Press.

Kansas v. Crane, 534 US 407 (2002).

Kansas v. Hendricks, 521 US 346 (1997).

La Fond, J. Q. (2003). The costs of enacting a sexual predator law and recommendations for keeping them from skyrocketing. In J. Q. La Fond, & B. J. Winick (Eds.), *Protecting society from sexually dangerous offenders: Law, justice, and therapy*. Washington, DC: American Psychological Association.

Lieb, R. (1996). Washington State Sexually Violent Predators: Profile of Special Commitment Center Residents. Olympia, WA: Washington State Institute for Public Policy.

Lieb, R. (2003). After Hendricks: Defining constitutional treatment for Washington state's civil commitment program. *Ann NY Acad Sci, 989*(1), 474–488.

Lieb, R., & Matson, S. (1998). *Sexual predator commitment laws in the United States : 1998 update*. Olympia: Washington State Institute for Public Policy

Lieb, R., & Nelson, C. (2001). Treatment Programs for Sexually Violent Predators -- A Review of the States. In A. Schlank (Ed.), *The Sexual Predator*. Kingston, NJ: Civic Research Institute. Maier, G. J. (1999). Taking issue: Sexual predators and the abuse of psychiatry. *Psychiatric Services: A Journal of the American Psychiatric Association, 50*(3), 295 (1 page).

Marques, J. K. (2001). Professional standards for civil commitment programs. In A. Schlank (Ed.), *The sexual predator*. Kingston, NJ: Civic Research Institute.

Martin v . Reinstein, 987 P.2d 779 (Ariz. App. 1999)

Mental Health America. (2006). *Confining "sexual predators" in the mental health system*. Alexandria, VA: Mental Health America.

Miller, N. (2002). *Sex-crime panic: A journey to the paranoid heart of the 1950s* (1st ed.) Alyson Books.

Minnesota Department of Human Services. (2006). *Addressing growth in civil commitments of sex offenders*. Minnesota Deptartment of Human Services.

National Association of State Mental Health Program Directors. (2007). *FY 2005 state mental health revenue and expenditure study results*. No. 07-03 National Association of State Mental Health Program Directors Research Institute.

National Conference of State Legislatures. (2006). *State crime legislation in 2005*. National Conference of State Legislatures.

Otto, R. (1994). On the Ability of Mental Health Professionals to "Predict Dangerousness": A Commentary on Interpretations of "Dangerousness" Literature. *Law and Psychology Review*, 18(43).

Overholser, W. (1935). The history and operation of the Briggs law of Massachusetts. *Law and Contemporary Problems, 2*(4), 436–447.

Petrila, J., & Otto, R. (2001). Admissibility of expert testimony in sexually violent predator proceedings. In A. Schlank (Ed.), *The sexual predator*. Kingston, NJ: Civic Research Institute.

Rogers, R., & Jackson, R. L. (2005). Sexually violent predators: The risky enterprise of risk assessment. *Journal of the American Academy of Psychiatry and the Law Online, 33*(4), 523–528.

Seling V. Young 531 U.S. 250 (2001)

Siegel, B. (1990, May 10). Locking up sexual predators. *Los Angeles Times,* p. A1.

Simon, J. (1998). Managing the monstrous: Sex offenders and the new penology. *Psychology, Public Policy, and Law, 4*(1/2), 452.

State v. Carpenter, 197 Wis. 2d 252, 541 N.W.2d 105 (1995)

State v. Laxton (2002 WI 82)

Steadman, H. J., & Cocozza, J. (1974). *Careers of the criminally insane: Excessive social control of deviance.* Lexington, MA: Lexington Books.

Sutherland, E. H. (1950). The diffusion of sexual psychopath laws. *American Journal of Sociology, 56,* 142–148.

Turay v. Seling, 108 F. Supp. 2d 1148 (WD Wash. 2000)

Washington Dept. of Social and Health Services (2000). *Special Commitment Center: Secure Community Housing Criteria and Site Selection Process.* Olympia: Washington Dept. of Social and Health Services

Washington Dept. of Social and Health Services. (2006). *Special commitment center: Strategic plan 2007–2011.* Olympia: Washington Dept. of Social and Health Services.

Wettstein, R. (1992). A psychiatric perspective on Washington's sexually violent predator statute. *University of Puget Sound Law Review, 15*(3), 597–633.

Zonana, H. (1997). The civil commitment of sex offenders. *Science, 278,* 1248.

Zonana, H. V., & Norko, M. A. (1999). Sexual Predators. *Psychiatric Clinics of North America, 22*(1), 109–127.

---

[i] Legislatures have adopted varied terminology to designate Individuals subject to civil commitment, the most prominent being "sexually violent predators" (SVPs) and "sexually dangerous persons" (SDPs). For consistency purposes, this chapter collectively refers to series of policies under discussion as "SVP civil commitment."

[ii] States with currently active SVP civil commitment laws are: Washington, Kansas, Minnesota, Wisconsin, Iowa, New Jersey, California, Texas, (outpatient only), Arizona, Illinois, North Dakota, Missouri, Florida, Massachusetts, South Carolina, Pennsylvania ("aging out" juveniles only), Virginia, New York, New Hampshire, and Nebraska.

[iii] For a history of the Briggs Act and a period perspective on its significance, see Overholser (1935).

[iv] The singular impact of the Shriner case on shaping the precedent-setting Washington law can be most prominently seen in the detailed history of the policy's genesis provided by David Boerner, the law's principal legal architect. In his narrative (1992), Boerner stated, "From the beginning, we knew that any reform proposals would be tested against one fundamental question. If the reform had been in effect in 1987, would it have given the state the power to act to prevent Earl Shriner from committing future violent acts?" (p. 530)

[v] The profound role of citizen advocacy on the political process is perhaps best reflected in the statement of Ida Ballasiotes—the mother of Gary Kane's victim—who sat in the gallery observing the final vote on Washington's Community Protection Act on February 5, 1990: "We were watching to see if anyone opposed the bill. We were prepared to publicize the names of those who voted against it" (Siegel, 1990).

[vi] Beyond meeting the new penology's demands for the empirical evaluation of risk, psychology has also emerged as the primary discipline in sex offender treatment, which has embraced cognitive behavioral and psycho-education as the dominant paradigms. The promises and limitations of both treatment and risk assessment technology are discussed later in this chapter.

[vii] The double jeopardy and ex post facto arguments connected to SVP civil commitment laws have figured prominently in several cases. Notable examples include *Kansas v. Hendricks* (1997); *State v. Carpenter* (1995); *Martin v. Reinstein* (1999); *Seling v. Young* (2000)

[viii] For offense profiles of committed SVPs, see Lieb and Nelson (2001), Janus and Walbeck (2000), and Lieb (1996).

[ix] For a summary of state provisions associated with juveniles and psychiatric patients, see Lieb and Matson (1998).

[x] See, for example, *State v. Laxton* (2002 WI 82); In Re Leon G. (26 P. 3d 481); Commitment of W.Z. (173 NJ 109).

[xi] See *Turay v. Seling:* Findings of Fact, Conclusions of Law, December 20, 2000, U.S. District Court (Western District of Washington).

[xii] Analysis of caseload data from California Department of Mental Health, accessible at http://www.dmh.ca.gov/Services_and_Programs/Forensic_Services/Sex_Offender_Commitment_Program/Facts_&_Figures.asp , Accessed May 2, 2008. For details on statutory changes, see report of the California High Risk Sex Offender and Sexually Violent Predator Task Force (2006).

12

The Death Penalty

Corey Rayburn Yung

The use of the death penalty for sex offenses has a long and complex history in the United States. Issues of race, gender, and justice have shaped the cultural debate about the use of the ultimate penalty in such cases. For most of American history, certain sex crimes have been punishable by death. However, no one has been executed in the United States for committing a sex crime in nearly 50 years (*Kennedy v. Louisiana*, Petitioner's Brief, 2008, p. 6). The latter part of this period without executions is the result of the 1978 United States Supreme Court decision in *Coker v. Georgia* (1977). In *Coker*, the Court held that executions for rape were cruel and unusual punishment in violation of the Eighth Amendment of the Constitution. That decision seemingly foreclosed the possibility of applying the death penalty in sex crime cases.

However, efforts to revive the death penalty for sexual violence gained a foothold in Louisiana on June 17, 1995. On that day, Governor Edwin Edwards signed into law provisions that allowed capital punishment for those convicted of raping a child (La. Stat. Ann. §14:42, 1997, 1998; *State v. Wilson*, 1996, p. 1067). Louisiana argued that its statute was constitutional because *Coker* only addressed capital punishment for the rape of an adult woman. The passage of a child rape death penalty statute in Louisiana set off a series of debates in state legislatures throughout America. In early 2008, six states, Georgia (Ga. Code Ann. §16–6–1, 2007), Louisiana, Montana (Mont. Code Ann. § 45–5–503, 2007), Oklahoma (Okla. Stat. Tit. 10, § 7115(K), 2007), South Carolina (S. C. Code Ann. §16–3–655(C)(1), 2007), and Texas (Tex. Pen. Code Ann. §12.42(c)(3), 2007), had statutes that allowed for capital punishment in certain child rape cases.

Despite this legislative activity, Louisiana was the only state in which a person was sentenced to death wholly for a sex crime conviction. Only two persons in Louisiana, Patrick Kennedy and Richard Davis, were sent to death row for sex offenses after the decision in *Coker*. Kennedy was the first person so sentenced, and his death penalty appeal was heard by the United States Supreme Court on April 16, 2008.

On June 25, 2008, the Supreme Court issued its opinion in *Kennedy v. Louisiana* (2008) and held that Louisiana's capital child rape statute was unconstitutional. As with *Coker*, the Court in *Kennedy* held that the application of the death penalty for a sex crime violated the Eighth Amendment's prohibition of cruel and unusual punishment. Since the decision in *Kennedy*, several politicians have vowed to fight the Supreme Court's ruling (Ramstack, 2008, p. A01). However, given the scope and clarity of the opinion, as long as the *Kennedy* decision is not overturned, there is little opportunity for any political body to revive the death penalty for sex crimes.

Historical Application of Capital Punishment to Sex Crimes

Before examining the current state of capital child rape law, it is essential to have an appreciation for the history of the application of the death penalty in sex offense cases. The use of capital punishment for sex crimes predates the founding of the United States. American jurisprudence on the issue was generated from a complex set of legal and cultural norms from Western societies.

The earliest documented accounts of death penalties for the crime of rape were found in ancient Babylonia (Mello, 1997, p. 166). When a married female was raped by someone other than her husband, she and her attacker were bound and thrown into a river (Driver & Miles, 1955, pp. 51–53). This system gave no allowance for a women's lack of consent and treated the rapist and person raped in the same manner. Early Jewish and Saxon law treated rape as an offense punishable by death but did not punish women who were raped (Blackstone, pp. 210 211). The rationale behind these early laws was that rape was a property crime against a man's interest in preserving his wife's chastity (Brownmiller, 1975, p. 18). The patriarchal structure of these laws rested on the belief that preserving the "purity" of women was a proper function of criminal justice (Mello, 1997, p. 167). Death was an appropriate punishment because a husband's exclusive sexual access to his wife was threatened by rapists (Brownmiller, 1975, p. 18). Thus, the only way to guarantee exclusive control of women by husbands was to threaten the ultimate punishment: death (Mello, 1997, p. 166).

Early common law treated rape as a crime "against nature" and allowed for capital punishment in such cases (Boorstin, 1941, pp. 143–144). The "against nature" belief was again premised on the "natural" order of having a husband own his wife (Ibid, p. 177). Blackstone ( )noted that the overriding historical trend in Saxon, old Gothic, and Scandinavian law was toward executing rapists (p. 211). When criminal statutes were implemented in the Americas, the common-law conception of rape was imported into the legal codes (Friedman, 1993, p. 42).

Early American History

The first written code of death penalty offenses in the Americas was in the Massachusetts Bay Colony (*Furman v. Georgia*, Marshall, concurring, 1972). The list of death penalty-punishable offenses was derived from the Old Testament and included the crimes of idolatry, adultery, blasphemy, and witchcraft (Bedau, 1997, p. 7). Under this system, rape was punished as a crime of adultery, and notions of consent were notably absent from the legal structure (Ibid). Other American colonies were not so indirect in punishing rape. The list of crimes for which the death penalty could be applied included murder, arson, rape, robbery, and counterfeiting (Isenberg, 1977, p. 29). The original "Capitall Lawes of New-England" listed rape and statutory rape as capital offenses (Ibid, pp. 28–29). Rape and other nonhomicide crimes were included in many early colonial death penalty laws (Ibid).

Not all of the legal regimes in early America considered rape a capital crime (Ibid, p. 29). There was a notable North/ South split regarding the application of the death penalty for rape. As Michael Mello (1997) observed,

> States which had authorized the death penalty for rape, justified the sanction by claiming it was for the protection of women. A review of the impact of the death penalty for rape reveals that instead, capital punishment served as a symbol of white man's outrage over the defilement of their property. This property tradition was especially evident in Southern death penalty states. (p. 166)

The difference between northern and southern states also reflected differences in race relations (Ibid, pp. 166–167). The fear of black men raping white women was a common justification for rape executions in early America. As a result, early capital rape statutes became vehicles to further subjugate free and enslaved black Americans (Ibid).

It is virtually impossible to discuss capital rape statutes without addressing the issue of race in sentencing. There is substantial evidence that the driving force behind the statutes was to prevent black men from raping white women. Further, the use of the death penalty for rape was derived from lynch mobs in the South. As a result, the application of capital punishment for rape has also fallen disproportionately on blacks (Ibid).

In the early 19th century, a prominent countermovement slowed the momentum toward executing people for nonhomicide crimes. Between 1810 and 1850, a coalition of groups formed to abolish the death penalty and had remarkable success (Krivosha, Copple, & M'Donough, 1982–1983, pp. 26–27). As a result, a few states limited the death penalty to the crimes of treason and murder (Ibid,

p. 27), whereas others, including Maine and Iowa, adopted total bans on capital punishment (*Furman v. Georgia* , Marshal, concurring, 1972, p. 339). Some states maintained their preexisting statutes, and a few states continued to expand the list of death penalty crimes (Ibid, p. 338). By 1897, there were only three federal capital offenses: treason, murder, and rape (Ibid, p. 339).

Twentieth Century

The early 20th century saw the overall trend toward abolition reversed as state legislatures began adopting new death penalty statutes that expanded the list of capital offenses (Ibid, pp. 339–340). In 1925, capital punishment was authorized for rapists in much of the United States. At the time, rape was a capital offense in the states of Alabama, Arkansas, Delaware, Florida, Georgia, Kentucky, Louisiana, Maryland, Mississippi, Missouri, Nevada, North Carolina, Oklahoma, South Carolina, Tennessee, Texas, Virginia, and West Virginia (*Coker v. Georgia*, 1977, p. 593). The federal government and the District of Columbia also authorized capital punishment for rape (Ibid, 593). In addition, Alabama allowed for capital punishment for statutory rape (Gray, 1998, pp. 1447–1448), and South Carolina and Virginia permitted executions for attempted rape (Bye, 1926, p. 242). Ultimately, the movement to abolish the death penalty did almost nothing to slow the number of executions for rape during the 19th and early 20th centuries (Ibid). And racism continued to serve a critical role in determining who was sentenced to death. One of the amicus curiae briefs in *Kennedy* detailed the horrific details:

> The scourge of racial bias continued unabated through much of the 20th century, when black men convicted of rape in the South received death sentences in grossly disproportionate numbers, especially when they were convicted of raping a white woman or child. Between 1930 and 1972, 455 people were executed for rape in the United States; 405, or 89.1 percent, were black, and 443 were executed in former Confederate states. During this period, Louisiana, Mississippi, Oklahoma, Virginia, West Virginia, and the District of Columbia did not execute a single white man for rape, but together these jurisdictions executed 66 blacks. Arkansas, Delaware, Florida,

Kentucky, and Missouri each executed one white man for rape during this period, but together they executed 71 blacks. (*Kennedy v. Louisiana*, amicus curiae brief on behalf of the American Civil Liberties Union, et al., p. 3)

The Legal History of Capital Punishment for Sex Crimes

In 1910, the Supreme Court held, in *Weems v. United States* (1910) that the "cruel and unusual punishment" clause of the Eighth Amendment required that a punishment be proportionate to the crime charged. The Court wrote, "It is a precept of justice that punishment for crime should be graduated and proportioned to offense" (Ibid, p. 367). In 1958, the Court, in *Trop v. Dulles* (1958), expanded upon the finding in *Weems* and held that even though jurisdictions had the authority to apply the death penalty, they were not free "to devise any punishment short of death within the limit of [that] imagination" (Ibid, p. 99). The Court then added the phrase that would shape death penalty jurisprudence for some time when it concluded that the Eighth Amendment must be defined "from the evolving standards of decency that mark the progress of a maturing society" (Ibid, p. 101).

To this end, in 1972 in *Furman v. Georgia* (1972), the Supreme Court reversed several death penalty convictions in a decision prohibiting arbitrary and capricious applications of the death penalty (*Godfrey v. Georgia*, 1980, p. 427). This rule in *Furman* was in contrast to the method of allowing an undirected juror to reach a decision as to whether death was a proper punishment (*Furman v. Georgia*, 1972, p. 295). Because the statutes at issue in *Furman* were similar to almost every other state law, the decision effectively invalidated every death penalty provision in the United States at that time (Diamond, 1999, pp. 1164–1165). Further, the sentences of all 629 persons on death row at the time were vacated (Mello, 1997, p. 141). The *Furman* decision was composed of five separate concurring opinions, but each one established the "arbitrary and capricious" (*Furman v. Georgia*, 1972, p. 248) rule for death penalty sentences.

In response to *Furman*, a number of state legislatures quickly passed new capital punishment statutes in an attempt to comply with the decision (Paternoster, 1991, pp. 19–20). The Supreme Court reviewed these hastily drafted new laws in *Gregg v. Georgia* (1976) and four companion decisions: *Proffitt v. Florida* (1976), *Jurek v. Texas* (1976), *Woodson v. North Carolina* (1976), and *Roberts v. Louisiana* (1976). In three of the five cases, the Court upheld the new death penalty statutes because they met the *Furman* test by providing for a narrowing of the class of defendants subject to capital punishment that required consideration of each individual defendant in sentencing (*Gregg v. Georgia*, 1976, pp. 162–164). In general, this meant that a death penalty statute that provided for bifurcated proceedings, where the sentencing authority received all relevant information and standards to review that information, would meet the *Furman* "arbitrary and capricious" rule (Ibid, p. 195). The Court also established a proportionality test that required courts to "look to objective indicia that reflect the public attitude toward a given sanction," to determine if it was unconstitutional (Ibid, p. 173). To determine the "public attitude," the Court looked at many factors in *Gregg*, including history and precedent, legislative judgments, jury decisions, basic human dignity, and whether the statute was consistent with the goals of deterrence or retribution (Ibid, pp. 173–186).

When the Court reached its decision in *Furman*, 16 states and the federal government allowed the death penalty for the rape of an adult female (*Coker v. Georgia*, 1977, p. 593). After *Furman*, three states—North Carolina, Louisiana, and Georgia—reenacted the death penalty for the rape of an adult female (Ibid, p. 594). Of those three states, both North Carolina and Louisiana had their statutes invalidated because the Supreme Court found that the laws were mandatory in application in violation of the Eighth and Fourteenth Amendments (*Roberts v. Louisiana*, 1976, pp. 637–638; *Woodson v. North Carolina*, 1976, pp. 304–305). At the time the Court heard *Coker*, Georgia's capital rape statute was the only law in effect that applied when the victim was an adult female (*Coker v. Georgia*, 1977, p. 594). In the post-*Furman* era, three other states—Tennessee, Mississippi, and Florida—allowed the death penalty for the rape of a child (Ibid, p. 595). Tennessee's law was later invalidated because of its mandatory application provisions (*Collins v. State*, 1977, p. 646).

Coker v. Georgia

In December of 1971, Ehrlich Anthony Coker raped a female and then stabbed her to death. Several months later, he kidnapped a 16-year-old female, raped her twice, beat her, and abandoned her. Coker was arrested for his crimes and pleaded guilty to all charges against him. He was sentenced to three life terms, two 20-year terms, and an 8-year term, to run consecutively, for the crimes of murder, rape, kidnapping, and aggravated assault (*Coker v. Georgia*, 1977, p. 605). Eighteen months after being incarcerated, on September 2, 1974, Coker escaped from the Ware Correctional Institution in Georgia. During his escape, Coker broke into the Carver household and committed acts similar to those for which he had been incarcerated. He tied up Mr. Carver and raped Mrs. Carver, threatening them both with a knife he found in the kitchen (Ibid, 587). Coker took Mrs. Carver as a hostage and told police he would kill her if they tried to stop him (Ibid, p. 609). When Coker was eventually apprehended, the state decided to seek the death penalty against him (Ibid, p. 587). In compliance with the *Gregg* and *Furman* decisions, Coker's trial was bifurcated into separate guilt and punishment phases (Ibid, pp. 587–592). The jury found Coker guilty of armed robbery, escape, motor vehicle theft, kidnapping, and rape (Ibid, p. 587). He was then sentenced to death by electrocution (Ibid, p. 591). Subsequently, the Supreme Court of Georgia affirmed Coker's conviction and sentence (*Coker v. State*, 1975, p. 797). He appealed the Georgia Court's decision to the Supreme Court (*Coker v. Georgia*, 1977, p. 586).

The Supreme Court heard Coker's appeal of his sentence and, in a plurality opinion, decided that the death penalty for the rape of an adult female was "grossly disproportionate and excessive punishment" in violation of the Eighth Amendment (Ibid, p. 592). Although the Court's reasoning in *Coker* was premised on the analysis developed in *Gregg*, the opinion differed significantly from other *Gregg* cases because the Court was not concerned with the sentencing procedures used in applying the death penalty (Ibid, pp. 591–592; *Gregg v. Georgia*, 1976, pp. 206–207). Rather, the Court found the death penalty excessive for the crime of rape regardless of the procedures used to reach that determination (*Coker v. Georgia*, 1977, p. 592).

In applying the objective test, the plurality decision evaluated five factors that they felt indicated a social trend against capital punishment for rape (Lormand, 1999, pp. 996–997). First, that only 3 of the 60 major nations applied the death penalty for rape was indicative of a global stand against capital punishment for rape (*Coker v. Georgia*, 1977, p. 596). Second, that only 16 states provided for the death penalty for rape in the pre-*Furman* era was viewed as a trend in America against allowing executions in such cases (Ibid, pp. 593–594). Third, the Court considered the fact that, post-*Furman*, only 3 of those 16 states revised their statutes to include rape as a capital offense as evidence of changing social standards (Ibid, p. 594). Fourth, the Court noted that because only three other states post-*Furman* passed laws making rape of a child a capital offense, those statutes were not indicative of a larger trend (Ibid, pp. 595–596). Fifth, the fact that 9 of the 10 Georgia juries that had considered whether to apply the death penalty under the rape statute did not do so was further evidence of limited societal support for the death penalty in these cases (Ibid, pp. 596–597).

The plurality considered the above factors as indicative of a legislative and public intolerance of the death penalty for rape cases (Ibid, pp. 596–597). One of the oddities exhibited in *Coker* was that the Court had engaged in a form of legislative "bean counting" as a proxy for determining social consensus regarding cruelty in punishment (Mello, 1997, pp. 153–155). It was unclear whether such a method truly reflects consensus or instead is actually related to the Court's vacillation on the issue of the death penalty prior to *Coker*. Given the narrow time frame in which the post-*Furman* statutes were written, the legislatures were probably more concerned with making sure their new laws were not struck down rather than with which crimes to include (Ibid, pp. 157–158). Without a more sophisticated understanding of the reason for the omission of rape from state statutes, the indicators used by the Court in *Coker* were hardly clear signals of a burgeoning trend against applying the death penalty to rape (Ibid, pp. 146–155).

Until *Coker*, the Supreme Court had never heard a case concerning the constitutionality of applying the death penalty to the crime of rape. In 1963, in *Rudolph v. Alabama* (1963) the Supreme Court denied a writ of certiorari to a man sentenced to death for raping a female (Ibid, p. 889). Three justices dissented from the decision to deny certiorari because they felt there was a substantial constitutional question as to whether it was cruel and unusual to execute a person convicted solely of rape (Ibid, p. 889). In 1970, the Fourth Circuit, in *Ralph v. Warden* (1970) applied the *Weems* proportionality test and found that the death penalty for rape was cruel and unusual in violation of the Eighth Amendment (Ralph v. Warden, 1970, pp. 789–790, 793). Still, the *Ralph* holding was limited to rape where no life was endangered and did not set a national precedent regarding the use of capital punishment in rape cases (Ibid, p. 793). Thus, *Coker* was a case of first impression for the Supreme Court.

In an amicus brief for *Coker*, on behalf of the National Organization for Women, the American Civil Liberties Union, and other women's groups, Ruth Bader Ginsburg argued that applying the death penalty for rape was premised on an ancient, patriarchal view that treated women as property who needed chivalric protection (*Coker v. Georgia*, brief amicus curiae of the American Civil Liberties Union, et al., 1977, pp. 11–12). Although the Court reached the outcome advocated by the brief, it effectively ignored the arguments about the nature of rape and the role of patriarchy (Mello, 1997, p. 162). The Court was unwilling to examine how rape had been construed as a "fate worse than death" as the key rationale for the application of the death penalty (Rayburn [Yung], 2004, p. 1160). Such an equivalence to death was a Victorian notion that elevated chastity above survival (Ibid.). Although the Court seemed willing to listen to the feminist arguments in the ACLU brief, it was not willing to put such reasoning into law.

The Aftermath of Coker

After *Coker*, Tennessee, Florida, and Mississippi maintained laws that allowed for the death penalty for the crime of raping a child (Higgins, 1997, p. 30). It remained unclear whether these statutes were at odds with the decision in *Coker* because the holding did not clearly extend beyond the rape of an adult to the rape of a child (Palmer, 1999, p. 857). Of those three states, only Florida's statute was invalidated because of an Eighth Amendment challenge before its highest court (*Buford v. State*, 1981, p. 951). Tennessee's statute was found unconstitutional because the application of the death penalty was mandatory, in violation of the *Furman* test (*Collins v. State*, 1977, p. 646). The Mississippi law was struck down because the state's sentencing guidelines for death penalty crimes required an attempt to kill, an intention to kill, that someone be killed, or that lethal force be contemplated—none of which were elements for the conviction of rape (*Leatherwood v. State*, 1989, p. 403).

During the same time period, extending the reasoning in *Coker* to other crimes, the Supreme Court applied the proportionality test and found the death penalty to be unconstitutional for the crimes of aggravated robbery (*Enmund v. Florida*, 1982, p. 797) and kidnapping (*Eberheart v. Georgia*, 1977, p. 917; *Eberheart v. State*, 1974, p. 247). The Court also continued to use the methods of *Coker* in evaluating other cruel and unusual punishment cases (Gray, 1998, p. 1461). Chiefly, the Court has evaluated "the evolving standards of decency that mark the progress of a maturing society" (*Trop v. Dulles*, 1958, p. 101) by looking to historical developments, international opinion, legislative changes, sentencing jury decisions, and legislative history (Gray, 1998, p. 1461).

Revival of the Death Penalty for Rape in Louisiana

From 1989 to 1995, no jurisdiction in the United States allowed for the death penalty for the crime of rape (Lormand, p. 1002). In 1995, Louisiana ended this short historical break from applying the death penalty in cases of rape when it passed legislation that allowed capital punishment for aggravated rape when the victim was under the age of twelve (La. Rev. Stat. Ann. 14:42(D)(2), 2004). The relevant part of the statute passed was this:

1. Whoever commits the crime of aggravated rape shall be punished by life imprisonment at hard labor without benefit of parole, probation, or suspension of sentence.
2. However, if the victim was under the age of twelve years … the offender shall be punished by death or life imprisonment at hard labor without benefit of parole, probation, or suspension of sentence, in accordance with the determination of the jury.

The statute passed the Louisiana House of Representatives 72 to 22 (Shuler, 1995). The Senate did not debate the bill and approved it by a 34 to 1 margin (Wardlaw, 1995). There was almost no legislative history articulating the underlying rationales for the new effort to apply capital punishment. Governor Edwards signed the bill into law on June 17, 1995, and it went into effect in August of 1995 (*State v. Wilson*, 1996, p. 1067).

Prosecutors did not immediately seek the death penalty in child rape cases, but it was not long before they found candidates for execution. Before the trials had even begun, the capital child rape statute was tested before the Louisiana Supreme Court in *State v. Wilson* (1996, p. 1064). The test case was the result of a consolidation of two separate cases before the court (Ibid, pp. 1064–1065). One defendant, Patrick Dewayne Bethley, was charged with the aggravated rape of three girls, ages 5, 7, and 9 (Ibid, p. 1065). The other defendant, Anthony Wilson, was charged with aggravated rape of a 5-year-old girl (Ibid, p. 1064). It was also alleged that Bethley was HIV-positive at the time of the rapes and that he was aware of his HIV status (Ibid, p. 1065). Both defendants moved to quash their indictments, and their motions were granted (Ibid, pp. 1064–1065). Upon appeal, the Louisiana Supreme Court consolidated the two cases and reversed the lower court decision, holding the death penalty was constitutional for those convicted of raping a child under the age of 12 (Ibid, p. 1064). Bethley petitioned the United States Supreme Court for a writ of certiorari but was denied on jurisdictional grounds because he had not yet been convicted or sentenced (*Bethley v. Louisiana*, 1997, p. 1259). Neither Wilson nor Bethley was ultimately sentenced to death under the Louisiana statute.

Other States Following Louisiana's Lead

After Louisiana adopted its child rape statute in 1995, many states debated similar bills making the rape of a minor a capital crime. California lawmakers considered providing for the death penalty when a twice-convicted offender committed a "lewd and lascivious act on a child under the age of [14] years" in 1999, but the effort ultimately failed (A.B. 35, 1999 Leg., Reg. Sess.,1999). Pennsylvania legislators proposed a statute that would "impose the death penalty for repeated sexual assaults on children" (Palmer, 1999, pp. 869–870). Massachusetts considered a bill to make child rape a capital crime (Mulvihill, 1997, p. 17). Alabama's legislators repeatedly pushed a bill that would have allowed executions of child molesters, but the measure never became law (Cockburn, 2002, p. 8). Virginia debated a bill to apply the death penalty to repeat sexual violence offenders (Hardy, 1998, p. A-8). Additionally, Mississippi lawmakers considered a bill to impose the death penalty upon conviction for rape of a child under the age of fourteen years (H.B. 1331, 2004 Reg. Sess., Miss. 2004).

As mentioned earlier, of these various efforts, only six other states actually adopted capital child rape statutes: Georgia, Louisiana, Montana, Oklahoma, South Carolina, and Texas. Interestingly, of the six states, only Louisiana's statute provided for capital punishment for first-time sex offenders. The other states required a prior conviction and sentence served as a prerequisite for capital punishment. The states varied concerning the age of the victim as well as with aggravating factors.

These legislative actions were strongly supported by a public that overwhelmingly favored the use of the death penalty for sex crimes against children. According to one poll, 65% of those surveyed supported the death penalty for child molesters (Barrett, 1997, p. A21). Americans came to believe that rape is the most heinous crime "worthy of the most serious punishment" (LaFree, 1989, p. 62). Politicians sensed the growing public fervor and placed the death penalty for the rape of a child at the center of their law and order platforms (Zambrano, 1998, p. 1268). "The death penalty [was] vigorously touted as the best way to deal with child molesters" (Cockburn, 2002, p. 8). Society and many of its leaders made clear that they favor applying the death penalty for aggravated sex crimes against children (Gray, 1998, p. 1467; Palmer, 1999, p. 870).

Although the trend toward capital punishment for child molestation was in its relative infancy, efforts to apply the death penalty for other nonhomicide crimes were very successful. In 1993, 36 states authorized the death penalty (Mello, 1997, p. 160). Of those 36, only 6 allowed for capital punishment for nonhomicide crimes (Ibid, p. 160). By 1997, 14 states and the federal government allowed the death penalty for crimes that did not result in death (Ibid, pp. 160–161). Currently, at least nine states—Arkansas, California, Colorado, Georgia, Illinois, Louisiana, Mississippi, Missouri, and Washington—and the federal government provide the death penalty for treason (18 U.S.C. § 794, 2000; Ark. Code Ann. § 5-51-201, 1997; Cal. Pen. Code § 37,

2004; Colo. Rev. Stat. § 18-11-101, 2003; Colo. Rev. Stat. § 18-1.4-102, 2003; Ga. Code Ann. § 16-11-1, 2003; Ill. Comp. Stat. Ann. 720 § 5/30-1, 2003; La. Rev. Stat. Ann. § 14:113, 1986; Miss. Code Ann. § 97-7-67, 2000; Mo. Ann. Stat. § 576.070, 2003; Mo. Rev. Stat. 557.021, 2001; Wash. Rev. Code. Ann. § 9.82.010, 2004).

At least five states—Colorado, Idaho, Illinois, Missouri, and Montana—consider aggravated kidnapping a capital crime (Colo. Rev. Stat. § 18-3-301, 2003; Idaho Code § 18-4505, 1997; Mo. Ann. Stat. § 565.110, 1999; Mont. Code Ann. § 45-5-303, 2003; Mo. Rev. Stat. 557.021, 2001). At least two states, Florida and Missouri, and the federal government, permit the death penalty for drug trafficking (18 U.S.C. §§ 3591 & 3592, 2000; Fla. Stat. Ann. § 921.142, 2004; Mo. Ann. Stat. § 195.214, 2004). Two states, Georgia and Mississippi, allow executions for aircraft hijacking (Ga. Code Ann. § 16-5-44, 2003; Miss. Code Ann. § 97-25-55, 2000).

Missouri considers placing a bomb near a bus terminal to be a capital crime (Mo. Ann. Stat. § 578.310, 2003; Mo. Rev. Stat. 557.021, 2001). New Mexico permits a death sentence for espionage (N.M. Stat. Ann. § 20-12-42, 2003). Montana provides the death penalty for aggravated assault by incarcerated, persistent felons or murderers (Mont. Code Ann. § 46-18-303, 2003; Mont. Code Ann. § 46-18-220, 2001). Even beyond the case of child rape, the trend in America has been to expand the use of the death penalty to an array of crimes other than murder (Mello, 1997, p. 160).

Outside of state efforts, there are also relics of the older system that treat the rape of adult women as a capital crime. Article 120 of the United Code of Military Justice (2000) holds, "Any person subject to [the code] who commits an act of sexual intercourse, by force or without consent, is guilty of rape and shall be punished by death or such other punishment as a court-martial may direct." The military has maintained this provision despite *Coker* because of its unique status under American law (Chamallas, 1998, p. 307). Further, in Georgia, the Senate never actually removed the death penalty language applied to the rape of an adult woman from the statute at issue in *Coker*, and it remains "on the books" 30 years later (Ga. Code Ann. § 16-6-1, 2007). At least one scholar has noted that Georgia's intransigence on this issue reflects the legislature's belief that, for the crime of rape, the death penalty is still the appropriate punishment (Silversten, 2001, p. 158).

Kennedy v. Louisiana

On March 2, 1998, Patrick Kennedy called 9-1-1 to report that his stepdaughter had been raped (*Kennedy v. Louisiana*, Respondent's Brief, 2008, p. 6). The stepdaughter's injuries were horrific and required substantial medical attention. Kennedy reported that two neighborhood boys had brutally raped the 8-year-old girl and fled on a bike. The stepdaughter initially confirmed Kennedy's account of what had happened. When the police investigated Kennedy's story, holes soon emerged. After an investigation with a few twists and turns, Louisiana authorities arrested Kennedy and charged him with the aggravated child rape.

After a trial before a jury, Kennedy was found guilty. Following the sentencing phase, the jury recommended the penalty of death. Kennedy appealed his sentence to the Louisiana Supreme Court. In *State v. Kennedy* (2007), the Louisiana Supreme Court, in addition to rejecting Kennedy's other arguments, held that the death sentence did not violate the Eighth Amendment's prohibition against cruel and unusual punishment. Consistent with the approach that the court had taken in *State v. Wilson*, the court held that *Coker v. Georgia* only applied to capital adult rape statutes.

Following the Louisiana Supreme Court's ruling, Kennedy filed for a writ of certiorari with the United States Supreme Court. In January of 2008, certiorari was granted. The Supreme Court heard arguments in the case on April 16, 2008, and issued its opinion on June 25, 2008. The Court utilized the same methodology employed in *Coker* to evaluate whether America's "evolving standards of decency" supported a finding that the death penalty for child rape constituted cruel or unusual punishment.

The Court concluded its analysis of the objective criteria underlying the "evolving standards" by finding,

> After reviewing the authorities informed by contemporary norms, including the history of the death penalty for this and other nonhomicide crimes, current state statutes and new enactments, and the number of executions since 1964, we conclude there is a national consensus against capital punishment for the crime of child rape. (*Kennedy v. Louisiana*, p. 23)

The opinion of the Court was by five votes to four. The dissent by Justice Alito was pointed and in sharp opposition to the majority (*Kennedy v. Louisiana*, 2008, p. 1). Although the holding in *Kennedy* makes clear that it is unconstitutional to apply the death penalty to any sex crime against an individual, if the makeup of the Court changed, it would be possible that the opinion might be overturned at some future date.

Policy Considerations in Applying The Death Penalty

The constitutional problems posed by capital (child) rape statutes were not the only reason to question the desirability of such laws. In the many public discussions and legislative debates about the use of the death penalty for sex offenses, there was surprisingly little mention of how these new capital child rape statutes would affect children. It was taken for granted that bringing "justice" to child rapists would be better for the children who were targets of molesters. Below, I discuss the various incentives, consequences, and other effects of the application of the death penalty to child rape cases.[i]

The Problem of Underreporting

The threat of a long trial and the guilt associated with testifying to put someone to death may discourage reporting of the crime. A review of convicted child rapists provides substantial evidence that the majority of rapists are known to the child before the crime (Greenfeld, 1997). When the offender is a friend of the family or actually a member of the family, reporting rates for the crime are significantly lower (Diamond, 1999, p. 1189). Adding the death penalty to the family's decision on whether to report will further discourage them from coming forward. As an amicus curiae brief in the *Kennedy* case argued,

> The threat of capital punishment for sexual abusers of children will greatly amplify the concerns that already prevent many victims and relatives from reporting abuse. Victims who love their abusers may be all the more reluctant to report abuse to police when the possible consequences include lethal injection. The reluctance may also be a product of the victim's own sense of

responsibility for the abuse ... The stigma of a possible death-penalty prosecution of a relative and its attendant publicity—as well as their feelings for the abuser—can only feed the fears that already inhibit non-offending family members from coming forward. Instead of encouraging the best-positioned witnesses—the victim and other family members—to report abuse, Louisiana's law will reinforce the internal constraints that many victims and their family members already feel. (*Kennedy v. Louisiana*, amicus curiae brief on behalf of the National Association of Social Workers, et al., 2008, pp. 11–12) [*hereinafter* "NASL Brief"]

If reporting decreases for aggravated child rapes, the deterrence and retribution goals of applying the death penalty will be completely undermined (Palmer, 1999, p. 865). The *Wilson* court's reply to this concern was simply to note that the child was an innocent victim and the offender was responsible and should have been punished accordingly (State v. Wilson, 1996, p. 1073). This was a non sequitur to the very real concern that the death penalty would actually discourage reporting of sexual violence against children. The *Wilson* court's counterargument was a disservice to the debate over the death penalty and indicative of shortsighted, retribution-oriented politics that would blind policymakers to the insidious effects of the statutes they supported.

Dangerous Messages to Child Rapists

A necessary portion of any deterrence discussion is to examine the signals sent to and incentives understood by would-be criminals. In the case of applying the death penalty, a policy maker hopes the ultimate penalty, death, will create a high disincentive toward committing rape even when the probability of being punished is low (Jun, 1996, pp. 1099–1100). Such an optimistic view misses the other incentives created by a system that treats murder and rape the same in regards to punishment.

When death is the penalty for rape and murder, a rapist has an increased incentive to kill the person he or she has raped. Under a statutory system where the death penalty is applied to the aggravated rape of a child, the rapist has every incentive to kill the child victim because the child is likely to be the only witness (Fleming, 1999, pp. 742–743). If murder does not incur additional punishment, then the motivation to kill the primary witness to the crime is strong.

The notion of a "freebie" in crimes is not unique to the crime of rape. Similar debates were had for statutes that applied capital punishment to the crime of kidnapping (Ala. Code § 13A-6-44 cmt., 1994). In that context, the application of the death penalty was viewed as an "invitation to the criminal to kill the victim" (Konradi, 1997, p. 3). The pervasive view regarding capital punishment and kidnapping thus turned to disfavoring death as a penalty (Diamond, 1999, pp. 1186–1187). A similar effect should dissuade those who seek to execute convicted rapists. Kidnapping does not have the same social resonance as rape, but the incentives created by applying the death penalty in either case are remarkably similar. Both are crimes with generally only one witness that have a low probability of successful prosecution when the person kidnapped or raped is also murdered (Ibid).

The risk of a rapist taking a "freebie" is especially high when the person being attacked is a minor. Sexual abuse cases are already among the most difficult for prosecutors to try (Ibid, p. 1187). As G. Russell Nuce has argued (1990), the "child victims are usually the key witnesses ... [and] their testimony is likely to be indispensable to the conviction of the person who committed the crime" (p. 607). Given that the rapist of a child would not incur an extra penalty when he or she is already eligible for execution, the incentive to kill the sole witness to the crime is a low-risk, high-reward scenario. This equation is fundamentally depraved, but it is the notion that underlies deterrence. That is, a would-be criminal assesses consequences and risk versus "reward" before engaging in criminal behavior (Dressler, 2001, pp. 14–15).

Proponents of death penalty statutes for child rape have advanced two major arguments against the "freebie" theory (Glazer, 1997, pp. 106–107). First, they have argued that the theory "assumes that the rapist is contemplating the consequences of his act at the time of its commission" (Ibid, p. 106). This argument allows death penalty proponents to play both sides of the deterrence debate. For the death penalty to have a deterrent effect, a criminal *must* consider his or her actions in light of the consequences, or deterrence fails to work. To then argue that the "freebie" theory is bankrupt because it assumes the criminal is thinking about those same consequences is contradictory nonsense. If a potential child rapist does not perceive the death penalty as a deterrent, then the primary argument in support of it is lost.

Second, proponents argue that murder of a child is unlikely because most rapists in these cases are friends or family who would be reluctant to kill the boy or girl (Ibid). Of course, one would probably have to ask how a friend or family member would rape a child they know in the first place. It hardly seems unreasonable to argue that someone willing to torment, abuse, and rape a known child would also be willing to kill him or her to avoid a death sentence. Further, the argument that offenders would not murder or seriously injure a child is in contrast to evidence of a higher rate of murder among child rapes (Greenfeld, 1997, p. 29) and the fact that one quarter of rapes where the attacker is the parent of a child cause "major injury" (Ibid, p. 12). It seems that many rapists have no qualms about killing their victim in the present environment. Adding the threat of execution will increase the incentives to do so.

It is also notable that the only study to examine whether capital punishment deters rapes did not find any strong correlation (Bedau & Pierce, 1976, p. 18). The authors of the study admitted that the issue was especially difficult to study given the small time frame, sample sizes, and control factors (Ibid.). Nonetheless, there has not been any contrary empirical evidence produced by those favoring capital punishment for rape.

The Ordeal of the Trial and Sentencing

There are important procedural differences in the context of a capital crime. Because a death penalty trial is usually very long and must be bifurcated into guilt and sentencing phases, children who have been raped would almost certainly have two long periods on the witness stand (Paternoster, 1991, p. 212). Further, the possibility of a death sentence makes a guilty plea highly unlikely. Thus, whereas a plea bargain might prevent a child victim from having to testify, if prosecutors push forward with the use of capital punishment, trials may be more common for the most severe crimes.

This is of significant consequence to a child who has been raped. Children who testify at rape trials are usually attacked by defense attorneys who allege that the children have fabricated their stories (Myers, 1992, pp. 30–31). Studies have shown that the emotional effects on children who testify in rape trials are severe (Diamond, 1999, pp. 1187–1188). The healing process that children must go through is delayed during the trial and trauma from the long process will inevitably cause more psychological damage to the child (Ibid). As Meryl Diamond (1999) has noted, "as important as it is to protect children from child rapists, it is equally important to protect them from any further emotional trauma (1188)." Capital trials may also bring in better defense lawyers who will, as part of their ethical duties, make the experience much more difficult for the child victims.[ii]

This associated trauma can discourage victims from testifying. In such cases, the underlying prosecution will fail even before it gets to the sentencing phase. If victims persevere and do take the stand, the psychological effects will be substantial. Almost every major study that has examined the effect of trials on children has shown that the process severely impedes recovery (NASL Brief, p. 18). If, after the entire process is complete, the defendant is sentenced to death, this can also have negative psychological effects on the child. Feelings of guilt for the resultant execution along with the impending death delayed through appeals can continue to work against psychological recovery (Ibid, p. 20). Obviously, this guilt can be even greater if, as is often the case, the defendant is a family member.

These various negative policy effects of applying the death penalty to sex crimes are substantial. They substantially undermine the case for capital child rape statutes. Goals of deterrence and retribution are not likely to be fulfilled. Further, the child may be put in psychological and physical danger by virtue of introducing death into the penalty equation.

Conclusion

The use of capital punishment for sexual violence has been quite common in American history. However, over the last 50 years, even though punishments on sex offenses have substantially increased, states have moved away from using death to punish sex crimes. Against this larger trend, Louisiana and five other states attempted to revive the use of capital punishment for certain child rapes.

This decision was against substantial evidence that the statutes would not serve any policy aims. The statutes could not achieve the goal of deterrence because they would decrease reporting, decrease convictions, and increase the incentives to murder rape victims. Whatever retributive function would be served by executions would be similarly undermined because the death penalty would likely decrease the number of rapists caught and convicted.

However, a policy being unwise does not make it unconstitutional. After remaining silent on the capital child rape statutes for over a decade, the U.S. Supreme Court decided the future of such laws in *Kennedy v. Louisiana*. With the issuance of that opinion, the constitutional question seems to be settled. If *Kennedy* remains "good" law, then there is no room for policy makers to enact death penalty laws for sex crimes. However, as evidenced by the Court's vacillation in a relatively narrow time frame concerning the capital punishment of juveniles,[iii] there is a possibility that *Kennedy* could be reversed. Nonetheless, as of now, the United States has decided to close the chapter on using death as a punishment for sex offenses.

References

A.B. 35, 1999 Leg., Reg. Sess. (Cal. 1999).

Ala. Code § 13A-6-44 cmt. (1994).

Ark. Code Ann. § 5-51-201 (1997).

The Babylonian Laws 1. (Vol. 2). G.R. Driver & John C. Miles trans. (1955).

Barrett, J. Q. (1997, August 18). Death for child rapists may not save children. *National Law Journal*, A21.

Bedau, H. A. (Ed.). (1997). *The death penalty in America*. New York: Oxford University Press.

Bedau, H. A. & Pierce, C. M., (1976) *Capital punishment in the United States*. AMS Press.

Bethley v. Louisiana, 520 U.S. 1259 (1997).

Blackstone, W. Commentaries (Vol. 4). *210–11.

Boorstin, D. J. (1941). *The Mysterious Science of the Law*. Cambridge: Harvard University Press.

Brownmiller, S. (1975). *Against our will: Men, women and rape*. New York: Ballatine.

Buford v. State, 403 So. 2d 943 (Fla. 1981).

Bye, R. T. (1926). Recent history and present status of capital punishment in the United States. *Journal of the American Institute of Criminal Law and Criminology, 17*, 234–245.

Cal. Penal Code § 37 (Deering Supp. 2004).

Chamallas, M. (1998). The New Gender Panic: Reflections on Sex Scandals and the Military. *Minnesota Law Review, 83*, 305–375.

Cockburn, A. (2002, May 20). Extreme Solutions; Capital Punishment for Child Molesters. *The Nation*, 8.

Coker v. Georgia, 433 U.S. 584 (1977).

Coker v. Georgia, 433 U.S. 584 (1977), Brief Amici Curiae of the American Civil Liberties Union et. al. (No. 75-5444).

Coker v. State, 216 S.E.2d 782 (Ga. 1975), *rev'd by* 433 U.S. 584 (1977).

Collins v. State, 550 S.W.2d 643 (Tenn. 1977).

Colo. Rev. Stat. § 18-3-301 (2003).

Colo. Rev. Stat. § 18-11-101 (2003).

Colo. Rev. Stat. § 18-1.4-102 (2003).

Diamond, M. P. (1999). Assessing the Constitutionality of Capital Child Rape Statutes, *St. John's Law Review, 73,* 1159–1190.

Dressler, J. (2001). *Understanding Criminal Law* (3rd ed.). Lexis Law Publishing.

Eberheart v. Georgia, 433 U.S. 917 (1977).

Eberheart v. State, 232 Ga. 247 (1974).

Enmund v. Florida, 458 U.S. 782 (1982).

Fla. Stat. Ann. § 921.142 (West Supp. 2004).

Fleming, A. F. (1999). Comment, Louisiana's Newest Capital Crime: The Death Penalty for Child Rape. *Journal of Criminal Law & Criminology, 89,* 717–750.

Friedman, L. M. (1993). *Crime and Punishment in American History.* New York: Basic Books.

Furman v. Georgia, 408 U.S. 238 (1972).

Furman v. Georgia, 408 U.S. 238 (1972). (Marshall, concurring).

Ga. Code Ann. § 16-11-1 (2003).

Ga. Code Ann. § 16-5-44 (2003).

Ga. Code Ann. § 16-6-1 (2003).

Ga. Code Ann. § 16-6-1 (2007).

Glazer, Y. (1997). Child Rapists Beware! The Death Penalty and Louisiana's Amended Aggravated Rape Statute. *American Journal of Criminal Law, 25,* 79–114.

Godfrey v. Georgia, 446 U.S. 420 (1980).

Gray, E. (1998). Death Penalty and Child Rape: An Eighth Amendment Analysis. *St. Louis University Law Journal, 42,* 1443–1469.

Greenfeld, L. A. (1997). *Sex Offenses and Offenders: An Analysis of Data on Rape and Sexual Assault.* Washington: U.S. Department of Justice.

Gregg v. Georgia, 428 U.S. 153 (1976).

Hardy, M. (1998, January 29). Committee Kills Death Penalty Bill, *Richmond Times-Dispatch,* A-8.

Higgins, M. (1997). Is Capital Punishment for Killers Only? *American Bar Association Journal, 83,* 30–31.

Idaho Code § 18-4505 (1997).

Ill. Comp. Stat. Ann. 720, § 5/30-1 (2003).

Isenberg, I. (1977). *The Reference Shelf, No. 2, The Death Penalty.* (Vol. 49). New York: H. W. Wilsons.

Jun, D. Y. (1996). *Bribery Among the Korean Elite: Putting an End to a Cultural Ritual and Restoring Honor, Vanderbilt. Journal of Transnational Law,* 29, 1071.

Jurek v. Texas, 428 U.S. 262 (1976) (plurality opinion).

Kennedy v. Louisiana, 07-343 Amicus Curiae Brief on behalf of the National Association of Social Workers, et. al. (2008).

Kennedy v. Louisiana, 07-343 Amicus Curiae Brief on behalf of the American Civil Liberties Union, et. al. (2008).

Kennedy v. Louisiana, 554 U.S. ___, slip. op. (2008).

Kennedy v. Louisiana, Petitioner's Brief, 07-343 (2008).

Kennedy v. Louisiana, Respondent's Brief, 07-343 (2008).

Konradi, A. (1997). Too Little, Too Late: Prosecutors' Pre-court Preparation of Rape Survivors, *Law & Social Inquiry,* 22, 1–54.

Krivosha N., Copple, R., & M'Donough, M. (1982-1983). A Historical and Philosophical Look at the Death Penalty—Does it Serve Society's Needs? *Creighton Law Review,* 16, 1–46.

La. Rev. Stat. Ann. 14:42(D)(2) (West Supp. 2004).

La. Rev. Stat. Ann. § 14:113 (West 1986).

La. Stat. Ann. §14:42, West 1997 and Supp. 1998.

LaFree, G. D. (1989). *Rape and Criminal Justice: The Social Construction of Sexual Assault.* Belmont: Wadsworth.

Leatherwood v. State, 548 So. 2d 389 (Miss. 1989).

Lormand, P. J. (1999). Proportionate Sentencing for Rape of a Minor: The Death Penalty Dilemma, *Tulane Law Review,* 73, 981–1015.

Mello, M. (1997) Executing Rapists: A Reluctant Essay on the Ethics of Legal Scholarship, *William & Mary Journal of Women and the Law,* 4, 129

Myers, J. E. B. (1992). *Legal Issues in Child Abuse and Neglect.* Thousand Oaks: Sage Publications.

Miss. Code Ann. § 97-7-67 (2000).

Miss. Code Ann. § 97-25-55 (2000).

Mo. Ann. Stat. § 195.214 (West 2004).

Mo. Ann. Stat. § 565.110 (West 1999).

Mo. Ann. Stat. § 576.070 (West 2003).

Mo. Ann. Stat. § 578.310 (West 2003).

Mo. Rev. Stat. 557.021 (West 2001).

Mont. Code Ann. § 45-5-303 (2003).

Mont. Code Ann § 45–5–503 (2007).

Mont. Code Ann. § 46-18-220 (2001).

Mont. Code Ann. § 46-18-303 (2003).

Mulvihill, M. (1997, October 26). Grieving Families Spare No Energy in Campaign for Capital Punishment. *Boston Herald,* 17.

N.M. Stat. Ann. § 20-12-42 (Michie 2003).

Nuce, G. R. (1990). *Child Sexual Abuse: A New Decade for the Protection of Our Children? Emory Law Journal,* 39, 581–618.

Okla. Stat. Tit. 10, § 7115(K) (West 2007 Supp).

Palmer, B.M. (1999). Note, Death as a Proportionate Penalty for the Rape of a Child: Considering One State's Current Law, *Georgia State University Law Review,* 15, 843–878.

Paternoster, R. (1991). *Capital Punishment in America.* Hoboken: Jossey-Bass Inc.

Proffitt v. Florida, 428 U.S. 242 (1976).

Ralph v. Warden, 438 F.2d 786 (4th Cir. 1970).

Ramstack, T. (2008, July 3). Louisiana Seizes on U.S. Oversight. *Washington Times,* p. A01.

Rayburn [Yung], C. (2004). Better Dead than R(ap)ed?: The Patriarchal Rhetoric Driving Capital Rape Statutes. *St. John's Law Review,* 78, 1119–1165.

Roper v. Simmons, 543 U.S. 551 (2005).

Roberts v. Louisiana, 428 U.S. 325 (1976).

Rudolph v. Alabama, 375 U.S. 889 (1963).

Shuler, M. (1995, April 27). House Passes Death Penalty for Child Rape. *The Advocate*, 1B.

Silversten, M. (2001). Sentencing Coker v. Georgia to Death: Capital Child Rape Statutes Provide the Supreme Court an Opportunity to Return Meaning to the Eighth Amendment. *Gonzaga Law Review, 37*, 121–166.

S. C. Code Ann. §16–3–655(C)(1) (Supp. 2007).

Stanford v. Kentucky, 492 U.S. 361 (1989).

State v. Kennedy, 957 So. 2d 757 (La. 2007).

State v. Wilson, 685 So. 2d 1063 (La. 1996).

Tex. Penal Code Ann. §12.42(c)(3) (West Supp. 2007).

Trop v. Dulles, 356 U.S. 86 (1958).

U.S.C., 10 § 920, Art. 120 (2000).

U.S.C., 18 § 794 (2000).

U.S.C., 18 §§ 3591, 3592 (2000).

Wardlaw, J. (1995, June 6). Death Penalty for Child Rape Gets Final OK. *Times-Picayune*, p. A4.

Wash. Rev. Code. Ann. § 9.82.010 (West Supp. 2004).

Weems v. United States, 217 U.S. 349 (1910).

Woodson v. North Carolina, 428 U.S. 280 (1976).

Zambrano, P. (1998). The Death Penalty is Cruel and Unusual Punishment for the Crime of Rape—Even the Rape of a Child. *Santa Clara Law Review*, 39, 1267–1293.

Portions of this chapter previously appeared in Corey Rayburn [Yung] (2004).

[i] One of the issues that is not discussed is the problem of race in relation to the application of the death penalty. Given the historical application on racial lines, this omission might seem surprising. However, given the relative paucity of cases because of the decisions in *Furman, Gregg, Coker*, and now *Kennedy*, it is unclear if race continued to play a key role in applying capital punishment.

[ii] The trauma on a child can be lessened in jurisdictions that allow children to testify through closed-circuit television. However, it is unclear whether such protections would be afforded in capital trials.

[iii] In *Roper v. Simmons* (2005), the Court struck down the juvenile death penalty after previously upholding a similar law in *Stanford v. Kentucky* (1989), with just 16 years having passed.

Policy
Alternatives

13

Leaders in Sex Offender Research and Policy

Alissa R. Ackerman &
Karen J. Terry

As with all policy efforts geared toward controlling sex offenders, rigorous and routine evaluations must be done to assess the impact and efficacy of these policies. In Part II of this book, authors have presented a critical and empirical assessment of specific sex offender laws. As documented throughout, there is often a disconnect between the scientific understanding of sexual assault prevention and the political trends of sex offender controls.

What the last decade of sex offender policies has also created are programs and governmental agencies geared toward prevention, the complexities of risk assessment, utilization of evaluation data, and comprehensive approaches to sex offender management. Some states and communities have taken the opportunity that sex offender laws present and have pursued their policies with significant attention to the evaluative testing, scientific underpinnings, and multidisciplinary collaboration. Although not an evaluative assessment, this chapter will highlight and summarize a few of these ideal approaches.

Modern Sex Offender Laws

In 1989, Earl Shriner, a sex offender with a long history of violent behavior, was released from prison in Washington State despite the knowledge of correctional staff that he was a high-risk offender who would likely recidivate. Not surprisingly, he sexually assaulted and tortured a 7-year-old boy. At the time, there was no legislation that allowed authorities to warn the community about high-risk sex offenders. In response to the public outcry regarding Shriner's acts, Washington implemented the first modern registration and notification statute as part of the Community Protection Act of 1990 (Berliner, 1996).

Other high-profile cases of sexual abuse and murder followed in other states over the next 5 years, including the cases of Polly Klaas, Jacob Wetterling, and Megan Kanka. Parents, community members, and the media demanded that politicians do something to protect children. Eventually, they did: New Jersey enacted Megan's Law in 1994. President Clinton signed it into federal legislation on May 17, 1996, amending the Jacob Wetterling Crimes Against Children and Sexually Violent Offender Registration Program Act of 1994 (which only required registration). This act was the first federal program that would mandate notification procedures of registered sex offenders.

Today, all 50 states have registration and notification statutes. In the dozen years since Megan's Law was enacted, new laws have been implemented at the federal, state, and local levels in an effort to better manage sex offenders in the community. Most recently, the Adam Walsh Child Protection and Safety Act (Adam Walsh Act) (Pub. L. 109–248) was signed into law by President George W. Bush in 2006. This act is broad in its scope, enhancing sex offender registration and notification and providing provisions for civil commitment and deportation for immigrant sex offenders. The goal of Title I of the Adam Walsh Act, the Sex Offender Registration and Notification Act (SORNA), is to strengthen the nationwide network of existing registration and notification programs. States that do not comply with the legislation willingly forfeit 10% of federal government funding under the Omnibus Crime Control and Safe Streets Act. Similarly, a proposed bill is currently (as of the writing of this chapter) being discussed before the U.S. Congress that would abolish parole for all sex offenders who commit a crime against a child or who are deemed sexually violent predators (SVP) (H.R. 2106). If passed, the bill would mandate state compliance to avoid forfeiting federal funding.

Sex offender legislation aims to protect the community, and community members think they are safer by knowing who and where sex offenders are. Unfortunately, at the time these laws were passed, there was little preliminary research conducted considering their effectiveness or whether they were even based on valid assumptions (Lotke, 1997; Thomas, 2003). It is quite possible that legislators did not ask the proper questions to obtain a better understanding of how this legislation could be effective in its goal of community protection (Terry, 2003).

The research that has been conducted since the enactment of the various sex offender laws has shown that they may not be the panacea the community anticipated (e.g., Cohen & Jeglic, 2007; Levenson & Hern, 2007). The body of research is nascent but growing; and so far, few policy evaluation studies have shown empirical support for current community mandates. Some studies even have indicated that the legislation may increase the risk of recidivism or at least cause unintended consequences, such as the inability to find adequate housing, unemployment, isolation, strain, and decreases in social support (Lees & Tewksbury, 2006; Levenson & Cotter, 2005; Tewksbury, 2004, 2005).

Policies that regulate the behavior of sex offenders differ by state. Although federal law mandates that states abide by certain rules, such as maintaining registration and notification, the federal rules are broadly defined and states draft legislation that suits their constituents. That is why various agencies at the federal and state level, both public and private, are working to better understand what works and what does not, and for whom legislation is most effective. It is important to understand the research and policy efforts of these organizations; though their goals are similar, their structure and research questions differ. The organizations discussed in this chapter represent the vanguard of sex offender research and policy, because their empirical findings are the basis for policies designed to keep communities safe through eliminating risk and balancing the rights of offenders and the community.

National Organizations

The Center for Sex Offender Management

The Center for Sex Offender Management (CSOM) was formed in 1997 after the Office of Justice Programs (OJP), U.S. Department of Justice, held a national summit called "Promoting Public Safety Through the Effective Management of Sex Offenders in the Community." This meeting brought professionals from different fields together to determine the most effective ways of managing sex offenders in the community. After listening to the experts who attended the summit, CSOM was created by OJP, the National Institute of Corrections (NIC), and the State Justice Institute (SJI). CSOM became a national effort to support various jurisdictions as they aimed to supervise, treat, and manage sex offenders in their communities. Today, CSOM is administered through a joint collaboration of OJP and the Center for Effective Public Policy.

The primary goal of the organization is to "enhance public safety by preventing further victimization through improving the management of sex offenders in the community" (CSOM, 2008a). There are three basic ways that these goals are achieved: an information exchange, training and technical assistance, and support to select resources sites and OJP grantees (CSOM, 2008a). Through these activities, CSOM does the following:

- It provides access to the most up-to-date knowledge and effective practices by obtaining, collecting, and synthesizing research and policy from the field.
- It follows the work of communities around the country that have demonstrated that they effectively manage sex offenders while increasing public safety. This information is disseminated so that other jurisdictions can benefit.
- It provides opportunities for other jurisdictions, through training and technical assistance programs, to better their practices.

CSOM has become an important resource for legislators and other policy makers, academic researchers, and community members. This is because of the vast array of resources CSOM has developed and disseminated over the past decade. The organization has accomplished this in a number of ways. First, CSOM has developed numerous training manuals and curricula that can assist different jurisdictions in developing a "best practices" approach to managing sex offenders. The curricula can be used by one organization, such as a parole agency or probation department, or can be used to bring various stakeholders together to have a uniform approach in a given community. CSOM delivers these training sessions at statewide and nationwide conferences, as well as at the local level (individual cities or counties) and provides the content of all curricula on their Web site for download. The content of these training sessions varies from an introduction to the etiology of sexual offending and how to manage the juvenile sex offender in the community to the role of the victim in sex offender management.

In a different role, CSOM provides technical assistance to various jurisdictions in support of establishing evidence-based, effective supervision strategies. These jurisdictions have been dedicated to exploring innovative methods of delivering these strategies. The information gathered from these jurisdictions and other agencies is crucial to the *Information Exchange* program. Here, CSOM is able to act as a moderator; individuals or organizations send inquiries to the Center and in return, CSOM distributes policy updates and answers to these questions, often using information collected from agencies around the country. Similarly, CSOM has identified 19 jurisdictions that they define as "resource sites." Each site comprises various agencies that have shown innovative practices to be effective. CSOM has "inventoried, documented, and analyzed the accomplishments of the Resource Sites" (CSOM, 2008b) and has made this information public for other jurisdictions or agencies to model.

Aside from providing technical assistance and training, and partnering with jurisdictions that show promising results of effective sex offender management, CSOM has also published 20 policy and practice briefs that are available on the CSOM Web site. Additionally, all these documents are distributed nationally through mailings and placement in criminal justice libraries. These documents cover a variety of topics, such as the following:

- Myths and facts about sex offenders
- Recidivism of sex offenders
- Understanding treatment for adults and juveniles who have committed sex offenses
- Female sex offenders

Finally, CSOM works in partnership with the Bureau of Justice Assistance (BJA) Comprehensive Approaches to Sex Offender Management (CASOM) Discretionary Grant Program, which was created as part of the Violent Crime Control and Law Enforcement Act of 1994 (Pub. L. 103–322). This program awards funds to help individual jurisdictions effectively manage sex offenders in the community by creating or enhancing programs. To this end, each grantee must develop a multidisciplinary team. Stakeholders include people from community and institutional correctional agencies, law enforcement, the courts, sex offender treatment providers, victim advocates, the state's attorney, the criminal defense bar, and various other agencies. CSOM has a role in developing the sex offender management policies that are utilized by grantees. In 2007, CSOM awarded $4.6 million in grant funds.

Stop it Now!

Stop It Now! was founded by Fran Henry in 1992. As a survivor of child sexual abuse, Henry had the goal of preventing abuse before it occurred, rather than trying to address the problem afterwards. At that time, public discourse on the issue of child sexual abuse was typically only related to sensationalized cases covered by the media, even though these only constituted a small minority of sexual abuse cases. At the time, Stop It Now! had two primary goals (D. D. Rice, personal communication, 2008):

- Widespread acceptance of child sexual abuse as a pervasive and important national issue by the public and as a preventable public health problem by the relevant health authorities
- The development of concrete strategies and programs to help adults take responsibility and action to prevent child sexual abuse

Since then, this community-based child sexual abuse prevention organization has been working with survivors, offenders, and the community at large to prevent sexual abuse. The national headquarters is located in Massachusetts, and community-based programs are located in Virginia, Minnesota, Georgia, and Philadelphia. Affiliate sites are located in the United Kingdom and Ireland. This international organization believes that by providing adults with accurate information, support, and guidance, child sexual abuse will decrease. Over the years, Stop It Now! has organized focus groups with different stakeholders to create effective media campaigns and educational material to disseminate to the public. Aside from these media campaigns, the agency runs a prevention help line (1-888-PREVENT). Callers receive guidance on preventing the sexual abuse of children, support in cases of actual or suspected abuse, referrals to local resources and Stop It Now! materials, and approaches to taking positive next steps.

In addition to their work on education and empowerment, Stop It Now! and its programs are involved in various research efforts that lead to policy development, evaluation, and change. This work is primarily based in a public health paradigm. There has been an important and growing body of literature that has focused on the effects of sexual abuse on both children and adults, as well as on treatment of sex offenders. However, it was not until the late 1990s that research focused on sexual abuse from a public health point of view.

Prior to the 1990s, child sexual abuse was framed primarily as a criminal justice issue. When someone disclosed that he or she had been the victim of molestation or sexual assault, the alleged offender would be investigated, charged, and if convicted, sentenced under some criminal justice sanction. However, many researchers, academics, and practitioners felt that this method did not address the root causes of the sexually abusive behavior. As it was, the abuse would continue to occur, and attempts to decrease abuse were through deterrence and punishment. Proponents of the public health model argued that addressing the sexual abuse issue from a prevention standpoint, we could stop the offense before it ever occurred. In this paradigm, child sexual abuse is considered a disease. Mercy (1999) argued that just as other diseases have gained national attention through prevention campaigns, so too should child sexual abuse. However, this has not been the case, and he argued that, as a society, we have underestimated the effects of sexual abuse on children.

Similarly, the Association for the Treatment of Sexual Abusers (ATSA) acknowledges sexual abuse as a public health issue. When we look at statistics regarding the issue, it is understandable why many people agree with this stance. For instance, in a study by MacMillan et al. (1997), 12.8% of the females and 4.3% of the males reported a history of sexual abuse during childhood. An earlier study by Moore, Nord, and Peterson (1989) found similar results. Approximately 15% of the females and 5.9% of the males experienced some form of sexual assault. In 1999, Bolen and Scannapieco conducted a meta-analysis of prevalence studies and found the overall prevalence of male children who are sexually abused to be 13%, compared to between 30% and 40% for female children. Finally, Finkelhor and Jones (2004) have used data from the National Child Abuse and Neglect Data System (NCANDS) to provide an estimate of cases substantiated by child protective services on a national level from 1992 to 2000. They found that the number of substantiated cases peaked in 1992 but continually declined through 2000.

Importantly, though the numbers speak for themselves, it is the effects of this "disease" that enable supporters to place it in the public health paradigm. When compared to other diseases or public health problems that affect children, one can see why child sexual abuse fits in this model. With regard to childhood diseases, autism affects 1 in 150 children and 1 in 94 boys (Autism Society of America, 2008); over 300,000 American children live with epilepsy (Epilepsy Foundation, 2008); 23% of high school students and 8% of middle school students smoke cigarettes (Centers for Disease Control and Prevention, 2005, 2006), with almost 4000 minors beginning to smoke each day (Substance Abuse and Mental Health Services Administration, 2005). Alarmingly, recent research indicates that as many as one in three girls and one in seven boys are sexually abused before they turn 18 (Stop It Now!, 2008). Although each of these issues has widespread prevention initiatives that provide prevalence statistics and helpful information for parents and caregivers to decrease the problem, until Stop It Now!, no such campaign existed for child sexual abuse.

Stop It Now! is engaged in the prevention of child sexual abuse using a public health model, through the use of ad campaigns and education that challenge social norms and bring the topic to the forefront. Addressing the issue in the open and challenging adults to take responsibility for their actions might prevent abuse. To determine whether their efforts were effective, several studies have evaluated the public health approach used by Stop It Now!, both in the United States and in the United Kingdom and Ireland.

The Stop It Now! prevention program was piloted in Vermont in the mid-1990s. To determine the effectiveness of the program, researchers conducted a pre-post evaluation (Chasan-Taber & Tabachnick, 1999). A random-digit-dialing telephone survey was conducted in 1995 to obtain baseline data. Although the majority of people said they were familiar with the term *child sexual abuse*, most could not define it. Many participants stated that they feared disclosing the abuse, as they thought it would bring more harm to their child. The prevention program was launched soon after, and encompassed three components: (1) a broad media campaign, (2) a one-to-one communications strategy that included a help line, and (3) an educational component aimed to educate decision makers and community leaders.

Two years after the implementation of the program, a follow-up telephone survey was conducted. Results from the follow-up were promising: more people could define child sexual abuse. Unfortunately, the percentage of people who did not know the warning signs associated with child sexual abuse did not change. With regard to the help line, calls increased from 100 calls in the first year to a total of 241 calls in the second year. Almost one fourth of the calls were from abusers, and over 50% were from someone who knew the abuser (Chasan-Taber & Tabachnick, 1999). An evaluation of the United Kingdom and Ireland Stop It Now! program (Kemshall, Mackenzie, & Wood, 2004) suggests that their help line is also growing, as evidenced by an increase in the volume of calls. Additionally, the help line continues to exceed its target number of calls. The research team agreed that the media campaign is reaching the public at a local level and that it is received in a positive light.

As innovative as Stop It Now! is, as with all programs and policies, critical, rigorous, and routine evaluations must continue to be conducted. It is also important to ensure that the applicability of the public health model be continually empirically assessed. As with the political underpinnings of sex offender laws, there is no program or policy with 100% efficacy.

State Agencies

Since the beginning of the 1990s, the federal government and various states have enacted legislation in an attempt to effectively manage sex offenders in the community. All 50 states currently have registration and community notification laws, and many states have included laws for residence restrictions and GPS tracking of certain sex offenders. However, there has been some research in the field suggesting that these types of mandates may not be effective (Colorado Department of Public Safety, 2004a; Levenson & Cotter, 2005; Minnesota Department of Corrections, 2003; Welchans, 2005). Public policy organizations in three states—Minnesota, Washington, and Colorado—have been at the forefront of research assessing the effectiveness of such community mandates, making evidence-based policy and programmatic decisions. Their research has also focused on civil commitment of sexually violent predators, risk assessment, and best practices in treatment. The remainder of this chapter addresses the best practices of these states, as well as an overview of their response to the Walsh Act and a discussion on how each has initially dealt with its implementation.

Minnesota Department of Corrections

As in most states, the Minnesota Department of Corrections (MDOC) is responsible for operating each of the state's public prisons and jails. The MDOC is a vast organization responsible for more policy and practice than is discussed in this chapter. Sex offenders are a key concern of the MDOC because they are often seen as a special group because of the many mandates placed on them. Registration, community notification, Internet registries, residence restrictions, and GPS tracking are all considered civil sanctions aimed at protecting the community—but do they work?

Sex Offender Policy. In the 1999 legislative session, Minnesota directed the commissioner of corrections to make recommendations on a variety of issues related to supervision of sex offenders in the community. Recommendations were to be made to the legislature by February of 2000. Subsequently, the MDOC created the Sex Offender Supervision Study Group to create a report that included such recommendations, because they would improve supervision of sex offenders (Minnesota Department of Corrections, 2000b). The study group reported on the following: methods of supervision-intensive supervised release (ISR), methods of supervision-specialized caseloads, optimum caseload size, suitable housing for sex offenders, classification and risk assessment, sex offender supervision training, and probation and postrelease programming funding. Recommendations were provided, including these: decrease caseload size for probation officers, create adequate housing for sex offenders, and create a risk assessment tool that can be use in pre-sentence investigations to assess risk of recidivism, among others.

Then, during the 2000 legislative session, a law was passed giving permission to the MDOC, in collaboration with various other agencies, to conduct a study on sex offender issues. The report would be updated every 2 years and would be presented to the legislature and would include studies of sex crime statutes and sentencing practices, supervision, treatment, predatory offender registration, community notification, risk assessment, fiscal impact, and recommendations. In 2004, the Governor's Commission on Sex Offender Policy convened to provide recommendations and a set of best practices on five broad areas related to sex offenders. These legislative mandates are evidence of Minnesota's commitment to evidence-based practices regarding sex offender management. Findings from their evaluations of sex offender policies are discussed below.

Sex Offender Recidivism. In 2007, two reports regarding sex offenders were published by the MDOC. The first was an analysis of sex offender recidivism in the state, and the second detailed residence proximity and recidivism. This was one of the largest studies on sex offender recidivism to date, using a state sample of offenders (Minnesota Department of Corrections, 2007a). Researchers analyzed data on 3,166 sex offenders released from prison between 1990 and 2002. The independent variables presented in the study were consistent with the literature on risk of reoffense. For instance, the

Static-99 (Hanson & Thornton, 1999), one of the most widely used risk assessment instruments for sex offenders, utilizes gender of victim, relationship with victim, age at release, and prior sex offenses as major predictors of risk of reoffending.

The dependent variable was recidivism—a concept that is often tricky to measure because of its variable definitions (e.g., another arrest for the same crime, a reconviction for that same crime, or a reconviction for any new offense). Because of the difficulties in operationalizing what recidivism is, the researchers measured recidivism nine different ways: sex crime rearrest, sex crime reconviction, sex crime reincarceration, non–sex crime rearrest, non–sex crime reconviction, non–sex crime reincarceration, any crime rearrest, any crime reconviction, and any crime reincarceration. Therefore, nine statistical models were used in this study to account for the nine different definitions of recidivism. Significant predictors of timing to sex offense recidivism were prior sex crimes, stranger victims, male child victims (i.e., male victims under the age of 13), failure in prison-based sex offender treatment, and a metro-area county of commitment.

Findings from this study supported those from previous research in the field. For instance, having a male victim or a stranger victim and having a previous sexual offense conviction are significant predictors of sexual recidivism (Hanson & Bussiere, 1998). Further, factors affecting nonsexual recidivism were different than those that increased risk for sexual recidivism. The study found that the more intensive supervision a sex offender had, the less likely he or she was to have a sexual reoffense; and the length of supervision was negatively correlated with nonsexual offending (Minnesota Department of Corrections, 2007a).

The policy implications that emerged from this study are crucial to the effective management of sex offenders in the community. First, the intensity of the supervision decreased sexual recidivism. Therefore, it might be beneficial to increase resources for probation and parole agents to provide intensive supervision. However, the researchers were quick to point out that *intensity* of supervision only decreases sexual recidivism. It is the *length* of supervision responsible for decreasing nonsexual recidivism, which accounts for three quarters of the recidivism in this study. The researchers further cautioned that increasing the length or intensity of supervision (e.g., lifetime supervision or registration) would produce diminishing returns and would not be worth the resources. A second key finding from the study is that sex offender-specific treatment might decrease risk of recidivism. Again, the authors warn that the cost of providing the resources for the treatment may not produce the intended outcomes, as rates of recidivism, at least in regard to sex crimes, are already low (Minnesota Department of Corrections, 2007b).

Residential Proximity and Recidivism. As discussed in chapter 9, over the past few years, many states and municipalities have enacted residence restrictions under the assumption that such restrictions (typically between 500 and 2,500 feet from a school, park, day care, or other place that children congregate) prevent child molesters from coming in contact with potential victims[i]. However, to date, studies have not found residence restrictions to be effective in reducing child sexual abuse (Colorado Department of Public Safety, 2004a; Levenson & Cotter, 2005). Minnesota conducted a study of its own to address whether residential proximity affects sexual recidivism (Minnesota Department of Corrections, 2007b). Data were collected on 224 recidivist sex offenders who were incarcerated in Minnesota between 1990 and 2002. The measure of recidivism used was reincarceration for a sexual offense, and all offenders were sentenced to prison for a new sex crime before January 1, 2006. Four criteria were used to determine if a residency restriction might have prevented a sex offense from occurring:

- The offender had to establish direct contact with the victim.
- Contact had to occur within 1 mile of the offender's home.
- The initial contact had to occur near a school, park, day care, or other prohibited place.
- The victim had to be less than 18 years of age.

The researchers found that residence restrictions would not be an effective measure in reducing recidivism. Of the 224 offenders, direct contact with a child victim within 1 mile of the offender's home occurred in only 16 instances. Additionally, none of those 16 cases involved contact with the victim near a school, park, or day care. Although this is a very brief description of their findings, this study is extremely important because of its policy implications. Minnesota opted not to enact a one-size-fits-all mandate restricting where sex offenders can live. Instead, the MDOC determines if protection from residential proximity is necessary on a case-by-case basis.

The Minnesota Sex Offender Screening Tool — Revised. Evidence-based practices for community mandates have not been the only focus with regard to sex offenders in Minnesota. In the early 1990s, the MDOC expressed concern about how violent and predatory sex offenders were identified. At the time, very few empirically based screening tools existed and most often, risk was determined based on clinical judgment (Epperson, Kaul, Huot, Goldman, & Alexander, 2003). From a review of the existing literature, the authors obtained 14 items that could predict risk, and the original Minnesota Sex Offender Screening Tool (MnSOST) was created. A revised edition with 21 items, known as the MnSOST — Research Edition, was the result. However, this instrument was best at predicting recidivism for rapists and extrafamilial child molesters.

By 1996, Webster, Harris, Rice, Cormier, and Quinsey (1994) had created the Violence Risk Appraisal Guide (VRAG), an assessment tool that could predict general, serious, and sexual recidivism. Relying on this literature, the researchers in Minnesota further refined their assessment tool, and it was then that the MnSOST-R, or revised edition, was born (Epperson, Kaul, & Hesselton, 1998). This revised version contains 16 items, and the developers maintain that it performs significantly better than the original edition. The latter version utilized clinically based scoring methods for each item. However, the revised version used empirically based item selection and scoring (Epperson et al., 2003). The MnSOST-R is brief and only uses information typically available in offender correctional files (Ibid) and is a popular assessment tool used not only in Minnesota, but in various other states as well.

Electronic Monitoring. In 2006, the legislature appropriated over $600,000 for the monitoring of sex offenders in the community, whether on supervised release, conditional release, parole, or probation. In a report to the legislature, the MDOC provided the advantages and disadvantages of electronic monitoring and will study its use over an 18-month period (Minnesota Department of Corrections, 2006). Global Positioning Systems (GPS) monitoring is thought to be a tool to assist law enforcement in supervising and tracking offenders. There are two types of GPS, active and passive. Active monitoring tracks and monitors offenders' movements throughout the day and provides constant information for law enforcement. Passive monitoring is different, in that at the end of each day the offender places the GPS monitor in a device that uploads the information to the supervising agency. However, there are disadvantages to GPS monitoring, as well. For instance, it is very costly—it costs approximately $10 to $14 a day per offender, not including the salary of the supervising agent. Using GPS monitoring would require the expansion of supervising staff to be available 24 hours a day. For their study, GPS monitoring will be used with high-risk offenders in the community, 24 hours a day for 60 days. The study will assess the effectiveness of electronic monitoring with regard to community supervision and will provide the state with 18 months' worth of data (Ibid). To date, this evaluation has not been published.

Minnesota and the Adam Walsh Act. As of the writing of this chapter, Minnesota has not implemented the Adam Walsh Act, and no proposed legislation has been written in regard to incorporating it into state law. Minncsota focuses on utilizing evidence-based practices when managing sex offenders in the community. Under this approach, the state's recidivism rate for sex crimes has continued to decrease for more than 15 years (Minnesota Department of Corrections, 2007a). Given the state's advanced efforts in sex offender management, some stakeholders envision various challenges in implementing the Adam Walsh Act. Therefore, until there is evidence that the act is effective in reducing recidivism, Minnesota does not plan on incorporating it into the sex offender management policies.

Washington State Institute for Public Policy

In 1983, the Washington State Institute for Public Policy (WSIPP) was created by the state legislature. Although the institute provides its own research and policy analysts and economists, it also works closely with many of Washington's public universities and other state agencies to ensure that sound research is conducted and that important policy questions are answered correctly. Research at WSIPP is conducted at the direction of the state legislature when significant, state-level issues arise.

Topics of research include health issues, education, welfare, government, and a variety of criminal justice issues. Washington was a leader in the implementation of sex offender policies, in the previously discussed Community Protection Act of 1990. In 1991, Felver and Lieb reported on initial compliance with the act and found that 57% of sex offenders had complied with the new law. Also in 1991, Berliner, Miller, Schram, and Milloy reported on factors associated with the decision to sentence certain sex offenders to the "Special Sex Offender Sentencing Alternative."[ii] Since that time, the WSIPP has been engaged in various studies related to sex offenders and sex offender management/policy. The institute has also compared sex offender laws within the state to laws that have been enacted in other jurisdictions.

In the mid-1990s, when there was widespread implementation of registration and community notification statutes, WSIPP charted and compared these laws on a consistent basis. The involuntary civil commitment of SVPs also became a controversial but politically popular topic in the 1990s. Again, Washington was at the forefront of enacting such a policy. Sexually violent predator legislation was developed and implemented (Washington RCW 71.09.010). Other states soon followed these legislative criteria and as of 2007, 20 states had SVP (civil commitment) legislation in place.[iii]

WSIPP examined how various states operate involuntary civil commitment (Gookin, 2007; Lieb, 1996a, 1996b, 1998, 2003; Lieb & Gookin, 2005; Schram & Milloy, 1998). Additionally, researchers for the institute have been following released sex offenders, who were recommended for civil commitment, but where no actual petition for commitment was filed (Milloy, 2003; Milloy, 2007). Other studies have focused primarily on female sex offenders (Song, Lieb, & Donnelly, 1993) and juvenile sex offenders (Milloy, 1994). Overall, WSIPP has published 58 reports related to sex offenders since 1991.

In 2004, the state legislature directed WSIPP to study the impact and effectiveness of current state policies regarding sex offenders. A directive such as this requires an extensive study, and 22 of the 58 reports mentioned above are all part of a series describing the results of this 2004 directive. Accordingly, the major goal of this undertaking was to "examine whether changes to sentencing policies and sex offender programming can increase public safety" (Barnoski & Lieb, 2004, pg. 1). To this end, at least 12 research questions in six major topic areas have been addressed, and research for this project continues today. As indicated in Table 13.1, these topic areas include measuring recidivism, initial sentencing decisions, the Special Sex Offender Sentencing Alternative, the Sex Offender Treatment Program in Prison (SOTP), actual recidivism, and end of sentence review (ESR).

13.1	Washington State Institute for Public Policy—2004 Directive from the Legislature
Research Questions	
Measuring Recidivism	How do we measure recidivism for sex offenders? Why use convictions rather than arrests? How does plea bargaining influence the crime of conviction?
Initial Sentencing Decision	How do sex offenders differ by age, gender, and criminal history from other felony offenders? How well can we account for the type of sentence a sex offender will receive?
Special Sex Offender Sentencing Alternative	How well can we predict who will be revoked from SSOSA? Based on recidivism, is SSOSA potentially appropriate for additional types of sex offenders?

Continued

Washington State Institute for Public Policy—2004 Directive from the Legislature (Cont'd)

13.1

Sex Offender Treatment Program in Prison	How do sex offenders in the treatment program differ from those who are not in the program? Does the SOTP reduce recidivism, when participants are compared with similar offenders who did not enter the program? How do the length of treatment and other treatment variables affect recidivism?
Recidivism	When and how often do sex offenders recidivate? How do age, nature of sex offenses committed, and juvenile record affect recidivism? How well can we predict the recidivism rates of offenders? How well can criminal history predict, at sentencing, which sex offenders will recidivate?
End of Sentence Review	How valid are the DOC's risk assessment instruments: Level of Service Inventory Revised (LSI-R), Sex Offender Screening Tool (SOST), Rapid Risk Assessment for Sexual Offense Recidivism (RRA-SOR), etc.?

Adapted from Barnoski (2005). Sex Offender Sentencing in Washington State: Introducing the Study Series. Washington State Institute for Public Policy.

In 2006, Drake and Barnoski assessed various trends about sex offenders in Washington state, including sentence length, types of offenses, trends in offending, and typologies of offenders. Many of the key findings are important to policy implementation at the state legislature level:

■ Since the 1997 enactment of sex offender legislation, sex offender recidivism has declined in Washington State. However, due to the correlating national crime decrease, the authors noted that any claims of causation were speculative (p. 15).
■ Since 1991, the use of the Special Sex Offender Sentencing Alternative (SSOSA) has decreased, but jail or community supervision has increased.

- Offenders who have adult victims have longer average prison sentences than those convicted of offenses against children.
- When compared to other felony offenders, sex offenders have the lowest recidivism rates for felony offenses and violent felony offenses—13% and 6.7%, respectively.
- Sex offenders have the highest rates of recidivism for felony sex offenses, 2.7%, when compared to other felons.
- Sex offenders convicted of failing to register have higher subsequent recidivism rates than those without a conviction.

Though this research, as well as other work, is still being conducted, the work that WSIPP has published is key to informing policy makers about what works and what does not. As the Walsh Act evolves, the work of WSIPP will need to be supported and integrated into state compliance.

Washington and the Adam Walsh Act. As of the writing of this chapter, Washington has not implemented the Adam Walsh Act, and no proposed legislation has been written in regard to incorporating it into state law. In the summer of 2007, participants representing various agencies commenced a meeting to discuss how this new act would affect the state. Specifically, the focus was based on concern about the change of intent between the state's current practices of registration and notification being based on risk to the community versus that of the Adam Walsh Act, which is based primarily on offense type. There was talk of concern regarding how this change would impact communities across the state (D. Ashlock, personal communication, 2008).

One of the provisions of the Adam Walsh Act is making "failure to register" a federal charge. When an offender has failed to register, federal law enforcement officers have requested that local authorities in the state provide the necessary documentation to support a criminal charge. In these instances, Washington has cooperated. The Washington Department of Corrections and members of other state agencies have met with staff from the federal government to further discuss "failure to register" (Ibid).

Though awaiting the signature of the governor, the state legislature recently passed a bill creating a Sex Offender Policy

Board (SSB 6596). If the bill officially passes, the duties of the board will be to stay up to date with "research and best practices related to risk assessment, treatment, and supervision of sex offenders; community education regarding sex offenses and offenders; prevention of sex offenses; and sex offender management, in general" (SSB 6596, p. 5, section 6). It has been suggested that at the time the governor signs the bill, the state might begin discussion on implementing the Adam Walsh Act (D. Ashlock, personal communication, 2008).

Colorado Department of Public Safety

The Colorado General Assembly created the Sex Offender Management Board (SOMB) in 1992. Under the auspices of the Division of Criminal Justice, members of the SOMB represent various state-level agencies, including the Department of Corrections, the Department of Public Safety, the Department of Human Services, the Public Defender's Office, district attorneys, treatment providers, and other relevant stakeholders. The main purpose for the development of the SOMB was to develop "standards and guidelines for the evaluation, treatment, and behavioral monitoring of sex offenders" (Colorado Department of Public Safety, 2008).

In 1996, the SOMB published standards and guidelines for adult sex offenders and followed up with 2002 guidelines for juvenile sex offenders (Colorado Department of Public Safety, 1996, 2002). Since 1996, various revisions to these guidelines have been made and as research develops, more updates will become available. In 2004, the revised document included guidelines for pre-sentence investigation, standards for evaluation, practices for treatment providers, and best practices for management of sex offenders on probation in the community.

The only way to assess the effectiveness of these guidelines was to conduct an evaluation of how they were utilized and whether practitioners found them to be easy to use. As part of a legislative mandate,[iv] the SOMB was required to conduct a process evaluation. In addition, the SOMB had to develop a system to track sex offenders who had been "subjected to evaluation, identification, and treatment" (Lowden, English, Hetz, & Harrison, 2003, pg. 14) pursuant to the guidelines. Overall, practitioners found the guidelines to be useful and felt that a standard practice throughout the state was

beneficial. However, although treatment was readily implemented for sex offenders, the evaluators found that individualized treatment plans were lacking, and they offered
suggestions about how to promote better execution of such
plans to align the practice with the guidelines and standards.
The most important finding, however, was in regard to the
tracking of offenders who were released from prison. Offenders who received both supervision and treatment were less
likely to be arrested for a violent crime when compared to
offenders who did not receive either supervision or treatment. Evaluation and revisions of the guidelines continues,
and both the SOMB and the state of Colorado are committed
to maintaining research-based, best practices in an effort to
manage offenders and promote public safety (Lowden, English, Hetz, & Harrison, 2003).

More recently, the debate regarding residential proximity grew, as various states and local jurisdictions implemented restrictions. The Colorado Department of Public Safety
and the SOMB embarked on a large-scale study of residence
restrictions to analyze safety issues related to the living
arrangements of sex offenders and to determine if such a
law would be effective in preventing sexual offenses.[v] At the
very least, the report had to discuss findings from the study
and offer suggestions for future policy. Table 13.2 shows the
major findings from the study.

Colorado and the Walsh Act As of the writing of this chapter,
Colorado has not implemented the Adam Walsh Act, and no
proposed legislation has been written in regard to incorporating it into state law (C. Lobanov-Rostovsky, personal communication, 2008). Colorado assembled a task force of all the
relevant stakeholders who participate in the management
of sex offenders throughout the state. For over a year, this
committee has met monthly to discuss the implementation
of the act. The main focus of these meetings is to compare
where Colorado is now with what the state would have to do
to implement the Adam Walsh Act. One step of this process
has been a cost-benefit analysis to establish whether the cost
of implementing the act is more than what the state would
lose if it chose not to implement it. Ultimately, the decision
rests with the legislature and the governor, but the task force
will make recommendations to both parties.

13.2 Major Findings and Recommendations from the Colorado Department of Public Safety (2004)

Finding	Recommendation
High-risk sex offenders living in Shared Living Arrangements had significantly fewer violations than those living in other living arrangements.	Shared Living Arrangements appear to be a frequently successful mode of containment and treatment for higher risk sex offenders and should be considered a viable living situation for higher risk sex offenders living in the community.
Shared Living Arrangements had one of the shortest amounts of time between when a sex offender committed a violation and when the probation officer or treatment provider found out about the violation.	
Roommates of sex offenders living in Shared Living Arrangements called in violations of probation and treatment requirements to the sex offender's treatment provider and probation officer more times than roommates in any other living arrangement.	
In urban areas, a large number of schools and child care centers are located within various neighborhoods, leaving extremely limited areas where sex offenders could reside if restrictions were implemented.	Placing restrictions on the location of correctionally supervised sex offender residences may not deter the sex offender from reoffending and should not be considered as a method to control sexual offending recidivism.
Sex offenders who have committed a criminal offense (both sexual and nonsexual) while under criminal justice supervision appear to be randomly scattered throughout the study areas.	
There does not seem to be a greater number of these offenders living within proximity to schools and child care centers than other types of offenders.	

13.2 Major Findings and Recommendations from the Colorado Department of Public Safety (2004)	
Finding	**Recommendation**
Those [sex offenders] who had support in their lives had significantly lower numbers of violations than those who had negative or no support.	Efforts should be made to ensure that the sex offender's support in the home is positive in order to aid in his or her treatment.
When support was examined for high-risk offenders, those with no support and living with a family member or friends had the highest numbers of violations (criminal, technical, and total). These findings suggest that although a high-risk sex offender may be living with a family member or friends, it does not necessarily mean that he or she is living in a supportive or healthy environment.	Although the findings in this report suggest a link between a sex offender's support in the home and performance in the community, more research in this area should be conducted to further inform this important finding.

Source: Colorado Department of Public Safety (2004a)

The SOMB is very interested and concerned about the Walsh Act. The board formed a committee to create a white paper that will not only discuss the cost-benefit analysis, but will also look at evidence-based practices from a policy perspective. The paper will discuss the relevant literature regarding what has been shown to be effective in sex offender management (Ibid).

Conclusion

Each state enacts laws for various reasons, but the goal of all sex offender policies is to protect communities from high-risk offenders. However, in order to know whether such policies will be effective at achieving such a goal, it is imperative to evaluate the effectiveness of the policies and determine whether they may increase rather than decrease potential harm. Although many other states also have research agencies or organizations that study criminal justice policy, Minnesota, Washington, and Colorado have done extensive research to guide current and future policies. As these states continue to inform policy through research, organizations such as CSOM and Stop It Now! work in tandem with them, not only with policy efforts, but with providing pertinent information to the public.

Although the organizations discussed in this chapter do not represent the only agencies that support evidence-based policy and practice, in our assessment they do represent the leaders in this field. Many states are beginning to follow their lead and conduct research as they enact sex offender policies and initiatives. As they do, they should look to the agencies discussed here, whose efforts are a vanguard in the area and can provide the basis for other states to follow.

References

Adam Walsh Child Protection and Safety Act (Walsh Act) (Pub. L. 109–248)

Autism Society of America. (2008). *About autism.* Retrieved on May 22, 2008, from http://www.autism-society.org/site/PageServer? pagename=about_home

Barnoski, R. (2005). *Sex offender sentencing in Washington State: Introducing the study series.* Olympia: Washington State Institute for Public Policy.

Barnoski, R., & Lieb, R. (2004). *Impact and effectiveness of Washington State's current sex offender sentencing policies: Research design.* Olympia: Washington State Institute for Public Policy.

Berliner, L. (1996). Introduction to the commentary. *Journal of Interpersonal Violence, 13,* 287.

Berliner, L., Miller, L., Schram, D., & Milloy, C. (1991). *The special sex offender sentencing alternative: A study of decision-making and recidivism.* Olympia: Washington State Institute for Public Policy.

Bolen, R., & Scannapieco, M. (1999). Prevalence of child sexual abuse: A corrective metanalysis. *Social Service Review, 73,* 281–313.

Centers for Disease Control and Prevention. (2005). Tobacco use, access, and exposure to tobacco in media among middle and high school students—United States, 2004. *Morbidity and Mortality Weekly Report, 4,* 297–301.

Centers for Disease Control and Prevention. (2006). Cigarette use among high school students—United States, 1991–2005. *Morbidity and Mortality Weekly Report, 55,* 724–726.

Center for Sex Offender Management. (2008) *Promoting Public Safety through the Effective Management of Sex Offenders in the Community.* Retrieved on May 22, 2008, from http://www.csom.org/about/about.html.

Center for Sex Offender Management (CSOM). (2008a). Welcome page. Retrieved on May 22, 2008, from http://www.csom.org/

Center for Sex Offender Management (CSOM). (2008b). Activities: Identifying and building capacity of resource sites. Retrieved on May 22, 2008, from http://www.csom.org/resource/resource.html.

Chasan-Taber, L., & Tabachnick, J. (1999). Evaluation of a child sexual abuse prevention program. *Sexual Abuse: A Journal of Research and Treatment, 11,* 279–292.

Cohen, M., & Jeglic, E.L. (2007). Sex offender legislation in the United States: What do we know? *International Journal of Offender Therapy and Comparative Criminology, 51*(4), 369–383.

Colorado Department of Public Safety (1996). *Standards and guidelines for behavioral monitoring of sex offenders.* Denver: Sex Offender Management Board.

Colorado Department of Public Safety. (2002). *Standards and guidelines for the evaluation, assessment, treatment and supervision of juveniles who have committed sexual offenses.* Denver: Sex Offender Management Board.

Colorado Department of Public Safety. (2003). *Standards and guidelines for the assessment, evaluation, treatment, and behavioral monitoring of juvenile sex offenders.* Denver: Sex Offender Management Board.

Colorado Department of Public Safety. (2004a). *Report on safety issues raised by living arrangements for and location of sex offenders in the community.* Denver: Sex Offender Management Board.

Colorado Department of Public Safety. (2004b). *Standards and guidelines for the assessment, evaluation, treatment, and behavioral monitoring of adult sex offenders—Revised.* Denver: Sex Offender Management Board.

Colorado Department of Public Safety (2008). *Sex Offender Management Board.* Retrieved on May 22, 2008, from http://dcj.state.co.us/odvsom/sex_offender/.

Community Protection Act 1990 (Washington RCW 71.09.010)

C.R.S. 16-11.7-103(4)(d)(I) and (II). Sex Offender Management Board – creation - duties

C.R.S. 16-11.7-103(4)(j). Safety Clause.

Drake, E., & Barnoski, R. (2006). *Sex offenders in Washington State: Key findings and trends.* Olympia: Washington State Institute for Public Policy.

Epilepsy Foundation. (2008). *Epilepsy and seizure statistics.* Retrieved on May 22, 2008 from http://www.epilepsyfoundation.org/about/statistics.cfm.

Epperson, D.L., Kaul, J.D., & Hesselton, D. (1998). *Final report on the development of the Minnesota Sex Offending Screening Tool – Revised (MnSOST-R).* St. Paul: Minnesota Department of Corrections.

Epperson, D.L., Kaul, J.D., Huot, S., Goldman, R., Alexander, W. (2003). *Minnesota Sex Offending Screening Tool – Revised* (MnSOST-R)

Technical Paper: Development, Validation, and Recommended Risk Level Cut Scores. St. Paul: Minnesota Department of Corrections.

Felver, B. & Lieb, R. (1991). *Adult Sex Offender Registration in Washington State: Initial Compliance, 1990*. Washington State Institute for Public Policy. Olympia, WA.

Finkelhor, D. and Jones, L.M. (2004). Explanations for the Decline in Child Sexual Abuse Cases. *Juvenile Justice Bulletin*. Washington, DC: U.S. Department of Justice, Office of Juvenile Justice and Delinquency Prevention

Gookin, K. (2007). *Comparison of State Laws Authorizing Involuntary Commitment of Sexually Violent Predators: 2006 Update*. Olympia: Washington State Institute for Public Policy.

Governor's Commission on Sex Offender Policy (2004). Commission Work Plan.

Hanson, R. K., & Bussiere, M.T. (1998). Predicting relapse: A meta-analysis of sexual offender recidivism studies. *Journal of Consulting and Clinical Psychology, 66*, 348–362.

Hanson, R.K. & Thornton, D.M. (1999). STATIC-99: Improving actuarial risk assessments of sexual recidivism. Ottawa: Office of the Solicitor General of Canada.

Kemshall, H., Mackenzie, G., & Wood, J. (2004). Stop it Now! UK & Ireland: An Evaluation. Executive Summary.

Lees, M., & Tewksbury, R. (2006). Understanding policy and programmatic issues regarding sex offender registries. *Corrections Today, 68*, 54.

Levenson, J.S. & Cotter, L.P. (2005). The Impact of Sex Offender Residence Restrictions:1,000 Feet From Danger or One Step From Absurd? *International Journal of Offender Therapy and Comparative Criminology, 49*, 168–178.

Levenson, J.S. & Hern, A.L. (2007) Sex offender residence restrictions: Unintended consequences and community reentry. *Justice Research and Policy, 9*, 59–73.

Lieb, R. (1996a). *Washington's sexually violent predator law: Legislative history and comparisons with other states*. Olympia: Washington State Institute for Public Policy.

Lieb, R. (1996b). *Washington State Sexually Violent Predators: Profile of Special Commitment Center Residents*. Olympia: Washington State Institute for Public Policy.

Lieb, R. (1998). *Sex offenses in Washington state: 1998 update*. Olympia: Washington State Institute for Public Policy.

Lieb, R. (2003) *After Hendricks: Defining constitutional treatment for Washington state's civil commitment program*. Olympia: Washington State Institute for Public Policy.

Lieb, R. & Gookin, K. (2005). *Involuntary commitment of sexually violent predators: comparing state laws*. Olympia: Washington State Institute for Public Policy.

Lotke, E. (1997). Politics and irrelevance: Community notification Statutes. *Federal Sentencing Reporter, 10*, 64–68.

Lowden, K. English, K. Hetz, N. & Harrison, L. (2003). *Process evaluation of the Colorado Sex Offender Management Board standards and guidelines*. Denver: Sex Offender Management Board.

MacMillan H.L., Fleming J.E., Trocmé N., Boyle M.H., Wong M., Racine Y.A., et al. (1997). Prevalence of child physical and sexual abuse in the community: results from the Ontario Health Supplement. *JAMA, 278*, 131–135.

Mercy, J.A. (1999) Having new eyes: Viewing child sexual abuse as a public health problem. *Sexual Abuse: A Journal of Research and Treatment, 11*, 317–321

Milloy, C. (2003). *Six-year follow-up of released sex offenders recommended for commitment under Washington's sexually violent predator law, where no petition was filed.* Olympia: Washington State Institute for Public Policy.

Milloy, C. (2007). *Juvenile sex offenders recommended for commitment under Washington's sexually violent predator law, where no petition was filed.* Olympia: Washington State Institute for Public Policy.

Milloy, C. (1994). *A comparative study of juvenile sex offenders and non-sex offenders.* Olympia: Washington State Institute for Public Policy.

Minnesota Department of Corrections, (2000a). *Sex offender supervision: 2000 report to the legislature.* St. Paul: Minnesota Department of Corrections.

Minnesota Department of Corrections, (2000b). *Sex offender policy and management board study: December 2000.* St. Paul: Minnesota Department of Corrections.

Minnesota Department of Corrections (2003). *Level three sex offenders residential placement issues.* St. Paul: Minnesota Department of Corrections.

Minnesota Department of Corrections, (2006). *Electronic monitoring of sex offenders: 2006 report to the legislature.* St. Paul: Minnesota Department of Corrections.

Minnesota Department of Corrections (2007a). *Sex offender recidivism in Minnesota.* St. Paul: Minnesota Department of Corrections.

Minnesota Department of Corrections (2007b). *Residential proximity & sex offense recidivism in Minnesota.* St. Paul: Minnesota Department of Corrections.

Moore, K.A., Nord, C.W., & Peterson, J.L. (1989). Nonvoluntary sexual activity among adolescents. *Family Planning Perspectives, 21,* 110–114

Schram, D. & Milloy, C. (1998) *Sexually violent predators and civil commitment.* Olympia: Washington State Institute for Public Policy.

Song, L., Lieb, R., & Donnelly, S. (1993). *Female sex offenders in Washington state.* Olympia: Washington State Institute for Public Policy.

Stop It Now! (2008). *About Stop It Now!* Retrieved on May 22, 2008 from http://www.stopitnow.org/asit_howwework.html.

Substance Abuse and Mental Health Services Administration. (2005). *Results From the 2005 National Survey on Drug Use and Health.* (PDF–1.41MB) (Office of Applied Studies, NSDUH Series H-27, DHHS Publication No. SMA 05–4061)

Terry, K.J. (2003). Sex offenders: Editorial introduction. *Criminology and Public Policy, 3,* 57–59.

Tewksbury, R. (2004). Experiences and attitudes of registered female sex offenders. *Federal Probation, 68,* 30–33.

Tewksbury, Richard. (2005). Collateral consequences of sex offender registration. *Journal of Contemporary Criminal Justice, 21* (1): 67–81.

Thomas, T., (2003). Sex offender community notification: Experiences from American. *The Howard Journal, 42,* 217–228.

Violent Crime Control and Law Enforcement Act of 1994 (Pub. L. 103–322)

Webster, C.D., Harris, G.T., Rice, M., Cormier, C., Quinsey, V.L. (1994). *The violence prediction scheme: Assessing dangerousness in high risk men.* Toronto: Centre of Criminology, University of Toronto.

Welchans, S., (2005). Megan's Law: Evaluations of sexual offender registries. *Criminal Justice Policy Review, 16,* 123–140.

---

[i] As of 2006, 18 states had statewide residence restrictions in place for certain sex offenders (Alabama, Arkansas, California, Florida, Georgia, Illinois, Iowa, Kentucky, Indiana, Louisiana, Missouri, Michigan, Ohio, Oklahoma, South Dakota, Tennessee, Washington, and West Virginia).

[ii] The Special Sex Offender Sentencing Alternative was made available in 1984 for first-time sex offenders convicted of a felony other than first- or second-degree rape. Typically the offender's sentence would not exceed 7 1/2 years, and most often a judge would require the offender to attend treatment.

[iii] Arizona, California, Florida, Illinois, Iowa, Kansas, Massachusetts, Minnesota, Missouri, Nebraska, New Hampshire, New Jersey, New York, North Dakota, Pennsylvania, South Carolina, Texas, Virginia, Washington, and Wisconsin.

[iv] C.R.S. 16-11.7-103(4)(d)(I) and (II),

[v] Pursuant to C.R.S. 16-11.7-103(4)(j)

14

The Containment Approach to Managing Sex Offenders

By Kim English

Thinking about the management of known sex offenders begins with thinking about victims of sex crimes. According to the Rape in America study by the Medical Center of the University of South Carolina (Kilpatrick, Edmunds, & Seymour, 1992), four out of five rape victims do not report the crime to authorities (Kilpatrick et al., 1992; Tjaden & Thoennes, 2000).[i]

Certain types of sexual assault victims, including younger victims and victims who know the perpetrator, are especially unlikely to report offenses to law enforcement (Smith, Letourneau, Saunders, Kilpatrick, Resnick, & Best, 2000). Not surprisingly, Hansen, Resnick, Saunders, Kilpatrick, and Best (1999) found that stranger perpetration, physical injury, or life threat increased victims' disclosure.

The most recent Violence Against Women survey in the United States found that only 19% of rapes of adult women and 13% of rapes of adult men are reported to law enforcement (Tjaden & Thoennes, 2006). Of these, only 3% resulted in a conviction. Child victims and victims who know the perpetrator are least likely to report their victimization: 28% of child rape victims never reported the crime(s) until the researcher asked (Smith et al., 2000). Peters (1988 found rape-related trauma is related to the frequency and duration of the abuse, and victims with perpetrators who live with them are frequently abused for years. In further analysis of the data generated by the Rape in America study, nearly 42% of those who were assaulted in childhood were raped more than once (Sanders, Kilpatrick, Hanson, Resnick, & Walker, 1999). Half (55%) of the series assaults were perpetrated by brothers, and 77% were committed by fathers or stepfathers (Ibid).

Because most rape victims are children and/or know the perpetrator, reporting the crime becomes a complicated process. Over two thirds (71%) of the women in the Rape in America study said they were concerned about their family knowing; an equal percentage said they were afraid of r being blamed for the assault (69%). Nearly all of the women in the Rape in America study said that they thought these things would increase reporting: Public education about acquaintance rape (99%) and laws protecting the victim's privacy (97%).

Officially recorded low recidivism rates of sex offenders[ii] are—to some unknown but significant extent—a function of this lack of reporting by victims. The likelihood, then, of convicting an individual of sexual assault is relatively rare, given the low incidence of reporting.[iii, iv, v] It becomes vital, then, that those offenders who *are* convicted of this crime be managed by the criminal justice system in ways that seek to eliminate their opportunities to rape again.

In light of the rapid growth of civil commitment laws that attempt to significantly delay imprisoned sex offenders from returning to the community, it may come as a surprise to many that most convicted sex offenders remain in or return to the community rather than being held in prison. Aware of the risk sex offenders in the community present to past or potential victims, criminal justice professionals in many jurisdictions have begun to reform the traditional methods of managing these cases. Many professionals working with this population recognize that inconsistencies and gaps in the case management of sex offenders often inadvertently give sex offenders opportunities to reoffend.

Through a series of research studies, researchers at the Colorado Division of Criminal Justice[vi] identified a promising approach for protecting victims by making it difficult for sex offenders to reoffend.[vii] Labeled the *containment approach,* this model is being adopted by jurisdictions nationwide. The containment approach operates in the context of multiagency collaboration, explicit policies, and consistent practices that combine case evaluation and risk assessment, sex offender treatment, and intense community surveillance—all designed specifically to maximize public safety.

This paper summarizes the five-part containment approach to managing adult sex offenders. The five components were identified from comprehensive field research in dozens of jurisdictions across the country.[viii] The containment approach consists of the following aspects:

1. A philosophy that values victim protection, public safety, and reparation for victims as the paramount objectives of sex offender management
2. Implementation strategies that depend on agency coordination and multidisciplinary partnerships
3. A containment-focused case management and risk control approach that is individualized based on each offender's characteristics
4. Consistent multiagency policies and protocols, and
5. Quality control mechanisms, including program monitoring and evaluation

Victim-Centered Philosophy

"What's best for the victim and the community?" This question lies at the crux of this approach. The containment approach is based on an explicit philosophy that defines victim protection and community safety as primary objectives of sex offender management. Research on the effects of sexual assault on victims has confirmed that the consequences of this crime are often brutal and long lasting (see Wyatt & Powell, 1988).[ix] Because most sexual assaults occur in the context of a relationship established and manipulated over time, the victim is often confused and made by the perpetrator to feel responsible. Experts on sexual abuse explain that this violation of a trusting relationship causes great confusion and nearly unbearable trauma to the victim (Herman, 1992). Summit (1988, p. 55) pointed to the psychological damage inherent in the full range of sexually abusive behaviors when he emphasized not just rape but touching: "Sexual touching, so often trivialized by words such as fondling or molestation (annoyance), is only the physical expression of a climate of invasion, isolation and abandonment." A victim-centered philosophy, then, assumes that every sexual assault, from a violent stranger-rape to voyeurism by a family member, represents a significant act resulting in fear and a sense of betrayal. The victim's need for safety and empowerment thus becomes a priority in the management of the offender's case.

If the societal or criminal justice system response to an attack is to place the victim at fault, the trauma is magnified and recovery may be delayed (Hindman, 1988). Explaining that sexual abuse is a complex process rather than an act or series of acts, Finkelhor (1988, p. 77–78) noted, "Clinicians have often observed that the harm of some sexual abuse experiences lies less in the actual sexual contact than in the process of disclosure or even in the process of intervention." Understanding this point is vital for professionals interested in implementing the containment approach. The power and authority of police officers, lawyers, judges, and social workers can weigh as heavily on the victim as on the perpetrator.

For example, even well-intentioned community notification laws may have a devastating effect on the victim if the perpetrator is a family member. Recognizing this, an Oregon statute explicitly directed probation and parole officers to develop and implement the notification plan on a case-by-case basis to guard against revictimization of family members. This process required that the supervising officer understand the full impact of notification and other policies on the victims of sex crimes. In an effective containment approach, the healthy recovery of the victim and the well-being of the community guide policy development, program implementation, and the actions of professionals working with both sexual assault victims and perpetrators.

Adopting a victim-centered philosophy sometimes requires a significant shift in management values because every case management decision will require considering the risk the offender presents to past and potential victims. Probation and parole agencies may be challenged to dissolve usual job and agency boundaries so that risk management decisions can be made quickly and in an ongoing fashion. New information about the offender's risk of reoffending is revealed in the first months and years of supervision, so intervention strategies and policies must encourage an elastic response to risk. Although most sex offenders do not have an extensive arrest or conviction record, research indicates that many sex offenders have a long history of hurting many types of victims (Ahlmeyer, Heil, McKee, & English, 2000). The lack of officially recorded contacts with the criminal justice system can cloud risk assessments conducted with actuarial scales because these usually depend on past (documented) criminal history to predict future criminal behavior.

Multidisciplinary Collaboration

The containment model for managing sex offenders in the community calls for the creation of intra-agency, interagency, and interdisciplinary teams. These teams can overcome the fragmentation that usually results from the multilayered nature of the criminal justice system. These teams are valuable for several reasons:

- They vastly improve communication among the agencies involved.
- They allow for quicker and less intrusive responsive responses to victims (Epstein & Langenbahn, 1994);
- They promote the exchange of expertise and ideas;
- They facilitate the sharing of information about specific cases;
- They increase team members' understanding of what everyone on the team needs to do his/her job well;
- Perhaps most importantly, they foster a unified and comprehensive approach to the management of sex offenders.

Collaborating agencies should include sex offender treatment programs, law enforcement, probation, parole, schools, social services, rape crisis centers, hospitals, prisons, polygraph examiners, researchers, and victim advocate organizations. In a call to collaborate across disciplines and within communities for the purpose of addressing the epidemic of sexual assault, the American Medical Association (1995) added the following to the list above: attorneys, emergency room staff, universities, and victim assistance centers.

Interagency and multidisciplinary collaboration can occur in many ways. In Colorado, for example, a state-level Sex Offender Management Board with multidisciplinary membership is defined in legislation and meets monthly. The board has issued guidelines for the evaluation, treatment, and behavioral monitoring of adult sex offenders, including sex offenders with developmental disabilities. It also developed release criteria for sex offenders serving lifetime probation or parole sentences, a sentencing strategy undertaken in lieu of civil commitment. In Oregon, a quarterly meeting is held for all the probation and parole officers from across the state who specialize in the supervision of adult sex offenders. In Ohio, a parole officer took it upon herself to meet her colleagues working in the local police department's sex crime unit, and they subsequently worked together to solve cases.

As in Ohio, line staff frequently initially forges these types of relationships, with one committed professional seeking out the expertise of another. Regular meetings and communication ensue. These small acts of collaboration are changing the way this work gets done in many jurisdictions across the country.

Containment-Focused Risk Management

Case processing and case management in a containment approach must be tailored to the individual sex offender and his or her deviant sexual history. The approach depends on obtaining and sharing key pieces of information about the abuser. Professionals must be prepared to consistently respond to that information to minimize the offender's access to victims and high-risk situations. Most jurisdictions consider community supervision to be a privilege, and a condition of this privilege in the context of sex offender containment is the offender's waiver of confidentiality. The waiver allows the sharing of important information about risk and treatment progress (or lack thereof) with the judge, probation and parole officer, offender, and family members or significant others (sometimes including the victim's therapist).

When a sex offender first begins to serve a sentence of probation or parole, sources of information about the offender are usually limited to police reports, the pre-sentence investigation, sometimes a psychosexual evaluation or risk assessment, and some criminal history information.[x] To manage risk effectively, the team needs to know much more: information about the offender's preferred victim types, sexual assault history (including age of onset), the frequency and extent of deviant sexual arousal and behaviors, and events, behaviors, or emotional states that are precursors to reoffense. Many offenders have more victims and have committed more sex crimes than the crime of conviction and the offender's self-report would suggest.

Additional, crucial information about a sex offender's *modus operandi (MO)* will be obtained though sex offense–specific treatment, validated and expanded by postconviction polygraph examinations performed by specially trained examiners. Like urinalysis testing with drug offenders, the polygraph examination is a tool to gauge an offender's progress and compliance with treatment and supervision expectations. Many offenders report a lengthy existence of secretive, assaultive behaviors, and the use of the postconviction polygraph exam assists them in making the transition to honesty (English, Pullen, & Jones, 1996). Its use should be officially required by the criminal justice system (in the form of supervision conditions), whose representatives can issue consequences for noncooperation.

The key to understanding the MO is working with the offender to assist him or her disclose the details of what is often a lifetime of sexual obsessions and abuse history. Early in the treatment process, the offender will be assigned the job of writing a sex history log detailing all sexual activity, consenting and nonconsenting; a description of the victim (age, gender, relationship to offender); and the circumstances surrounding the assault. In this exercise, the offender reveals the lifestyle he or she has carefully designed to deceive others and promote deviant sexual activity, including methods of victim selection and efforts to keep the abuse a secret. The information is verified using a polygraph examination, and deceptive findings on the exam require further investigation by the supervising officer and the therapist, and can also lead to a variety of consequences for the offender, most commonly payment for a second polygraph examination.

This information, not readily disclosed by the perpetrator, will be used to manage current and future risk and also to assure that the offender receives treatment that is appropriately directed at real patterns of behavior.

There are three anchors in containment-focused risk management: (1) supervision, (2) therapy provided by a specialist, and (3) polygraph examinations conducted by a specially trained examiner. Each benefits from the distinct functions of the others. "The criminal justice supervision activity is informed and improved by the information obtained in sex-offender-specific therapy, and therapy is informed and improved by the information obtained during well-conducted post-conviction polygraph examinations" (English, 1998, p. 225). Each anchor must be perceived by the offender as separate yet aligned with the other. Each of these three components is discussed below.

Criminal Justice Supervision

First and foremost, sexual assault is a crime that gives the criminal justice system jurisdiction over convicted sex offenders. The containment team-consisting of the supervising officer, therapist, and polygraph examiner-is empowered primarily by the authority of the criminal justice system. The system, via the probation or parole officer, can exercise its containment powers in a number of ways including specialized terms and conditions for sex offenders, lengthy probation and parole sentences, restrictions on high-risk behaviors, restriction on contact with children, random home visits, urinalysis testing, electronic monitoring, and verified law enforcement registration. Ideally, these strategies are applied based on an individualized case assessment and supervision/treatment plan that focus on each offender's unique assault patterns.

The criminal justice system can also invoke consequences against the offender for nonparticipation in treatment, violation of supervision conditions, and behaviors that represent a risk to any potential victim. Consequences for failure to follow the directives of treatment and supervision can take a variety of forms. At a minimum, surveillance can be increased (e.g., house arrest, electronic monitoring, additional home visits by the supervising officer, requirements to phone the officer or others with location information) and, equally important, orders for additional treatment sessions can be imposed. Intermediate sanctions include community service activities, short-term jail sentences, or placement in a halfway house for sex offenders. At the extreme end of the sanction continuum is revocation of the community sentence and placement in prison.[xi] The anticipation of these potential consequences provides incentive for an offender to participate actively in treatment, obtain regular polygraph examinations, and comply with conditions of supervision.

Not surprisingly, sanctions must be invoked immediately to encourage compliance. Many treatment providers and polygraph examiners have reported that without the leverage of the criminal justice system's consequences for noncompliance, they could not work with sex offenders. Change is difficult. When the offender engages in a long-term process to change a lifetime of behaviors and fantasies that have been self-gratifying and exciting, this effort can be expected to ebb at times. The dangerousness presented by an offender's inconsistent effort to change is obvious and is intolerable in terms of public safety. The availability of a variety of consequences invoked quickly, then, is a vital and ongoing aspect of risk management. Without consistent pressure on the offender to adhere to the behavioral expectations detailed in the conditions of supervision and treatment contract, community safety must depend on the offender's good will. According to trauma expert Dr. Judith Herman of Harvard (1989, p. 188), "Vigorous enforcement of existing criminal laws prohibiting sexual assault might be expected to have some preventive effect since both the compulsive and opportunistic offenders are keenly sensitive to external controls." Vigorous enforcement translates into supervision and surveillance strategies that are customized to each offender's individual assault patterns. Once these patterns are known, the officer can design specific restrictions in terms of employment (e.g., working around children), limit leisure time activities (e.g., cruising the streets in an automobile), monitor the offender's internet use and telephone bills for use of 900 numbers,[xii] restrict the offender's use of alcohol and drugs, and/or confiscate items used to entice children (toys and video games, kittens or puppies) or stimulate deviant fantasies.

Pithers' (1990, p. 334) description of the assault pattern was a reminder of the need to be alert to what may, at first, appear to be accidental or occasional victim access: "Many aggressors, seeking to minimize their responsibility for offenses, would also have us believe their behaviors are the product of irresistible impulses overwhelming their self-control … In reality, many offenders carefully plan offenses so that they appear to occur without forethought." Hudson, Ward, and McCormack (1999, p. 179) stated, "Much of the optimism that has pervaded the treatment of sexual offenders in the last 15 years has come from the notion that the processes that these men follow are comprehensible and, therefore, under ideal circumstances, at least controllable." To this end, they described three potential types of planning in the "seduction process" (p. 783): covert planning, explicit planning, and chance contact.

This very attention to planning increases the likelihood of detection once case managers have complete information about the offender. Equipped with such information, the criminal justice agent is well positioned to identify precursor behaviors that can be managed by applying appropriate restrictions.

The intensity of supervision required of the probation or parole officer is significant, and collaboration with other professionals takes time and care. Case-specific supervision requires planning, documentation, and on-site meetings with the offender at home and work. Often, safety considerations require that fieldwork be conducted in teams of two officers. Ongoing training is also necessary to keep professionals at the top of their game. Probation and parole officers should have caseloads limited to 20 or 25 sex offenders, and they should have flexibility in work hours to monitor the offenders' activities at night and on weekends. Halfway houses with 24-hour monitoring of the facility and the offenders' locations should be available in all jurisdictions so that a safe residential option is available to criminal justice officials managing these cases. Criminal justice policy makers must explore the real-location of resources if they intend to take the leadership role necessary to implement a containment approach.

Sex Offense–Specific Treatment

Sex offender treatment targets the thoughts, feelings, denial, minimizations, motivations, justifications, and lifelong behaviors and thought patterns that are, in fact, fused to the sexual assault itself. The supervising officer works closely with the treatment provider to learn the offender's long-term patterns that *precede* actual assaults. This vital information, necessary for risk management but historically outside the scope of criminal justice system intervention, is the stuff of therapy.

Sex offense–specific treatment of offenders differs from traditional therapy in a number of important aspects.[xiii] First, in sex offense–specific treatment, the therapist best cares for the client by not accepting the client's description of his or her sexual past as complete or even true. In addition, the therapist's primary commitment is to the community at large; public safety is paramount.[xiv] The focus of treatment is on assaultive behavior that harms others: substance abuse, the offender's abusive childhood, and the feelings the offender has toward therapy are secondary (although still important) concerns that the therapist must manage. The offender's manipulation and rationalizations that precede the assault are considered part of the crime, not an explanation for the assault. Treatment providers help the offender to disclose the full extent of his or her deviant sexual history. Holding on to these powerful secrets is not therapeutic and, if allowed by the therapist, may perpetuate the secrecy at the core of the offender's lifestyle.

Sex offense–specific treatment occurs primarily in group therapy settings. Working in a group, therapists are less likely to succumb to the subtle manipulations that offenders have perfected over a lifetime. A group of offenders, coached by the therapist, can often recognize and confront others' familiar manipulations. Descriptions of cognitive distortions and psychological defense mechanisms, the step-by-step sexual assault cycle that clients use to set up opportunities to assault victims, and the development of a concrete prevention plan are the material of treatment.

One essential role of treatment in the containment approach is to obtain the details needed by criminal justice officials to develop risk management plans as well as to assist sex offenders in developing internal controls over their offending behaviors. Offenders are expected to assume full responsibility for the damage they inflict and to take measures to prevent future abusive behaviors. The threat of criminal justice consequences helps motivate these nonvoluntary clients to engage fully in treatment.

Postconviction Polygraphs

The postconviction polygraph examination is the third element of the containment strategy. The polygraph examination strengthens sex offender treatment and supervision by verifying the accuracy and completeness of self-reported sexual history information gained in treatment and by periodically monitoring the offender's compliance with criminal justice and treatment conditions. An examiner who specializes in this type of exam conducts regular polygraph examinations. This use of the polygraph, although nontraditional, is not uncommon. Our 1998 telephone survey of a nationally representative sample of more than 600 probation and parole supervisors across the nation found that the postconviction polygraph was used in jurisdictions in 30 states.

Sex offense–specific treatment, criminal justice supervision, and postconviction polygraphs have a synergistic effect on each other. The threat of the polygraph increases the scope and accuracy of the sexual history information obtained by the treatment provider. Conversely, the polygraph examiner uses the information obtained in treatment and supervision to design test questions that verify the accuracy of this information. The criminal justice supervisor uses this information to manage risk, and the therapist uses the information to design a meaningful treatment plan that is informed by the full scope and variety of the offender's sexual deviancy.

Studies of sex offenders' self-reports of sex crimes reveal that most offenders have engaged in a considerable number of lifetime sexual assaults. Abel, Becker, Cunningham-Rathner, Mittleman, and Rouleau (1988) and Abel and Rouleau (1990) studied 561 men seeking voluntary treatment. The researchers found the ratio of arrest to self-reported (anonymous) sex crime was approximately 1:30 for those who engaged in rape and child molesting, and 1:150 for exhibitionists and voyeurism. Further, Abel et al. (1988) also found that exhibitionists were highly likely to engage in additional sexually assaultive behaviors: "46 percent had been nonfamilial female pedophilia, 22 percent in male nonincestuous pedophilia, 22 percent in female incestuous pedophilia and 25 percent in rape" (p. 163). A more recent study (English, Jones, Patrick, & Pasini-Hill, 2003, pp. 419–420) of 180 convicted adult sex offenders' self-reports of sex crimes obtained in conjunction with the polygraph examination found the following:

■ 56.5% of the 23 offenders who assaulted boys ages 5 and younger also assaulted girls in the same age category, and 26% of this group reported assaulting adult women.

- ▨ 64.3% of 28 offenders who disclosed assaulting boys 6 to 9 years of age reported assaulting girls in the same age category; 39.3% reported assaulting adult women.
- ▨ Eighty cases were convicted of incest, but 104 admitted family victims. Of the 104, 34.8% self-reported assaulting strangers and 56.7% said they also had victimized another from "a position of trust." Two thirds (64.4%) disclosed assaulting victims outside the family.

The point here is not that sex offenders crossover from one category of victim to another; this phenomenon has been understood for many years. Rather, the assault history of each offender must be understood so that the duration, frequency, and variety of dangerous behavior are fully known by those who intend to provide treatment and supervision. Studies of cohorts of sex offenders can be used by those without the benefit of the polygraph examination to generalize the possibility for crossover. For example, among the incest perpetrators discussed above, two thirds reported assaulting victims outside the family. For professionals managing incest perpetrators, this is a reasonable generalization. Since only one third of the offenders in the English et al. (2003) study were found non-deceptive on the polygraph exam, it is likely that the extent of crossover found in that sample remains an underestimate.

The polygraph must be used in conjunction with sex offense–specific treatment. These two components, acting together and consistently supported by criminal justice supervision and consequences for noncompliance, provide a powerful incentive for an offender to be truthful and to refrain from behavior for which he or she will surely be caught. Without the use of the polygraph examination process, the information necessary to manage the risk of offenders is incomplete, and the offender's risk to the community remains uncertain.

The use of the postconviction polygraph is best described as a process because it requires the collaborative efforts of the examiner, the therapist, and the criminal justice supervisor. The examiner must understand the case and be prepared for the test by conferring with the therapist and the case manager. The examiner remains completely neutral, that is, with no vested interest in the outcome of the exam. This role differs from the other two professionals in the team. The therapist may hope that the offender has revealed all during group treatment, and the supervising officer may be continually suspicious. The polygraph examiner focuses on the technical and physiological requirements of the exam itself, threats to validity, and the careful construction of questions. The examiner also undertakes a methodical execution of the pre-test (where every question is reviewed with the offender), the test itself (measuring heart rate, blood pressure, respiration, and perspiration), and the post-test (review of test results with the offender). Communication among the supervising officer, the treatment provider, and the polygraph examiner is absolutely key to the successful implementation of this management tool. Lack of communication, or too much focus on "passing the polygraph" rather than being honest and trustworthy, will eventually undermine the use of this containment strategy.

Responding to Previously Undisclosed Offenses

In the containment approach, responding to previously unknown sex offenses disclosed through polygraph tests becomes a critical issue. Containment team members generally inform offenders that there will be no confidentiality or immunity from prosecution for new offenses committed since they were convicted of the current crime.

Admissions of prior offenses are handled in one of three ways in the United States. The first method involves granting the offender no immunity for any disclosures. All admissions of previously unknown offenses are disclosed to law enforcement or child protective services, or both. This approach allows victims to be identified and to receive treatment, which some communities have prioritized, but because it subjects the offender to further prosecution, it likely discourages admissions of additional offenses. A common variation of this method involves reporting only offenses that fall under mandatory reporting laws. That is, reporting to law enforcement and social services those offenses involving minors. This, also, likely discourages admissions.

The second method commonly used is granting limited immunity on prior offenses. Using this method requires the cooperation of the prosecuting attorney. Offenders sign a limited immunity agreement with the prosecutor's office that specifies that all crimes will be reported to the prosecuting attorney's office. This allows victims to be identified and referred for treatment. The agreement is limited in this sense: As long as the offender successfully completes treatment and supervision, he or she will not be prosecuted for prior sex offenses. If the offender drops out of or fails treatment and supervision, the crimes can be prosecuted. This approach has the significant advantage of providing an incentive for complying with treatment and supervision.

But arranging immunity agreements with prosecutors can be difficult. As an elected official, a prosecutor may be concerned that the public will view such agreements as excusing sex offenses. Moreover, offenders may disclose crimes that occurred in jurisdictions outside the purview of the prosecutor. Without similar agreements with prosecutors in all jurisdictions where crimes may have occurred, the limited immunity provision is compromised.

The third method entails no immunity for prior offenses, but offenders are asked to disclose prior sex offenses without providing details such as the name of the victim or location of the offense. Consequently, sufficient facts are not provided to evoke requirements for mandatory reporting. Typically, the age, gender, and general relationship category (relative, position of trust, acquaintance, or stranger) are recorded, providing the containment team knowledge of the variety and frequency of past offending behaviors. This method has the obvious disadvantage of telling offenders to conceal the truth at the same time we are trying to teach them to live an open and honest lifestyle. More importantly, past victims who are currently at risk remain unidentified, and past victims cannot be referred for treatment.

Nevertheless, as case law evolves in this field, it appears that there will be increased pressures to use the second or third method to handle past offense admissions because those methods sidestep self-incrimination concerns. In 2005, the Ninth Circuit Court, in the *United States v. Antelope*, determined that Antelope's supervised release could not be revoked after he invoked his Fifth Amendment rights in connection with required participation in a treatment program that included completing a sexual history polygraph examination. This forced the third option described above on jurisdictions in the Ninth Circuit Court.

Informed and Consistent Public Policies

The fourth component of a sex offender containment approach requires local criminal justice practitioners to develop public policies, at all levels of government, that institutionalize and codify the containment approach. These policies should be based on research; should hold offenders accountable; and, to be effectively implemented in the field, must empower those who work closely with these cases. Policies must define and structure the discretion authorities need to manage each offender individually. Criminal justice practitioners must also codify local and agreed-upon practices that support a victim-oriented approach to sex offender risk management. According to English et al. (1996), written guidelines for the uniform processing of sex assault cases should include, at a minimum, the following:

- The acceptance or rejection of plea agreements in cases of sexual assault
- The weight given in sentencing to an offender's denial of the crime
- The use of polygraph information
- Family reunification assessment protocols
- Pre-sentence investigation report information
- Failure to progress in treatment
- Revocation procedures
- Third-party liability/duty to warn potential victims
- Employment restrictions for sex offenders under criminal justice supervision
- Length of community supervision (i.e., lifetime)

Two important reasons for clearly stating policies include (1) the offender deserves to know what is expected of him or her and what to expect from the criminal justice/mental health system, and these clear expectations will help keep the focus on the offender "working his program" rather than complaining about the system; and (2) some policies undermine sex offender containment and minimize the seriousness of the crime. Policies that undermine sex offender containment include allowing plea bargains to lesser charges, to nonsex crimes, or to misdemeanor sex crimes *when the evidence exists to fully prosecute the case*. Lowering the charge, granting diversion, or issuing a deferred judgment at best facilitates the minimization of the case to the offender ("It wasn't that bad, I won't do it again") and the victim ("I'm not important to the court"), and, at worst, eliminates the sexual assault history in the official record. Prosecutors and judges who specialize in sex crimes and receive regular training from national entities understand the power of the court to set in motion the healing process (therapeutic jurisprudence as discussed elsewhere in this issue). Aiding in the minimization process will ultimately make it harder for the offender to begin and sustain the lifelong changes required to ensure public safety.

Clear, consistent, and documented agreements on sex offender polices, combined with the cooperation of agencies responsible for managing sex offenders, then, are essential to enable the containment process outlined here to proceed. Written procedures and protocols should describe how and when team interactions occur. The range of activities that require such documentation is quite large, but primary among them is the need for open communication and information sharing at all stages of the process of managing sex offenders in the community.

Quality Control

The containment approach requires broad discretion on the part of the criminal justice system professionals, treatment providers, polygraph examiners, and others collaborating to protect public safety. This discretion allows for quick responses to the ongoing assessment of risk and progress, and it recognizes that these cases often involve complicated relationships between the perpetrator and the victim. Such discretion must be systematically monitored to ensure fairness and justice. For this reason, quality control is fundamental to the administration of any sex offender management program, project, or system-wide process. Quality control activities should include, at a minimum, the following:

- Monthly, multiagency case review meetings to ensure that prescribed policies and practices are implemented as planned
- The requirement of annual training on the topics of sexual assault, conflict resolution, teaming,

victimization, trauma, family reunification, treatment efficacy, and research related to each of these

- Developing and tracking performance measures associated with the policies and procedures specified in the jurisdiction
- Videotaping all polygraph examinations to avoid recanted statements and to facilitate periodic review of examinations (including chart reviews) by a quality control team
- The collection of case data describing the characteristics of offenders who fail in treatment or commit new sex crimes so gaps in containment can be identified and closed

Sexual abuse cases are difficult to manage, and offenders attempt to manipulate the management system just as they did their victim(s). Containment professionals can burn out, get soft, miss "red flags," become cynical, and otherwise become ineffective. Empathy toward victims and repeated exposure to traumatic material can also result in compassion fatigue (Figley, 1995; Stamm, 1995). Police, firefighters, and other emergency workers have reported that they are most vulnerable to compassion fatigue when dealing with the pain of children (Beaton & Murphy, 1996). In addition, "trauma is contagious" (Herman, 1992 p. 180). Compassion fatigue, a near certainty in this work, presents a significant threat to the quality of the program, and the well-being of the dedicated professionals who are working to make our world safer.

Working together as a team is the first line of defense against this common phenomenon. Honest communication among team members is the first step in developing a continuum of quality control mechanisms. The next step is a process that brings together agency administrators who actively support the protocols and stand behind the staff that enforce the protocols and make difficult decisions in the field. Ongoing training, flexible hours, a supportive environment, and safe working conditions are important ways that administrators can help fight compassion fatigue.

A final aspect of quality control consists of clearly defined and agreed-upon measures of success. It is challenging to identify measures of detection, detention, and revocation that target offenders *before* the commission of a new assault. Addressing these issues requires the allocation of resources for monitoring and evaluation. Indeed, resource allocation is a key component of quality control.

Conclusion

The five-part containment model process for managing adult sex offenders summarized here establishes a framework within which agencies and communities can develop specific practices to promote public safety and victim protection. Just as the containment triangle itself must be tailored to the individual characteristics of the sex offender, so should the method of implementing this model process vary based on the context and needs of each community.

References

Abel, G. A., Becker, J. V., Cunningham-Rathner, J., Mittleman, M., & Rouleau, J.-L. (1988). Multiple paraphilic diagnoses among sex offenders. *Bulletin of the American Academy of Psychiatry and the Law, Vol. 16,* No. 2, 153–168.

Abel, G. G., & Rouleau, J.-L. (1990). The nature and extent of sexual assault. In W. L. Marshall, D. R. Laws, & H. E. Barbaree (Eds.), *Handbook of sexual assault: Issues, theories and treatment of the offender* (pp. 9–20). New York: Plenum Press.

Ahlmeyer, S., Heil, P., McKee, B. and English, K. (2000). The impact of polygraphy on admissions of victims and offenses in adult sexual offenders. *Sexual Abuse: A Journal of Research and Treatment, 12,* 123–138.

American Medical Association. (1995). Sexual Assault in America. American Medical Association position paper.

Beaton, R. and Murphy, S. A. (1995).Working people in crisis: Research implications. In C. R. Figley (Ed.), *Compassion fatigue: Coping with secondary traumatic stress disorder in those who treat the traumatized.* New York. Burnner/Mazel.

Becker, J. V., and Coleman, E. M. (1988). Incest. In V. B. VanHassett, R. L. Morrison, A. S. Bellack, & M. Hersen (Eds.), *Handbook of family violence* (pp. 197–205). New York: Plenum.

Becker, J. V., Cuningham-Rathner, J., & Kaplan, M. S. (1986). Adolescent sexual offenders: Demographics, criminal and sexual histories, and recommendations for reducing future offenses. *Journal of Interpersonal Violence,* 431–445.

Beitchman, J. H., Zucker, K. J., Hood, J. E., daCosta, G. A., Akman, D., & Cassavia, E. (1992). A review of the long-term effects of child sexual abuse. *Child Abuse and Neglect, 16,* 101–118.

Briere, J., and Runtz, M. (1988). Post sexual abuse trauma. In G. E. Wyatt & G. J. Powell, (Eds.), *Lasting effects of child sexual abuse* (pp. 85–99). Newbury Park: Sage.

Colorado Sex Offender Treatment Board. (1999, rev.) *Standards and guidelines for the assessment, evaluation, treatment, and behavioral monitoring of adult sex offenders*. Denver: Colorado Division of Criminal Justice, Department of Public Safety.

Dupre, A. R., Hampton, H. L., Morrison, H., & Meeks, G. R. (1993). Sexual assault. *Obstetrics Gynecological Survey* 48.

English, K. (1998). The containment approach: An aggressive strategy for the community management of adult sex offenders. *Psychology, Public Policy, and Law, 4,* 218–235.

English, K., Jones, L., Pasini-Hill, & Patrick, D. (2000). *The second national telephone survey on the community management of adult sex offenders: Appendix B. The value of the post-conviction polygraph*. Washington, DC: National Institute of Justice, U.S. Department of Justice.

English, K., Jones, L., Patrick, D., & Pasini-Hill, D. (2003). Sex offender containment: Use of the postconviction polygraph. *Annals of the New York Academy of Sciences, 989,* 411–427.

English, K., Pullen, S., & Jones, L. (Eds.) (1996). *Managing adult sex offenders: A containment approach*. Lexington, KY: American Probation and Parole Association.

Epstein, J., & Langenbahn, S. (May 1994). *The criminal justice response to rape*. Washington, DC: National Institute of Justice, U.S. Department of Justice.

Figley, C. R. (Ed.) (1995). *Compassion fatigue: Coping with secondary traumatic stress disorder in those who treat the traumatized*. New York: Brunner/Mazel.

Hansen, R., Resnick, H., Saunders, B., Kilpatrick, D., & Best, C. (1999). Factors related to the reporting of childhood rape. *Child Abuse and Neglect, 23*(6), 559–569.

Herman, J. (1992). *Trauma and recovery*. New York: Basic Books.

Hindman, J. (1988) Just before dawn. Boise, ID: Northwest Printing.

Hudson, S. M., Ward, T., and McCormack, J. C. (1999). Offense Pathways in Sexual Offenders. *Journal of Interpersonal Violence, Vol. 14, No. 8,* 779–798.

Kilpatrick, D. G., Edmunds, C. N., & Seymour, A. (1992) *Rape in America: A report to the nation*. Medical University of South Carolina, National Victim Center and Crime Victims Research and Treatment Center. Charleston, NC.

Langan, P. A., Schmitt, E. L. and Dunse, M. R. (November 2003*). Recidivism of Sex Offenders released from prison in 1994*. Bureau of Justice Statistics, U. S. Department of Justice, Washington, D. C.

Peters, S. D. (1988). Child sexual abuse and later psychological problems. In Wyatt, G. E. & Powell, G. J. (Eds.), *Lasting Effects of Child Sexual Abuse,* pp.101–117. Newbury Park: Sage.

Pithers, W. D. (1990). Relapse prevention with sexual aggressors: A method for maintaining therapeutic gain and enhancing external supervision. In W. L. Marshall, D. R. Laws, & H. E. Barbaree (Eds.), *Handbook of sexual assault: Issues, theories, and treatment of the offender*. New York: Plenum Press.

Saunders, B. E., Kilpatrick, D. G., Hanson, R. F., Resnick, H. S., Walker, M. E. (1999.) Prevalence, case characteristics, and long-term psychological correlates of child rape among women: A national survey. *Child Maltreatment, Vol. 4,* No. 3,187–200.

Smith, D., Letourneau, E., Saunders, B., Kilpatrick, D., Resnick, H., & Best, C. (2000). Delay in disclosure of childhood rape: Results from a national survey. *Child Abuse & Neglect, Vol. 24*, No. 2, 273–287.

Stamm, B. H. (Ed.). (1995). Secondary traumatic stress. Lutherville, MD: Sidran Press.

Steadman, H. J., Mulvey, E. P., Monahan, J., Robbins, P. C., Appelbaum, P. S., Grisson, T., Rother, L. H., and Silver, E. (1998) Violence by people discharged from acute psychiatric inpatient facilities and by others in the same neighborhood. *Archives of General Psychiatry, Vol. 55*, 393–401.

Summit, R. C. Societal Avoidance of Child Sexual Abuse. In Wyatt, G. E. & Powell, G. J. (Eds.), *Lasting Effects of Child Sexual Abuse.* Pp. 39–60, Newbury Park: Sage.

Tjaden, P. and Thoennes, N. (2000). *Full report of the prevalence, incidence, and consequences of violence against women: Findings from the national violence against women survey.* Washington DC: U.S. Department of Justice, National Institute of Justice (NCJ 183781).

Tjaden, P., & Thoennes, N. (2006). *Extent, Nature, and Consequences of Rape Victimization: Findings from the National Violence Against Women Survey.* Washington DC: U.S. Department of Justice, National Institute of Justice (NCJ 210346).

United States v. Antelope, 395 F.3d 1128, 1132 (9th Cir. 2005).

Wyatt, G. E., & Powell, G. J. (Eds.) (1998). *Lasting Effects of Child Sexual Abuse*, Newbury Park: Sage.

---

[i] An earlier version of this article was originally published in Seton Hall Law Review, Vol. 34, No. 4, 2004.

[ii] In a recent study, the U.S. Bureau of Justice Statistics found that only 3.5% of nearly 9,700 sex offenders released from prison were reconvicted for a sex crime in a 3-year follow-up period. However, 38.6% were returned to prison for other crimes during this period. Further, convicted sex offenders were four times more likely [than whom?] to be rearrested for a sex crime in the 3 years following release from prison (Langan, Schmitt, & Dunse, 2003).

[iii] Additional problems occur at the points of arrest and prosecution also but will be not addressed here.

[iv] Grotpeter and Elliott (2002) [Add to References section, please], in a longitudinal crime study of a general population sample of more than 1,700 subjects over 25 years, found 80 self-reported committing a serious sexual assault; only two (1.1%) were arrested for a sex crime, and neither were convicted.

[v] Agency records of postdischarge violence among psychiatric patients were found to underestimate actual reoffending by a factor of more than six (Steadman et al., 1998).

[vi] This agency is located in the state Department of Public Safety.

[vii] English, K., Pullen, S., & Jones, L. (Eds.). (1996). *Managing adult sex offenders: A containment approach.* Lexington, KY: American Probation and Parole Association. [Please put this reference in the References section with a citation here. Delete endnote.]

viii Much of this research was funded by the National Institute of Justice, U.S. Department of Justice. The findings reported here represent the views of the author and not the Department of Justice.

ix Sexual assault victims, compared to non–rape victims, are at significantly higher risk to abuse alcohol and drugs; to suffer from depression, anxiety, nightmares, and social isolation; and to attempt suicide (Kilpatrick et al., 1992; Peters, 1988; Briere & Runtz, 1988).

x Information on parolees may be even less available, if the conviction records and prison records do not accompany the offender's release onto parole. Ideally, when offenders are on parole, information on prison treatment and behavior, as well as information on the crime of conviction, will accompany the offender's movement into the community.

xi Prison sentences are, of course, not the end of risk management concerns. Most prisoners eventually are released into the community.

xii We have been informed of sex offenders who have generated telephone bills in the thousands of dollars by using 900 numbers. Although this is not a crime, for sexual abusers, compulsive phone calling represents out-of-control behavior, a likely prelude to more dangerous acts. Also, the additional financial burden creates a level of stress that may seduce the offender into psychologically escaping into an assaultive fantasy—the first step in the next assault.

xiii In fact, many sex offender treatment professionals do not refer to this intervention as *therapy*, since it differs significantly from what they were taught in graduate school. Rather, it is typically referred to simply as sex offense–specific treatment.

xiv "Public safety is paramount" is one of a dozen guiding principals that introduce the Colorado Standards for the Assessment, Evaluation, Treatment and Behavioral Monitoring of Adult Sex Offenders. This publication is available from the Colorado Division of Criminal Justice, 700 Kipling, Denver, Colorado 80215.

Sexual Violence and Restorative Justice

Jo-Ann Della Giustina

Sexual violence is unlike most other violent acts in that it is an intrusion into a person's very private world. It violates not only a person's body but also her/his psyche. Because the offense is often committed in private by someone the victim knows and even trusts, the effect is uniquely traumatic. Instead of recognizing the realities of sexual violence, media efforts often sensationalize sexual violence (especially against children), glamorize stranger violence, and repeatedly promulgate the falsehood that sexual offenders cannot be treated and will always reoffend. Moreover, the harm that is caused by acquaintance rape or incest gets ignored and trivialized.

What is justice for sexual violence? What do survivors/victims[i] need to heal from the pain? How can offenders be held accountable? How can the survivor/victim continue to live in the same community as the offender? How can the survivor/victim, the offender, and the community heal? Given the prevalence of sexual violence committed by known offenders, a strategy examining if and how victims and offenders can coexist needs further analysis.

The existing criminal justice approach, which focuses on punishment instead of healing, treats sexual violence as a crime against the state. But an offender does not rape "the state" or molest "the commonwealth." The survivor/victim is a real person with real needs who is arguably treated by the criminal justice system as nothing more than a means to a successful prosecution and conviction. The focus is on apprehending and convicting the offender, not on helping the survivor/victim heal from the trauma. Part of the healing process involves the survivor/victim telling her/his story and hearing the offender accept responsibility for the harm caused. Those needs are not recognized as important by prosecutors who focus on obtaining a conviction and punishment.

Offenders are often equally mishandled by the system. Instead of focusing on rehabilitation and reintegration into the community, vengeance and retributive justice stigmatize and isolate the offender from the community, which often leads to further sexual violence.

This inherently flawed approach ensures that survivors/victims will not have their needs met, offenders will not understand the personal impact of their actions, and the state will inevitably focus more on its goals than on the process of justice.

In response to the criminal justice system's failure to meet the needs of survivors/victims, offenders, and communities, there is a growing interest in developing an approach to justice that is restorative and transformative. Can restorative justice be used to control the threat of future sexual victimization by repairing the harm to the survivor/victim, the community, and the offender instead of the traditional criminal justice system's sole focus on punishment of the offender?

Despite the growing use of restorative justice for a variety of crimes, controversy surrounding its use in sexual violence cases remains. The main concerns center on survivor/victim safety, offender accountability, and the effectiveness of its use to minimize future sexual violence.

This chapter explores whether restorative justice is appropriate to address sexual violence. A critique of the use of the criminal system for sexual violence cases is followed by a discussion of restorative justice and its possible use with these cases. The controversy surrounding using restorative justice in sexual violence cases is then assessed. Finally, several programs that implement restorative justice with sexual offenders are discussed.

Definition of Sexual Violence

As has been documented throughout this book, sexual offenders are not a homogeneous group. Sexual violence includes a wide range of behaviors against females and males, children and adults. There is a continuum of sexual offenses, which range from indecent exposure to more serious offenses, such as sexual abuse, sexual assault, and rape. In this chapter, *sexual violence* is used as an overall term for all sexual offenses, and specific sexual delineations are made when important.

What is Restorative Justice?

Restorative justice is a justice model that aims to transform the community's role in addressing crime. It emphasizes the harm caused by the offense instead of the violation of a law. The offender is held accountable for the harm caused and is supported in taking responsibility for the offense, and the survivor/victim is offered support and aid in the healing process (Sullivan & Tifft, 2005; Yantzi, 1998; Zehr, 1995). It focuses on the survivor's/victim's needs while also addressing the needs of the offender and the community so that the relationships among all the parties can be healed and reconciliation can occur (Koss, Bachar, & Hopkins, 2003).

The potential benefits of a restorative justice approach include improving survivor/victim safety and healing, providing assistance to the community, and transforming and reintegrating the offender into the community in an effort to prevent future sexual violence.

Restorative justice practices include community conferencing, family group conferencing, victim–offender mediation, and circles (Sullivan & Tifft, 2005; Van Ness & Heetderks Strong, 2002). The following are descriptions of these restorative justice models:

- In community conferencing, victims, offenders, and their key supporters voluntarily meet to decide how to handle the aftermath of the crime. A trained facilitator guides the process, which includes offenders taking responsibility for their behavior and victims being involved in the decisions about offender sanctions.
- Family group conferencing is a form of community conferencing that involves the family groups of the victim and offender.
- In victim–offender mediation, victims meet with their offenders in a safe setting with the guidance of a trained mediator, who facilitates discussion of the crime and provides victims and offenders the opportunity to determine a plan that alleviates harm.
- Circles provide a safe place for people to connect positively with others, strengthen bonds, and solve community problems through sharing.

These practices can be utilized in numerous settings and at various points in the traditional criminal justice process: as an alternative to prosecution, within pre-sentencing or post-sentencing programs and procedures, in prison programs, in pre-prison release programs, or in community reentry programs (Hopkins & Koss, 2005; Koss, et al., 2003; McAlinden, 2005, 2007; McWhinnie & Wilson, 2005).

Restorative justice is a justice model that is an alternative to retributive justice, which stigmatizes both the offender and the survivor/victim. Within a retributive framework, the adversarial criminal system is organized around the concept that the state is the aggrieved party that seeks punishment of the defendant, who has violated a criminal law. After a law is violated, an adversarial legal contest decides who is to blame. Because defendants are innocent until proven guilty, they usually plead not guilty, which discourages them from taking responsibility for their actions. Survivors/victims, on the other hand, are often seen as an instrument in efforts to prove defendants guilty. Their needs are often overlooked.

In contrast to the traditional legal system, the restorative justice model frames crime as a violation of people and relationships. It seeks to restore the damaged community fabric, to heal the survivor/victim, and to restore and transform the offender to the community (Sullivan & Tifft, 2005; Yantzi, 1998; Zehr, 1995). It creates obligations for the offender to right the wrong. Central to restorative justice is the idea that the offender has committed harm and must take responsibility for that behavior so that the relationship of the offender to the survivor/victim and to the community can be healed.

For survivors/victims, the goal is to enable them to ask the offender why the crime occurred, and to participate in determining the sanctions against the offender (Daly, 2006). To begin to heal the harm, the offender must recognize the wrong committed and accept responsibility for the harm caused (Dickey, 1998; Sullivan & Tifft, 2005; Zehr, 1995). Once that occurs, reconciliation of important connections and relationships can begin (Dickey, 1998; Pranis, 2002). Reconciliation may be between the offender and the individual survivor/victim, between the offender and the community, or between the survivor/victim and the community.

Restorative justice is based on the philosophy that a just system requires a community that values and practices social and individual healing through interpersonal connections and relationships. Justice involves the survivor/victim, the offender, and the community in the search for solutions that promote healing and a sense of security. Apology, forgiveness, and restitution are crucial elements of that reconciliation (Zehr, 1995). Future sexual violence may be reduced by restoring wholeness to those whose lives and relationships have been damaged (Dickey, 1998).

Failure of the Traditional Criminal Justice Approach

Since the 1970s, the movement against sexual violence has focused on a "law and order" approach. Major legal and policy reforms have focused on expanding the definitions of sexual assault; establishing rape shield protections; eliminating corroboration requirements at trial; and increasing punitive measures, including longer prison terms, mandatory minimum sentences, and special surveillance measures such as sexual offender registration, community notification, and naming and shaming practices for those convicted of sexual offenses.

None of these actions, however, have resulted in lower rates of sexual violence (Koss & Achilles, n.d.).

The legal system does not prevent sexual violence. It intervenes only after the violence has been reported, which occurs for only a minority of sexual violence offenses. Estimates of rape reporting have ranged from 8% to 33% of all assaults (Herman, 2005; Hopkins & Koss, 2005), and recent research indicated that less than 5% of sexual offenders are ever apprehended (Salter, 2003). Underreporting may occur because the survivor/victim is ashamed or embarrassed and may even blame herself/himself for the violence. This is particularly true if the survivor/victim knows the offender, especially if it is a trusted family member or intimate partner.[ii] Nearly 90% of sexual assault survivors/victims know their attacker, and 76% of women who are raped are victimized by an intimate partner (Greenfeld, 1997; Tjaden & Thoennes, 1998). Moreover, 80% to 90% of child sexual assault victims are abused by someone they know, most often by a family member. Furthermore, sexual offenders often use grooming techniques to gain the child's trust so that the offense is not discovered (McAlinden, 2007).

Prosecution and Conviction

In addition to the underreporting of a majority of sexual violence cases, the legal system does too little to protect the survivor/victim or to effectively hold offenders accountable. Only 50% to 75% of reported rapes are prosecuted (Hopkins & Koss, 2005), and conviction rates are very low (Daly, 2002; Herman, 2005).

Once the offense has been charged, the prosecutor must prove the defendant guilty beyond a reasonable doubt, which encourages defendants to plead not guilty instead of accepting responsibility for any harm they have caused. Even when a guilty plea is made, it is often considered a compromise. It makes the defendant legally responsible, but not necessarily morally accountable.

How does the legal system treat survivors/victims? They must endure interrogation by medical personnel, law enforcement officers, and prosecutors, who often disbelieve them and question their credibility (Koss et al., 2003). Once the case goes to court, the adversarial structure of the legal system does not favor survivors/victims, often revictimizing and stigmatizing them instead of protecting them. Many survivors/victims feel that the legal system humiliates them by marginalizing them and treating them with casual indifference and disrespect (Herman, 2005). As for date rape and acquaintance rape, the criminal system often views these as minor offenses even though they traumatize the survivor/victim and may be part of a damaging pattern of sexual offending (Koss et al., 2003).

Courtrooms can be intimidating and present a complex set of rules and procedures that survivors/victims often do not understand (Daly, 2006). When they tell their story in court, they are often limited to answering the lawyers' questions instead of explaining the trauma caused by the sexual violence. Further, they often feel that the questions posed by defense attorneys aggravate their self-blame (Koss et al., 2003).

Evidentiary problems exacerbate this negative atmosphere. Most sexual offense cases do not include eyewitnesses, so the survivor's/victim's credibility is often questioned, leading to embarrassment and shame. Moreover, the survivor/victim may still be afraid of the offender. No wonder that some survivors/victims do not want to testify or take part in the legal process.

If there is a conviction, the survivor/victim has no say in the punishment. Although a victim impact statement may be allowed, the judge is not obligated to consider the survivor's/victim's wishes when imposing a sentence.

What do survivors/victims want? They want acknowledgement, support, and a renewed sense of power and control over their lives. They want the opportunity to tell their stories in their own way. They want validation and vindication from those close to them, but also from the community and the legal authorities. Although they also have economic needs such as housing and employment, education, retraining, or help with immigration problems, their overriding need is to feel safe (Herman, 2005; Koss, Bachar, Hopkins, & Carlson, 2004).

Survivors/victims want offenders to accept responsibility for the harm they caused and to apologize for the assault (Hopkins & Koss, 2005). Situations that involve sexual violence by an intimate partner or trusted family or friend are particularly complicated. In these cases, the survivor/victim wants the violence to stop, but may not want the offender to be punished within the criminal legal system. The survivor/

victim may want to heal the relationship rather than to sever all ties to someone they may still love (McAlinden, 2007).

How are sexual offenders treated within the criminal legal system? Punishment for convicted sexual offenders has evolved from rehabilitation and indeterminate sentencing to punishment and vengeance (Dickey, 1998). Judicial sentencing discretion has been limited by mandatory minimum sentences and state and federal legislative sentencing grids, which are influenced by the law-and-order policy of a retributive system. Instead of trying to deter offenders from reoffending through treatment and transformation, the legal system focuses on shaming the offenders (Koss et al., 2003; McAlinden, 2007).

Although evidence has suggested that treated sexual offenders do better than those who do not get treatment and completing treatment is one of the best predicators for successfully controlling sexual offending, little treatment occurs within prisons (Ibid). Of the approximately 710 sexual offender treatment programs in the United States, only 90 are in prisons (McAlinden, 2007).

Naming and Shaming Practices

Current public policy favors a disintegrative shaming of sexual offenders within a retributive criminal justice framework rather than efforts to successfully reintegrate sexual offenders into the community as productive citizens. Braithwaite (1989) defined shaming as "all social processes of expressing disapproval which have the intention or effect of invoking remorse in the person being shamed and/or condemnation by others who become aware of the shaming" (p. 100).

Disintegrative shaming practices include postrelease control mechanisms, such as sexual offender registration, community notification, residency restrictions, global positioning systems (GPS) monitoring, and other parole/probation conditions, many of which are discussed elsewhere in this volume (Hudson, 2003; McAlinden, 2005; Robbers, 2008). Despite the stated aim of public protection, these shaming sanctions function to stigmatize and humiliate offenders. Moreover, these laws have no impact in preventing first-time offenders and repeat offenders not captured by the criminal justice system.

Community notification laws have been passed in all states. Notification can occur through a variety of methods, including door-to-door visits, newspaper ads, community meetings, Internet databases, wanted posters, special license plates, and lawn signs (McAlinden, 2007). For example, in Louisiana, sexual offenders must go door to door to inform their neighbors that they are convicted sexual offenders (Ibid). Legislators in Wisconsin, Ohio, and Alabama have proposed special license plates for convicted sexual offenders (Jones, 2007).

Research has shown that community notification does not reduce reoffending (Hopkins & Koss, 2005). Not only do these tactics deflect attention from nonstranger sexual violence, which features in the majority of sexual offense cases, but they also give the community a false sense of security (McAlinden, 2007; Presser & Gunnison, 1999).

In addition, naming and shaming of sexual offenders fuels the public's fear, anger, and hostility toward the sexual offenders living in the community, creating a public hysteria, which has led to harassment and vigilante attacks on suspected pedophiles (McAlinden, 2005; Ronken & Lincoln, 2001).

Moreover, sexual offender laws depend on full compliance, which does not occur if offenders "go underground" in an effort to avoid stigmatization and humiliation (Ronken & Lincoln, 2001). The unwanted consequence of disintegrative shaming may be an increase in sexual offending, because offenders feel socially isolated (Braithwaite, 1989; McAlinden, 2007; Ronken & Lincoln, 2001). Once a person is stigmatized as a sexual offender, others respond to the offender as deviant, which leads to the offender being marginalized. Once marginalized by society, the offender uses isolation as a coping mechanism, which can result in denial, retaliation, defiance, and reoffending (Presser & Gunnison, 1999). It inhibits rehabilitation due to lower motivation to seek and/or maintain treatment. Isolation can ultimately increase the risk of recidivism by impeding successful reintegration into the community because of fewer employment opportunities as well as a loss of housing, ineligibility for public assistance, and disenfranchisement (McAlinden, 2007; Robbers, 2008; Ronken & Lincoln, 2001). As a result, the labeling of the sexual offender can make it easier for the offender to live within the deviant label instead of breaking from that label (Becker, 1990).

Restorative Justice and Sexual Violence

Since the traditional retributive legal system has not adequately addressed sexual violence, restorative justice is being explored as an alternative approach that would promote the survivor's/victim's recovery, increase offender accountability, and provide for safer offender reintegration into the community (Hopkins & Koss, 2005; Hudson, 2002; McAlinden, 2007).

The restorative justice paradigm presents an opportunity to change how sexual violent offending is addressed by our society. Although there is no single definition, restorative justice can best be understood as a paradigm that promotes community cohesion. When an offense occurs, society's fabric is torn apart. In addition to the harm committed against the individual victim, everyone around that person is negatively affected. As a consequence, the offense breaks down society, which can lead to further offenses. Restorative justice is an approach that can bring together those affected in an effort to heal the wounds and reconcile the parties. Crucial to restorative justice is the reduction of trauma in the survivor/victim. Survivors/victims want vindication and validation for the wrongs that were committed against them. They want offenders to take responsibility for the offense. They want a process that acknowledges that they, as survivors/victims, were not to blame for the offense. They want to avoid the feeling that they, not the offender, are on trial (Daly, 2006; Herman, 2005). A system which features these components may encourage increased reporting of sexual violence crimes.

For survivor/victims, healing depends on the opportunity, ability, and success in telling their stories, including the offense's impact on their lives. Narrative is a powerful tool in helping the victim face the trauma and transform from a victim into a survivor. Also crucial are the community's validation and support; survivors/victims need to feel believed and to have the community listen with compassion and understanding. In restorative justice, survivors/victims get the chance to be heard, to confront the offender, and to participate in the decision making process regarding punishment (Daly, 2006; Herman, 2005).

Survivors/victims also need to make their own choices regarding their future relationship (if any) with the offender (Yantzi, 1998). A key concept includes giving the survivor/

victim the choice of reconciling the relationship. If the survivor/victim wants to repair the relationship with the offender, (which may particularly be true in the case of an offense committed by a family member) the restorative justice process may be the mechanism. Since sexualized violence is often a secretive and private offense, disclosure and reconciliation in a safe, controlled environment can be powerful and effective for both the survivor/victim and the offender, but only if the survivor/victim chooses to participate (Yantzi, 1998). The survivor/victim should never be pressured into participating. The survivor's/victim's safety is tantamount to the process. The community must show sensitivity and respect for the survivor's/victim's wishes (Yantzi, 1998).

Restorative justice principles are also designed to strengthen sexual offender treatment (Koss, Bachar, & Hopkins, in press). Family group or community conferences, either preconviction or postconviction, are forums in which survivor/victims can discuss the impact of the offense, and in which offenders can hear how their behavior has affected others, which can lead to their taking responsibility for their actions. This process sets the stage for offenders to take steps to repair the harm and then to restore themselves to family, friends, community, and in some instances, the survivor/victim.

Reintegrative Shaming

In contrast to the harmful effects of disintegrative shaming discussed earlier, reintegrative shaming can be a powerful healing sanction. Braithwaite (1989) proposed that shaming, which can be disintegrative or reintegrative, is a form of social control. Reintegrative shaming involves the explicit disapproval of the delinquent act (shaming) by socially significant members, labeling the act without stigmatizing the offender, and the ongoing inclusion of the offender within the interdependent, reintegrative relationship (Makkai & Braithwaite, 1994; McAlinden, 2005). The shaming ends with gestures of acceptance and forgiveness, which allows the offender to become a fully contributing member of society (Braithwaite, 1989; McAlinden, 2005). For example, good parents can shame their child's bad behavior without rejecting the child (Braithwaite, 1989). This approach expands the possibilities of personal development and strengthens the offender's bonds to society (Hudson, 2002, 2003).

Reintegrative shaming schemes may have the added benefit of protecting the offender from retaliatory vigilante attacks. They may also help the offender to adjust to demands of living in the community. It is important to understand that these programs are not suited for all sexual offenders (i.e., not for high-risk repeat offenders). However, they may provide an effective alternative for low- to medium-risk offenders, particularly those who have perpetrated intra-familial abuse (McAlinden, 2005).

Empirical tests of Braithwaite's theory have shown that reintegrative shaming has been effective in reducing drunk driving and bullying (Robbers, 2008), but there has been limited empirical evaluation of its use with sexual offenders. Although reintegrative shaming theory was developed in response to the negative effects of disintegrative shaming, it is only one theory within the restorative justice paradigm.

Role of Apology and Forgiveness

Another restorative justice concept is the power of apology and forgiveness. Whether apology and forgiveness are part of the restorative justice process varies from case to case. If an offender apologizes to the survivor/victim, the survivor/victim is empowered to either accept or reject the apology. However, the evidence has suggested that survivors/victims usually accept apologies, which allows them to be less angry and bitter (Koss et al., in press). Survivors/victims alone get to decide whether forgiveness will be given; they should never be pressured to forgive. Even if an apology and forgiveness are given, the process of repairing the harm caused by the offender remains difficult.

What is forgiveness? Yantzi (1998) described forgiveness as a process that includes confession of the wrong, remorse, repentance, restitution, and reconciliation. Others (Dickey, 1998) have considered forgiveness an act by the survivor/victim that may or may not include the offender's remorse.

Although forgiveness is part of restorative justice, restorative justice goes beyond forgiveness to include healing. Healing is a process, a journey. For offenders, it means acknowledging the wrong and accepting responsibility, which leads to a change in behavior and orientation. Acknowledgment is merely the beginning. For survivors/victims, healing means regaining power and control over their lives.

Although victim–offender mediation is one of the most widely used restorative justice practices in the United States, it is not the only model that is being used. Other restorative justice approaches include sharing circles, victim impact panels, community reparation boards, circles of support, sentencing circles, conferencing with juveniles and adults, and restorative justice discipline in educational settings (Umbreit, Vos, Coates, & Lightfoot, 2006). The following are descriptions of these restorative justice models:

- Sharing circles offer a safe place for people to connect positively with others, strengthen bonds, and solve community problems through sharing. They occur in various settings.
- Victim impact panels allow a victim to meet with offenders who have committed a related crime (not against this particular victim, however) in an effort to promote healing and closure as well as to allow the offenders to understand the extent of the damage their actions may cause.
- Community reparation boards are composed of trained citizens who hold public, face-to-face meetings with offenders who are court ordered to participate in the process. The boards develop sanctions, plans, and agreements in which the offenders make reparations for their offenses, ensure that the agreements are honored, and issue compliance reports to the courts.
- Circles of support can be created at any time during the restorative justice process to support the victim and the offender.
- Sentencing circles are circles that involve victims, offenders, judges, prosecutors, defense attorneys, and interested community members, who meet after a conviction to discuss and determine the appropriate sanctions for the harm caused.
- Conferences with juveniles and adults are community conferences or family group conferences.
- Restorative justice discipline in educational settings typically involves conferencing circles that address discipline for harm caused within a school.

Many of these approaches promote appropriate forms of reparations by the offender toward the survivors/victims and the community, seeking reconciliation between the offender and survivor/victim, where appropriate, and reintegrating the offender into the community (McAlinden, 2007).

Community

Whereas many existing sexual offender policies emphasize stranger-based sexual assault, encouraging community members to constantly fear unknown predators, restorative justice focuses on the actual harm done to the actual victim. Changing the community's awareness of the problem is the first step in reducing sexual violence (Hopkins & Koss, 2005). The community needs to take ownership of the divisive, harmful actions by providing an environment supportive of reconciliation and healing through balancing support and confrontation of the offender (Dickey, 1998; Yantzi, 1998). Increased community awareness and education are necessary to prevent future sexual violence (Hopkins & Koss, 2005).

Critiques of Restorative Justice Approaches

Experience with restorative justice processes in response to sexual violence has been limited. There are inadequate empirical studies to evaluate whether it can be used safely and effectively. Thus, it is important to maintain a balance between prudence and hope of success in using restorative justice. One must always be mindful of potential risks of harm to survivors/victims.

Some feminist scholars have raised important questions about whether restorative justice is a safe and effective response to violence against women. These concerns include the survivor's/victim's physical and emotional safety and well-being, as well as whether any intervention is balanced and effective (Coker, 2006; Stubbs, 2002). Although these concerns have been raised mainly in the context of intimate-partner violence, they also should be considered for all sexual violence.

First, survivor/victim safety is a major concern because restorative justice is an informal process that may put survivors/victims at risk of continued violence. It could permit power imbalances to go unchecked and reinforce abusive behavior, especially in intimate-partner violence cases (Stubbs, 2002). However, acquaintance sexual assault cases may be at a significantly lower risk of repeat violence because the assault typically ends whatever relationship existed between the parties (Hopkins & Koss, 2005). To avoid potential problems, it is important to maintain a tightly controlled process where the survivor's/victim's safety is of utmost concern. If there is any question about safety, the restorative justice process should not be used.

Next, survivors/victims may feel pressured to accept certain outcomes, such as an apology, even if they feel they are inappropriate or insincere (Daly, 2006; Stubbs, 2002). For that reason, the survivor/victim should control the process, including the participants, who should include people with whom the survivor/victim feels safe.

Another concern is that some communities may not have the necessary resources to utilize restorative justice approaches effectively. They may lack resources to reintegrate offenders into the community, lack treatment resources for offenders, and lack appropriate support and assistance for survivors/victims (Daly, 2006). These are issues of policy and financial priorities. As a society, we need to focus our resources on restoring the community, which includes the survivor/victim and the offender.

Although these concerns are legitimate, one could argue that restorative justice approaches represent a preferable alternative to the traditional legal system, which often retraumatizes the survivor/victim, stigmatizes the offender, and fails to reconcile the community and eliminate further sexual violence. Nevertheless, it is crucial that restorative justice programs be carefully prepared and implemented. Given the limited empirical evidence about efficacy, it is still worthwhile to examine a few restorative justice programs that address sexual offending.

Restorative Justice Programs

The programs discussed briefly in this section have been implemented in a variety of settings. Unfortunately, there has not been extensive empirical evaluation of these programs. As a consequence, they are not presented here as programs with proven success, but simply as examples of restorative justice programs attempting this new approach.

Stop it Now! Program

As discussed in chapter 13, the Stop It Now! program was established in Vermont by Fran Henry, a survivor of sexual abuse. It is a prevention program that encourages abusers and potential abusers to recognize that their behavior is abusive and to seek help. Although it does not operate with a restorative justice framework, per se, its central thesis is a nonpunitive approach, emphasizing the offender's ability to change. The evaluative findings of Stop It Now! are discussed in chapter 13.

Circles of Support and Accountability (COSA)

One of the best known restorative justice reintegrative programs for sexual offenders is Circles of Support and Accountability (COSA), which was started in Canada in 1994 by Reverend Nigh when sexual offender Charlie Taylor was released from federal prison. COSA's philosophy is that the community must accept responsibility for addressing sexual violence by caring for the offender while considering the community's safety (McAlinden, 2007).

COSA is an intensive and individualized volunteer project that incorporates a holistic response to assist released sexual offenders to reintegrate into the community and lead responsible, productive, and accountable lives (McWhinnie & Wilson, 2005). This occurs through support circles with selected high-risk sexual offenders who are reentering the community. Practical and emotional support is given to these offenders, including matching them to needed resources (Correctional Services Canada, 2002).

Sexual offenders are recommended to the COSA program by their treatment providers after they have made significant progress in their treatment (Center for Sex Offender Management [CSOM], 2007). They are aided by volunteers from COSA, who are professionally trained in restorative justice principles, the dynamics of sexual offending, and concepts of specialized treatment. Five to seven volunteers are then matched with a sexual offender to create a circle of accountability and support that is assisted by a professional staff (Ibid).

The COSA model has spread across Canada and exists in the United States, in the United Kingdom, and around the world. What started as an ad hoc response to a difficult situation has become an international approach by innovative communities for managing sexual offender risk (McWhinnie & Wilson, 2005). In Canada, local COSA projects are guided by an advisory panel or steering group, usually sponsored by a local faith organization. However, in the United Kingdom, COSA is a more treatment-focused project working with individuals still within the criminal justice system. There, they use the Church of England's Board of Social Responsibility as well as local police and probation units (CSOM, 2007; McWhinnie & Wilson, 2005).

Although there is limited empirical evidence, there has been some evidence that the program has been effective in reducing reoffending (McAlinden, 2007). Research has shown that reoffending was lower for COSA's sexual offenders in comparison to a matched comparison group. One example of COSA's success is that Charlie Taylor spent 11 years, 6 months in the community, completely free of any sexual or violent offending. Until his death, Charlie kept in contact with his circle volunteers (McWhinnie & Wilson, 2005).

Responsibility and Equity for Sexual Transgressions Offering a Restorative Experience (RESTORE)

RESTORE is a community-based program that implements a restorative justice community conferencing model for misdemeanor sexual offenses in which there has been a guilty plea. The program started in 2001 in Pima County, Arizona, with three local sheriffs' offices, the offices of Tucson and Pima County, two victim service centers, and the University Of Arizona College Of Public Health. RESTORE is a victim-driven, postarrest, preconviction program limited to adult offenders charged with date and acquaintance rape, indecent exposure, and peeping (Hopkins & Koss, 2005). Specifically excluded are cases where the offender had prior domestic violence arrests or the assault was part of an ongoing pattern of intimate-partner violence so that the cases do not involve ongoing emotional and physical violence (Hopkins & Koss, 2002; Koss et al., in press; Koss et al., 2004).

The RESTORE program has four stages: (1) referral, (2) preparation, (3) conference, and (4) monitoring and reintegration. In the first stage, referrals are made by prosecutors after the survivor/victim and offender have already agreed to participate as part of a sentencing/plea bargain. Free legal counsel is provided to the survivor/victim, who voluntarily participates after consenting in writing to the offender's participation (Koss et al., 2004).

In the preparation stage, the facilitator considers the complex nature of the sexual victimization. The facilitator meets with the survivor/victim to assess safety, identify the conference attendees, identify the impacts of the offense, and develop appropriate reparation expectations. After extensive preparation, the survivor/victim, her/his community support network, the offender, and his/her community support network meet face-to-face (Koss, Bachar, Hopkins, & Carlson, 2004).

The conference stage is held in a police station and is facilitated by a trained human services provider. The survivor/victim is given a full opportunity to describe the offense and the resultant harm, after which the offender acknowledges the wrong committed and the harm done. Then, the facilitator presents a preliminary redress plan developed by the survivor/victim and agreed to by the offender. The plan may consist of a psychosexual forensic examination, psychotherapy, no contact with the survivor/victim, community service, weekly supervision by program staff, and regular supervision by the community board. The typical survivor/victim requests restitution, a role in shaping of the community service, and input into the counseling plan.

The final stage includes monitoring the survivor/victim, generating support from family and friends, and monitoring and reintegrating the offender. Successful completion of the agreement results in the charges being dismissed (Hopkins & Koss, 2005).

Most cases in the RESTORE program are still ongoing, so there is no empirical evidence of its success or failure. There has been only one report of a rearrest of an offender who completed the program. Two offenders were terminated for noncompliance. In both cases, no further action was taken or likely to be taken by prosecutors (Koss et al., 2004).

Community conferencing brings together survivors/victims, offenders, and their supporters for a face-to-face meeting where they are encouraged to talk about the effects of the incident and to make a plan to repair the damage and minimize the likelihood of further harm. This approach emphasizes accountability and acceptance of responsibility. Providing trained facilitators experienced in sexualized violence who incorporate a supportive system for survivors/victims recognizes the importance of relationships and community (Hopkins & Koss, 2005; Koss et al., 2004).

Conclusion

Restorative justice does not have all the answers and remains controversial. However, there is a need to continue to assess if and how restorative justice can be used to address sexual violence. Restorative justice procedures can improve survivor/victim safety, transform offenders, and protect communities. For survivors/victims, restorative justice promotes healing within a supportive and caring community. Restorative justice can allow offenders to earn back a place within the community. As a result, offenders can develop pro-social concepts of self and identity, which can motivate personal change.

The community must take ownership of the problem. Community cohesion needs to be developed so that working relationships can be strengthened to informally manage sexual offending. When restorative justice principles are applied to sexual violence, it is important that a community leadership exists to ensure public support for survivors/victims as well as the reintegration of offenders into a community that does not accept or allow sexualized violence. We must move away from the current punitive policy approach to effective reintegration absent stigma and prejudice. Such reintegration can lead to transformative motivation for personal change and a safer society.

References

Becker, J. V. (1990). Treating adolescent sexual offenders. *Professional Psychology: Research and Practice, 21*, 362–365.

Braithwaite, J. (1989). *Crime, shame and reintegration.* Sydney, Australia: Cambridge University Press.

Center for Sex Offender Management. (2007). *Managing the challenges of sex offender reentry.* Washington, DC: Center for Effective Public Policy.

Coker, D. (2006). Restorative justice, Navajo peacemaking and domestic violence. *Theoretical Criminology, 10*(1), 67–85.

Correctional Services Canada. (2002). *Circles of Support and Accountability: A guide to training potential volunteers: Training manual 2002.* Ottawa, Ontario: Correctional Service Canada.

Daly, K. (2002). Sexual assault and restorative justice. In H. Stang and J. Braithwaite (Eds.), *Restorative justice and family violence* (pp. 62–88). Cambridge, UK: Cambridge University Press.

Daly, K. (2006). Restorative justice and sexual assault: An archival study of court and conference cases. *British Journal of Criminology, 4,* 334–356.

Dickey, W. J. (1998). Forgiveness and crime: The possibilities of restorative justice. In R. Enright & J. North (Eds.), *Exploring forgiveness* (pp. 106–120). Madison, WI: University of Wisconsin Press.

Greenfeld, L. (1997). *Sex offenses and offenders: An analysis of data on rape and sexual assault.* Washington, DC: Department of Justice, Bureau of Justice Statistics.

Herman, J. (2005). Justice from the victim's perspective. *Violence Against Women, 11*(5), 571–602.

Hopkins, C. Q., & Koss, M. P. (2005). Incorporating feminist theory into a restorative justice response to sex offenders. *Violence Against Women, 11*(5), 693–723.

Hudson, B. (2002). Restorative justice and gendered violence. *British Journal of Criminology, 42,* 616–634.

Hudson, B. (2003). Restorative justice: The challenge of sexual and racial violence. In G. Johnstone (Ed.). *A restorative justice reader* (pp. 438–450). United Kingdom: Willan Publishing.

Jones, B. (2007). Sex offenders may get special tags; Eye-catching license plates proposed by lawmakers in Wisconsin, Ohio, Alabama. *USA Today.* Retrievedo n November 19, 2008 from http://www.usatoday.com/printedition/news/20070502/a_licenseplates02.art.htm

Koss, M. & Achilles, M. (No Date). Restorative justice responses to sexual assault. Retrieved on June 29, 2008 from http://new.vawnet.org/category/Main_Doc.php?docid=1231

Koss, M. P., Bachar, K. & Hopkins, C. Q. (2003). Restorative justice for sexual violence: Repairing victims, building community, and holding offenders accountable. *Annals of the New York Academy of Sciences,* 989, 364–477.

Koss, M. P., Bachar, K. & Hopkins, C. Q. (in press) Disposition and treatment of juvenile sex offenders from the perspective of restorative justice. In H. Barbaree (Ed). *Handbook on the treatment of juvenile sexual offenders.* Retrieved on June 29, 2008 from: http://restoreprogram.publichealth.arizona.edu/research/.

Koss, M. P., Bachar, K., Hopkins, C. Q., & Carlson, C. (2004). Expanding a community's justice response to sex crimes through advocacy, prosecutorial, and public health collaboration: Introducing the RESTORE program. *Journal of Interpersonal Violence,* 19, 1435–1463.

Makkai, J. & Braitwaite, J. (1994). Reintegrative shaming and compliance with regulatory standards. *Criminology,* 32, 361.

McAlinden, A. (2005). The use of 'shame' with sexual offenders. *British Journal of Criminology,* 45, 373–394.

McAlinden, A. (2007). *The shaming of sexual offenders: Risk, retribution and reintegration.* Portland, Oregon: Hart Publishing.

McWhinnie, L. & Wilson, R.J. (2005). Courageous communities: Circles of Support and Accountability with individuals who have committed sexual offenses. *International Institute for Restorative Practices*. Bethlehem, PA: Author.

Pranis, K. (2002). Restorative values and confronting family violence. In H. Stang and J. Braithwaite (Eds.). *Restorative justice and family violence* (pp. 23–44). Cambridge, U.K.: Cambridge University Press.

Presser. L & Gunnison, E. (1999). Strange bedfellows: Is sex offender notification a form of community justice? *Crime and Delinquency,* 45(3), 299–315.

Robbers, M.L.P. (2008). Lifers on the outside: Sex offenders and disintegrative shaming. *International Journal of Offender Therapy and Comparative Criminology, XX, XX*.

Ronken, C. & Lincoln, R. (2001). Deborah's law: The effects of naming and shaming on sex offenders in Australia. *Humanities & Social Sciences papers, Griffith University*. Retrieved on June 29, 2008 from http://epublications.bond.edu.au/hss_pubs/85

Salter, A. (2003). *Predators, pedophiles, rapists, and other sex offenders: Who they are, how they operate, and how we can protect ourselves and our children*. New York, NY: Basic Books.

Stop It Now! (No Date). Retrieved on June 28, 2008, from http://www.stopitnow.org/asit_pubarticles.html

Stubbs, J. (2002). Domestic violence and women's safety: Feminist challenges to restorative justice. In H. Stang & J. Braithwaite (Eds.), *Restorative justice and family violence* (pp. 42–61). Cambridge, UK: Cambridge University Press.

Sullivan, D. & Tifft, L. (2005). *Restorative justice: Healing the foundations of our everyday lives*. Monsey, N.Y.: Willow Tree Press.

Tjaden, P., & Thoennes, N. (1998). *Prevalence, incidence, and consequences of violence against women: Finding from the National Violence Against Women survey*. Washington, D.C.: Department of Justice, Bureau of Justice Statistics.

Umbreit, M.S., Vos, B., Coates, R.B. & Lightfoot, E. (2006). *Restorative justice in the twenty-first century: A social movement full of opportunities and pitfalls. Marquette Law Review*, 253–304.

Van Ness, D. & Heetderks Strong, K. (2002). *Restoring justice*, 2nd ed. Cincinnati, OH: Anderson Publishers.

Wilson, R.J., Huculak, B. & McWhinnie, (2002) Restorative justice innovations in Canada. *Behavioural Sciences and the Law*, 20, 363.

Yantzi, M. (1998). *Sexual offending and restoration*. Waterloo, Ontario and Scottsdale, PA: Herald Press

Zehr, Howard. (1995). *Changing lenses: A new focus for crime and justice*. Scottdale, PA: Herald Press.

---

[i] The term survivor/victim is used to maintain the empowerment expressed by the word survivor while at the same time recognizing that recovery from victimization is an individual experience.

[ii] Intimate partner relationships are those romantic relationships that exist between spouses and ex-spouses (legal and common law), girlfriends/boyfriends, ex-girlfriends/-boyfriends, and same-sexualpartners.

The Impact of Sex Offender Policies on Victims

Rachel Kate Bandy

Established elsewhere in this collection is a thorough examination of data that substantiate what victim advocates have long known: sexual violence is pandemic in U.S. society. One in 6 women and 1 in 33 men has been the victim of a completed or attempted sexual assault (Tjaden & Thoennes, 2000). Most victims know their perpetrators (Ibid) and, therefore, would be able to identify them to the authorities; yet "rape is the most underreported crime in America" (Kilpatrick, Whalley, & Edmunds, 2007 Abstract ¶ 1).

The impact of sexual assault on the health and well-being of its primary victims has also been well established in research. Sexual assault victims are three times more likely to suffer from depression, four times more likely to have suicidal ideations, six times more likely to suffer from posttraumatic stress disorder, 13 times more likely to abuse alcohol, and 26 times more likely to abuse drugs (Kilpatrick, Edmunds, & Seymour, 1992).

The impact of sexual violence on secondary victims such as the family, partner, and/or friends of a sexual assault victim has also been studied (e.g., Motta & Kefer, 1999; Schneider, 2001). Research has suggested that the stress and trauma secondary victims experience as the result of a loved one's victimization has significant and potentially long-lasting negative effects on their well-being and/or ability to provide support to the primary victim (Remer & Ferguson, 1995; Schneider, 2001). The aforementioned statistics have led scholars and practitioners alike to conclude that "rape is a problem for America's mental health and public health systems as well as for the criminal and juvenile justice systems" (Kilpatrick et al., 2007 Other Mental Health Problems ¶ 6). Therefore, public policy actors have multiple imperatives in efficiently addressing issues of sexual violence.

The past two decades have seen a tremendous growth in the enactment of sexual assault legislation. In 2005 alone, more than 100 laws aimed at identifying, treating, punishing, or otherwise controlling sex offenders were passed in the United States (Abner, 2007). Largely, these types of laws have intended to accomplish two ends: (1) public safety by controlling or containing sex offenders, and (2) public articulation of outrage and disdain for a specific criminal class while simultaneously acknowledging the loss suffered by its victims (Garland, 2001; Wood, 2005). Although much research has been conducted on the various ways in which these legislative initiatives have affected sex offenders (e.g., Glaser, 2003; Logan, 1999), virtually no research exists on the impact of sex offender laws on victims; specifically, research that explores victim-reported benefit—or harm—as a result of offender registration, notification, residency restrictions, and/or electronic monitoring.

The goal of this chapter is to explore what victims of sexual violence have reported needing and/or wanting from various stakeholders and to ascertain how well—if at all— various sex offender laws have addressed these needs and wants. To this end, 18 survivors of sexual assault were interviewed, as were representatives from five state coalitions against sexual assault. Additionally, as articulated in chapter 4, the story of one victim elaborates on her views of sex offender laws. In that chapter, Patricia Wetterling's views as activist, parent, secondary victim, and policy maker, provide a unique perspective on the evolution of these laws.

To frame this research, first presented is a historical account of rape law reforms from a victim-centered perspective, followed by a brief introduction to the history of crime victims' rights. The existing empirical research on the impact of sex offender laws on victims and the criminal justice system is then presented, followed by an explanation of the research methods employed in this study and the subsequent findings. This chapter concludes with a discussion of possible policy implications for sex offender laws.

Background

Victim Construction and the Legal Redress of Sex Crimes

The social control of sexual behavior is not a new endeavor. Throughout history, societies have sought to establish rules to govern sexuality, rules informed by social norms, values, customs, and sensibilities (Thomas, 2000). Yet, across time, sexual behaviors determined to be morally repugnant or otherwise illegal have not been uniformly defined, policed, or punished (Hamilton, 2004; Thomas, 2000). The development of guidelines for unacceptable sexual behavior and its consequences, while not linear, has long been driven by the goal of controlling a population of offenders believed to be inherently more problematic than other offender types: sex offenders (Thomas, 2000).

Societies have employed various techniques over time to identify, rehabilitate, and/or punish sex offenders. To understand socio-legal changes in the social control of sex offenders—and by extension, sexual assault victims—Garland (1990, 2001) argued that we must begin by understanding the culture in which the social control takes place. It is here, he posited, that we find the necessary context in which to understand the underlying principles and goals of our systems of punishment and control; that a society's system of punishment is reflective of its culture. Punishment illustrates what a culture despises and, conversely, what it values (Ibid).

Arguably, most Americans value both public and personal safety. However, precisely how this value manifests

itself into policy and practice is widely disparate among key
stakeholders charged with addressing sexual violence. Two
groups have been identified as having prominent—and competing—influence in both the redress of sex crimes and the
socio-legal construction of sexual violence: the criminal justice system and feminist organizations.

By design, the criminal justice system sets as its foci
criminal acts and actors. The state is legally identified as the
victim; by default, the true victim is relegated to the status
of witness to her[i] own victimization, her injuries treated as
evidence in bureaucratized criminal proceedings. Under the
legal system model, the state also assumes the role of dispas-
sionate arbiter (Herman, 2005). However, under this same
legal system, there has been little historical consistency in
how, exactly, sex crimes have been adjudicated (Pratt, 2000).
Moreover, identifying who qualifies as a real victim and a real
perpetrator within this system has been largely informed by
misconceptions and cultural stereotypes (Bachman & Paternoster, 1993; Estrich, 1987; Largen, 1988).

Historically, broader structural relations and cultural
systems of gender, race, and power went unexamined and,
therefore, were reinforced (Belknap, 2007; Madriz, 1997).
Under the traditional legal system model of social control,
'real' sex offenders were men who preyed on strangers
and/or belonged to a suspect class (poor, person of color).
'Real' victims were children or virtuous others (white, middle
class, virginal, feminine) whom the public deemed worthy
of compassion and justice (Estrich, 1987; Wood, 2005). As
a result, the first modern wave of legislative action against
sex offenders was foreseeably directed at a class of offender
that would harm these 'real' victims (Lieb, Quinsey, & Berliner, 1998). The first wave of action against sex offenders
was prompted by the rape and murder of two girls, 4 and 8
years old, respectively, in the late 1930s (Ibid). A moral panic
about sex offenders was touched off by the intense attention these crimes received from the media and politicians.
J. Edgar Hoover described this time as one marked by rapidly increasing sex crimes and stated that this was a time
for "sex crimes to be placed under the spotlight and its evils
disclosed" (as quoted in Lieb et al., 1998, p. 53). Moreover, he
urged an "aroused public opinion" of crimes of this nature
and the criminals that commit them (Ibid).

Sexual offenses and offenders had long been studied by criminal justice experts, psychologists, and psychiatrists, but prior to this intense interest in sexual offenses by mainstream society, relatively little attention was paid to these crimes. After these two high-profile sex crimes against children, popular, nonscientific magazines began to run stories about sex crimes and their victims, and people with little to no exposure to information about sexual criminals were now able to read about them regularly (Ibid; Robertson, 2001).

A second moral panic was touched off in 1949 when two girls, this time 6 and 7 years old, were raped and murdered (Lieb et al., 1998). The perception of a wave of sexual crimes prompted officials to seek out advice from psychiatric experts. Robertson (2001) noted the role of the media and politicians in the furor around sex crimes:

> The press and public officials created a type of offender labeled the "sexual psychopath" from what psychiatrists told them. Legislators placed the sexual psychopath at the heart of new laws that provided for psychiatric examinations to identify those dangerous individuals and for the committal of such men for treatment until psychiatrists determined they no longer posed a threat to society. (p. 12)

Sexual psychopathy laws were considered the first social experiment in the United States to merge psychiatry and criminology and were "touted as a scientific, enlightened response to dangerous sex offenders" (Lieb et al., 1998, p. 55). California's sexual psychopathy laws, some of the earliest passed in the United States as well as the most utilized (Dix, 1976), originally applied only to child molesters (Lieb et al., 1998).

Under this model of sex offender redress, the public expressed less sympathy for the majority of adult, female victims. Sutherland (1950) remarked about this unfortunate hierarchy of victimization, "The ordinary citizen can understand fornication or even forcible rape of a woman, [but] a sex attack on an infant or girl must be the act of a fiend or a maniac" (p. 143). As a result of this general societal acceptance of male aggression against females, few offenders who attacked adult females were identified as sex offenders.

Therefore, few laws offered potential victims any protection against a more common and more "socially acceptable" offender type (Robertson, 2001, p. 31). In fact, sexual assault is the one crime for which victims historically have had to prove their innocence before the perpetrator was expected to defend his (Spohn & Horney, 1992; Estrich, 1987). As a result, there has been little incentive for victims to come forward with reports of sexual assault, for fear that they might be subjected to the legal system's "theater of shame" (Herman, 2005, p. 573).

Rape Law Reform and Victims' Interests

For the most part, the criminal justice system operated under this paradigm until the 1970s, when feminists challenged the assumptions underlying this system. Feminist groups began to speak out against more common types of sexual offenses and sexual victimizations. They organized victim rallies, at which they told stories of incest and date rape. They moved the dialogue past the idea of the stranger-rapist and towards the more common intimate-partner violence and intra-familial violence experienced by many (Lieb et al., 1998). The theory of "rape culture"[ii] was introduced to explain the United States' relatively high rates of sexual victimization and offending; that is, sexual violence as the result of institutionalized sexism and objectification of women. This view argued that the only way to adequately stop sexual assault was to stop patriarchy and male privilege in society. This ideology ran counter to that of stopping sexual violence through the increased power of the state via rape laws, policies, and criminal justice practices.

Due to the newly increased visibility of sexual violence, criminal justice system entities such as law enforcement and prosecutors joined feminist efforts for rape law reform. While ideologically misaligned, both camps were invested in advocating for sweeping legislative initiatives aimed at improving crime victim reporting, cooperation, and satisfaction (Bryden & Lengnick, 1997). As co-advocates, they pushed for legal changes to sex crime laws and won them (to varying degrees) in all 50 states (Spohn & Horney, 1992). As a result, rape laws and the treatment of rape victims were reformed through the efforts of a "fragile alliance [of] feminist groups, victim's rights groups, and organizations promoting more general 'law and order' themes" (Bachman & Paternoster, 1993, p. 554).

By the early 1980s, emphasis was given to educating the public on the more prevalent types of sexual assaults, and policy initiatives reflected this. Since 'respectable' men (e.g., fathers, husbands, boyfriends, pastors) were now being identified as sex offenders, more treatment-based sentencing alternatives were advocated under the assumption that this would increase crime victim reporting and cooperation (particularly with child victims) within the criminal justice system; ergo, the victims' needs would be met while simultaneously holding offenders accountable (Lieb et al., 1998). For example, at the urging of treatment providers for both sex offenders and sexual assault victims, the Washington State Sentencing Guideline Commission, in conjunction with the state legislature, created the Special Sex Offender Sentencing Alternative, which allowed for certain offenders to receive community-based treatment and supervision, rather than serve time in prison (Berliner, Schram, Miller, & Milloy, 1995).

Victims' Rights and Roles in Sex Offender Policy

Rape law reform efforts sought to "reflect and legitimate the changing status of women in American society" (Marsh, Geist, & Caplan, 1982, p. 3). This movement to redefine sexual assault and sexual assault victims also called into question the very role of the victim in the criminal justice process. Public discourse during the 1970s and 1980s on the issue of formalized victims' rights was an extension of the public discourse on rape law reform. As Americans came to identify crime as a top-priority social problem, a larger conversation about the appropriate role of victims in informing criminal justice policy began to take place in earnest.

In 1975, the National Organization for Victim Assistance (NOVA) was formed to be a clearinghouse for information for victim service providers. By 1982, the first federal victims' rights legislation, the Victims and Witness Protection Act (VWPA), was passed (Glynn, 2000). Through VWPA, Congress acknowledged the historically poor manner in which victims were treated by the criminal justice system. The purpose of VWPA was

(1) to enhance and protect the necessary role of crime victims and witnesses in the criminal justice process; (2) to ensure that the Federal Government does all that is possible within limits of available resources to assist victims and witnesses of crime without infringing on the constitutional rights of defendants; and (3) to provide a model for legislation for State and local governments. (Pub. L. No. 97-291, § 2)

VWPA charged the U.S. Attorney General's Office with the responsibility of developing and implementing services to victims including case updates, protection, private and secure waiting areas within courthouses, and the return of personal property, while also mandating training for law enforcement on victim issues (U.S. Department of Justice, 2005). VWPA and subsequent legislation, including the Federal Victims of Crime Act of 1984 (VOCA), created a legally recognized victims' bill of rights which includes the right to make a victim impact statement at sentencing, mandatory financial restitution to sexual assault victims, and the establishment of a funding stream for victim service providers (Glynn, 2000; U.S. Department of Justice, 2005). Through VOCA, the Office for Victims of Crime (OVC) was created under the auspices of the Department of Justice as a federal initiative that was "committed to enhancing the Nation's capacity to assist crime victims and to providing leadership in changing attitudes, policies, and practices to promote justice and healing for all victims of crime" (U.S. Department of Justice, July 2000).

Within 10 years of VWPA's passage, no fewer than 7,000 victim advocacy groups had been formed throughout the United States (Glynn, 2000). Today, NOVA has over 5,500 member agencies, including criminal justice agencies, service providers, health professionals, and survivors/victims (Martin, 2005). Approximately 32 states have victims' rights amendments in their constitutions (Herman, 2005). Dozens of crime bills have been passed into law that are named in honor of victims, serving as a symbolic act to recognize their suffering while demonstrating a legislative commitment to the prevention of future victimizations (Wood, 2005).

The victims' rights movement has played a key role in the development of the bevy of sex offender laws that have been enacted over the past 20 years. A combination of high-profile sex crimes, the public's perception of high crime rates, and a growing distrust of the criminal justice system to adequately protect society from criminal threats fueled a legislative era marked by get-tough-on-crime policies; policies that would serve to honor crime victims while simultaneously acknowledging public outrage at the offenders (Garland, 2001).

Sexual violence became more freely discussed than it had been in previous eras, because of the efforts of the women's movement and victim advocacy organizations. Moreover, it was viewed as an increasingly serious crime—one worthy of immediate attention and redress in the name of justice—particularly when it came to child victims. Similar to the intense public attention given to sex crimes during the late 1930s through the 1940s, the 1980s and 1990s saw several high-profile sexual assault cases introduced to the American public in minute detail due to their extensive coverage by the media. As was the case in the 1930s and 1940s, many of these cases involved child victims and gruesome acts of violence. Examples of such high-profile cases include the abduction and murder of Adam Walsh in Florida; the abduction and presumed murder of Johnny Gosh in Iowa; the alleged ritualistic sexual abuse of children in day care centers spanning from California to Massachusetts; the abduction and presumed sexual assault and murder of Jacob Wetterling in Minnesota; the abduction, sexual assault, and murder of Polly Klaas in California; and the sexual assault and murder of Megan Kanka in New Jersey. Despite the rarity of such cases, America again turned its attention back to the rare offender and focused primarily on the child victim.

These cases were the catalyst for the current era of intense and increased attention on sex offenders and victims' rights. Members of the public, particularly survivors of sexual violence and their families, began to look to state legislatures and Congress—not to prison officials or the psychiatric profession as they previously had—to address their concerns (Lieb et al., 1998). The political voice of sexual assault victims grew and was given great deference when determining policy choices. When it came to discussions of what constituted justice, the offender was no longer the sole consideration (Logan, 1999).

The strides made in public policy concerning sexual victimization have been enormous. However, the impact of these laws on victims and victimization trends remain largely unexamined. The following is a discussion of the limited existing research on the impact policy efforts have had on sexual assault victims and the systems that address their needs.

Empirical Research

The Impact of Rape Law Reform on Victims and Criminal Justice Outcomes

According to Herman (2005), victims need "social acknowledgement and support ... a sense of power and control over their own lives ... [and] an opportunity to tell their stories in their own way" (p. 574). The degree to which sex offender laws and rape law reform have adequately addressed these needs has not been widely researched. The research that does exist has identified three key metrics to assessing the effectiveness of sexual assault law reforms: increased comfort and confidence in the reporting of an assault, decreased case attrition rates, and increased conviction rates.

Research findings have been largely inconsistent. Caringella-MacDonald (1984) found a postreform decrease in attrition rates and an increase in conviction rates. Marsh et al. (1982), too, found an increase in conviction rates, but Spohn and Horney (1992) did not. Neither Marsh et al. (1982) nor Polk (1985) found an increase in reporting of sexual assault victimization, but Spohn and Horney did. Overall, Spohn and Horney (1992), whose study was the most extensive at the time, concluded, "The ability of rape reform legislation to produce instrumental change is limited" (p. 173). Moreover, they noted, "Victim-oriented reforms are unlikely to facilitate the smooth and efficient flow of cases through the system, and are likely to conflict with officials' values" (Ibid). While their research did not provide evidence of systemic behavior change, they did proffer that "the passage of reforms sent an important symbolic message regarding the treatment of rape cases and rape victims ... [therefore] this symbolic message may be more important than the instrumental change" (p. 175). As evidence of symbolic change, they noted that several key players in the criminal justice system reported that they no longer felt that victims' sexual histories or social status should be taken into account when determining an official course of action.

Bachman and Paternoster (1993) took this body of research a step further by examining the overall impact of rape reform laws in reporting, sentencing, and the extent to which the more common sexual offense (acquaintance rape) is actually adjudicated when compared to other violent crime types. Using both official and unofficial data, they concurred with Spohn and Horney's (1992) conclusion that rape law reform has had little impact on either victim behavior or criminal justice system practices. Bachman and Paternoster (1993) did find a slight increase in the likelihood of an offender (including an acquaintance rapist) being sentenced to prison. They also found a slight increase in victim reporting of sexual assault and speculated that this may indicate a symbolic effect of rape law reform "[in] a reduction ... in rape victims' perceptions that the legal process would stigmatize them" (p. 574).

What is the victim's perspective on the impact of these laws on their experiences, needs, and desires? As sex offender legislation has continued to grow over the past two decades in both numbers and scope—with justice for victims as the ostensible goal—very little is known about how this new class of sexual assault laws impacts victims' needs or desires. The following is a presentation of the research methods and findings from the present study that sought to address this question.

Methodology

Within the past two decades, various rape law reforms and sexual assault laws have attempted to redress sexually criminal behavior, ostensibly from a more victim-centered perspective than in the past. This assumes that victims' needs and desires are understood and accurately represented by these laws. However, given this unchecked assumption, justice assumed may be justice denied.

In order to better understand what victims need and/or want, 18 sexual assault victims were interviewed in depth. Additionally, representatives from five state coalitions against sexual assault (CASA) were interviewed to ascertain how well they believed sex offender laws assisted or impeded victim services.

Sample Demographics

An initial convenience sample of 21 victim participants was secured through professional and personal acquaintances. After three subjects declined to complete participation, 18 victim interviews were conducted. Most interviews took place in face-to-face meetings lasting approximately 1 1/2 hours. Eight interviews took place over the telephone. Victim participants were asked a series of open-ended questions about their experiences with sexual victimization, what they wanted and needed from informal and formal support networks, and what adjudication they wanted for their offender(s). They were also asked their opinion on the effectiveness of various sex offender laws to help past victims or to prevent future victimizations.

The group consisted of two men and sixteen women, ranging in age from 18 to 71 years old. The group was racially and ethnically homogeneous, except for one African American, one Latina, and one Middle Eastern person. All others identified as white. Nine were married or otherwise partnered, one was engaged, seven were single or dating, and one was divorced. Nine participants were parents. Two participants held high school degrees, eight had some college or were college graduates, four were pursuing college degrees, and four held advanced degrees. Four were retirees, with the rest actively involved in either paid labor or unpaid, family-related labor. For two participants, victimization influenced their chosen professions, social work and victim advocacy. Three participants were involved in volunteer work serving sexual assault survivors.

Victimizations took place in childhood for five participants, for four during adolescence, for five during college, and for two in post college adulthood. Two participants had been victimized at multiple times throughout their lives, by multiple assailants. Eight participants survived ongoing acts of abuse. Ten survived one-time acts of sexual violence. Almost all of the participants knew their assailants. Only one subject was sexually assaulted by a stranger. One was assaulted by a man she had met on the day of her attack. Eight were assaulted by family members. Three were assaulted by neighbors or family friends, and five were assaulted by husbands, boyfriends, dates, or acquaintances.

Seven state sexual assault coalitions were invited to participate in this study, as well. In selecting coalitions to solicit for interviews, criteria included geographic dispersion, population size, and varied sex offender legislative initiatives (past and present). Five state coalitions accepted the invitation to be interviewed, one each from the West Coast, the Southwest, the Midwest, the Northeast, and the Southeast. All victim respondents in this research are identified by a pseudonym, and state coalitions are simply referred to as "CASA" to retain each participant's confidentiality.

The following sections describe key elements that have been identified by sexual assault victims and/or by victim advocacy organizations in both adequately meeting victims' needs and desires and in coordinating an effective social response to addressing sexual violence.

Results

Supportive Disclosure Opportunities

Without exception, respondents identified disclosure as a critical element in both assisting sexual assault victims in their recovery and preventing future victimizations by making it acceptable to talk publicly about something about which they feel immense shame. Participants identified as a key need of victims the opportunity to disclose their victimization without feeling judged or rejected by family, friends, or the criminal justice system. Additionally, they wanted to have control over how, when, and to whom this information was shared.

The National Women's Study (NWS), a longitudinal survey of over 4,000 adult women, reported that 71% of sexual assault victims fear their families finding out about their assault; 68% fear friends or others finding out (Kilpatrick et al., 1992). Victims were concerned because they feared they would be blamed—at least in part—for their own victimization (Ibid). Daane (2005) reported that the response victims receive from the first people to whom they disclose greatly impacts their recovery process. If a victim discloses to a supportive, nonjudgmental source, she is more likely to seek out support services to aid in long-term recovery and less likely to blame herself.

Blame, Shame, and Labeling

Throughout victim interviews, respondents reported that they dreaded disclosure to any party because they believed they would be harshly judged and/or blamed for their own victimization. This fear was well-grounded, as many did receive harsh judgment from family, friends, and/or the criminal justice system. While most participants (12) reported disclosing their victimization to family members, most also identified this as a painful experience made worse by family members' reactions, which ranged from lukewarm to hostile. Some loved ones implied or overtly alleged guilt on the part of the victim (especially if the assault involved another family member). Others focused on why the victim waited to disclose the information, rather than on why the victim was disclosing in the first place.

Sharice, a 25-year-old graduate student from Mississippi, was assaulted repeatedly by a neighbor when she was 8 years old. Not knowing exactly what was happening to her, she assumed that the behavior was wrong because it involved nudity. Being raised in a strict household with a Baptist preacher for a father, she decided to disclose the abuse. Because of his response, she reported that she never talked about the abuse again until after taking a women's studies course in college:

> My daddy was quiet at first when I told him. He's a Baptist preacher so he tried to turn this into some kind of learning exercise. He told me that since I was so grown [physically developed] at such a young age I needed to mind myself like a lady; that what had happened to me was a message to "get right with God." I didn't know I was "wrong" with him. (Personal interview, January 4, 2008)

Sharice explained that for several years she assumed that she had brought violence upon herself. In high school, she experienced both emotional and physical abuse at the hands of boyfriends. She stated in her interview that she accepted this behavior as "just the way it is" (Ibid). In her women's studies course, she read about the prevalence and incidence rate of sexual violence. She was introduced to theories of violence that did not place her at the center of explanation or blame. Armed with this knowledge and new language to discuss what she experienced, she talked about her victimization with a few college friends and learned that they, too, had either been molested as children or knew someone who had. She reported taking great comfort in knowing that she was not alone in her experience, but also being saddened by this fact. She is convinced that if more victims felt comfortable disclosing their assaults, that fewer assailants would "get away with it" (Ibid). To her knowledge, her abuser was never turned in to the authorities, and he lives in the same house he did when she was growing up. She still identifies as a devout Baptist.

Four participants disclosed their victimization to law enforcement agencies. Rebecca, a 44-year-old professor, was sexually assaulted by a date in college and immediately reported it to the local police. She explained the police's response to her disclosure:

> They looked me up and down, incredulous and disinterested at the same time. They told me I didn't "look" like I'd just been raped and wondered if it wasn't just a misunderstanding between me and my date. They asked if I really wanted to "cry rape" on "some poor guy." I have never recovered from that. I don't know what's worse: the rape or the insulting way I was treated afterwards. (Personal interview, December 1, 2007)

Rebecca is open about her experience with sexual assault and occasionally uses it as a teaching tool in her classes. As a result, not infrequently, students come to her with disclosures of sexual victimization. She stated that because of her negative experience with the police, she cautions students against filing a formal complaint with the police without having with them a support person who can forcefully advocate for their rights. Rebecca believes police reaction to assault allegations depends on the personality of the local police department—not sex offender laws—observing that law enforcement agencies in college towns handle sexual violence differently than do police departments that serve a different demographic. She does not believe that, generally, the sex offender legislation of the past decade has provided any improvement of victim treatment or rights that she would define as "meaningful" (Ibid). She clarified her opinion by stating,

It's complete political bullshit to say that these so-called get-tough-on-crime sex offender laws are supposed to somehow help victims. If they [politicians] wanted to help victims, they'd address issues like free or affordable [mental health] services ... access to safe housing, and comprehensive sex ed[ucation] in the schools. They just pass these laws to get reelected. (Ibid)

Ashley, a 23-year-old advertising assistant who was sexually assaulted during an off-campus mixer between her sorority and a fraternity, had a much more positive experience with law enforcement. She immediately disclosed the assault to the privately hired security personnel who were working the mixer. They informed the local police department, and an investigation was instigated. Ashley reported that she received both support from her sorority sisters and simultaneous pressure from them to drop the charges. She stated,

They were all, like, "We totally believe you and love you but he was drunk and so were you." They didn't want there to be bad feelings between the [sorority] house and the [fraternity]. Even though it's a huge campus, everyone in the Greek system knows everyone else at [this university]. I didn't want to be known as the girl who got [offender] in trouble. (Personal interview, December 2, 2007)

According to Ashley, because she was a freshman at the time of the assault, she was convinced that her remaining college years would be marred by this experience if she pursued criminal charges. Her family agreed with her and encouraged her to "just move on and put this behind me" (Ibid). She remained in the sorority for a short time following the assault but decided to deactivate after feeling that her sisters had betrayed her by showing tacit support for her perpetrator. She stated that the police treated her very well and listened carefully to her. She appreciated the way her case was handled by the detectives.

Others who disclosed their victimization to family, but not law enforcement, were often advised by loved ones to move on and to put the assault behind them, as Ashley had been. Three respondents, two women and one man, had been molested as children by uncles. When they told their parents about the abuse, each was told the same thing: we will make sure the abuse will stop, we will get you therapy or support, and we do not want to continue to talk about this because it is upsetting to the family.

Piroz, a male, 27-year-old business professional whose family is from Iran, explained that he was told that the punishment for the uncle would far outweigh the harm he, as the victim, experienced. He was told that he should just be quiet and not dishonor the family:

> Family is everything in our culture ... I was raised in the States, but everyone else in my family still follows Iranian culture and customs. If I were to go against [these customs], I would have been seen as the problem, not my uncle. Mostly, I was just afraid that [the sexual abuse] made me gay, but I couldn't talk about it with anyone because in my family's culture you do not talk about sexuality and certainly not homosexuality. I think they still kill people in Iran for being gay. (Personal interview, December 11, 2007)

Piroz felt that as a result of his victimization, his sexuality and masculinity were questionable or suspect, a common fear among male sexual abuse survivors (Dumond & Dumond, 2002). In college, Piroz spoke with a college professor about his experiences and stated that he was relieved to have someone tell him that his assault did not have anything to do with his sexual orientation, which he identified as heterosexual. He stated that throughout high school and college he felt as though he always needed a girlfriend to "prove to myself that I'm straight" (Ibid). He reported that he does not seek out information about the prevalence of male sexual assault victims or support services because he fears that "people will find out and I'll have to explain myself" (Ibid).

Molly, an 18-year-old college student who was sexually assaulted at the age of 15 by a young man whom she had met earlier on the day of her assault, concurred with Piroz about wanting support to help understand the victimization, but not wanting to disclose or to be labeled a sexual assault victim:

> Anytime sexual assault would be brought up on TV or in school, I always wondered if I had a big red flag on my face that said "rape victim" ... I wondered, "Do they know something is wrong with me?" I sort of got the message

that a rape victim was a victim because they were doing something wrong and the consequence was rape. (Personal interview, February 29, 2008)

Conflicting Loyalties

When a family member or loved one is the perpetrator, disclosure—and what will come of it—becomes more complicated for victims. Conflicting loyalties are a serious concern for many sexual assault victims and their families. Many victims know—and even love—their offenders. Consequently, they fear disclosing because they are unsure what will come of it. Some families do not support disclosure because any sanctions against the offender may negatively impact the entire family in profound ways. According to two CASAs, sex offender laws such as residency restrictions and juvenile offender registration have inadvertently created a disincentive for victims to disclose. A Midwest CASA said,

> We're predicting a decrease in reporting due to the various sex offender laws ... [The laws] disallow discretion and discretion is needed ... [Sex offending] disrupts the entire family ... There needs to be a middle ground. We've lost focus on treatment and only focus on punishment. (Personal interview, March 4, 2008)

Those victimized by family members want the abuse to stop—not necessarily for their abuser to be imprisoned. Because legal sanctions have been elevated in profound ways for almost every sexual offense category, some victims and their families are hesitating to disclose because they fear that there are no intermediate interventions available. Victims and/or their families fear that the offending family member will go to prison, thereby depriving their loved ones of a breadwinner. In families where the abuse was at the hands of a juvenile, they fear that the youth will be required to register as a sex offender and will, therefore, be "branded" for life despite being potentially amenable to treatment. As a byproduct, then, victims receive less or no supportive services, and perpetrators go untreated and unaccountable. The West Coast CASA noted an increase in defense attorneys counseling their clients to refuse plea bargains and/or guilty pleas "because the stakes are so high" (Personal interview, March 5, 2008).

Amelia, a 28-year-old lawyer from a prominent family, was molested by her uncle when she was approximately 11. When her parents learned of the abuse, they put her in therapy but did not press charges or cease contact with the perpetrator. During her teens, she developed an eating disorder and was hospitalized. Because she refused to continue with therapy and her parents refused to cut her uncle out of her life, the juvenile courts ordered her into a residential treatment center (RTC), where she lived for over a year with youth adjudicated for crimes ranging from armed robbery to drive-by shootings. Her placement in the RTC reinforced to her that she, not her abuser, did something wrong. Amelia explained her reaction to her family's handling of her abuse:

> I'm pretty sure what messed me up the most was the fact that my parents picked him over me ... They showed more loyalty to him ... They were so afraid that if anyone found out [about the molestation], our "good name" would be ruined ... [My uncle] was in business with my dad, so if he went to jail, the family's finances would collapse ... I didn't want his life to be over—I just wanted him to admit what he did was wrong. (Personal interview, March 2, 2008)

Iris, a 29-year-old doctoral candidate, was sexually assaulted when she was 12 by her brother's best friend, during a sleepover. She was conflicted about the assault, she explained:

> I didn't want it to happen, but I was afraid and didn't know what to do ... I was embarrassed and didn't want to get in trouble and I didn't want to get him in trouble ... If he had been held accountable, I would have felt bad because he was a friend. (Personal interview, February 7, 2008)

Overwhelmingly, respondents offered that providing victims with supportive and varied opportunities and outlets for disclosure was the most crucial need yet to be adequately met for sexual assault victims. Moreover, they wanted some control in deciding what sanctions to impose against their perpetrator, whether that be court-ordered therapy or prison. Respondents largely agreed that expanding statutes of limitations on sexual abuse cases was beneficial, but none thought this legal reform would have made a difference in their cases. In fact, most victim respondents were unaware what specific laws and/or legal reforms have been initiated over the past two decades on behalf of sexual abuse victims.

When given examples of these reforms (e.g., Megan's Law, Jessica's Law), several subjects nodded to acknowledge familiarity with what these laws attempt to accomplish. Others rolled their eyes, seemingly in exasperation. Tammy, a 41-year-old, stay-at-home mother who was molested repeatedly by her father, explained her dissatisfaction with laws that attempt to restrict where a sex offender can live: "I get why people care about where an offender lives. I've got kids and I care, but my offender lived in my house. No law was going to change that—at least not one that was being enforced" (Personal interview, February 10, 2008). Two CASAs proffered that the general expansion in size and scope of sex offender laws was unnecessary, that the laws that already existed were sufficient—they were simply poorly implemented. They attributed this poor implementation largely to criminal justice actors who were uninformed or misinformed about sexual assault, in general, and about sex offenders and victims, in particular.

Accurate Public Education and Awareness

Victim participants in this study observed that a well-informed and accurately informed public would be more likely to believe victim disclosures and to respond to the effects of sexual abuse. Victims, in turn, would feel more comfortable asking for the support and help that they needed. Tammy stated, "All the signs [of molestation] were there, I was just waiting for someone to notice them ... to save me ... for someone—anyone—to ask the right questions" (Ibid).

Carol, a 63-year-old retiree, was sexually assaulted when she was 21, while on a date with a man who was considered in her hometown to be "quite a catch" (Personal interview, December 30, 2007). She reported that some years later she learned,

> Apparently, everyone in town knew he had his way with women—that's what they called it—but no one ever did

anything about it. He was from a nice family and was so handsome ... If that boy had been forced to list his whereabouts [on a public sex offender registry], I doubt anyone would have acted any differently towards him or his family. It's like because he didn't look like a rapist, he wasn't one. (Ibid)

All CASAs interviewed for this study observed that one of the most confounding impacts of sex offender laws is their power to misinform the public about the issue of sexual violence. As a result of these laws, several coalitions believe that the public is actually less safe from sexual abuse. The Southeast CASA noted, "[These laws] shift the focus from the majority of offenses to the minority" (Personal interview, March 28, 2008). The Southwest CASA observed, "[These laws] intended to keep people safe, but they don't work ... Now the public is afraid" (Personal interview, March 24, 2008). Coalitions identified two areas in which sexual assault education has been done a disservice by sex offender laws: (1) the construction of sexual assault risk—who poses it, who faces it, and how to mitigate it—and (2) the reinforcement of a victim hierarchy that demeans most victims.

Misunderstood Victimization Risk

By drawing public attention and scrutiny towards the most egregious offenders and offenses, sex offender laws detract attention and scrutiny from the most common type of offenders and victims. It is this detraction that potentially decreases public safety and increases victimization risk. The Northeast CASA offered, "If these sex offender laws have done anything, they have confused the public by emphasizing the least common offender" (Personal interview, March 21, 2008). The West coast CASA stated, "Vulnerability [for sexual abuse] is actually reinforced by these laws because it turns the attention [of the public and the criminal justice system towards] one-percent of the crime" (Personal interview, March 5, 2008). The Southwest CASA argued that laws such as sex offender notification, offender GPS tracking, and residency restrictions have actually impeded public safety because they have reinforced to the public grossly inaccurate depictions of the type of sexual assault risk one is most likely to face. The Southwest CASA noted that by focusing on the "stranger danger" myth, people are less aware of a more likely assailant: a person they know. These myths, in turn, have created a public demand for sexual assault risk mitigation (e.g., residency restrictions, offender registries and notification) aimed at particularly scary, but unlikely, threats.

All five CASAs interviewed have independently and publicly denounced residency restriction laws, describing them as "irresponsible," and "counterproductive," on the grounds that they provide the public with a false sense of security and serve to reinforce stereotypes about the typical offender and the typical victim. The Midwest CASA noted that some family members of well-known victims, such as Megan Kanka and Jacob Wetterling, have acknowledged the harm of the unintended consequences of the laws named on behalf of their loved ones. The majority of the victim respondents in this study knew their offenders and disclosed to family their victimization; yet most victims maintained (by force or default) at least some contact with the offender, either because he was family or because their accusation was not entirely believed. None of the research subjects' offenders were ever prosecuted or convicted; therefore, none would have been subject to sex offender residency restrictions, registration, or public notification. This finding is consistent with the literature, which finds systematic underreporting of sexual violence. Therefore, these laws would have done nothing to assist these victims or the potential future victims of their assailants.

Various CASAs stated that, while public discourse on sexual victimization has increased (in part due to sex offender laws), the way sex offenders are discussed is problematic. All of the CASAs interviewed offered that sex offenders are often publicly depicted "as if they are all the same." Sex offender laws have been widely applied to a variety of offender types, with little public education of the various aggregates and the various risks each poses. As an example, the Midwest CASA observed that the blanket label of "sex offender" does not take into account the important differences (in response to treatment, recidivism, etc.) between offenders on a public registry, one of whom is a diagnosed pedophile and the other a 19-year-old statutory offender. Without receiving accurate information and education on the variety of offender types, the public is left at a disadvantage as to how to best mitigate sexual victimization risk. Consequently, hypervigilance is used against those who are the least likely to offend (strangers) and guards are dropped around those most likely to offend (nonstrangers).

While casting a broad net over all sexual offenses, sex offender laws simultaneously reinforce a narrow construction of what sexual behavior is inappropriate and unacceptable: that only forced sexual contact with a stranger that results in grave bodily harm is a 'real' assault, and that only child victims are 'real' victims. Thereby, a social blind spot to the most common types of victimizations is sustained. According to the Southeast CASA,

> Victims need to be heard about a broad range of victimizations. If they don't, it makes it harder to come forward ... [The laws] reinforce the notion that [the justice system, public, and service providers] are only interested in a specific offender type ... [Advocates] need to say, "What you're seeing is only one piece of the issue." (Personal interview, March 28, 2008)

Reinforcement of the Victim Hierarchy

Some sex offender laws have served to reify a victim hierarchy—that is, a spectrum of victim types categorized according to the sympathy (or lack thereof) each evokes from the public and policy makers. Laws named in honor of certain sexual assault victims inadvertently prioritize the suffering of one victim type over the suffering of another (Wood, 2005). The victims for whom these laws have been named do not reflect the common story of victimization or victim type. The implication is that these were truly innocent victims and, therefore, their victimization is deserving of public acknowledgment, more so than that of other victim types (Ibid). As a result, several CASAs reported that they and the service providers they support have heard from victims that they do not see any reflection of self in many of the sex offender laws named for victims. This has made it hard for some victims to acknowledge and act upon their needs for support and self-care because their assaults were not as 'bad' as those suffered by victims for whom laws were named. The West Coast CASA stated, "Individual stories need to be honored, but balanced with what we know about all victims ...

We shouldn't have a law that simultaneously honors one victim type while disregarding other victim types" (Personal interview, March 5, 2008). The Southeast CASA noted, "The victim hierarchy is reinforced with [these laws] ... A secondary victimization is that the majority of victims do not see their experiences reflected in sex offender laws" (Personal interview, March 28, 2008).

Nine years ago, Rose, now 51 years old, was brutally beaten and raped by a stranger after leaving her second job as a janitor at an office building late one evening. She was duct taped to a dumpster and assaulted at knifepoint. Her assailant carved a sign into her upper thigh with a coat hanger and told her it was so "you'll never forget me." When police arrived on the scene, they did not immediately free her hands or cover her exposed body; they were concerned with preserving evidence. Only after the crime scene was recorded was she cut free, covered, and then transported to the hospital. After several hours of receiving medical treatment and giving statements to the police, she was left to find her own ride home. Three months after the assault, she learned that during the attack, her perpetrator infected her with HIV.

During her attack, she was instructed to make sexual comments to her perpetrator, comments that she was instructed to repeat to the detectives who interviewed her. She stated that these comments were "indecent and vulgar" (Personal interview, February 13, 2008). She was so disturbed by having to say them and then repeat them to the police that she reported brushing her teeth repeatedly afterwards. While she stated that repeating these vulgar comments to investigators was humiliating, she was bothered more by the way the investigators responded to her:

> I was brought up to be a lady ... It bothered me to be treated as less than that. I was raised to never use that kind of language; in fact, a lot of what was said to me I had never heard before that night ... The police looked at me like I was crazy for being embarrassed to use this type of language with them or for being unfamiliar with it ... I took this as an assumption about my character ... They acted like they didn't believe me when I told them that I just don't talk about my body in that way ... They were so used to dealing with things like this, they couldn't understand why their questions were so hard for me. (Ibid)

According to Kilpatrick et al. (2007), "Victims are most likely to receive sensitive treatment when they are 'good victims,' meaning that they were raped by a stranger who used a weapon and were sober at the time of the assault" (Scope and Key Characteristics of Rape Cases ¶ 2). Despite fitting this description, Rose did not feel that she was treated with sensitivity or compassion by law enforcement or other criminal justice actors. She suspects that the officers thought they were doing their job well by vigorously investigating her case. She believes that it never occurred to the investigators that she was not "a case," but a human from whom "the soul [was] taken" (Personal interview, February 13, 2008). She explained what she wanted and needed from the police after her victimization:

> I wanted them to treat me like an individual, like a human being—not some case number or opportunity for career advancement. I wanted them to explain to me why they were doing what they were doing, and asking what they were asking. I wanted them to ask my permission to ask me certain questions—I just wasn't ready or prepared when they were ready. (Ibid)

Ironically, because Rose was identified by law enforcement as a 'good' victim, and by prosecutors as a 'good' case, her experience was processed by the criminal justice system with the offender in mind, not her. Even though the circumstances of her assault placed her somewhere near the top of the victim hierarchy, the 'sensitive' treatment she received from the criminal justice system was focused on catching her perpetrator— with little attention paid to her recovery. Eighteen months after her assault, her perpetrator was identified while being held on another criminal offense. Rose reported that she wanted desperately to confront her attacker, to ask him why he picked her. She wanted him to take responsibility for his actions and for the criminal justice system to hold him accountable. Before he could be tried, he died of AIDS complications. She noted, "Before he died his defense attorney asked the prosecuting attorney, 'Well, how do we know that *she* didn't give *him* HIV?'" (Ibid). Rose's attack and subsequent HIV infection took place before mandatory HIV testing and reporting in sexual assault cases. She strongly supports mandatory testing and enhanced penalties for offenders who knowingly expose their victims to HIV. She also thinks that restitution should be paid by the offender to a community-based AIDS foundation or support service. Moreover, she supports the development of services specifically designed for people infected during the course of a crime: "I tried to get services from the local AIDS support group but it was mainly geared towards gay men ... They didn't really know how to treat me ... I felt even more alienated" (Ibid). Rose did not express concern for the privacy rights of the offender; rather, she holds as a paramount priority the need for victims to receive immediate and adequate health care to prevent further physical and mental harm:

> [The offender's HIV status] is a base to go off of ... It's informational and can offer some relief to the victim. If [the offender's HIV status] is known, [the victim] is maybe spared one less intrusive procedure ... She doesn't have to go back [to the hospital]. (Ibid)

She explained that whereas it took her time to talk openly about her victimization, she still keeps her HIV status private. On occasions when she selectively disclosed being HIV-positive, she was rejected by some family members. Additionally, she was dismissed by a long-time employer, an act she believes was the direct result of her HIV status disclosure.

Again, being the 'good' victim had its disadvantages for Rose; it meant that her case was scrutinized throughout various stages in the criminal justice process, scrutiny that introduced her to more avenues for secondary assaults. Rose eventually became a victim advocate, in part to educate criminal justice actors on how *not* to treat a sexual assault victim. She did not believe that her treatment as a victim or the processing of her case indicated that rape reform efforts or sex offender laws made criminal justice actors more victim oriented or better educated about the impact of sexual assault on victims—even for someone at the top of the victim hierarchy.

Immediate and Long-term Victim Services

Respondents in this study identified a strong need for both immediate and long-term, sustainable support services for both themselves and for loved ones traumatized as secondary victims. Immediately after her assault, Ashley received a medical exam by a Sexual Assault Nurse Examiner (SANE) who she described as "someone who seemed really safe" (Personal interview, December 2, 2007). SANE programs, while not widespread, were identified by many of the CASAs interviewed to be exceptionally important agents in providing compassionate victim treatment and in assisting criminal justice processes by their careful collection of forensic evidence. Several CASAs noted that SANE programs were developed before widespread sex offender legislative initiatives, but that these initiatives may have improved SANE visibility. Still, the Northeast CASA explained why some hospitals are hesitant to get involved with SANE programs:

> No one wants to be affiliated with sexual assault victims ... Hospitals want to be known as centers for excellence in cardiac care—not for excellence in sexual assault care ... There is a stigma even amongst the medical profession about sexual assault victims. (Personal interview, March 21, 2008)

Sustainable Access to Services and Support

Several participants observed that their healing has been a process, noting that although immediate assistance from a victim advocate is helpful, access to free, confidential, long-term therapy services and/or support groups was more helpful. Rose, a woman of strong religious faith, reported that she felt God had left her during her assault. Some well-intentioned but uninformed members of her religious community made unhelpful and hurtful comments about her assault and recovery process, such as, "God doesn't give anyone anything more than they can handle" (Personal interview, February 13, 2008). She did not find informed or sustained support within a community she considered to be primary in her life. Despite this, she reported that "my pastor was my "rock" (Ibid). She found a support group through her county's victim service agency, a group she described as something that "became sacred to me" (Ibid). She observed:

> Most of my initial supporters didn't last ... They kept expecting me to "get over it." For 1 to 2 years after my assault, I couldn't make decisions ... I thought I was

going nuts ... My pastor formed what he called "a circle of love" consisting of people who stayed with me on and off ... Others wrote down directions or maps or grocery lists to help me do the mundane things I needed to do ... My long-term support network helped me focus on "celebrating" a year, 2 years, etc., of success rather than focusing on it being 1 year, etc., since my assault. (Ibid)

Molly did not tell anyone about her assault or seek therapeutic services until 1 year after her assault, when she went from a straight-A student to a struggling one. In therapy, she came to realize that she had internalized the message that she was to blame for her victimization. Her school work suffered, and she assumed it was her fault that boyfriends were unfaithful. Over months of counseling, she came to believe that she was not to blame—that her offender took something away from her that was hers alone to give. While therapy was helpful in teaching her how to communicate her feelings, she did not find in it the support she needed to deal with the day-to-day effects of sexual assault. She credits her volunteer work as a victim advocate as the key to her long-term recovery success:

At first, volunteering was about meeting my own needs ... clandestinely ... The more I learned [in training], the better I felt ... Now whenever I work with a victim, I tell her all the things I wish someone would have told me, I do the things I wish someone would have done for me ... When I hear someone's story, it's reassuring to know that I'm not alone. I try to put myself in their shoes and treat them the way I wish I had been treated. (Personal interview, February 29, 2008)

By finding a sustainable support network, Molly has slowly become more comfortable talking about the victimization she suffered 3 years ago. She noted that every time she talks about her assault, "There is a little less weight on my shoulders" (Ibid).

Donald, a 71-year-old, retired social worker, was physically abused by his father and sexually abused by his mother, by a hired hand on his parent's farm, and by a neighbor. He did not receive any supportive services to help him work through these experiences until well into his career as a social worker. He attributed this to a combination of being both ashamed about and uneducated on sexual abuse. He said,

> In those days, no one talked about anything like that; it was all hush-hush. You practically had to kill someone to get into trouble. A man basically owned his family and had the right to use physical control ... I came to grips about the physical abuse much earlier than I did about the sexual stuff ... I was already a practicing social worker when during a professional workshop where I had to talk about some personal information, a colleague said to me, "You're a sexual abuse victim, you just don't realize it." At first I denied it, but then it all made sense. (Personal interview, February 19, 2008)

Donald reported that because of a lack of support services and education about the effects of sexual abuse, he spent a lot of his adult life feeling angry, inadequate, and primarily interested in his own needs. He confessed that he participated in sexual activities "that I'm ashamed of ... stuff that probably could've landed me in jail" (Ibid). He wondered aloud during his interview what his life would have been like if he had received the services he needed to appropriately deal with his abuse. His first marriage, which ended after 18 years, was by his description completely unhealthy. He feels that he was not the father to his children that he would have liked to be, and that when his children were born, "I did not know what love was, so I didn't know how to give love" (Ibid). After receiving the support and treatment that he needed to aid his recovery from both physical and sexual abuse, he reported, he remarried and now enjoys a healthy marriage, which has lasted several years. He acknowledged that although he cannot change the way he parented his children when they were young, he has come to terms with his relationships with them as adults. He identified two key figures in helping him begin his long journey toward recovery before he was even aware of his recovery needs: a schoolteacher he had as a teenager and a college administrator he met in seminary. Although he never disclosed his abuse to either party, he stated that they told him what he longed to hear his whole life: that he was a person of value who deserved good things in life. He stated, "When you grow up abused, you assume there is something wrong with you. [These two people] didn't just *not* reject me like every other adult in my life; they *accepted* me" (Ibid). Donald stated that if victims do not feel that they can disclose their experiences and seek out therapeutic services or do not have access to services, they have little hope for a healthy life. He stated that in his practice as a social worker, he saw first-hand the impact of sexual abuse on a person's trajectory in life.

Secondary Victims

Although some respondents reported that their disclosures were met with initial support from friends or family, several stated that eventually they felt pressured to get over it. Their initial support systems were frustrated and/or fatigued by their continual needs for emotional support and reassurance. Many faced questions such as "How long was I going to 'let' this [victimization] control me?" "Why can't I just forget about the whole thing?" or "Why can't I just move on?"

Several subjects attributed these responses to a lack of general understanding of sexual abuse; others observed that their loved ones were also impacted by their victimization but did not realize it and, therefore, did not receive any services to address their own trauma. As a result, several victims reported being put in a caretaker role for *their* caretaker. Some participants reported feeling as though they needed to comfort their confidant because he or she was upset at learning of the victimization.

Rose stated that her weekly support group meeting was the only place where she did not have to worry about taking care of other people. Several respondents reported having to jockey for control over what the confidant would do with the information. Iris noted, "I never got the right reaction … I wanted them to be concerned with me, but they kept focusing on him … He's not the person I wanted to talk about" (Personal interview, February 7, 2008).

Some respondents reported well-intentioned boyfriends or fathers wanting to hunt down their attacker and beat him up. Although some victims appreciated the sentiment, none thought that it would have benefited them. Patricia, a 38-year-old, stay-at-home parent, was molested by a boy in her neighborhood when she was 11 years old. She noted,

When I told my dad [about the assault] I thought he was going to go through the roof. He was so mad, stomping around, saying stuff like, "I'll kill him—I don't care if I do go to jail!" At first, this made me feel safe, like he would really protect me, but then I was sick with worry that he would do something [to the assailant] and would go to jail, leaving me alone. (Personal interview, January 2, 2008)

Some resented having to refocus their confidant's attention away from their offender, and back onto them. Veronica, a 21-year-old college student, was sexually assaulted by an acquaintance. She explained the impact of having to meet the emotional needs of her fiancé: "He was a secondary victim ... and had a Superman complex ... He wanted to fix everything ... He wanted revenge ... This didn't help me heal ... His actions just brought it all back up ... I was afraid he would retaliate [against the offender]" (Personal interview, February 14, 2008).

Veronica speculated that her fiancé's strong reaction was due in part to the judgmental and/or nonsupportive reaction she received from campus security, college administrators, medical personnel, and local law enforcement. She was surprised that despite all of the energy and attention given to sex crimes, by both policy makers and the media, she still struggled to find support within the criminal justice system: "The nurse was hostile ... The cop who interviewed me treated me like I was a suspect ... He was blunt and demanding ... The college just wanted it to go away ... He got away scot-free, and this will stick with me forever" (Ibid). She takes some comfort in knowing that because she refused to be silent about how as a sexual assault victim she was failed at every turn, her college has instituted sweeping changes in how sexual assaults are now handled on campus.

Resources for Services

According to several of the coalitions interviewed, the majority of state funds earmarked to address sexual violence are directed to agencies that provide services to offenders, thereby leaving fewer resources available for victim services. The West Coast CASA offered that an enormous number of resources are used for initiatives such as offender GPS tracking, with absolutely no corresponding increase in material support for victim services—yet these are the very laws named for victims:

> [Sex offender laws] have provided zero increase in support for victims in material forms. [These laws] didn't add victim funds ... Victims have not benefited from most sex offender laws ... [These laws] haven't done for sexual violence what O.J. did for domestic violence. (Personal interview, March 5, 2008)

The Midwest CASA reported that its state is outside the norm in that it has seen an increase in funding streams for victim services, but noted that the funding opportunities are not on par with funding for offenders: "The money for victim services is a drop in the bucket compared to the money for offenders ... Legislators believe that sex offender laws are inherently victim focused ... [By passing them] they can 'check off' that constituency" (Personal interview, March 4, 2008).

The West Coast CASA noted the exorbitant amount of state money—$25 million—spent in 2007 on a class of offender deemed the most rare: the sexually violent predator. This spending in turn created some tension between those who treat offenders and those who treat victims. This CASA observed, "Victims aren't necessarily aware of the exact money spent on sex offenders, but they do know that [victim] services aren't available and that there is a long wait to process their evidence" (Personal interview, March 5, 2008). The Northeast CASA explained that the reason victim services are not adequately funded is that there has not been the public outcry to do so. Despite a lack of evidence supporting the notion that sex offender laws actually achieve their intended outcomes, the Northeast CASA has been cautious when publicly opposing sex offender legislation for fear that it may lose funding in retaliation:

> If a policy is problematic, we'll say so; we're not afraid to do that, but we have to be very specific about why we're against it. We're a nonprofit, grant-funded entity. A number of state agencies are our funders; some of these agencies have contrary relationships; it's adversarial

sometimes. This has the potential to create a funding issue. We can't be too political, but by doing that, we *are* being political. (Personal interview, March 21, 2008)

In light of expensive offender initiatives, victim services in some states have had to turn to unexpected sources to generate funds. According to the Southwest CASA, in 2007 a bill was passed in its state to tax the adult entertainment industry in order to fund sexual assault programs aimed at prevention, research, and treatment. It has been estimated that this will generate approximately $40 million annually, with the first $12.5 million earmarked for sexual assault victim services. Similarly, the Illinois state legislature is currently considering a bill that would require patrons at strip clubs to pay a tax, referred to as a "pole tax," to fund victim services. This initiative was introduced in an effort to ease the burden of a looming budget crisis at rape crisis centers because of a $1.4 million cut in federal funding (Colindres, 2008). The Southeast CASA noted that its state is considering a similar initiative to complement the limited funds currently available for sexual assault victims and their service providers. The Southeast CASA observed that its state lags behind other states in providing services to victims and in showing a commitment to supporting victim services in any sustainable manner. It was as recent as 2003 that its state created a fund to finance sexual assault victim services. This CASA observed, "Sexual violence is a tough sell in [this state] ... In a conservative state we don't even want to talk about consensual sex, so how can we begin to talk about nonconsensual sex?" (Personal interview, March 28, 2008).

Policy Implications

Victims and CASAs largely agreed that the most effective ways in which policy makers and the public could assist victims and prevent future victimizations included the following: (1) providing opportunities to talk about victimization without being judged, (2) demanding and supporting accurate and widespread sexual violence prevention education, and (3) funding and otherwise supporting access to both immediate and long-term, sustainable services for both

		Major Sex Offender Laws' Impact on Addressing Sexual Assault Victim Needs			

16.1

	Registration	Notification	Residency Restrictions	Electronic Monitoring	Mandatory HIV Testing
Supportive Victim Disclosure Opportunities	NA	NA	–	NA	NA
Accurate Public Education	–	–	–	–	NA
Immediate and Long-Term Victim Services	NA	NA	NA	NA	+

+ positive impact, per victims and CASAs

– negative impact, per victims and CASAs

0 no discernible impact, per victims and CASAs

NA not applicable

victims and offenders. The research findings presented here indicate that the host of sex offender laws passed in recent years have had little to no impact on the aforementioned victim- and CASA-identified needs. As illustrated in Table 16.1, victims and CASAs consistently identified only one sex offender policy as having a positive impact on victims' needs: mandatory HIV testing. Other policies were viewed as negatively impacting victims and/or having no discernible victim impact.

Several CASAs observed that sex offender laws really have nothing to do with victims. They argued that victims may be used as a political tool to pass the law but in reality, few—if any—tangible benefits are realized by victims. Garland (2001) identified the naming of laws in honor of victims as

The new political imperative ... [These named laws] purport to honor them ... though there is undoubtedly an element of exploitation here, too, as the individual's name is used to fend off objections to measures that are often nothing more than retaliatory legislation passed for public display and political advantage. (p. 143)

CASAs are invested in the outcomes these laws have on offenders, as well. According to several CASAs, these expensive laws have demonstrated little to no discernible impact on reducing recidivism. Instead, they eat up scarce resources, scare victims into not reporting a perpetrating loved one, and reinforce to the public stereotypes about what sexual violence is and who perpetrates it. The West Coast CASA believes, "These policies are about a *sense* of safety, not *real* safety" (Personal interview, March 5, 2008). The unintended byproduct of these laws, then, may well be the creation of more victims. Although victims and CASAs believe that these laws have increased public discourse on sexual violence as a social problem, the laws have also managed to highlight the most sensationalistic types of offenders, thereby reinforcing stereotypes that only serve to decrease public safety.

It appears as though the fragile alliance between victims' rights groups and criminal justice actors has been reconstituted as of late, as more and more of these groups have come together to publicly oppose sex offender legislative initiatives. Although at first blush it may seem strange that victim advocates, sexual assault coalitions, and some victims themselves would oppose laws ostensibly aimed at increasing public safety, they are actually best suited to know the real impact these laws have on the public, the criminal justice process, and sexual assault survivors. Fittingly, several respondents in this study advised against policies in which a zero-sum relationship is falsely created between victims and offenders. Although offenders are understandably unsympathetic characters, true public safety demands policies that will most vigorously and effectively address all sexual violence—not just the rare types most frequently explored by the media and elected officials.

The public conversation about how best to address the social problem of sexual violence may be headed back to the future. Over the past several decades, the policy pendulum has swung from focusing on the rare offender, to focusing on intra-familial and acquaintance victimization, back to the rare offender. The respondents in this study—both victims and CASAs—believe that the policy pendulum must swing back again if victims' needs are to be adequately and compassionately addressed. In order for this to happen, policy makers must not presume to know what victims need and want; they must ask victims how they can best be served through legislative initiatives that seek to redress sexual violence as a social problem. This will require that policy makers engage in an ongoing dialogue with many and varied sexual assault survivors to better understand the often complicated relationships between the abuser and the abused. But most importantly, "victims must be key stakeholders rather than footnotes in the justice process" (Zehr, 2001, p. 195).

References

Abner, C. (2007). Waging war on sex crimes: States target sex offenders through policy and practice. National Legislative Briefing, The Council of State Governments. Retrieved November 29, 2007, from http://www.csg.org/pubs/Documents/sn0604WagingWar.pdf

Bachman, R., & Paternoster, R. (1993). A contemporary look at the effects of rape law reform: How far have we really come? *Journal of Criminal Law and Criminology, 84*(3), 554–574.

Belknap, J. (2007). *The invisible woman: Gender, crime, and justice*. Belmont, CA: Wadsworth Publishing.

Berliner, L., Schram, D., Miller, L., & Milloy, C. D. (1995). A sentencing alternative for sex offenders. *Journal of Interpersonal Violence, 10*(4), 487–502.

Bryden, D. P., & Lengnick, S. (1997). Rape in the criminal justice system. *The Journal of Criminal Law and Criminology, 87*(4), 1194–1388.

Buchwald, E., Fletcher, P., & Roth, M. (2005). *Transforming a rape culture*. Minneapolis: Milkweed Editions.

Caringella-MacDonald, S. (1984). Sexual assault prosecution: An examination of model rape legislation in Michigan. *Women & Politics, 4*, 65–82.

Colindres, A. (2008, March 1). Strip club tax designed to aid rape-crisis centers. *Springfield Journal Register*. Retrieved from http://www.sjr.com/news/statehouse/2008/03/01/strip_club_tax_designed_to_aid_rape_crisis_centers/

Daanne, D.M. (2005). Victim response to sexual assault. In F. Reddington and B. Wright Kreisel (Eds.) *Sexual assault: The victims, the perpetrators, and the criminal justice system* (pp. 77–106). Durham, NC: North Carolina Academic Press.

Dix, G.E. (1976). Differential processing of abnormal sex offenders. *Journal of Criminal Law, Criminology, & Police Science, 67*, 233–243.

Dumond, R.W. & D.A. Dumond. (2002). The treatment of sexual assault victims. In C. Hensley (Ed.) *Prison sex: Practice and policy* (pp. 67–88). Boulder, CO.: Lynne Rienner Publishers.

Estrich, S. (1987). *Real rape: How the legal system victimizes women who say no*. Cambridge, MA: Harvard University Press.

Garland, D. (1990). *Punishment and modern society: A study in social theory*. Chicago: University of Chicago Press.

Garland, D. (2001). *The culture of control: Crime and social order in contemporary society*. Chicago: University of Chicago Press.

Glaser, B. (2003). Therapeutic jurisprudence: An ethical paradigm for therapists in sex offender treatment programs. *Western Criminology Review, 4,* 143–154.

Glynn, K. (2000). *Tabloid culture: trash taste, popular power, and the transformation of American television.* Durham, NC: Duke University Press.

Hamilton, M.A. (2004). Religious institutions: The no-harm doctrine and the public good. *BYU Law Review, 2004*(4), 1099–1126.

Herman, J.L. (2005). Justice from the victim's perspective. *Violence against Women, 11*(5), 571–602.

Kilpatrick, D., Edmunds, C., & Seymour, A. (1992). *Rape in America: A report to the nation.* Arlington, VA: National Crime Victims Research and Treatment Center at the Medical University of South Carolina.

Kilpatrick, D., Whalley, A. & Edmunds, C. (2007). Sexual Assault. In A. Seymour, M. Murray, J. Sigmon, M. Hook, C. Edwards, M. Gaboury, & G. Coleman (Eds.), *National victim assistance academy textbook* (ch.10). Washington, DC: US Department of Justice, Office for Victims of Crime. Retrieved November 19, 2007, from www.ojp.usdoj. gov/ovc/assist/nvaa2002/chapter10.html

Largen. M.A. (1988). Rape law reform: An analysis. In A. Wolbert Burgess (Ed.) *Rape and sexual assault, II* (pp. 271–292). New York: Garland Publishing, Inc.

Lieb, R., V. Quinsey, & L. Berliner. (1998). Sexual predators and social policy. In M. Tonry (Ed.) *Crime and justice: A review of research,* vol. 23 (pp. 43–114). Chicago and London: University of Chicago Press.

Logan, W.A. (1999). Liberty interests in the preventative state: Procedural due process and sex offender community notification laws. *Journal of Criminal Law and Criminology, 89*(4): 1167–1231.

Madriz, E. (1997). *Nothing bad happens to good girls: Fear of crime in women's lives.* Berkeley, CA: University of California Press.

Marsh, J. C., A. Geist, & N. Caplan. (1982). *Rape and the limits of law reform.* Boston: Arbor House Publishing.

Martin, P. Yancey. (2005). *Rape work: Victims, gender, and emotion in organization and community context.* New York: Routledge.

Motta, R. W., & J. M. Kefer. (1999). Initial evaluation of the secondary trauma questionnaire. *Psychological Report, 85*(3), 997–1002.

Polk, K. (1985). Rape reform and criminal justice processing. *Crime & Delinquency, 31*(2), 191–205.

Pratt, J. (2000). Sex crimes and the new punitiveness. *Behavioral Sciences and the Law, 18*(2/3), 135–151.

Pub. L. No. 97–291, § 2

Remer, R., & R. A. Ferguson. (1995). Becoming a secondary survivor of sexual assault. *Journal of Counseling and Development, 73*(4), 407–412.

Robertson, S. (2001). Separating the men from the boys: Masculinity, psychosexual development, and sex crime in the United States, 1930s–1960s. *Journal of the History of Medicine, 56*(1), 3–35.

Spohn, C., & J. Horney. (1992). *Rape law reform: A grassroots revolution and its impact.* New York and London: Plenum Press.

Sutherland, E, (1950). The diffusion of sexual psychopath laws. *American Journal of Sociology, 56*(2), 142–148.

Schneider, H. J. (2001). Victimological developments in the world during the past three decades: A study of comparative victimology. *International Journal of Offender Therapy and Comparative Criminology*, 45(5), 539–555.

Thomas, T. (2000). *Sex crime: Sex offending and society*. UK: Willan Publishing.

Tjaden, P. & N. Thoennes. (2000). *Full report on the prevalence, incidence and consequences of violence against women* (NCJ 183781). Washington, DC: National Institute of Justice, Centers for Disease Control and Prevention. Retrieved February 2, 2008, from http://www.ncjrs.gov/pdffiles1/nij/183781.pdf?PHPSESSID=9b0f266925c06211980333e713e2e399

U.S. Department of Justice, Office of Justice Programs, Office of Victims of Crime. May 2005. Attorney General Guidelines for Victim and Witness Assistance. Retrieved May 29, 2008 at http://www.usdoj.gov/olp/final.pdf

U.S. Department of Justice, Office of Justice Programs, Office of Victims of Crime. July 2000. Retrieved May 29, 2008 at http://www.ojp.usdoj.gov/ovc/welcovc/mission.htm.

Wood, J. K. (2005). In whose name? Crime victim policy and the punishing power of protection. *NWSA Journal, 17*(3), 1–17.

Zehr, H. (2001). *Transcending: Reflections of crime victims*. Intercourse, PA: Good Books.

---

[i] Although we recognize that males experience victimization and that females perpetrate sexual offenses, here feminine pronouns are used for victims and masculine pronouns used for perpetrators to reflect the gendered patterns of these statuses.

[ii] The phrase "rape culture" cannot be attributed to any one author, as it was used widely and, apparently, simultaneously by many writers beginning in the early 1970s.

Index

NOTE: Footnotes are indicated by lower case roman numerals.

D

H

I